Preaching
with
Passion

Preaching
with
Passion

*Sermons from the
Heart of the
Southern Baptist
Convention*

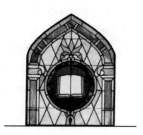

JAMES T. DRAPER, JR.

BROADMAN
& HOLMAN
PUBLISHERS

Nashville, Tennessee

Published by Broadman & Holman Publishers
Nashville, Tennessee

Dewey Decimal Classification: 252
Subject Heading: SERMONS

1 2 3 4 5 6 7 8 9 10   09 08 07 06 05 04

Contents

111084

Part 3: Preaching from a Heart of Encouragement

Part 4: Preaching from a Heart for the Kingdom

Preface

MY HEART'S DESIRE FOR THIS VOLUME is to be a blessing and a benefit to ministers and Bible teachers across our nation and beyond. This is a unique volume, as you will see. The sermons in these pages show the heart of some of Southern Baptists' best-known and most-loved preachers. Also included are sermons from some of the best of the younger preachers among us.

Each sermon is different. Approaches to content, outline, and emphasis vary. There are literally hundreds of ideas for messages for the searching preacher. These pages will challenge, bless, and inspire.

The thread that ties them all together is an unquestioned confidence in the sufficiency and perfection of God's Word, a passion to declare the truth of God's Word, an unashamed surrender to the Lordship of Jesus Christ, and a deep desire to give honor and praise to Him.

This volume is unprecedented in its contents. You have these messages not only in the printed book but also in electronic form on a CD-ROM (inside back cover). This will give you an easy way to copy a portion of the book into your word processor when you find something that is particularly meaningful to you.

It is especially gratifying to me that rather than provide this electronic copy in a traditional way, B&H is including a fully functioning copy of its new Bible Navigator Bible-study computer program.

This product has been receiving extraordinarily good comments from users. It is the very latest Bible-software technology for Microsoft Windows-compatible computers.

All Scripture references in the sermons appear as "links" called SmartLinks. Simply hover your computer's mouse pointer over a SmartLink and the Scripture text will pop up, or click on the SmartLink and a Bible window will open to allow you to browse the scriptural context.

While B&H asks that you register to receive some of these free reference helps, all of the above is yours to keep along with the Holman Christian Standard New Testament. Installing Bible Navigator will also give you a fully functional thirty-day preview of twelve other Bible translations and forty other reference helps. After the preview period expires, these additional Bible and reference works may be purchased at an additional cost from WORDsearch Corporation using the built-in Bible Navigator catalog.

I would encourage you to install the Bible Navigator CD without delay and review the brief video tutorials that are included as an option on the startup screen. It is probably the easiest, most powerful way to begin using Bible-study software. You'll become an instant expert, and Bible Navigator will become a time-saving resource to you.

Enjoy these pages and the electronic tools included. It is a tremendous pleasure and blessing for me to be part of this unique book. Special thanks go to John Landers, George Williams, and the B&H team, and to Aubrey Parish, who worked tirelessly to make the electronic provision possible.

In His love,
James T. Draper, Jr.

Part 1:

Preaching from the Heart of SBC leadership

1

The Life-Changing Power of the Gospel

1 Corinthians 2:1–5 NKJV

Jerry Rankin
President, International Mission Board
of the Southern Baptist Convention

I WANT TO REFER TO AN ANNIVERSARY over thirty years ago, when, with my wife and two small children, I arrived in Indonesia in response to a sense of God's call compelling us to go and share the gospel with people who had never heard of our Lord Jesus Christ. I was under the illusion that I would arrive in that Far Eastern country, and the pages of Acts would just unfold once again. I envisioned identifying with my hero, the apostle Paul, as he swept across the nations declaring the gospel, planting churches, reaping the harvest.

And I indeed did identify with the apostle Paul, in his testimony in the second chapter of 1 Corinthians when he said, "I, brethren, when I came to you, did not come with excellence of speech or of wisdom declaring to you the testimony of God. . . . I was with you in weakness, in fear, and in much trembling. And my speech and my preaching were not with persuasive words of human wisdom" (1 Cor. 2:1, 3–4).

When we face the opportunity and mandate to witness to the lost on the streets of our city, when we participate in those volunteer mission projects, cross-culturally, among those strange sights and smells, and people speaking languages we don't understand, we

3

stand before them in fear and trembling, not with fluency of speech to communicate the wisdom of the gospel. But you are aware that Paul went on to exclaim, "For I determined not to know anything among you except Jesus Christ and Him crucified . . . that your faith should not be in the wisdom in men but in the power of God" (1 Cor. 2:2, 5).

I discovered, as did Paul, and all of our missionaries discussed, that as they go out to share the gospel with the lost world, to reach the nations with the saving message of salvation, it is not their abilities. It's not their skills. It's not their programs and their ministries. But as Paul expressed in Romans 1:16, "It is the power of God to salvation for everyone who believes." It's the gospel of Jesus Christ that is our power for winning a lost world.

God has clearly defined His purpose for us, His people. Even before the foundation of the world, it was born in the heart of God that redemption would be provided through the gospel of Jesus Christ. He called Abraham to leave his home and his family, that through his seed all the families of the nations would be blessed. He called apart the Jews as His chosen people so they would be a priestly nation to draw the Gentiles and the nations to know and exalt the name of our Lord. And He has given us to that mandate to go into all the world and disciple the nations.

Jesus came in fulfillment of that vision and the heart of God to bring redemption to empower His people. He died on the cross and rose again that whosoever would call upon the name of the Lord should be saved. He said, "As the Father has sent Me, I also send you" (John 20:21). We go only in the power of the gospel of Jesus Christ, with a vision to reach the nations and a lost world to the glory of the heavenly Father.

God is saying to us as Southern Baptists, as He said to Isaiah about the Messiah, "It is too small a thing that You should be My Servant to raise up the tribes of Jacob, and to restore the preserved ones of Israel; I will also give You as as a light to the Gentiles, that You should be My salvation to the ends of the earth" (Isa. 49:6). We dare not be disobedient to the mandate, to the mission, to the purpose that was born in the heart of God and given to us almost two thousand years ago. Yes, it's a challenging world out there. Our newspapers, our television screens, and our newscasts are filled with warfare, bombing, ethnic violence around the world, economic deterioration sweeping Asia, political disruption, natural disasters, and human suffering.

What do we have in our hands? What do we have with which to respond to the awesome needs of humanity and suffering in a lost world? It's not our Western diplomacy and United Nations peace-keepers. It's not humanitarian sociologists. It's not even the programs of our denomination and the strategy of the International Mission Board. The only thing that we have to share is the message that Jesus died and rose from the dead and is coming again. The gospel of Jesus Christ—that sin-conquering, life-changing, redeeming message that Jesus saves—is our weapon to combat evil. That's what empowers us for our mission and our task.

Paul is reflecting on the power of the gospel in 1 Thessalonians. He is reflecting on the gospel and the power of that message that has been received and planted in the hearts of the Thessalonican believers. He observes:

Our gospel did not come to you in word only, but also in power, and in the Holy Spirit and in much assurance, as you know what kind of men we were among you for your sake.

And you became followers of us and of the Lord, having received the word in much affliction, with joy of the Holy Spirit, so that you became examples to all in Macedonia and Achaia who believe. For from you the word of the Lord has sounded forth, not only in Macedonia and Achaia, but also in every place. Your faith toward God has gone out, so that we do not need to say anything. For they themselves declare concerning us what manner of entry we had to you, and how you turned to God from idols to serve the living and true God (1 Thess. 1:5–9).

Do you get the picture of what's happening here? As Paul continued on his itinerate preaching ministry, he found that he didn't have to explain the gospel of Jesus Christ. He didn't have to tell people who Jesus was. They already knew. They had heard. It had swept not only the province and into the neighboring provinces but on beyond them. People had seen the reality and power of the gospel; they had seen how these people had turned from idols to serve the living and true God. It was the power of that life-changing message that was the hope of sweeping the world with the saving message of Jesus Christ.

It reminds me of visiting in the southeast corner of Bangladesh a few years ago, where one of our missionaries had been working among the people for several years. When he got there, he found that they had never heard of Christianity. They had never heard the name of Jesus. He told me about two men who came running down a roadway, down a hill into the roadway, stopped his car, and said, "Are you the man who is telling about a religion that provides the forgiveness of sin?"

Where had they heard that? It was sweeping from village to village. They had seen how those who embraced faith in Jesus Christ had cleaned their villages. They no longer got drunk. Their children were being educated. Others would come to these converted people and ask, "What is it that has made a difference? Why is it that you no longer worship those little clay idols?" And they would tell them about the life-changing message of Jesus Christ.

When I visited a couple of years later, there were already eleven churches, fourteen other villages worshipping our Lord Jesus, where believers were baptized. Just last year this missionary was on furlough, and I recalled this experience. And I said, "How many churches are there among the Tripura today, eight years later?" He said, "We lost count after two hundred churches because the villages are just so remote!"

It wasn't our missionary who reached over two hundred villages with the gospel. It was the power of the gospel of Jesus Christ changing lives. You have heard others tell about eight years ago, when our missionaries first went into the killing fields of Cambodia. And two years later, in 1993, there were three little Baptist churches. Four years later there were eighty churches. And now there are over two hundred churches. That is not the work of our missionaries. It is the power of the gospel of Jesus Christ. It's not ministry and rehabilitation work. It's the power of the gospel of Jesus Christ.

If we are going to be empowered for the mission that God has given us, if we are going to seize the opportunity in the twenty-first century, we must realize our only power is that message—a story, or an experience of what Jesus has done in our hearts, and that life-changing experience. God is at work today in unprecedented ways. And God has blessed Southern Baptists in numbers and resources. We are not to take pride in being a great denomination but only in being His servants and His instruments to reach the Gentiles, the nations.

Last year we saw 885 new missionaries commissioned by the International Mission Board. We have more than 5,400 missionaries overseas. This last year we saw more than half a million baptisms reported on mission fields. We are seeing that last frontier of the Great Commission. Those nations and peoples who have never had an opportunity to hear the gospel are systematically being penetrated and touched by the gospel of Christ. We are in the midst of the greatest opportunity God has ever given His people to fulfill His mission.

We must be compelled and driven by that vision. John saw in Revelation 7:9 a multitude that no man could count, from every tribe and people and tongue and nation, gathered around the throne and worshiping our Lord. But if we are to be compelled by that vision, if we are to be empowered by that message, if we are to be empowered for tomorrow, we cannot limit our international missions work to the organizational potential of the International Mission Board. We have one missionary unit for every 2.8 million people overseas. My native state of Mississippi has 2.7 million people. What if there was only one pastor, one family to share the gospel with that entire state? We cannot do it simply with the potential of the International Mission Board. We must mobilize the resources of our entire denomination and involve every church and every denominational entity in fulfilling the Great Commission.

If we are to be empowered to do God's mission tomorrow, we can no longer be satisfied with incremental growth. We cannot be satisfied with anything less than the global impact of all the nations knowing Jesus Christ. As Southern Baptists, we are good at measuring ourselves by ourselves and commending ourselves to ourselves. As long as we can report a few more new churches than last year, a few more baptisms than last year, appoint a few more missionaries than we had a few years ago, we pat ourselves on the back and are so happy with incremental growth.

But when we reached five thousand international missionaries, that represented only 0.03 percent of Southern Baptists. Not even one-tenth of one percent! If we took seriously the call and mission of God, the empowerment of the message of the gospel that He has given us, compelled by that vision that all the nations and peoples of the world would have an opportunity to hear and respond to that message of Jesus Christ, and called out only one from among a thousand in the churches in your associations, we would be talking about not five thousand but sixteen thousand missionaries to carry the gospel around the world.

We cannot be satisfied with incremental growth, but we must reach for having a global impact. If we are to be empowered for tomorrow, we cannot be confined to man-sized goals but a God-sized vision. The psalmist said, "All the ends of the world shall . . . turn to the LORD, and all the families of the nations shall worship before You" (Ps. 22:27). That's the goal. That's the vision. To have such a passion in our relationship with God is a compulsion that all the world would know Him and worship Him.

I have often shared the experience of coming into our headquarters in Richmond after twenty-three years overseas, and trying to get up to speed on all the technology we were using in our mission administration, to discover that they had just put a new word-processing program on our computer system. Now if you work with computer word processing software, you know as I discovered that it has an automatic spell-check. If you misspell a word, it will highlight it right there on the screen. You can't deny it.

It blinks right there before God and the office and everybody. But amazingly you don't have to know how to spell. All you have to do is click the mouse, and it will just spell it automatically for you.

I quickly discovered that not all of my vocabulary was in that spell-check dictionary. It had never heard of Turkestan and Azerbaijan. I didn't know if I spelled it right, and it didn't either. It had never heard of Lottie Moon. The first time it highlighted "Lottie Moon" and I clicked the mouse, it changed it to "Little Moon." I found that you could add those words to the program, and it wouldn't keep doing that. But a word I was amazed wasn't in that spell-check dictionary on my computer was a word I often used—the word *unreached*. Unreached people. Unreached nations. Thinking that was a misspelled word when I clicked the mouse, it changed it to what it presumed should be the correct spelling—the word *unrelated*.

I don't think there is a theological basis for word-processing software. But it's right on target here. Who is it that is unreached? Whether in your community or in the last frontier of unreached people groups the other side of the world, those who are unrelated to our heavenly Father. And the greatest tragedy is not just their lostness; it's not just the fact that many have never even heard the gospel. The greatest tragedy is that He alone who is worthy of all praise and worship and honor and glory is not receiving the worship and praise and glory from those He loves and died to save. I have often wondered why we are no more diligent in sharing the gospel, in witnessing to the lost around us, in responding to God's call to go to those who have yet to hear of our precious Lord.

I read a paragraph in a book that just jumped off the page that helped me to understand it. The author said the Great Commission is the efficient authority to send us after the lost, but it's not sufficient motivation. And I thought if we are not motivated by the command of our Lord to go, what will motivate us? But he went on to say that it's not the authority of an external command that sends us after the lost but the impulse of an indwelling presence.

It's only when we enter into a relationship with our Lord Jesus Christ and worship and honor and praise Him, that there springs up something within our hearts that compels us to share our Lord Jesus Christ with those who are lost, that compels us to go to the nations to declare the message that draws people to Himself. But this will not happen through program promotion. It's not all about promoting the International Mission Board. But it's only through a spiritual motivation of knowing God and God's heart for the nations.

It will come not through generic support of missions but through personalized involvement, adopting unreached people groups, working along with strategy coordinators. We have been identifying and mobilizing churches that will say, "We are not going to draw a circle around our community and say, 'This is our mission.' We realize our mission as a local church is the entire world."

We have been talking about global priority churches. We received a letter from a young man in a small church in Texas. He explained that he was their missions coordinator. He was a volunteer layman. And he said that they had been reading about the global priority church network, and they wanted to be part of that. He said that they thought they qualified. He went on to explain that they were a new church, less than three years old. He said they didn't even have their own facilities. They met in a school building. But they were giving 40 percent of their offerings to missions. He said they seldom had as many as one hundred in Sunday school and worship. But last year they sent volunteer teams to Guatemala, Mexico, Romania, and the Ukraine. They had adopted a people group in North Africa and a city in China to pray for until the strongholds of Satan are broken and until they come into the kingdom.

He went on to say that last year the IMB appointed two couples from their church to go as missionaries. He asked if they could be a global priority church. Absolutely yes! Praise God, you don't have to be big. You don't have to have big resources. But you do have to have a heart for God because He has given us all the message of the gospel. That's what empowers us for His mission today and tomorrow.

Recently Jerry Sutton talked about Two Rivers Baptist Church in Nashville, Tennessee, linking up with a strategy coordinator in southwest China. He said their church has been revitalized with a sense of ownership and responsibility for providing the prayer support, the volunteers, and the resources to impact that people group with the gospel. And we are thrilled that he invited a thousand churches to a missions summit for this new millennium.

What will empower us for tomorrow as we move into the twenty-first century to share the gospel of Jesus Christ? More resources? New strategies? More denominational programs? No. It's only when we return not to the twenty-first century but to the first century and stand by Peter as he declared, "Let all the house of Israel know assuredly that God has made this Jesus, whom you crucified, both Lord and Christ" (Acts 2:36). It's the power of that message of the gospel that empowers us as Southern Baptists, as God's people, to fulfill His mission tomorrow as we move into the twenty-first century.

If there is any verse of Scripture that any Southern Baptist knows next to John 3:16, it would be the Great Commission. We are told to "go therefore and make disciples of all the nations, baptizing them in the name of the Father and of the Son and of the Holy Spirit, teaching them to observe all things that I have commanded you" (Matt. 28:19–20). But we must never forget that the Great Commission is framed by two very important verses. Jesus said, "All authority has been given to Me in heaven and on earth," and "lo, I am with you" (Matt. 28:18, 20).

Let that sink into our hearts. There is no power in all the universe that exceeds the power and authority of our Lord Jesus Christ. He has the authority to do whatever He plans and determines to do. And He tells us in the next verse exactly what that is—that we are to go and disciple the nations. But then He closes by reminding us, "But don't forget, I go with you." May we go in obedience with the assurance that the Lord Jesus Christ goes with us, as we go in the power of the gospel of Jesus Christ, to fulfill God's mission and reach a lost world for Jesus Christ.

2

Sent to Be on Mission

ACTS 8 NIV

Robert E. Reccord
President, North American Mission Board
of the Southern Baptist Convention

SEVERAL YEARS AGO BILLY GRAHAM WAS TOLD of a man who had criticized his evangelistic efforts in crusade methods. In fact, the man had indicated that Dr. Graham, in his opinion, had set back the church in America a hundred years.

With a twinkle in his eye and his normal gracious demeanor, Dr. Graham responded, "Only one hundred years? I've been trying to set it back two thousand years!"

What was it about the first-century church that made it so contagious? As it exploded on the scene of a pluralistic society with a tremendous bent toward secularism (much like our own), it grew by leaps and bounds. It was a church on the cutting edge!

It is that contagious kind of Christianity that North America needs so desperately in our day. It seems frighteningly clear that we are following in the tracks of modern England. For it was in that great bastion of civilization that the church of the 1800s was contagious—the home of the Wesley brothers and George Whitfield. England has seen its society impacted with the Christian message like few nations in the world. Tutored and taught later by the prince of the pulpit, Charles Hadden Spurgeon, they reached a climax of Christian impact.

Historians tell us that the Victorian age in England may well have been one of the most significantly "churched" populations of history. That is to say, that the greatest percentage of the population somewhat regularly attended some type of church service.

By 1987 there had been a marked change in the religious demographics of England:

- One-third of the Baptist churches had significant difficulty finding a pastor.
- The average Sunday school attendance was thirty-four.
- The average baptismal rate was one-half person per year.
- Every nine days a church closed its doors for good.
- Every fourteen days a Muslim mosque or learning center opened its doors to the future.

In seeing this frightening trend, I asked our research department at the North American Mission Board and study when the highest percent of the population in the United States somewhat regularly attended church. The answer came back—1958 and 1959. In eighty years England fell from a society greatly impacted by the church to an incredibly secular society. The United States now stands approximately halfway through that journey of eighty years since our high point of percentage of population being involved in church.

So let's take a look at what impacted the church in the first century to change its world and turn it right side up. As the church exploded in the city of Jerusalem, the whole city became aware of this new life-changing movement. On the day of Pentecost, three thousand people placed their faith in Jesus Christ as their Savior and Lord. Not many days hence, great numbers were being added daily as they put their faith in the risen Christ (Acts 2:47). Within weeks we are told that many who had heard the message believed and that the number of men placing their faith in Christ as Savior grew to about five thousand (Acts 4:4). With such great success it is no surprise that the Jewish leaders and the Roman government looked with alarm on this life-impacting set of beliefs.

As the church exploded, there had to be incredible excitement. However, success can also breed comfort zones. And God never called us to comfort zones but rather to conviction and commitment and to be *on mission* as a way of life. But there was one sure cure for the comfort of success—persecution.

Acts 8 tells us that as persecution came against the church at Jerusalem, the apostles stayed there, and Jerusalem served as the nerve center of the new church. However, godly men who had come to know Christ and had been discipled for Him spread out into the far reaches of the known world. The church had already penetrated Jerusalem and Judea; now it would bridge into Samaria—where it would have to cross economic, social, cultural, and linguistic barriers.

And of all people to be thrust into Samaria, we find a Jewish layman by the name of Philip being the chosen agent of change. This is significantly important because Samaria is the last place a Jewish man would have wanted to be sent on mission. Great racial and cultural tensions strained life between Jews and Samaritans. The Samaritans were the result of the Assyrian invasion of Israel in Old Testament times. When many of the people were carried off into bondage, Assyrians moved in and intermarried with those who were left. The results of those marriages were children who would become Samaritans—half-breeds. And the true Jews resented and despised Samaritans.

Yet it was here that God and His unpredictable strategy sent Philip to proclaim the good news of Jesus Christ. The Scripture tells us in Acts 8 that the equivalent of a Billy Graham Crusade broke out. What a marvel it must have been to Philip to see God move in the midst of a people whom Philip's own kin despised. How could this be happening, and how could the gospel bridge such deep chasms?

Yet there it was, before his very eyes, in reality.

But once again God would do the unpredictable. In the middle of this major awakening in the city of Samaria, God's Spirit came with a new assignment for Philip.

> Now an angel of the Lord said to Philip, "Go south to
> the road—the desert road—that goes down from Jerusalem
> to Gaza." So he started out, and on his way he met an

Ethiopian eunuch, an important official in charge of all the
treasury of Candace, queen of the Ethiopians. This man had
gone to Jerusalem to worship, and on his way home was sitting in his chariot reading the book of Isaiah the prophet.
The Spirit told Philip, "Go to that chariot and stay near it."

Then Phillip ran up to the chariot and heard the man
reading Isaiah the prophet. "Do you understand what you
are reading?" Philip asked.

"How can I," he said, "unless someone explains it to
me?" So he invited Philip to come up and sit with him.

The eunuch was reading this passage of Scripture:

"He was led like a sheep to slaughter, and as a lamb
before the shearer is silent, so he did not open his mouth. In
his humiliation he was deprived of justice. Who can speak
of his descendants? For his life was taken from the earth."

The eunuch asked Philip, "Tell me, please, who is the
prophet talking about, himself or someone else?" Then
Philip began with that very passage of Scripture and told
him the good news about Jesus. As they traveled along the
road, they came to some water and the eunuch said, "Look,
here is water. Why shouldn't I be baptized?" And he gave
orders to stop the chariot. Then both Philip and the eunuch
went down into the water and Philip baptized him. When
they came up out of the water, the Spirit of the Lord suddenly took Philip away, and the eunuch did not see him
again, but went on his way rejoicing. Philip, however,
appeared at Azotus and traveled about, preaching the gospel
in all the towns until he reached Caesarea (Acts 8:26–40).
There are four powerful aspects about this story.

I. There Was a Perplexed Seeker

I want to tell you a few things about this perplexed seeker that
are very relevant to our day and time.

This perplexed seeker was born ethnic. He was not of the same
race or cultural background as Philip. Philip was having to extend

even further across cultural, linguistic, and social barriers. This man most likely came from an area of what is today called the Sudan. The racial and cultural differences between Philip and this leader from the continent of Africa could not have been greater.

In similar ways our culture in America today is dramatically changing ethnically. I recently spoke in Houston, and a leader of the city told me that by the year 2020, the population will grow in a number equivalent to the entire population of San Antonio and that one out of every two people moving to Houston will be Hispanic. If you look at the 1990s in the demographics of our nation, you will find that the Anglo population experienced zero growth. This means there were as many deaths as there were births. At the same time, Asian, Hispanic, and African-American populations grew in double-digit percentages. It is estimated that by the year 2050 just under one-half of the United States will be white Anglo-Saxon. With that ethnicity comes a vastly different religious background.

Likewise today, our American society has seen a radical religious shift. The Muslim population seems to be superseding Judaism as the second largest religious body in our land, growing by 25 percent between 1989 and 1998.[1] With more than one million Hindus, this religion is the second fastest-growing religion in North America. And Buddhism is growing nearly three times faster than Christianity.[2]

This leader from Africa whom Philip baptized had also been to the big city. Going into the 1900s, some 30 percent of the population of the United States lived in cities. Today, a full 85 percent live in the top 276 metropolitan areas of our land. Taking just the top fifty cities, 57 percent of the U.S. population would be located in them. And one out of three people lives in the top-ten cities of our nation. And in these cities 81 percent of the African-Americans will be found. Eighty-eight percent of the Hispanics live in them. Ninety percent of the Asians make the cities their home. And a startling 48 percent of Native Americans are found in our cities.

In addition, the convert from Ethiopia had been to the big church. It says in Acts 8:27 that he had been "to Jerusalem to worship." But unfortunately, he evidently didn't find what he was looking for. George Barna tells us that today "people are desperate for spiritual truth—but they can't find the answers they need in Christian churches.[3] He further states, "Those have turned to Christianity and churches seeking truth and meaning and have left empty-handed, confused by the apparent inability of Christians themselves to implement the principles they profess."[4]

As I moved from being a senior pastor to being the president of the Southern Baptist North American Mission Board, I had a very difficult challenge. For the first time in years, I was looking for a church rather than a church looking for me. My wife Cheryl and I were amazed at how many churches we visited and the reception we experienced. Often, even when the church had greeters, they were spending more time talking to one another or other church members than they were greeting guests. Not once did we attend a Bible study class in which people invited us to sit with them during the worship service. No one ever asked us out for lunch or to join them. Overall, we found it to be a very lonely and troubling experience and couldn't help but wonder how often this was happening across America.

Then we see that this perplexed seeker came away with big questions. Reading a scroll of the book of Isaiah, he was trying to sort out for himself a message he had evidently missed in worship. There must be a number of people like that in our land. In the research department of the North American Mission Board, we estimate that there are 224 million people in the United States and Canada who do not claim a personal relationship with Jesus Christ (200 million in the U.S. and 24 million in Canada). Tom Clegg and Warren Bird in their book *Lost in America*, report that in the year 2000 one-half of all churches in America did not add one new person through conversion growth.[5] Theologian and religious analyst Tom Rainer, in collecting data for his book *The Formerly Unchurched*, found that it takes eighty-five Christians in the United States working over one year to produce just one convert! While the church is the primary institution in society which was created to exist for those who are not there yet, it seems that too often the church has fallen to the temptation of turning in on itself.

The amazing thing is that there are perplexed seekers like this, much like the searching man from Africa, all around us. I know that from personal experience. When Cheryl and I moved to the North Atlanta suburb to take this new position in 1997, we determined we must do what we asked others to do—reach out evangelistically to those surrounding us. We determined to begin a neighborhood Bible study. As we put together the flyer, we made it as attractive as possible and planned the launch for five weeks down the road. Passing out the flyers to neighbors in the surrounding several streets, we began to pray that God would do something special through this time.

I got busy traveling and sooner than expected, the five weeks were upon us. On the Thursday night we were to begin the Bible study, I had been gone for five days and arrived home at approximately five o'clock. Putting my luggage down in the hallway, I must honestly say there was a part of me that wished nobody would show up. I had been with people without stop for five days, and I was ready for a break! I just wanted to be brain-dead! In addition to that, I hadn't eaten all day, and Cheryl told me I would just have time to grab a quick bite. Sitting down at the table, I smiled and suggested to Cheryl that if we turned out the lights in our house, nobody would know we were there. As usual, she just shook her head and went about her work getting my dinner ready. As I sat down and took the first bite, suddenly there was a knock at the door. Even as Cheryl made her way to the front of the house, I was calling out, "It's still not too late to turn out the lights!"

But when she opened the door and we heard that voice, the night took on a whole different meaning. A mellow young voice in a female New York accent said, "Hi, I'm Toni Ann, and I need God! I've been to over ten churches trying to find Him, and none of them could tell me how to do that. I got your flyer a few weeks ago, and I thought this was my last hope. If I don't find Him here, I'm giving up the search. Can I please come in? I've been sitting outside your house for over an hour."

As Cheryl brought Toni Ann into the house, we had the privilege of sharing Christ with her. During the following day, Cheryl had the joy of seeing Toni Ann accept Jesus Christ as Savior.

But that's not the miraculous part alone! In the following weeks her son came to know Jesus Christ. Her Jewish husband started asking a lot of questions. Her Jewish mother-in-law got involved in a Bible study in Mississippi on the book of Romans because of the change in Toni Ann's life. Her sister made a renewed commitment to Jesus Christ. And at a bar mitzvah for her niece, her sister-in-law came up and exclaimed, "Toni Ann! What in the world has happened to you? You are just not the same person!"

As Toni Ann recounted the event to us, she said with a big grin, "And you know me, I couldn't keep quiet so I just told her about Jesus right there in the midst of the bar mitzvah!"

My wife discipled Toni Ann for a year. When they finally moved to California, we were elated to get our first call from them. It seems that God had used Toni Ann to establish a brand-new Bible study and prayer group for mothers of school kids who gathered weekly in her new home to pray for students, the administration and faculty, and one another.

Are *you* looking for the perplexed seekers around you?

II. A Prepared Messenger

But second, in this passage, there is a prepared messenger. Never once does it indicate that Philip had to wonder what he should say or which approach to take. Instead, the message of Jesus Christ simply flowed out of him.

That's exactly how the Bible says it ought to be with us. First Peter 3:15 clearly implores us, "In your hearts set apart Christ as Lord. Always be prepared to give an answer to everyone who asks you to give the reason for the hope that you have. But do this with gentleness and respect." This is the fulfillment of the Great Commission and Christ's charge to the church in Acts 1:8. He has charged us with making disciples, not just counting decisions. And it is to be accomplished by our being simple witnesses. It is important for us to remind ourselves that to be a witness is simply to be a person who honestly and straightforwardly testifies to what he has personally experienced.

It is in the context of being a witness that we simply take the initiative to share Jesus Christ and the power of the Holy Spirit. Then we leave the results to God! And as we do, we will never be the same. Paul made this clear in Philemon 6 when he said, "I pray that you may be active in sharing your faith, so that you will have a full understanding of every good thing we have in Christ." This tells us that if we are active in sharing our faith, we will increasingly come to know every good thing we have in Christ. The opposite, however, is also true. If we aren't regularly sharing Christ, we will not grow into a full understanding of everything we can experience in Christ. That's why the Old Testament says, "Let the redeemed of the LORD say this" (Ps. 107:2).

But too often I find Christians who are like Magelina DeVrie. As Magelina came through security checks at the airport in Milan, Italy, security was concerned. She just didn't look right. There was something about her that gave off clues that they had been trained to be on the lookout for. Yet every check seemed to indicate that everything was fine. When a complete check of her baggage and her clothing provided nothing as evidence, the head of security took a significant gamble—he asked that she be X-rayed. This was a great challenge because he knew if he was wrong he could be fired.

Amazement was the only word that could be used for what everyone felt when they saw the X-rays. In small balloons, Magelina DeBrie had swallowed a total of 10,999 small-cut diamonds and 217 emeralds. She was a walking treasure chest!

It reminds me of a lot of Christians. God has said He has put His treasure into the earthen vessels of our lives so that we in turn might give it away to others. But too often, we are simply trying to sneak the treasure through by keeping our lips sealed.

Far too often I hear people in churches say, "But, Bob, that is not my gift." Though some would disagree with me, I do not find strong biblical evidence that evangelism is primarily a spiritual gift. Ephesians 4 makes clear that it is a spiritual leadership office of the church. I do not find strong evidence that evangelism is primarily a gift. Rather, I find an indication that it is a responsibility—a responsibility of every Christian!

Too often, also, well-meaning church members say, "But I witness by my life." The difficulty with that is when we witness by our lives alone, the only thing we witness about is our own goodness. People cannot know what is making a difference within us. That is why Samuel Shoemaker, a converted layman of years ago who fell madly in love with Christ and giving Him away to others, said, "I cannot witness by my life alone; I must include my lips. For if I witness by my life alone, I proclaim too much of me and too little of Him."

III. A Powerful Savior

The message in the text that Philip shares with the man from Ethiopia is that of a powerful Savior. Notice that when Philip had the opportunity to give the man understanding about what he was reading in Scripture, he never proclaimed a message about a pastor of a church. While the pastoral role of leadership is critically important, it is never to be the main message of the church.

Nor did Philip lift up some Christian personality. In our day Christian performers and entertainers have too often become front and center. I am thankful for the marvelous gifts of such talented people. But they must not be the central message or image of the church.

Nor did Philip tell this perplexed seeker about some special program that the church was having. In our day we are blessed with churches that have ministry upon ministry addressing every need imaginable. Yet even despite those kinds of resources, the message of Philip was not a program. Instead, the message of Philip, beginning from the very Scripture that the eunuch was reading, was *Jesus!*

It is the same message that Peter preached on the day of Pentecost when he stood boldly before the throngs of people and proclaimed, "Therefore, let all Israel be assured of this: God has made *this Jesus,* whom you crucified, both Lord and Christ!" (Acts 2:36). Paul, proclaiming the focus of his message in 1 Corinthians 2:2, said, "I resolved to know nothing while I was with you except *Jesus Christ* and him crucified."

The church's message is not to be about a pastor; it is not to be about a personality or even a program—it is to be about a Savior! And His name is Jesus Christ! That is why Paul proclaimed, "I am not ashamed of the gospel, because it is the power of God for the salvation of everyone who believes" (Rom. 1:16). That is the fulfillment of Christ's prayer in the Garden of Gethsemane when He prayed, "Now this is eternal life: that they may know you, the only true God, and Jesus Christ, whom you have sent" (John 17:3).

Jesus alone must be the focus of the message in the New Testament church.

- For those who are hungry, He is the Bread of life.
- For those who are spiritually thirsty, He is the fountain of living water.
- For those who are sick, He alone is the Great Physician.
- For those who are troubled, He is the wonderful counselor.
- For those who are lonely, He is a friend who sticks closer than a brother.
- For those who are lost, He is the Shepherd looking for the lost sheep.
- For those who feel shut out, He alone is the open door.

IV. A Permanent Reminder

And lastly, you find in the account of Philip and the Ethiopian that there was a permanent reminder. Remember, God is not looking simply for decisions but for disciples. And the first step of discipleship in the New Testament church of the first century was believer's baptism.

I wear a wedding ring on my left hand. I wear it proudly because it is a symbol of an act of commitment I have made. I want everybody to see it because it says, "I am taken." I am not looking for another relationship, nor am I open to anything else. By an act of my will, I have given my life to a woman whom I love very much, and her name is Cheryl. I have made a public statement for the world to see that this commitment, having been made in the past, is ongoing in the present. In the same way, believer's baptism is an outward picture of an inward reality of commitment. Once a believer in the New Testament church accepted Christ, he followed by believer's baptism to publicly proclaim to the world that he had given his life to Jesus Christ and had invited Him into his life as Savior and Lord.

But there is a divine order in how it must happen. According to Scripture, there must be first a conviction of our need of Jesus Christ; next, a conversion by placing our faith in Him alone for a relationship with God; third, a public confession of that conviction and conversion by believer's baptism.

If a person's baptism is out of that order, it is out of divine order. That happened to me early in life. When I was ten years of age, my best friend went forward in a Sunday morning worship service. As I watched him walk down the aisle, numerous adults patted him on the back and gave him wonderful words of encouragement. It didn't take me long to figure out that this must be a very good thing to do. I immediately fell in behind him.

Up in front of the church, a well-meaning and loving pastor greeted me. He asked me if I had come to make a decision, and I responded, "Yes." He asked me if I wanted to make that decision that very day, and I responded, "Yes." He asked me if I wanted to pray with him, and I responded (you guessed it), "Yes."

And then we sat down on the front row and prayed. There was only one problem. The pastor was the only one who prayed. Soon I filled out a card, and two weeks later I was baptized. For over ten years I lived with the presumption that because I had gone forward and been baptized, I was a Christian. It was not until I was a young adult that I came to the point of knowing Romans 10:9–10. This passage plainly proclaims that everyone must make his own decision, with his own heart, and express his confession with his own lips. No one can do it for you.

Suddenly I had a dilemma. Now as a young adult having accepted Jesus Christ, I had already been baptized when I was ten years old. What was I to do? Due to embarrassment I decided to do nothing. It was not until I was thirty-five years of age and serving as a copastor of a church that I realized that I was out of divine order. While I had gone through the water at age ten, it had not been believer's baptism because I was not a believer at that point. As a result, I had to humble myself and admit to my church that this was something God convicted me of, and as a result I needed to get it in proper order. And it was a key changing point of my life. You can't obey Jesus Christ and take Him at His word and not see your life radically change.

So it was with this new believer from Africa. Seeing the water, and evidently understanding that this was the first act of discipleship in the New Testament church, he asked that the chariot be stopped and that he be baptized. And as Philip baptized him, suddenly the Spirit of God led Philip away. The gentleman from Africa would never see Philip again. The Ethiopian went on his way rejoicing. He evidently took the message of Christ back to his continent and became the first seed of a great future harvest

How great was that investment of Philip? *Amazing!* Statistics tell us today that in the continent of Africa, twenty thousand people per day are coming to know Jesus Christ as Savior! Not a bad return on the investment of one man who, hearing the direction of Christ, obeyed it immediately and approached a perplexed seeker as a prepared messenger and shared with him a powerful Savior that led him to the experience of baptism, which would become a permanent reminder.[6]

What perplexed seeker is God leading you toward today? Are you prepared?

1. Wendy Murray Zoba, "Islam, USA," *Christianity Today,* April 2000, 40.

2. Justin D. Long, "North America: Decline and Fall of World Religions, 1990–2025," at www.gem-werc.org.

3. George Barna, *The Second Coming of the Church* (Nashville: Word Publishing, 1998), 2.

4. Ibid., 5.

5. Tom Clegg and Warren Bird, *Lost in America, 2001* (Loveland, Colo.: Group Publishing, 2001), 27.

6. Statistics from "Catch Division!" *Mission Frontiers* (November-December 1996), www.missionfrontiers.org.

3

Beware of Satan's Weapons: A Heads-up for God-Called Ministers

EPHESIANS 2:8–10 KJV

Richard Land
President, The Ethics & Religious Liberty Commission
of the Southern Baptist Convention

AS I HAVE MOVED INTO MY MIDDLE YEARS, one of the things I regret is that I did not stop and smell the roses and appreciate special moments more. I was always in a hurry, and I know that if God has called you to be a preacher, you are in a hurry. You want to get through seminary. You want to go out there and do what God has called you to do, to go on to the next thing, the next degree, the next church, and the next challenge. And that's good. Paul said that we are to press toward the mark, to run the race, stretching toward the finish line (Phil. 3:14). But stop and savor the moment.

This is a special moment. In the providence and grace of God, you are graduating from a seminary as fine as any that has existed on the North American continent since the fall of Princeton Theological Seminary into liberalism in the 1920s. I was a seminary student at New Orleans Baptist Theological Seminary in the late

27

1960s and early 1970s. It was a topic of conversation every day in the student lounge. There was not a seminary—certainly not a seminary in our great Southern Baptist Convention—that was as committed to the bedrock issues of the faith and the inerrant, infallible Word of God as the seminary from which you graduate today.

I praise God for all of those who have invested in your lives, for the investment that they have made in your ministry, and thus in the kingdom of God. You stand here today better prepared than any generation of seminary graduates for at least the last three-quarters of a century to go forth and do battle with the devil.

Paul declared, "By grace are ye saved through faith; and that not of yourselves: it is the gift of God: not of works, lest any man should boast. For we are his workmanship, created in Christ Jesus unto good works, which God hath before ordained that we should walk in them" (Eph. 2:8–10).

What this clearly means is that once you become saved, God has a plan and a purpose for you, a pathway that is marked out for you. And it is your pathway, not anybody else's. Nobody else can do as good a job of being the minister of God and the servant of God that God has called you to be. God has a plan and a purpose for your life, and it's not a one-size-fits-all design, not just a suit off the rack. It's made just for you. You may need a size 48 long coat and 40 short pants. God knows that. God has His divine scissors out, and He has cut a role that is tailor-made for you.

There is great rejoicing in heaven as you stand here this morning. And there's great consternation in Satan's region because he knows that the settled goal and purpose of this seminary is to train Green Berets, Seals, and Special Forces soldiers for Jesus, not just occupation troops, not just the shore patrol, and certainly not just Remington Raiders with their typewriters.

The devil doesn't waste his time trying to subvert the ministry of moderates and liberals. They are like Pekinese puppies yapping at the heels of a Great Dane. Make no mistake about it. The devil is a Great Dane. If you do warfare against the devil in your own power, you are going to lose. I don't fear him, but I respect him. And so should you. You don't struggle against flesh and blood but against principalities and powers of spiritual darkness (see Eph. 6:12). We are engaged in spiritual warfare, but greater is He that is in us than he that is in the world (see 1 John 4:4). You have that personal relationship with Jesus Christ. You have trusted Him as your Savior.

I spend a lot of time in Washington. That means I spend a lot of time with lost people. I have spent a lot of time with reporters, which *certainly* means I spend time with lost people. Sometimes they don't have any idea what we are talking about. One time I was talking about the article on the family that Southern Baptists had added to the Baptist Faith and Message, and I said the reason we put it in there was because the family was in crisis. I pointed out that only half of our children are being reared in an intact family.

A reporter from the *Boston Globe* asked, "What's that?"

I said, "What's what?"

He said, "What's an intact family?"

Thinking I had better speak very slowly, I said, "An intact family is a family in which the husband and wife are married to each other, and the children are their children, not his, mine, and ours."

Only then did this reporter realize what I was talking about.

The church today is under assault, and I find that I sometimes have to explain what I mean when I talk about a personal relationship with Jesus Christ.

My dad is a fifth-generation Texan. That means that I am a sixth-generation Texan. I am grateful to God—probably more grateful than I ought to be—but I am grateful to God that I grew up a Texan. I'm a sixth-generation Texan living in exile in Nashville, Tennessee, by the command of God Almighty. Now that means, brothers and sisters, that you may not get to serve the Lord where you want to serve Him—but where He wants you to serve. I tell you right now, that's where you want to be.

My mother is from Boston, Massachusetts, and I come from a bicultural background. I got that most rare gift. I got that wonderful Texas heritage with a Bostonian mother whispering in my ear that biggest was not always best and loudest was not always wiser.

But having that background, I grew up with a healthy interest in the Civil War because I had ancestors who fought on both sides.

Out of that interest I came to have a great admiration for two men—two men who in their own very different ways typify much of what is best about the American character. Those two men are Robert E. Lee and Abraham Lincoln. I have been to many of the significant places in their lives. I have sat in the church pews where Robert E. Lee worshiped every Sunday when he was at home in Arlington, Virginia. I have stood on the place at Gettysburg where historians tell us that Abraham Lincoln stood to give what is still the greatest speech ever given by an American president. I have read multivolume biographies of their lives. I have memorized parts of their speeches.

But you would think that I had lost my mind or I had been smoking something illegal, if I were to say to you that I *know* Robert E. Lee and that I *know* Abraham Lincoln. Both of them died more than eight decades before I was born. I know *about* Robert E. Lee. I know *about* Abraham Lincoln. But I *know* my mom and dad. I *know* my wife. I *know* my children. I have a personal relationship with them. It makes all the difference for all of time and eternity whether you know Jesus Christ as *your* Savior, not just *the* Savior. As *your* Lord, not just *the* Lord. I would be remiss in my responsibility as a minister of the gospel of Jesus Christ if I did not say to you that you should make certain you have a relationship with Jesus Christ. This should be as real as your relationship with your spouse, your relationship with your mom and dad, and your relationship with your children or your siblings.

The devil is already at work. He is painting a target on your back, on your front, or anywhere else you have a weak spot. I could name a few. He is already making plans to do everything he can with his demon accomplices to devastate, denigrate, and destroy your ministry if he can. I want to talk to you for a few moments about some of the powerful weapons in his arsenal that he will use to diminish your ministry, if not destroy it.

I. Femme Fatale—or the Opposite Sex

The first is femme fatale. I am talking about women other than your wife. To you who are female graduates, I am talking about men other than your husbands. If David is not one of the most frightening characters in the Bible to you, he ought to be. David was a man after God's own heart, but he fell victim to his own lust. David was in trouble a long time before anybody else knew it. If he had been where he should have been, he would have been out in the battlefields with his soldiers. But instead, he was relaxing back at the palace, enjoying the luxuries of an oriental potentate and the lust of the eye, which led to the lust of the flesh, which led to a conspiracy to commit murder. Let me tell you that if the devil could use a woman to get to David, he can use a woman to get at you. Be wary of femme fatale. It's a greater temptation today than ever before.

There are more women in your church today who are not married and who are not living with their parents than at any time in the history of the Christian faith. I want you to think about that a minute. There are more adult women in your church, in our society, who are not living with their parents, and are not married any longer—or never were married—than ever before in the history of the Christian faith. You cannot be too cautious in this area. One of the nicest things people can say about you is that you are over-cautious and foolish about contact with women. They may criticize you because you won't ride in the car with a woman other than your mother, your wife, and your daughter. They may think that it is a little odd, but they will be comforted by it.

II. False Finances

The second weapon of Satan is false finances. The Bible calls it "filthy lucre." Peter said that we should serve the Lord willingly, not for filthy lucre (1 Tim. 3:3). I once turned down a 100 percent salary increase, and I had people all over the Convention calling me and asking what was wrong. What happened? Something had to be wrong. They couldn't comprehend that it was God's will that

I would turn down a 100 percent salary increase. It was a little hard for me for a while to comprehend it.

Don't do what you do in the ministry for money. Don't adjust what you say because the big givers may not like it. Utterly and totally reject the devil's golden rule, which is, "Those that have the gold rule." They are not the best source of the Lord's will. There may be too much money between them and God. You preach what God wants you to preach. Sooner or later it will make everybody mad. That is really liberating. There is something in the Bible to convict everybody sooner or later.

III. Fleeting Fame

Don't let the devil destroy you with femme fatales, and don't let him destroy you with false finances. In addition, don't let him entice you with fleeting fame. I have seen ministers who couldn't be corrupted by money. They couldn't be corrupted by women. But how they craved having that honorary doctorate, that prestigious degree. How they craved being named alumnus of the year. They reasoned that they had to be careful what they said because they might not be elected moderator of the association. Ministers like this are lovers of the first place of honor.

You will see your brother preacher, and you know in your bones that you are better on your worst day than he ever was. And let's just go ahead and be honest—every one of you would rather be up here than me. I understand that. No preacher worth his salt wants to hear somebody else preach when he could be preaching! But if you become lovers of the first place of honor, you will carefully adjust what you say. You will just cut the edges off, cut the sharp corners off, and you will become a butter knife instead of a scalpel in the Lord's service.

IV. Fearless Familiarity with Holy Things

Finally, don't let the devil defeat you with what perhaps is the most subtle weapon of all—to develop fearless familiarity with the holy things of God. You will become content just to know more than anybody in your congregation does about God's Holy Word. You want to have God's power in your life, and you want to have God's good hand upon you. Reflect back on Ezra. Why did God put His hand on Ezra? The Israelites were coming back to rebuild Jerusalem after the exile. We are a nation in exile. We have been in exile as a nation and as Christians for half a century. We have been bound up in lifeless liberalism. God wants to send revival. God wants to send reformation to America. But it won't come unless we have Ezras among us.

Ezra had prepared his heart. He had made it the settled goal of his life always to seek the law of God. You ought to know something about God's Word at the end of the day that you didn't know when the day began. God doesn't hold you responsible for knowing everything. But He wants you to know more today than you did yesterday, and He wants you to know more tomorrow than you do today. Don't ever get to the place where you are not in awe when you stand behind the sacred desk, when you are not in awe when you hold in your hand the sacred Word of God. When you stand as God's instrument, you proclaim His Word to His people.

So beware of femme fatale. Beware of false finances. Beware of fleeting fame. Beware of fearless familiarity with the Word of God. And the only inoculation against these weapons of the devil is to practice faithfulness to God. Stay close to God, and God will ward off the fiery darts of the evil one.

Some of you know the story of the person who served as the head football coach at Notre Dame for a week. He was a good football coach, and he fulfilled his life's ambition to be the head coach at Notre Dame. So much for some people's taste. You see, I have two favorite teams—actually three favorite teams every week: the University of Texas, whoever is playing Oklahoma, and whoever is playing Notre Dame! If Notre Dame and Oklahoma are playing each other, I just root for them both to lose! This man was the head coach at Notre Dame for one week, and then he had to resign because he had falsified his résumé. And as he got off the phone with a reporter who broke the story, he was overheard to say, "What am I going to tell my mother?"

When the devil gets close and you feel all alone, ask yourself: *If I do this, what am I going to tell my Father?*

God bless you. God bless your ministry. And God bless the United States of America.

4

Search the Scriptures

JOHN 5:39 KJV

Morris H. Chapman
President and Chief Executive Officer,
Executive Committee of the Southern Baptist Convention

YOU NEVER KNOW HOW PEOPLE are going to respond to a message. All of us who preach the gospel have had various responses. I read a story about Dr. George Stewart, who preached a sermon one Sunday morning. In the message he used the word *britches.* Now I suppose that was in the day before the word was commonly used as we use it today. After the service Dr. Stewart, as was his custom, stood in the vestibule of the church. One of the dear ladies of the church came by to greet him. As she took his hand, she said, "Dr. Stewart, I can't understand it. A man of your dignity, a man of your grace, a man of your sophistication, using the word *britches.*"

He replied, "Did you hear anything I said before I said *britches?*"

She responded, "Well, no."

He asked, "Did you hear anything I said after I said *britches?*"

She said, "I guess not."

He declared, "Then I'm glad I said *britches,* or you wouldn't have heard one word of my sermon."

Listen, God has a word for Southern Baptists. That word is our chart and our compass. That word is our pillar of cloud by day and pillar of fire by night. That word is our lamp and our light. That word is pure and precious. That word is the full and final authority. Jesus was talking to religious scholars of His day when He said,

"Search the scriptures; for in them ye think ye have eternal life: and they are they which testify of me" (John 5:39).

He was talking to highly intelligent men who counted every letter, weighed every word, and scrutinized every sentence of the Scriptures. But they were still strangers to the truth. They had spent their lives searching the Scriptures, but they had failed to find the Savior. What a waste! What a tragedy! Men have spent their lives in the pursuit of truth, but they have found themselves in bondage to their own thoughts and their own theories. But I tell you the truth, the theories of men come and go but "the word of the Lord endureth for ever" (1 Pet. 1:25).

I. The Performance of God's Word

You ask, "Why search the Scriptures?" To know the truth. Jesus said, "If ye continue in my word, . . . ye shall know the truth, and the truth shall make you free" (John 8:31–32). As we search the Scriptures, I want us to see the performance of God's Word. As we do, I want to be certain we refocus our thoughts upon the vital issue of the holy, written Word of God. The Bible is its own best commentary, and it builds verse by verse, truth upon truth. The Bible says, "For ever, O LORD, thy word is settled in heaven" (Ps. 119:89).

Now what is settled in heaven ought to be settled on earth. What is settled with God ought to be settled with Southern Baptists. We have long said we have no creed but the Bible and no need to defend the Bible. It needs no defense. I agree, but we do need to defend how the Bible is represented to the people, by the people, and for the people called Southern Baptists. Some people divide us into liberals and fundamentalists. Others divide us into moderates and conservatives. Still others talk about the left and the right. But it is not a matter of the right turn or the left turn; it is a matter of the right turn or the wrong turn.

Years ago, J. Sidlow Baxter warned about the weakened condition of the modern church. He said, "The root cause is a defective attitude toward the Bible. If we are shaky there, we are shaky everywhere." He forecast division within denominations over this issue.

In expressing his belief in the plenary inspiration of God's Word, he said, "There will never be unity of purpose and action until there is unity of conviction about the Bible. That is not to limit the right of every man to interpret for himself what is in the Bible. There has never been complete uniformity of interpretation, but there must be unity of attitude toward the Bible, or there is simply no final authority."

May I say to you from the depths of my heart that we will never get beyond our discord until we with one accord search the Scriptures. God is calling us today to a collective conviction and to a cooperative spirit. They should go hand in glove. The Bible is the inspired Word of God, the very breath of God. The Bible is the infallible Word of God, for God cannot lie, and the Bible never misleads or deceives. The Bible is the inerrant Word of God because God breathed out His perfect Word. The Bible says, "The law of the LORD is perfect" (Ps. 19:7). All Scripture is given by inspiration of God. When God breathed out the Bible, He breathed a perfect Word. Just as our Lord Jesus was conceived to be without sin, God's written Word, the Bible, was breathed upon this earth without error.

Some people say, "I believe in functional inerrancy." Functional inerrancy is a figment of someone's imagination. God decided to breathe out His Word without error. He breathed out the substance of Scripture. Whether we allow it to function in our hearts is a separate matter. God gave us the Bible without error and—make no mistake about it—when He inspired the Holy Word of God, He inspired not only the men; He inspired the very substance of His message.

II. The Permanence of God's Word

In light of the permanence of God's Word, what must we do? We are to *profess the Word*. Jesus said to those Pharisees, "Had ye believed Moses, ye would have believed me: for he wrote of me" (John 5:46). And He said, "If ye believe not [Moses'] writings, how shall ye believe my words?" (John 5:47). We know Jesus had the highest respect and love for the Old Testament. He believed it implicitly. He constantly quoted Old Testament Scripture. He obeyed

God's Word perfectly. The Lord knows the way through the wilderness, and that way is the Word of God. During His temptation in the wilderness, Jesus quoted from the book of Deuteronomy. Three times Jesus said, "It is written."

In response to the first temptation, Jesus said, "Man shall not live by bread alone, but by every word that proceedeth out of the mouth of God" (Matt. 4:4). Proverbs says, "Every word of God is pure" (Prov. 30:5). Never has there been a generation that more desperately needs the truth than our generation. We must raise up generation after generation of our young people to *hear* the Word, to *heed* the Word, and to *herald* the Word to the next generation. In generations past, some have said, "Thus saith Bruner." Others have said, "Thus saith Barth." Still others have said, "Thus saith Bultmann." Some have even said, "Thus saith Beethoven!" But the Bible says, "Thus saith the LORD God."

In recent years there has been a cry for us to return to our Southern Baptist heritage, our historic Baptist principles and practices. Therefore, I have a question. What did our forefathers intend in the establishment of colleges which would bear the Baptist brand? Now I know that Southern Baptists have only indirect influence on our college campuses because they are owned by our state Baptist conventions, but listen to what the Convention said in the 1913 annual session in St. Louis. It comes from a report by the Christian Education Committee.

The report says, "If we hope to bring this world to the foot of the cross and the glory of the crown, let us not undervalue our work in Christian education. The denomination ought to have such control of its colleges as will make speedy correction possible when the college begins to veer from the doctrine or spirit of the New Testament." The report goes on to say, "The Baptist preacher who does not keep himself informed as to the educational interests of his denomination and who does not take a deep, abiding and intelligent interest in the same, needs to grow in the grace and in the knowledge of our Lord and Savior Jesus Christ."

In the Convention session in 1922 in Jacksonville, Florida, the "Report of the Committee on the Report of the Education Board" said, "If textbooks *cannot* be found which are not destructive of the faith of the students in the inspiration and inerrance of the Bible, the teachers in such departments ought to be of such pronounced faith in the Bible and of such learning in their departments as to be able to so explain the defects of the textbooks as to magnify the message of the Bible rather than to discredit it."

In 1925 Southern Baptists said, "Because we have solidified ourselves according to the beliefs of God's Holy Word, we need to find a way to cooperate together. We need to establish the distinctives of our faith." And in that year both our Baptist Faith and Message and our Cooperative Program were born. To this day these commitments of faith and practice have run on those parallel tracks. We must never allow either of them to be derailed.

I thank God for the professors I had in the Baptist college I attended and in the Baptist seminary I attended. I want to say to the professors of this great Southern Baptist Convention, I thank God for you and encourage you to teach the Word of God as nothing but the truth. A professor is one who professes, and there is nothing greater than to profess the Lord Jesus Christ as Savior and as Lord of our lives. Every Baptist college professor ought to be a Christian, born again into the kingdom of God.

We are a people of the faith who believe in the inspired, infallible, inerrant Word of God. We need professors in our Baptist schools, colleges, and seminaries who believe in the inspired, infallible, inerrant Word of God. Isaac Newton said, "If all the great books of the world were given life and were brought together in one convention, the moment the Bible entered, all other books would fall on their faces."

On this day we must stay the course that was blazed in the past by our fathers in the faith. Then our young people will have the joy of sitting at the feet of professors who believe in the historicity of the first eleven chapters of Genesis; in the miracles of the Old and New Testaments; and in the virgin birth, the sinless life, the sacrificial, substitutionary death, the bodily resurrection, and the literal return of our Lord Jesus Christ. Vance Havner said, "You can't tell it like it is if you don't believe it like it was."

It is not uncommon for faith to flounder in the academic classrooms of higher education, but let it not be so with those who are called Southern Baptists. Unwavering faith must forever flourish on the campuses of our Baptist schools. R. G. Lee once said, "We have the higher education, but it is evidently not high enough to get us where we ought to be. We have the new chemistry and the new psychology, but they do not give us a new heaven and a new earth." Do you want to know the importance of education, the right kind of education? You only need to read the book of Daniel.

King Nebuchadnezzar had a plan to win over the allegiance of the most brilliant young people of Judah who had been captured by the Babylonian army. He determined to accomplish his scheme through education. He ordered Daniel and his three friends—Hananiah, Mishael, and Azariah—to be taught the language and the literature of the Babylonians. In other words, he attempted to undermine their faith.

He sought to confuse them; he changed their names because all of them in some way incorporated the name of the true God.

Daniel: El-Elohim
Hananiah: Ah-Yahweh
Mishael: El-Elohim
Azariah: Ah-Yahweh

Nebuchadnezzar said, "I'm changing your names," and Daniel became Belteshazzar, Hananiah became Shadrach, Mishael became Meshach, and Azariah became Abednego (see Dan. 1:6–7). He sought to confuse them and to compromise them. He attempted to get them to eat food that was against Levitical law under which they had been trained. But notice their defense. Daniel purposed in his heart that he would not defile himself. Do you know why? Because these four young men, before Nebuchadnezzar ever seized them, were taught as boys to walk by faith and not by sight. They were men of conviction. They were men of courage. Dear Southern

Baptists, we not only need our conviction; we need the *courage* of our conviction. There is nothing to lose and everything to gain.

These four young men stood before the king, and their faith set them apart. The Bible says none were quite like them. They stood fast in their faith. But notice the subtlety of Satan. Generations later in the Christian church, we teach our children to sing the pagan names of Shadrach, Meshach, and Abednego. We still have the Babylonian gods at our doorsteps. Let us sing about Hananiah, Mishael, and Azariah—those names associated with the living God.

Our hope for world missions lies in our students who are worshipping in our churches and who are walking on our campuses. Yet the hour is late. Other world religions are pouring millions of dollars into Africa, Asia, and South America to reach people, especially young people, and to disciple them. But I believe we are poised and ready for the greatest mobilization of missionaries in human history.

Not only are we (1) to profess the Word, we are (2) to practice the Word. The Bible says, "If we live in the Spirit, let us also walk in the Spirit. Let us not be desirous of vain glory, provoking one another, envying one another" (Gal. 5:25–26). The Resolutions Committee considered a one-year moratorium on resolutions this year. We have a greater need. We need a resolution that declares a moratorium on name bashing and character assassination. This denomination is not a demolition derby. Conviction and compassion are not mutually exclusive. A person's conviction must never be compromised, but they can be expressed in the spirit of unconditional love. Both absolute truth and unconditional love were born in the heart of God and must abide in the hearts of Southern Baptists.

We need more personal conferences with one another and fewer press conferences. We make our decisions in a democratic form of government. We must not have friend against friend and brother against brother. I know there are some who have the spirit of fear, but let me appeal to you: The Bible says, "God hath not given us the spirit of fear; but of power, and of love, and of a sound mind" (2 Tim. 1:7). If there is any fear in your heart, the Bible says, "God is our refuge and strength, a very present help in trouble" (Ps. 46:1).

"Be still, and know that I am God" (Ps. 46:10). When we do that, He says, "I will be exalted among the heathen, I will be exalted in the earth" (Ps. 46:10). That phrase "be still" literally means "cease striving."

III. *The Person of God's Word*

I have shown you the permanence of God's Word. It is settled in heaven, and it will endure forever. There is the person of God's Word. "They are they which testify of me" (John 5:39). Jesus and the Bible are inseparably linked together. When you love the written Word, you will love the Living Word. When you love the Living Word, you will love the written Word. The person of the Word is our dear Lord Jesus Christ. The Bible says, "His name is called The Word of God" (Rev. 19:13). Whose name? The name of Jesus. Jesus is saying, "Search the Scriptures and search again until you find the scarlet thread through the Bible."

IV. *The Power of God's Word*

There is the person of the Word as well as the permanence of the Word, and then there is the power of the Word. Jesus said, "All power is given unto me in heaven and in earth" (Matt. 28:18). He is the sovereign power. We see Jesus as the sovereign King, the suffering Savior, and the compassionate Shepherd. As the sovereign power, "The earth is the LORD's, and the fulness thereof; the world, and they that dwell therein" (Ps. 24:1). Regardless of what we face, our Lord Jesus Christ reigns supreme. "He is before all things, and by him all things consist" (Col. 1:17). Whether it is now or whether it is later, "every tongue should confess that Jesus Christ is Lord" (Phil. 2:11). I tell you, Jesus Christ is Lord of all. He is Lord of heaven above; He is Lord of earth beneath; He is Lord of hell below.

To know the sovereign power of God, we must guard every day against any personal pride that may come into our lives. We must surrender any desire for prominence, prestige, position, or power. The words on our lips must be, "He must increase, but I must decrease" (John 3:30). He is sovereign power, and He is the saving power. As Abraham and Isaac marched up Mt. Moriah, Isaac asked his father, "Where is the lamb for a burnt offering?" (Gen. 22:7). And in a trembling voice Abraham said, "The Lord will provide an offering." That is the first mention of the Lamb in the Bible. And the question is raised, "Where is the Lamb?"

The Old Testament is a search for the Lamb. As lambs were laid upon the altars of sacrifice, thousands upon thousands asked the question, "Where is the Lamb?" The question is not answered until you go through Matthew, Mark, Luke, and you finally come to the Gospel of John. For the first time in the New Testament, the Lamb is mentioned. As John the Baptist stands on the banks of the River Jordan and sees the Lord Jesus Christ coming, he says, "Behold the Lamb of God, which taketh away the sin of the world" (John 1:29). When Jesus died upon the blood-stained cross of Calvary, He paid for our sins.

Let us tell the old, old story that Jesus saves. Let us stand before those walls, those Jericho walls of doubt and disbelief, and let all the people send out the great shout. Let all the people shout the sounds of salvation, and the walls will fall down flat! God said in His Word, "My word . . . shall not return unto me void . . . it shall prosper in the thing whereto I sent it" (Isa. 55:11).

Jesus is also the sustaining power: "The LORD is my shepherd; I shall not want. . . . Surely goodness and mercy shall follow me all the days of my life" (Ps. 23:1, 6). I don't know what you're facing, but whatever the disappointment, whatever the discouragement, whatever the distress, whatever the depression, Jesus says, "Come unto me, all ye that labour and are heavy laden, and I will give you rest" (Matt. 11:28).

Goodness takes care of our steps, and mercy takes care of our stumbles, and we need a touch of glory. We need a touch from God. We need to pray, "Restore unto me the joy of thy salvation" (Ps. 51:12).

The Spirit of God ignited the fires of revival in Wales one day in February 1903 at a youth church meeting. A little girl who had just been saved stood up and said, "I love the Lord Jesus Christ with all my heart." Her unrehearsed testimony electrified the meeting, and in three months one hundred thousand people had come to Christ.

Jesus says, "Search the scriptures; for . . . they are they which testify of me" (John 5:39). And God's Word says, "Ye shall seek me, and find me, when ye shall search for me with all your heart" (Jer. 29:13). God has the answer. We must be on our faces before Him so that when we stand for our convictions, we stand with an unconditional love that says to the world, "I love the Lord Jesus Christ with all my heart." May it be so with each of us, with all of us.

5

Our No-Fear Culture

ACTS 9:31 NKJV

O. S. Hawkins
President, Annuity Board of the Southern Baptist Convention

NO FEAR. Those two words seem to be tattooed across our culture. In fact, they even appear as the brand name of a popular apparel company. The phrase, "no fear," speaks volumes about who we have become in our current culture.

Unfortunately, in a day when the culture of a secular society has infiltrated the church, it has brought with it a "no-fear" philosophy. When was the last time we heard a message in the modern church cover a topic like the fear of the Lord? When was the last time we even heard anyone mention such a thing as the fear of the Lord? And yet, this phrase, "the fear of the Lord," is woven throughout the fabric of more than three hundred verses in the Bible.

Our Western culture is in the midst of a serious credibility and integrity crisis. Our leaders have descended to such a level that past public moral scandals seem to be more commonplace than out of the ordinary. This climate says more about the American people than it does about the American politician. It says more about the American pew than it does about the American people. The salt has lost its savor. But, in reality, it says even more about the American pulpit than it does the American pew.

What is missing in the church today? The difference between the modern church and the early church can be found in two words, *influence* and *power*. The early Christians did not have enough influence to keep Simon Peter out of jail, but they had enough power to pray him out. Today the church seems to speak less of any kind of spiritual power while it prides itself on its influence. The early church engaged its culture and transformed it.

What did those believers have that we seem to have lost? In many ways we have much more than they did. We are far more educated. We have far more in the way of technological methods to be used in the kingdom expansion. We have television, radio, air travel, e-mail, computers, the Internet, and our personal Web pages. But along the way we have lost something very important: we have lost the concept of "walking in the fear of the Lord." It is said of the early church that they "had peace and were edified. And walking in the fear of the Lord and in the comfort of the Holy Spirit, they were multiplied" (Acts 9:31).

What an incredible insight! They were "walking in the fear of the Lord." Who is doing that today? Who even knows what it means, much less gives it a thought? So much of the church in the Western world today is anemic in confronting the culture. Many modern church growth gurus encourage us to minister according to polling data and popular opinion. We often criticize those in politics for abdicating true leadership in favor of leading by popular polling data they have obtained and then simply furnishing their constituents with what they want instead of what they need. But the church often does the same thing. One church recently revealed how its musical selections for worship were selected by doing a survey of which radio stations their congregants most enjoyed. The church's music style was then determined by the wants of the people. Such completely man-centered ministries may ultimately dethrone doctrinal truths related to the nature of God, the nature of man, and the nature of sin in favor of a self-help, feel-good-about-yourself philosophy that is void of the idea of "walking in the fear of the Lord."

Many churches today are filled with "felt-need" hearers and how-to motivational messages. Some even refer to this as a new reformation centered on the importance of self-esteem with little mention of things such as sin, judgment, or the fear of the Lord—and consequently less mention of the need of anything as drastic and archaic as repentance. In many circles the pastor is looked upon more in terms of a corporate executive whose main concern lies in the realm of marketing and sales.

We have raised several generations in America who do not know the "rest of the story." We are convinced that people prefer to hear about God's love, mercy, kindness, and His unconditional acceptance regardless of our lifestyles. When the subject of God's wrath, judgment, or fear surfaces, many people are quick to respond, "Oh, my God is not like that." The monthly periodical *Current Thoughts and Trends* gives the following quote from a well-known popular pastor: "I don't think anything has been done in the name of Christ and under the banner of Christianity that has proven more destructive to human personality, and hence counterproductive to the evangelistic enterprise, than the unchristian, uncouth strategy of attempting to make people aware of their lost and sinful condition."[1]

In the midst of a modern "no-fear" culture, some churches are emerging into what appears to be nothing more than impressive self-help clubs and motivational assemblies. Much of what takes place in church growth philosophy today is foreign to the New Testament pattern of church growth. "Walking in the fear of the Lord" is one of the lost elements in modern church growth mentality and methodology. Why is "the fear of the Lord" the lost phrase in our church vocabulary? What is the "fear of the Lord"? How can it be rediscovered in our generation? Why? What? How?

I. A Why Question

Why is it that we live with a no-fear mentality in our culture? Perhaps it is because our generation knows little of the nature of God. We have lost a sense of the holiness of God. This reverence has been exchanged for a "good buddy" image of God. Some of us are out of balance in our market-driven approach to church health and growth. We often tailor our church ministries to appeal to the selfish, self-centered desires of those we are striving to reach.

There is little mention of the nature of a holy God in the modern church. We have replaced Him with the idea of a sort of contemporary "buddy" who is into backslapping and giving high fives. Job did not see God on this level. When confronted with the holiness of God he said, "I abhor myself, and repent in dust and ashes" (Job 42:6). When John saw God's holiness and glory on Patmos, the Bible says he "fell at His feet like a dead man" (Rev. 1:17 NASB). We have developed an ecclesiastical no-fear-of-God culture primarily because, in a dearth of doctrinal truth, we have lost our concept of the holiness and awesomeness of our Creator God.

We have lost our way and have such little discernment that we compliment the Hollywood elite for such television offerings as *Touched by an Angel*. Christians clamor about how wonderful it has been to have had such a prime-time television series. But its "angels" are a far cry from angels we read about in the Bible. They are a mixture of New Age deceptions. One angel in the program tells us, "There is a piece of God in each of you." Any "angel" who denies the necessity of the cross and promotes a feel-good, no-condemnation approach to human problems is often, and sadly, embraced by a world that is searching for spiritual truth. Should we be surprised that the Bible warns of those who masquerade as "angels of light," twisting the Word, hiding the gospel, and offering false promises that blind the eyes of unbelievers and believers alike?

The Lord Jesus came to bring forgiveness to sinners, not to tell them that they are all right and that they simply have a self-esteem problem. He said the world hated Him because He testified that its works were evil (John 7:7). While more and more churches place doctrinal truth on the bottom shelf in favor of self-help, market-driven approaches, the church knows less and less of a holy God and never even thinks of "walking in the fear of the Lord."

This concept of the fear of the Lord held a prominent place in Old Testament worship. We remember how Noah "moved with godly fear," built the ark (Heb. 11:7). Before dying on Mt. Nebo, Moses challenged the Israelites with a question, "Now Israel, what does the LORD your God require of you, but to fear the LORD your

God" (Deut. 10:12). Then years later, after conquest of the promised land, his successor, Joshua, assembled the people and said, "Now fear the LORD and serve him with all faithfulness" (Josh. 24:14 NIV). This element of "walking in the fear of the Lord" winds its way throughout the experiences of the Old Testament saints.

This same emphasis found its way into the Gospels during the ministry of Christ. The virgin Mary herself, with the Christ alive in her womb, reminds us of this in her sweet song as she sings, "His mercy is on those who fear Him" (Luke 1:50). When Zacharias's speech returned after the birth of John the Baptist, it is said that "fear came on all who dwelt around them" (Luke 1:65).

This attitude of fear, a holy reverence, is prevalent among believers throughout the Gospels. After the Lord healed the paralytic man, the Bible records that those who observed this miracle "were all amazed, and they glorified God and were filled with fear" (Luke 5:26). Again, when Jesus visited the city of Nain and healed the widow's son, the Bible records that "fear came upon all, and they glorified God saying, 'A great prophet has risen up among us'; and 'God has visited His people'" (Luke 7:16). When the Lord Jesus sent out the Twelve, he said, "Do not fear those who kill the body but cannot kill the soul. But rather fear Him who is able to destroy both soul and body in hell" (Matt. 10:28). And the women who came to the empty tomb after the resurrection "went out quickly from the tomb with fear and great joy, and ran to bring His disciples word" (Matt. 28:8).

Not only do we find the concept of "walking in the fear of the Lord" woven through the Old Testament and the Gospels; it also appears on practically every page in the book of Acts, describing the early church. It was there at the birth of the church. After Peter's remarkable proclamation at Pentecost, "fear came upon every soul, and many wonders and signs were done through the apostles"(Acts 2:43).

In Acts 5, when Ananias and Sapphira met their untimely death at the hands of the Holy Spirit, the Bible records that "great fear came upon all the church" (Acts 5:11). After the conversion of Saul of Tarsus, we read that the early church ceased growing by addition and began to multiply and went forward "walking in the fear of the Lord" (Acts 9:31). When Simon Peter preached to Cornelius's household in Caesarea by the Sea, he proclaimed that "in every nation whoever fears [God] and works righteousness is accepted by Him" (Acts 10:35). In the great apostle Paul's first recorded sermon, at Pisidian Antioch, he addressed his hearers with these words: "Men of Israel, and you who fear God, listen" (Acts 13:16). When Paul visited Ephesus and performed miracles, we are told that "fear fell on them all, and the name of the Lord Jesus was magnified" (Acts 19:17).

One cannot read the accounts in the book of Acts without seeing the prominent part that "walking in the fear of the Lord" played in the explosive growth of the first-century called-out ones.

When we close the pages of the Acts of the Apostles and move into the Epistles, we find this theme continuing to weave its way throughout the whole Bible. Paul spoke often of it to the first-century churches and to us. To the Romans he lamented about a people who had "no fear of God before their eyes" (Rom. 3:18). He admonished us in this dispensation of grace to "stand by faith. Do not be haughty, but fear [the Lord]" (Rom. 11:20).

To the Corinthians Paul said, "Therefore, having these promises, beloved, let us cleanse ourselves from all filthiness of the flesh and spirit, perfecting holiness in the fear of God" (2 Cor. 7:1). He continues by reminding them that Titus's "affections are greater for you as he remembers the obedience of you all, how with fear and trembling you received him" (2 Cor. 7:15). In an often-quoted passage to the believers at Ephesus, he reminds us to submit "to one another in the fear of God" (Eph. 5:21).

Other New Testament writers beat this same drum. The writer of Hebrews sums it up by saying, "Therefore, since we are receiving a kingdom which cannot be shaken, let us have grace, by which we may serve God acceptably with reverence and godly fear" (Heb. 12:28). Simon Peter in his epistle admonishes us to "honor all people. Love the brotherhood. Fear God. Honor the king" (1 Pet. 2:17). In one of the most personally challenging passages in the Bible, Peter calls upon believers to "sanctify the Lord God in your hearts, and always be ready to give a defense to everyone who asks you a reason for the hope that is in you, with meekness and fear" (1 Pet. 3:15).

Not only is the idea of the importance of "walking in the fear of the Lord" woven throughout the Old Testament, the Gospels, the Acts of the Apostles, and the Epistles; but it is also there in the Apocalypse. In that coming grand and glorious day when the amens and alleluias are heard around the throne, we are told there will be a great voice coming from the throne saying, "Praise our God, all you His servants and those who fear Him, both small and great!" (Rev. 19:5).

The modern church is faced with a *why* question. Why do we have a no-fear culture in the modern church? The Old Testament saints, those in the Gospels, those in the early church, and those gathered around the throne in heaven—all have something in common that is separate and apart from much we see in the church today. What is the missing element? Those before us were all found "walking in the fear of the Lord." Our church culture has little concept of the holiness and awesomeness of God. We have forgotten that God is watching, that "the eyes of the LORD are in every place, keeping watch on the evil and the good" (Prov. 15:3). Do we really believe that truth will win in the end? Our no-fear culture scoffs at the idea of future divine judgment. It is seldom, if ever, mentioned in modern pulpits.

The concept of the fear of the Lord could well be the single most important missing element in the church of the Lord Jesus Christ in our day. The answer to the question of *why* lies in the fact that many of us have lost our sense of reverence and awe in our relationship with our sovereign Lord. When we rediscover the holiness of God, which comes in understanding the great doctrinal truths, we will have the same healthy and wholesome fear that characterized the Old Testament saints, those who followed Christ in the Gospels, and those who made up the early church. Then we too will know the power and peace that comes with "walking in the fear of the Lord."

II. A What Question

What is the fear of the Lord? Does it mean we must live in constant fright and flight? Does it mean that we must live in fear of God in the way one might who is terrorized by a gang leader in the neighborhood? Is it living with the idea that God has a big hammer and is just waiting to smash us at the slightest sin we might commit? People who have grown up with physically or emotionally abusive parents might confuse the fear of the Lord with the unhealthy fear of an abusive father or mother. Sadly, perhaps too few of us really know what it means to be walking in the fear of the Lord, as did those in Scripture who came before us.

In the Old Testament, the most common Hebrew word translated into our English word *fear* means "to stand in awe with reverence and respect." This word describes a person who recognizes the power, purity, and position of another and offers him respect. This concept is hard to find in an ecclesiastical culture that prides itself on portraying God as "one of the boys," who is often addressed in prayer like one would address another over a hamburger. Some of us seem to be losing our sense of reverential awe in our relationship with the Father.

The most common word used in the New Testament to translate this word *fear* can best be described as a reverential fear of God as a controlling motive of life in matters both spiritual and moral. This is not so much a fear of His awesome power and righteous retribution as it is a wholesome fear of displeasing Him. When you read of the fear of the Lord in Scripture, it does not make you feel like you have to cower down in God's presence for fear of being hit or slapped down or embarrassed. It is the thought of bowing before Him in awe and reverence for who He really is, an awesome Creator God in total control of His creation and worthy of all respect, love, praise, and worship. Walking daily in the fear of the Lord moves us to a submissive recognition of His lordship and results in a passionate longing to live in trust and obedience.

The fear of the Lord is a healthy concept for the believer. It is a reverential awe, a sense of being afraid of offending our holy God in any way. It is not simply intellectual assent to an idea. It is a consciousness that the believer lives with continuously. It comes from a daily surrender of our lives to Christ.

Surrender. Now there is a word we seldom hear today. Preachers of old used to call men and women to "surrender" their lives to Christ. We used to sing, "All to Jesus I Surrender." Not today. We are too self-sufficient for such a concept. We speak of flexing our own spiritual muscles. Today we speak of "committing" our lives to Christ. "Walking in the fear of the Lord" does not come from a pumped-up kind of self-induced commitment but from a surrender to Jesus Christ as Lord.

What happens to a church culture when walking in the fear of the Lord is a forgotten concept? There emerges a sort of antinomian attitude that exhibits little restraint of evil. Paul speaks of a people who had "no fear of God before their eyes" (Rom. 3:18). Moral failures by pulpit ministers are epidemic in our generation. Within a short period before this writing, several Southern Baptist pastors of my personal acquaintance have shocked their churches and devastated their families. One left his family and his church for a woman in his wife's prayer group. Another left his family and his church in favor of his former secretary. Another returned from a mission trip to announce he had fallen in love with a fellow traveler. Then he resigned his church and walked away from his family. Another left his wife and children and pulpit to move in with a woman he had met on the Internet. Still another resigned his church after being arrested for picking up a prostitute in his city. And the beat goes on! How does this happen? Could it be we are reaping the results of a generation of church leaders who have "no fear of God before their eyes"?

There are other by-products of one who does not "walk in the fear of the Lord." There is little respect for submission to authority. Paul admonishes us to be "submitting to one another in the fear of God" (Eph. 5:21). Do we wonder why there is such a problem with submission to authority in the home, at school, in the workplace, in the civic arena? When the salt loses its savor, when the church ceases to engage its culture, when we have no concept of walking in the fear of the Lord, a lack of submission is the natural result.

The church we read about in Acts saw corruption and attack from without. They came under great persecution at the hands of the Roman Empire. As we live in the third millennium, our danger no longer is from without so much as from within. We seem to be living in Jude's day. Jude spoke of a church that would become corrupt from within. He metaphorically presents a shocking picture of what is taking place in much of modern church growth. He speaks of a day when churches would be led and attended by those who are "without fear" (Jude 12). He describes the individual who has no fear of God before his eyes as a hidden reef, a cloud without rain, a tree without fruit, a wild wave of the sea, and a wandering star out of orbit.

Jude cites in verse 12 several characteristics of those in the church who manage and minister "without fear." He says they *lack peace*. He uses the metaphor of "spots [hidden reefs] in your love feasts." The picture is one of hidden rocks or reefs below the surface of the water and unnoticed by the naked eye. These unexpected dangers can cause a boat to be grounded and to begin to leak. Many churches sailing across the waters of love and fellowship have been "grounded" by individuals who lived "without fear" and who destroyed the unity of the fellowship of faith.

Jude also indicates that these types of people within the church also *lack* productivity. They are, in his words, like "clouds without water, carried about by the winds." They appear to be full of wonderful prospects for the future. However, they are filled with empty promises. They never produce spiritual results. They look good and say all the right words, but they possess nothing of substance, and they are blown around by the next thing that comes out of a success magazine.

Jude says these people who live "without fear" are exposed not only by a lack of peace and a lack of productivity but also by a *lack of* proof. They are like "autumn trees without fruit." The Lord Jesus said, "You will know them by their fruits" (Matt. 7:16).

Jude continues by showing another characteristic by which these disrespectful people may be known. They also *lack* purity. In Jude's words, they are like "raging waves of the sea, foaming up their own shame" (v. 13). That is, they will eventually expose themselves.

For fifteen years I lived on the Atlantic coast. When the weather is calm, the ocean is crystal clear. But when the storms come and the winds of the hurricane season begin to blow, the ocean begins to churn. Those raging waves bring up filth and debris from the ocean floor and deposit it with its foam upon the shore. A beach stroll in the aftermath of a storm reveals a multitude of rotting fish and all sorts of trash from the ocean floor now on the beach for all to see. Jude says that those who live "without fear" are eventually exposed by their lack of purity.

Finally, Jude illustrates one other characteristic—a lack of purpose. He says these people are like "wandering stars for whom is reserved the blackness of darkness forever." Those who are not "walking in the fear of the Lord" have no real direction, no purpose in life. Who of us has not seen a shooting star, a piece of the cosmos gone wrong, out of orbit, racing across the night sky. Its brilliance is dazzling. And then, as quickly as it appeared, it disappears into the darkness of the night. God placed the stars in their courses in the heavens. Stars have orbits in which they operate. They have direction and purpose. Those "without fear" are like these wandering stars out of orbit. They do not want any structure. They do not like things like statements of faith. They do not want to play within any boundaries.

In a no-fear culture that has invaded the church of the Lord Jesus Christ, we need more than ever "to contend earnestly for the faith which was once for all delivered to the saints" (Jude 3). When the church is "walking in the fear of the Lord," the result is vibrant and productive.

Recently my home church had a reunion of hundreds of us who were active during our high school and college years. It had been a quarter of a century since some of us had seen one another. I had no real church background until I was converted at the age of seventeen.

My life was radically transformed, and I immersed myself in the life and ministry of Sagamore Hill Baptist Church in Fort Worth, Texas. Our pastor and role model, Dr. W. Fred Swank, was pastor there for more than forty years. Over one hundred young men surrendered to the gospel ministry and are preaching around the world today as a result of God's call and our pastor's example and encouragement.

Going back "home" after all those years brought back a myriad of memories. I saw several girls I had dated as a young man—now middle-aged like myself—whom I had not seen in years. I was thankful I could look them all in the eye with no regrets. I had remained morally pure. How? We were all tempted in our day as young people are today. But we had something few young people seem to have today. We had a healthy and wholesome concept of the fear of the Lord. It was not the fear of being beaten down by God for any little slip along the way. It was a reverence, an awe of His presence and holiness that we acquired from hearing Him lifted up and exalted from a Bible preacher whom we loved and respected and who was himself a paragon of faithfulness. My fear was not that God might lay a hand on me but that He might take His hand off me! I feared disappointing God who had done so much for me.

When we are walking in the fear of the Lord, there is imparted to us a power to overcome our sinful desires and habits. Solomon reminds us that "by the fear of the LORD one departs from evil" (Prov. 16:6). After receiving the law on Sinai, Moses told his people that "God has come to test you, and that His fear may be before you, so that you may not sin" (Exod. 20:20).

When we are "walking in the fear of the Lord," we receive supernatural wisdom and understanding. The wisest man in the Old Testament put it like this: "The fear of the LORD is the beginning of wisdom" (Prov. 9:10). It is also the avenue into true worship. David said, "In fear of You I will worship toward Your holy temple" (Ps. 5:7).

Walking in the fear of the Lord was a constant theme of the psalmist. He relates how it can bring supernatural deliverance: "The angel of the LORD encamps all around those who fear Him, and delivers them" (Ps. 34:7). It is a channel through which the mercy of the Lord can flow to you. The psalmist says, "Great is His mercy toward those who fear Him" (Ps. 103:11). When we "walk in the fear of the Lord," it brings joy to the Father's heart as the psalmist reveals when he says, "The LORD takes pleasure in those who fear Him" (Ps. 147:11).

Recently my wife Susie and I were in a department store in one of our favorite shopping malls. As we were picking out a few items, I noticed a small security video camera mounted high on a wall and pointed in my direction. I mentioned it to the sales attendant and asked if we were being watched or if we were on television! He chuckled and replied, "Oh, it is not real, but just the fact that people think they are being observed in what they are doing is a deterrent to theft and crime."

God's camera is everywhere you go. "His eyes are upon everyone, observing the good and the bad" (see Prov. 15:3). If you are conscious of this, it will bring a healthy fear that will keep you from trouble and disgrace. How is it that fallen preachers have become an epidemic in our generation? Could it be that the church has lost something? Could it be that we are not walking in the fear of the Lord as did so many of those who went before us?

The question for us is not simply a *why* question but a *what* question. The fear of the Lord is a conscious awareness that God is watching and that we can only approach Him in reverence and awe, not so much for what He has done but for who He is. It is not the fear that He might put His hand on us in retribution. It is the fear that He might take His hand of anointing and blessing off us! This is the real essence of walking in the fear of the Lord.

III. A How Question

How can we walk in the fear of the Lord in the midst of a no-fear culture that has infiltrated not only our society but also many of our churches? We begin with the one who has been given the responsibility of leading the only group in the world that lives with a cultural mandate from the One who created it all and who is controlling it all. We begin with the leadership of the local New Testament church. When the church of the Lord Jesus Christ has a healthy concept of the fear of the Lord, it then becomes salt and light to its community. Then walking in the fear of the Lord, we will be "multiplied" (Acts 9:31) like the Jerusalem church. We will begin to engage our culture and raise high the standard of righteousness, which is the only thing that truly exalts a nation.

In order to maintain a wholesome and healthy fear of the Lord, we must recapture the concept of the seriousness of sin. Tolerance is not only the buzzword for our secular society but for many churches as well. Many people simply ignore the seriousness of sin. Some simply laugh it off as though it were of their small vices. Others excuse it by insisting that everyone else is doing it, and that it is just a part of living in a twenty-first-century world. Still others minimize it by convincing themselves that their sin is not as bad as some things others are doing.

But God said He would destroy man because of sin. Yes, He waits with great mercy and patience for the sinner to repent, but in the absence of repentance, God ultimately will destroy the sin and the sinner with it. He is serious about our sin, so serious that He sent His Son to a Roman cross. Satan is at work in our world to destroy everyone. When we live with no fear of God, we play right into Satan's hands.

So where do we begin to recover this vital concept of walking in the fear of the Lord? We begin with the Word of God. Before the Israelites entered the land of promise, God instructed Moses to gather the people and read to them from the law "that they may hear and that they may learn to fear the LORD, . . . and that their children, who have not known it, may hear and learn to fear the LORD your God as long as you live in the land which you cross the Jordan to possess" (Deut. 31:12–13). Our spiritual ancestors made their conquest of the land by learning to walk in the fear of the Lord, and they learned it through the hearing of God's Word.

The major reason walking in the fear of the Lord is a lost concept in the modern church is that exposition of the Word is not a high priority. Many modern church growth gurus are forecasting that sermons of the twenty-first-century church should be no more than fifteen minutes in length to accommodate attention spans of biblically illiterate hearers and should be entirely topical in nature. Thus, we will raise another generation that knows little of the Word of God, much less the seriousness of sin. The fear of the Lord is imbedded in us only by the planting of the Word in our hearts.

How do we learn to fear the Lord? By hiding the Word of God in our hearts. Moses recounts how God instructed him to "gather the people to Me, and I will let them hear My words, that they may learn to fear Me" (Deut. 4:10). God desires that His people hear His words. Why? So they may learn to fear Him! The primary reason the church lives with so little fear of God today is the dangerous lack of doctrinal truth emanating from the modern pulpit. Not enough pulpits lift up the awesome majesty of the Lord Jesus Christ before the people.

Walking in the fear of the Lord is a choice. Solomon tells of people who "did not choose the fear of the LORD" (Prov. 1:29). It is a choice. We must make a decision to fear Him. The Word of God always brings us to a crisis decision, a choice between right and wrong, good and evil.

When I was in high school, my dad always wanted to know where I was, what I was doing, with whom I was doing it, and when I would be home! Although I did not admit it at the time, I was really glad he cared. My parents made a lot of personal sacrifices for me, one of which was the acquisition of my 1956 Chevrolet. The fact that the year was 1965 did not really matter to me. I was so proud of that old car!

Unlike a lot of my friends, I had a curfew. On a given night I was gathered with my friends at the local drive-in restaurant and had forgotten about the time, which was about an hour after I had been instructed to be home. Into the parking lot drove my dad. He parked his car, got out, and then caught my eye across the parking lot. Without saying a word, he simply stared at me and then pointed to his wristwatch. He got in his car and drove off. I beat him home! Why? I feared my dad. Oh, not physically. The truth is, I could most likely have handled him physically at the time. What I really feared was that after all he had sacrificed for me, after all he had done in a thousand ways to show his love for me, I might disappoint or dishonor him.

As I think about that, I am convinced that this is the kind of fear and reverence that came upon the early church. It was more of a fear of disappointing the One who had given His all for them. Their passion was not so much to be made happy in His sight but to be made holy. For them, walking in the fear of the Lord was a conscious choice that came from an abiding love, knowledge of His Word, and a deep appreciation for His sacrifice.

When we speak of walking in the fear of the Lord, we are not talking about living with an unhealthy fear of retribution. You will not get very far trying to raise a kid like that. An atmosphere where one dodges in fear of a slap every time he spills the milk is far from the biblical concept. As children of God, we should live in the fear that something we do or say might bring dishonor to Him and might disappoint the One who loves us so much that He gave Himself for us.

Balance is the key. There are two extremes at work today that need to be avoided. One extreme develops in the mind an attitude of tolerance and permissiveness so that "anything goes." This extreme makes a mockery of God's holiness and judgment. The other extreme overemphasizes the "fire and brimstone" passages in the Bible and knows little of God's tender mercies and lovingkindness. This can develop into a psychosis of fear that has no room for compassion and grace.

The good news is that God loves us so much that He has provided a way for us to obtain forgiveness. We do not have to pay the penalty for the sins we have committed. The sacrificial, atoning death of the Lord Jesus Christ has covered our sins. Thus, we do not live with the fear of God in the sense of being condemned. But we do walk in the fear of the Lord in the sense of acknowledging His worth and refusing to do or say anything that might disappoint or dishonor Him.

The writer of Ecclesiastes sums it up beautifully in the conclusion of his book. "Let us hear the conclusion of the whole matter: Fear God, and keep his commandments: for this is the whole duty of man" (Eccl. 12:13 KJV).

1. Quoted in *Milk & Honey,* December 1997, 4.

6

Mission and Missions

MATTHEW 9:35–38; 10:1, 5 HCSB

James T. Draper, Jr.
President, LifeWay Christian Resources
of the Southern Baptist Convention

THE RECENT EXPLOSION of the space shuttle *Columbia* continued a long list of tragedies that made headline news. A few weeks before the loss of *Columbia,* Jerry Rankin, president of our International Mission Board, announced the murder of three missionaries in Yemen. All of this reminds us of the danger of our day, the issues at stake, and the fragile nature of life. *Life* is not a necessity; *death* is a necessity. Life is a prolonged miracle, and every day that God gives us is a gift from Him. It must be handled with care as we respond to God and seek to be what He would have us to be.

There is a difference between *mission* and *missions*. Mission is God's purpose for the world. Mission is what God is about. Mission is the heart of God that does not desire that any person should perish but that all should come to repentance. Mission is what God was about when He sent Jesus Christ in the incarnation into this world as the Savior of the world to die on the cross. That was God's mission. The purpose of God's invasion of history in the person of Jesus was that people might know of the grace of God, the love of God, and the offer of forgiveness and salvation that is so desperately needed by every person.

That is God's mission. That has not changed. God is still on mission. His mission is that everyone might hear the gospel of the kingdom. Matthew 24:14 says the gospel "will be proclaimed in all the world as a testimony to all nations. And then the end will come." So whenever God concludes history and whenever the Lord comes back, it will be in fulfillment of His purpose, of His mission.

Now we do missions, but it is God's mission. This passage in Matthew 9 is the greatest characterization, the greatest description of how God sees His mission as it relates to His church, how God looks at what we're to be about. When we grasp that, we will begin to accomplish the mission that God has for us.

"Then Jesus went to all the towns and villages" (Matt. 9:35). Now Matthew is talking about Galilee. You will recall that Jesus had set up His headquarters, His command post, in Capernaum. You remember the account of Jesus' healing Simon Peter's mother-in-law? That was in Capernaum. That's where Jesus had His headquarters, but He didn't stay there.

Jesus went to all the towns and villages of that region. He got up from the comfort zone of His headquarters, and He went to all the towns and villages in Galilee, "teaching in their synagogues, preaching the good news of the kingdom, and healing every disease and every sickness" (Matt. 9:35). When He saw the crowds, He had compassion on them because they were worn out like sheep without a shepherd. Then He said to his disciples, "The harvest is abundant, but the workers are few. Therefore, pray to the Lord of the harvest to send out workers into His harvest" (vv. 37–38). Chapter 10 of Matthew begins simply by saying that Jesus summoned His twelve disciples and gave them authority. Then verse 5 tells us that He sent out the Twelve "after giving them instructions."

I want us to see five things that result from our understanding of God's divine mission as seen in this passage. It results from our understanding of what God is about.

I. The Divine Mission Demands That We Go as Jesus Went

Jesus did not stay in Capernaum. He got up and went to where the people were. Whatever else that means for us, it means that we do not fulfill our purpose by going to a church building. It is not the purpose of the church to see how many people we can get into the church building. Our purpose is to go where the people are. There is no such thing as "come and hear" in the gospel mandate. It's always "go and tell." We're to go where the people are.

We find that pattern throughout the New Testament. When the disciples began to witness and preach in Jerusalem following the resurrection of Jesus, they went to the temple. They went to the place where the people were. They always went where the people were. If we're going to be on God's divine mission, if we're going to understand our part, it means that we have to go. We have to get out into our communities and into the neighborhoods, the housing projects, and every place. Out there—that's what the gospel is for. It is not just for us to enjoy. It is a sacred trust for us to share. So the divine mission demands that we go as Jesus went.

II. *The Divine Mission Demands That We See as Jesus Sees*

This passage says very simply, "When He saw the crowds" (Matt. 9:36). How something is seen differs with each person or thing that sees. I'm told that a hawk can see a dime on the sidewalk below from the top of the Empire State Building. I'm not sure what a hawk would be doing in New York or why it would need a dime, but nevertheless, people claim that its vision is so good that it can see a dime from that great distance.

On the other hand, the kingfisher bird has two kinds of seeing. When he soars over the water looking for fish, he has a lens that will allow him to see into the water. When he dives into the water, the lens changes, and he can see underwater so he can grab the fish.

Soldiers, military people, police officers, and firefighters often wear infrared goggles so they can see in smoke or in the dark. That is a way of seeing. There are electron microscopes that doctors use to see on an atomic level. And though it's an oxymoron in language, there are radio telescopes that allow us to probe the outer reaches of space.

Seeing varies from person to person, but the question comes back to us: How do we see people? When you are late getting to work or school and all those people are crowding the highways, how do you see them? As people who are in your way? As people who are obstructing your progress? Do you see them as a nuisance? Perhaps you just wish they would get out of the way! How do you see people?

The retailer sees people as individuals whom he wants to sell something to. A doctor may see people as patients and someone whom he needs to treat. An artist may look at people and see individuals he wants to paint. A writer or an author may see people as objects of a story. How do you see people? Jesus saw the multitudes in their desperate condition. He saw them weary and worn out. He saw them distracted, damaged, attacked, isolated, hurting. Jesus saw them as they were. As His followers, we have to see people as Jesus saw them.

We have to begin to look at the exploding population of this world the way Jesus looks at it. Right now there are 6.2 billion people in the world. By the year 2050 there will be 8.9 billion people. Now a billion is more than any of us can imagine. I doubt if any of us will ever have to worry about that amount in our bank accounts. If we had one billion dollars in one-thousand-dollar bills, and if we stacked them straight up one on top of the other, the stack would be one hundred and twenty feet taller than the Washington Monument. That is incomprehensible! That's just one billion. But there are 6.2 billion people in the world.

Our International Mission Board tells us that there are 1.7 billion people in the "last frontier," people who have never heard the gospel. Let me tell you how critical that is. If we took all our missionaries with the International Mission Board who are career missionaries—about 5,500 of them, and if we doubled that this year, so that next year we would have 11,000—and if we assigned them to these last frontier people, we would have only one missionary for every 177,000 people.

Let me put it in perspective. Let's say there's half a million people in a specific metropolitan area of the United States. If this half a million people represented the last frontier people, we would have only two or three people preaching the gospel in that entire metropolitan area.

That is the real world we live in. Jesus wants us to see the world as He sees it. And it's not just a shame that people don't have the gospel. It matters as to eternity that they have never heard the gospel, because the gospel is the good news of hope for forgiveness and salvation. The gospel is the good news of God's gift, the offer of eternal life. We're going to have to see as Jesus sees the world. So the divine mission demands that we go like Jesus went, and it demands that we see like Jesus sees.

III. The Divine Mission Demands That We Feel as Jesus Feels

The Scripture before us says simply that Jesus "felt compassion" (v. 36). Your translation may say that He was "moved" with compassion.

I provided transportation for a missionary from Japan to a retreat years ago when I was a college student. We got to talking about this verse. I remember vividly what he said. He said there was no word in the Japanese language for *compassion*. So the translators of the Japanese Bible rendered this verse as, "Jesus loved them until it hurt."

Recently I pulled out my Greek New Testament, and I looked to see what word from the Greek language is translated as "compassion." It is a technicolor word. It is an explosive word in its meaning. The root word means "the chief intestines," the viscera of the human body, the bowels. It hurt Jesus through His whole being. Jesus saw these people, and He didn't just see their need. He didn't just observe their pain. He *felt* their pain. He hurt through His innermost being in the depths of His body. Jesus hurt for those people. He felt for them. The divine mission demands that we not share the gospel with detachment, that we not simply observe the suffering of the world with interest but that we empathize, hurt with, feel with people.

There is a difference between sympathy and empathy. If I sympathize with you, I observe your pain, and I feel sorry for you. But if I empathize with you, I *feel* your pain. And that's what Jesus did. Jesus felt the needs of the people. He not only saw the needs; He felt the needs. It was something that moved Him to the depths of His being. This was so different from others in His day. The religious leaders of Jesus' day didn't react to needs like that. Annas and Caiaphas, high priests, would literally drive people with whips out of the temple to keep them away. How differently Jesus looked at these people. He felt for them, hurt deeply for them.

We live in a world that conspires to insulate us from feeling. Everything about our culture tends to make us calloused. Everywhere we see violence, murder, war, disease, tragedy, and devastation. We see so much of it that we often just observe it casually. Our whole culture has insulated us. Perhaps it started for many of us during the Vietnam War when Walter Cronkite would give us blow-by-blow descriptions during the supper hour of what had happened in Vietnam that day. We began to be exposed to all of the tragedies and horrors faced by our soldiers and our men and women who were fighting for freedom.

Add to that everything we see today, and it is devastating. An explosion in Lagos, Nigeria, an explosion at a plant in South Carolina, the explosion of the space shuttle *Columbia*, the murder of missionaries, suicide bombers, and on and on it goes. These are things that we see or hear about every day! And it blunts our sensitivity. If the church is going to accept its part in the mission of God, we're going to have to feel as Jesus feels.

What would have to happen to us to make us feel the way Jesus felt? We've had many opportunities. We wept with the families of those who were killed on September 11, 2001. We wept with families of our missionaries who were killed in Yemen. Our daughter called us recently and asked if we had seen the news. We had not turned on the news that morning. That was the day the space shuttle

Columbia exploded. She told us about it and then burst into tears. She didn't know those people, but something in her identified with what had happened.

What would have to happen to us to make us feel again? What would have to happen to us so we didn't just casually observe a world around us, but somehow we saw people as they really are—human beings who are distracted, devastated, hurting, and dying? When Jesus saw the multitudes, He was moved with compassion. From the depths of His being, He felt for them.

IV. The Divine Mission Drives Us to Pray to the Lord of the Harvest

So the divine mission demands that we go; it demands that we see; it demands that we feel. But the divine mission also demands that we pray to the Lord of the harvest. That's what Jesus said, and this is really not our natural tendency. Our response to almost anything is to appoint a committee or a task force. But Jesus saw the people. He was moved because they were weary, worn out, devastated, isolated, attacked, and hurt. So He said, "The harvest is abundant, but the workers are few. Therefore pray to the Lord of the harvest to send out workers into His harvest" (Matt. 9:37–38).

Beseech or pray the Lord of the harvest. This is the distinction I made at the beginning. This is God's mission. We have to understand that. The whole emphasis on reaching a world with the gospel—that's God's idea. That's God's mission. If we don't understand that, we'll look at all the needs around us and grow despondent because we're helpless to meet those needs.

I remember the first time I went to New York City as a young pastor. I drove down the streets of Manhattan and up into Long Island, then over into New Jersey. I realized that from the top of the Empire State Building I could see the rooftops of 22 million people, which was one-tenth of the population of the nation at that time. Suddenly I was overwhelmed! "God, how can we reach these people?" I prayed. We can look at the world like that, and we can become despondent because we don't know what to do. Or we can take the other extreme and become frantic in our activity, doing this and that, running here and there, trying somehow to meet the need. But Jesus said, "No, you're not supposed to do either one of those things. You should pray the Lord of the harvest."

Notice that Jesus didn't tell us to pray *for* the harvest. I don't know how many times as a pastor I asked God to give us a great harvest. And people prayed, "God, give us a harvest." God never told us to pray for the harvest. God says that the harvest is already there. It's out there ready to be gathered. Pray that the Lord will send laborers into the harvest.

I want to tell you something. There is a harvest all around us. We don't have to pray for the harvest, but we have to pray that God will send people to gather the harvest. It's there! It's always ripe! Jesus said to the disciples, "Don't you say, 'There are still four months, then comes the harvest'? Listen to what I'm telling you: Open your eyes and look at the fields, for they are ready for harvest" (John 4:35). We must pray that the Lord of the harvest will send laborers into the harvest.

We are in the greatest era of mission opportunity that the world has ever seen. There's never been a time like this. We can connect to the world easily. I get e-mail from all around this globe—from people everywhere! We have the opportunity through the technology of our day, through the travel that is available, and the open doors that we have to share the gospel as it has never been presented before. We have to be willing to make whatever changes are necessary to meet the challenges before us. We need to tell God that our answer is yes to whatever He calls us to do.

We need to pray, "Lord, send laborers into the harvest," and "Lord, here am I, send me." We must pray out of a sense of surrender to His will, out of a sense of surrender to His purposes for our lives, because it's His mission. We pray the Lord that He will send laborers into the field.

Perhaps it would help us if we viewed this great mission movement as a mighty river. Our missions are carried along on God's mighty mission river. That mission river flowed out of a rock in the highlands of Galilee when Jesus gave the Great Commission to His church. It flowed through Pentecost and the early disciples, Peter and the other disciples. It flowed through the early years of Christian history, and then there was a period of time when it seemed to flow underground. It was almost unseen through the dark times of the Middle Ages, but then it emerged again with groups like the Moravian Brethren in Europe and the Baptists of England. And there were William Carey and Hudson Taylor, and this great river emerged in more modern times. Throughout the history of this great mission river, it has swept thousands and thousands of people along its course.

But we must remember that this is God's mighty mission river. We do not carry the river; the river carries us. It is His mission river. It was here before us, and without us. If the Lord tarries, it will be here after us and without us. It is His mission. He does not depend on us. We depend on Him. It is God's great mission river that carries us along in its course.

Sometimes we ask the wrong question. Sometimes we ask what the place of missions is in our lives. We look at missions as if it is a piece of a puzzle, and somehow that piece is missing. So we try to find where we can place that piece. Where does missions fit into our lives? But the real question is, Where does my life fit into missions? That's the real issue. For God's people, for those of us who know Jesus Christ, it's not a question of trying to fit God's mission into our busy lives. It is how do we fit our lives into God's mission, or even better, how does God fit our lives into His mission? Pray the Lord of the harvest that He will send laborers into His harvest.

V. The Divine Mission Ultimately Demands That We Do Missions

So the divine mission demands that we go as Jesus went, see as He sees, and feel as He feels. It also drives us to pray the Lord of the harvest. And it ultimately demands that we do missions ourselves. After Jesus had gone, seen, felt, and prayed, He sent forth the Twelve. There comes a time when we have to quit talking about it and do it, when we have to quit dreaming about it and do it. The divine mission ultimately drives us to do missions.

Jesus *did* something. That's what the incarnation is all about. When God loved the world, He sent His Son. Jesus came from heaven to earth. God's Son, a missionary—God's Son fulfilling God's great mission to reveal His love, His grace, and His mercy. Jesus came to where we are; it was incarnational. And missions, our part in God's mission, is incarnational. That's why we don't just send videos and books overseas to people who need to be reached. We go because nothing can take the place of being there and doing missions in the flesh.

The divine mission ultimately means that we must do missions. John 3:16 does not say that God so loved the world that He appointed a committee or He assigned a task force. No, He sent His Son. In one of the most dramatic pictures in the Bible, God speaks to Moses and says, "I have observed the misery of My people in Egypt, and have heard them crying out because of their oppressors, and I know about their sufferings. I have come down to rescue them" (Exod. 3:7–8). That's the heart of mission.

The divine mission ultimately demands that we do something. God is not a God of remoteness. He is a God of nearness. It is not that God is everywhere; it is that God is where I am. God is here. He is within. He is with us. He is Emmanuel, God with us. And we're to be the extension of the nearness of God in His great mission to reach this world.

One of the great, mostly unknown chapters in missions history involves the first missionaries to the Caribbean. When we talk about missions history, we hear that the modern missionary movement began with William Carey going to India in about 1792. What is not as well known is that sixty years before that, in the 1730s, two laymen, Moravian Brethren, came from Denmark to St. Thomas in the Caribbean as missionaries to share the gospel.

That fact in itself is startling, but the story is even more impressive. King Christian VI was going to have his coronation as king of Denmark. A delegation came from St. Thomas to Denmark for the coronation of the king. Among that delegation was an African man who had been brought to St. Thomas as a slave. He was a Christian slave. He approached the Moravian Brethren while he was in Denmark, and he begged them to send some missionaries to St. Thomas to preach the gospel. He mistakenly told them that if they came, they would have to sell themselves into slavery in order to preach the gospel.

Two laymen, Leonard Dober, a potter, and David Nitschman, a carpenter, felt in their hearts that God wanted them to go to St. Thomas, sell themselves into slavery, and begin to witness among the people on the island of St. Thomas. It was one of those dramatic moments that historians love because the announcement came at 3:00 A.M. It was a foggy, drizzly, cold morning when Count Zinzendorf, who headed up the Moravian Brethren at that time, stepped out on the balcony of his apartment and spoke to those gathered, including Leonard Dober and David Nitschman, and gave them permission to go to St. Thomas to preach the gospel.

Leonard Dober and David Nitschman came to St. Thomas. To their surprise they discovered that they did not have to sell themselves into slavery. Their passion to follow the call of God to do missions was so great that they came prepared to become slaves. Before there was ever another missionary, before anyone ever came to establish churches or to preach the gospel, there were thirteen thousand converts who were baptized in the Caribbean basin. Churches were begun on St. Thomas, St. Croix, St. John's, Jamaica, Antigua, Barbados, and St. Kitts. All across that area the gospel was proclaimed, thousands were saved, and churches were established. But it all happened because two laymen, understanding that we do missions as part of God's mission, came to St. Thomas to sell themselves into slavery if necessary so they could share the gospel of Jesus Christ.

We have to go, and we have to see as Jesus did. We have to feel as He felt. We have to pray the Lord of the harvest to send laborers into the harvest. But ultimately the divine mission demands that we *do* something.

Now I want to ask you to do something. I want to ask you to come before God in your heart to say, "Lord, my answer is yes. Whatever that means, I'll be praying and giving. If You open the door for me to go, I'm willing, Lord. My answer is yes. I want to do missions as part of Your great mission. It's Your mission, and I want to be part of what You're doing."

7

No Ordinary God: Why the Biblical Doctrine of God Matters

DANIEL 4:28–37 NASB

R. Albert Mohler, Jr.

President, The Southern Baptist Theological Seminary

THROUGH THE PROPHET JEREMIAH, God spoke these words: "Let not a wise man boast of his wisdom, and let not the mighty man boast of his might, let not a rich man boast of his riches; but let him who boasts boast of this, that he understands and knows Me, that I am the LORD" (Jer. 9:23–24). The highest aspiration of the human soul and mind must be to know the one true and living God, to enjoy Him, and to serve Him with gladness.

The good news is that a vast majority of Americans report a belief in God. Indeed, pollsters indicate that only a bare fraction of Americans are atheists or agnostics. If you take these data at face value, you would think America must be experiencing a great revival and spiritual recovery. This is hardly the case, however. Do Americans live as if they believe in a God of holiness who hates sin? Do Americans fear a God of wrath who shall surely judge sinners? Do Americans find their security in a God of omnipotence who holds all creation by the power of His might and the exercise of His providence? Do Americans believe in a God who created the heavens and the earth? Do Americans find their hope in a God who is rich in mercy? I think not. The bad news is that the God in whom millions of Americans believe is not the God of the Bible.

A remarkable insight into the contrast of this apparent religious belief with genuine faith in the living God is found in a study of the British population. Like Americans, the great majority of Britons report a belief in God. The pollsters then asked a revealing question: "Do you believe in a God who can change the course of events on earth?" One man's response was taken as so indicative of the public's general view that his answer became the title of the study. Do you believe in a God who can change the course of events on earth? "No," he replied, "just the ordinary one."[1]

Just the ordinary God, he said—meaning a God in whom you believe for a pollster but not a God who rules the universe, not a God who can change your life, surely not the God of Abraham, Isaac, and Jacob, clearly not the holy Trinity of the Father, the Son, and the Holy Spirit.

This man's response is sadly indicative of modern belief in God. It is not a true belief at all but superstition at best. We are standing once again where the apostle Paul once stood at Mars Hill in Athens. Acts chapter 17 tells us that Paul stood in the midst of the Areopagus and said, "Men of Athens, I observe that you are very religious in all respects. For while I was passing through and examining the objects of your worship, I also found an altar with its inscription, 'TO AN UNKNOWN GOD.' Therefore, what you worship in ignorance, this I proclaim to you" (Acts 17:22–23).

Our message must be the same: "Men and women of America, we observe that you are very religious in all respects. We have seen your altars and your crystals; we have heard your prayers and have watched your lives; we have observed your worship and heard your conversations. What you worship in ignorance, this we proclaim to you."

The unavoidable truth is that most modern Americans do not know God. Ignorance of basic biblical truth is rampant and now expected. People are perishing because of a lack of knowledge. Remarkably, this is a problem inside, as well as outside, the church. Many church members are as ignorant of the true and living God as is the general public. Too many pulpits are silent and compromised. The "ordinary God" of popular belief is the only God known by so many. The God of the Bible is as unknown in many pews as He is unknown in the world at large.

The problem is rooted in the godlessness of our age and in the secularization of our culture. The disease is also present in much of what is called "modern theology." For too long we have had theologians who have told us that God is doing the best He can under the circumstances. For too long we have been told that we must outgrow the primitive belief in God found in the Bible. For too long we have been told that God lacks the power to effect His will. For too long we have seen the God of the Bible replaced with the God of the modern theologians—a God who generally means well but cannot accomplish His will. This God is a spectator, not a sovereign.

I want to bring in a witness to set this case with clarity. This is an unlikely witness but a man with a powerful testimony. His name is Nebuchadnezzar. Once of the greatest kings of all history, one of the most effective builders, one of the most illustrious warriors, one of the most brutal tyrants ever to sit on a throne—Nebuchadnezzar, king of Babylon. Three times he attacked Judah. Three times he defeated the children of Israel. Historians record that Nebuchadnezzar took the Jews into captivity. The Bible records that God raised up Nebuchadnezzar in judgment against His own chosen people.

The book of Daniel records that Nebuchadnezzar was troubled by dreams, and that the prophet Daniel faithfully interpreted these dreams as warnings from God that Nebuchadnezzar would be judged. The judgment surely came, as we find in Daniel 4:28–37:

All this happened to Nebuchadnezzar the king. Twelve months later he was walking on the roof of the royal palace

of Babylon. The king reflected and said, "Is this not
Babylon the great, which I myself have built as a royal residence by the might of my power and for the glory of my
majesty?" While the word was in the king's mouth, a voice
came from heaven, saying, "King Nebuchadnezzar, to you it
is declared: sovereignty has been removed from you, and
you will be driven away from mankind, and your dwelling
place will be with the beasts of the field. You will be given
grass to eat like cattle, and seven periods of time will pass
over you, until you recognize that the Most High is ruler
over the realm of mankind and bestows on it whomever He
wishes." Immediately the word concerning Nebuchadnezzar
was fulfilled; and he was driven away from mankind and
began eating grass like cattle, and his body was drenched
with the dew of heaven until his hair had grown like eagles'
feathers and his nails like birds' claws. But at the end of
that period, I, Nebuchadnezzar, raised my eyes toward
heaven and my reason returned to me, and I blessed the
Most High and praised and honored Him who lives forever; For His dominion is an everlasting dominion, and His
kingdom endures from generation to generation. And all
the inhabitants of earth are accounted as nothing, but He
does according to His will in the host of heaven and among
the inhabitants of the earth; and no one can ward off His
hand or say to Him, "What have You done?" At that time
my reason returned to me. And my majesty and splendor
were restored to me for the glory of my kingdom, and my
counselors and my nobles began seeking me out; so I was
reestablished in my sovereignty, and surpassing greatness
was added to me. Now I, Nebuchadnezzar, praise, exalt
and honor the King of heaven, for all His works are true
and His ways just, and He is able to humble those who
walk in pride.

Nebuchadnezzar—whose very name invoked a pagan deity—
came to know and worship the one true and living God—the Most

High—and to bear witness to His power and glory. The God of Daniel, the God who reduced the proud Nebuchadnezzar to the state of a wild beast, the God who restored Nebuchadnezzar's power and reign—this is no "ordinary God." Nebuchadnezzar was among the world's most successful kings. It was he who built the great hanging gardens of Babylon—one of the seven great wonders of the ancient world. He had defeated all the known powers of his day, from Egypt to Judah and to every point on the compass. He had built an empire, and millions of people were under his sovereignty. As he walked on the walls of the royal palace that fateful day, he was filled with a pride the world could easily understand. "Is this not Babylon the great, which I myself have built as a royal residence by the might of my power and for the glory of my majesty?" (v. 30).

Nebuchadnezzar is a fitting example of the egotistical pride that has so thoroughly infected our own society and age. America—and much of the modernized world—is experiencing a "Nebuchadnezzar moment" of self-centered pride. Is not this America the great, which we ourselves have built by the power of our own might, and to the glory of our own democratic majesty? Are we not the world's only superpower? Did we not split the atom, wage war against our enemies, and rule the forces of nature? Are we not the center of the information revolution, the capital of economic energy, the exporter of culture, the protector of freedom?

The same pride can infect our smaller kingdoms as well. Is this institution, this corporation, this congregation, this denomination not what we have built? And to whose glory?

Nebuchadnezzar discovered that the living God will allow no competitors, and will eventually make His will known. The word from the sovereign of all creation was this: "King Nebuchadnezzar, to you it is declared: sovereignty has been removed from you" (v. 31). The proud king was reduced to eating grass like the cattle, roaming with the beasts, and appearing as a wild and wet bird. He was driven from mankind and expelled from his royal palace. The king's humiliation was complete. But the same God who humbled Nebuchadnezzar brought him back to his senses when he raised his eyes toward heaven. With his reason restored, Nebuchadnezzar praised and honored the Most High.

Listen to his testimony: "For His dominion is an everlasting dominion, and His kingdom endures from generation to generation" (v. 34). Nebuchadnezzar came to know what a real dynasty was like. He also discovered the One who rules all creation. "All the inhabitants of earth are accounted as nothing, but He does according to His will in the host of heaven and among the inhabitants of the earth" (v. 35). What about real power? "And no one can ward off His hand or say to Him, 'What have You done?'" (v. 35).

The Christian doctrine of God is rooted in this most fundamental truth—that God and God alone is sovereign. The Bible reveals so much about the true and living God, and without this revealed knowledge we would know nothing of Him, for He is incomprehensible and beyond the reach of our creaturely investigation. There is much we cannot know of God, for as the apostle Paul said, "How unsearchable are His judgments and unfathomable His ways" (Rom. 11:33).

There are questions we should not ask. Martin Luther, the great reformer, reminded his own students of this truth. In his "Table Talk" he told his students this story: "When one [student] asked, where was God before heaven was created? St. Augustine answered: He was in himself. When another asked me the same question, I said: He was building hell for such idle, presumptuous, fluttering and inquisitive spirits as you."[2] I can assure you that every seminary professor has been tempted to answer some irritating and troublesome students the same way!

This God is one, and He is the only God. That most basic truth is found in the Shema—that central verse in the Old Testament (Deut. 6:4): "Hear, O Israel! The LORD is our God, the LORD is one!" This great revelation set the true worship of Israel over against the myriad of paganisms all around them. That great central truth is followed by the great commandment: "You shall love the LORD your God with all your heart and with all your soul and with all your might" (Deut. 6:5).

This God who is one is also three persons: Father, Son, and Holy Spirit. The Trinity is not an accessory doctrine to Christianity; it is our most central doctrine. This great doctrine sets the worship and witness of the church of the Lord Jesus Christ over against all the rampant paganisms of our own day. The doctrine of the Trinity is the most fundamental starting point in which everything else we know of God is rooted. As the early church confessed, the Father, the Son, and the Holy Spirit are three persons, each "very God of very God," fully divine—of one essence—*one true God.*

The God revealed in the Bible is a personal God, not an impersonal force. He is Spirit, but He is not only a vague Spirit who animates the universe; He is both Spirit and person. The God of the Bible relates to His creatures, and that relationship is genuine and personal.

God is self-existent and self-sufficient. He depends upon nothing and is complete in Himself. God is the only uncreated being, and He brought all creatures into being. He is eternal—there never was a time when He was not; there never will be a time when He is not; and He himself is the Creator of time. When Moses asked His name, God responded: "I AM WHO I AM" (Exod. 3:14). His name establishes His eternity and self-existence.

This is a good reminder to us that God does not need His creatures, but He chooses to glorify Himself through them. Our God is a God of glory. The Bible is rich with passages about the glory of God—the radiance of His deity and the effulgence of His majesty. There is no one like Him and no one to whom He can be compared. The more we know Him, the more we see His glory, and the greater we glorify Him.

God never changes. As the great hymn resounds, "There is no shadow of turning"[3] in Him—He is not forced to change His will or His ways. God's character is also unchanging. This is a great comfort to His people. Our God is not quick to anger, and He keeps His promises. As the Lord stated in Malachi 3:6, "For I, the LORD, do not change; therefore you, O sons of Jacob, are not consumed."

Words fail to express the greatness and majesty of God, but we must do our best with the words at our disposal. Several key words describe important attributes of God—truths about Him we must know and confess.

God knows all things—past, present, and future. There is nothing hidden from His sight. God never learns anything, for He has no need of learning. We describe this as His *omniscience*. God's knowledge is all-encompassing and perfect. As A. W. Tozer has written: "God knows instantly and effortlessly all matter and all matters, all mind and every mind, all spirit and all spirits, all being and every being, all creaturehood and all creatures, every plurality and all pluralities, all law and every law, all relations, all causes, all thoughts, all mysteries, all enigmas, all feeling, all desires, every unuttered secret, all thrones and dominions, all personalities, all things visible and invisible in heaven and in earth, motion, space, time, life, death, good, evil, heaven, and hell."[4]

God's infinite and comprehensive knowledge is also a *foreknowledge*. God does not wait to see what will happen; He rules by the power of His will and by the determination of His foreknowledge. As Nebuchadnezzar boldly stated: "He does according to His will in the host of heaven and among the inhabitants of earth; and no one can ward off His hand" (Dan. 4:35). This should come as great comfort to God's people, for we are safe in the care of the One who knows the future, and rules the future as well as the past and present. God knows all the people of the earth, and He knows us better than we know ourselves.

As David expressed this truth: "O LORD, Thou hast searched me and known me. Thou dost know when I sit down and when I rise up; Thou dost understand my thought from afar. Thou dost scrutinize my path and my lying down, and art intimately acquainted with all my ways. Even before there is a word on my tongue, behold, O LORD, Thou dost know it all" (Ps. 139:1–4).

God not only knows all, but He is everywhere at once. God is always near us, and we cannot escape His presence. We refer to this as God's *omnipresence*. David knew this and asked: "Where can I go from Thy Spirit? Or where can I flee from Thy presence? If I ascend to heaven, Thou art there; if I make my bed in Sheol, behold, Thou art there. If I take the wings of the dawn, if I dwell in the remotest part of the sea, even there Thy hand will lead me, and Thy right hand will lay hold of me" (Ps. 139:7–10). God's omnipresence reminds us that all creation is His and that He is never far from us.

Stephen Charnock set this right when he explained that "God is essentially everywhere present in heaven and earth. If God be, He must be somewhere; that which is nowhere, is nothing. Since God is, He is in the world; not in one part of it; for then He would be circumscribed by it: if in the world, and only there, though it be a great space, He were also limited."[5]

There is far more to say, for God is not only omnipresent and omniscient, He is also *omnipotent*. The Lord is almighty and holds all power. In the Old Testament He is revealed as *El Shaddai*—God Almighty. As Nebuchadnezzar reminds us, "No one can ward off His hand" (Dan. 4:35). He is the source of all that is, and of every power. There is no power in heaven or on earth that can thwart His plans, frustrate His will, or force His hand.

Kings may think themselves powerful, but like Nebuchadnezzar they will discover their limits. Nations exult in their power, but as the prophet Isaiah stated, "All the nations are as nothing before Him, they are regarded by Him as less than nothing and meaningless" (Isa. 40:17). This is a cogent and prophetic word to our own nation. The Lord is the only all-powerful One, and all the nations will bow before Him one day. No force, no power, no king, no president, no nation, or even all the powers of the universe combined, can stay His hand or force His action.

In his vision, the apostle John saw the great multitude of heaven "as the voice of many waters, and as the voice of mighty thunderings, saying, Alleluia: for the Lord God omnipotent reigneth" (Rev. 19:6 KJV).

God is revealed to us in terms of these biblical attributes. To these already listed must be added His faithfulness, goodness, patience, love, mercy, supremacy, grace, glory, infinitude, majesty, wisdom, and wrath.

At the foundation of all these attributes are two great truths of which we must be ever mindful. The first of these is God's total, final, and undiluted sovereignty. Our Lord is not only the Creator of all; He rules over all. God's sovereignty is the exercise of His rightful authority. His omnipotence, omniscience, and omnipresence are the instruments of His sovereignty. Nebuchadnezzar's great discovery was that there is one true sovereign of all creation—and His name is not Nebuchadnezzar. The one true and living God is the sole sovereign, and He shares His sovereignty with no other power. What was Nebuchadnezzar's response? "Now I, Nebuchadnezzar, praise, exalt and honor the King of heaven, for all His works are true and His ways just, and He is able to humble those who walk in pride" (Dan. 4:37).

Job discovered this when he was called to answer God. Was God really able to rescue Job, and was He really sovereign after all? Job knew, and he rightly answered, "I know that Thou canst do all things, and that no purpose of Thine can be thwarted" (Job 42:2). The sovereignty of God is one of the most compromised doctrines within the church, and this is to our everlasting shame. So many who think themselves Christians believe in a God who means well, but cannot seem to make His will determinative—or a God who is needy and requires our help to accomplish His will—or a God who is not quite sure what He wants done in certain circumstances. This is not the God of the Bible.

As A. W. Pink famously observed: "The conception of Deity which prevails most widely today, even among those who profess to give heed to the Scriptures, is a miserable caricature, a blasphemous travesty of the Truth. The God of the twentieth century is a helpless, effeminate being who commands the respect of no really thoughtful man. The God of the popular mind is a creation of a maudlin sentimentality. The God of the present-day pulpit is an object of pity rather than of awe-inspiring reverence."[6]

Pink's words were written almost seventy years ago, and the situation is far worse today. Some theologians who dare to call themselves evangelicals now speak of the "openness of God" and deny His omnipotence and omniscience. These theologians must revise their understanding of divine sovereignty, and what is left is no sovereignty at all. As one former Southern Baptist states: "God sets goals for creation and redemption and realizes them ad hoc in history. If Plan A fails, God is ready with Plan B."[7] This is a denial of God's sovereignty. The God revealed in the Bible needs no Plan B.

The other fundamental truth about God refers to His character. God is holy. Isaiah heard the seraphim cry, "Holy, Holy, Holy, is the LORD of hosts, the whole earth is full of His glory" (Isa. 6:3). God does not and cannot sin. He is absolute righteousness, for He is the standard for righteousness and holiness. There is not the slightest imperfection in God, for He is pure and perfect.

Since the Hebrew language has no comparatives or superlatives, words are repeated for emphasis. From Isaiah's vision we learn that God is not merely holy or even holy, holy; but He is holy, holy, holy—infinite holiness. All that belongs to God is holy. His presence marks holy ground. His temple is a holy place, and His altar was in the holy of holies. The church of Jesus Christ is a holy nation, and we preach God's holy Word, the holy Scriptures.

Holiness is the quintessential attribute of God's moral character, and it defines all other attributes. God's power is the power of holiness; His omniscience is a holy knowledge. God's love is a holy love, even as His wrath is a holy wrath. The doctrine of the wrath of God has been banished from far too many pulpits, but God's holiness cannot be understood apart from His determination to punish sin. There are few doctrines as thoroughly grounded in Scripture as the doctrine of God's wrath. Jesus Himself taught that God would judge all persons and that He must punish sin. Paul reminds us that "the wrath of God is revealed from heaven" (Rom. 1:18). John the Baptist warned that we should "flee from the wrath to come" (Matt. 3:7). Yet God has made a provision for us through the shed blood of Jesus Christ, who for sinners bore God's wrath against sin.

A holy God demands and deserves a holy people, and thus we are called to be holy as well.

Nebuchadnezzar came to know the Lord Most High, the one true God. There is coming a day when every creature will come to know God, when every knee shall bow and "every tongue [will] confess that Jesus Christ is Lord, to the glory of God the Father" (Phil. 2:11). In the meantime it is our task and glory to bear witness to the true and living God. As our Lord prayed in His final hours on earth: "This is life eternal, that they may know thee the only true God, and Jesus Christ, whom thou hast sent" (John 17:3 KJV).

While others may preach a dehydrated deity, let us bear witness to the God who revealed Himself in the Bible—the God who is our Creator, our Redeemer, our Deliverer, and our King. Let us tell of His greatness and power, of His sovereignty and majesty, of His sufficiency and omniscience, of His omnipresence and His eternity, of His glory and His grace.

Let us bear witness to the God of Abraham, Isaac, and Jacob—to God the Father, God the Son, and God the Holy Spirit. No matter what the world may say, let us tell of His greatness, of His holiness, and His sovereignty.

A. W. Tozer rightly observed that "what comes into our minds when we think about God is the most important thing about us."[8] What comes to your mind? The God of the Bible shows mercy to sinners through the grace of our Lord Jesus Christ. His greatest demonstration of His own glory is seen in the redemption of sinners. To truly know Him is to know His saving power. May you know the one true God and find salvation by His grace.

"Thus says the LORD, . . . let him who boasts boast of this, that he understands and knows Me, that I am the LORD" (Jer. 9:23–24).

1. Grace Davie, "An Ordinary God: The Paradox of Religion in Contemporary Britain," *British Journal of Sociology* 41 (September 1990), 395.

2. Martin Luther, *A Compend of Luther's Theology*, ed. Hugh T. Kerr (Philadelphia: Westminster Press, 1953), 28. Alternate version found in

Luther's Works, vol. 54, "Table Talk," ed. Theodore G. Tappert (Philadelphia: Fortress Press, 1967), 377.

3. "Great Is Thy Faithfulness," words by Thomas O. Chisholm, in *The Baptist Hymnal* (Nashville: Convention Press, 1991), no. 54. See James 1:17.

4. A. W. Tozer, *The Knowledge of the Holy* (San Francisco: HarperCollins, 1961), 56.

5. Stephen Charnock, *The Existence and Attributes of God,* 2 vols. (London: Robert Carter & Brothers, 1853), 1:366–67.

6. Arthur W. Pink, *The Sovereignty of God* (Grand Rapids: Baker Book House, 1930), 20.

7. Clark Pinnock, et. al., *The Openness of God* (Downers Grove, Ill.: InterVarsity Press, 1994), 113.

8. Tozer, *The Knowledge of the Holy,* 1.

8

Women: Are They Equal with Men?

GENESIS 2:18–25; 1 TIMOTHY 2:12–15 NKJV

Paige Patterson
President, Southwestern Baptist Theological Seminary

ARE WOMEN EQUAL WITH MEN? What can a woman do in the church of God? I will address two texts: Genesis 2 and 1 Timothy 2.

And the LORD God said, "It is not good that man should be alone; I will make him a helper comparable to him [Heb. *'ezer kenegdo*]." Out of the ground the LORD God formed every beast of the field and every bird of the air, and brought them to Adam to see what he would call them. And whatever Adam called each living creature, that was its name. So Adam gave names to all cattle, to the birds of the air, and to every beast of the field. But for Adam there was not found a helper comparable to him.

And the LORD God caused a deep sleep to fall on Adam, and he slept; and He took one of his ribs [Heb. *tsela*], and closed up the flesh in its place. Then the rib which the LORD God had taken from man He made into a woman, and He brought her to the man (Gen. 2:18–22).

Elsewhere in the Old Testament, the Hebrew word *tsela* is translated "side." Although some people would say that for this reason men have one less rib than women, that is not true. If I am in an automobile accident and lose one arm, all of my kids are not going to be born one-armed. The genetic code is in place.

> And Adam said: "This is now bone of my bones and flesh of my flesh; she shall be called Woman [Heb. *'ishsha*], because she was taken out of Man [Heb. *'ish*]." [A play on the words translated "man" and "woman" occurs here in the Hebrew text. Even with the English translation, you can see that there is a linguistic similarity both visually and phonetically.] Therefore a man shall leave his father and mother and be joined to his wife, and they shall become one flesh.
>
> And they were both naked, the man and his wife, and were not ashamed (Gen. 2:23–25).

During the almost two decades I served the First Baptist Church of Dallas, Texas, many people came to look at the facilities of that historic place. Tours were regularly given. Many of the staff were involved in hosting these tours on Sunday mornings. Included in the tour was the chapel where many wedding ceremonies were performed.

One day I saw something lying in the corner while taking a group of people through Slaughter Chapel—a surprising name for a wedding chapel. I was quite surprised because the custodial staff always took excellent care of the facilities. A yellow sack was in the corner. Thinking that someone had failed to see an item left behind, I determined to do my part and be a good groundskeeper, and I reached over and picked up the sack to throw it away. When I did, I saw an inscription on the sack, which obviously had something inside. First, I emptied the contents, finding what was left of a man's wedding ring. Seemingly it had been beaten with a heavy object (perhaps a hammer) until the ring was broken and gnarled. Curious as to the meaning of such destruction, I read the inscription:

> I returned this broken ring to where it was blessed. Pray God forgive her that broke it, but pray that He will grant me the grace to forgive her as I ask Him to forgive me. Use this metal as you will in God's work. If you would, say a prayer for me because I hurt.

There was no signature—only the date of the marriage and the date of its dissolution. As I stood holding that ring, I thought, *What has gone wrong in our country? What has gone wrong in the church of God?*

Long since, I have concluded that among the most serious threats to the spiritual lives of our churches and our nation is the dissolution of God's first and greatest institution—the home. Who will speak a word for the home? Will it be government officials—the Congress or your local school board? I hope you won't hold your breath. Who is going to speak a word for the sanctity of the home? Of all the destructive forces that are tearing at the foundations of that home life today, I have become unalterably convinced that feminism is perhaps the greatest enemy of all.

Look at what God's Word says. First, when God created the man, He affirmed that under no circumstances is it good for a man to be alone (Gen. 2:18). The strong negative indicated in the Hebrew text suggests an emphatic tone because for a man to be alone violates God's plan. God's plan is for one man to marry one woman and to stay with her for all of their lives. That is God's plan for everyone except the few people who have the gift of celibacy.

Is celibacy a gift? Oh, yes. First Corinthians 7:7 describes singleness as a grace gift (Gk. *charismata*). I do believe that God gives to some people, as He did to the apostle Paul, the gift of celibacy. Unless God has given you the gift of celibacy, then God's plan for your life is to find someone of God's choosing with whom you are to spend your lives united together as one. In this case, men, you are not complete until you find the one with whom God has prepared to link you. So it is not good that man should be alone.

God says that He is going to create for man "a helper comparable to him." You already know the Hebrew word *'ezer* better than you think! You have sung the hymn, "Come Thou Fount of Every Blessing." The second verse contains the phrase, "Here I raise mine Ebenezer." I know you would not sing anything you do not fully understand! Actually what you raise is your *'eben 'ezer*, a Hebrew phrase referring to an event that transpired on the field of battle when the children of Israel were fighting the Philistines. Suddenly they decided to pray and seek the Lord. God came through for them, and they defeated the Philistines. The Israelites determined to memorialize this place. They built an altar of unused stone as a memorial and called this structure "a stone of help" or *'eben 'ezer*.

The Hebrew phrase *'ezer kenegdo* is best translated "a helper corresponding to or just like him." Are women equal with men? Would the world please get it straight? Evangelicals should not be designated "male chauvinists." They absolutely believe what the Bible teaches: A woman is fully equal with man. God affirms that in describing her as "corresponding to him." Just as man is in the image of God, so the woman is in the image of God. They are equally created in the image of God in every conceivable way. Evangelicals want the world to know that God says women are equal with men.

"Out of the ground the LORD God formed every beast of the field and every bird of the air" (Gen. 2:19). Here we have what may have been the first recorded Ringling Brothers, Barnum and Bailey parade as God had all these animals walk by Adam. The prevalent idea that men in antiquity were suffering from an advanced degree of mental limitation is very interesting to me. Only those among us with Ph.D.s are considered to be the advanced ones. But I think Adam must have been pretty sharp. He named every one of these critters. There goes a hippopotamus. That is not bad. There goes a pachyderm. That's pretty good, too. There goes a rhinoceros. And the amazing thing is that apparently Adam remembered when he saw the animal the second time what he called it the first time. However, "a helper comparable to him" was not found.

Did the Lord expect that man would take up with a female orangutan? Of course not. But by the time the parade was over, Adam understood clearly that he was the only one around who did not have his other half. He was alone. He needed somebody. After the parade was over, he understood that he was still incomplete— half a man.

What are you going to do, God? He "caused a deep sleep to fall on Adam, and he slept" (Gen. 2:21). While Adam slept, God took one of his ribs, closed up the flesh, and from this rib He made a woman.

Ladies, you ought to underline this word *made*. There are several Hebrew words describing God's creative activity in these first two chapters of Genesis. One of them is the word *barah*, which suggests creation out of absolutely nothing. Then there is *'asah*, which describes making something out of existing materials. *Yatsar* is also used, meaning "to mold or fashion." Each of these words is used repeatedly. But the word in this verse from the root *banah* is used only here in the entire passage. The word has the sense of beautifully and artistically constructing. Can you believe that? More literally the word may be translated God "built" the woman. God "built" her and brought her to man.

Adam then had something to say. The Bible does not tell us the whole conversation, but it records everything you need to know for redemptive purposes and godly living. But you can imagine that more was said than what is recorded here. Can you put yourself back there? As the anesthetic was wearing off, Adam looked up and saw Eve. Whoa! I would not even attempt to fill in the conversation, but I would love to have heard it. This much you do know from Scripture. Adam said, "This is now bone of my bones and flesh of my flesh" (Gen. 2:23). In other words, "Whatever it is that I am, look, there's another one." He declared the same thing that God said, "Whatever it is that I am, there's another one right over there." But "she shall be called Woman, because she is taken out of Man (Gen. 2:23). By the way, that appellation did not derive, as is commonly rumored, from the murmuring "woe is man."

> Therefore a man shall leave his father and mother and be joined to his wife, and they shall become one flesh (Gen. 2:24).

These words express clearly and succinctly God's divine order for marriage. If you reverse the order, you will pay the price for it. You cannot reverse God's divinely ordered plan and have the blessings of God upon your marriage. Anyone who does marriage counseling knows that one of the major problems in marriage is maladjustment in physical intimacy. When a couple comes to me for marital counseling, I have come to the point of asking the question (and I get into a lot of trouble doing it): "Have either one or both of you been involved in premarital sex?" You would be amazed how many couples who are having trouble with sexual adjustment admit that one or both were involved in premarital sex.

Do you see God's divine order? You leave your father and mother. Does that mean desert your parents, forget them, have nothing to do with them? No, of course not. As a matter of fact, as mom and dad get older, you become responsible for them. God said to honor your parents. This reference is to the civil authority, the religious witness to the commitment ceremony of marriage. You say during your wedding that you are committing yourself to your mate as your new first loyalty until death do you part.

Then, having left father and mother, you cleave to your mate. You establish a spiritual oneness. On the basis of that spiritual oneness, you enter into the sexual union and act out physically the spiritual union that has already taken place as you become one flesh. God says, "Do it My way, and I will bless your socks off! Do it the other way, and I will turn My face, and it will never be what it ought to be."

If women are equal with men, then can women do anything they desire in the church of God? "And I do not permit a woman to teach or to have authority over a man, but to be in silence. For Adam was formed first, then Eve. And Adam was not deceived, but the woman being deceived, fell into transgression. Nevertheless she will be saved in childbearing if they continue in faith, love, and holiness, with self-control" (1 Tim. 2:12–15).

If the church of God is actually going to be bound by biblical revelation, if believers genuinely want to be a people of the Book, then they had better make up their minds to be bound by the Book and find out what this passage means. It does mean what it says: "I do not permit a woman to teach or to have authority over a man, but to be in silence." Does that mean a woman cannot say anything in the church of God?

No, it does not mean that. In 1 Corinthians Paul already has said that when a woman prays or prophesies in public in the church of God, she is to do so with authority on her head because of the angels. The essential point is that under certain circumstances (if her head is covered), a woman may pray or prophesy in the church. Although space does not allow time for an exegesis of this passage, I will give a brief comment. The clear statement of male headship in this passage is a timeless principle, while the reference to a head covering is a timely manifestation of that principle.

Two times in 1 Corinthians women are told to be "silent." In 1 Corinthians 14:34, the best understanding I can give you for "silent" (Gk. *sigatosan)* is "hush, not a peep, don't say a word." What is the subject of 1 Corinthians 14? From the first to the last verse, the entire chapter is about "tongues." The clear teaching is that a woman is forbidden to speak in tongues in the church of God. Paul delivered these words under the inspiration of the Holy Spirit of God. Women here are told not to speak a single word of *glossolalia*. But in 1 Timothy 2 another word is used for "silent" (Gk. *hesuchia)*. The latter word speaks more to a woman's attitude than to her verbal outpouring.

God honors in women the attitude of a gentle and quiet spirit, which He counts as beauty. To be a beautiful woman, don't be boisterous and rambunctious. Nobody likes that in a woman. Develop a gentle and quiet spirit, and God will say, "There goes a beautiful woman." This verse does not mean that a woman cannot say anything at all. The passage rather affirms God's desire for a gentle and quiet spirit in every woman who is committed to Him.

"I do not permit a woman to teach or to have authority over a man" (1 Tim. 2:12). Don't extrapolate the phrase and try to put it in another setting. This phrase does not necessarily mean that Margaret Thatcher cannot be prime minister of Great Britain. It doesn't speak about the role of women in government. In the church of God, however, a woman should not instruct men or exercise authority over men. Why is that? How can you maintain that women are equal with men and turn around and deny them any such opportunity?

I have a confession to make. I love to drive fast. I hate slow! The German autobahn may be the greatest creation under God's heaven. There are no speed limits. The first time I drove on the autobahn I could not afford to rent anything but an Opal. But I had the pedal on the floor and the door open, pushing with one foot, to get as much as I could out of that car. You can imagine my frustration as people flew by me. I was doing 110 miles per hour in that vehicle, and I had people passing me as if I were standing still. What fun!

There is one problem associated with that sort of thing. I had it happen one day in Garland, Texas. A young state trooper pulled me over. He walked up to the window and said, "All right, buddy, where's the fire?" I replied, "In hell; are you going there?" Before he could get his breath, I added, "Why don't you go fight crime? Here I am a law-abiding citizen. The whole world is involved in drug traffic, murder, rape, theft. Why don't you go fight crime? Why do you bother me just because I was going seventy in a forty-miles-per-hour zone?"

You know good and well that I did not say any of that. I did the same thing you would do. I stood on the side of the road and looked down at my shoes. I prayed, "Dear God in heaven, please don't let anybody from First Baptist, Dallas, drive by."

Why did I not say the first words? Is that trooper any better than I am? Is he worth any more before God than I am? Am I not equal with him? Friend, you and I are totally equal in our creation. But God, according to the book of Romans, has made the policeman a magistrate in my life; and I have a commandment from God to obey him and to submit myself to him. It is no put-down of me that I am expected to obey the express Word of God.

May I go a step further? What does God have against children? Think about it. Children are to obey their mothers and fathers. Isn't that irritating? Are children not people of worth? Children are people, and they are fully in the image of God and thus equal with their parents and all adults. But being equal does not mean that you do not have a role assignment of subordination.

The apostle Philip said, "Lord, show us the Father, and it will be enough." Jesus said, "Philip, Philip, if you have seen Me, you have seen the Father. I and the Father are one" (see John 14:8–12). Turn a few pages, and you will see that same Jesus saying, "The Father is greater than I. And I subordinate Myself to the Father's will" (see John 14:28). Folks, if it is not too good for Jesus, it is not too good for us. Yes, there is equality of essence, but there is also subordination of office.

"I do not permit a woman to teach or to have authority over a man" (1 Tim. 2:12). Paul then gives three historical-theological reasons for his position. Reason number one is the primacy of Adam in creation. Adam was first created, then Eve. Reason number two looks like a put-down to women when you first read it: "Adam was not deceived, but the woman being deceived, fell into transgression" (1 Tim. 2:14). Before you take that verse to mean something it does not mean, you need to remember that when Paul got ready to describe human depravity, he said, "In Adam all sinned" (see Rom. 5:12). These words sound like the condemnation of man, not of woman. Eve was deceived; Adam wasn't. Adam's act was raw, unmitigated rebellion against God.

So God says to the man, "You blew it for the whole race. Now go and be the spiritual leader to guide the race back to God." Then verse 15 says, "Nevertheless she will be saved in childbearing" (1 Tim. 2:15). In all these years, I thought you were saved by Jesus!

That word *saved* has different connotations in the Bible. I was at a Dallas Cowboys football game many years ago, and the Cowboys were behind going into the last play of the game. Quarterback Staubach threw a Hail Mary pass, and one of his receivers caught the ball on the one-yard line and flipped over into the end zone. They won the game. The guy in front of me had a cigar in one hand and a beer can in the other. He stood up and said, "Saved!" I don't think his thoughts or words had anything to do with personal salvation. But I did tap him on the shoulder and ask, "Are you sure?"

The word *saved* means "to keep from disaster." In its most significant form, the word is used to describe the rescue of a lost life. The phrase suggests here that a woman will find her greatest contribution in the bearing and rearing of her children. I got on an airplane, and a woman was sitting in front of me. She was in a business suit. The hairdo was perfect. Her nails were perfectly painted. Jewelry was in place, and she had a *Wall Street Journal* with her. She was in high cotton. She was moving on to a business appointment.

Right across the aisle there was a young mother with three children—all under six years of age. There was not a single hair where it was supposed to be. Those kids were in the cockpit and in the tail of the airplane and all over me. The whole world today would say that this mother was a failure and that the businesswoman across the aisle was a success. God looks down from heaven with a different view. He sees that mother as pouring out her life in the most important assignment a woman can have.

Let me introduce you to two women who have been dead a long time. Susanna Wesley. She was a remarkable person. She had eighteen children. She was a prolific woman. She did not merely clean up after kids and wash dishes. She was brilliant. She was fluent in several languages. She would have made a great preacher, or she could even have been prime minister of England.

"Susanna, I want to ask you a question: Don't you wish you could be alive in modern America instead of living back there in the Dark Ages? Why, you might have been the pastorette of the First Baptist Church of Dallas?"

Susanna would say, "You see that boy over there. He looks a lot like that kid over there. Those are my boys John and Charles Wesley. If I had another lifetime, I would not do anything different, because through those two sons I helped to shake three continents—most of which I never visited myself—for Christ. Until this day when you come into a service of worship and the minister of music asks you to open your hymnbook, chances are good that you will be singing one of the hymns written by my boys. Although they and I are dead, yet they, and even I, continue to speak because I poured my life into those two boys."

Can I introduce you to one more? Anthusa lived about three hundred years after Christ's death. They said that Helen of Troy would have paled in beauty when compared to her. Anthusa was as smart as she was beautiful. When she was six months pregnant with her first child, her husband was killed in a tragic accident. As a widow, she bore that little baby boy and named him John. As soon as she had weaned the boy, suitors began to come from all over the ancient Roman world to try to persuade her to marry, because she was known everywhere for her beauty and intellect. She responded that she already had a full-time assignment. God had given her a boy named John, and she determined to devote the best of her abilities and energies to rearing this child for God. That boy's name was John Chrysostom—John, "the golden-mouthed" orator of Antioch and later of Constantinople.

Anthusa would say, "That boy preached to untold hundreds of thousands of people and saw them come to Christ. Even today, if you go to any evangelical seminary in the land, you will have to read the sermons of my son John, because until this day they stand as the epitome of what good expository preaching is all about. I had a part of all he did for God because of my investment in his life."

Dear precious mother and grandmother, I have made a major shift in my theology. I used to believe, as I have heard Vance Havner and others say, that being called to be a Baptist pastor is the highest calling in the world. I used to believe and preach that. I don't believe that anymore. It is the second highest calling. But the first and highest calling is to be a mother and a grandmother. I want to plead with you today from the bottom of my heart: Don't let an unbelieving, cynical world entice you to take the fruit offered to your foremother Eve. Don't take it. Don't take second best. Do it God's way, and let Him bless your life forever.

When I was nine years old, I had been a typical bad little preacher's kid. My mother used some applied psychology to the seat of the problem. She wasn't big enough to hurt me, and her punishment didn't matter much. But then she said something that did matter, "And furthermore, when your father gets home, I'm going to tell him, too." Serious stuff! I decided it was a great time to go to bed early.

So although it was only five in the afternoon, I went on to bed. Dad came home about ten o'clock that night, and I still hadn't gone to sleep. I was too terrified. But I was relieved because they did not talk very long. They went right into the master bedroom, and all the lights went out. I breathed a sigh of relief, but they kept talking. I could hear them talking but could not understand their words. After about an hour, I wondered, *What is the woman saying to him?*

Do you know anything about nine-year-old boys? Curiosity will outrun fear every time. As stealthily as an American Indian in the forest, I crawled out of my bed and on hands and knees across the hall and into the master bedroom, and I lay down at the foot of the bed and listened. I came to find out that my father wasn't in the conversation; he had gone to sleep. It was just mother and Jesus.

The conversation is more vivid to me than if it had happened this morning. It went something like this, "Thank You, Jesus, for our son. The doctors said we couldn't have another child, but You gave us a son. Lord, I just have one concern. He's nine, and he hasn't been saved. Lord, he knows how to be saved. Lord, I couldn't take it if he died and went to hell. I pray that You will save my son." Then she said, "Lord, he is Yours. And like Hannah I bring him to You. Lord, if You take him and he dies somewhere on a mission field before his thirtieth birthday, it is OK, God, because He is yours. Just save him and call him into Your work." I went back to bed that night, but I did not sleep much.

On Friday night, Fred Brown from Chattanooga, Tennessee, was doing the revival preaching in our church. I would like to tell you that his sermon left a great impression, but I don't remember any of it. What I do remember was sitting on the third row when God spoke to my heart while Mother stood there as she always did with tears staining the back of the wooden pew in front of us. I knew what she was doing. She was praying for me.

I said, "Enough of this. I am going to God." I ran to the front where my pastor father caught me. He hugged me for a moment and sat me down on the front pew. I couldn't talk, and he knew that. He asked, "Are you coming to be saved?"

I shook my head affirmatively.

"Do you want to be baptized?"

Same response. I don't know why he didn't ask me the third question, because he made me have to come forward again. He could have said, "Do you surrender to preach?" I would have said, "Yes."

On that Sunday night I was baptized, and on the following Wednesday night I was back at the front again. My father asked, "Why are you coming, son? Is something wrong?" I said, "No, but you didn't ask the other question, and I need to tell the people I am surrendering to preach, also." He said, "Well, I had no idea, but I will tell them." All the sweet little old ladies in the church came by and patted my red head and said how sweet it was, but they thought I would get over it. *I didn't!*

However long God gives me to preach the unsearchable riches of Christ, I want you to know that wherever I go, I am going to be praising God that He gave me a mother who wasn't out running for vice president of the United States or building some corporate enterprise. Rather, she understood that the most important assignment she had was to rear her children in the nurture and admonition of the Lord and to win them to Christ—and through them she could change the world.

9

The Suffering Servant of the Lord

ISAIAH 52:13–53:12

Daniel Akin
President, Southeastern Baptist Theological Seminary

ISAIAH 53 HAS CAPTIVATED THE HEARTS and imaginations of those who study the Bible like few other texts in Holy Scripture.

Kyle Yates, Old Testament professor at Southern Seminary, called it "the Mount Everest of Old Testament prophecy"; Polycarp, "the golden passional of the Old Testament evangelist" and Spurgeon, "a Bible in miniature, the gospel in its essence." Delitzsch called Isaiah 53 "the most central, the deepest, and the loftiest thing that the Old Testament prophecy, outstripping itself, has ever achieved. . . . It looks as if it had been written beneath the cross upon Golgotha." Engnell adds, "Without any exaggeration, [it is] the most important text of the Old Testament."

The text, which actually begins at 52:13, is the fourth of the Great Servant Songs of Isaiah and the climax of the section (cf. 42:1–7; 49:1–6; 50:4–9). It is divided into five stanzas of three verses each, with each stanza being longer than the previous one. By means of creative contrast and regular repetition, the twin themes of exaltation and humiliation are woven into a beautiful tapestry of theological truth. Interestingly, exaltation is prominent in stanzas 1 and 5, while suffering and humiliation dominate stanzas 2, 3, and 4.

Because priestly and sacrificial imagery permeate the passage, some, such as S. Lewis Johnson, believe the five stanzas are intentionally structured to match the five Levitical offerings:

- Burnt offering, 52:13–15
- Meal offering, 53:1–3
- Peace offering, 53:4–6
- Sin offering, 53:7–9
- Trespass (guilt) offering, 53:10–12

The first verse of each stanza captures the theme of that stanza and summarizes beautifully its content. [Read the first of each.]

As we prepare to enter this Holy of Holies and bask in its glories, a crucial question must be addressed: "Who is the Suffering Servant?" While many suggestions have been put on the table, three main interpretations have eclipsed the rest. Some say the text should be understood:

1. *Corporately:* the Suffering Servant is national or a remnant or ideal Israel (cf. 49:3). This view was developed in medieval Jewish thought, but fails on (1) the historical tradition of interpretation and (2) the work accomplished by this Servant. Israel could not atone for her own sins, much less the sins of the nations.

2. *Individually:* the Suffering Servant is Isaiah himself, Hezekiah, Jeremiah, Zerubbabel (in John D. W. Watts's view), or Moses. Yet what is said of the Servant scarcely fits the life or ministry of any of these, nor could what is said in 53:9b be said of even one .

3. *Messianically:* the Suffering Servant is the coming Messiah, the royal Davidic King, the ideal Israelite who is totally committed and consecrated to Yahweh's will and work, plan and purpose for His life. The German scholar Gerhard von Rad, professor at Heidelberg, catches a glimpse of what the chapter is all about when he writes, "We may rule out those interpretations—some of which are grossly fanciful—that see in the Servant a figure in the past." "The Servant embodies all that is good in Israel's existence before Yahweh." ". . . the expressions used go far beyond biography, indeed they go far beyond anyone who might have existed in the past or the present. The picture of the Servant of Yahweh, of his

mission to Israel and to the world, and of His expiatory suffering, is prophecy of the future. . . . and belongs to the realm of pure miracle which Yahweh reserved for himself."

However, the New Testament reveals, as does the intertestamental period, that prior to the cross, Isaiah 53 was not uniformly interpreted or identified with the Messiah. This view of a suffering Messiah finds support from only two books in the prophetic literature: Isaiah and Zechariah. Indeed, the idea of a suffering Messiah was rejected outright by the followers of Jesus, as Peter's perspective in Mark 8:31–34 makes abundantly clear.

Yet following the cross and resurrection, a *new interpretive key* was provided that opened the eyes of the early church and opens our own eyes to the true identity of the Suffering Servant. Jesus Himself, together with Paul and Peter, Matthew and Mark, Luke and John, are in agreement as to who the Servant is. Philip the evangelist likewise joins their chorus when in Acts 8:35 he makes plain to the man from Ethiopia that *the Suffering Servant is Jesus*. This text is directly cited no less than seven times in the New Testament with more than forty allusions.

It is my strong conviction that Jesus, in Mark 10:45, weds Isaiah's Suffering Servant to Daniel's Son of Man (Dan. 7:13–14) and thereby redefines for us who and what the Messiah would be. He is the Suffering Servant of Isaiah 53:

- Who bore our griefs (v. 4)
- Who carried our sorrows (v. 4)
- Who was wounded for our transgressions (v. 5)
- Who was bruised for our iniquities (v. 5)
- Who was chastised for our peace (v. 5)
- Who heals us by His stripes (v. 5)
- Who bore our iniquities (vv. 6, 11)
- Who was oppressed, afflicted (v. 7)
- Who was slaughtered (v. 7)
- Who was cut off (v. 8)
- Who was stricken for our transgressions (v. 8)
- Who was bruised by the Lord (v. 10)

- Who was put to grief (v. 10)
- Whose soul was made a sin offering (v. 10)
- Who poured out His soul unto death (v. 12)
- Who was numbered with the transgressions (v. 12)
- Who bore the sin of many (v. 12)
- Who made intercession for the transgressors (v. 12)

This is Isaiah's Suffering Servant. This is the Lord Jesus.

As we survey the five stanzas, we shall see five significant facets of the Servant's career.

I. See the Servant's Exaltation (52:13–15)

This stanza serves as the prologue to the song. In fact, it serves as a summation of the entire prophecy. Von Rad is again on target when he notes, "It is unusual in that this great poem begins with what is really the end of the whole story of the Servant's glorification and the recognition of His significance for the world." The initial song of chapter 42 gives us the *origin* of the Servant's mission, while this text provides the *culmination* and *exaltation*.

1. He is exalted because of His success (52:13). The text begins with "behold" or "see" (NIV)—look, take notice, pay attention (cf. 42:1 for the same introductory word). Whom do we see?

"My Servant," the Lord's Servant and our Savior! Interestingly, the Servant never speaks!

"He shall deal prudently," or "will act out wisely" (NIV), will accomplish His purpose. He will act so wisely that He will certainly succeed in His mission. He shall (1) "be exalted" (raised, high); (2) "be extolled" (lifted up); and (3) 'be very high" (highly exalted).

"Exalted" and "extolled" (high and lifted up) are used in combination four times in Isaiah and no place else in the Old Testament (see 6:1; 33:10; 57:15). In the other three instances they describe God.

Some scholars find in these three terms Christ's resurrection ("raised"), ascension ("lifted up") and session ("be very high/exalted"). There is little doubt that this text was in the mind of Paul when he penned his great Christological hymn in Philippians 2:5–11, especially verse 9.

God knows, and the world should know, that the Servant will not fail. He will succeed.

2. He is exalted because of His suffering (52:14). People are astonished, appalled, shocked at His appearance. "Exalted" in verse 13, the Servant is "humiliated" in verse 14. This word *astonished* is used in Ezekiel 27:35 to describe men's reaction to the ruins of Tyre.

His "visage" (appearance) and "form" (outward features) are "marred," or "disfigured" (though some believe the word could be "anoint"). Peter Gentry of Southern Seminary translates the verse, "Just as many were astounded at you, so His appearance was a superhuman anointing; His form more than humanity." If this is correct, He is exalted not because of His *suffering*, but because of His *splendor*. Oswalt's translation in contrast is, "Such a disfigurement! His appearance is hardly human!" Thus people are paralyzed with wonder (1) at the horror of His suffering and at the extent of the cruelty inflicted upon the Servant, or (2) at the magnificence of His splendor.

3. He is exalted because of His service (52:15). There is debate concerning the Hebrew verb *yazzeh*, translated "sprinkle" in most English versions. Contextually there is support for this translation. Priestly and sacrificial currents run throughout the song. However, rhetorically there appears to be something of a comparison with verse 14. In verse 14 they are shocked at the Servant's *abuse*. In verse 15 they are shocked at the Servant's *accomplishment*. Indeed they are so surprised that the mightiest "kings shall shut their mouths," an utterly unimaginable thought. Furthermore, what was previously hidden to the Gentile nations will be revealed to them. They had never heard or considered "that it was through the loss of all things that the Savior will conquer all things." Paul made such an application of this verse in Romans 15:21 as he carried the gospel to those who did not know.

II. See the Servant's Rejection (53:1–3)

Isaiah 53:1 flows naturally out of 52:15. The speaker appears to be the redeemed eschatological community, led no doubt by redeemed Israel through the voice of her prophet. They "look back" and lament and mourn over the fact they misjudged the Lord's Servant and did not believe the message about Him. The nations did not believe, because they did not know. Israel knew, and yet she did not believe, because she failed to recognize the "arm of the LORD" when it was revealed in the Suffering Servant. Both John (John 12:38) and Paul (Romans 10:16) saw in the unbelief of Israel a fulfillment of verse 1. English translations that use the past tense throughout these verses accurately reflect the fact that 700 years before Christ, the work of the Servant was a signed, sealed, and settled reality. Men may misunderstand Him, but God is made known by Him.

In what way did they misunderstand Him?

In what context did they reject Him?

1. He appeared to be insignificant, not important (53:1). Two rhetorical questions are put forth:

Who has believed our report? Answer: very few. The emphasis is on human responsibility.

To whom has the arm of the LORD *been revealed?* Answer: Not many. Here the emphasis is on divine sovereignty.

The message about the Servant impressed few. But their evaluation will spiral further down.

2. He appeared to be a nobody, not a somebody (53:2). He is like a "tender plant" (better "tender sprout or shoot"). This recalls Isaiah 11:1 and connects the Servant to the Davidic Messiah. All of this takes place "before Him," before God. The Lord directs the entire course of His earthly life and mission. The world may think He is a nobody, but God's estimate is something altogether different. He is "a root out of dry ground"—unimpressive; it appears he will not even make it. He has "no form" (beauty) or "comeliness" (splendor, majesty); "when we see Him, no beauty" (appearance) "that we should desire Him."

The Servant lacked the regal splendor necessary to attract the nations. He arose out of humble circumstances and lowly conditions (from a poor nation, of impoverished parents, had a stable for His birth and a carpenter for His vocation). The verse is not saying he was ugly, just unimportant. His was the stuff of a nobody, not a somebody! This is not what "the arm of the LORD" should look like!

3. He appeared to be a loser, not a winner (53:3). "Despised" means to be considered worthless (repeated for emphasis, forming an inclusio in the verse). He is quickly dismissed. "Rejected" literally is "a ceasing by men." He is a loser, so why waste any time with Him? "A man of sorrows" addresses both physical and mental pains. "Acquainted with griefs" means he is familiar with sickness.

What can such a weakling do for us? This is "the arm of the LORD?" "We hid our faces from Him"; we would not even look on such as He. We "despised . . . did not esteem Him." We loathed Him and paid Him no attention. He was a loser, not a deliverer. This man had His own problems. What could He possibly do for us?

He's insignificant, a nobody, a loser. See the Servant's rejection.

III. See the Servant's Passion (53:4–6)

These verses involve a dramatic turn revealing a new perspective all together. Now we discover why the Servant had pain and sickness. We find out it was all for us. At least ten times in these three verses the personal pronouns *our, we,* or *us* appear. The suffering of the Servant was not His fault; it was ours.

1. He bore our sorrows (illness) (53:4; cf. Matthew 8:17). "But surely" expresses not only certainty but also contrast. Do you wish to get an accurate picture of how things really are? Clearly "He bore" (took up) "our griefs" (sicknesses) "and carried our sorrows" (pains) looks back to verse 3.

"We esteemed" (reckoned, considered) "Him stricken." "Stricken" is sometimes associated with the disease of leprosy. It may be the basis for the tradition in the Babylonian Talmud that described the Messiah as a leper (*Sanhedrin 98a*).

"Smitten by God and afflicted" tells us they thought this was the Lord's doing. Many in ancient Israel believed suffering was the result of one's own sins, and therefore they assumed (wrongly!) that the Servant was getting what He deserved. The griefs and sorrows He carried were indeed deserved, but not by Him, but by us.

2. He bore our suffering (53:5). He was "wounded" (pierced through) "for our transgressions" (rebellions), "bruised" (crushed, broke into pieces, pulverized, ground into dust) "for our iniquities" (twistedness). "The chastisement" (punishment) "for our peace" (shalom) "was upon Him, and by His stripes" (welts, wounds, blows that cut) "we are healed."

- He takes our disease and gives us health.
- He takes our punishment and gives us peace.
- He takes our wounds and gives us healing.

3. He bore our sin (53:6). H. A. Ironside called this "the most wonderful text in the Bible."

"All we like sheep" informs us that none are excluded (Rom. 3:23). We have gone astray like dumb sheep: prone to get lost, ever unaware of the danger that is about us, oblivious to the consequences of wrong choices.

"We have turned, everyone, to his own way." Each of us has chosen our way over God's way. "And the LORD has laid on Him" (caused to land, caused to fall) "the iniquity of us all."

Jesus in John 10 taught us that "the Good Shepherd lays down His life for the sheep." Could Isaiah 53:6 provide, at least in part, this image to explain His ministry?

Since verse 4 we have been immersed in the language of sacrifice and atonement, of substitution and salvation.

1. Recall the contrast between *He* and *our*.

2. Examine the words descriptive of our sin: griefs, sorrows, transgressions, iniquities, gone astray, his own way.

3. Meditate on the words of His work: borne, carried, wounded, bruised, punishment, stripes, laid on Him (and by the Lord!).

The language of substitution, of penal substitution, could not be clearer. I am convinced that theologians, myself included, should not speak of "the theory" of penal substitution. There is nothing theoretical about it at all. It is biblical through and through.

Feminist theologian Delores Williams could not be more wrong when she says, "there is nothing divine in the blood of the cross."

John Spong is without hope when he says, "I do not want a God who would kill His own Son."

No, Calvin saw it correctly when he wrote, "In order to interpose between us and God's anger, and satisfy His righteous judgement, it was necessary that He [the Son] should feel the weight of divine vengeance."

Theories known as Example, Moral Influence, Governmental, and *Christus Victor* all have their place in a holistic theology of atonement, but as Paige Patterson well says, "neither good example nor moral influence ever gets men to God and to heaven. Sin and its penalty must be addressed. The primary significance of the atonement from which all other meanings draw their dynamic is that of penal substitution." Jesus suffered in my place. He paid the penalty I owed.

What grace, O Lord, and beauty shone around Thy steps below!
What patient love was seen in all Thy life and death of woe!
Forever on Thy burdened heart a weight of sorrow hung;
Yet no ungentle, murmuring word escaped Thy silent tongue.
Thy foes might hate, despise, revile; Thy friends unfaithful
  prove;
Unwearied in forgiveness still, Thy heart could only love.

IV. See the Servant's Submission (53:7–9)

Here is the exemplary dimension of the Servant's work. The apostle Peter accurately draws upon this aspect of Christ's work in 1 Peter 2:18–25.

1. He was submissive in His silence (53:7). He was "oppressed" (harsh, physical treatment at the hands of others) and "afflicted" (or "He was humbling Himself"), "yet He opened not His mouth." He does not protest His treatment. He does not resent His destiny.

"He was led as a lamb to the slaughter and as a sheep . . . is silent."

"So He opened not His mouth" is repeated for emphasis. The theme of "the lamb" runs from Genesis to Revelation (Isaac, Gen. 22; Passover, Exod. 12; Jesus, John 1:29; the Warrior Lamb, Rev. 5:6).

No doubt this verse formed the basis of the declaration by John the Baptist, "Behold, the Lamb of God who takes away the sin of the world" (John 1:29).

2. He was submissive in His suffering (53:8). "Taken from prison and from judgment" teaches that an unfair and unjust trial was His. His treatment was wrong from beginning to end.

"Who will declare His generation? For He was cut off from the land of the living." The Servant of the Lord is executed with no offspring left behind. In that day to die childless meant you were cursed by God and your life was virtually useless. Has anyone given a second thought to what this terrible injustice means?

But again we need to see "the rest of the story."

"For the transgressions of My people He was stricken" (the blow is His, cf. v. 4). For the transgressions of the people, a blow has fallen on the Servant. That which should have hit me hit Him. That which should have hit you hit Him.

3. He was submissive in His shame (53:9). "He was assigned a grave with the wicked and with the rich in His death" is a form of Hebrew parallelism and carries the idea that He was buried among the wicked rich. He was a good man, yet He is buried with the wicked. He was a poor man yet He is buried with the wealthy. It should not have ended this way. "He had done no violence. Nor was any deceit found in his mouth." Both by word and deed His life should have turned out differently. This is how we, from our human perspective, would see it. Oh, but how different is the perspective of heaven! He died like a criminal but was buried like a prince. Here is a hint that things may not be as they seem.

Why Was He Silent?
Why is He silent when just a word would slay His accusers all?
*Why does He meekly bear their taunts when angels await His
    call?*
"He was made sin," my sin He bore upon the accursed tree.
And sin has no defense to offer at all, His silence was for me!

V. See the Servant's Salvation (53:10–12)

The death of the Servant was not a murder or a martyrdom. It was nothing less than a divine appointment! Spurgeon was exactly right: "the blood-stained Scriptures were written by the Lord as much as any other!" Who killed Jesus? Pilate, Herod, the Jews, the Romans, you and me? We all played our part, but ultimately it was God who sacrificed His Son.

1. It is purposed by the Lord (53:10). The Servant was the *right person* at the *right time* at the *right place* following the *right plan.* "It pleased the LORD to crush Him," better "it was the LORD's will" (NIV). "God wanted this to happen. It was no accident; it was a divine appointment.

It was His Father who "put Him to grief" (sickness) "making His soul a guilt offering for sin" (Lev. 5:1–19). It was God's will that the Servant become an atoning sacrifice for sin.

Now we see that His death was not the end. If verse 10b does not teach resurrection, its glorious shadow looms large just behind us. The Servant's life and sacrifice was not a waste, a loss, after all. In fact, "He will see His seed (offspring), His days will be prolonged" (lengthened) and the best of all: "the pleasure" (will, desire) "of the LORD shall prosper" (be accomplished) "in His hand." Yes, He was "bruised" by God, but He is also "blessed" by God. This is purposed by the Lord.

2. It is pleasing to the Servant (53:11). Verse 11 should read, "From the anguish of His soul, he will see light, and be satisfied by His knowledge. My righteous Servant shall justify many, bearing their iniquities." It thematically links with Jeremiah 23:5–6 and the righteous Davidic branch, a king who will reign, prosper, and execute judgment and righteousness in the earth. The Servant can rejoice. Though the cost was great the outcome is greater still. Anguish is replaced by joy. Darkness is vanquished by light. The Servant is satisfied by the knowledge of what has been achieved. The Servant, by what He did, will make guilty persons righteous. And what did He do? He bore their iniquities.

3. It is provided for many (53:12). The picture in verse 12 is that of a victory parade with the Servant marching out front in the role of conqueror, bringing home the spoils of battle. God will give the Servant those He redeemed as well as those who rejected Him. Indeed, every knee will bow! (Phil. 2:10–11). Why does He deserve such honor? Isaiah brings it to a beautiful and appropriate summation:

- Because He poured out His soul unto death,
- He was numbered (listed) with sinners.
- He bore the sin of many.
- He made intercession for the transgressors. ("For their rebellions He intervened" (Oswalt).

He died not just *with* sinners. He died *for* sinners.

Dan Block wonderfully puts it all together: "The Messianic hope is a single line that begins in broadest terms with God's promise of victory over the serpent through the seed of woman (Gen. 3:15), then is narrowed successively to the seed of Abraham (Gen. 22:18), the tribe of Judah (Gen. 49:10), the stem of Jesse (Isa. 11:1), the house/dynasty of David (2 Sam. 7), and finally the suffering and slain Servant of Yahweh (Isa. 53)."

Rejection was His. Acceptance is ours.

The wounding was His. The healing is ours.

The stripes were His. The salvation is ours.

The price paid was His. The forgiveness is ours.

The death was His. But life is ours.

Hallelujah! What a Savior!

Conclusion
"O Sacred Head Now Wounded"
by Bernard of Clairvaux (1090–1153)

O sacred Head, now wounded,
*   with grief and shame weighed down.*
Now scornfully surrounded, with thorns your only crown.
How pale you are with anguish, with sorrow, abuse and scorn!
How does your visage languish, which once was bright as morn!
What you, my Lord have suffered, was all for sinners' gain.
Mine, mine was the transgression, but yours the deadly pain.
O, here I fall, my Savior! It's I who deserve your place.
But you showed me your favor! It is all because of grace.

I thank God for Isaiah's Suffering Servant. I thank God for Jesus!
What a Servant! What a Savior!

10

Evangelism Lessons from a Pouting Prophet

JONAH 1:1–4:11 NASB

Chuck Kelley
President, New Orleans Baptist Theological Seminary

I'VE BEEN A SOUTHERN BAPTIST ALL MY LIFE. I started going to church nine months before I took my first breath and have been going pretty much ever since. And in all of my years as a Southern Baptist, I've come to learn what most Southern Baptists believe about evangelism. For most Southern Baptists, evangelism is one of the most important jobs in the church—for someone else to do. I mean we're so excited when people get saved; we love it when folks are born again, but we're absolutely convinced somebody can do a better job of witnessing than we can—somebody who knows more Bible, somebody who has more organizational skills, somebody who has a more outgoing personality, somebody who is better at closing the deal, somebody who is better at witnessing than we are. And whether the person speaking is a pastor or a layman, I can't tell you the number of times I've heard that expressed in one way or another. Evangelism is one of the most important jobs in the church—for somebody else to do.

But as we study God's wonderful Word, we learn that this attitude is not an option. The word about the Great Commission, the word about evangelism, the word calling us to tell everybody we know about Christ is not for the few, the proud, the spiritually elite!

117

In fact, the word about evangelism is a word that God gives to all of us. What I want to do in the few moments we have together is to walk you through some things God has been teaching me about evangelism from the book of Jonah. This is a book that God has used probably more than any other to help me understand why I must be about the Father's task of telling this lost world about Jesus Christ. To drive these lessons home, we're going to use your hand.

How many of you have a hand? Would you raise it, please, if you have a hand? That's very good. Many of you have a spare, don't you? Well, we're going to use your hand, and I'm going to see if we can teach you how to give a hand to Jonah for showing us the biblical basis of evangelism.

I. God's Passion

We'll start with the first finger. Do you have a finger, everybody? Hold up one finger, OK? This finger stands for God's passion. Can you say that with me? God's passion. I think these words in the book of Jonah would be rated as one of the most stunning statements in the Bible by the children of Israel, by the Hebrew people who heard it when it was written for the first time. Look at Jonah chapter 1 verse 1. Have you ever noticed it? And noticed how stunning this verse must have been in the eyes of the people who heard it first? "The word of the LORD came to Jonah the son of Amittai saying, 'Arise, go to Nineveh the great city, and cry against it, for their wickedness has come up before Me'" (Jon. 1:1–2).

That may not sound very stunning to you. That may not sound dramatic or unusual to you. God is calling a preacher to go to a place that needs to repent and to call them to repentance. But you don't know much about Nineveh. This city was the home of the Assyrian people, one of the most cruel, barbaric peoples on the face of the earth. They were in the process of trying to conquer all the known world of that day. They were making war against city after city, and they would stay at war as long as it took until they finally conquered that city. They camped outside the walls of the city of Samaria for three solid years until they finally starved them out. Stubborn people, those Assyrians. They would have made great Baptists, don't you think?

And not only that: When they finally took the city, they would take the mayor and city council and impale them alive on giant stakes outside the walls of the city as a warning, "Don't mess with the Assyrians." If you go to the British Museum today, you can visit the Assyrian Halls in the British Museum. There you will see gates, gigantic gates from an ancient Assyrian city. There you will see stone carvings from the walls of the palaces of the Assyrian kings.

Now what you carve in stone is what you're real proud of. What you carve in stone is what you want people to remember forever about you. If you were to go to the walls of the British Museum and see the stone carvings from the palaces of the Assyrians, what you would find are scenes of Assyrian soldiers at the end of a battle playing catch with the heads of their victims. These were not nice people. They were very cruel. They were very militaristic, and they were literally attempting to wipe God's people off the face of the earth.

That God would call a preacher to go and warn the Ninevites to repent so they could avoid judgment was unthinkable. The great, passionate love of God is deeper than any of us can ever reach in our understanding. It is a love not inclined solely to those who are searching after God. It is not a love only for those who are somewhere along the way toward faith in God. It is a love to those who are the farthest away and the least interested and the most opposed to everything God stands for. And the attitude of God toward all of those who are the opposite of everything He values is not an attitude of judgment; it is an attitude of love.

As a matter of fact, we will never understand how much God loves us until we understand how much God loves people like the Assyrians. It's so easy in our subconscious mind to think what I am occasionally tempted to think when I stand in front of the mirror getting dressed to go out for a day of serving God and His kingdom: "God loves me, and I'm not surprised! If I were God, I'd love me too!" I'm thinking about all the time I give to His kingdom's work, all the things I do for the church, all the hours I've logged in church.

But the love that God has for me is exactly the same in its depth and passion as the love God had for the people of Nineveh. It has no respect to my character, no respect to my actions, no respect to my family or my background. God loves me because He has chosen to love me. The reality of God's love is most clearly illustrated in the passion of His love for the most unlovable. It means He must love you and me as well. And we can never begin to understand why the Bible calls all of us to the Great Commission task if we don't understand—what's that first finger?—*God's passion!* The passionate love of God for the lost and those who need the gospel.

I don't have to spend too much time on that point because the truth of the matter is, systematic theology for most Americans is a one-point systematic theology: *God loves me.* That is a lesson we have learned well in American churches. This is the message preached from more pulpits than any other message. This is a message you will find in more religious writings than any other message. We are indeed a culture saturated with the idea that God loves us. Unfortunately, systematic theology for many people stops with that first finger.

II. God's Penalty

But how many of you have more fingers on your hand? OK, do you have a second one? Hold that one up. That second finger stands for God's penalty. Would you say that with me? God's penalty. We have God's passion, but we also have God's penalty. The truth of the matter is, God not only loves us with an everlasting love, but He is also a righteous God. He will uphold the righteousness of His character and His ways. If we, though we are loved by God, violate and ignore His Word and His way, God will bring judgment upon us.

I had to learn as a child growing up in Beaumont, Texas, the reality of both love and judgment, for my parents loved me as much as parents could ever love a child. My parents provided for me; my parents encouraged me; my parents loved me. There was never any doubt about whether my mom and dad loved me and would have given their lives for me. But I began to understand that they had a standard called *Kelleyness*. I had an obligation because I was a Kelley to live like a Kelley.

"Mom, Dad, can I go do so and so?"

"No."

"But David's doing that, or Tommy's doing that, or Bobby's doing that. . . ."

"But their name isn't Kelley."

If I heard that once, I heard it a million times. Their name wasn't Kelley, and I began to realize that being a Kelley meant there was a standard of conduct, there was a way of living that I was expected to embody in my own life, and if I ever fell short of that mark—we won't get into that! Let's just say that I learned love and judgment are not opposites. They are extensions of the same thing. The God who loves us with an everlasting love is a God who will hold us accountable to the standards of His character.

What was the message that God gave to Jonah to go and call Nineveh to repent? *Lest He had to judge them and destroy them.* But you must understand it was a warning not simply to the people of Nineveh; it was a warning to Jonah as well. You know the story, don't you? Jonah heard that call from God. Jonah heard that assignment to go and tell the people of Nineveh to repent and to call them to repentance lest judgment come. But Jonah, being a Baptist, went the other way, refused to accept God's commission. He got as far away from that as he could.

That's when God had to cause a great storm to come up around Jonah. That's when God helped those men on the boat know Jonah was the cause of it. That's when God prepared that big fish and they threw Jonah overboard. He became the first submarine commander in the Bible! And for three days he was in the stomach of that fish.

Now look at Jonah chapter 2. We have here a prayer that Jonah prayed while he was in the stomach of that fish. Have you ever noticed the prayer of Jonah? Look at Jonah chapter 2, verse 2: Jonah said, I called "out of my distress to the Lord, from the belly of hell itself, I cried out to you." Jonah, what's it like to be in the stomach of that fish? It's like being in hell. This was the preacher, this was the prophet who had a call from God, but he disobeyed.

Friends, Romans, and countrymen, lend me your ears. I need to bury an idea and not praise it. God has not, is not, will not tolerate sin in the life of any of His creation. It does not matter if you're a lost person or if you're a saved person. There will be judgment when you refuse the ways and Word of God. There is a penalty for disobedience. There is a penalty for sin, and this penalty is severe.

For the Ninevites, it would have been total destruction. For Jonah, it was as though he were living in hell itself. God loves us with an everlasting love, but God also holds us accountable to live in His Word and in accordance with His way. To hear the call from God, to know what God expects and what God wants, and to fail to obey will mean God's judgment. It is because the lost are lost and will spend eternity in hell that we must go and tell them and warn them, but it is also because the saved know what God wants and will be judged if we fail to obey that we must go and tell.

Do I need to remind you of the story of the children of Israel? They knew they were the people of God. They knew that every other nation on the earth worshiped false gods and idols. They knew that they and they alone worshiped the one true God. But when the prophets came and warned them that judgment would come, when the prophets came and called them back to the word and ways of God, they said, "Well, God might get a little mad. God might get upset, but after all, we're God's only hope. We're God's only voice. We're God's only representative. We have God's only temple. Surely the judgment of God can't be that bad."

But they found out, didn't they? Because of their consistent and persistent refusal to be the bearers of the gospel and not the keepers of it, because of their consistent and persistent refusal to live out the gospel instead of simply knowing it in their head, God sat on the sideline one day while the Babylonians took the city apart literally stone by stone. Yes, God has a passionate love, but there is also that second finger—God's penalty.

III. God's Patience

But I am so glad my hand has three fingers. It's my favorite. Now what was that first finger? God's passion. What was that second finger? God's penalty. The third finger is God's patience. Can you say that with me? God's patience. The Bible tells us that God loves us with an everlasting love. The Bible tells us that this does not preclude His judgment. The God who loves us with an everlasting love will always sustain and uphold His character and His righteousness in His people and in those who are outside the fold, those who are lost. We as believers must also heed His command lest we be judged. But the Bible thankfully tells us that God is a patient God.

Can you imagine how it was for Jonah in the stomach of that fish? We hear his prayer, and we hear the agonizing moment of his aloneness and his suffering. As far as Jonah was concerned, he was never again going to see the light of day. But God in His patience, God in His mercy had that big fish cast Jonah out on the beach. The Bible tells us in Jonah chapter 3, verse 1, "Now the word of the LORD came to Jonah a second time." God gave the prophet another opportunity to be obedient.

I have been on the campus of New Orleans Baptist Theological Seminary continuously since 1975. I'm in the slow-learner track. In all those years I've talked with many people who said God called them to preach years ago, but they kept running, avoiding, hiding, and finally said yes. I'm so glad that God is a patient God.

He was patient with the Assyrians in all of their wickedness and evil. He sent them a prophet. He wanted them to repent, and He gave them time to repent. He was patient with Jonah when Jonah refused to obey. When Jonah was too good to spend his time doing mission work with the Ninevites, God gave him a second chance. God's patience is a wonderful thing, but here's what you have to remember about God's patience. You never know how long it will last—and that's the rub.

When I was growing up, I had four sisters and no brothers. Even our dog was a girl. I had no chance at all! But thank goodness, our next-door neighbor had five sons. So you can imagine how much time I spent with those five boys next door. And late in the afternoon when I had been playing out there with them, our kitchen door would open, and my mom would cry out, "Chuck, come in. It's time for supper."

But we were in the middle of a game. The good guys were winning, and we couldn't stop yet. We'd play a little longer. That back door would open again. "Chuck, come in, it's time for supper." We'd keep playing. I told myself, *I'll be through soon. It will just take a few moments, just a little bit longer. We're almost finished.* But then that back door would open, and a voice would float out saying something like this: "Charles Seymour Kelley, Junior, get in here!" And when she got to "Charles Seymour Kelley, Junior," I knew there was more than supper waiting inside! That from the mother who loved me with an everlasting love.

God does love, and He is patient, but He will uphold His character and His ways. God has called all of us to be witnesses. It's not good enough to bring an evangelist in, to do the revival in your place. It's not good enough to let somebody else do the witnessing for you. It's not good enough to be good at moving paper clips around on your desk and forming them into beautiful shapes. All of us must be witnesses, and God is calling us to the task. He is patient. But you never know how long that patience will last.

I suppose all of us have a story like this. It's a story that I never like to tell. A story of somebody who called my office when I was teaching evangelism at the seminary. I had preached in their church. They said their mom was sick and in the hospital and was not a Christian. Would I go by to see her? "Please tell her about Jesus. I've told her. She's getting interested; she was more responsive the last time than she has ever been before. She's very sick. I think she's ready to make a decision. Would you go by?"

"Sure, I'll go by." But I was busy, and I didn't go by that day, and I didn't go by the next day, and then I had a preaching assignment over the weekend, and I didn't go by the next day. I didn't go by the next day. Things finally settled down. After about ten days, I called the hospital to ask for the room number of the woman—and she had died the day before. I know God still loves me. I got down on my knees by my desk that day and repented of my foolishness, but I'll never get that opportunity back. Now that's the reality we live with in evangelism. The stakes are too high for our disobedience to linger long. We must understand how critical it is for us to obey *now*.

God has a passionate love. This passionate love does not preclude the reality of the penalty for our sin. God is patient, but you never know how long that patience will be extended.

IV. God's Power

Let's hurry on to the fourth finger: God's power. Would you say that with me? God's power. This is one of the most important things about evangelism that God has taught me from the book of Jonah, and it has made a big impact on my life. Jonah finally got out of that fish and went to Nineveh. The Bible tells us that for forty days and forty nights he preached all up and down Nineveh. He had a warm, loving, pastoral kind of message: "Yet forty days and Nineveh's going to be destroyed!"

Can you imagine preaching that message all day, every day, for forty days? People would come out of the Winn-Dixie, and there was Jonah in the parking lot: "Yet forty days and Nineveh is going to be destroyed!" The kids would come out of high school and head to their cars or to football practice, and there was Jonah: "Yet twenty-nine days and Nineveh's going to be destroyed!" The people would be coming out of a movie or stopping off at a Starbuck's for a cup of coffee, and there was Jonah: "Yet seventeen days and God's going to destroy the city."

For forty days Jonah preached that message, and what happened at the end of forty days? Everybody in that city, from the king on the throne to the drunk in the gutter, cried out to God for forgiveness. Isn't that unbelievable? Isn't God a powerful God? He can change any city, any time, anywhere, any place, with anybody. And Jonah was so pumped and so excited, this is how we know he was a Baptist. How did Jonah respond to Nineveh's repentance? He went up on a hill and pouted! He had to be a Baptist.

He went up to the top of that hill and said, "Oh God, how could you spare Nineveh? I knew this was going to happen. I knew if I preached they would repent. I knew if they repented you would forgive them. I knew if you forgave them you wouldn't destroy the city. I told everybody you were going to destroy the city. You're not going to destroy the city. I'll never be accepted as a prophet again. I just want to die."

What an awful thing to have on your résumé as a prophet! An entire city of pagans repented. And God didn't destroy them! You failed. Can you imagine the dilemma of God? All these people in repentance, the prophet, who ought to be down there following up and beginning to teach them about the God who forgave them, on top of a hill pouting!

So what does God do to try to teach Jonah a lesson? He calls a great big old gourd tree plant to cover Jonah with shade while he pouted under the hot Middle Eastern sun. Then God got rid of the gourd tree plant, and Jonah said, "Lord, I sure miss the shade of that plant." And God said, "If you miss the shade of a plant, don't you think I would miss the lives of all those people of Nineveh? I love everybody, no matter who they are or what they've done."

God tried one last time to teach Jonah. What did God use to teach Jonah a lesson? He could have used any of the great angels in glory. He could have used any person on the face of the earth, but what did God use to teach Jonah a lesson about how important people are? You find it in my favorite verse in the Bible—Jonah 4:7: "God appointed a worm when dawn came the next day and attacked the plant and it withered." Can you imagine? I mean, can you imagine that little worm when God came and knocked on his door! He opened the door, and there was God. He probably dropped his worm teeth.

The story of Jonah is a perfect illustration of the instrumental power of God. Now let me say that again. This is important. The story of Jonah is the story of the instrumental power of God, a vivid illustration that God is able to do anything He wants to do with whatever He chooses to use.

Think about the things that God used and appointed in the book of Jonah. He used a great storm. He used a great fish. He caused a gourd tree plant to grow. He used a little worm to get rid of that gourd tree plant. The story of Jonah is more than the story of a great city's miraculous repentance; it is the story of God demonstrating He can use anything, from a reluctant prophet to a little worm—and He doesn't care who or what He uses.

What are the implications of this for us? You just ran out of excuses about being a witness. It doesn't matter how smart you are. Do you think your IQ might be higher than that of the worm? It doesn't matter how much Greek and Hebrew you know. It doesn't matter if you can handle people's objections or questions that they may raise. It doesn't matter what kind of personality you have. It doesn't matter what your background is. It doesn't matter what you're good at. It doesn't matter what you enjoy. God is able to use you for His intended purpose. The question in evangelism is not what *you* are able to do; the question is, What is *God* able to do? And the answer is, Anything He wants.

That's why all of us can be witnesses. Not one of us can ever save a soul. Jesus saves. Not one of us can reduce a lost person to repentance and tears. The Holy Spirit alone brings conviction of sin. Evangelism is not the human work of God's servants; it's the supernatural work of God's Spirit. He has the power to use any one of us.

V. God's Problem

So far we've looked at four fingers. God's passion. God's penalty. God's patience. God's power. Now we're down to the thumb. They tell us the thumb is perhaps the single most distinguishing characteristic of us as human beings. It is the thumb that haunts me nearly every day I live. And there are not many days that go by when I don't think about the book of Jonah and the thumb. When we get to the end of Jonah, it finally dawns on us that the thumb stands for God's problem. Can you say that with me? God's problem.

It finally dawns on us what God's biggest problem in the book of Jonah was. Was God's biggest problem the wicked Ninevites? No.

Was God's biggest problem their evil ways and their pagan idolatry? No. God's biggest problem was Jonah. And what we see is that as soon as Jonah obeyed, God brought repentance to Nineveh. The bottom line is that Nineveh was only a Jonah away from repentance.

Could it be that God's biggest problem is not a stubborn church but an intimidated pastor who doesn't think he can handle personal evangelism? Could it be that God's biggest problem is not a bunch of ornery deacons, but a bunch of ornery preachers who don't want to do anything they're not good at? I wonder, is there a community in your state that is just a Chuck, a Bill, a George, a Jim, a Susan, or a Mary away from revival? God has no problem bringing repentance to the hardest heart. God has no problem saving the lost. God's biggest problem is me.

My prayer for you is that you will experience the fullness of God's love. That you will come face-to-face with the reality of God's penalty; that you will cherish, more than you have ever cherished, God's patience; that you will have a confidence and a hope in God's power that will back down any fear in your soul. But may you never forget that there's only one person to whom you are accountable to God for your response—and that person is you. Don't be the thumb on God's hand.

11

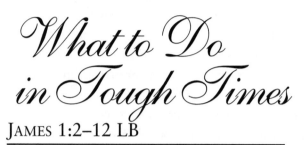

*What to Do
in Tough Times*

JAMES 1:2–12 LB

William Crews
President, Golden Gate Baptist Theological Seminary

ON MAY 22, 1997, at three o'clock in the morning, the doctor came out of the intensive care unit at our local hospital to tell me that our thirty-seven-year-old daughter, Rhonda, had succeeded in doing what she had been trying to do since she was sixteen years of age. Rhonda was beset with severe depression early in her life. And at age sixteen for the first time, she took an overdose of prescription drugs, attempting to take her own life. And in the succeeding twenty-one years, more times than I can count, Rhonda tried over and over and over again to end her life. That morning at three o'clock the doctor came out to tell me that our daughter was dead.

I went into the room where the body of my daughter lay and said good-bye to the little girl who had always been daddy's girl, the little girl whom I had held in my arms only hours after she was born. But she was gone. Our family was ushered into what was for us a new experience. As a pastor, I had always been with other people in times like that, and often faced the struggle of knowing exactly what to say or what not to say, but our family had never experienced loss like that.

About three weeks later, the Southern Baptist Convention was meeting in Dallas, Texas, and I had been invited by a friend to preach

129

in his church that Sunday morning. When he heard about Rhonda's death, he called and offered to release me from preaching in his church. I thanked him for his consideration, but I said I would preach again, and it probably would be better if I preached in front of people I did not know. So I agreed to preach that Sunday morning in his church. But as I thought about that, I wondered, *What will I preach about this first time since Rhonda's death?*

Then I remembered a sermon I had prepared in a class at Southwestern Seminary, "What to Do in Tough Times." I had preached that sermon many times across the years, and God had always seemed to use it to benefit the people who heard it. It was something that I knew to be true because it was in Scripture, though I had never actually experienced in my own life. I realized as I thought through that sermon prepared in a seminary classroom that what I had discovered in that text in seminary many, many years before was something God was trying to do in my life at that very moment.

And I shared on Sunday morning with this church that message and how God was helping me with the toughest time that I had ever faced in my life. Some of you even now are facing a tough time. Others of you have, and most of you will. What I share with you comes from Scripture, but it also comes out of my own experience. I believe God wants us to handle tough times His way.

One day many years ago in a time when it wasn't easy to be a Christian, a pastor stood and spoke to a small group of people on that Lord's day, and here is what he said:

Dear brothers [and sisters], is your life full of difficulties and temptations? Then be happy, for when the way is rough, your patience has a chance to grow. So let it grow and don't try to squirm out of your problems. For when your patience is finally in full bloom, then you will be ready for anything, strong in character, full and complete.

If you want to know what God wants you to do, ask him, and he will gladly tell you, for he is always ready to give a bountiful supply of wisdom to all who ask him, and will not resent it. But when you ask him, be sure that you really expect him to tell you, for a doubtful mind will be as unsettled as a wave of the sea that is driven and tossed by the wind; and every decision you then make will be uncertain, as you turn first this way and then that. If you don't ask with faith, don't expect the Lord to give you any solid answers.

A Christian who doesn't amount to much in this world should be glad, for he is great in the Lord's sight. But a rich man should be glad that his riches mean nothing to the Lord, for he will soon be gone, like a flower that has lost its beauty and fades away, withered and—killed by the scorching summer sun. So it is with rich men. They will soon die and leave behind all their busy activities. Happy is the [person] who doesn't give in and do wrong when he is tempted, for afterwards he will get as his reward the crown of life that God has promised to those who love him (James 1:2–12).

God is doing four things in my life to help me through a tough time.

I. Trials Have a Godly Purpose

First, if I am to get through a tough time, I must agree with God that all trials have a godly purpose in my life.

When I was pastor in Portland, Oregon, our church went through what we preachers would call a time of renewal or a time of revival. It wasn't a meeting. It wasn't about a person. It was one of those times when God's Spirit blows across a congregation, and the kinds of things that God alone can do begin to happen—families put back together and folks being saved whom we had prayed for for many years, and just that wonderful reconciling way in which God's Spirit moves among His people and does the thing that God alone can do. As that was happening in our church, I began as the pastor to think, *How did this happen? What did we do?* Maybe if I could discover some secret to this thing, I could write a book and become famous.

So as I began to try to analyze that and discover how all this got started, I discovered that it actually started in my own home, and I had been unaware of it. My wife, Jo Ann, to whom I have been married for forty-six years, was diagnosed about thirty-five years ago with what was called then manic depression. It is called bipolar disorder now. It is a chemical imbalance in the brain that causes excessive mood swings. Persons can be high, or they can be low. Because they are not balanced, it can go back and forth, and you never know exactly where they are going to be. And we discovered in Seattle, Washington, that she was manic-depressive. As a part of the process of dealing with that, someone suggested to her that she read a book.

I went home one day for lunch to our home in Portland, and she said, "I am reading this wonderful book that I think you would enjoy reading."

I said, "Well, what is it? I like to read books."

And she said, "It's a book by Hannah Smith entitled *The Christian's Secret of a Happy Life*."

"Well," I said to her rather proudly, "I have that book. In fact, I have had that book for many, many years. In fact, I have a hard-back copy of that book." She had a paperback. I said, "I've not found that book to be particularly interesting." And I did what most men do with their wives' suggestions: I ignored it. I did not read the book.

I was home for lunch a couple of days later, and she asked, "Have you read that book?" Well, rather indignantly, I said, "You know, you brought that up several days ago, and I told you then and I will tell you again that I have a hardback copy of that book. And I have not found that book to be of any particular interest." Again, I did what I had done the first time: I did not read the book.

I came home the third time for lunch, and she brought the subject up again. She said, "Have you read that book?"

Well, I didn't have to do anything about the indignation. It was all over me then. I said, "I'm telling you for the third time. I have a hardback copy of that book. And I have not found that book to be particularly interesting."

She said, "Sit down! I am going to read it to you." She began to read the book to me, and it is a great book if you can get past the first chapter. Forget the first chapter; get to the second chapter and move on through it. It was a great book, and out of that book some small groups were formed in our church. In reading that book, this thing that God was doing in our church began to happen.

My wife liked that book except for one chapter. It is entitled "Is God in Everything?" In that chapter, Hannah Smith quotes that little Bible verse that you and I learned in Sunday school that "all things work together for good to them that love God, to them who are the called according to his purpose" (Rom. 8:28 KJV). She said that is more than a Bible verse for kids to learn in Sunday school. She said that is literally true. Nothing happens in your life that does not pass through the hands of God. He has His own purpose for allowing it to take place in your life.

My wife had a hard time with that. Her father had been murdered when she was five. Her mother died when she was eight. She had been pushed from family to family, and here now she was suffering from an illness for which there seemed to be no cure. She had a hard time believing God had anything good to bring out of that. But I want to tell you that you will never, ever successfully handle a hard time until you agree with God. You don't have to understand God. You don't have to like what He says. But you must agree with God that all trials have a godly purpose in your life.

James said that God is doing two things when He allows us to be tested with a tough time. First, He is trying to teach us patience. That's not a good word for our day. Our culture is geared for action. We don't want to wait on anybody or anything. But the word *patience* means "the ability to stand up under pressure." God is not trying to see if we will fall. God is trying to help us stand up when tough times come. James said that God is trying to make us stronger, and He is trying to give us the ability to stand up under the pressure by allowing us to be tested. James says that the first thing God is doing is trying to make us stronger, trying to put some muscle in us.

Then he says that if we let patience do what it can do, then we will be perfect or complete. Well, if you have been a Baptist more than a week, you know that isn't going to happen in this world. We are reminded constantly by our songs and by our sermons that we are sinners; we are saved by grace, but we are sinners nonetheless. So perfection is out of the question in this life.

Well, the word *perfect* has nothing to do with sinlessness. It is a word that means "to be grown up." It means to be mature. It means to be more and more like Jesus Christ. And what James is saying is that God allows us to be tested—first, by building up our spiritual muscle, and then by helping us become more and more like Jesus Christ. Agree with God that all trials—not some, not most, but all—have a godly purpose in our lives.

II. Ask for God's Help

Second, I'm learning to pray and ask for God's help. James 1:5 says, "If any of you lack wisdom, let him ask of God, that giveth to all men liberally, and upbraideth not" (KJV). It's unfortunate that the verse begins with "if," because *if* implies that maybe I have it and maybe I don't. It probably should be translated "since" you lack wisdom. James is not assuming—and neither is God—that any of us knows how to handle tough times. So since we don't know how to respond when a tough time comes, James says God will tell us what to do.

By the way, the word *wisdom* has an Old Testament background. My definition of *wisdom* is "the ability to see the right way and the wrong way to handle a tough time, and the courage to choose the right way." James says that since we don't have that, God will tell us how to get it. What he says is something very simple. He says, "ask." Is there anybody here who does not know how to ask?

My wife and I had two children, and we tried to teach them many things. We succeeded in a few and did not succeed in others. But there were some things that we did not have to teach our children. One of the things we did not have to teach them was to ask. In their mother's womb they were kicking around asking and saying, "Give me, give me, give me." They came into the world with their hands out. Though they could not speak, I knew what they meant. "Give me, give me, give me." We didn't teach them that. They came by that naturally.

It's simple to ask. We all know how to ask. But the issue is: Whom are we going to ask? And James says, "Why don't you ask God?" Now some of us will eventually get around to that after we have asked everybody else. But James suggests that we start there. Ask God. And he points out some things about God that ought to encourage us to ask God. He says we should ask God first because it is His nature to give. God enjoys giving. He delights to give. It is a godly thing that God does when He gives. God does not have to be begged or pled with to give us answers. God is a giving God. He wants to give us answers. So ask God, the One who gives.

Who does God give to? He gives to *all*. That's an interesting word. It's a word that means God doesn't look at our faces. God gives to all. How does God give? He gives liberally. That means God gives more than we expect, more than we ask. I have always found that to be true in my experience. I go to God with a little cup, and He fills it to overflowing. God wants to give. God gives liberally. He may hold back in some areas of His nature, but not when He is giving. God gives liberally.

That last phrase is one that I didn't understand for a long time: "and upbraideth not." The phrase actually means "no scolding lecture." If you hear nothing else, hear this: When you ask God for help in facing a tough time, God is not going to give you a scolding lecture and make you feel stupid because you have asked Him for help. The devil may do it, and your friends may do it. But God is not going to make you feel silly and stupid when you ask Him for help.

When I was growing up as a little boy, my father was a truck driver, and my mother did not drive. My dad was gone all the time, driving these big trucks across the country.

My earliest goal that I can remember was to learn how to drive the family car. I didn't have a lot of goals early in life. I just wanted to drive the family car. I remember my father taking me down to the department of motor vehicles office, and I got my driver's license before everybody else in my class. I knew how to drive the family car, and I had a license to drive. Well, I lived two blocks from school and across the street from church. That was about the extent of my world, and you don't really need a car when you live in a world that small.

But I can remember saying to my father on a number of occasions, "Dad, I want to go down to the school, and I'd like to take the car." It was just two blocks. And my father would launch into this rather passionate explanation of what life was like when he was a boy going to school. You know, he walked five miles to school. The next time he told that story, it was six miles. The school moved every time he told that story. Or I said, "I have a date to go to church, and I want the car." Well, he would go into a horse-and-buggy routine—the whole thing about what life was like when he was a boy. This was his way of scolding me for asking. He was trying to make me feel silly for asking for the car. It didn't work, but he tried. God does not do that to us when we ask for help. So learn to pray and ask for God's help.

III. Have Total Faith in God

The third thing I am learning is this: If I am going to make it through tough times, I must have total faith in God. In verses 6–8 James talks about a double-souled or double-minded person. I've decided he's talking about a spiritually bipolar person, a spiritual manic-depressive. I have lived with manic depression so long that I know what it's like. You have seen people like that. You will have some in your church. One week they will be higher than a kite, and the next week lower than a snake's belly. You never know where they are going to be. They are up and down, in and out. You never know exactly where they are.

People like this haven't found that solid rock of faith upon which to build their lives, a place where they can stand when the storms come. James says we need to find that rock. We must find that rock, and that rock is absolute, total trust and faith in Jesus Christ. We have to find that rock if we are going to make it.

One of my favorite characters in the Bible is Job. You know his story well; it's the oldest story in Scripture. Job was a man whom heaven could look upon and smile. God could look down and say, "Of all the people on the face of the earth, Job is one who fears God, who has good relationships with his family, with his fellow man." God was proud of Job. The devil came and accused Job of serving God only because of what he got out of it. By the way, that's what the devil thinks about us, too. He thinks the only reason we serve God is because of what we get out of God.

So the devil said that if God took away all the things that God had blessed Job with, Job would curse God to His face. God gave Satan permission to take it all away. So Job lost it all. He lost all his money. His children were killed in a storm. He lost everything. Even his wife urged him to curse God and die. His body was wracked with sores that oozed day and night—an incurable disease from which no relief came. All of that happened to Job (see Job 1:1–19). The thing that bothers me the most about Job was his friends. To their credit, they did come, and they sat silently.

That's what friends can do—sit silently when we are in trouble. I used to think that Job's friends were a Rotarian, a Kiwanian, and a member of the Chamber of Commerce. But I have since discovered that Job's friends were theologians. And you really don't want friends who are theologians when you are in real trouble! The reason is that theologians by their very nature feel compelled to provide answers. Even if they don't know what the questions are, they are to provide answers. And when they do give answers, their answers are based primarily on their theology. And if their theology is wrong, their answers will be wrong.

And Job's friends had a bad theology. They said to Job, "If you will just get right with God, just pray more, just do more for God and do what's right, God will bless you again." But Job could not accept that counsel. God said in chapter 2 of Job that there was no reason in Job's life for what was happening to him. Job concluded that his friends were miserable comforters.

Did you ever have friends like that? You know, you feel better after they are gone. I want to tell you from experience that all of Job's friends are not dead. You just get in trouble, and they will show up. They may not say it, but they will indicate that if you just get right with God, everything will be OK again. Well, Job's friends left, and Job decided he wanted to write a book. He had something he wanted to say. In fact, he said he would like to do better than that. He would like to find a granite mountain and carve these words in stone, cast them in lead, so that everybody could see them for years to come. God did better than that! He put it here in the book of Job, and it will be here even when the mountains are gone.

Here is what Job said: "I know that my redeemer lives. And I know that one day He is coming back to this earth. And I know that one day I am going to see Him for myself" (see Job 19:25–27). Job said "That's all I know." But that is all he needed to know, and that's all we need to know. We have to have complete and total faith in God.

IV. Keep Your Eyes on the Goal

The fourth thing I am learning is that you have to keep your eyes fixed on the goal that is ahead. In verses 10–12, James begins to talk about rich people and poor people. And you could get lost in that and think that he is advocating poverty or saying there is something wrong with riches. But that's not it at all. James is reflecting about human nature that causes most of us to live our lives looking at other people. If we are poor, we look at the rich, and we wish we had what they have. If we are rich, we look at the poor, and we feel sorry for them. And James says, "Don't look around you, but look up." Look up to Him who stands at the end of the way, ready to give a crown of life to those who endure. Keep looking up.

When I was at Hardin-Simmons University, I was pastor of a little church near Stanford, Texas, called Plainview Baptist Church. It was called that because it was in "plain view." You could see it for miles and miles.

In that church there was a faithful couple. He worked for the gas company. He was a deacon, Sunday school superintendent, and tither. They were always there when the church doors were open. She taught Sunday school. It was a wonderful family. They had a little eight-year-old girl named Celia, who was their only child. One Saturday night as I was preparing to drive up to the church on Sunday, the phone rang. It was another deacon of the church. He said, "Pastor, Celia died this afternoon. You need to come as quickly as you can."

We packed up, and we went to that home where we had been on so many happy occasions. We went into the bedroom, and the mother was lying on the bed, and the father was sitting at the head of the bed, and other friends were gathered around. I went over and took their hands, and I prayed to God they would not ask me that question that every pastor hates to hear. But the father asked, "Pastor, why did God let our little girl die?" I didn't know then, and I don't know now the answer to that man's question.

On Wednesday, I conducted my first funeral service for that little eight-year-old girl. I asked God to help me give that family something that would help them, and He reminded me of the story of David and Bathsheba, the child of their adultery. And you remember that David was praying for his son. The news came that his son was dead, and David got up and said, "I know that my son can't come back to me, but I know that some day I am going to be with him" (see 2 Sam. 12:23). And while it may not be hermeneutically correct, I shared that word with that family that afternoon. We went out to the cemetery and put the little body in the ground, and I went back to school. And I prayed for that family like I had never prayed for a family in all my life because I had no idea what this would do to their faith.

But I didn't have to wait; the next Sunday they were right back in church, over there on the second row in the first two seats, dark glasses on because the tears were still there. And when I gave the invitation, they came forward. Cecil said he would like to say something. So when the invitation was over, I had the people sit down. And here this precious couple stood. And I stood with them. Here is what he said:

"When our little girl died, our first thought was to turn away from God. But then we thought if we turn away from God, who do we turn to? We are here to say to you that we know our little girl can't come back to be with us, but some day we are going to be with the Lord and with her. And until then we are going to keep serving Him." It wasn't long until the wife died, and she went to be with the Lord and with that little girl. And I hear from that deacon almost every Christmas. He is still serving God.

You ask, "How can he do that?" The same way we can. Just understand that trials have a godly purpose in our lives. Learn to pray and ask for God's help. Find that rock of faith to stand on. But above everything else, keep looking up—and God will bring you through.

12

A Report Card for Southern Baptists

REVELATION 2:1–5 HCSB

R. Philip Roberts
President, Midwestern Baptist Theological Seminary

"A REPORT CARD FOR SOUTHERN BAPTISTS" is a fitting title for this sermon. In a similar vein, John R. W. Stott, in his homiletical commentary on Revelation 1–3, entitles that volume *What Christ Thinks of the Church*. Why? Because these verses offer an opportunity for us to stop and ask ourselves, "What does Jesus think about us? What's His opinion about who we are and what we are doing and the motivation for our service and ministry to Him?"

The message of Christ to the seven churches of Revelation reveals His careful, critical, and constructive analysis of the church's work, fruitfulness, and motivations. His analyses offer us a fabulous opportunity for self-examination. Especially does this first letter to the church at Ephesus provide for Southern Baptists a reflecting mirror in which, with the Holy Spirit's help, we can see how we might be measuring up to what Jesus expects from us.

The modern church seems determined to press on with issues, objectives, and attitudes regardless of whether they may or may not be pleasing to the Lord. This text speaks to each Christian, to each Southern Baptist to every congregation. It asks us, Are we doing what Jesus wants us to do? And perhaps more importantly, *Are* we what Jesus wants us to *be*?

The Word of God says:

To the angel of the church in Ephesus write: "The One who holds the seven stars in His right hand and who walks among the seven gold lampstands says: I know your works, your labor, and your endurance, and that you cannot tolerate evil. You have tested those who call themselves apostles and are not, and have found them to be liars. You also possess endurance and have tolerated many things because of My name, and have not grown weary. But I have this against you: you have abandoned the love you had at first. Remember then how far you have fallen; repent, and do the works you did at first. Otherwise, I will come to you and remove your lampstand from its place—unless you repent (Rev. 2:1–5).

It is interesting, is it not, that in these seven letters to the seven churches, each one begins with a preamble that is an extract of the vision of Jesus Christ revealed in Revelation chapter 1? The Revelation of Jesus Christ given there is lifted out of that text, and is applied to each of the seven churches in a particular way that has significance for them, their great needs, as well as their opportunities. So let us review briefly the preamble given in Revelation 2:1. Then we will examine the message itself. Afterwards, we will note three marvelous compliments that Jesus pays the church at Ephesus. Then we will turn our attention to the one complaint He has about them found in verse 4. Finally, we will review Jesus' loving and compassionate word of correction in verse 5.

Interestingly, out of the seven messages to the seven churches of Revelation 2 and 3, only two have no word of complaint. Five of them do. It is very important to notice that whenever Jesus has a complaint or a criticism about a church, He always gives a word of correction. He doesn't leave them to stumble along or to languish and wonder what to do next. He always tells them what they ought to do and provides a measure of guidance.

There are Christians who believe that the New Testament era was the golden age of the church, an age where there were no problems and everything was perfect. That was hardly the case as any cursory reading of these inspired pages will reveal. Such an attitude reminds me of that anecdote attributed to Charles H. Spurgeon. A woman came up to him one Sunday morning and said, "Well, Pastor Spurgeon, I would join your church except that it is not the perfect New Testament church." Spurgeon knew a bit about the character of this dear woman. He looked her up and down, and in his wit and wisdom said, "Well, Madam, let me just suggest something to you. When you find the perfect New Testament church, please don't join it because you'll ruin it."

There is a word of correction after the word of complaint because the church of Ephesus, despite all of its redeeming qualities, possessed a fatal flaw which, if left uncorrected, would destroy the vitality of the fellowship. Jesus gives them clear direction on how to avoid the problems which could mar and eventually eliminate their witness.

It is interesting that the name of Jesus is not mentioned in any of these letters. It doesn't have to be. It's very clear who is sending this word because the One who sends the word is the One who is described as holding the seven stars in His right hand, walking in the midst of the seven golden lampstands. "The One who holds the seven stars in His right hand" (Rev. 2:1) speaks vividly to us of Jesus' omnipotence. Those stars symbolized the churches, and most biblical exegetes would say that those seven stars signify to us that Jesus is the Lord of the church. But we also know in ancient and even modern thought that the stars were representative of the entire cosmos, reminding us that He who is Lord of the church is *Lord of all*. He has *all* power and *all* authority (see Matt. 28:18). By Him all things were made, and without Him there is not anything made that was made (John 1:3). He is the Lord of lords and the King of kings (Rev. 19:16).

Note that old cliché which says, "If He is not Lord of all, then He is not Lord at all." His omnipotence must be utmost in our minds. He is not just a religious mystic we are following. He is the Lord of lords and King of kings. Some people have said to me, "Do you believe that Jesus is superior to Buddha and Mohammed and all the other religious leaders?" And I reply, "Of course, He is. He made them. While He did not create their religion, He is their God and Creator. He is Lord of all."

A few years ago when my family was living in Atlanta, some of our neighbors got interested in astrology. One of the neighboring ladies came to me and asked, "What do you think of astrology?" I replied, "There is a good Greek word for it, and that word is *baloney*." Astrology is actually built on a false view of physical reality because it holds that the earth is the center of the universe and that the stars are fixed in their place. It also teaches that they emanate spiritual powers and influence. Astrology claims that these physical suns dotting our universe shape the character of people, depending on the time and season of the stars under which they are born. Absolute superstition and nonsense! Astrology projects not only a false view of physical reality but of spiritual claims as well.

But here is the point. Let's just say, for the sake of argument, that astrology is true. The point about this text is: Who cares? Because through having a personal saving relationship with the Lord Jesus Christ, you can know the One who made the stars and who holds them in His right hand, who has all power in heaven and earth, and who is our Lord and Savior, Lord of lords and King of kings.

Second, Jesus wants the churches to be reminded of His omnipresence. The text notes that the Lord Jesus walks among the seven golden lampstands. This perspective debunks the old worldview known as deism, the view that God is a divine watchmaker. He created the world like a watchmaker crafted a watch, this perspective claims. Then He walked away from His creation as well as those who bear His image—human beings. That's certainly not the biblical view of God, because the Bible reminds us that Jesus, while He is omnipotent, is also omnipresent. He walks among His people. He has fellowship with us. He desires to know, bless, encourage, and when necessary, to correct and redirect us. He is present with His people—His church. His ultimate desire is to bless us with His wonderful grace and mercy.

Not only is He omnipotent. Not only is He omnipresent, He is also omniscient. Why? In the heart of the message after the preamble, the first words Jesus says to them are, "I know your works" (Rev. 2:2).

Jesus knew every last detail about this church and its members. He knew their failings, their successes, their ups and downs. Their hearts, their motives, and their intentions were an open book for Him. Jesus knows everything about us. He knows everything about our works, our labor for Him, our motives, everything that we do in His name. He knows our sins and shortcomings as well. In fact, the Word of God reminds us that even the hairs on our heads are numbered by Him (Matt. 10:30; Luke 12:7). And what we will rediscover in this text is this: Not only does He know our works externally, what we are doing for His name's sake, but He also knows our motives, why we do certain things.

He knows infallibly when we are motivated rightly and when we are not. He knows everything! Jesus is omniscient! With all of this important revelation and reminder about Jesus as background, let's look at three wonderful compliments he pays to the church at Ephesus.

A Compliment for Their Perspiration

The first compliment is, "I know your works, your labor." He commends the church at Ephesus for their perspiration. He compliments them because they were a hardworking, diligent fellowship.

We might ask, "Why were they a hardworking church?" It is easily discovered when we examine their history. It was written in their DNA. According to Acts 19 and 20, Paul spent approximately three years in Ephesus. It was a great imperial city in Asia Minor, probably the most influential city in the region. Paul spent those years there engaged in excruciating labor. What did he do? First, he did what he always did when he went to a Mediterranean city with Jewish inhabitants. He headed for the Jewish synagogue. He took the Hebrew Scriptures, opened them up, and from the Hebrew explained and argued that Jesus is the Messiah, the Christ, the Savior of Jews and Gentiles. Then he went down to the school of Tyrannus and met with the leaders of the city and presented the gospel of the Lord Jesus Christ to them (see Acts 19:19).

Then in Acts 20, when he says good-bye to the elders of Ephesus on his final visit there, he reminds them that he had gone from house to house sharing the gospel. He calls to their attention the fact that he was not reluctant to share the gospel with anyone who would listen. It didn't matter to Paul whether a person was the mayor of the city or a slave in the household. He was interested in whether they had heard the good news of the Lord Jesus Christ. His objective had been to evangelize the entire city!

The church at Ephesus followed that model so faithfully that before Paul left town, so pervasive and powerful was the presentation of the gospel that the silversmiths, the idol makers, began to lose business. The impact of truth had undercut those merchants profiteering on paganism.

Paul was a hardworking servant! The church he founded in Ephesus was a hardworking, evangelizing congregation.

Many times when I sound this note and emphasis in Southern Baptist churches, people look at me with this blank stare as if to say, "You don't understand Southern Baptists very well. You don't realize how busy we are." Some of these congregations are so busy that their calendars look like an airline flight schedule. There is something going on or taking off every fifteen minutes.

A church where my wife and I were members began reviewing how they were going to admit new members into the church. They asked me if I had any suggestions. I said, "I just have one. Before you admit anyone into membership, they should go to the doctor and have a physical exam and see if they have the stamina and strength to be an active participant in this congregation." It reminds me of that little poem someone wrote:

Mary had a little lamb.
She thought he was a sheep.
They both joined a Baptist church
And died for lack of sleep.

But why isn't the church in North America more productive in reaching our continent for Christ? Could it be that we are spending our energy on nonessentials? Most of our activity, much of our resources and energy are spent doing "church work." What is church work? Church work is all the essential ministry, organization, and administration necessary to keep the church going, to keep it "active" and "healthy." But how much of our time do we spend doing *the work of* the church? And what is the work of the church? The work of the church consists of all those things the Lord Jesus Christ gave us to do in the Great Commission—evangelism, discipleship, and missions.

If you ask why churches have plateaued or are declining in North America today, I would argue that it's because we are out of focus. We are spending most of our time and energy doing church work and very little time doing the work of the church. If you don't believe me, I challenge you to take out your calendar from this past year and ask yourself this question: In my church responsibilities, what percentage of my time is spent doing church work versus the work of the church? Sharing the gospel with the lost and needy world around us is *the work of* the church.

Can you imagine a company like Delta Airlines suddenly deciding not to serve all people who aren't a part of the Delta family? "For the next six months," they might say, "we are only going to sell tickets and have passengers who are our employees, our stockholders, and other members of the Delta family. In this way we will encourage one another, and we will be happy and so gratified by the service we are receiving from one another that things are going to be much better in six months." In six months the company would be bankrupt.

In regards to the church in our land we ask, "Why is it that so many make so little impact with so much?" The answer is, "We are probably focusing on the wrong thing. Our priorities are askew." This Ephesus church, however, was complimented for their perspiration. They were busy doing evangelism and discipleship.

A Compliment for Their Perseverance

Note that Jesus Christ compliments the Ephesian church for its perseverance. Verse 2 says, "I know your works, your labor, and *your endurance.*" And then he reiterates this matter again in verse 3: "And you have persevered and have patience." The picture here from the original language is not of the church sitting back passive in their approach to the needs of the world. We just saw that they were a very hardworking church. What is implied here is that this was a church under pressure. They were persevering under pressure. In the midst of persecution, they were faithful to the Lord.

The groups that Jesus is addressing here are those who pretend to represent true Christianity.

The Book of Revelation is the last book in the New Testament canon. It was written sometime in the closing years of the first century A.D. By this time in the great empire of Rome, there had already been several empirewide waves of persecution against Christians. There were also local outbreaks of intimidation and oppression against believers. We know that even before Paul left Ephesus, the silversmiths had lost or were losing business. So what did the silversmiths do? They rented the city football stadium or the chariot rink and had a pep rally for the pagan goddess Diana of the Ephesians. They gathered all the people of the city who were opposed to the gospel. For several hours there was an outcry of support for the pagan worship of Diana that surely agitated the masses against the believers in that metropolis (see Acts 19:21–41). Consequently, in the years that followed, many followers of Jesus Christ possibly lost their health, their wealth, and even their own lives for their testimony to Jesus.

Don't ever believe that if you have an effective ministry, there won't be opposition. If you are unwilling to stand for the gospel, you will never experience it. But if you stand for the gospel and its values, you can expect opposition. You will be persecuted. Paul wrote Timothy, "All those who want to live a godly life in Christ Jesus will be persecuted" (2 Tim. 3:12). If you have not already experienced persecution, I'm worried about you because you are not living for Jesus in a world that's opposed to the gospel. There will be some opposition along the way. The point is that you should deal with opposition in a godly, biblical fashion. Don't let it make you bitter; let it make you better.

It has been my privilege over the years to meet and to work with some of God's truly great saints. Many of them have suffered deeply for their faith. One such dear friend is president of a seminary in the heart of a Muslim country. During a time of horrific warfare, he pastored a Baptist church in a great city in that country. There were actually occasions when, during Sunday worship, members of the congregation would be wounded by exploding shells or hand grenades. During a visit together I once asked, "What keeps you in the pastorate?" He said it was the call of God to uphold the Word of life in a city where death is a regular occurrence.

Imagine that a man truly gifted could serve the Lord just about anywhere, but is faithful to His calling to suffer the consequences in a place of great danger and sorrow. The Lord truly rewarded his efforts and his faithfulness to the gospel. It is that kind of perseverance for which Jesus commended the church of Ephesus. They were a persevering, faithful congregation.

A Compliment for Their Perception

But not only did Jesus compliment the church at Ephesus for their perspiration and perseverance; He also complimented them for their perception. His exact words were, "You have tested those who call themselves apostles and are not, and you have found them to be liars" (Rev. 2:2). Do any of us think that we need theological and doctrinal perception in the church today?

We live in a pluralistic country with a plethora of religious options. Over 1,650 major religious groups exist here in the United States. Perception is an extremely important characteristic that is often missing from our churches. It is an essential ingredient of Christian maturity that is sorely needed in today's church.

When members of cultic groups come knocking on your door on Saturday mornings, they are not going to say, "We are the local heretical cult down the street." They are going to say, "We are the witnesses of Jehovah. We are from the Church of Jesus Christ of Latter-Day Saints. We are members of the Church of Christ, Scientist." And they are going to use the same religious terms we use. They are going to use biblical words and terms. They are going to refer to the Bible. They are going to tell you how much they love Jesus. They are going to talk about the gospel and how you can have eternal life, but it's not going to be anything like the message in the Bible. They are false prophets. And the gospel they have is not the one true gospel that we know from the pages of the Bible. We need people who understand the essence of true Christianity and who can spot spiritual counterfeits.

One of my friends is a Secret Service agent. He confirmed for me an illustration Walter Martin uses in his book, *Kingdom of the Cults,* regarding counterfeit cults, their exposure, and the Secret Service. The Secret Service has two main responsibilities. One is protection of VIPs along with the leadership of our nation. The other responsibility is uncovering and destroying false currency operations. When the Secret Service trains their agents for counterfeit operations, they don't expose them to phony currency. Instead, they take them up to Philadelphia to the Bureau of Printing and Engraving. There the trainees spend several weeks examining the genuine article. They touch, feel, smell, and examine authorized U.S. currency. After this exposure to real money the new agents could spot a counterfeit a mile away.

Part of our purpose in seminary education at Midwestern Seminary is to get so well acquainted with the real thing, the real gospel, to develop theological perception, a perception that can be passed on to other Christians and followers of Jesus Christ. The Lord knows we need this ability in the American church today!

A few years ago I clipped an Associated Press article from the newspaper. It was entitled "Family Ditches Clothes in Pursuit of the Lord." It read, "People were surprised when a driver wearing only a towel got out of a car, then got back and sped off. They were dumbfounded when the car hit a tree and revealed twenty people wearing nothing at all. The Lord told them, they said, to get rid of all their belongings and go to Louisiana. So they got rid of all their clothes, wallets, identification, and the license plate on their car, and they came to Louisiana. The police said they didn't have any money, not even a dime." Of course they didn't. Where would they have put it?

The article goes on to say that "all 20 people were from Floydada, in the Texas panhandle." But here is how it ends and the point that it makes: "The car was totaled, but all injuries were minor. The entire group was *released into the custody of a Baptist church.*" I appreciate that! There are a lot of folk with doctrinal loose ends running around out there who need to be released into the custody of a good Bible-believing, Bible-teaching Baptist church.

A Word of Concern

So Jesus complimented the church of Ephesus. He congratulated them that they were hard workers. They were persevering under pressure. They were perceptive. We could say, "Amen, hallelujah, there was revival in Ephesus!" But verse 4 reveals that there was something seriously amiss in the church at Ephesus. Jesus said to them, "But I have this against you: you have abandoned the love you had at first" (Rev. 2:4). Let me ask you something. Do you think it's possible for a person to get involved in Christianity, to do many great things in the name of Christ, to sacrifice and suffer in the name of the gospel, even to have great insight in every manner of doctrine and theological concern, yet somehow be losing his or her love for Jesus?

Paul wrote in 1 Corinthians 13 some words to this effect. He said, "If I give all that I have to the poor, if I give my body to be burned, if I have all wisdom, understand all mysteries, have all knowledge, to speak them and articulate them with the tongues of an angel, and have not love, it is nothing." It's zero without the rim around it. And to whom is this great love to be expressed? This great love is necessarily and primarily to be love for the Lord Jesus Christ.

Why are you here today? Why did you accept the call to ministry? Why did you leave family and home? Why are you willing to take the hard way and prepare and to give your life in service to Christ? Why are some of you willing to leave these shores and invest your life in foreign missions, or accept the pastorate of a struggling church, or move into a city where there is no church? Or go to a troubled church and stand faithfully proclaiming the Word of God? Why are you willing to do that? It must be because you love Jesus that you are doing those things for Him. That's what it's all about. After all, Christianity is, at its most basic level, a relationship—a love relationship between you and the Lord Jesus Christ.

Recently in my devotional readings I read through 1 Corinthians 15 and 16. Do you know how Paul closes First Corinthians? Do you know what verse 22 of 1 Corinthians 16 says? "If anyone does not love the Lord, a curse be on him." Do you know why? Because that's the essence of the Christian faith. Christianity is not just a matter of doing good work. It's not just sacrifice in the world's greatest cause. It's not just learning and absorbing truth. It is, in its essence, a personal relationship with Jesus Christ. Without that relationship the reality of Christianity is lost

Let me tell you about the most dangerous false religion in America today. It is not a cult based in Salt Lake or Brooklyn or even a non-Christian world religion. It is social, cultural, traditional Christianity without a saving personal relationship with Jesus Christ. It is the most dangerous false religion, because there are so many good things about it, including a wonderful ethic, a great tradition, a wonderful worship experience, friends, and every sort of intellectual challenge you could ever face. But without a personal relationship with Jesus Christ it is zero. It is nothing.

A Word of Correction

When the Lord Jesus gives the word of concern or criticism in any of these several letters, He also has a word of correction to go with it. His desire is to change the church for the better and to redirect it in a constructive manner. There, Jesus says to the fellowship at Ephesus, "Remember then how far you have fallen" (Rev. 2:5).

Now let me ask you a question. If your love for Jesus Christ has diminished, whose fault is it? Who has changed?

The text says, "Remember therefore from *whence you have fallen.*" It reminds me of a story of an old farmer on a country road with his wife. He is behind the wheel of his pickup truck. She is over by the door. They pull in behind a convertible. The top of the convertible is down, and a woman on the passenger's side is leaning so far over on the driver's shoulder that it looks like a two-headed man driving the car. The couple is in love and is showing it. After a few minutes of following that convertible, Grandma looks at Grandpa and says, "That's the way we use to be." The farmer looks back at her and says, "Well, I ain't moved."

If something has happened to your love relationship with Jesus Christ, He hasn't moved. He hasn't changed. He is the same yesterday, today, and forever. He loves you as much today as when He suffered, bled, and died for your sins on the cross of Calvary.

Jesus then prescribes a solution to the problem. He goes on to say, "Do the works you did at first" (Rev. 2:5). Whenever I have a conversation with a person who says, "My spiritual ardor, my zeal, my love for Jesus has grown dim," I am prone to ask, "When did you stop reading the Bible and feeding your own soul? When did you stop having private prayer time?" Take some time out and spend the morning with the Lord. Have an hour of prayer. We come to church and sing "Sweet Hour of Prayer," but how many of us have spent an hour in prayer recently? When was the last time you told somebody about Jesus' love? When did you stop worshiping and fellowshipping in the company of God's people?

I have never had one person who complained about spiritual laxity say to me that he or she was doing any of those things. They had at some point grown lax about doing the first works. Do you know that is always the case? They stopped praying, haven't read the Bible for their spiritual health like they should have, haven't witnessed regularly like they should have, haven't been consistently in the fellowship of God's people like they used to be. In every case, lack of discipline and consistency are evident.

We need to remember these words of Jesus, "If you love Me, you will keep My commandments" (John 14:15). Do the work that you did at first. It's all about Jesus. It's all about loving Him, walking with Him, and experiencing His love for us fresh and anew every day.

D. L. Moody was probably the most effective evangelist in the late nineteenth century. He preached in every major city in America. Urban evangelism was his emphasis. He had a fabulous preaching tour in England and rocked that nation for Christ. But Moody was a sixth-grade dropout. He was won to Christ while selling shoes in a store in Boston. His grammar was horrible. He didn't say "ain't," he said "hain't." His grammar was that bad. But God would greatly use D. L. Moody.

Moody did not, however, start out as a great evangelist. He began his ministry as a Sunday school teacher. He loved young people because He knew Jesus loved them. He got a little group together in Chicago and nurtured them and taught them the gospel. He led them to Christ and discipled them. When the Civil War broke out, he volunteered to be a chaplain in the Union army. He went and ministered to wounded and dying soldiers. He visited them, comforted them, and read the Bible to them. Many of them he led to faith in Jesus Christ. He gave of himself. Later God created a national and international platform for him. His willingness to be used of God in any arena was the key to Moody's life and ministry.

One hot, dusty, unpleasant Saturday afternoon in Chicago, a couple went to see Moody teach his Sunday school class. He had a roomfull of ragamuffin boys in a little room on the second floor of a building in central Chicago. He was pouring out his heart to them about God's love for them. They sat quietly and listened. After the class was over, the couple came up to him and said, "Mr. Moody, we are going to pray for you. God is going to use you wonderfully. You have many talents and gifts. God is going to use you in an effective and dynamic way."

Moody replied, "Oh no. You don't understand. I don't have any great gifts. I don't have any great skills. But I have one great passion, and that is that I love Jesus Christ will all my heart. Pray for me that I will always love Jesus with all my heart."

Is that the prayer of your life? If it isn't, then when there is disappointment, and there will be, and when there is discouragement, and there will be, you will begin to say, "It's not worth it. I can't take it. I don't want to go down this path any more." But if Jesus is at the center of your life, and if your passion is to love him with all your heart, mind, and strength, and if you fellowship in the wonderful presence of the Holy Spirit, God will use you. And you will find joy in His work and delight in serving in His great name.

Part 2:

Preaching
from the Heart
of a Family

13

What Jesus Does for the Sinner
LUKE 19:10 KJV

James T. Draper, Sr. (1913–1966)
Pastor, First Baptist Church, Warren, Arkansas

THE MISSION OF JESUS into this world in human form was primarily in the interest of lost men. He did not come for personal gain, for honor to Himself, to prove that He could do it, or for any other purpose, other than to seek and save those who are lost (Luke 19:10).

It seems very appropriate therefore that we inquire into just what He does for lost men. Since He subjected Himself to the limitations of the flesh and suffered pain and embarrassment, shame, ridicule, and agony, for man's sake, then surely it must have been something marvelously wonderful that He came to do for the sinner. One, even God, would not go to trouble and suffer so much, unless it were something vital that He would be able to do through this suffering.

Jesus does three things for the sinner though His life, death, and resurrection. These three things explain His mission and make all His sacrifice as clear as the noonday sun and as glorious as all the riches of the Triune God.

I. Jesus Loves the Sinner in Spite of Sin

God's Book tells us that He is love. Then Christ made the startling claim in John 10:30 that "I and my Father are one." When we read over and over in His Word that God loves the sinner, we must be constrained to say that Jesus loves the sinner also, since He is God Himself. So wherever we find in the Word the great fathomless love the Father for sinning humanity, we can say, "Yes, that expresses the love of Jesus, the Son, for lost men too, because He and the Father are one."

As a matter of fact, Jesus is the supreme manifestation of love. Men might doubt the love of the Father for lost men if He remained in His heavenly kingdom and only sent down messages through men to the effect that He loved them and never did anything for them. But the Father forever hushed the mouths of the gainsayers along that line when He sent His Son, His only begotten, dearly beloved Son, heaven's most precious jewel, onto the earth in human form, allowed Him to be subjected to torture, ridicule, opposition, pain, suffering, and even a criminal's death, to prove that He does love lost men. If those who deny that God loves lost men will take one good look at Jesus, the Father's Son, they will be forced to admit that God does love lost men, because Jesus provided it in His work.

With all of our imperfections, we often fail to love folks with no tangible reason for so feeling. Because we don't like the language they use, or the way they dress, or the look they have on their faces or their attitude towards us, we dislike them very strongly. And most of us would raise our hands in unholy horror at the suggestion that we love someone who had wronged us. All this in spite of the fact that our Savior has commanded us to love our enemies and those who despitefully use us. But picture Jesus if you will, wronged terribly by those who broke His law, slighted, mocked, ridiculed, shunned, opposed, and finally murdered. Yet hear Him as He says to the disciples, "As the Father hath loved me, so have I loved you" (John 15:9), and as He prays on the cross for His enemies, "Father, forgive them, for they know not what they do" (Luke 23:34).

There are numerous examples in the Gospels of Christ's love for sinners. We will notice only two of them. You will recall the incident in Mark 10 of the rich young ruler who came to Jesus, seeking spiritual light. He affirmed that he had kept the commandments but was unwilling to obey Christ when He commanded him to sell his possessions, give the proceeds to the poor, and follow Him. He was unwilling to surrender himself in obedience to the Master. He went away sorrowful, unsaved. The significant statement in the record of that incident is to be found in verse 21a: "Then Jesus beholding him, loved him."

The other incident may be found in the fifth chapter of Mark. Jesus and the disciples crossed the Sea of Galilee, landing in the country of the Gadarenes. Scarcely had they set foot on land when old Legion ran to meet them. Old Legion was a crazy man. He was possessed of many demons. He tortured himself, terrified the neighborhood, and lived alone in the cemetery. Many times his countrymen had bound him with ropes or chains, thinking to keep him in solitary confinement and thus lift the dread of him that rested on everyone. They had been unable to do so, so strong was he. Now he runs to meet the great Nazarene teacher. The people around must have thought this to be the end of the Great Dreamer, the Radical teacher from across the lake. Imagine their amazement and that of the disciples when, instead of running as others did, Jesus walked serenely on toward the man, as if unaware of his condition.

The disciples must have tried to turn him aside and make Him return to the boat, but it was no use. The Master was determined to meet the man. Imagine their utter amazement when the man did not offer to harm Jesus. They must have thought themselves dreaming when they heard this terrible demon-possessed man pleading with Him, pleading with another when others had been accustomed to pleading with him. Hear his beseeching tones as he pleaded with Jesus to let him alone. The demons in the man had so possessed him that he didn't want Jesus, the supreme demon enemy, around him. Determined to cast the demons out, Jesus allowed them to enter a herd of swine that immediately plunged to their death in the sea. It is significant that two thousand swine died when one man who had demons in himself had lived with them for years.

Let us follow the story on to its conclusion. Jesus remained a short time there, cutting his visit short because the people who had lost the hogs didn't want Him around them. When He came to leave, however, the demon-possessed man begged to go with Him. Legion was clothed, in his right mind, and turned missionary. Jesus told him to tell his own people what He had done for him. Imagine the stir that created in that land. What a missionary that man must have made. And why? Simply and only because Jesus loved the man. The man was a lost sinner, and Jesus loved that lost sinner.

Jesus loves sinners in spite of their sinfulness. He hates sin with all the force of a holy and righteous God, who knows no sin, but He loves the sinner in spite of his imperfections and transgressions.

Jesus loves you today—you who are the farthest from God and the deepest in sin—Jesus loves you with the undying, perfect love of a great God.

II. Jesus Lifts the Sinner out of Sin

In John 12:32, Jesus made this striking claim, "And I, if I be lifted up from the earth, will draw all men unto me." If Christ draws men to Him when He is lifted up, then they too must be lifted up in order to be drawn to Him. Psalm 40:2 expresses this lifting power of Christ: "He brought me up also out of an horrible pit, out of the miry clay, and set my feet upon a rock, and established my goings." He does by His atoning sacrifice what the combined learning of many scholars could not do. He does in response to a man's faith what that man could not do after a lifetime of much striving and toil. Yes, Jesus does not save the man in his sin but lifts him out of his sin. He saves a man from sin and not in sin.

Now what does this mean? It means three things. First, it means that *sin is powerful,* else man would not need an external, divine force to lift him out of it. If sin, as some men say, were something not very bad, then man could shake it off, get out of it with little effort, and that with his own power, without any other help. But if what Jesus said is true, and if it takes Jesus to lift a man out of sin, then sin must be powerful. Even other men cannot do it—it takes the perfect Son of God.

Then second, it means that *man must be willing to be lifted,* as God does not force His salvation on anyone. The old idea that God will save a man in His good time, in His season, irrespective of that man's own desires and will, is a dangerous doctrine. I have heard of people who have died without Christ, simply because they were waiting for God to knock them down and reveal to them His salvation, and that time didn't come. All the way through the Word of God, His invitation is to "whosoever will," and His promises are to those who will accept them. It is true, very true, that salvation must come from God and that man cannot produce one iota of it, but it is likewise true that God will not place that salvation in the heart of a single individual without first that individual opening his heart and by faith allowing God to save him.

Then in the third place, it means that *Christ is more powerful than sin,* else the sinner could not be lifted out of sin by Him. Unless Jesus had more power than Satan and sin, He couldn't save one single soul from sin unless Satan voluntarily gave in to him. Christ is all-powerful. He has not been shackled or bound by sin, and thus is over and above it, not in it. Hence, through His marvelous power, sinners can be lifted out of sin.

This is one of God's most glorious truths: that men bogged down in sin can be lifted out of sin by the crucified Savior. Truly, He did do some wonderful things for lost men through His matchless sacrifice! He lifts the sinner out of sin.

III. Jesus Leads the Sinner Away from Sin

He does not leave the newborn soul on the brink to slide back into the mire. He takes him as one takes a toddling child and teaches him to walk in his newfound world. He leads him step-by-step away from sin toward God.

Jesus guides him in such a way that he may overcome temptation. Concerning this we read in 1 Corinthians 10:13 that "there hath no temptation taken you but such as is common to man; but God is faithful, who will not suffer you to be tempted above that ye are able; but will with the temptation also make a way to escape, that ye may be able to bear it."

Jesus leads him in paths of service. For every child of God in the world, there is some sphere of service and usefulness, a sphere that will not be covered unless that child finds and fills it. Churches have been planted for that purpose. It is our glorious, God-given task to take these newborn babes in Christ and lead them into paths of service, for in so doing we will be in a measure filling our places, pleasing the Savior, and helping to support the kingdom of God long after we have passed off the stage of action.

Jesus directs his steps in the way of obedience and sacrifice. John says in I John 2:6, "He that saith he abideth in him ought himself also so to walk, even as he walked." As Christ obeyed the Father and sacrificed Himself for the benefit of others, so we are also to obey Him and sacrifice for others and for Him. The newborn babe in Christ is to walk in the way of obedience and sacrifice; Christ would lead him in that way, and He would have us to allow ourselves to be used as instruments in His hands to accomplish that purpose.

And then, one day, when death claims His child, Jesus will not relinquish His hold but will lead him right into the Father's presence, away from all sin—perfect and eternally happy and useful. Then He will have led His child, the sinner, so far away from sin that He has led him right into the presence of God, away from all sin and out of the presence of sin for all eternity.

What a marvelous Savior! He begins with a love for a poor deluded sinner and ends up with that sinner free from all sin, in the Father's presence, having the approval of the Father, and clothed in the righteousness of Him who loved him and died for him.

IV. Lessons for You

There are four lessons to be learned:

1. Christ is intensely interested in you as an individual. Ours is a Great God, a God of unlimited power, wisdom, and grace. Yet the most outstanding element of His greatness is the fact that He is vitally concerned about each one of His creatures.

2. He offers you the only avenue of escape from sin. There is absolutely no other way out, save the way of the cross. The path to

glory lies over the sacrifice of Calvary. Try as you will, philosophize as you please, theorize all you can, read the works of the masters, study with the diligence of a Luther, search with the determination of a Diogenes, travel as widely as those who sail the seven seas, and yet with it all you must come back to this eternal truth, this life-giving truth: that Jesus offers you the only escape from sin.

3. You must accept it while He offers it. God says, "My Spirit shall not always strive with man" (Gen. 6:3), and again, "Behold now is the accepted time, . . . now is the day of salvation" (2 Cor. 6:2). God is under absolutely no obligation to offer you salvation at all, let alone to leave His offer open indefinitely. It is dangerous to delay. You have no assurance of any time to call your own. You can't write down on a piece of paper how long God will let you live. And besides all that, you do not know how many more, if any, opportunities you will have to give your heart to the Lord. If ever Jesus, who loves you in spite of sin, will be able to lift you out of sin and lead you away from sin, He will be able to do it only if you accept salvation while He offers it.

4. What you do is a matter of individual choice. No one else can decide for you. If I could, I'd trust Christ for you, but that is a matter of absolute impossibility. You have your own account to give to God. You will not be responsible for what others do, but on the other hand, you will be responsible for your own actions. It is a fearful thing to fall into the hands of the living God—*unprepared!*

14

Knowing God as He Really Is

EXODUS 3:1–14 HCSB

James T. Draper, Jr.

ONE OF THE GREAT DANGERS for all of us in the Lord's service is that we become very familiar with what we're doing. We become very mechanical. Our service becomes habitual. We get used to being saved. We get used to the message. This is amazing when we think about the incredible message of a God who created us. He gave us choices, and He saw those choices separate us from Him. He knew that the only way we could correct those choices would be to be separated from Him forever. So the God who demanded holiness and demanded that sin be atoned for sent His own Son to die on the cross.

We often speak about that like we would talk about something we have read in the newspaper. Yet it is an incredible truth! It's a wonderful story that God loves us and has sent His Son to die for us. And God not only sent His son to die for us, but when Jesus ascended back to heaven, He sent the Holy Spirit so He could live in us. The very life of God can dwell within us. We often forget that. We lose sight of the fact that God wants us to know Him.

We never can reach perfect knowledge of God. We never can say that we have learned everything there is to know about Him. There's always something new. God wants us to know Him, and it takes a lifetime of relationships and a lifetime of discovery. The more we discover about God, the more we find there is to know about God. It is tragic how matter-of-fact and apathetic we are about our relationship with God and the message of His gospel.

Turn with me to the book of Exodus. I want us to spend some time looking at one of the most remarkable encounters any person ever had with God. You are familiar with the context. Moses is on the back side of the desert. He's away from everything familiar, everything that holds his dreams and hopes. On the back side of the desert, as he's tending his sheep, he sees a bush burning. The bush is an unusual bush because it burns, but it is not consumed. It does not burn up. That is a curiosity to him, and he turns to look at the bush.

> Meanwhile Moses was shepherding the flock of his father-in-law Jethro, the priest of Midian. He led the flock to the far side of the wilderness and came to Horeb, the mountain of God. Then the Angel of the LORD appeared to him in a flame of fire within a bush. As Moses looked, he saw that the bush was on fire but was not consumed. So Moses thought: I must go over and look at this remarkable sight. Why isn't the bush burning up?
>
> When the LORD saw that he had gone over to look, God called out to him from the bush, "Moses, Moses!" "Here I am," he answered.
>
> "Do not come closer," He said. "Take your sandals off your feet, for the place where you are standing is holy ground." Then He continued, "I am the God of your father, the God of Abraham, the God of Isaac, and the God of Jacob." Moses hid his face because he was afraid to look at God (Exod. 3:1–6).

Then follows some conversation back and forth as God assigns Moses a task and Moses asks God to reveal His name. "God said to "God replied to Moses, 'I AM WHO I AM.' This is what you are to say to the Israelites, 'I AM has sent me to you'" (Exod. 3:14).

There is a great deal of difference between knowing about God and knowing God. One of our great dangers is that we may know a lot of things about God but we would lose intimate knowledge of

God. God wants us to know Him and to know Him personally and intimately. The difference between knowing about God and knowing God is like the difference between studying electrical engineering and grabbing a hot wire! There is a dramatic difference between simply knowing about God and knowing God.

In this passage Moses is coming into an encounter with God. I don't know whether this is his conversion or not. Certainly Moses knew much about God. Forty years before this time, his defense of an Israelite who was being mistreated by an Egyptian slave master indicates some of his knowledge of the plans and purposes of God, and certainly the purposes of God for the children of Israel. Yet he's been forty years in the wilderness, forty years away from Egypt, forty years away from any apparent plan and purpose of God. This could be a conversion experience, but it certainly is a time when God is reminding Moses that He wants to know him and wants to know him personally.

God is always in the process of drawing us to Himself. Every day God is trying to bring us to Himself. Every day God is trying to break through whatever wall we may have built, whatever activity may screen us away from His presence. God is always trying to bring us to Himself. He is always preparing us to encounter Him. He is always moving us toward that confrontation.

We may not know it. Moses didn't. This was the last day Moses would ever be a shepherd, and he didn't know it. He wasn't looking for this. It was God appearing to him. We need to be reminded that there is a wind blowing that always brings us toward God. There is an invisible hand reaching out that is always endeavoring to draw us to God. I want us to see some things that I hope will be challenging and encouraging. I want us to see how God prepared Moses for this encounter, and I want to suggest that God will use one or more of these same things to prepare us to meet Him in a fresh, new way.

I. Preparation for Knowing God

First of all, God used *devastating events.* Have you ever had any of those? Any disappointments, any reversals, any things you didn't want but you got anyway? Plan B, not Plan A; things that discourage, that disappoint; things that would threaten your well-being and threaten your understanding of the purposes of God? Moses certainly experienced devastating events.

He spent forty years in pharaoh's court, where he was the crown prince of Egypt. It would be difficult to exaggerate the luxury and the privilege in which Moses was raised. He had the finest of everything. He lived in the palace of the pharaoh. He was taught by the best teachers in that country. He was a child of privilege. He was the fair-haired boy of all of Egypt. Everyone looked to Moses. He might have been the next ruler of Egypt. He was a privileged and incre-dibly blessed young man.

Then something happened. He saw an Egyptian abusing an Israelite. He went to the defense of the Israelite, and in the struggle the Egyptian was killed. Now he's got a dead Egyptian on his hands. He digs a hole and tries to bury him, but before long the body is discovered. And now Moses goes from being the prince of Egypt to running for his life. He now has been expelled from the palace.

He who was one of the most recognized and blessed people in all of Egypt is now a fugitive. He is now a criminal, running for his life. He had a devastating change in circumstances. He went from the palace to the pasture. He went from the fellowship of royalty to the fellowship of peasants. He went from a royal diet to a subsistence diet. He went from the crown room of Egypt to the wilderness of the desert. Devastating events! Nothing could have been more devastating than that.

Every one of us knows devastating events, don't we? Every one of us has experienced those. We know what it is like to see our lives plunged into turmoil. We know what it is like to see our plans dashed. We know what it is like to see our dreams crushed. Every one of us has had that. Maybe we were fired. Maybe we were told we were not wanted anymore. Maybe there was a devastating report on our health. Maybe there was some event that changed the make-up of our family. Maybe it was the casket that we stood beside that was so unexpected and certainly undesired. Every one of us knows what it is like to have devastating events overwhelm our lives.

When those things happen to us, they will either make us bitter or they will make us better. It will be one or the other. If we look carefully into the devastating events of our lives and into those things that threaten our well-being, we will find that there is a bush burning, and God is endeavoring through those devastating events to bring us to Himself.

Some people are going through tough times. Some are experiencing great pressures in life. I want you to see God in the midst of that. These things didn't happen outside the understanding of God. They don't surprise God. These devastating events that Satan may have meant for our ill, God means for our good. He will bring us through those devastating events into an encounter with Him. He is preparing us to meet Him in a special way. God used devastating events in Moses' life.

Second, God used isolated places. Moses is on the back side of the desert. The word *back side* (KJV) is a Hebrew word that literally means "beyond or behind." It reflects the fact that Moses is further out in the wilderness than he has ever been. He is the greatest distance away from home that he has ever been. The word *Horeb* means "dry, sterile, bleak, rocky." It speaks of a place of solitude, silence, and isolation. Absolute quietness. No sound, no airplane overhead, no automobile engine sounds, not even the sound of a newspaper plopping on the driveway early in the morning. Nothing. Isolation and silence. And in the silence Moses met God.

Most of us are afraid of quiet. We don't like silence. The first thing we do when we get in our car is turn on the radio, the CD, or the tape player. The first thing we do when we get home is turn on the radio, CD, or television. We don't want silence. We don't like isolation. We are inundated with words. Words form the walls and the ceiling and the floor of our lives. They scream to us on television and radio, on billboards, on the Internet, and even in sermons! Words are always pounding at us. We hate to be quiet.

But notice that Moses found God not in the noise but in the silence. Not in the crowd but alone. You may find yourself isolated today. Sometimes we find ourselves in forced isolation. We've been forced to be isolated from things that are familiar and people whom we love, and it's not by our choice. But I want to suggest to you that if you have never known isolation, you'll never know God. God will meet us in the quietness of isolation. If we really want to know God, we must have some time of quiet. We must have times when we shut out the world around us. And here is Moses on the back side of the desert with not a sound of a human voice—only the bleat of sheep— and yet God used that isolated experience to prepare Moses to meet Him.

So God used devastating events and isolated places. Third, He used humiliation, humbling activities. In the first verse we read that Moses was tending the flock of Jethro, his father-in-law. In those days you could tell the value of a person's estate by how many flocks he had and how many animals he had in his flocks. Now here is Moses, eighty years old, and he doesn't own a flock. He's taking care of someone else's sheep. He's a consummate failure. He's bankrupt. He is helpless. Can you imagine that? Going from the prince of Egypt to taking care of somebody else's sheep. How humiliating!

God uses devastation, He uses isolation, and He uses humiliation to prepare us to meet Him. Have you ever been humiliated? Ever been told you weren't needed anymore, weren't wanted? Ever been fired? Ever heard someone say, "I don't love you anymore?" One way or another, all of us have been through those times of humiliation. I want you to realize that when devastation, isolation, and humiliation come, if you look closely, you'll see a bush burning. And God is in the process of preparing you to meet Him.

Jesus knew the same trilogy of devastation, isolation, and humiliation. Devastation: He was run out of the country when he was a baby, and his family had to take him to Egypt. Isolation: He was from Nazareth. Remember the reaction of the disciple who was told that the Messiah was Jesus from Nazareth. His response was, "Can anything good come out of Nazareth?" (John 1:46). Nazareth was a nowhere village, a no place. And humiliation: death on the cross. Jesus understood these three things.

I want you to see that when these things happen in your life, it is not as though God has forsaken you. Rather, God is preparing you to meet him in a fresh, new way. So God prepares us to know Him.

II. *The Reality of Knowing God*

Our encounter with God rarely happens when we expect it. Moses wasn't looking for it that day, but God was in all the circumstances that brought him to that place. God took the initiative. God always takes the initiative in calling us. That bush exploded with fire. It was an incredible experience, but it didn't burn up. Now note carefully: There was a decisive moment when Moses saw that the bush was burning with fire but was not consumed. Here at that strategic moment Moses said, "I will now turn aside and see" (Exod. 3:3 NKJV).

What if Moses hadn't turned aside? What if he had said, "That is a strange bush, but I have so many sheep to take care of. I'm by myself. I don't have any help, and something might happen to the sheep. I don't really have time to pay attention to this"? What if he had just turned away?

The key is that God had prepared Moses for this moment, but there was a choice that Moses had to make. Every one of us has that same choice. In the midst of all the devastation, isolation, and humiliation of life, there comes that divine moment. There comes that moment when we have to turn aside. We have to stop and look. I wonder how many bushes have burned in our lives and we missed them because we didn't turn aside to see them. Many of us never encounter God in richness, in fullness because we never turn aside to see. God takes the initiative. He took the initiative with Moses, and He takes the initiative with us. He takes the initiative by instructing us through what we see. The bush was burning, but it was not consumed.

We are told by scholars that the bush was just a common bush. It was just a bramble bush. If this had happened in Texas or

New Mexico, the bush might have been a tumbleweed—a nothing bush. It was burning, and it perhaps was not unusual to see something burning in the wilderness. A lightning flash might start a fire. Perhaps it was not unusual for Moses to see something burning, but this was an unusual bush. It was burning, but it wasn't burning up.

I used a cedar tree as a Christmas tree one year when I was in seminary. When Christmas was over, I thought I would get rid of it by burning it. I lived out in the country, and I thought that would be the easiest thing to do. I took it out into the backyard, and I got a match and lit the tree and nearly burned my hair off! When I took a match and put it to that dry cedar bush, it exploded with flame. Flames went everywhere. That's what you would expect from a dry bush that was burning in the wilderness.

This bush was burning, but it wasn't being consumed. God was teaching Moses a lesson. God enters into the most common things and reveals Himself through them. Major Ian Thomas in one of his books has a chapter entitled "Any Old Bush Will Do." It wasn't the bush that was important. It was God in the bush! That's a good lesson for us. God doesn't use any of us because we're gifted or good or talented. He uses us because He chooses in His sovereignty to do so.

Moses was that bush that burned. Here is Moses, a consummate failure, an eighty-year-old man, out in the wilderness. But when he died forty years later, the Scripture says that "his eye was not dim, nor his natural force abated" (Deut. 34:7 KJV). He was a healthy male at 120 years of age because God was burning in him and through him without burning him up or burning him out. Scripture declares, "Even though our outer person is being destroyed, our inner person is being renewed day by day" (2 Cor. 4:16). That's what we need. We need that inward renewal day by day.

We have a vivid illustration of this in the person of Billy Graham. He is over eighty years old. Gone is the Hollywood-handsome good looks of his youth. Gone is that piercing voice and those dramatic gestures. He is quiet. He speaks slowly. But in recent crusades more people, percentage-wise, have responded to the invitation to receive

Christ than at any other time in his ministry. He is a bush who is burning without being burned up.

That is the way God does it. God wants to work in us and through us. When we talk about burning out, we're talking about serving God in our own energy. But if we come into these encounters with God where we have that fresh moment with Him and that fresh encounter with Him and know Him in a fresh new way, God will burn through us without burning us up or burning us out.

God takes the initiative and instructs us through what we see and what we hear. Moses is there, he sees the bush, and then he stops and turns aside to see this phenomenon. Then God says, "Moses." It's hard to ignore God when He calls you by name. I remember when as a little boy, over sixty years ago, God tapped me on the shoulder and called me by name. I understood I needed a Savior. He came into my heart. I remember when I was fourteen years old that God tapped me on the shoulder and called me to preach. He could not have made it any more plain if He had sent me a special delivery letter. He said, "I want you to preach the gospel." It is hard to ignore God when He calls you by name. He instructs us through what we hear.

We need to understand that when God speaks to us, we need to respond. We spend too much time listening to our critics and listening to the things that go wrong, the plans that don't quite materialize. We need to learn to see what God is doing and listen to the voice of God in our lives. God takes the initiative. He always does. He always has. He always will. Wherever you are, whatever you're experiencing, God is drawing you to Himself. Whether you are experiencing the high of an exhilarating ministry and God is blessing in ways far beyond your imagination, or whether you are experiencing devastation, isolation, or humiliation, God is endeavoring to bring you into a fresh, new encounter with Him.

When He does, you're going to discover that He is the God of history. He told Moses, "I am the God of your father Abraham, Jacob, Isaac." He is the God of history. He is the God of our fathers. He is the God of my grandfather, who preached for fifty-four years in Arkansas. He is the God of my father, who preached for thirty-six years in Texas and Arkansas. He is the God of history. He's the God who has revealed Himself all down through the aeons of time, and He's the God who still reveals Himself today. He is the God of history.

He is the God of activity. He said, "I AM WHO I AM" (Exod. 3:14). He is so vital and vibrant and so alive that He had to take a noun and make a verb out of it. "I Am" is a verb, but that is His name. He is the God of activity. He is the God who moves and acts and lives in our lives.

And He is the God of immediacy. He is the God who will meet you right now. If you ever meet God, it will not be yesterday. It will not be tomorrow. It will be on the razor-thin edge of that moment we call *now*. "Now is the accepted time," the Scripture says (2 Cor. 6:2 KJV). That means now is the time God accepts. This is God's time.

There is no moment that compares with that encounter with God when God tells us His name. To know someone's name is a powerful thing. It singles that person out; it takes that person out of the mass and links that person with me. To know God's name is a powerful thing. It means more than God's ID. It speaks of His character, His integrity, His reputation, His ability, and His power. God at this very moment is explosive with life, mercy, and immediacy. Until you feel that immediacy and urgency, you do not encounter God. Knowing God blows apart all of our categories. Nothing in our language can handle Him. He is the God of immediacy, the great *I Am*.

I met my wife Carol Ann forty-eight years ago. I was a Baylor student, and she was a senior in high school. The first thing I wanted to know was her name. But you would readily recognize that was not all I wanted to know. I've spent the last forty-eight years getting to know her. We've been married forty-seven years now. We courted through the mail. Two hundred and fifty miles was a long way back in 1955. We would see each other on weekends. We had known each other for four months when I bought her a ring. I brought the news back to my roommate. He asked, "How many carats does the diamond have?"

I asked, "What's that?"

"Well," he said, "that's how you measure the diamond."

I said, "I don't know." So I had to go back down to the jeweler and ask, "Would you mind getting that ring out of the safe and let me look at it so you can tell me how many carats it has?"

Eight months later we were married, six weeks after she graduated from high school. But the important thing was not that we just knew each other. We have spent these last forty-eight years really getting to know each other.

The greatest tragedy I see in people is that we seem to meet God and then we don't want to know Him. We don't seem to want to get to know what His character is like, what His presence is like. And we get tired. We not only get tired *in* the work, we get tired *of* it. And we not only seem to burn *up*; we burn *out*. That won't happen if we understand that God is a God who is always bringing us into an encounter with Him.

There is a blowing wind bringing us toward God that we are not even aware of. I want to suggest to you that God has a bush burning in your life. If you will stop and look, you may hear Him call you by name.

15

Joy for the Journey
HEBREWS 12:1–2 HCSB

James T. Draper, Jr.

THE WRITER OF HEBREWS has concluded that wonderful hall of fame of faith in chapter 11. All the great heroes of the faith are spotlighted along with the things they endured and the faith they demonstrated. He reminds us that "faith is the reality of what is hoped for, the proof of what is not seen," and "without faith it is impossible to please God" (Heb. 11:1, 6a).

Chapter 12 begins, "Therefore." Now anytime you see a "therefore" in the Bible, it means to look back on what has just been said. He has been talking about faith. He's been talking about the faithfulness of God in bringing His people through all of the trials and difficulties that he cataloged for us in chapter 11. "Therefore since we also have such a large cloud of witnesses surrounding us, let us lay aside every weight and the sin that so easily ensnares us, and run with endurance the race that lies before us, keeping our eyes on Jesus, the source and perfecter of our faith, who for the joy that lay before Him endured a cross and despised the shame, and has sat down at the right hand of God's throne" (Heb. 12:1–2).

There is a dual focus here. In verse 1, the writer of Hebrews challenges us to look back at those wonderful saints of the Old Testament. They are a part of a great cloud of witnesses who now observe us and challenge us and encourage us. Then he says that he wants us to look beyond that. Not only does he want us to look at these who have passed before; he wants us to look to Jesus and see the perfect One, the author, or source, and the finisher, or perfecter, of our faith. These verses focus us on the journey that we're on in life, the course of life. They speak to us about the race of life. Verse 2 points us to the captain that we must have during this race of life. It talks to us about Jesus, our leader.

First, think about this race of life that we're in. Life is seen as a great endurance race. It's not a hundred-yard dash; it's a marathon. It's an endurance race that we're on. In this race we are surrounded by a great host of witnesses. We see the three things the writer of Hebrews says about our race of life.

I. The Observers for Our Race of Life

There is a great cloud of witnesses. Normally we think of a great grandstand full of people, and they're watching us run the race. I don't think that's the meaning of this verse. If I thought that all the saints of all the ages, my dad, my granddad, and everybody were just sitting there watching everything I did, I'd be petrified with fear. It would scare me to death. Now I know they know, and I do believe they see, but that's not really what this verse says.

What is a witness? There are at least two things necessary for a person to be called a witness. He has to have seen something, and he has to tell about it. So a witness is somebody who has seen something and who is testifying to it. These witnesses, these observers to our lives, this great cloud of witnesses are there for one basic reason—they testify to the faithfulness of God. They testify that they have experienced the work of God; they saw firsthand the hand of God in the midst of difficult circumstances.

God proved Himself faithful to them, and they are saying, "We testify that God is faithful. You can trust Him. God will see you through. We made it through, and you can make it through. We want you to live trusting God as we trusted Him. Don't give up; we didn't give up. No matter what obstacles or what hardships you face or what the cost may be, God is a faithful God, and you can trust Him."

That's a needed word for us. Sometimes we feel like we're all by ourselves. Sometimes we feel like no one understands, that no one can know or feel the experience we're going through. And many times

Satan tells us because of what we're going through that God is embarrassed about it. He's ashamed of us and not interested in us. This great cloud of witnesses rises up as one to say, "God is faithful."

Look again at what these faithful witnesses faced. They were persecuted, they were afflicted, they were rejected, they were cast down, they were killed and martyred, they were sinners. Here is Rahab the harlot who was a temple prostitute for a pagan religion, and yet God reached down and touched her in her sin and guilt. We find in the Gospels that Rahab is in the lineage of Jesus because of the touch of a loving God. It doesn't matter whether we're facing persecution, or some affliction, or some unraveling relationship, or something else that threatens our lives. God is faithful and will meet us at the point of our needs.

These witnesses stand to testify that we can trust God. Don't feel forsaken. We are never alone. God says, "I will never leave you or forsake you" (Heb. 13:5). God will be there. He is adequate; he is faithful. Here rises a great cloud of witnesses who testify to the faithfulness of God. This verse speaks to us about the observers in this race of life.

II. The Obstacles We Face in the Race of Life

Life is not easy. It is difficult. There are many things we don't understand. The curious thing about life is that by the time we've figured out how to do something, it's too late. We start things without any experience. For instance, when we first get married, we've never had a wife or a husband before. When we have our first baby, we've never had one before. It's hard; it's not easy. And some things are obstacles in the race of life.

The writer of Hebrews describes them here in two ways. He says that we must lay aside the weight and the sin. What weight could he be talking about? Well, there are many things that are weights that keep us from functioning in this race of life. They need to be put aside. We never see Olympic athletes running in their sweat suits, because they want to win. They take off the things that will hold them back. Those sweat suits will gather too much wind; they will impede them. They won't run a good race. They won't get a good time. They strip down to the bare essentials. Everything they wear is the lightest possible. They lay aside the weights.

God says that in the race of life we are to lay aside the weights. Many things can be weights to us. Anger hinders us. Nearly all the problems we face are from unresolved anger. That's why the Bible has so much to say about bitterness and anger. Lay it aside. If we are angry with someone about something, then we are slaves to that person or that thing. We must refuse to let anybody or anything enslave us. We must not keep anger. It is a weight that keeps us depressed and discouraged and beaten down. Lay aside anger, jealousy, pride, and those other things that are obstacles for us. We know there are many things that are inherently wrong. We must lay them aside.

In this race we have a faithful God who is able to take us in every circumstance and see us through. We can finish. We can come through these things because God is faithful. The great cloud of witnesses testifies to that. We need to lay aside those things that keep us from running that race well.

And by the way, these could be good things. The greatest threat we face is not bad things. The greatest threat we face consists of the good things that keep us from the best things. For most of us the danger is not that we'll take a gun and rob a store or kill someone. Our greatest danger may be that we neglect the things that are precious to us. Our families and relationships will be destroyed because we didn't give attention to them. Sometimes good things can keep us from the best. And what the writer of Hebrews is saying is that this race of life is a tough race. We need to lay aside the weights—both evil and good things—so we can concentrate on the best.

Then he says to lay aside sin. In this context it should be obvious what this is. In the original language there is a definite article here. It is the sin. Lay aside the sin. He's talking about a particular sin. What sin could he be talking about? In this context of faith, it is obvious. The great enemy of faith is doubt. The great enemy of trusting a faithful God is a lack of trust, a lack of belief. So the sin he is talking about is the sin of unbelief, the sin of disbelief. God tells us to stop disbelieving Him. Stop failing to believe in God. Trust Him.

Now that's not going to make the headlines, and we won't get arrested for it, but we'll destroy our lives if we don't live with trust in God. That's the message that is given here. Lay aside the things that keep us from trusting God and cause us to stop disbelieving God. Lay aside the weight and the sin that hinders us.

III. The Obsession in Our Race of Life

We are to run with patience or endurance the race set before us. Run with persistence, stay with it, keep at it, don't stop, finish the race. That is to be the obsession of our lives. God wants us to finish the race. I don't know how long I have to live, but I want to finish the race. God will tell me when it's over. Until He sends down His messenger to take me to be with Him, I want to finish the race. Stay with it. That's the witness and the testimony of Hebrews 11 and the challenge of this first verse. Run with patience, stay with it, don't give up.

I preached my first sermon when I was fourteen years old. I began to preach in revival meetings in Houston, Texas, when I was seventeen. We were crazy enough to believe that we could win Houston to Christ. We really thought we could. It never occurred to us that we couldn't do it. I remember kneeling beside a car with a teenage preacher friend, and we prayed for God to give us Houston, Texas. Then we started preaching in revivals all across that area. We had a great evangelistic team. We were enthusiastic.

But let me tell you, I am more enthusiastic today than I've ever been to preach the gospel of Jesus Christ. I am not going to let others rob me of my passion. I'm glad others have it, but God wants us to stay with it, finish the race. Don't give up, don't turn back. Sometimes I think of people I have known who gave up on life, gave up on love, and gave up on faith. It breaks my heart. Think about what it does to the heart of God.

Here we see our faithful Father. There is a great cloud of witnesses who testify to His faithfulness. He will be faithful to us. He saw them through; He will see us through. Now lay aside the weight and the sin that knocks you off stride and keeps you from running that race. Stay at it with persistence and perseverance and finish the race.

Verse 2 switches the focus to Jesus: "Keeping our eyes on Jesus, the source and perfecter of our faith." It mentions the accomplishments of Jesus. He is the author, or source, and finisher, or perfecter of our faith. The word *author* (KJV) or *source* (HCSB) is a Greek word which means "trailblazer." It speaks of someone who takes a machete and hacks through the underbrush so that everybody behind him can find his or her way through the underbrush. It is a word in classical Greek to refer to a person who founds a city so that others could come and live in the city. Jesus is the first, He is the trailblazer, He is the author. He is the one who initiated our salvation.

He is the finisher (KJV) or perfecter (HCSB) of our faith. That word is the Greek word *telios* that means He's the concluder, the completer of our faith. He finished it. Listen to me! There is nothing left for us to do. Jesus did it all. He completed it. When He cried from the cross, "It is finished" (John 19:30), that cry rang through the halls of heaven. There were millions of people like these in Hebrews 11 who were in heaven on credit. They had trusted that something would be done. They had trusted that a price would be paid. They must have hung with bated breath as they observed the drama of Calvary.

I'm convinced Satan did everything he could to get Jesus to come down off that cross. He did everything he could to get Him to call ten thousand angels to rescue Him from the cross. The tormentors cried, "If you're the Christ, prove it; come down and we'll believe in you." Satan did everything to get Jesus to come down. I imagine those saints in heaven, by faith on credit, hung with bated breath as they watched that drama unfold.

Then that cry rang out, "It is finished." Down through the halls and corridors of heaven rang that word, "It is finished, it is finished!" Imagine the rejoicing that went through heaven as those saints knew their salvation was completed.

Jesus paid it all.
All to him I owe.
Sin had left a crimson stain.
He washed it white as snow.

We don't have to do anything but receive what Christ has done. We don't contribute anything to our salvation. He's the source and perfecter of our faith.

Jesus sat down at the right hand of God. That speaks of His majesty. He is sitting at the right hand of majesty. His task is completed. The Book of Hebrews shows the supremacy of Jesus, the great high priest, over the Jewish high priest. The Jewish high priest never sat down because his work was never done. But Jesus sat down. He finished His work. It is done.

See not only His *accomplishments* but see His *actions*. Hebrews says that He "endured a cross" (v. 2). He persevered; He remained constant. He didn't have to, but He did. Jesus demonstrated for us that perseverance, that persistence to finish what was before Him. He endured the cross, and He despised the shame. That means He disregarded the shame. It was unimportant to Him.

He despised the shame, He endured the cross, and He did it with joy. "For the joy that lay before Him" (v. 2). What was the joy that was before Him? God gave me an answer to this question, but I need to explain a couple of things. I want to paint a picture for us. There is a theological concept known as the *transcendence* of God. It is a term that means that God is not bound by the same laws we are. He transcends natural laws, and He is different from us.

For instance, we are bound by a law of physics, which dictates that we can't be in two places at the same time. That is impossible for us to do. We are limited to this body, and we can only be in one place at a time. Not only that, two of us can't occupy the same place. I can't sit where you sit unless I sit on you! Even then we do not occupy the same space. God is not bound by that law. God can be in me and in you at the same time. God is not bound by the law of gravity. We're bound by that law. The law of gravity says that if we step off one level we will go down. We might like to go up, but we're going to go down.

Now there's another law. It is a law of chronology. We're bound by that. Let me put it in even simpler and more vivid terms. We are in a time tunnel. We're not born sixty years old. We are born, and we begin life, and we proceed through in this chronological timetable. I am almost sixty-eight years old. You would agree that on my next birthday, I'll be sixty-nine. I won't be sixty-six or sixty. I'm trapped in this thing, though I would like to reverse it. I would like to work up to sixty-eight and then start back. I can't do that. I'm in a chronological trap. All of us are trapped in a time warp.

God is not trapped by time. God is not bound by time. So here's what happens. When God looks at my life, He not only sees me, present tense, where I am today; He sees the day I was born and the day I'll die. He sees it all. Psalm 139 tells us that before we were ever conceived, God recorded every day of our lives in a book. How could He do that? How could God record every day of my life in a book, even before I was conceived or had even been born?

That is easy for God. He sees all of time in one sweep. That's why prophecy is just as sure as history: all prophecy is history that God sees is going to happen before it takes place. The study of prophecy is wonderful because it helps us to know the things that will come to pass. God sees it all. He's not bound by time, so He sees all of time at once—past, present, and future.

Now, we can't do that. Let's pretend. Imagine how strange it would look if we saw only the tip of a leaf. We would wonder, *What on earth is that?* And then we would see a little bit more and more and more. Before long, we would see something yellow and something red until we would recognize it as a leaf. Life is full of surprises for us. But it's not for God. Did it ever occur to you that nothing ever takes God by surprise? He sees it all.

So here's what I believe happened. Knowing that God transcends human laws and natural laws, I believe that on the cross, Jesus, God's perfect man, was dying, shedding His sinless blood for us, dying an excruciating death. The Roman cross was the most cruel form of punishment, the most painful way in the world to die. He's agonizing physically. Then add to that the fact that He who was holy is now becoming sin for us. Everything He hated, He's becoming. Can we somehow see something of the anguish and the agony of the physical suffering and the spiritual pain that poured in upon Jesus?

Yet the writer of Hebrews said there was joy set before Him. It's astonishing—suffering an incredible, indescribable death, yet there was joy. What was that joy? I believe that in that moment God the Father, who transcends time, who sees all of time in one package, allowed Jesus the Son, the perfect man, to see everybody who would ever get saved as a result of what He was going through. Do we get happy when somebody gets saved? Sure we do. I want you to think about somebody getting saved that really made you happy. Remember how full of joy your heart was?

Imagine the joy of Jesus when He sees not one, not two, but millions and millions of people being saved. He saw Saul of Tarsus get saved on the Damascus Road. Wow, what joy! He saw all the faithful witness of those disciples. And He saw Martin Luther getting saved. He saw Charles Wesley getting saved while a missionary in Georgia. He saw Billy Sunday and Billy Graham. He saw you and me.

I was just a kid almost ready to go to the first grade when I knelt on the back porch of a parsonage in Arkansas with my mother and dad and asked Jesus to come into my heart. That was part of the joy set before Jesus. All of a sudden Jesus saw each person who would ever be saved.

Come to the book of Revelation. We find before the throne of God in God's great millennial kingdom that there were multitudes of people, so many that they couldn't be counted. God showed Jesus Christ in that split second the joy of the multiplied millions who would be saved, and there was joy before Him.

That word *joy* is an interesting word. It's not something like being happy. It's an expressive joy, an explosive joy. This word means a visible outward expression of joy. This helps me understand something else in Luke 15:10. It is said that "there is joy in the presence of God's angels over one sinner who repents." I used to think all that meant was that the saints up there were rejoicing in the presence of the angels. I believe now that Jesus is rejoicing. I believe there are holy hallelujahs ringing out from the lips of our Savior as an afterglow of the joy that was set before Him on the cross.

Now listen. Jesus was on a journey that climaxed in the cross. It was not a pleasant thing for Him. It was a hard thing, but as He finished His journey there was joy. You and I are on a journey. We want to finish with joy. Just as Jesus needed joy for the journey, so do we. And we're going to get our joy the same place that Jesus got His. He got His joy trusting in the faithfulness of God the Father.

By the way, I know we understand that we are saved by a covenant, but I want to make sure that we understand that the covenant is not between God and us. The covenant is between God and Christ. They have made a covenant. Salvation is God opening up that eternal covenant between the Father and the Son and letting us be part of it. We get our joy from entering into that same covenant. Jesus trusted in the faithfulness of God. And we, too, can trust in the faithfulness of God. Whatever we are experiencing, it doesn't matter. God is faithful. He will give us grace, strength, and guidance. He will give us comfort and wisdom. He will give us everything we need for the moment so we can proceed on our journey with joy.

If we get our joy anywhere else, we're going to crash in life. If we get our joy from our business success, either our business will fail and we will be forced to retire, or our job will be deleted and we'll be forced to go somewhere else. If we get our joy from our families, they will disappoint us at some point. There will be some time of great disappointment. We need joy for the journey, but our joy will not come from anything or anybody else. Our joy comes only from God—the joy of the faithfulness of God and the joy of seeing people get saved.

There are a lot of unhappy Christians. What an oxymoron! But I'm convinced that if every unhappy Christian would become a soul winner and a witness and see people give their hearts to Christ, they would have joy for the journey. That's where Jesus got His joy— seeing people receive and respond to His offer of grace.

We are in a race. Great witnesses urge us to trust in the faithfulness of God. Hebrews 11 is the hall of fame of faith. Most halls of fame are hard to get into. I have good news for us: we don't have to be voted into God's hall of fame. Verse 1 says, "Therefore . . . we also." This means that this hall of fame is still open. We can get in, too. We can put our trust in God just like these other people did. We can finish the race just like they did. Sometimes we revere these biblical characters as being untouchables, people unlike us, people of superhuman piety and spirituality. They were people just like us. They were bound by the same limitations and passions, yet their faith in God, their trust in God, and their joy in God brought them into God's hall of fame.

I want you to know that we can get in there, too. We can exercise the faith God has given to us. We can place that faith and trust in Him, and we can anchor our hearts in the faithfulness of God. We, too, can be a part of that great hall of fame of faith. And we can have joy for the journey.

I want you to know that God is faithful. I don't know what burden you're carrying, but I want you to know you can give it to the Lord, and He will carry that burden with you. There's not any testing, any temptation that has come your way that others have not faced— and God will see you through it. God will give you victory in it. He will allow you to overcome it. He will give you joy for the journey.

I want to ask right now, whatever your burden, that you simply say, "Father, I want to receive Your strength and Your sufficiency. I trust You. I believe You." By doing that you allow Him to take that burden that has so dominated your life and give you joy for the journey.

16

Laughing on the Rooftops
ISAIAH 22:1–14 HCSB

James T. Draper, Jr.

FIDDLER ON THE ROOF is one of the most beloved musicals of all time. The protagonist and hero is an Eastern European Jew named Tevye. A chronic sufferer from a shrewish wife, the burdens of persecution, and finally a daughter who marries a non-Jewish radical, Tevye sings some of the most beloved music in Broadway musical history. The title of the play suggests that the rooftop was a place of retreat from all of life's troubles, a place where the fiddler could play his simple instrument without being interrupted by the harshness of life below. The image of a fiddler on the roof sticks in the mind, does it not?

The prize-winning playwright, Tennessee Williams, wrote *Cat on a Hot Tin Roof*. The image evoked by that title befits the sultry play of discontented characters and alienated people. Once again the image of a surprised cat suddenly thrown onto a blistering tin roof stands out in the mind, does it not?

Sometimes a rooftop may be a place for one-of-a-kind encounters. The late and legendary Dr. R. G. Lee told an amusing anecdote from his storied life. There was a man in Memphis whom Lee wanted to win to Christ. Lee usually made ten visits a day, and among those calls were persistent attempts to reach this certain man. The man eluded Lee by going out the back door when Lee came in the front. On a day when the man was repairing his roof, Lee climbed up the ladder to the roof, kicked the ladder away, and sat down with the astonished man on the rooftop. He won the man to Christ on the roof. That gives a new meaning to the phrase "captive audience."

Sometimes a roof was a place of lust and moral compromise. It was while walking on the rooftop that David saw Bathsheba and their immoral affair began (2 Sam. 11:2).

Something humorous, strange, or improper often characterizes a person on a rooftop; it is not where you generally expect someone to be. That was not the case in eighth-century Israel. The flat rooftop of the typical residence was a place where people did go. In that sweltering land, people climbed to their roofs to catch any of the cool breezes that might blow their way. People went to the rooftops for other less-innocent reasons. Rooftops gave an observatory to those Israelites who practiced the abomination of astrology. Also, rooftops were places where faithless Israelites who practiced auguring the entrails of animals might look into the remains of birds or beasts and seek to find some sign of the future. Isaiah 22 describes still another unseemly scene on the rooftops.

Inhabitants of Jerusalem in 701 B.C. had experienced a terrorizing invasion of their homeland by a foreign enemy, the dreaded Assyrians. Doom seemed unavoidable. The walls of Jerusalem were filled with gaps, the water supply was limited, and the city was in no position to withstand an attack. For some reason lost in the dusty history of antiquity, the Assyrians retreated after an initial attack. Perhaps the tribute paid to the Assyrians satisfied them momentarily.

Relief swept over the city like warm butter on pancakes. One moment a life-threatening invasion stalked the very gates of the city; the next moment it was gone. So what did the suddenly delivered people of God do? Did they fall on their knees in prayer? Did they go to the temple to worship? No. They went to the rooftops and partied! Dancing and laughing at an unlikely deliverance.

It remains as a timeless truth: God's people may quickly fall into reckless celebration because of God's initial deliverance and totally forget their complete dependence upon God. This is a word for all times—Isaiah's time and our time.

God's prophet for this day was Isaiah. His ministry lasted for approximately sixty years and spanned the reign of four kings in Judah. He was well educated and highly respected with great influence on each of the kings and among the people. What Shakespeare was to literature, what Spurgeon was among the Victorian preachers, what Billy Graham is in our day among preachers of the gospel, Isaiah was among the prophets.

He stands out for his courage and matchless message and his steadfast devotion to the Lord. He was bold whether before the king or the people. He never tried to engender compliments or curry favor. He was an ardent patriot who was the enemy of all that was against the best interests of his nation. But he also had a tenderness and sympathy that reached out to other nations. He had a fiery indignation with compromise that was often expressed with satire and sarcasm. But throughout his prophecy he displayed a deep reverence for God, and he portrayed a vivid sense of the majesty of God. He was the voice of God to the nation at that time.

Isaiah warned his generation to depend on God, not to live a life of riotous, heedless, hedonistic celebration after God's gracious initial deliverance. King Sennecharib of Assyria would be back.

The enemies of the gospel and of our nation have attacked us today in many ways. The events of September 11, 2001, are forever etched in our minds and have revealed the physical danger we face today. The continuing hostility and bias against Christian faith and principles is a growing menace that will not relent. The challenges before us are more than we can count. As never before we need to respond to God, to return to Him in repentance and trust. Isaiah's message is a message for us today.

I. An Inappropriate Celebration after a Divine Intervention

Nearly everyone else in Jerusalem was partying, but not Isaiah. The lonely prophet sat in quiet introspection while the exultant residents of Jerusalem raucously celebrated on their roofs. The ricocheting catcalls and drunken shouts of carousing men and women echoed down the narrow lanes of the City of David. In light of that, the prophet sadly, rhetorically asked, "What's the matter with you? Why have all of you gone up to the rooftops?" (22:1). At a moment when everyone in Jerusalem should have been in quiet reflection and thanksgiving that God had snatched them from utter destruction, they were instead in the middle of a party.

What a contrast between their jubilation and their situation. This was merely a brief pause, a momentary break, an interlude in the relentless march of the Assyrians. Already the bloodthirsty Assyrians had ended the history of the northern tribes (the Northern Kingdom) in 722 B.C. There was nothing to celebrate.

Further, those of their Hebrew kinsmen who had perished in battle had not done so valiantly or as heroes (v. 3). They had died running from the enemy in panic and confusion; not an arrow had been shot. They had been cowards who gave up without a fight. Some escaped "far away" but were still captured. The troops did not cover themselves with glory. They should have been humiliated and the people embarrassed.

If anything, the situation should have been one that called for grave national reflection and prayer. There was every reason to pause before God and meditate. Yet such is the nature of human flesh that we look for any reason to escape the situation and fall back into an unseemly, inappropriate celebration.

We saw this vividly portrayed in post-September 11 America. The front page of the *Wall Street Journal* for October 5, 2001, gave ample illustrations of how quickly we may forget any lessons learned after critical events—or never learn them at all. In the aftermath of 9/11, while acknowledging that some people were turning to family, faith, and friends, the *Journal* went on to add:

> With the country on the verge of war and fear of bioterrorism mounting, many are wondering what's the point of being good anymore. The abstemious are drinking alone and before noon. Homebodies are dancing all night. Calorie counters are hitting the Doritos. During the week after the attacks, David Blend, a Texas native living in New York, spent his days watching the news and his nights at candlelight vigils for the victims. Then the 29-year-old freelance writer for men's magazines went on a 16-hour bender.

Robert Wheeler, a Seattle psychotherapist, started smoking again. Alli Steinberg, a 28-year-old actress and waitress in New York, used to go out twice a week, but now parties every night. "I'm literally living each day like it is my last," she said. In addition, she had a long-distance e-mail flirtation with a Chicago man. She decided to meet him immediately. Diet manuals have stopped selling, and people are binging on rich foods.

At least for some people, the post-September 11 world has turned into a party. What should have driven us to God seemed to drive us to pleasure and craving for physical satisfaction.

Instead of returning to God, the people of Isaiah's day turned to laughter and jubilation. "The noisy city, the jubilant town is filled with revelry" (22:2). Loud, careless, raucous, clamorous, strident laughter filled the narrow lanes of Jerusalem. On their roofs, happy with wine, perhaps the full moon shining brightly on their festivities, the residents of Jerusalem partied into the night.

Evidently the crowd catcalled to Isaiah, half inviting him to join the revelry and half deriding him for not doing so. In response to their derisive mock invitations, Isaiah replied, "Therefore I said, 'Look away from me! Let me weep bitterly! Do not try to comfort me about the destruction of my dear people'" (22:4). There is a time when God's man or woman must sit silently and alone while others celebrate and laugh.

Jesus proclaimed, "Blessed are those who mourn, for they will be comforted" (Matt. 5:4 NIV). He did not pronounce a blessing on grief generally. Grief makes many people hard and bitter and others softer and better. Jesus' blessing in this Beatitude belongs to those who mourn over the poverty of spirit that belongs to them and their generation. Ultimate comfort belongs to those who ultimately feel deeply and grieve genuinely over the spiritual emptiness of their times.

Richard Foster, in his masterpiece on the inward life, *Celebration of Discipline*, states that American Christianity is a mile wide and an inch deep because of our addiction to noise, hurry, and crowds.

There are times when we must shut out the noise of our culture's perpetual party, stop our obsessed hurry, get off our "rooftops," and recognize the reality of our situation. We need God. While we are celebrating the successes of our war against terrorism, we need to be reminded that this is no time for celebration, but a time that calls for repentance.

These times for the prophet called for bitter tears of grief over the deluded people. He wanted to weep in solitude away from the extravagant revelry of the people.

II. A Misunderstanding of the Danger Ahead

Isaiah declared, "The Lord GOD of hosts has a day" (Isa. 22:5 NASB). These words in Scripture inevitably refer to the future. The prophet sees that the nation's riotous reaction will bring doom and destruction.

It is a picture of chaos, confusion, and violence in Jerusalem. Verses 5–6 envision the enemy already in place around the wall with a precisely executed attack. Men from Elam, who were renowned as skilled archers, are getting their bows ready. Chariots carrying armed soldiers are seen in the field. Cavalry riders appear. Warriors from Kir are preparing for battle by taking the protective covering off their shields.

But that is not all. Verse 7 shows that the valleys are full of chariots and horsemen are at the gate. With such a future, how could the people be so lighthearted and riotous? Not accurately understanding the danger they were in, they made the rooftops ring with laughter.

Today we do not understand the dangers that lie ahead. Threats from a determined Islam will only intensify. The god of Islam is not the God of our faith. These are opposing theologies with deep convictional positions about the authenticity of each. Islam sees only Allah and his prophet Mohammad as valid expressions of God. The Koran is the inerrant book of Islam. Christianity sees Jesus Christ alone as the way to Jehovah God and the Bible as God's inerrant

Word to us. These two opposing philosophies can never come together.

The way of Islam has always been the way of violence. Christianity does not grow through violence but through compassion and witness of believers. Wherever Islam has spread, it has always spread through coercion, and that is directed by the Koran. Whenever Christianity has resorted to violence, as in the Crusades, it has always been against the very teachings of Scripture. We face the greatest threat in history to our faith in the continual assault of militant Islam. Yet we continue to "play church" and go about "business as usual," seemingly unaware of the danger before us.

We face increasing danger from the rise of secularism and the new religion of tolerance. Belief in God is accepted but not the God of the Bible or the uniqueness of Jesus Christ in salvation. There is a profound hunger in America for spiritual satisfaction and fulfillment. Yet, any testimony about Jesus Christ and the faith of God's Word inevitably brings hostility and opposition. We face the growing threat of these elements in our society yet seemingly are unable to understand the dangers that confront us.

The people in Isaiah's day did not understand the danger that would soon return to them. Neither do we!

III. A Miscalculation of Resources Available

We like to believe that when God is our protector, we are always ultimately protected. This verse could mean that. But when God takes away the cover, there is no protection, regardless of our resources (22:8). Or this verse could mean that God took away the blindness of the people and let them see what was coming. However we interpret these words, one thing is obvious: The people of Isaiah's time looked to their own weapons for security. They relied upon human strength and not divine strength.

In the face of the coming enemy, the celebrating Israelites looked at their weapons, walls, and water but refused to look at their own ways. They evaluated what they could do by themselves offensively and defensively. They inventoried their own resources, but they never really considered their own ways in the light of the Lord.

This did not drive the people to God. It is interesting that no spiritual awakening has been precipitated by a national tragedy or crisis! Human nature is bent on turning away from God!

Divine aid was not invoked. The need for it never seemed to occur to the people. Almost feverish activity characterized the city. All the weaknesses became apparent at once. Their weapons were inadequate. The walls around Jerusalem were incapable of keeping the enemy away. The water supply was insufficient for the needs of the people.

We do not face the Assyrians today; we face an assembly of threats to our national existence and our way of life unlike any we have seen before. We face obsessed terrorists who will blow themselves up to kill others. Continued terrorism in the Middle East and elsewhere around the world stalks us. We live with faceless copycat terrorists who will send anthrax spores and kill unsuspecting postal workers and elderly women. We face the most precipitous unemployment in three decades. We face a declining interest rate that makes borrowing money easy, but may shatter the retirement dreams of millions who hoped to live on the return from certain levels of interest that may never be the case again. We face the relentless attack of Islam and secularism. Where do we turn in such times?

The people in Isaiah's day looked at their weapons. They depended on the weapons of the "House of the Forest" (v. 8). The famed King Solomon had built an armory in Jerusalem filled with expensive weapons (1 Kings 7:2–5; 10:17, 21). While pausing in their heedless partying, the Israelite crowd fiddling while Jerusalem was about to burn, they inventoried the armory of Solomon to discover weapons available "just in case." They were ready to go on the offensive if necessary. They did not grasp that they were no match for the enemy they faced, regardless of the weapons in Solomon's armory.

Yet God brings us to foes we cannot face, threats we cannot target, and adversaries we cannot attack. Regardless of our energy, network, connections, or strategies, we cannot go on the offensive without God. The misguided generation of Isaiah's time thought they could grab the weapons of another day and fight the enemies of today. We might as well combat the missiles and bombs of our enemies today with Revolutionary War muskets as to think that yesterday's weapons can fight today's battles. Past strengths are not sufficient for today's battles. When God removes the cover (v. 8), our offensive initiatives are nothing without Him.

Then the people of Jerusalem looked to their walls: "You saw that there were many breaches in the walls of the city of David. . . . counted the houses of Jerusalem so that you could tear them down to fortify the wall" (22:9–10). Pausing in their party, some inhabitants of Jerusalem noticed the ominous gaps in the defensive walls around the city. Had the people been prepared, those gaps would never have been permitted. But now the celebrants break their bash and defer from their drinking to make a strange assessment: how many of their own houses would they have to tear down in order to mend the gaps in the walls? (v. 10). In a time of emergency, hungover revelers argued about whose house to level for stones to stuff in the gaps of the city wall.

How often do we think of shoring up our defenses in the midst of an attack on our lives? Illness, loss of job, sudden business reversals, unexpected defections of friends or family—and we are on the defensive. We want to close the gaps in the walls of our lives. We should recognize that it is too late to repair the walls at the last minute when we have failed to trust God in the situation. Crisis time is no time to make repairs!

When I was a youngster, Peggy Lee made famous a song called "Mañana." It was a catchy tune and popular at that time. The last verse of that song goes:

> The window she is broken and the rain is comin' in.
> If someone doesn't fix it, I'll be soaking to my skin.
> But if we wait a day or two the rain may go away,
> And we don't need a window on such a sunny day!

Then the refrain went, "Mañana, mañana, mañana is soon enough for me!" We must not put off until another day what needs to be done today. When the crisis comes, it will be too late to prepare.

The people of Jerusalem would soon find that crisis is no time to make repairs. Many of us make that same sad discovery. When the crisis comes, it is too late to shore up our defenses. When we lose our cover, our first response should be to seek the Lord. The inhabitants of Jerusalem trusted in themselves and not in the Lord.

A city suddenly under siege must consider its water resources: "You made a reservoir between the walls for the waters of the ancient pool" (v. 11). Pausing in the perpetual party, some of the more sober celebrants wandered down to the old pool, a reservoir or cistern, to collect water. They stroked their beards and mumbled to one another about whether the old pool would hold enough water for the siege they faced. They assessed old resources and pondered whether they would suffice for a new situation. They checked out the Pool of Siloam, or perhaps the Tyropoeon Valley of the city where two walls already existed, and constructed a reservoir between those walls.

How often do we do just that in the midst of a crisis? We stop our own personal parties just long enough to assess whether our own old resources will meet our new situation. The Jerusalemites would find that old resources are not sufficient when God removes the cover. How plaintive are the words of Isaiah: "But you did not depend on Him who made it, nor did you take into consideration Him who planned it long ago" (22:11 NASB). In all their feverish activity, there was no time to look to God—the sovereign Lord, who alone could protect them.

While the people looked at their dwindling water supply, the Lord who made the waters of the earth waited to help them. While they shored up their walls with fragments of building stone, the Lord who made the everlasting hills, the Rock of Ages, waited to be their mighty Fortress. What an irony. All the resources of Almighty God were at their disposal, but they could only think of the pitiful old pool, the diminishing resources of another day.

IV. A Life of Self-Sufficient Celebration Can Lead to Final Condemnation

This is not a popular message to bring in our culture. Much Christian preaching is of the "feel good" variety. Few preachers want to be prophets, and few hearers want to hear one. Isaiah would not likely get a sermon published in the annual volume of favorite sermons. Yet the fearless prophet told the truth: "On that day the Lord GOD of Hosts called for weeping, for wailing, for shaven heads, and the wearing of sackcloth. But look: joy and gladness, butchering of cattle and slaughtering of sheep, eating of meat, and drinking of wine—'Let us eat and drink, for tomorrow we die!' The LORD of Hosts has revealed this in my hearing: 'This sin of yours will never be wiped out.' The Lord GOD of hosts has spoken" (22:12–14).

At a time of national calamity when the people should have been repentant in the extreme, they kept on partying. They thought they had escaped the army of Sennacherib, but they were about to deal with the Lord of Hosts, whose invisible heavenly army always stands at attention to execute God's judgments.

The crowd mouthed the words of hedonists in every generation: "Let us eat and drink, for tomorrow we die!" (v. 13b). There was no sense of a meeting with God at His throne of judgment; only the immediate, existentialist's delight in pleasures of the flesh and the heedless hedonistic pursuits that blot out the urgency of the current crisis. Such an unabated sensual life ultimately renders a person impervious to the voice of God and too hard to repent. God had literally whispered in the ear of Isaiah, who heard the Lord's whisper. God could not even get the attention of that generation when He shouted at them through dramatic events. A life that parties endlessly without pausing for God moves beyond the ability to hear God. Has that happened to America today?

In light of everything that prophets had proclaimed, every Israelite should have known that repentance was called for. Some might express repentance with weeping and lamenting aloud, confessing their sin against God. Others might adopt the Oriental custom of shaving their heads and sitting in sackcloth to express repentance.

But all of this was conspicuous by its absence. No one gave any evidence of having taken God's deliverance to heart. How did this untimely celebration express itself? Primarily with excessive feasting. They killed animals from their meager supply, using the meat that had been set aside for important festivities. They drank wine. Still there was no background of true happiness to celebrate. There was no reason to celebrate.

The people could not even be serious in the face of death! "Let us eat and drink, for tomorrow we die!" (v. 13b). They even made light of the approaching death that awaited them. For Israel to have such an unworthy attitude in light of the opportunities to repent and cry out to God was unpardonable. No wonder pardon was out of the question. The people would not and could not repent! Such heedless living in the light of personal and national crisis may in some strange way be akin to the dreaded "sin against the Holy Spirit." The withering words of warning, "This sin of yours will never be wiped out" (22:14), holds the same frightening thunderbolt as do the warnings in the New Testament about the unpardonable sin and the sin unto death.

In light of this warning, each of us must ask, "Lord, is it I?" The safest harbor to anchor your soul is to plead with God at this very instant that you personally not be guilty of such a deadly, mortal, inexcusable spiritual neglect that it can never be atoned for until you die. We don't want to hear this message, this call to repentance. We wish this sermon were over. We want to get out of here to go about our normal activities.

And many of us today are more interested in hearing some profound answer to our questions and some new biblical insight than we are in meeting intimately with God. Christians, preachers and laity alike, may heedlessly "party" while playing church and miss the call of God for our lives. That is the very attitude Isaiah warns against. This is not child's play. This is not merely a lesson or a lecture. It is a message of warning for us at this very moment.

At 7:05 P.M. on July 17, 1981, 114 people suddenly fell to their death on skywalks while laughing and dancing high above the floor of the Hyatt Regency Hotel in Kansas City. Only one year old, the hotel had already become a scene of Kansas City nightlife. Two 120-foot-long walkways collapsed from their impressive height above the lobby onto the people on the floor below. The walkways collapsed because of a design flaw. The collapse triggered multi-million-dollar lawsuits and stunned the city and nation.

Those who witnessed the horrific sight of the crashing walkways found their lives changed forever. Think of it. Heedless revelers dancing to swing music on narrow walkways suspended by rods over the lobby far below. One moment enjoying their cocktails and swirling around in a dance . . . the next moment crashing to the floor below.

No one could fail to sympathize, empathize, and feel deeply for the shattered lives in the tragedy. Yet that moment could very well be a symbol for our text. Are we like the prophet's crowd, laughing and dancing on the roof? Has our nation become an overentertained crowd on a walkway suspended by slender rods that barely hold us up? Are the rods about to break and our party about to come suddenly crashing down?

Could that Kansas City tragedy of 1981 be a metaphor, a figure, a symbol of a nation dancing precariously around its own destiny and judgment at sunset—heedless, swirling, circling, mindless, hedonistic, unknowing, thinking this will go on forever, never considering that the party should stop long enough to assess whether we are standing on safe ground or dancing on something about to collapse beneath us.

It is the sober responsibility of our generation of proclaimers to warn a nation, either literally or metaphorically, that they are laughing and dancing on the rooftops while judgment awaits.

17

One Thing for Sure

NUMBERS 32:23 HCSB

James T. Draper, Jr.

I WANT TO ADDRESS AN AREA that is often overlooked, but it is the key to understanding the failures we have in our lives. Whatever that failure may be, in business or home, spiritually or emotionally, whatever failure we have, this is the reason. Look with me at Numbers 32. Leave your Bibles open because we will look at other verses in that chapter. My text is very familiar. You have heard it preached before. My It is a simple statement. The last portion of verse 23 is, "Be sure your sin will catch up with you."

I have heard that text used all my life. Normally it is preached to lost people. Normally it is preached to those who may be involved in some great sin. And the point is always that "you can't get away with it." You can be sure your sin will find you out. Now, that is true, but that's not what this verse is about. To get that meaning out of it, you take it out of context.

When you study the Word of God, it is important to study it in context, to see what it meant in the original setting. Who was it written about? What were the circumstances in which it was written? What was the counsel, the warning? What was it for? What was there in society that caused this kind of warning to be issued? We need to examine the context of the verse. Manley Beasley used to say that the greatest heresy is a falsehood that sounds the most like the truth. For instance, to say "there is no God" isn't a heresy; it's stupidity! Heresy is to take a truth like the reality of God and twist it so that God becomes our errand boy instead of the Sovereign of the universe. He becomes our servant instead of the holy, holy, holy God. We twist it just enough to take truth and turn it and make heresy out of it. So it's important for us to stay in context.

This verse is a classic example of that. The children of Israel have been wandering around in the wilderness. They have come now to the Jordan River. They are ready to cross into the promised land. They are ready to claim what God had promised them hundreds of years before. The tribes of Reuben and Gad were cattlemen. They had lots of herds, lots of flocks. When they came up on the east side of the Jordan, they found that it was a lush bottomland. It had fertile fields with lots of grass. It was a great place for livestock.

So when the leaders of Reuben and Gad saw this land, they concluded that it was a great place for cattle (32:1). In other words, it was great range land. This was wonderful. This was what they had been dreaming about. There couldn't be anything better than this. So they came to Moses and said, "Moses, we have an idea. We have cattle. God is with us. There are plenty of you guys. There is really no need for us to cross the Jordan. There is really no need for us to go into the promised land. We think we will just settle down here. We think we will just stop right here, and you give us this land. When you proportion out the land for the tribes, you give us this land here on the east side of the Jordan."

God had said that the Israelites were to go across the Jordan and to possess the land. As a nation they were to go and conquer the land. God pledged to be with them, to fight their battles for them. This land would be theirs. God would give their enemies into their hands. But now Reuben and Gad were considering backing out. They were considering letting others go on without them. All the twelve tribes together had secured that land east of the Jordan. Now these two tribes wanted the other ten to secure their own land. "They helped us, but we won't help them," seemed to be their attitude.

In this context we find this verse: "Be sure your sin will catch up with you." But the sin that will find us out is the sin of omission.

It is the willful, deliberate, premeditated, intelligent decision not to do what God has told us to do. The sin that will find us out is the sin of refusing to obey God. There is a tremendous responsibility when God speaks to our hearts. There is a tremendous responsibility for us to be obedient to God.

Listen to what God says. God spoke through Moses and said to the tribes of Gad and Reuben, "Should your brothers go to war while you stay here?" (v. 6). In other words, "Are you going to forsake your responsibility and let others do it?" That's what Moses asked them. He indicated that their proposal was not all bad because he told them that if they would obey God, then they could come back and have the land. But if they insisted on disobeying God, then they would be forsaking their responsibility.

It gets worse. "Why are you discouraging the Israelites from crossing into the land the LORD has given them?" (v. 7). Moses said that if they didn't obey God, they would discourage the rest of the people from obeying God. We never disobey God in a vacuum. We never disobey God in isolation. There is no private sin. Sin always has an impact on others. When we do not do what God has commanded us to do, then we make it easy for somebody else to be disobedient.

Let me show you how that works out. Have you ever wondered why we have a hard time on Sunday morning getting people to respond? Who of us has not had the experience of the minister preaching his heart out from the Word of God and know that there are people there who need to respond, yet nothing happens during the invitation? Why does that happen? The reason is that the great majority of the people in that service have disobeyed God, and that makes it easy for other people to disobey God.

There is an incredible responsibility that we have to others in our obedience or lack of it. We cannot disobey God in a vacuum. We cannot disobey God and have it affect us only. If we do not obey God, then we encourage other people not to obey God. We discourage them. It should not be any surprise that we have difficulties in our homes. If the man is not actively, aggressively, intelligently, willfully obeying God, it sets off a chain reaction of discouragement. Rather than making it easy for the family to obey God, it makes it easy for them to disobey God. Rather than making it easy for the family to follow God, it makes it easy for the family to rebel against God. What a responsibility we have!

Sometimes Satan whispers in our ears that our disobedience doesn't make much difference. Yes, it does! It doesn't matter what the disobedience is. There are not any "big" sins and "little" sins. Certainly, there are sins that have a more devastating effect on society than others. But God says that the sins we commit issue from an attitude of sin in our hearts. And what is sin? It is to disobey God, to disregard God. When we do not obey God in even small things, we make it easy for others to disobey God.

Look at the cost of that. Look at verse 15. Notice the pronouns in this verse. "If you [Reuben and Gad] turn back from following Him [God], He [God] will once again leave this people [the whole nation—all twelve tribes] in the wilderness, and you [Reuben and Gad] will destroy all of them." Moses said if these two tribes didn't obey God, then God was not going to bless the entire nation. He would leave them in the wilderness, and it would be their fault. These two tribes would have destroyed the rest of the nation.

That is a heavy, incredible responsibility. Apply it to the family. Dad, if you don't obey God, your family may be destined for the wilderness. You will have done it. Apply it to the church. If you don't obey God, He may write "ichabod" across the church and leave it in the wilderness. And it will be your fault. You will have destroyed it. Apply it to a denomination. Apply it to a nation. Apply it to the world. When we don't obey God, the consequences are incredible.

Let me back up and be sure you understand what I am talking about. I don't want you to miss where I am headed. I'm not talking about adultery. I'm not talking about murder. I'm not talking about embezzlement. I'm not talking about slander. I'm not talking about gossip. I'm not talking about lust. I'm not talking about deceit. I'm not talking about lying. I'm talking about not doing what God tells you to do, failing to obey Him, being unresponsive to Him.

That is the essence of sin. We sometimes think that "sin" is synonymous with "sins." That is not true. Sin is a spirit, an attitude. Sins are actions or inactions. Sin is the attitude that says to God, "I don't need you. I'm doing quite fine, thank you," and pushing God out of our lives. That is sin.

In the New Testament, the writer of James says, "So, for the person who knows to do good and doesn't do it, it is a sin" (James 4:17). It's the same principle we are talking about here. The sins of these two tribes would cause God to leave all of Israel in the wilderness, and the blame would be squarely on their shoulders. There is a devastating effect when we refuse to obey God. When we fail to do what God wants us to do, we keep others from doing what God wants them to do. It is a sin against God, but it is also a sin against others.

I said earlier there is no private sin. Every sin that we commit is against the family. It is against the fellowship of believers. It is against the church. It is against God. Every sin is significant. When we do not do what God tells us to do, we make it easy for others to disobey. We discourage them from doing what they ought to do. You can be sure your sin will catch up with you.

When we do not do what we should, it leaves a gap. God intended for our lives to be filled with positive response and obedience to Him. And when we don't do that, it leaves a void. It leaves an emptiness. But it will not remain empty long. It is into that void, into that emptiness that sins rush and tragedy comes. I want to illustrate that with the most vivid illustration I can imagine.

Turn with me to 2 Samuel. If I were to ask you what was the sin of David, you would probably say it was the sin of adultery. But that was not his primary sin. David's sin that led him away from God, that caused him to embarrass a nation, was not the sin of adultery. You say, "Well, it must have been murder, then. He had Uriah killed." No, it was not murder. "Well, it must have been lying; he lied to the people and tried to deceive them by marrying Bathsheba." No, it was not that.

Look at 2 Samuel 11:1. "In the spring when kings march out to war." That has always struck me as being rather humorous. The Middle East didn't have an NBA, an NFL, or an NCAA during those days. So once a year they went to war. They lined up all their troops to see which nation had the best army. You will find the phrase, "at the time when kings go to war" several times in the Old Testament. Underline the word *kings* there. "David sent Joab and his servants with him, and all Israel" (NASB). Do you see what was happening? David was the defending champion, and he had a great army. He had the best troops. So when the kings went to battle, David told Joab to take the troops and fight for Israel. And so they did. "They destroyed the children of Ammon, and besieged Rabbah."

Notice the last sentence in this verse: *"But David tarried still at Jerusalem."* In ancient times it was the king's responsibility to be with his troops in battle. That was his job. That was his assignment. It was his national assignment. It was an assignment that had been given to him by God. He was the leader. He led his troops. But David decided one year not to do that. He knew he was supposed to be leading the army. But he knew he had a good army. It wouldn't matter. They would win the battle. Besides that, he reasoned that he needed some R&R. He had burnout and needed some rest. So the troops went into battle, and David rested in Jerusalem.

Now listen to me. I want to be sure that you get the picture. I am not saying that it's wrong to rest. I believe the Bible teaches us that we need to come apart, come aside from daily activities, that we need to have a time of recreation, a time away from the normal demands of life. I believe that the Bible is replete with commands and illustrations for us to spend time alone with God in a time away. The problem was not that David was away, and it was not that he was resting. The problem was that he was away and he was resting while his troops were in battle. And he forsook his responsibility. He remained in Jerusalem.

While he was tarrying, he was out one day on the roof. He stands up. He stretches. He looks around, and he sees a beautiful woman sunbathing on another roof. Here is what happened. He refused his responsibility. He forsook his position. He had sent his troops into battle without him. He allowed somebody else to do what he was supposed to do. And, thus, he was vulnerable. He never would have seen Bathsheba if he had been in battle. He never would have seen her if he had been doing what he was supposed to do. He never would have seen her if he had been fulfilling his responsibility. But he was tarrying, just avoiding his responsibility. That wasn't bad. He was just not doing what he was supposed to do.

That's innocent enough, isn't it? That's not so bad. Who is going to know? Who is going to know if we have our time with God? Who is going to know? Who is going to know if it's just something private and quiet? Nobody is going to know. That's all David did. His sin was neglecting to do what God had assigned him to do. In his disobedience he saw Bathsheba. He liked what he saw, and he moved into acts of sins of disgrace.

All of us are capable of doing exactly what David did. When we think we are not vulnerable, we are closer to it than we ever imagined. Satan will blindside us and show us how weak we are. David was disobedient, neglecting his responsibility, not doing what God wanted him to do. In that moment he lusted. He sent his servants and said, "Bring her to me." They did. She came. They committed adultery together. But the adultery wasn't where it started. It started with something far more innocent than that—something that is seldom mentioned and something we seldom guard against. It started when he simply refused to do what he was supposed to do, when he neglected his responsibility.

Now the complications come. That was a sensuous day for David. But a few weeks later, a messenger comes with a note. Bathsheba says, "King, I hate to tell you this, I am pregnant." Now David is in a quandary. What is he going to do? In this experience we see the way that we rationalize our sinfulness. We see how one sin leads us into another and how it gets deeper and deeper. We see how it gets like tar baby. We can't turn loose of it. We get more and more involved.

David was also the spiritual leader of the nation. He knew what to do. He should have cried to God for forgiveness. He should have confessed his sin. He should have dealt with it like a person who loves God and walks with God. But remember, he was not walking with God. He had neglected to obey God. He had pulled away from God. So he devises a plan. He sends a message to Joab to send Bathsheba's husband Uriah back home. Just think of the hold Joab had on David the rest of his life! Joab did all of the dirty work. For the rest of his life, David had to know that Joab knew.

So Joab sends Uriah home. David tells Uriah that he has been a faithful servant, he has fought in battle, and he wants him to have some R&R with his wife. Here is what David thought. Uriah would spend the night with his wife, then when it turned up she was pregnant, everybody would think that it was no big deal, that the child was Uriah's.

But Uriah was a man of convictions greater than David at this point. Uriah said, "King, it is not right for me to be having this time with my wife while my troops are sleeping in the field." And he wouldn't go in to sleep with her. He lay down in the hall outside and would not take advantage of David's offer. Uriah refused to enjoy something that his troops did not enjoy. The troops were out there fighting and sleeping in the field. He had a sense of responsibility that David did not have.

That should have been David's speech. David is the one who should have determined that he should not have been in Jerusalem. But he didn't, and now he was trying to cover a sin. Uriah reasoned in his heart, "I can't spend the night with my wife while others are out there. I need to be there." And he refused to go in to be with his wife.

Now David has a problem. What is he going to do with Uriah? So he devises a scheme. He tells Joab to go out to battle tomorrow and form the troops like an arrow. He was to place Uriah right out on the point of the arrow. Then at a certain point in battle, Joab would give a signal and all the other troops would fall back, leaving

Uriah by himself to be killed by the enemy. That was the plan. David was scheming in the flesh to cover up a sin.

Let me tell you that you can't cover up your sin. It will come back, and it will be found out. The plan seemed to work to perfection. The troops pulled back, and Uriah was killed. Now David plays the part of the benefactor. They had Uriah's funeral. The king said, "My faithful servant Uriah served me so well. He worked so hard, labored so well. I'll take his wife into my house, and I'll take care of her in memory of my faithful servant, Uriah." Good, faithful king David! But look at the last sentence in 2 Samuel 11:27: "However, the LORD considered what David had done to be evil."

If you are determined to displease somebody, choose someone besides the Lord. If you are going to pick a fight, pick one you can win. You can't win that one. You are not going to defeat God! David had an ingenious plan to cover his sins. Everything was done in the flesh, and when it was reported in heaven, God said He was displeased. David thought he had gotten away with it. That night when Bathsheba came, and the months they lived together, and when the baby was born, I can see David saying, "Whew, I got away with it. I put one over on them." He may have even thought, *I won't let it happen again.*

But remember our text: "Be sure your sin will catch up with you." Lying, adultery, murder—all began in a simple refusal to obey God. You can be sure your sin will catch up with you. I don't have time to go into all the details of the rest of the story, but you know it. God sends a prophet by the name of Nathan. God told Nathan what had happened. Nathan came to the king and told him a story about a rich man with a lot of flocks and many sheep who had company arrive at his house. He had a poor neighbor, a little sharecropper, who lived next to him. The neighbor had just one lamb. The rich man had company arrive, and he wanted to feed them. He sent his servants over, and they stole the one lamb from the poor man, killed it, and fed it to his guests.

Nathan asked, "What do you think ought to happen to that rich man?" David grew livid with rage. His veins bulged; his face turned red; and he said that the man ought to be killed. Then Nathan pointed a finger right at the king and said, "You are the man" (2 Sam. 12:7). The sword of the Lord pierced the heart of David, and he cried out, "I have sinned against the LORD." Nathan said to David, "The LORD has taken away your sin; you will not die" (2 Sam 12:13).

The wages of sin is always death. The only reason we escape the immediate wages of physical death is by the grace of God. By Jewish law, David should have been killed, but he repented. Thank God for repentance. Nathan said that because David had repented, God would not kill him. And David may have thought again, "Whew, I dodged another bullet." But he didn't. Remember our text: "Be sure your sin will catch up with you."

Nathan continued to reveal God's punishment of David. Disgrace and violence would follow him the rest of his life. "It's not over, David. What you did innocently and quietly, what you thought nobody knew, God knew. And because God knew it, you are going to live with the consequences the rest of your life."

You know the story of David's life. He was plagued with rebellion and disgrace within his own family. David had a son named Amnon. He had a daughter named Tamar. Tamar was beautiful. Amnon saw Tamar and lusted after her. Sound familiar? Where do you suppose he learned that? Like father, like son. He lusted after Tamar. He so lusted after her that he contrived a scheme. He pretended he was sick, and he sent word to his half sister, Tamar, that if she would just come and feed him some broth, just come and take care of him, he would be better.

So she came to Amnon's tent. When she did, he grabbed her, raped her, disgraced her. In the Hebrew tradition, if he did that, he should keep her and care for her. But as often happened, once he had satisfied his lust, he despised Tamar and drove her out of the house. Now she is disgraced. She is no longer a virgin. She is no longer pure. She has been disgraced, and she runs from the tent in tears and runs into her brother, Absalom. He asks why she is crying, and she tells him. Absalom brought his sister Tamar into his tent, to be part of his family, and he took care of her. But the Scripture says that Absalom burned with hatred toward his brother, Amnon. He knew in his heart that Amnon had abused and disgraced his sister. He swore that someday he would take revenge on him.

It's not over, David. What you did innocently and quietly, you thought was not significant. You just refused to do what God told you to do. It's all so innocent. But it's not over, David. You can be sure your sin will catch up with you. We may ask, "Didn't he repent?" Yes. Repentance cleanses us of the penalty of sin, but it doesn't remove the consequences of sin. So rebellion and disgrace persist.

Absalom burned with hatred for his brother Amnon. Months later he planned a great barbecue. Everybody was to come. He got some of his friends and shared his plan to have this celebration. At a certain point, there would be some chaos, some confusion, and Absalom instructed them to attack Amnon and kill him. It all happens as planned. At the appointed time the men turn on Amnon and kill him. You can be sure your sin will catch up with you.

David may have said, "Thank God, it's over. It's finally over." But it wasn't over. Absalom now becomes a rebel against his father. He leaves the city, gathers a band of outlaws around him, captures the imagination of the people, and leads a rebellion against his own father. There is a time in which the battle favors Absalom. David is driven from Jerusalem and hides in the hills from his own son. You can be sure your sin will find you out.

Then the battle turns and David comes back to Jerusalem and his army gets the upper hand. David calls Joab, the commander of his military forces, into his quarters. Remember Joab? He's the conspirator in this. He said, "Joab, I want you to go out and destroy the armies of my enemies, but my son, Absalom, don't touch him. Don't take his life. Watch out for my son, Absalom" (see 2 Sam. 18:5). But why should Joab obey David? He knows the dirty laundry. He knows the truth. What could the king do to him if he did just the opposite of what David commanded? And the battle rages.

At one point in the battle, some of the men of Joab came upon Absalom, who had long golden hair. And he had ridden his horse under a tree, and his hair had become tangled in the branches. He is ripped from his horse, and he is hanging helpless. The men call Joab. They know David has instructed that no harm should come to him. But Joab leads the charge, and they toss darts into the body of Absalom until he is dead. Then they take his body and throw it in a gorge and cover it with rocks.

And it all started when David tarried in Jerusalem! If you want to know the agony, the anguish, the despair of disobeying God, watch this scene. I am not talking about murder. I am not talking about adultery. I am not talking about embezzlement. I am talking about the willful, deliberate, premeditated choice not to do what God has told you to do. You nowhere see the consequences more graphically pictured than in this scene.

When the battle is won and the messenger comes to David, David asks how the battle is going. The messenger reports victory. David asks, "What about my son Absalom?" And the messenger says, "Would God that all your enemies were as he." He was dead. In that moment we see the concentrated hell of disobedience pouring in upon the soul and spirit of David. As he begins to ascend the steps to his chamber, the Scripture says he cried, "My son Absalom! My son, my son Absalom! If only I had died instead of you" (2 Sam. 18:33).

And it all started when David tarried in Jerusalem. I don't want to be guilty of not applying this message. I hope you have gotten the message. But I am telling you that God has given each of us an assignment in our home, in the church, in society. Every problem in your home, every emotional problem you face, every difficulty in your church, your family, every relational disruption that you have had can be traced directly to some point in time when you refused to do what God commanded you to do.

If you are not saved, you may have thought, "Well, I have a right to live my own life." Yes, that would be true if it were your life, but you don't live in a vacuum. You have no right to lead your children, your family, your neighbors to hell. You have a responsibility to respond to God's call for your life. If you could reject God and go to hell and do it by yourself and nobody would be the worse off, it would be one thing. But you can't. When you don't obey God, it has a ripple effect, and it makes it easier for other people not to obey God, and on and on it goes.

That's why we have a chaotic society today. The ripple has extended until our society has erupted in violence, because we have lost our respect for authority. This begins when we refuse to become what God wants us to be. We must be obedient to God. If we aren't, we can be sure that our sin of refusing to obey God will find us out.

18

Rivers of Living Water

JOHN 7:37–39 HCSB

James T. Draper, Jr.

JOHN CHAPTER SEVEN is a remarkable passage of Scripture. Beginning in verse 37: "On the last and most important day of the featival, Jesus stood up and cried out, 'If anyone is thirsty, he should come to Me and drink! The one who believes in Me, as the Scripture has said, will have streams of living water flow from deep within him.'" And then in verse 39, John, in a parenthesis, said, "He said this about the Spirit, whom those who believed in Him were going to receive, for the Spirit had not yet been received, because Jesus had not yet been glorified."

The setting for that saying is the Feast of Tabernacles. It was a dramatic feast. In fact, it may have been the most dramatic of all the feasts of the Jews. The Feast of Tabernacles was the third of a trio of great Jewish feasts. There were Passover and Pentecost and Tabernacles. The Feast of Tabernacles is sometimes called the Feast of Booths. Originally in the Old Testament it lasted seven days, but by the time of Christ, it had been expanded to run Sabbath through Sabbath, so it was an eight-day celebration. It was the original Thanksgiving celebration. It was a thanksgiving time to God for His mighty deliverance and provision.

God wanted the people to be thankful. God wanted the people to be grateful. He wanted the people to remember the provision that He had made for them. He wanted them to remember that there was a time when they didn't have a roof over their heads. They had been nomads, wandering in the desert. They had no abiding place, no home or permanent dwelling place of their own.

During the Feast of Tabernacles, or Booths, the people were required to build booths outside their permanent dwelling. They had to come outside, in the street, or on the roof. And booths sprang up everywhere. Leviticus 23 gives many of the details about how they were to do this. They were instructed to bring willow branches and palm branches and construct these booths in such a way that the people could see through the branches and see the stars, the sun, and the moon, and the breeze could still blow through. It was a reminder to them that there was a time when they did not have permanent homes. They were to be thankful for God's provision for them while they wandered without permanent homes.

It was a very significant feast, a very festive feast. Every day they had special celebrations or ceremonies. It was an incredible time. It was really the most joyous feast of the Jews and one of the most significant. The prophet Zechariah envisioned a day in the millennial kingdom when all the nations of the world would observe the Feast of Tabernacles (Zech. 14:2–10). It was a wonderful celebration. It was so important that every Jewish male within twenty miles of the temple was required to participate. They were required to come to the Feast of Tabernacles, to the celebration, the ceremony.

All over Jerusalem the booths would spring up, even in the temple area itself. In the streets there would be booths. And every day they would have this wonderful ceremony. A white-robed priest carrying a golden pitcher would lead a procession of priests with pitchers. They would take these pitchers and walk down from the temple area. They would go down to the pool of Siloam, where they would fill those golden pitchers with water. Then the white-robed priests would lead the procession back into the city of Jerusalem to the temple area. They would come through the water gate. As they did, they would chant Isaiah 12:3, "You will joyfully draw water from the springs of salvation."

As they came through the water gate, the procession would wind its way back up to the temple, where the city of Jerusalem would be filled with thousands of people. The people began to sing the hallel, from Psalm 113 to Psalm 118. The procession came through the water gate and into the temple area. As they came, temple trumpeters stationed on the perimeter of the temple would blast triumphantly twenty-one times. When the people came to verse 1 and verse 29 of Psalm 118, "Give thanks to the LORD," they would wave those branches and shout with a roar. It was enough to make the hair on the back of your neck stand up. Children would be wild-eyed with wonder and amazement. It was an incredibly exciting, spine-tingling time.

The procession would come into the temple area, and the priest with the golden pitcher would come to the altar. At the great altar there was a silver funnel. The priest would pour water into that silver funnel. It would go around and around until it splattered all over the altar. When the water splashed over the altar, the people would cheer and wave their branches. It was a marvelous time of remembering the providence of God, the goodness of God, the provision of God while the Israelites wandered in the wilderness.

It commemorated God's miraculous deliverance of the Israelites out of Egypt but especially the miracle of providing water in the desert for two million people. Unbelievable! God did it, and this was the reason for the celebration. This ceremony was repeated every day for eight days. On the last day the ceremony was repeated essentially as I have described it, only in much more detail, with much more grandeur, and with much more vividness than I could ever tell you. The procession would come into the area of the temple with thousands of people crowded together all along the way.

On the last day the ceremony was repeated with two exceptions. When the priests came to the altar carrying those golden pitchers, they would circle the altar seven times as a reminder of the sevenfold march around the city of Jericho when the walls fell down (see Josh. 6:15–20). Then the priest would turn the pitcher to pour water into the silver funnel. But on the last day, there was no water in the pitcher. It was a symbol of the incompleteness of all past provision. Their fathers had drunk water in the wilderness but they died. And the Messiah had not yet come. The promises of God had not yet been fulfilled. Instead of the spine-tingling roar that reverberated through the city of Jerusalem, when the priest turned the pitcher and nothing came out, a hush fell over the crowd. The Messiah, God's ultimate provision, had not yet come.

At precisely that moment in the ceremony, Jesus stood. And in that moment of solemn quietness, Jesus cried, "If anyone is thirsty, he should come to Me and drink! The one who believes in Me, as the Scripture has said, will have streams of living water flow from deep within him" (John 7:37–38). What a dramatic moment! At that moment which spoke of the incompleteness and the lack of fulfillment of God's promised Messiah, Jesus spoke of the water of life that He came to give to all people. What an incredible moment!

I. An Intense Proclamation

We are arrested by the words *stood* and *cried* in John's description of this event. These are very forceful words. John reports that "Jesus stood." Jewish teachers never stood; they always sat. If I were a typical Jewish teacher in those days, I would never stand. Teachers always sat. The only people who stood were imperial heralds who brought a message from Caesar, the king, or the governor. Standing and speaking like that was reserved for an imperial proclamation.

It is interesting that one of the words for preaching in the New Testament is *kerrusso,* which comes from the Greek word *kerux,* which referred to an official herald. It referred to someone who delivered a proclamation from the king. That's one of the things about preaching. We are delivering a message from King Jesus. It's a wonderful thing to be able to proclaim the message of Jesus. This verse said that Jesus stood. It was remarkable that in that moment when a teacher would normally sit, Jesus stood.

Then John reports that He "cried" (v. 37). This word *cried* is a unique word. It only appears in the Gospel of John in the New Testament. And it only appears in three chapters in the Gospel of John. It appears in chapter 1 where it says that John the Baptist came "crying out in the wilderness" (1:23). And it appears in chapter 11 when Jesus was at the grave of Lazarus. The Gospel of John says that "Jesus wept" (11:35), and then He shouted out with a loud voice, "Lazarus, come out!" (11:43). Those are the only times other than chapter 7 where that word is used. It is a word of emotion, a word of passion, a word of intensity, a word of enthusiasm.

This tells me that that those of us who have been entrusted with the message of the gospel need to give an intense proclamation. For heaven's sake, don't serve God like you are half asleep. Don't serve God like you have no enthusiasm for it. Give it your all. Be intense, passionate, and energetic. This intense proclamation is a reminder to us that we need to be intense, passionate, and energetic about the proclamation of the gospel. Serving God ought to be exciting. Serving God ought to be energetic. It ought to be passionate. It ought to call for all of our energy. Why should we give more energy to secular pursuits than we do to the things of God? The gospel deserves an intense proclamation.

II. An Inclusive Provision

We see an inclusive provision in verse 37: "If anyone is thirsty he should come to Me, and drink." There are two important things about this provision. First, it is important for us to see the absence of something specific. Jesus just says that if *anyone* thirsts. It's a vague yet descriptive term. Jesus is comparing physical thirst to the longing of the human heart. These people understood thirst. The Feast of Tabernacles came at the end of the dry season. During the Feast of Tabernacles, there was an enacted and dramatic prayer for rain. The farmers needed additional rain for the latter crops. All these people understood thirst. They knew what it was like. They had seen people die of thirst.

Thirst is the most powerful craving of the human body. You can live for weeks, even months, without eating a lot, but you can't live very long without water. You have to have water. It's the strongest craving of our physical bodies. And Jesus compares all the needs of the human heart to physical thirst. Whatever the thirst of your life is, whatever craving you have, Jesus Christ declares that He can provide satisfaction for that craving.

We're living in a pleasure-crazed age. Could Jesus possibly provide the longing of the human heart for pleasure? Psalm 16:11 says, "In Your presence is abundant joy; in Your right hand are eternal pleasures." What about the longing for recognition and acceptance? Ephesians 1:4 declares that we're accepted by the Lord. Revelation 1:5–6 says that God has made us to be kings and priests through Christ Jesus. Whatever the longing of the human heart, Jesus Christ says, "I can satisfy that longing." He describes human need in terms of thirst. And He says, "I can quench that thirst."

Notice the universality of this provision. He says, if *anyone*—not just certain people, not just certain classes, or races, or cultures, or people who speak certain languages. If anyone—anyone, anywhere, anytime—thirsts, the gospel is the answer. Anywhere the gospel is preached, Jesus Christ brings salvation and satisfaction. I have seen this happen all over this world. I have been in areas of East Africa where people have never seen a white face, where they've never heard the gospel. When you tell them about Jesus Christ, the vast majority of the people receive Christ as Savior.

It doesn't matter whether you're in the backward Pokot tribe of western Kenya or whether you're a sophisticated suburbanite in an upper-class suburban area of an American city. It doesn't matter where you are, who you are, what you are. If there's a thirst in your life, Jesus declares that He can supply the answer for that thirst. This is a universal invitation that He gives. It is an unlimited provision that Jesus offers. That's the message we have to give to this world— that Jesus saves. Tell the world. Whatever the problem, however deep in sin they have gone, Jesus' love reaches down to pick them up and draw them back. However far away from God and decency they may have gone, Jesus' love reaches out to bring them back. There is an answer for the thirsty heart, and His name is Jesus.

You can verify that fact. You can prove it if you just look at history. At the end of the first century, the beloved apostle John wrote a letter to the churches of Asia Minor. He was probably the last living eyewitness of the earthly ministry of Jesus Christ. John says, "What was from the beginning, what we have heard, what we have seen with our eyes, what we have observed, and have touched with our hands, . . . we also declare to you" (1 John 1:1, 3). It is almost like John the beloved apostle was passing the torch on to the second-century martyrs. And it's as though he said, "Jesus offered us this cup of the water of life and we drank, and we want you to know that the cup is still full." And John passed the cup to the martyrs of the second century.

When those second-century martyrs drew their last breath, their dying testimony was, "The cup is still full." They passed it to the commentators and the Church Fathers of the third century, and their testimony was that the cup is still full. And the commentators and the Church Fathers of the third century passed it on to Augustine of North Africa, and their testimony was the same: "It's a strange thing. The more you drink, the more there is. The cup is still full." And Augustine passed it on to the Middle Ages. During the Middle Ages the Word of God was bound and was not proclaimed in the churches. The common people couldn't read the Word of God. Even then there was a silver stream that flowed down through the Middle Ages. Whoever drank of that stream found life through Jesus Christ.

That stream flowed until it came in the fourteenth century to John Huss and Jerome of Prague and in the fifteenth century to Martin Luther. While studying the book of Romans, Martin Luther read, "The just shall live by faith" (Rom. 1:17 KJV). He took that cup and found that the cup was real, that life was real, that water was real, that Jesus did give eternal life. He passed it on to John Calvin. And John Calvin passed it to John Knox of Scotland. The testimony was always the same, "The cup is still full." It came to John Smith and the Separatists and then to Cromwell and the Puritans.

Finally that message came across the Atlantic Ocean and landed on the eastern seaboard of the United States. And the testimony was always the same: There was a cup filled with the water of life.

Whoever drank of that water of life found eternal life and the quenching of their thirst, the craving of their hearts.

That message spread across the eastern seaboard, and it crossed the Appalachian Mountains in the frontier revivals. It made its way westward until over sixty years ago it came to the back porch of a little parsonage in central Arkansas, and a little boy took that cup and drank from it. I was that boy, and I want to tell you that the cup is still full!

"If anyone is thirsty, let him come to Me and drink." That's the message that God has entrusted to us. So there is an intense proclamation to us, and there is an unlimited provision.

III. An Incredible Promise

Jesus said in verse 38, "The one who believes in Me, as the Scripture has said, will have streams of living water flow from deep within him." Listen carefully because this is important. Lasting satisfaction does not come from drinking the cup; it comes from being a conveyor of living water to others. Jesus was focusing the people away from the ceremony to Himself. He was focusing people away from the shadow to the substance, from the promise to the fulfillment, from the ritual to the reality. He was saying, "I'm the fulfillment of the promise of God." He intended that we should drink from the cup, but He never intended that we should keep it. The gospel is ours to give away. It is ours to share. It is ours to pass on. How selfish we would be if we had something wonderful and did not share it with others who needed it. Our greatest satisfaction does not come from drinking the water Jesus offers but in being a conveyor of living water to other people.

How does one drink of this cup? John says it is very easy as he quotes Jesus saying, "The one who believes in me." For John, the worst sin was unbelief and the best obedience was believing and responding to Christ. So he said that those who believe would have rivers of living water flowing from deep within them. It is God's intent that we who have received the water of life should pass it on to others, that we should become conveyors of living water.

Some scholars get disturbed because they can't find any passage in the Old Testament that Jesus quoted in John chapter 7. Jesus said, "As the Scripture has said." I believe He was referring to Ezekiel 47. There is a picture in this passage of a great river flowing out of the throne of God. The Scripture says that at first it flows ankle deep, then knee-deep, then up to the waist, and then it is over the head and a person just has to swim in it. Then verse 9 of Ezekiel 47 declares, "There will be life everywhere the river goes." That's the way it is to be with us. Wherever the water of life flows, things come alive. Things live because Jesus is the water of life, and He desires that His church be a life-giving supply of water. He intends for us to minister grace to the world in which we live.

Our Lord did not intend for us to be absorbed and consumed with the world about us, but that we should shape the world—that we should change the culture in which we live, and that we should provide life-giving water. That was the intent of Christ. Everything lives wherever the water flows. God intends for the church to receive the water of life but also to give it to others.

That is the difference between churches that are alive and those that are dead. You show me a dead church, and I'll show you a church that is bound up in tradition and preoccupied with fellowship. "Me and my wife, my son John, his wife—us four, no more." You know the attitude. They are bound up in what they can get out of church, and the church is dead.

There are two bodies of water in Israel that illustrate this vividly. There's the Sea of Galilee and the Dead Sea. The Sea of Galilee is an incredibly beautiful body of water. I don't think I'll ever forget the first time we topped a hill and looked across the Sea of Galilee into Lebanon and Syria. The surface of this lake is above sea level, but the bottom is below sea level. It's supplied with water from the rivers that flow out of Mount Herman to the northwest. It teems with life. If you go to Tiberias today and stay in that beautiful city on the Sea of Galilee, you can eat St. Peter's fish. You can eat the same kind of fish that Peter caught. The Sea of Galilee still gives life.

To the south lies the Dead Sea. As its name implies, it is dead! The interesting thing is that the same water fills both bodies of water. The water in the Sea of Galilee flows out of the southeast end as the R\river Jordan flows down to the Dead Sea. It's the same water that's in the Sea of Galilee, but the Dead Sea is just what you think— it's dead. The Sea of Galilee receives and it gives—and thus stays alive. The Dead Sea receives and receives and never gives—and it dies. Many Christians are "dead" in their walk with Christ because they're takers and not givers.

Stewardship is not a scheme to raise money; it is God's plan to help us understand what life is all about. We're to be givers. As we give, we find that we give back to ourselves. God intended for us to receive the water of life but for us to give it. And as we give it, every- where the water flows, there is life.

That's the picture of the church. That's why we teach Sunday school. That's why we have Vacation Bible School. That's why we do children's church. That's why we prepare sermons and messages and write songs and lead worship. We do it so we can be transmitters of this wonderful water of life that comes from Jesus, and pass it on to other people.

There's a great mystery about the origins of the world's great rivers. You can find all kinds of ideas about how rivers originate. Zebulon Pike, who discovered Pike's Peak in Colorado, actually started out looking for the headwaters of the Mississippi River. He took a left turn at the Missouri River and ended up in Colorado. There is a mountain over there, but that wasn't what he was looking for. You go to Africa and you'll find that there's a mystery about where the Nile River comes from. Is it the White Nile or the Blue Nile?

Let me tell you about another river. High in the Andes Mountains in South America, way above the freeze line, up where the ice never completely melts, there is an ice-clad rock. And on a sunny day when the wind gets just right, under the ice on the face of that ice-clad rock, a little gurgle of water begins a hesitant course. That little gurgle of water moves across the face of the ice-clad rock and joins other little gurgles of water. They become droplets, then rivulets, and then streams. And they flow together until 3,600 miles later, the Amazon River flows into the Atlantic Ocean at a rate of 180,000 cubic feet of water per second. It is such a powerful flow that the Atlantic Ocean contains fresh water sixty miles out from the point where the Amazon flows in! Yet it all started with a little gurgle of water beginning a hesitant course across the face of a rock, 3,600 miles away and high in the Andes Mountains.

Sometimes we think, and Satan encourages us to think, "I'm just one person; what can I do? I'm just a little gurgle of water." Yes, but when that little gurgle of water joins with others and we come together in Christ, we become a mighty, rushing, roaring stream and everything lives wherever the water flows. When that water flows into the polluted society that we call our culture today, just like the saline solution of the Atlantic Ocean is cleansed by the Amazon River, so our culture is cleansed by the living water of Jesus Christ. The force of the water issuing forth from God's people purges and cleanses society wherever it goes. That is God's intent! That is why Jesus said that "streams of living water [shall] flow from deep within him" (John 7:38).

Notice this about a river. A river flows effortlessly. Did you ever see a river trying to flow? Did you ever go down to a river and say, "It's really struggling today; it's really having a hard time?" No, it just flows. Rivers flow effortlessly. That's the way believers in Christ are to flow. It's not to be a big deal. It's a result of our union with Christ. It's a result of our walk with Him. We live in such a relationship with Him that He flows naturally through us, just like rivers flow so effortlessly.

Rivers flow inwardly. There is a force within those rivers that causes them to flow. The source comes from within. The mighty Amazon River has its own headwaters, and those waters come together to produce the force that takes it all the way to the Atlantic Ocean. So there's an inward flow that originates from our relationship with Christ.

Something else about a river is that it flows abundantly. This passage from God's Word tells us that. It says, "streams," plural. Rivers of living water. That is what God wants to bring through us. He flows through us abundantly. God never does anything halfway. God always does things abundantly. Jesus told the disciples to let down their nets for a large catch of fish (see Luke 5:4). They didn't just catch a few fish. Their nets began to break, and their boats began to sink. Jesus took a boy's lunch and fed five thousand people. But notice that they had twelve full baskets left over after all these people had eaten (see John 6:1–14). Everything God does is abundant. The river flows abundantly. That is God's picture of the church. What Jesus said in this dramatic moment in the Feast of Tabernacles is His vision for His people, His church.

We come to Him with our thirst, our craving, our needs. We drink the water of eternal life that satisfies our craving and thirsting. Then from us, miraculously because of our union with Him, there flow rivers of living water that changes everything it touches. So take heart, pastor friend, Sunday school teacher, minister of education, church member. We are part of a mighty river that flows not from our energies, not from us, but from Him. Out of us will flow rivers of living water. Our world desperately needs the cleansing, healing flow of those streams.

19

Good News for the New Year

ISAIAH 43:18–21 HCSB

James T. Draper, Jr.

ON NEW YEAR'S EVE OF 2002, the news media reported that three American missionaries were killed and another wounded in a shooting at the hospital at Jiblah in Yemen. It capped off a year that contained a lot of bad news. Last year was a tough year. We faced not only the normal dangers that are inherent in our world today. The west coast has been searching for a mother-to-be who disappeared Christmas Eve. The mountains of east Tennessee are being scoured for a teenager who disappeared recently.

Every time we open a newspaper or watch a newscast, we're reminded that this world is a dangerous place. And we're reminded that there is no safe place, humanly speaking. The only real safe place is in the center of the will of God. The will of God makes any place a safe place, regardless of the danger involved, because God is always in control and is always present in the midst of every situation.

Last year was one of those hard years. We faced economic recession in the world. We all felt the pinch of the rise and fall of the stock market and of investments and savings. We pray for a recovery, but economically, it's been a hard year. Coupled with that, and contributing to the crisis, are the events coming out of September 11, 2001 and the scandals in corporate America. Scandals rocked Enron,

Arthur Andersen, WorldCom, and other big companies of America. Insider trading scandals erupted, with people getting tips and trading stock that would be worthless in a few days. All of these things contributed to an economic and business environment that was very negative and very difficult.

All the while, we're involved in the war on terror. It's a new kind of war for us. We're not sure who the enemy is, sure where they are. We don't know when we'll face another outbreak of terror. It's not a question of if, but when and where. We're living in a world where terror is now reality. What has been happening around the world has come to dwell in our country, and we have felt fear for our own safety.

Added to all this we have the war with Iraq. What's going to happen in the Middle East? What about North Korea? We are seeing a proliferation of nuclear and germ warfare capabilities. How do we deal with the diplomacy and all that is involved with the tensions that arise with these nations?

Who could forget those several weeks when we were riveted to the television and the radio with the sniper saga on the east coast, with John Malvo and John Muhammed. When we come to stand at the first weekend of a new year, we need some good news. We need something that is encouraging, something that is uplifting, something that will bless us and encourage us as we move through this year.

I learned a long time ago that the place to go for encouragement and good news is the Word of God. He has spoken words to us that are timeless. In Isaiah 43 we have a great illustration of this truth. Isaiah prophesied in the eighth century. His message had a great impact on a people who had gone into exile in the latter days of that century. It also had an application two hundred years later because it would be about two hundred years before the exile would be ended with a return home.

Even though this was spoken in the eighth century with application in the sixth century, it also has application to us. The Word of God is timeless and has application to each of us. Isaiah was preaching to discouraged people whose lives had been rearranged, whose lives were controlled and dominated. They needed some good news. Listen to these words from Isaiah 43:

"Do not remember the past events, pay no attention to things of old. Look, I am about to do something new; even now it is coming. Do you not see it? Indeed, I will make a way in the wilderness, rivers in the desert. The animals of the field will honor Me, jackals and the ostriches, because I provide water in the wilderness and rivers in the desert, to give drink to My chosen people. The people I formed for Myself will declare my praise" (Isa. 43:18–21).

This was good news to those people! God was going to do something new. God was about to break through into their experience in a new way. Isaiah was God's prophet to deliver this message to them. Of all the prophets of the Old Testament, Isaiah stands out as perhaps the greatest of the prophets. If one took a poll of Bible teachers, Bible scholars, and Bible students who seriously read the Word of God, it is likely that the name of Isaiah would rise to the top of the list.

Isaiah was an unusual prophet. He was a man who was extremely well educated. He was a man who walked with kings. The time of his ministry spanned about sixty to sixty-five years. It spanned four kings of Judah and five kings of Israel. He was the dominant prophet during this period.

Isaiah was a man of unfailing courage. He never failed to attack the wrong and the sin and whatever needed to be dealt with in his society. He never asked for a favor. He never curried a compliment. He never tried to get anyone to approve what he said. He simply delivered the message that God had given to him. He was a fiery patriot who was against anyone who was against his nation. Yet at the same time, he had great compassion for the surrounding nations. He was always indignant with compromise. He would not tolerate any compromise with the truth of God.

The thing that stands out most about Isaiah is his picture of God. Who could forget that awesome moment in Isaiah 6, after his friend

King Uzziah had died and the prophet came into the temple to worship. He describes his great vision of God with deep reverence and great emphasis on the majesty of God. Isaiah stood as a giant in his time to preach the Word of God to those people.

This man of God with the timeless, courageous message came to a discouraged, weary people and brought some good news. He reminded them that God would keep his promises. God would do what He said He would do. He would bring the captives back to Jerusalem. He would restore the people to their land.

They could scarcely believe that! These were people who looked around them, and all they saw was the ruin of their hopes, the crushing of their dreams. The great dream of being a nation for God that began with the call of Abraham to leave Ur of the Chaldees, the great movement of God in leading them out of Egypt, crossing the Red Sea, the survival in the wilderness, the conquering of the Promised Land—these were just memories of a remote past. It seemed that those days were gone forever. All the people could see was crushed dreams and ruin, rubble, and despair. And to those people Isaiah said, "God said to tell you He's going to do a new thing. He's going to keep His promise to you."

The people to whom Isaiah spoke lived in two worlds. They lived in a world of reality, the world of sight. What they saw, what they understood as reality was bondage and slavery. It was the world of Babylon. But faith was also a world in which they lived. God had said, "You are my chosen people. I have a place for you. I have a plan for you. I have a kingdom for you, and I'm going to bring you to that kingdom." Faith said that God would be true to His promises. Faith said, "God will keep His word to you," but sight said, "It won't happen." What they saw said that what they believed was not true.

The people of Isaiah's time lived in two worlds. Which would they believe? Would they believe the world of sight? Would they believe what they saw, or would they believe the world of faith? Did they dare believe that God would be true to His word, that God would do what He said He would do? Did they dare believe that in the midst of this barren bondage in which they lived, God was going to do a new thing in their lives?

That world is not so remote, is it? We also live in two worlds. We live in the world of sight. The world of reality, if you please. It is a world of danger, collapsing economy, deteriorating international relationships, war, terror, and violence. We live in that world too. Then we live in the world of church or the world of faith. It is the time of worship, study, praise, and preaching. It is the world of faith where we study the Word of God and encourage one another and fellowship with one another.

But then Monday comes. We move out of the world of faith into the world of sight. And like the people of Israel, we have to decide. Will we believe God, or will we believe what we see? Will we believe the conditions, the circumstances? The people to whom Isaiah spoke were faced with that kind of decision.

God wants to do a new thing in our lives. One of the great tragedies in our Christian world today is that we grow accustomed to being believers. We often get so comfortable in our religious life that we don't realize that the most important thing is not what has happened in the past, but what God is doing now and what He's going to do. God is the God of the eternal present tense. God is continually moving forward in history. It is a tragedy when we begin to focus in so much on where we are and what we have that we lose sight of what God is about to do. God is going to do a new thing, and this is some good news for the new year.

I want to suggest that there are five things that need to be kept in mind if we are to get good news in this new year.

I. We Need to Understand That We Were Created by Design

Our existence is not an accident. We are not victims of circumstances or happenstance. In verse 1 of Isaiah 43, God says, "I am your Creator. I am the One who formed you." We were created by design. God has a plan for our lives.

This is a very important thing for us to understand. If we are going to experience the new thing that God has for us in this day, we must remember that God has a plan for our lives. If there is no plan for our lives, then life is one extended tragedy. We cannot explain anything that happens. There is no reason, no rationale to life unless we understand that God has created us with a plan. The psalmist states that even before we were born, God had already recorded the days of our lives (Ps. 139:16–17). God has a plan and a purpose for our lives.

When we understand that God has a purpose for us, then we can face the uncertainties of life. We don't know what's going to happen. We don't understand all that has happened. But if we know God has a plan, that He has a purpose for our lives, it helps us to accept and to experience the new thing that God is doing in our lives. God has a plan. Sometimes we think that God only has plans for missionaries, preachers, or leaders in the church. But I want you to understand that God created all of us by design. He has a plan for every life.

Someone may say, "I don't know what God's plan is." I have good news for you. It's not up to us to figure out what God's will is. Our part is to bow our knees before Him and to accept His plan for our lives. "Lord, my answer is 'yes.' I will obey You, whatever You want me to do. I will serve You, I will live for You, I accept Your plan even before I know it."

If we understand that God has a plan for our lives, then we can know that whatever happens to us, God will use it to accomplish that plan. That's what Romans 8:28 is all about: "We know that all things work together for the good of those who love God: those who are called according to His purpose." It doesn't say everything is good. It says everything will *work together* for good. God doesn't lose control when tragedies occur. God doesn't lose control when circumstances change. God has a purpose and plan for your life. As we enter a new year, understanding and knowing that God has a plan for our lives will open us up to God's new thing that He wants to do in our lives.

II. We Need to Understand That
We Were Created to Know God

Look at the words that God uses. He says, "I have redeemed you; I have called you by name; you are Mine!" (Isa. 43:1 NASB). These are intimate words. God wanted the people to know Him. We were created to know God. There is an emptiness in our lives, a confusion about life, a disorientation about life until we know God.

There's a great deal of difference between knowing God and knowing about God. Everyone knows about God. Everyone has some concept of God. But it is important to know that we were created to know God. We were created for intimacy with Him. The promise of Jesus was that when He went away, the Holy Spirit would come, and He would dwell in us, and He would guide us into all truth. Jesus said, "The one who has seen Me has seen the Father" (John 14:9). Jesus told those disciples that because they knew Him, they could know the Father. We were created to know God. If we do not live with the daily awareness of the presence of God in our lives, we are missing one of the great joys and blessings of life. We were created to know God.

III. We Need to Understand That
We Were Created to Succeed

Isaiah didn't say in verse 2, "*If* you pass through the waters." He said, "I will be with you *when* you pass through the waters, and when you pass through the rivers, they will not overwhelm you. You will not be scorched when you walk through the fire, and the flame will not burn you" (Isa. 43:2, emphasis added). God created us to succeed. Nothing will defeat us; nothing will destroy us if we know God. If we are living in the awareness that we were created with a plan and created to know God, and if we are walking in an understanding of the presence of God, we will succeed. Later in this chapter Isaiah talked about God making a way through the sea, a path through mighty waters, a roadway in the wilderness, and rivers in the desert (vv. 16–20). Whatever this year holds for us, if we live in the awareness of God's presence and God's purpose, we will make it. We will succeed. God will make a way for us.

Jeremiah 29:11 is a great promise to us. God says, "For I know the plans I have for you . . . plans for your welfare, not for disaster, to give you a future and a hope." God says there is hope for us, there is a future for us. We will succeed. God will see that His purpose is realized through us.

When we understand that, we look at all of life differently. If we did not understand that, we could not look with optimism at what happened in Yemen on New Year's Eve. But we understand that God will take even the evil intent of the man who took those lives, and of those who encouraged him and trained him, and make it to be best, and make it to be good for us. I believe we'll see one of the greatest blessings come out of the death of these three servants of the Lord. That contradicts human logic. Human logic says that it was a tragedy, a waste. God says that He is in control and we will fulfill the plan, the purpose He has for us. Nobody can destroy it. Nobody can keep us from it. We will succeed.

Now if we're going to succeed, there are some things we need to do. First, we can't get trapped in our past. In verse 18, God tells us not to remember the things of the past. He is talking to people for whom everything was in the past. Everything God had done was in the past. Everything God had promised was in the past. God had done some mighty things in the past, but He told the people of Isaiah's day not to reflect just on the past.

The point is obvious for us. We must not go through life looking in the rearview mirror! Many times we look back and try to live in a past time. We just can't do that. It's not productive! It's not real! It is an illusionary world. The past is not what we think it was.

I have people say to me, "I just love to go back to the good old days." When was that? I was born in the thirties, a time of depression. Do you want to go back to the Depression? I grew up in the time of World War II and the Korean War. Do you want to go back to worldwide war, where children in school were having air-raid drills and being taught how to duck under desks and go to certain parts of the building in bomb drills? Is that what you want? Do you want to go back to the sixties with all of the craziness that happened in that time and the assassinations that took place? Where do you want to go back to?

We idealize and memorialize the past, but it's an unreal world. My favorite uncle had a saying: "I'm not the man I used to be, but then I never was." You know, the past is not what we make it to be. We lift up the past as if it were some kind of idol, and we worship and memorialize it. If we're going to succeed in life, we can't go through life looking in the rearview mirror. Don't just look back, even at the good things. If we look back and remember the good things that happened to us in the past, it will keep us from the new things that God is doing now. And if we look just at the bad things that have happened to us in the past, it will create depression and despair. So God reminds us that we must not be trapped in the past.

Second, God reminds us that He will make a way where there seems to be no way. He says He will make a roadway in the wilderness. Isaiah is speaking to people who would have to cross what is modern-day Iran, Iraq, and Jordan to get back to Jerusalem. There was just no human way they could do it.

But God declared that He is a God who makes a way where there doesn't seem to be a way. Do you find yourself in a situation where there doesn't seem to be a way out? Enslaved by a habit, tormented by guilt, confronted every day with the depression or despair of a meaningless life? There just doesn't seem to be any way out. You feel trapped in unhappy circumstances with no way out. The good news is that God says He will make a way where there is no way. If we understand that we were created for a purpose, that God has a plan for our lives, that He created us to know Him, then we can come to experience the fact that He wants us to succeed in the plan He has for us. Nothing will detour us from God's purposes if we understand that. God said that He would make a way where there is no way.

Third, God says that He will give us resources where there seem to be no resources. He will provide rivers in the desert. Several years ago I drove down the coast of Israel to Egypt. I drove by that wilderness that the Israelites wandered around in. Even on the coast, had it not been for the paved highway and the people who worked to keep it open, there would have been no way through there because it's just blowing sand like the Sahara Desert. There are not any rivers in the wilderness, but God says even when we find we are in a place where resources don't seem to exist, He will provide what we need.

What I want you to understand is that God has a purpose and a plan for your life. He created you to know Him, and He created you to succeed in the plan that He has for your life. In the midst of barren dryness, God says that He will give artesian wells of provision. The psalmist said, "[God] satisfies you with goodness" (Ps. 103:5). Heaven's banquet hall is always open, even in the wilderness. God created us to succeed.

IV. God Wants Us to Understand That He Created Us for Adventure

God says that He will do a new thing and we will be aware of it. We won't have to read a book about it. We won't have to buy a tape and hear someone describe it. We won't have to attend a seminar or a workshop. We will know it firsthand. God created us for adventure. Don't get trapped in the past. Don't be despondent about the present. God has a future that is exciting! "For I know the plans I have for you," declares the LORD, "plans for your welfare, and not for disaster, to give you a future and a hope" (Jer. 29:11). I'm grateful for my past. I have a wonderful heritage in the Lord—a preacher father, a preacher grandfather, two preacher brothers, a preacher son-in-law, two sons who are deacons, and a life of wonderful fellowship and ministry. I'm grateful for everything that has happened in the past, but the future is the best yet!

When the governor of the feast tasted the wine that Jesus turned from water into wine, he said to the host, "You have kept the fine wine until now" (John 2:10). The good news of the new year is that God has saved the best until now. The present and the past may be wonderful and significant. God may have moved in wonderful ways in our lives, but He is going to do a new thing—something significant, something fresh, something adventurous in our lives if we will let Him do it.

He created us for renewal, for adventure. Faith is not static. It's not just information. It's not just dull, hypothetical—or even logical—truth. It is an encounter with the God who created us. And He says He created us for adventure. When we understand that, every day is an adventure. Every day is a great day! "Thank You, God, that You're in my life, You're in control, and this is the day You have made. I'll rejoice and be glad in it because You created us for newness, for adventure."

V. God Wants Us to Understand That He Created Us for Eternity

One of the great verses in the Bible is Isaiah 43:25. God says, "It is I who sweep away your transgressions for My own sake and remember your sins no more."

God created us for eternity. That's why we can't be content with just the things we see, with the circumstances of life. We can't be content with that. We can't make enough money or have enough honors or successes to satisfy the longing of our hearts. That can come only with the presence of Christ, who comes into our hearts and brings forgiveness, cleanses us of sin, and removes our guilt. He offers the gift of eternal life. God created us for eternity.

This life is just preparation. Think about it. How long are you going to live? A hundred years? Probably a few of us will live longer than that. How long is eternity? When I was in the fifth grade, my principal told us that eternity could be illustrated by a block of granite a thousand miles square. If an eagle came by once every thousand years and brushed this block with its wing, whenever the friction of that brief brush wore that granite to the ground, then eternity would just be beginning. That was a vivid picture for a fifth grader, and it is still vivid.

How long is eternity? Have you ever asked what is the purpose of life? The answer is very simple: Prepare for eternity. God created us for eternity. We can never be satisfied with anything less than eternity. The only thing eternal is God. He created us for eternity.

Think about the good news He offers. It was good news to people of Isaiah's day, and it's good news for us today. God created us with a plan and a purpose. Our lives are not just haphazard, bounced around by circumstances. God created us with a design and purpose in mind. He created us to know Him. He created us to succeed. He created us for adventure. He created us for eternity. Now that's good news.

Whatever happens in this year, if we can understand that, if we can encounter Christ in the midst of this year, if we can come to know God's purpose in the midst of this year, then it will indeed be the best year yet. God has promised to do a new thing in our lives.

20

The Encourager

ACTS 4:36 HCSB

James T. Draper, Jr.

ONE OF THE GREAT WAYS for us to look at our lives and to determine what we are to be is by looking at individuals in the Bible, people whom God used and whose lives are patterns and examples for us. For instance, when we refer to Andrew, we will usually hear someone say, "Every time you see Andrew, he is bringing a person to Jesus." That's a wonderful example. It reminds us of the privilege that is ours to always be bringing people to Jesus.

I want us to focus on another man. I pray that our churches will be filled with people like this man. If we could become like this man, it would revolutionize our churches, transform our homes, and change our communities.

One simple verse introduces us to this man: "Joseph, who was named by the apostles Barnabas, which is translated Son of Encouragement" (Acts 4:36). The son of encouragement. Barnabas was a nickname. It reflected the kind of person he was.

In New Testament times the nickname was a special name given to someone that represented the kind of person they were. It was a characterization of who they were. Here was a man by the name of Joseph, whose nickname was Barnabas, "Son of Encouragement." He was the kind of man who encouraged other people everywhere he went. He brought out the best in other people. He lifted their spirits. He quieted their hearts. He brought joy and comfort to them. He was an individual who constantly encouraged other people.

He was also the kind of person who always sought out the one who was faltering, the one who had failed, the one who had stumbled. Barnabas helped them back on their feet and helped them to realize that failure is not final, that we don't have to live life on the basis of our mistakes. He demonstrated that the gospel is the gospel of beginning again. The gospel is the gospel of going on from where we are. The gospel is the gospel of transforming the mistakes and the tragedies of our past into the glories of God's grace in our lives.

That's the kind of person Barnabas was. Acts 9 gives us the account of the conversion of Saul of Tarsus. Saul was a man who hated the Christians. He viewed it as his call from God to wipe out the Christian movement. He went to the Jewish officials in Jerusalem and asked for authority to go to Damascus, find the Christians in that city, and bring them back to Jerusalem to punish them, to condemn them, to put them in prison, or perhaps to put them to death. So Saul was given the authority. He had the written authority to bring the Christians whom he found in Damascus back to Jerusalem as captives.

On the way to Damascus, in the hot Syrian sun, there appeared the blinding presence of the Son of God Himself. Saul was blinded, fell to the earth, and heard a voice saying, "Saul, Saul, why are you persecuting Me?" (Acts 9:4). Saul cried out, "Who are You, Lord?" He was introduced to Jesus Christ. We remember the story of the magnificent, transforming grace of God that saved Saul of Tarsus. What we may not remember is that after Saul goes back into town, his sight is restored, and he returns to Jerusalem.

What does the new Christian want to do? He wants to be with other Christians. He wants to tell somebody that he's been saved. That's what Paul did. He immediately began to preach Christ (see Acts 9:20). He shared his faith. When he got back to Jerusalem, he wanted to be a part of the Christian fellowship. But the people in Jerusalem knew what kind of man he had been, and they were afraid of him. He had been one of their chief antagonists. He was on his way to Damascus to capture Christians. He had the authority to condemn them and to bring them back as prisoners. They thought this was a ruse, that he just wanted to get in to see who was there. They did not want to have this man around.

It was Barnabas who came and put his arm around Saul and brought him before the Christians and said, "Brethren, this man met Jesus and gave his heart to Christ. He has been preaching and telling people about Christ, and we need to receive him as a brother" (see Acts 9:27). It was Barnabas who first brought Saul of Tarsus into the Christian church, and Saul became Paul, the great missionary leader.

In the eleventh chapter of Acts, we find that God began to do some unusual things. The early Christian movement was a Jewish movement. The Jewish Christians thought it was restricted to Jews. The Holy Spirit had come at Pentecost. There had been a great moving of the Holy Spirit through those believers at Pentecost. God had thrust them forward with great success, and they were rejoicing. But they thought Christianity was for Jews. They began to hear strange things from Antioch. The Holy Spirit began to move on Gentiles. They were puzzled, so they decided to investigate these things. They sent Barnabas to Antioch to check it out. Barnabas went up to Antioch and saw the moving of the Holy Spirit among the Gentiles. The record says that "he was glad" (Acts 11:23). He was glad, and he encouraged these new believers to go on in their faith, to continue to follow Christ. It was Barnabas who first encouraged the inclusion of Gentiles in the church.

Perhaps the most dramatic moment in the life of Barnabas came in the fifteenth chapter of Acts. We recall that Paul and Barnabas went on a missionary journey together. On the first missionary journey of Paul, he was accompanied by Barnabas. They established churches. It was a wonderful journey except that they had one problem. A young man named John Mark went with them. Somewhere on the journey John Mark got discouraged. He must have thought he could not go on. The trip was just not what he thought it would be. So he turned back and went back to Jerusalem. He left Paul and Barnabas shorthanded. They had to complete their journey and do their work with the new churches they were establishing without the support and help they had counted on. Paul was very rigid in his anger toward John Mark.

However, as they prepared for their second missionary journey, Barnabas said, "I've got a wonderful idea. Let's take John Mark" (see Acts 15:37). Paul refused, and heated debate followed. It resulted in Paul and Barnabas splitting up. The contention between Paul and Barnabas became so great that they could not go on together. Paul would not relent. Paul refused to forgive John Mark and would not welcome him back to the team. But Barnabas believed John Mark deserved a second chance. Sure, he failed, but he deserved a second chance. That's when Paul took Silas on the second missionary journey, and they went to check on newly established churches and to establish other churches.

But Barnabas also went on a missionary journey, and he took John Mark (see Acts 15:39). He put his arm around John Mark and said, "I know he failed. I know he didn't do what he said he would do, but he has repented. God has forgiven him, and I forgive him. I want to encourage John Mark. I want to give him a second chance." It was that arm around the shoulder of John Mark by Barnabas that saved John Mark for the ministry.

We have a permanent testimony of that in our Bible. The second Gospel is written by a man named Mark, whose first name was John. John Mark. He was saved for service because there was a man like Barnabas who encouraged him.

Now I submit to you that we desperately need to be individuals like Barnabas. We desperately need people like Barnabas in our churches who will be encouragers, who will reach out to those who have stumbled and fallen, those who are discouraged and oppressed, and will lift their hearts and draw them back to the Savior. We need redemptive, restoring individuals who will make it their task to be sons of encouragement, to be encouragers.

The New Testament uses the word *exhort*. The word literally means "to encourage." See how many times we are told to exhort one another, to encourage one another. Hebrews 3:13 says, "But encourage each other daily, while it is still called 'today,' so that none of you is hardened by sin's deception." If we are not encouragers, then Satan has an entrance into our lives. If we are not encouraging others, if we are not exhorting others and encouraging others, then we may be "hardened through the deceitfulness of sin" (NKJV).

In Hebrews 10, the writer says that we should not forsake the assembling of ourselves together, like some people do, but we should exhort one another, encourage and help one another (see Heb. 10:25). That's what it is all about. We need to encourage one another. The church ought to be a haven of strength. It ought to be a harbor of encouragement, a place where we find the strength to go on. We ought not to come to church to be beat up. We ought not to come to church to be condemned. We ought to be in the church, in the family, in the fellowship where there are people who are encouraging one another, helping one another.

If we don't have that kind of people in our churches, then we are going to continue to see those who were once very active in the service of the Lord drop out. They become stragglers in Christian service and Christian fellowship. The last seven years I served as a pastor, I preached three services every Sunday morning. And even with a membership of more than 3,500 people, I usually could tell where many people regularly sat. I couldn't always tell you who was there, but if you asked me if somebody was there, I could probably tell you whether they were there or not.

But every now and then I would find myself sitting on the platform, and a great sadness would come over my heart because I would remember the people who used to be there who were no longer there. They used to love God. They used to lift their voices in praise. They used to serve Him and study and walk with Him, but something happened. They became dropouts, stragglers in Christian service.

The old army infantry used to have a group called the rear guard. The purpose of the rear guard was to follow the troops in battle. And if someone was wounded, they would pick them up and take them back where they could be treated, to make sure that no one was abandoned on the field. In case of retreat, the rear guard was out between the retreating troops and the enemy gathering up those who may have been wounded. It was their purpose to make sure that no one was abandoned, no one was left out in the battlefield alone, but to bring them back to safety.

The church of the Lord Jesus Christ needs a rear guard. We need a group of people like Barnabas who will make it their task to be encouragers, to be looking for those who stumble, those who have fallen, those who have lost heart, who have lost faith, and bring them back into the family and into the fellowship of the Lord.

I. We Need to Encourage Those Who Are Hurting

I have never seen a time when there is more pain among God's people. It seems like it is getting worse. The pain, the hurt, is severe. When I was a young preacher, my father told me something that I have never forgotten. He said, "Son, be kind to everybody because everybody is having a hard time." No one is having an easy time these days.

Some time ago I was with the pastors of the largest churches in the Southern Baptist Convention. We had about fifty pastors around that table. On the last morning we went around the table and shared what God was doing in our lives. I sat there astonished as one by one these men began to share. It was obvious that all of them had pain. All of them had great hurts in their lives. I am satisfied that if we asked those around us to share, all of them would have hurts. We need to be like Barnabas to one another. We need to encourage those who are hurting.

So many things happen to cause hurt. Change takes place. Broken relationships. There is a suicide. There is a divorce. There is a relocation. There is a separation. Here is a pregnant teenager. There is a bankruptcy. Here is a wife dying of cancer or a child who is wayward. There is great hurt and great pain everywhere. We need to be like Barnabas and encourage those who are hurting. Often, there is misunderstanding, disappointment, depression, or discouragement. Our goals have been shattered. Our dreams and plans have been thwarted. We need a Barnabas in our lives to lift us up, to help us.

Thank God for men who have been like Barnabas to me over the years. I remember a dark night a number of years ago. My wife had cried herself to sleep, and I lay in the bed disillusioned, shattered. At two in the morning the phone rang. It was a friend. He said, "I have had you on my heart. I have been praying for you tonight. I know it's late, but I wanted to encourage you." Listen, if we walk with God, there should be a sensitivity in our hearts. God has put people in your life who desperately need you to encourage them in their hurt. God has put somebody in your life who needs your encouragement. If we all encourage the somebody that God has given to us, then everybody will have somebody. That's God's plan. We need to encourage those who are hurting.

II. We Need to Encourage Those Who Are Lonely

We are living in a world filled with lonely people. Over twenty million Americans live by themselves. They live totally alone. But there is a difference between aloneness and loneliness. You could be in a crowd and be lonely. It's possible to be lonely in the midst of thousands of people. There are many lonely people in the world, and we need to encourage them. There are people whose lives have become isolated. Circumstances have changed. There has been a death, divorce, or relocation. Nothing is the same. They try to go home, but it isn't there anymore. Have you ever tried to go home? You discovered that it wasn't there, didn't you? Nothing is ever the same. You can go back to the place you once called home, but it's not the same place. Everything changes, and our lives are filled with uncertainties and loneliness.

I was walking out the door of my home several years ago to go visiting on a Tuesday night. The phone rang just as I was out the door. For some reason I came back in and answered it. I don't usually do that. But on the other end of the line, a man in a deep, resonant voice spoke. I thought it was a recording at first; the voice was just too good. But he identified himself as the head of a suicide prevention center in Dallas. He asked, "Are you the pastor of First Baptist Church of Euless?"

I said, "Yes, I am."

He said, "There is a man who has barricaded himself in an apartment over in south Euless. He says he is going to kill himself. He has a gun. He won't let the police officers in, but he says he will talk to you. Will you come talk to him?"

Well, you know exactly what I did. Carol Ann and I drove over to that apartment complex. Police cars and SWAT teams were all around the place. In a few moments I was sitting in the living room of an apartment in that complex beside a sixty-seven-year-old man dressed in running shoes and shorts, and he was holding a 38-caliber pistol. He began to weep. "Pastor, I am lonely. My wife died some years ago, and a couple of years ago I married again, and she has left me and doesn't want to live with me. My kids don't care about me. I don't believe God wants me to live like this. I'm lonely, pastor, I'm lonely."

That story is repeated over and over and over again. There needs to be a Barnabas who will reach out to lonely people. We need to encourage those who are lonely.

III. We Need to Encourage Those Who Are Doubting

There are a lot of people who begin to question their faith. They are not bad people. They are not heretics. They are not people who have forsaken God. They just don't know anymore. Nothing seems to fit together, and somehow the pieces have fallen apart. They begin to doubt. They have become indifferent to the things of Christ. They are not bad people; they have just lost heart. We need to reach out to those people and encourage them. Tell them God loves them and help them restore their faith.

Do you remember the story of Thomas in John 20? When Thomas was told Jesus had been resurrected from the dead, he would not believe it. He said he would not believe it unless he could put his hand on the scars in Jesus' hands and on the scar in His side. If he couldn't do that, he would not believe. Those disciples could have abandoned Thomas. They could have driven him away. But they loved him. He remained in their circle. The Lord thought it was important enough that before long He came to stand before them. He looked right at Thomas and said, "Here are My hands. Handle Me and see" (see John 20:26–27). Jesus cared about someone who was doubting. We ought to care. We ought to encourage those who are doubting.

IV. We Need to Encourage Those Who Have Fallen

It happens all the time. Someone quits coming to church because he has sinned. Isn't that ironic? Isn't church about sinners? Listen, the church is not a country club for saints. It's a hospital for sinners. When people sin, when people fall, there needs to be a Barnabas who will reach out and pick them up and say, like Barnabas did to John Mark, "You deserve a second chance. You can start over again. You can move on from here."

Let me ask you a question. In the family, which child gets the most attention—the fast learner or the slow learner? Which child gets the most attention—the well child or the sick child? It's the slow learner and the sick child. Why? Because he needs it. When a person is stumbling and fallen, we need to encourage him. Isn't that what Paul said in Galatians? If a fellow believer stumbles, "you who are spiritual should restore such a person with a gentle spirit" (Gal. 6:1). By the way, he also said for us to consider ourselves lest we also be tempted. Only the grace of God keeps us from falling.

By the way, not any of us haven't fallen. There are no perfect people. There are no perfect churches. My father used to say, "If you are looking for a perfect church, don't join this one. It's not perfect." Then he always added, "By the way, if you ever find one, don't you join. You would spoil it!" We need to encourage those who have fallen.

My favorite pastime is to watch football games. I love football games. New Year's Day is my day. We have all those games, and the Rose Bowl always has the largest attendance. In the Rose Bowl game every year, one of the announcers will say something about "Wrong Way Riegels." You know the story, don't you? Roy Riegels played for a team in the Rose Bowl years ago that had the ball in its possession right at the goal line about to score. Regal got hit and got turned around. He didn't realize what had happened, but he started running in the wrong direction. He ran ninety-nine yards in the wrong direction. He was tackled on his own one-yard line by one of his own teammates to keep him from scoring two points for the other team.

Riegels said that when he was tackled by his own teammate, he got up angry and began to chew his teammate out: "Why in the world did you tackle me?" Then he realized what had happened. He realized he had almost scored for the other team. He may have cost them a score because they were about to score at the other end of the field. He said that he was so embarrassed, so humiliated, so disgraced, that he rushed from the field into the dressing room. After a while halftime came. The players came in and gathered in small groups all over that dressing room just whispering. He said he just knew everyone was talking about him. He said that he was so discouraged and so much in despair that at that moment he thought he would never leave the dressing room alive. He didn't want to live another day.

Then the coach came in and gathered the players around him. Roy said the coach looked right at him and pointed his finger at him and said, "Roy, when you go in this half . . ." Roy was crying. "Coach, I can't go in. I may have cost us the ball game. I have embarrassed my team. I have done a stupid thing. I can't go in." He said by this time the other players were crying. The coaches were crying. He said the coach stepped over through all those players and came over to him. He put his arm around his shoulder and said, "Roy, remember the game is only half over."

Roy said that hand around his shoulder at that most desperate moment in his life literally saved his life. Roy went on to become an outstanding high school football coach in the western United States, but it was because in the darkest moment of failure, there was one who cared enough to say, "Roy, remember the game is only half over."

Listen to me. You may have stumbled. You may have fallen. The game is not over yet. God's grace is big enough to lift you up. We need to encourage the fallen. Maybe the song we used to sing would be true once again if we did.

Down in the human heart, crushed by the tempter.
Feelings lie buried that grace can restore.
Touched by a loving heart, wakened by kindness,
Chords that were broken will vibrate once more.
Rescue the perishing, care for the dying,
Jesus is merciful. Jesus will save.

V. We Need to Encourage Those Who Are Lost

We have a good-news gospel in a bad-news world. We have the gospel of hope. Listen to that gospel. Never is it more clearly presented than in Psalm 103:11: "For as high as the heavens are above the earth, so great is His faithful love toward those who fear Him." How high are the heavens above the earth? We don't know, do we? Scientists keep telling us that there is more out there. We know that they discovered from an observation post at Santiago, Chile, several years ago a star that they had never seen before. Based on the earthly calculations, the light from that star would take 39,000,000 light years to get to earth. Light travels at the speed of 185,000 miles a second. That's nearly eight times around the earth every second. That's how fast light travels. Traveling that fast, it would take that light 39,000,000 years to get here. That's a lot of space out there. That's a lot of grace! God says that is how big His grace is.

Doesn't that make your problem seem small? It doesn't matter what you have done. A God with grace that is as high as the heavens are above the earth offers His mercy to us. He will cover us. He will forgive us. He will save us.

The psalmist goes on to say, "As far as the east is from the west, so far has He removed our transgressions from us" (Ps. 103:12). I ask another question. How far is the east from the west? When I first read that, being a Southern boy, I asked the question: "Why didn't he say north and south?" But then I got to thinking. There is a logical reason He didn't say north and south. That's a measurable distance. We start north; if we keep going, we will eventually come to the North Pole. Then we start going south. If we keep going south, we will eventually come to the South Pole. If we keep traveling in the same direction, we will start going north again.

But let me tell you something. If we start going west today and go west the rest of our lives, there never will come a time when we will stop going west and start going east. And if we started east today, there will never be a time no matter how many years—ten years, a million years, or an eternity—when we will stop going east and start going west.

God says we have a gospel that can say to a lost man, "I have mercy bigger than this universe. And I have grace that can take your sins and remove them so far that you will never see them again." In fact, God says He will forgive our sins and will remember them no more (see Heb. 10:17).

Colossians 2:14 says that when Jesus died, He took the ordinances that were against us and blotted them out. It was customary in New Testament times to post the crimes of a man who was executed. And when Jesus died, we died with Him, and He nailed our sins to that cross and then blotted them out. Forgiven. Removed. Life eternal. We need to encourage those who are lost. We have a gospel that can lift them from sin and lift them into salvation. We need to encourage those who are lonely, hurting, doubting, fallen, and who are lost. Like Barnabas, we need to be encouraging, redemptive people. God grant that we shall.

21

One Transforming Moment

ISAIAH 6:1–8 HCSB

James T. Draper, Jr.

THE ONLY THING THAT WILL SUSTAIN ANY BELIEVER is the indelible imprint of an encounter with God. The ultimate power for life rests in our vision of God. One of the reasons we see so much discouragement and wrestle with so many things in our lives is that we take our eyes off God. Isaiah had a world of problems. He was facing discouragement, heartbreak, and the death of a friend. Yet when we read in Isaiah 6, all he sees is the glory of God. That is what we need to focus on. When we focus on our circumstances, our own feelings, or our own experiences, we can often become very depressed, discouraged, and beaten down. But if we focus on God, it's amazing how everything else filters out. Everything else is obscure when He is clearly in focus in our lives.

Isaiah 6 is that incredible passage of Scripture where Isaiah is coming into an experience of seeing God, a vision of God.

> In the year that King Uzziah died, I saw the Lord seated
> on a high and lofty throne, and His robe filled the temple.
> Seraphim were standing above Him; each one had six wings:
> with two he covered his face, with two he covered his feet,
> and with two he flew. And one called to another:
> Holy, holy, holy is the LORD of Hosts;
> His glory fills the whole earth.

The foundations of the doorways shook at the sound of their voices, and the temple was filled with smoke. Then I said,

Woe is me, for I am ruined,
because I am a man of unclean lips
and live among a people of unclean lips,
and because my eyes have seen the King,
the LORD of Hosts.

Then one of the seraphim flew to me, and in his hand was a glowing coal that he had taken from the altar with tongs. He touched my mouth with it and said:

Now that this has touched your lips,
your wickedness is removed,
and your sin is atoned for.

Then I heard the voice of the Lord, saying:
Who shall I send?
Who will go for Us?
I said,
Here am I. Send me (Isa. 6:1–8).

The encounter with God is always a time of crisis. When that encounter comes, we can never be the same again. Whenever we have an encounter with God, a vision of God, the call of God upon our lives, we can never be the same again. We need to revisit that experience often and reflect upon that encounter with God.

That moment may come in different ways. For Isaiah it came in the form of a vision at a time of great turmoil in his own life, a time of great concern, a crisis moment. It may come in different times and different ways, but it always creates a crisis in our lives. The essence of what happens is that we get a vision of God. In some way we encounter the living God. This is what we find in Isaiah's life. He is facing one of those critical moments.

We don't know how old Isaiah was at this point in his life. We know that a definite crisis had overtaken him. The king had ruled for fifty-two years. He died suddenly. This shook up the nation. It left a tragic uncertainty about the future for Isaiah. It certainly was a personal crisis because he considered the king a very special friend. It was in that time that Isaiah had a personal vision of God high above his own circumstances. In that moment of crisis, he saw the eternal God high and lifted up. He had a vision of God as He really is, and that made all the difference for the prophet in this critical moment.

The purpose of a faithful, believing life is the expectation of a vision of God. Jesus said, "Blessed are the pure in heart, because they will see God" (Matt. 5:8). The expectation of every believer is that we will one day see the King, the invisible God whom we serve. We will be able to gaze at Him in all of His glory.

The occasion of seeing God in this passage is the death of King Uzziah, who died about 740 B.C. His reign had been a wonderful reign. It extended the boundaries of the nation to the maximum extent. Commerce and agriculture had flourished. The nation was at peace, but the death of Uzziah ended all of that. From the time of his death onward, Judah declined, decayed, and finally dissolved. So it was a time of crisis, and for Isaiah personally it was the most significant moment in his life.

For most of us, God has to empty some chair on earth in order to make us see by faith His throne in heaven. Life has its way of emptying those chief chairs, doesn't it? Parents, mentors, models disappear. Suddenly a chair is empty at work, at home, at church. Someone is gone. God can break through to us in those moments where we feel lost. And when a chair on earth is empty, we see the throne in heaven more clearly.

Someone asked me recently, "What have been the critical moments in your life? Those moments that changed your life?" For me the most significant thing that happened in my life was the death of my father. I learned for the first time what deep personal sorrow was. I learned for the first time how adequate God is. It was a moment of crisis. It is in those moments that God has a way of getting through to us in a significant way. And that is what happened with Isaiah.

I. The Manifestation of God Defies Description

We cannot describe what Isaiah saw in this passage. Suddenly, by God's initiative, the Lord invaded Isaiah's world with a vision of Himself. Isaiah wasn't seeking it. He wasn't expecting it. He could not have imagined it, but God broke through into Isaiah's world. Suddenly Isaiah was in crisis. He was in a passage of life in that moment of transition when God suddenly invaded his world. That's what we mean when we say God reveals Himself. God crashes into our world. He always does. He always moves first. He always seeks first. He always arrives first. He always calls first. God seeks us.

Sometimes we talk about seeking God. No, God seeks us. I love the way the prophet Jeremiah puts it. He says, "If you seek the Lord, you will find Him and He will be found of you" (see Jer. 29:13–14). God lets us find Him. When we find Him, we discover He has been seeking us all the time.

God takes the initiative. How it happens doesn't matter. We don't know exactly what happened here for Isaiah. This may have been an objective, external experience. It might have been subjective and internal. It doesn't really matter, but it was a real, vivid encounter with the living God at the most crucial moment in the prophet's life. This is an interesting thing—seeing God. The Bible speaks with one voice that the essence of God cannot be seen by mere human beings. John 1:18 clearly says no one has seen God. Paul puts it beyond all question: "The blessed and only Sovereign, the King of kings, and Lord of lords, the only One who has immortality, dwelling in unapproachable light, whom none of mankind has seen or can see, to whom be honor and eternal might. Amen" (1 Tim. 6:15–16).

The Bible asserts that the very essence of God Himself cannot be seen. Yet Jacob exclaimed, "I have seen God face to face, and I have been delivered" (Gen. 32:30). Jesus Himself promises, "Blessed are the pure in heart, because they will see God" (Matt. 5:8). Here is a paradox: God can't be seen, but He is seen. Jacob saw Him. Isaiah saw Him. Jesus says we shall see Him. God is pure spirit. He is omnipresent. He is present equally everywhere. There is not more of

God at one place and less of Him in another place. Even the heaven of heavens cannot contain Him.

How do we understand this paradox? Well, I notice in this passage that Isaiah describes nothing about God Himself. He saw His throne, His robe, His attendance, but the very essence of God he could not see. There was a radiance, a glory, an aura. I am going to give you a little prejudice of mine. I believe the only visible manifestation of God we will ever see is the person of Jesus Christ. We may see the aura of God, the radiance of God, but the only God we will ever see is Jesus. He is the one we will see in heaven.

When by faith we see God, what do we see? This passage tells us that the vision of God reveals His position and His praise. The first thing Isaiah sees is the throne. A throne indicates the absolute rule and sovereignty of God. God is a sovereign God. We may disagree about what that means but never doubt the sovereignty of God. God is the sovereign Creator, Preserver, Sustainer, and Controller of this universe. History will not come to a conclusion by accident. It will come to a conclusion of His choosing. It is still His story. God is still in control. God is still sovereign. God is still absolute. He is still Lord of lords and King of kings. And, by the way, He knows your zip code and your address. God is still important to everything we do.

It's not that God has just set us loose. Sometimes we think God is an absentee landlord. Some people say that He got this world started and then He said, "OK, you are on your own." Not at all. God knows every burden we bear, every crisis we face. And He says that all things work together for good to those who love Him (Rom. 8:28). What things? All things. How many things? All things. Everything. He tells us to give thanks in everything. Then He tells us to give thanks for everything (see Phil. 4:4–6). That's a little harder, isn't it? It's not too difficult sometimes to give thanks *in* everything, but to give thanks *for* everything is not easy.

God is still in control. He wants us to know that He is the Lord. Isaiah sees the exalted throne of God. Isaiah bends his neck and his eyes look up, and there is a towering, mountainous throne rearing itself higher and higher into the heavens. He describes it as "high and lifted up."

Second Chronicles 9:17–19 describes Solomon's throne. It was a beautiful throne. In fact, Scripture says there was none like it in all the earth (2 Chron. 9:17). Yet God's throne is more beautiful than that. The oldest throne still surviving is built in the walls of Kenosis on the island of Crete. It dates back to 1800 B.C.. but the throne of God survives forever. The most beautiful throne in history is said to have been the Peacock throne, the throne of Shah Jahan in the seventeenth century. It was a throne ascended by silver steps. It stood on golden feet set with jewels. It was backed with the representation of two open peacock tails gilded, enameled, and inset with diamonds and rubies and other precious stones. The dazzling throne was so beautiful that it was stolen from India by the Persians. But God's throne is even more beautiful than that.

When we have an authentic vision of God, we see Him on His throne. The throne is lifted up. It is above every earthly power and separated from everything that is merely human. Everything speaks of the power of the One on the throne. The long, loose, flowing robe that we find here fills every available space in the temple. Everything centers on the throne of God. His sovereignty, His rule, His lordship, His kingship. The vision of God reveals His position and reveals His praise.

His praise comes with action and confession from some interesting heavenly beings. We are introduced here to the seraphim. They are named only here in the Old Testament. Their name invokes awe and wonder. The name means "burning ones, flamelike beings, fiery ones." They are very personal beings. They have faces, feet, hands, and human speech. The only addition to their human form is that they each have six wings. These fiery ones are characterized by availability, activity, and humility. Their chief characteristic is their constant availability. They continually stand before God's throne. Many times we see this in Scripture.

In Daniel 7:10, God is seen as having ten thousand times ten thousand fiery beings standing before Him. In 1 Kings 22:19, the prophet Micaiah sees the Lord with all the Hosts of heaven standing around Him on His right and left. Our enthroned, exalted God is attended by countless numbers of spiritual fiery beings. They are always available to Him. If they are available to Him, what does that say to us? Our chief response to God is not our ability but our availability. Will we allow God to use us? Will we come to God and lay ourselves before Him with no strings attached? Will our answer be yes to whatever God asks us to do?

So many of us want to know the will of God in order to consider it. God only reveals His will for us in order for us to do it. These seraphs speak to us about availability. They are ready. They are available. The test of the genuineness of our faith is whether we can be available to Him in those unseen moments when nobody knows and nobody will ever be aware of the need of that moment and in that moment we are available to God.

These seraphs were available. That was their constant characteristic. And they were humble. Their humility is seen by the fact that they covered their faces and their feet. They covered their faces so they would not look directly at the One on the throne. They covered their feet because the lower part of the body is a symbol of humility and unworthiness. These creatures who stand here in the presence of God stand in transparent humility before Him. Each one of us must stand before God with that same kind of humility. There is no place for arrogance or pride in His presence. No place for competitiveness or measuring ourselves by one another. No place for entertainers or prima donnas—just servants. Humbly bowing before the eternal King.

With two of the six wings, these seraphim fly. This speaks of their activity—ceaseless, continuous, unstopped activity—on behalf of the One on the throne. Does that invoke from us any sense of wonder, awe, reverence, or response? This is the setting in which all believers of all ages will spend forever and forever. This is what we will see the moment after our last heartbeat. This is not myth. This is not saga. This is not fiction, legend, or invention. This is the throne of God, and it's that throne before which we will stand one day. We stand before it in an attitude of wonder.

Oswald Chambers has an interesting, poignant statement at this point of wonder. He says to beware of anything that takes the wonder out of your life. When we have lost wonder, we have lost life. One of our problems is that we have lost the wonder. We have lost the wonder and the awesomeness that God could choose us. And remember that. He did choose us. We did not choose Him. He chose us. We need to have a sense of wonder about that.

Isaiah gives us a vision of God. His posture is on the throne. His position is high and lifted up. His praise is seen in action and confession. The action is availability, humility, and activity of those around His throne. Then there follows a confession of praise. For the first time in this scene, we hear something. It's interesting what we see and what we hear. These beings called out three times, "Holy, holy, holy, is the LORD of Hosts; His glory fills the whole earth" (v. 3).

That's the word we sing: "Holy, holy, holy." The root of that word *holy* is separateness. It means God is different. God is not like us. God is God. He is unapproachable in a sense. There is always a distance between us and Him. There is a reminder that God is God. He is wholly other from human beings. That's the essence of worshipping God. We have made God too familiar. God is not our buddy. He is God. There is an awesomeness about God. It would remove the pain from many of our lives, and it would remove the conflict that we constantly find ourselves in if we focused on God. We are not people trying to tell other people about God the best we can. We are individuals who are being called by God, and God desires to reveal Himself through us.

He is an awesome God, not a common God. We need to magnify His holiness. Holiness is His basic characteristic. We don't find any other attribute of God that is given a threefold expression like this. We never hear, "Love, love, love is the God of Hosts." We don't ever hear, "Forgive, forgive, forgive" as a characteristic of God. But we hear, "Holy, holy, holy is the LORD of Hosts." We need to continue to focus on that.

What does that mean? Are we supposed to go around just saying, "Holy, holy, holy"? No, but it does mean something for our lives. First of all, we need to meditate often upon the nature of God. Do we do that very often? Do we take time just to dwell upon who God is? The nature of God? The attributes of God? We need to think about His eternal nature, His immutability, His presence, His knowledge, His power, His grace. We ought to think about those things, and we ought to come often into His presence. We must prepare for that. We don't just rush into the presence of someone in authority. We try to get ready for it.

I remember when I was president of the Southern Baptist Convention, I was invited to the White House to visit with President Ronald Reagan. I had met Governor Reagan before he was elected president, but now I was going to go to the White House. So I went to the White House and had my picture taken with the president. They sent it to me. I looked at it and thought, "Isn't that great! Here I am with Ronald Reagan."

Then I looked closely. My coat was kind of spread a little bit, and there with me with the president of the United States was my fifty-nine-cent ballpoint pen sticking out of my pocket. It's hard for me to look at that picture because here I was getting to meet the president, and I wasn't ready. How much more awesome to come into the presence of God. How much more careful we ought to be that we are ready when we come into His presence. If we would come into the presence of God more often, we will have the anointing of the power of God on us more often.

Most of us find ourselves running and running and trying to have time with God on the run. Martin Luther once said that he had so much to do that day that he needed to spend more time in prayer. That's not the way we think, is it? We have so much to do. We had better get after it. We have to get out our calenders and make sure we do everything on time and that we stay on schedule.

Our real need is to pause before the awesome vision of God, the presence of God, and be ready to meet Him. That defies description.

II. The Manifestation of God
Defines the Message We Deliver

There is a heavenly reaction to the need of mankind. This reaction comes at the initiative of God. While Isaiah was crying out, "Woe is me! . . . I am a man of unclean lips," God was already taking action. Maybe it was a nod from God. Maybe it was a gesture from the divine hand. Maybe it was a spoken command. We are not told. But one of the seraphim goes to the altar, takes the tongs, and lifts a coal from the altar and places it in his hand. What is he going to do with it? Is he going to hurl it at Isaiah in condemnation? Will he burn Isaiah as an act of judgment? Here is a man with unclean lips dwelling in the midst of a people of unclean lips. What will God's seraph do with that coal?

There is no condemnation. There is forgiveness because the coal touches the lips of the prophet. He had just confessed that he was a man of unclean lips. When the coal from God's altar touched Isaiah's lips, he was cleansed. The prophet does not touch his own lips. We don't have to have a message imposed by someone else upon us. God touches the lips of the prophet with a burning message of His truth.

The message of the believer is found in the holiness of God. It is seen in this passage. Every facet of the gospel is found in this great all-encompassing attribute of God. It is from this source that all of the great activity of God's redemption flows. It is from the holiness of God that the love of God flows. It is from the holiness of God that the grace of God flows. It is from the holiness of God that the sacrifice of Christ flows, the substitutionary, atoning death of Christ upon the cross. It is from the holiness of God that forgiveness flows.

Holiness finds a way to redeem the objects of its love. Our message is wrapped up in the holiness of God. The coal, the fire that touched the lips of the prophet purged him of his uncleanness, but it also anointed him with God's message, "Holy, holy, holy is the LORD of Hosts."

Our message is the Word of God. It's not up to us to try to find a message. It's up to us to declare a message. We need to remember that God called us to declare His Word. He doesn't call us to entertain people. He calls us to communicate the Word. He doesn't call us to try to cater to people's whims and desires. He calls us to reveal the Word. The world desperately needs a word from God. There is so much ungodliness in the church and outside the church.

One of the frightening things about our time is that every survey taken in the last twenty years that I have read indicates that there is no difference between the lifestyles, actions, and conduct of the people in the church and those who are not in the church. This ought not to be! We have failed to stand and declare, "Thus saith the Lord." This is what God says. "If any one is in Christ, there is a new creature; old things have passed away, and look, new things have come" (2 Cor. 5:17).

Either that is true or it is not true. Is it true? If it's true, we ought to say it. We ought to hold up the holiness and the purity of God. That's the message that we have to give. God expects us to be different. We are His children, and we are not the same. We are to be holy as He is holy. That means we are to be different. We are to march to the beat of a different drummer. We do not have something to prove. We have Someone to please. That's the passion of the believer, and the message that we have is the Word of God.

Paul told young Timothy, "Proclaim the message" (2 Tim. 4:2). That is the message that God has given to us to proclaim. Hebrews 4 has a vivid picture of this: "For the word of God is living and effective and sharper than any two-edged sword, penetrating as far as to divide soul, spirit, joints, and marrow; it is a judge of the ideas and thoughts of the heart. No creature is hidden from Him, but all things are naked and exposed to the eyes of Him to whom we must give an account" (Heb. 4:12–13).

The message we have to proclaim is the message of the Word of God. It alone can reveal the heart of God. How many stories could we tell of times and places where the Word of God has been planted in a pagan society. And out of the planting and teaching of the Word of God has emerged a great number of people being saved and churches being planted. No other book could do that. We could go out into a needy area of the world and leave a physics text or a great novel or a biography of a great man or a collection of short stories or poetry, and we would not expect dramatic changes in the people. But when we leave the Word of God, dramatic changes take place.

This passage tells us why. The Word of God lives. I often hear people say that we need to make the Word of God relevant. That's not true. The Word of God is relevant. We don't make it relevant; it *is* relevant. It lives. The Word of God is quick, or alive. The Greek text uses a phrase that literally says, "Alive, living is the Word of God." It is vibrant, vital, vivacious, moving, multiplying, enlivening. It is energetic. It is living. It is a living Word because it is a Word from the living God. God's Word is alive.

As my hand lives because it is connected to the source of life in my chest, so the book of God lives because it is filled with the life of the One who makes it live. It vibrates with life because it is inseparably connected to the life of God Himself. It never decays, decomposes, or disintegrates because it is alive. That is true of no other book in the world. You could not pick up any other book in the world and find that to be true, but you pick up this book, and Jesus Christ leaps off its pages. And confronts me. It's the living Word of God. It's the living Word because it gives life. A living thing is alive because it gives life.

How do I know this Book lives? Because it gives life. Peter says that we "have been born again—not of perishable seed but of imperishable—through the living and enduring word of God" (1 Pet. 1:23). This book has a strange, mystic vitality about it. It relates to me as a person. It wrestles with me. It convicts me. It comforts me. It smiles on me. It frowns on me. It clasps my hand. It grips my heart. It weeps with me. It sings with me. It whispers with me. It challenges me. It inspires me. It transforms me. The Bible never gets sick or old. Its eye never dims. Its ear never deafens. Its step never slackens. Its brow never creases with a frown. It lives. It breathes. It moves.

We do not bring life to the Scripture. We draw life from the Scripture. Even a single verse of it can give eternal life. The Bible is a judge of the "ideas and thoughts of the heart" (Heb. 4:12). The word *judge* means "critic." We are not the Bible's critic; it is our critic. It criticizes us. It confronts us. It is a living Word. It's living because it has power. It has inherent energy. It is quick. It is powerful. When Jesus Christ was arrested, He spoke a word, and his enemies fell to the ground (John 18:6). Just a word. And when He wins His final victory over all the opposition, it will be with His energetic word (Rev. 19:15). The Word of God has an energy that always yields results. It will never return void.

I learned this in so many ways. My grandfather preached for fifty-four years. He died just before my sophomore year in college. I went to spend a few days with him that summer. I was preaching youth revivals all over the gulf coast of Texas. My granddad was quite a tease. We were sitting looking out the window of his home there at 708 Battery Street in Little Rock, Arkansas. He knew I was preaching revivals. He looked at me and said, "Little Jimmy." My daddy was five feet six, but he was "Big Jimmy!" I was "Little Jimmy." He said, "Little Jimmy, would you like to know where you can find a good sermon?"

I said, "Granddad, I sure would. Boy, I need a good sermon."

He picked up his Bible and cradled it like a mother might cradle a new baby. He smiled with a twinkle in his eye and said, "From Genesis to Revelation."

In 1967, we lived in Kansas City, Missouri. My seven-year-old son went with me to a softball game. The first pitch was a foul ball. All the kids ran to get the foul ball. They ran across a narrow road. My son was the fastest and got there first. I saw the car. I heard the screech of the brakes. I heard the dull thud of that car striking the body of my son. I saw him flipped in the air. The car passed underneath him. He landed in a heap in the ditch. I set a world record from shortstop to the ditch. His leg was badly broken but miraculously there were no other injuries. We took him to the hospital. He had surgery. My wife Carol Ann stayed with him during the night. He was having a hard time sleeping, so she was trying to create a conversation. She said, "Well, Bailey, weren't you afraid?"

He said, "No, Mom, I wasn't."

She was kind of shocked. She said, "You weren't?"

He said, "No, Mom, you remember that Scripture we learned? Psalm 56:3 says, 'Whenever I am afraid I will trust in the Lord.'"

Now here is a seven-year-old boy. He didn't understand that. But the Word of God gave him grace and strength and peace in a critical moment.

We don't need to worry about the Word of God. We don't need to spend a whole lot of time defending it. We just need to turn it loose. Let it go. We need to proclaim the Word of God. It is the Word of God with energy and power. Charles Spurgeon once said, "Cut it into a thousand pieces, and every piece will live and move." Try to contain it inside a government or with church restrictions, and one copy will escape and you will find a Protestant Reformation. It's alive. God's Word lives. In order for me to live spiritually, I must come into contact with the Word of God. Contact it, and it will give life. It is the road to God.

This passage also tells us that the Word of God cuts. It is sharper than a "two-edged sword." God's Word is a cutting Word. A two-edged sword cuts in every direction, and the Bible is like that. It is the sword of the Spirit (Eph. 6:17). The smallest cutting device ever made consists of glass micropipette tubes used in intracellular work with living cells. These glass knives can cut an object 6,500 times thinner than a human hair.

But there is something that cuts even more precisely than that. It is the Word of God. It can slice through the deepest evasions. It can slice through the finest distinctions of a deceptive human heart. It is a cutting Word. And when it cuts, it must kill before it can heal. At the point of sin, the Word of God must cut and kill if there is going to be spiritual life. His living Word must be put to the throat of every sinful tendency, habit, and thought. It must be sacrificed to the cutting of the Word of God. It must first kill, but then it heals.

God's Word cuts thoroughly. It penetrates. It cuts even to the "dividing asunder of soul and spirit and joints and marrow." This simply tells us that the Word of God operates in such a way that it penetrates deeply. It strikes through us. Nothing is hidden from it.

No part of human nature is untouched. The very innermost parts of my being are touched by the Word of God. It cuts personally. It is a critic, a discerner of the thoughts and intents of the heart. The Word of God scrutinizes the emotions, the rational thoughts of life. It sifts through every impulse, every secret thought, every desire, every purpose. And it does this by getting through to the human heart.

The book of Hebrews warns us about the human heart. In chapter 3, it tells us, "Do not harden your hearts" (v. 8). The heart tends to stray (v. 10). Chapter 8 says that God is going to write His laws in our heart (v. 10). Chapter 10 says, "Let us draw near with a true heart" (v. 22). We can only do that with a heart strengthened by God's grace (Heb. 13:9). The Word of God speaks to the heart. It speaks personally to each of us. It speaks universally. There is nothing hidden from His sight. No created thing will escape its search. No archangel, no seraph, no demon, or any other being will escape the scrutinizing power of the Word of God.

God's Word exposes powerfully. Notice it says, "All things are naked and exposed to the eyes of Him to whom we must give an account" (Heb. 4:13). This is one of the most vivid pictures in Scripture. All things are "naked." It means uncovered. There is nothing obscure about this. Everything is naked before God. All is "exposed." The Greek word is *trachelos*. We get our word *tracheotomy* from this.

This word comes from a custom in ancient times when a criminal was arrested and was brought before the judge. Often people would hang their heads to avoid looking at the judge, just as they do today. In ancient times, when a criminal was brought before a judge, a dagger would be placed at his throat. He would be forced to keep his head up. He had to look into the eyes of the judge. If he lowered his head, he would cut his own throat. Here it says that "all things are naked and opened unto the eyes of him with whom we have to do." We will face our judge eye to eye! Everything is stripped away. We are experts at wearing masks, disguises, and cover-up. But when we stand before God, we will stand before Him looking full into the eyes of Him with whom we have to do.

The Word of God causes us to face the truth, the reality. It causes us to come before Him in openness. When God touches our lips with a coal from the fire on the altar, His Word becomes our message: "Holy, holy, holy is the LORD of Hosts; the whole earth is full of His glory." That's the vision of God that confirms our encounter with Him and defines His message.

22

The Fringes of His Ways

JOB 26; ISAIAH 40:12–17 HCSB

James T. Draper, Jr.

PRESIDENT THEODORE ROOSEVELT and industrialist Walter Bebee used to visit together at Sagamore Hill, the presidential home on Long Island at Oyster Bay. Roosevelt and his guest would walk out of the Victorian mansion onto the large, lush yard that surrounded it. One of them would point out the faint haze of the spiral galaxy called Andromeda, just barely visible to the human eye. The other would say, "That is the spiral galaxy of Andromeda. It contains a million, million stars larger than our sun. Do you think we are small enough? Let's go to bed."

Certainly one lesson from the size of the universe is how small we are. Another thing we learn from the immensity of the universe is how great God is. That is the way Job looked at it. We are only able to detect the outer fringes of God's ways, the mere whisper of His greatness.

There is a remarkable similarity in thought between Job 26 and Isaiah 40:12–17. Both passages emphasize the majesty of God as expressed in His natural works, and those passages may be considered in tandem together. At our best we can only touch the fringes of God's mystery. The created world suggests only a whisper of His power.

I. Consider the Magnitude of His Measurements

"He stretches the northern skies over empty space. . . . He enfolds the waters in His clouds" (Job 26:7–8). "Who has measured the waters in the hollow of his hand . . . ?" (Isa. 40:12).

To consider the magnitude of His measurements, consider the magnitude of the *seas*. We mortals can conceive of the greatness and glory of God only in terms we can understand. The theologians call this "anthropomorphic," conceiving of God in terms of human imagery. After all, we are humans, and that is how we must think about God. The prophet Isaiah and Job think of the oceans of the world—some sixty-six oceans in all in the world ocean system. Almighty God towers above them in such majesty and strength that it is as if He held them all in the cupped hollow of His hand (Isa. 40:12).

Consider the mighty Pacific Ocean with sixty-four million square miles of water at an average depth of 13,215 feet, or the Atlantic Ocean at thirty-one million square miles with an average depth of 12,880 feet. We cannot even conceive the immensity, power, depth, sea life, winds, waves, and currents in such massive bodies of water. To God, they are all as if He held them in the cupped hollow of His hand.

The might of the seas is a worthy study to understand the power of God. If we cannot even comprehend the power of the oceans of the world, how little can we understand the power of Almighty God, Maker of heaven and earth? Look at the tides of the sea ebbing and flowing every twelve and one-half hours. The power is irresistible. No amount of human work and planning can hold back the tides, any more than we could hold back the sun. Watch the surfer ride the waves at Huntington Beach, California; the waves hurl him forward with a force he cannot stop; he must ride or be swept under. That is only one wave of one sea at one place. The power of Almighty God, Maker of heaven and earth, can be expressed by the phrase, "He holds the oceans in the hollow of His hand." Surely we only approach the fringes of His power.

To consider the magnitude of His measurements, consider the magnitude of the *heavens*. Every discovery proves the truth of J. B. Phillips' famous book title, *Your God Is Too Small*. Recently astronomers using a radio telescope detected the furthest galaxy from the earth yet to be discovered. They estimate that the galaxy is 15 billion light-years from earth, on the fringes of the known universe. Light travels at a speed of 186,000 miles per second. The light leaving that distant galaxy today would take 15 billion years traveling at 186,000 miles per second to reach us. The immeasurable distances of the created universe proclaim ever more greatly the mercy of God.

The Hubble Telescope, launched into space to observe distant galaxies, continues to amaze us with what it sees on the fringes of the universe. It has observed halos of hot gas around distant galaxies. It has captured the image of two galaxies trapped by their own gravity, spinning around each other at the furious pace of 670,000 miles per hour. These galaxies are connected by what appears to be a pipe or a tube of enormous size. The Hubble has taken a picture of a space "hubcap," a cloud of galactic dust that is 6,700 light-years across. The black hole in the middle of the hubcap-shaped cloud of dust has a mass 300 million times the mass of the earth's sun. The gas and dust are rotating around the black hole at a speed of 341,000 miles per hour.

What light this throws on Job's revelation that we only know the fringes of God's ways! Every discovery in the universe only enlarges the majesty and the mercy of God. In contrast to the smallness of humanity, the actual emphasis rests on the greatness of God Himself. The emphasis here is on the omnipotence of God, the dominion of God, the wisdom of God, and the works of God.

As Isaiah says, God has "marked off the heavens with the span of his hand" (Isa. 40:12). Or as Job states, "He stretches the northern skies over empty space; He hangs the earth on nothing" (Job 26:7). The unfathomable distances and dimensions of the cosmic universe itself suggest to us that we only know the outer fringes of God's ways. The galaxy of which planet Earth is a part is the

Milky Way, a galaxy that is 100,000 light-years across. If you could harness and ride a beam of light, it would take you 100,000 years at 186,000 miles per second to cross the Milky Way. It contains 400 billion stars! During any twenty-four-hour period the rotation of the Milky Way galaxy carries the earth about 12 million miles. Over a century the earth travels around 400 billion miles in this rotation.

Yet astronomers tell us that our galaxy is only one galaxy in a group of about twenty in one corner of a universe that contains 100 billion such galaxies, each with millions of suns larger than our sun. Yet our great God measures these galaxies as if He were measuring them with the outstretched palm of His mighty hand. It is to Him a trivial measurement, as if He were measuring a two-by-four inch board for a small home improvement project. This is what Job means when He assures us that we only comprehend the outer fringes or outer edges of God.

II. Consider the Magnitude of His Mind

"Then Job answered: How you have helped the powerless and delivered the arm that is weak! How you have counseled the unwise and thoroughly explained the path to success! Who did you speak these words to? Whose breath came out of your mouth?'" (Job 26:1–4). "Who did He consult with? Who gave Him understanding and taught Him the paths of justice? Who taught Him knowledge, and showed Him the way of understanding?" (Isa. 40:14).

The measurement of human power, might, and authority is the number of humans who report to another human—counselors, advisers, consultants, and helpers. In the world of the corporation, the CEO is surrounded by his COO, CFO, ISO, and others. The CEO of a large corporation such as General Electric has the advice of 300,000 employees. In the same way, the president of the United States is surrounded by counselors in his cabinet. With the shortest memorandum he can demand information not only from his cabinet but also from the brightest and the best at Harvard, Yale, and MIT. Part of presidential power is the power to command knowledge.

Yet Job and Isaiah reveal God as the exact opposite. The Most Powerful One is the one-who-needs-no-counsel. In the ancient world every emperor of every empire was surrounded by those who were his closest counselors. Their every word was whispered only to the king, and they never whispered the king's business to anyone else. Almighty God needs no counselors, advisers, or helpers. He is omniscience itself. He is intellect. He is wisdom. He is knowledge. What mere humans discover, He already knows. When God called Abraham out of Ur of the Chaldees about four thousand years ago, He already knew all of the algorithms that make modern computer programs possible. It took the human race four thousand years to catch up with Him. All human knowledge is only catching up with what He already knows. There are no discoveries for God to make. He is absolute discovery.

All of the most recent work of cosmologists, those who study the origins of the universe, agree that mind is behind matter. For the universe to have developed as it has now developed, there had to be mind behind the matter, or there would never have been a universe. Sir Fred Hoyle, a former atheistic astronomer, made the following statement about the impossibility that the basic building blocks of life could have mindlessly arranged themselves:

> If only ten amino acids of particular kinds are necessary at particular locations in a polypeptide chain for its proper functioning, the required arrangement (starting from an initially different arrangement) cannot be found by mutations, except as an outrageous fluke. Darwinian evolution is most unlikely to get even one polypeptide right, let alone the thousands on which living cells depend for their survival. This situation is well known to geneticists and yet nobody seems prepared to blow the whistle decisively on the theory. If Darwinism were not considered socially desirable, and even essential to the peace of mind of the body politic, it would of course be otherwise. . . . Just as the brain of Shakespeare

was necessary to produce the famous plays, so prior information was necessary to produce a living cell.

That is, cosmologists are now admitting that it is impossible to account for the present universe without the presence of mind and intention behind the universe. For practical purposes, the probability of creating any particular average protein from a prebiotic supply of amino acids by random processes is as remote as the probability of a monkey typing a sentence; it would require more time than is available even at the highest imaginable rate of protein synthesis. Selection must have been involved.

Cosmologists know statistically that the presence of the world as we know it is impossible mathematically without the Mind behind it. Science is just now catching up to the assertion of Genesis 1:1. We are not even on the outer fringes of knowing the secrets that God has known from the beginning of history. As an excellent example of the mind of God, consider the human eye:

For the eye to function, many perfectly coordinated steps must occur simultaneously. It must be clean and moist (tear glands and movable eyelids). The cornea must be transparent and clear, for light to pass through it to the pupil—a self-adjusting aperture—to an automatic lens that focuses it on the back of the retina, where 130 million light-sensitive rods and cones cause extraordinary photochemical reactions that transform the light into electrical impulses. Some one billion of these are transmitted every second to the brain, which then takes appropriate action and lets us see an image. The eye either functions as a whole or not at all; it is either perfect or perfectly useless. How then, could it evolve by chance? Is it really possible, let alone plausible, that thousands of random mutations could have coincidentally evolved simultaneously to produce an organ which is a wonder of perfect synchronization? And nature abounds with such examples of amazing, mind-boggling coordination. For instance, the human brain has 12 billion cells with 120 trillion connections. Each neuron itself is marvelously complex, with 6 billion molecules of protein, 600 billion of RNA, and many unknown substances which somehow produce our "thoughts." The old argument from design (teleology) is now stronger and more compelling than ever.

We are forced to admit that the eye was perfected and started to improve from the moment it enabled the animal to see, even though in a deformed and crude manner. But it only served this purpose *after* it had been optically constructed and linked by nervous cells to a sensitive optical center in the brain. How can we explain the simultaneous evolution of the elements necessary for vision as long as vision did not exist? The simple sensitivity to light of a particular region of the epiderm in no way explains the ultimate formation of the lens, of the iris, and of the retina.[1]

When Job maintains that we can only trace the outer fringes of God's being and Isaiah maintains that no one can counsel God, every discovery of modern cosmology only further proves the point. There is no one beneath God who would dare give Him direction. There is no one alongside Him who could give Him direction. There is certainly no one above Him who might give Him direction. The massiveness of the divine Mind demonstrates our knowledge of only the outer fringes of His ways.

III. Consider the Magnitude of His Might

Job and Isaiah speak of God's power over nature and history. Job says, "By His power He stirred the sea" (Job 26:12). "I will teach you about God's power" (Job. 27:11).

He has power over the created world (Job 26:7). The "north" was considered by pagans to be the dwelling place of the gods. God suspends it "over empty space" (v. 7). It expresses His total mastery of the world, real or imaginary. He has power over all the processes of nature.

The clouds do not burst under the weight of water (Job 26:8). God is in control over celestial phenomena (v. 9). The reference to "boundary" (v. 10) speaks of the dividing point from the viewer's perspective between what can be seen (light) and what cannot be seen (darkness). It separates the visible world above the surface from the dark world beneath. The important thing is that God is the subject of the verb. The earth and the heavens are His design and His handiwork (Ps. 19:1; Prov. 8:27–29; Isa. 40:22).

God holds power over all the threats of nature (Job 26:11–13). He causes the rumblings of thunder (v. 11). He "crushed Rahab"—mythical monster of the deep, supposedly responsible for the tempestuous seas (v. 12). No creature, real or imaginary, is beyond God's control. The skies "gained their beauty" (v. 13) because His hand pierced the "fleeing serpent" (v. 13), thought to cause the turmoil in the ocean (v. 12). He put to death the source of the ocean's agitation!

Another measurement of the greatness of our God is His sovereignty over history. "Look, the nations are like a drop in a bucket; they are considered as a speck of dust on the scales; He lifts up the islands like fine dust" (Isa. 40:15). Isaiah considers the long march of empires and nation states through the millennia (40:15, 17, 23–24). Consider the ancient civilizations. There stands Egypt with its dynasties, its capitals at Thebes and Cairo, its Valley of the Kings and Queens, its pyramids and hieroglyphics—three thousand years of civilization before the birth of Christ. Yet to Almighty God it is as the drop that hangs precariously on the lip of the bucket about to disappear into the sands of the desert. Moses stood before Pharaoh. The only reason most of the planet even remembers the existence of the pharaohs is their confrontation with the living God in the exodus.

Consider the empires of the Assyrians, Syrians, Babylonians, and Persians. For thousands of years these empires ruled the earth, crushed their enemies, and created fear in the heart of humankind. Yet today we only remember these ancient imperial names because they came into contact with the people of God, ancient Israel, and the word of God through the prophets. Take Nebuchadnezzar as an example. Every brick in every building of ancient Babylon was stamped with his name. Around the walls of his palace two chariots could race side by side. His god was Marduk, and the ancient Babylonians cried out in the city of Babylon, "Great is Marduk." Yet you never would have heard of Marduk or Nebucadnezzar or ancient Babylon if this great power had never come into contact with a Jeremiah or a Daniel. They are as a drop in the bucket to God Himself.

Or consider the empires of Greece and of Rome. The mighty names of those empires stand out in history only because they came into contact with God and His people. Alexander the Great barged into the temple in Jerusalem and bolted into the holy of holies. It was for that one act that he is often remembered. The date of his death is 323 B.C., about 323 years before the coming of Christ. Even the great of the world are measured against the birthday of Jesus. Augustus is said to have found Rome a city of bricks and left it a city of marble, yet how many people would ever have heard the name of Augustus had he not come into contact with the name and the power and the purpose of God in Jesus Christ?

History is littered with those who have risen and fallen under the judgment of God, who alone remains great. Lenin and Stalin are now banished from the memory of the people of the former USSR, but the same Jesus who was Lord before them is Lord after them. Hitler and the Third Reich are now the shame of Germany, and all that he stood for is detested. But the same Jesus who was Lord before Hitler is Lord after Hitler. The British Empire over which Victoria reigned is now gone, and the present Queen Elizabeth II reigns over only a shadow of the once great British Empire. But the same Jesus who reigned before this great empire continues to reign. And we do not even comprehend the fringes of the greatness of God.

IV. Consider the Magnitude of His Mercy

"These are but the fringes of His ways; and how faint is the word we hear of Him! Who can understand His mighty thunder?" (Job 26:14).

This declaration of Job leads us to consider the nature of language about God. When the inerrant, verbally inspired, and totally perfect Word of God calls God *Father,* it means that God is more like a

Father than we poor, mortal, limited, finite humans can grasp. The best and closest thing we can compare Him to is a good human father. The inerrant Word of God does not mean, however, that we exhaust who God is by calling Him Father. Even Jesus suggested that.

In Luke, when speaking of a human father, Jesus said, "If you then, who are evil, know how to give good gifts to your children, how much more will your Father in heaven give good things to those who ask Him!" (Matt. 7:11). Jesus acknowledges that our understanding of God as Father is limited by our midget minds, our pygmy understandings of God Himself. He is better than the best of all human fathers, just as the universe itself is larger than we can comprehend. Expand the best of human fatherhood to the billions of light-years of space, and you have just touched the fringes of God's ways.

The psalmist tells us, "The LORD is my shepherd" (Ps. 23:1). God is better than any human shepherd. What we know about a human shepherd in his care for the flock does not even touch the outer fringes of God's care for His flock. The psalmist told us that God is our light (Ps. 27:1). Yet God as our light expresses only the outer fringe of all the light that God sheds on the universe, spiritually and physically. Human language tells us all that we can comprehend about God as God, yet we must always understand that human language only touches the fringes of who He is.

As Paul stated in 1 Corinthians, "We see indistinctly, as in a mirror" (1 Cor. 13:12). In the biblical world a mirror was made of metal; our modern silvered mirrors did not come along until the eleventh century A.D. at the earliest. A biblical person in the first century A.D. looked at a metal mirror that only barely reflected his image. What is more, he looked into that mirror in a room lit by a lamplight, not by an incandescent bulb. When you looked into a looking glass in the biblical world, you looked into a bad mirror in a dark room. Paul informs us that all of our knowledge of God as mortal men is just like that—looking into a bad mirror in a dark room.

How this should warn us, keep us humble, keep us from arrogance and pride when speaking of God. Some preachers speak of God as if they had mastered all there is to know of God. One minute on the other side of the life beyond, and we will want to repent of all of our theology because it will fall so short of His reality. Five minutes into glory, and we will blush to think of all of our sermons because they will fall so short of His glory.

We are like an explorer standing at the foothills of the Himalayas, with no comprehension of what their peaks are like. We are like children playing on the beach, with no understanding of the waters of the seven seas. We are like Christopher Columbus, thinking he had discovered islands off of India when he was still half a world away. We can only touch the outer fringes of who God is. We can only hear the faintest whisper. But a whisper is enough for us. Elijah did not encounter God in the earthquake, the fire, or the storm. He heard God in the still, small voice, the whisper of the eternal, and that was enough for Elijah.

All that we can see and observe are just the fringes of God.

- Fringes tell us God is powerful but not that He is loving.
- Fringes tell us God is creative but not that He is compassionate.
- Fringes tell us that God is purposeful but not that He has a plan for our lives.
- Fringes tell us that God is a God of order but not the reason for that order.
- Fringes tell us that God is worthy of worship but not that He desires worship.
- Fringes tell us that God is wise but not that He is redemptive.
- Fringes tell us that God is consistent but not that He is forgiving.
- Fringes tell us that God is mysterious but not that He makes Himself known to us.
- Fringes tell us that God demands to be acknowledged but not that His desire is to show mercy.
- Fringes tell us that God is intelligent but not that He is full of grace.
- Fringes tell us God is mighty but not that He is loving.

Just as each part of creation functions according to a wise plan, so each of us lives by God's plan and purpose for us. We do not see or appreciate what is behind the operation of the universe. They are only the "fringes" of God's ways. It is only a whisper. If we cannot understand the gentle whisper of God, how could we understand His full voice?

If the wonders of creation are too marvelous for us to comprehend, it is even more challenging for us to understand the purposes of God in redemption.

Seek the LORD while He may be found;
call to Him while He is near.
Let the wicked one abandon his way,
and the sinful one his thoughts;
let him return to the LORD,
so He may have compassion on him,
and to our God, for He will freely forgive.
"For My thoughts are not your thoughts,
and your ways are not My ways.
For as heaven is higher than earth,
so My ways are higher than your ways,
and My thoughts than your thoughts" (Isa. 55:6–9).

We are speaking of the mercy of God that brings pardon. Who can fathom that!

The powerful deeds of God in the created universe are mere whispers in comparison to the rest of the mighty acts of God. Clearly these acts are His activity in relation to the redemption of mankind. His redemptive acts are eternally greater and even more difficult to understand than His works in creation. We stand merely at the fringe of His majestic power. Who can begin to comprehend this, let alone fully realize the thunderous might of which He is capable?

God is mighty in creation but marvelous in mercy! We must declare this marvelous mercy to a world in desperate need.

1. Lecomte du Nouy, *Human Destiny* (1947), 96–97.

23

When God Delays

JOHN 11:1–46 HCSB

James T. Draper, Jr.

THIS IS A VERY FAMILIAR PASSAGE OF SCRIPTURE. It describes the death and resurrection of Lazarus. Mary and Martha, the sisters of Lazarus, sent for Jesus and told Him that Lazarus was sick. When Jesus comes, Lazarus has died, and Jesus raises him from the dead. It's a dramatic passage of Scripture, certainly one of those pivotal events in the life and ministry of Jesus. In these first verses there's a strange twist to it that doesn't seem to fit. There is a verse that just seems out of place.

Now a man was sick, Lazarus, from Bethany, the village of Mary and her sister Martha. Mary was the one who anointed the Lord with fragrant oil and wiped His feet with her hair, and it was her brother Lazarus who was sick. So the sisters sent a message to Him: "Lord, the one You love is sick."

When Jesus heard it, He said, "This sickness will not end in death, but is for the glory of God, so that the Son of God may be glorified through it" (Jesus loved Martha, her sister, and Lazarus.) So when He heard that he was sick, He stayed two more days in the place where He was (John 11:1–6).

Now this last verse is unusual and doesn't seem to fit. Jesus gets the message that one of His dearest friends is sick. He knows it is serious, but He doesn't do anything. He just stays where He is. We would have expected—and it's obvious that Mary and Martha expected—that as soon as Jesus got the message that Lazarus was sick, He would come running. And they knew everything would be OK if Jesus would just get there. But instead of hurrying to Bethany to the home of Mary and Martha, to the ill Lazarus, his friend, Jesus stayed where He was two days. Now Jesus was two days journey away from Bethany. When He finally arrived, it had been four days since He got the message. By then Lazarus was dead.

This passage sets before us something important. What do we do when God delays? Every one of us has had the experience of asking God for something and nothing happened. We asked for guidance and didn't seem to get a response from God. We asked God to heal a loved one, and he was not healed. In fact, he died. We asked God to help us with our job needs, and we didn't get the job or the request didn't come through. Perhaps we needed companionship or fellowship or friendship, and we asked God for these things, but God delayed. Business turned sour. Someone said, "Cheer up; it could get worse." Sure enough, we cheered up and it got worse! God does nothing. We needed a word from God, and there was only silence.

What do you do when that happens? What do we do when something we cannot explain, something we do not want enters our lives, and we ask God about it, and He doesn't seem to respond?

Most of us have had the experience of not understanding the ways of God, not understanding the silence of God, not understanding the delays of God. Why doesn't God do something quicker? Why doesn't God do something *now*? Why is He delaying? Why is He waiting? This passage sets before us this whole dilemma. From this passage we can learn why God delays and what we ought to do about His delays.

Why does God delay? Why does God not seem to respond when we ask Him to? Why does God not do what we ask Him to do? Why is He silent? This passage gives us two simple and clear reasons.

I. When God Delays, It Is Always for His Glory

In verse 4 Jesus said that this had happened "for the glory of God, so that the Son of God may be glorified through it." Then in verse 40 Jesus said to Martha, "Did I not tell you that if you believeed you would see the glory of God?"

The first reason God delays, God is sometimes silent, is that it is always for His glory. God is always interested in bringing glory to Himself. If any of us were trying to do that, it would be supreme egotism. For any of us to try to get credit, to get glory, to be acclaimed, to be honored would be egotistical and inappropriate. But not for God, since He is perfect in beauty, perfect in holiness, perfect in grace, perfect in mercy. Everything about God is perfect. His provision is perfect, and everything that God does is designed to let people see the perfection that is His and to enter into that perfection through Jesus Christ. Nothing comes into our lives that God does not allow. When God allows silence to shroud our lives, when He delays in our lives, it is always for His glory.

Jesus was showing that He knew perfectly well that to go to Bethany to raise Lazarus from the dead was to take a step that would end in the cross. And that's exactly what happened. When He returned to Bethany to raise Lazarus from the dead, it was the first step that ended in His death on the cross—and that was His supreme glory. That was the greatest glory that could ever come because it was at the cross that God provided redemption and forgiveness. It was at Calvary that God brought mercy and grace. At the cross the greatest glory God could ever bring to Himself was revealed.

Throughout all these days, Jesus' disciples showed that they understood the danger. In verses 8 and 16 we see that they knew that if He went to Bethany, the Jewish religious leaders would be hostile toward Him. "Then Thomas said to his fellow disciples, 'Let's go so that we may die with Him'" (v. 16). They knew that it would end eventually in His death. It took a great deal of courage for Jesus and the disciples to return. His delay is hard to explain on any other ground than His complete mastery, His complete control of life and death. It was just as easy for Him to raise the dead as it was for Him to heal the sick, and it was just far more necessary for His purpose in creating a fixed faith in the lives of those whom He loved. So Jesus delayed because He wanted to bring special glory to God. When God delays, it is always for the purpose of bringing glory to Himself.

II. *When God Delays, It Is Always for Our Good*

The second reason is easier for us to understand. God sometimes delays for His glory and for our good. Jesus told the disciples plainly, "Lazarus has died" (v. 14). "I'm glad for you that I wasn't there" (v. 15). It was for their good, for their sake. He allowed the agony of sorrow, the disillusionment of hope, and the anguish of the death scene, the grave, and the funeral to come into the experience of Mary and Martha because He loved them. His love for them and their thoughts of it were different at the time. They didn't really appreciate it right then. In verse 21 Martha almost sarcastically says to Jesus, "Lord, if You had been here, my brother wouldn't have died." But He allowed it to happen for their sake.

Most of us can look back over our lives and see times when things didn't happen the way we wanted them to, when life seemed to fall in around us, and when God didn't respond. Can we not look back and think of how much we learned during those times? What a blessing it was, how much patience it brought, and how it strengthened our faith?

Where would character be if there were no tribulation to test it or develop it? The truth is that our pain drives us to the Savior. And it often reveals some side of our Savior's character that we would never get to know any other way. Mary and Martha would never have known Jesus as the resurrection and the life if Lazarus had not died. David would never have known of God as his rock, his fortress, his deliverer if he had not been hunted in the hills of Engedi. It was the disappointing experiences of his life that made it possible for David to discover deep truths about God.

Jesus said, "It's for your sake; I delayed for your sake." He tarried because He loved Martha and Mary and Lazarus. He went because He loved them. He loved them deeply. When God delays in our lives, it's always for our good. It's always best for us.

That's the clear meaning of Romans 8:28: "We know that all things work together for the good of those who love God: those who are called according to His purpose." This verse does not say that everything is good but that everything *works together* for good. Our God is so perfect, so majestic, and so wonderful that He will take those things in life that would defeat us and turn them into things that are actually best for us. That's the way our God does it. Things we didn't want to experience, that we didn't expect, that we asked God to deliver us from, God didn't deliver us from them but delivered us in the midst of them. We discover in the long run that it is good for us. I'm sure Mary and Martha thought Jesus was being neglectful. But He was not. He knew perfectly what was taking place. He knew everything they were experiencing.

We can learn from this account the truth that the steps of Jesus may linger, but His watchful interest in us never falters. We never have a sigh, a tear, or a pain that He does not know about. He is there with us in the midst of every experience. Whatever He allows to come into our lives, He does for His glory and for our good. It's wonderful to have that kind of confidence, to know that God is always bringing glory to Himself and bringing what is best into our lives.

We can all think of times like that. I was just a young pastor when my father died suddenly. He was fifty-two years old. I can look back on that now and tell you the best thing that ever happened to my ministry was my father's death. That was the first time anybody close to me had died. It was the first time I understood the depth of emotion, sorrow, and grief that comes with the death of a loved one. It was the first time some of the songs I had sung rather mechanically had a real meaning and brought joy to my heart. Songs like "When We All Get to Heaven" had a new meaning for me. My mom and dad had been married only thirty-three years when he died. Carol Ann and I have been married for forty-seven years now, so we have far surpassed the length of time my mother and father had together.

My mother has always said they didn't have enough time together. Yet even though that was an undesirable thing, something we would not want, it was something God used to bring glory to Himself and to bring good to us.

If we will look at those experiences in our lives that were unwanted, those things that we considered unnecessary, those things that we dreaded happening, we can see that God revealed a part of Himself in a special way through those events. And He did it for our good. God allows the things that come into our lives. He is often silent, and He delays for His glory and for our good.

III. What Should We Do When God Delays?

What should be our response? We pray, and nothing seems to happen. We pray, and heaven seems silent. We ask God, and He does not seem to respond. He delays coming to our aid. What do we do? This passage gives us three clear things that we ought to do if we're going to respond appropriately to the silence of God, to the delays of God.

First of all, we need to display confidence in the love of God. Jesus received word that His beloved friend was ill. Then this passage remarks about how much "Jesus loved Martha, her sister, and Lazarus" (v. 5). Then we see Jesus as He wept before the tomb of Lazarus: "So the Jews said, 'See how He loved him!'" (v. 36). Whenever Jesus is silent in the midst of our life experiences, we can always be confident that He loves us. We are never for even a moment away from His love. The message that was sent to Jesus included no request for Jesus to come to Bethany. It was unnecessary. His friends knew that their need would bring Jesus. They had confidence in His love. They knew that if He found out there was a need, He would respond.

Jesus' love is seen in the words used to describe His heart in this passage. In verse 33 we see Mary weeping and the Jews weeping, and the words used are words in the original language that speak of a loud crying, a wailing, an almost hysterical expression of grief. But when we come to verse 35, it reads that "Jesus wept." This is a different word. It is a word that speaks of intensity of feeling rather than extravagant, uncontrolled wailing. Jesus was deeply moved in His soul, in His spirit. And we read that He was "angry" in Himself (v. 38).

This is an interesting term. It literally means "to snort like a horse." It speaks of indignation. Jesus was looking at the tomb where Lazarus was buried in Bethany. It was a silent testimony to the devastation of death that was brought on the human race, and He was angered by it; He was indignant at it. There was a deep groaning within His soul.

Death to Jesus was not an impassible barrier but a call to battle. He groaned within, in great indignation at the invasion of death upon those whom He loved. We read that He was "troubled." The word *troubled* is the same word used in John 14 when Jesus told the disciples, "Your heart must not be troubled" (v. 1). Now His heart is troubled. He could calm the agitation of His friends because He had passed through it Himself. He had been there. Jesus had known anger. He had known grief. He had known indignation. He had known the troubling of His spirit.

He stood there at the grave of Lazarus, and He understood all they were going through. He took into His own heart all the agony of death. He made Himself responsible, and He gathered up into Himself all the misery resulting from sin, represented in a dead man and a brokenhearted people around Him. Here was a voluntary identification with all the sorrow that issues from sin. It is a remarkable unveiling of the heart of Jesus as we see His spirit that revealed His love. We can go through many tragic experiences in our lives, and we can go through many unwanted experiences, but we need to always remember that God loves us. God always deals with us in love. We can display confidence in the love of God. Jesus didn't respond as Mary and Martha thought He should. But they knew He loved them, and we can have that same confidence.

Second, we need to declare submission to the authority of God. Thomas said to his fellow disciples that if Jesus was going back to Bethany, "Let's go so we may die with Him" (see v. 16). They knew if Jesus went back, the Jewish religious leaders would kill Him. But these disciples said, "If He goes, we'll just go die with Him." That's strong submission to the authority of Jesus. They knew that if they followed Him to Bethany, they could die themselves. But they went anyway. They were submissive to His authority.

Jesus told Mary and Martha to roll the stone away from the tomb where Lazarus was buried. That was not a normal thing to do. This was a cemetery. Bodies decay, and decaying bodies have an odor. The sisters said, "Lord, he's been dead four days; his body is already decaying." Jesus commanded them to roll the stone away. So they rolled the stone away. It is a picture of submission, a picture of obedience. We need to always remember in the midst of the silences and delays of God that He loves us. We need to display confidence in the love of God, and we need to have absolute obedience and submission to the authority of God in our lives.

We need to always remember that we must obey God. Our trouble is not with things we don't understand. It's with things we understand all too well and are not willing to do anything about. There are many things we know God has told us to do that we have not obeyed. We need to be obedient to God, submissive to Him and His will for our lives. We need to display confidence in His love, and we need to declare our submission to His authority.

Then we need to demonstrate faith in the power of God. Martha says, "Lord, if You had been here, my brother wouldn't have died" (v. 21). There's a mingling of faith and rebuke in her words. This indicates the kind of friendship they had. These were dear friends. We don't talk so frankly with someone we're not close to. Even though Martha was bereaved, she still had faith that God could do whatever Jesus asked Him to do. Jesus gave that wonderful statement that we cherish: " I am the resurrection and the life. The one who believes in Me, even if he dies, will live. Everyone who lives and believes in Me will never die—ever" (vv. 25–26).

This is a wonderful statement, and the response of Martha is the greatest confession in the New Testament. I know Peter said, "Thou art the Christ, the Son of the living God" (Matt. 16:16 KJV), and we always say that was a great confession. It was, certainly, but we need to understand that Simon Peter made his confession from the pinnacle of exhilaration, as the climax of having seen a series of wonderful works performed by Jesus Christ. Peter was riding the crest of excitement. Jesus had displayed His authority and His power. Coming off the emotion and excitement of that experience, Peter said, "Thou art the Christ, the Son of the living God."

But Martha's brother was dead. Her heart was broken. There was an empty place in her home. They had asked Jesus to come, and He hadn't come as quickly as they had hoped. She is still in despair. Yet from her despair, hear what she said. Jesus asked, "'Do you believe this?' 'Yes, Lord, she told Him, I believe that You are the Messiah, the Son of God, who was to come into the world'" (v. 27). From the depths of her grief, she demonstrated faith in the power of God. And her faith was rewarded.

It is a dramatic scene. Jesus prayed quietly to the Father. Then He spoke with a loud voice. Why did He cry with a loud voice? He raised His voice so the crowd would hear. He had prayed to His Father that they would believe. Now in order that all might hear what He says, He raised his voice. With a loud voice, He cried, "Lazarus, come out" (v. 43). I love what Dr. R. G. Lee said about this passage. He said that Jesus had to call Lazarus by name because if he had just said, "Come out," the whole cemetery would have been emptied of all its corpses! With a loud voice he cried, "Lazarus, come out." Here was absolute proof that the Lord Jesus had power over the material world as Lazarus came to life and walked out of the tomb.

How do we respond when God delays? We display confidence in His love. We know that He loves us. We declare our submission, our obedience to His authority, and we demonstrate faith in His power.

There is another picture here that may describe some of us. Jesus raised Lazarus from the dead, but he was still bound in his grave clothes. He was alive, but he wasn't free. Jesus had to tell those around Lazarus, "Loose him and let him go" (v. 44). There are many Christians who have been saved but don't know the liberty that is ours in Christ. They don't know the freedom that is ours in Christ. They are still bound by the same evil habits, still tormented by the same forces that created such devastation in their lives. They are bound by the grave clothes of tradition, misunderstanding, or unbelief. It's wonderful when we hear Jesus say, "Loose him and set him free." It's a beautiful picture.

Christ not only wants to give us life, He wants to give us abundant life. He not only wants to give us life, He wants to set us free to live that life in Him. We can have faith in the power of God. We can know that He loves us, and we can respond in faith to Him. So the bottom line is that we need to trust Him. When things happen that we don't understand, we need to know that there are lessons we can learn in the midst of those experiences that we would never learn otherwise. Lazarus had to die before he could be resurrected. The sorrow and anguish of death had to be experienced before the exhilaration of resurrection could come.

Can you imagine life being dull for Lazarus after that? I like to think about what it must have been like in the community where he lived. Imagine all the kids in the neighborhood bringing their new friends to see the man who was dead but was now alive. Can you imagine Lazarus sitting on his porch just rocking and reminiscing for the rest of his life? I have an idea things were different after that. He was raised, and he was set free. God had demonstrated His power. The sisters of Lazarus thought that if Jesus would come, their brother wouldn't die. But he died, and Jesus came and turned death into life.

When Jesus is silent or when He delays, we can trust Him. We can know that He is acting for His glory and for our good. We can have confidence that He loves us. We can know that we need to be obedient and demonstrate faith in Him. Someone said, "Never doubt in the dark what God told you in the light." There are many things we know that we have been taught and that we understand in the Word of God. Never let the darkness obscure the truth that God has revealed to us in the light.

You may find yourself in the midst of one of God's delays. Maybe you've asked God for something, and nothing has happened. Maybe there's perplexity, confusion, and misunderstanding in your life. Perhaps there's a crisis, and it has not been resolved. You don't know what to do. I want to tell you that you can trust God in the midst of that difficulty. Your part is to be submissive to Him. Surrender your life to Him, and God will bless and honor you as He brings glory to Himself and brings what is best in your life.

24

Chambers of Imagery

EZEKIEL 8:7–12 NASB

Charles W. Draper

Associate Professor of Biblical Studies, Boyce College,
a school of The Southern Baptist Theological Seminary

SUDDEN AND UNEXPECTED EVENTS can color our lives forever. Some of these are highly public and impact the popular consciousness of entire generations. We always remember where we were and what we were doing when such moments occurred. A shrinking number remember an otherwise uneventful Sunday morning, December 7, 1941, when the Japanese Navy attacked the U.S. Pacific Fleet, which lay at anchor in Pearl Harbor, Hawaii. More remember Friday, November 22, 1963, when President John F. Kennedy was struck down in an unprecedented public way. News of JFK's shooting circled the globe in eight minutes. Most remember the two disasters with NASA's space shuttles, the *Challenger* and the *Columbia*. All of us remember in traumatic detail September 11, 2001, when terrorists flew hijacked airliners into the twin towers of the World Trade Center, the Pentagon, and a field in Pennsylvania, killing thousands.

But the unexpected does not have to be of national or global significance to profoundly affect us personally. Often, with apparently stunning suddenness, people whose lives are devoted to Christ and the church collapse morally.

I remember a day when I was a seventeen-year-old pastor and learned that a man I knew, a respected denominational worker, was exposed as a pedophile. One day several years later, a prominent pastor failed to make an important national appearance, and soon it was known that he had been exposed after decades of immoral behavior. In my early thirties a minister I revered as much as I did my own father, a man whose children were effective ministers, left town with a coworker, abandoning his wife of over forty years. Another time, a bold evangelist who risked his life many times to preach the gospel announced that his young lover was God's reward for a life of faithful service and abandoned his wife, family, and ministry. Across my desk, prominent church members have beamed as they explained sincerely that God directly led them into adulterous affairs that scandalized the church and shattered their families. And on it goes with heartbreaking and sickening regularity. But no matter how often it happens, it still shocks and saddens.

We all know we are fully human, yet somehow we believe there are certain things we would never do. The reality is, however, that when we feel strongest we are most vulnerable and in greatest danger of moral collapse. Even the great King David, in an idle moment, was drawn into a web of immorality, deceit, and murder. How and why do these stunning and devastating tragedies occur?

Tucked away in a dusty corner of the Old Testament, Ezekiel 8, is the record of an unexpected moment from the sixth century B.C. that offers rare insight into the cause of these seemingly sudden moral collapses. The prophet Ezekiel was a man of passionate intensity toward God and the message God sent him to declare—an earnest and eccentric man, meticulous about details. Ezekiel was unusual in that he was both a priest and a prophet. He never lost his awe of God or his love for his people. He has been described as a sensitive soul caught in the crosscurrents of history, driven by his zeal for God and painfully aware of the tragedy of his people. His name means "God strengthens," and his ministry was to exiles in Babylon who needed to be strengthened and encouraged. Ezekiel's book contains predictive prophecy, much about sin and judgment. We glimpse the great, patient heart of God and the soul of this prophet.

In Ezekiel 2 and 3, Ezekiel was called and commissioned to stand before God, to stay true to God, to speak only God's words, and to surrender all his hopes and desires to the will of God. Just over a year after his commissioning, the elders of the exiles came to the prophet's house in Babylon. They hoped to hear that they could go home soon, back to lives of safety and security, near the temple in Jerusalem, where Almighty God dwelt among his people. As they waited, a devastating vision descended on Ezekiel (Ezek. 8–11), making it painfully obvious that judgment could be deterred no longer because of the grave nature of their spiritual corruption. God demanded that the character and conduct of His people be consistent with His own character. The abandonment of their covenant relationship demanded the sweeping consequences, including exile, which Moses had predicted. Beyond recovery, Jerusalem and the temple would be swept away.

We also live in a corrupt culture. Years ago Ruth Graham wrote that if God spared the USA, he would have to apologize to Sodom and Gomorrah. Indeed, few nations in history are more deserving of judgment than our own, and God's judgment begins with His own people (1 Pet. 4:17).

To understand sudden moral collapse, we must do a difficult thing and turn a critical eye toward ourselves. Let us examine the most secret and hidden places of our hearts, places no one else sees or knows, places we visit only in the dark. Our own secret delights have consequences too, even when we do not act on them. Unchecked fantasies condition us to entertain possibilities we would not otherwise even think about. And one day secret fantasies will work their way out of the dark for all the world to see. Only the Lord Jesus Christ can cleanse our hearts at the deepest level.

No matter how reflective of truth the forms of faith and worship are, when external forms become our main focus, spiritual and moral collapse loom on the horizon.

In Ezekiel 8 are five scenes from the prophet's vision. Ezekiel was carried to Jerusalem and the temple to see the spiritual reality of his people. In all five scenes are direct insults to God. The staggering thing about Ezekiel 8 is that all of these insults to God took place in the temple. But our own insults often happen in His house also.

Go with me long ago and far away to a distant but strangely familiar place. Let us look at only one of the five abominations of Ezekiel 8. We will learn how the best of people (including any of us) can act to contradict everything they believe, betraying the Lord and all those they hold dear in the process.

Ezekiel 8:7–12 tells us:

> Then He brought me to the entrance of the court, and when I looked, behold, a hole in the wall. He said to me, "Son of man, now dig through the wall." So I dug through the wall, and behold, an entrance. And He said to me, "Go in and see the wicked abominations that they are committing here." So I entered and looked, and behold, every form of creeping things and beasts and detestable things, with all the idols of the house of Israel, were carved on the wall all around. Standing in front of them were seventy elders of the house of Israel, with Jaazaniah the son of Shaphan standing among them, each man with his censer in his hand and the fragrance of the cloud of incense rising. Then He said to me, "Son of man, do you see what the elders of the house of Israel are committing in the dark, each man in the room of his carved images? For they say, 'The LORD does not see us; the LORD has forsaken the land.'"

In the majestic language of the King James Version, Ezekiel 8:12 says, "Then said he unto me, Son of Man, hast thou seen what the ancients of the house of Israel do in the dark, every man in the chambers of his imagery? for they say, The LORD seeth us not; the LORD hath forsaken the earth."

Notice these things from the text:

I. The Disintegration of the Wall (Ezek. 8:7–8)

Around the temple was a courtyard. Around the courtyard was a wall. Within that wall were several rooms that served various purposes. Ezekiel was taken to the temple compound, and the Spirit pointed out a place where the wall was crumbling and disintegrating. Ezekiel was told to clear the rubble and open the door. Notice that the damage to the wall was in plain sight. Prompted by the Lord, Ezekiel walked right in. The secrets cherished in the image chamber revealed what they really loved and the depravity of their native human nature. Solomon said, "The hearts of the sons of men are full of evil and insanity is in their hearts throughout their lives" (Eccles. 9:3). Jeremiah 17:9 asks similarly, "The heart is more deceitful than all else and is desperately sick; Who can understand it?"

There is a secret place in all of us. Its crumbling walls are more visible than we imagine. Most often we fool ourselves more effectively than we deceive others. What we are in our most secret place also will one day work its way out for the world to see, unless we act now to cleanse it. Unless God has control there, unless Christ cleanses it and cleans it out, one day we will be shamed as they were, and the name of God dishonored, as the light of day floods in. Jesus said, "there is nothing concealed that will not be revealed. or hidden that will not be known" (Matt. 10:26).

What these people were and what they did were two different things. They did all the right things. They were meticulous about their obligations of worship and service to God. But what they did was not consistent with what they were. Outside the entrance of the secret place lay the rubble of wasted lives and lost opportunities.

II. The Degradation of God (Ezek. 8:9–10)

Here is the greatest element of the tragedy. God is degraded in the image chamber. Notice again that Ezekiel did not have to break the door down or fight his way in. When the rubble was cleared away, he walked right in.

There is no fulfillment or value to our Christian lives until what we do is the product of what we are. What you crave, what you love, and what you cherish does matter greatly, and it matters every bit as much as what you do. Sin is destructive of our lives, even when it is internal and unperformed. Jesus raised the standard of righteousness from one of conduct to the thought life (Matt. 5:27–28).

The people of Ezekiel's vision were doing all the right things, but their hearts were not right, and judgment came. Though secret and remote from their daily lives, their true worship was now in the dark. Sometimes so is ours. What is in your image chamber, where memory embellishes and imagination paints beautifully and carves intricately? Whatever it is, for the glory of God, or to His shame, it will be revealed at some point. The fundamental reality remains unchanged. The Israelites practiced secret idolatry and so do we. Worship consists of more than what we believe. Idolatry lifts the creature above the Creator and the animal urge above the spiritual impulse. Our idols are no less destructive or abominable then theirs.

God told His people not to make images of any kind because no image of anything in the heavens, the earth, or the sea could describe Him or capture His glory. All the other nations had idols, physical representations of the gods they cherished. And here within the temple dedicated to the one true God, Maker of heaven and earth, was a pantheon of all the pagan gods. Daily their secret worship degraded God.

III. The Degeneration of Conscience (Ezek. 8:11–12)

The amplified product of secret sin is seen in the dark. The inhabitants of Jerusalem were worshipping earnestly, performing some elements reserved for the priests and the Levites in temple worship. But their true worship was in the dark, though they retained the outward practices of the proper worship of God. This is the key to understanding the full significance of the secret image chamber. Led by the priest Jaazaniah, the seventy chosen elders of Israel, the leaders of the nation were chanting before pagan idols: "The LORD does not see us; the LORD has forsaken the land."

But God does see! Always! The daylight and the darkness are the same to Him. Whether in behavior or in the hidden crevices of our souls, we are always before His face. He is always looking into our eyes.

Commenting on this passage, Joseph Parker of London said: "Is it not true now that in many enjoyments the whole delight is to be found in the secrecy of their participation? A man can hide himself from his fellowman in this matter, and can, in the very act of prayer, place himself within chambers of imagery, and delight himself with visions which no eye but his own can see." Isaiah wrote, "Woe to those who deeply hide their plans from the LORD, and whose deeds are done in a dark place, and they say, 'Who sees us?' or 'Who knows us?'" (Isa. 29:15).

Conclusion

Many lessons are taught in this passage. These are among the most important:

1. No matter how reflective of truth the forms of faith and worship are, when the forms are the main thing, spiritual decline and moral collapse have begun.

2. What we are in our secret place will one day work its way out for all the world to see. Each time we yield to temptation it becomes easier, until we can indulge our fantasies without pangs of conscience. Therein lies the danger. The delights of the image chamber will eventually be as easy to act out as they are to imagine.

3. There is no value to or fulfillment in our Christian lives until what we do is the product of what we are.

4. What we crave, love, and cherish does matter. It matters every bit as much as what we do.

5. Sin is destructive of our lives, even when it is secret and unperformed. Some may feel vulnerable, and others may feel invincible. The enemy of God tells us we can never be free of the things that inhabit the secret places. But that is a lie! Anyone can change and be free. That is the message of the gospel! No matter what your condition, God can create a new heart in you and set you free.

6. What we do is meaningless and empty until Christ is Lord in the image chamber, in the secret places of our souls.

Many of us have seen it happen. Suddenly and stunningly those we admire and respect collapse morally. I pray I will never see it or hear of it again, but I fear that I will. We must surrender even the most secret part of ourselves to Him, or else one day, as the wall crumbles, there may be a stirring outside the door. The door will open as the light floods in, and the voice of God will boom, "Hast thou seen what they do in the dark, every man in the chambers of his imagery!"

Pray now as David did, "Search me, O God, and know my heart; try me, and know my thoughts; and see if there be any hurtful way in me, and lead me in the everlasting way" (Ps. 139:23–24).

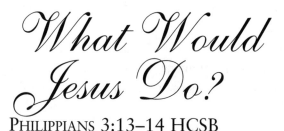

25

What Would Jesus Do?

PHILIPPIANS 3:13–14 HCSB

Randy Draper

Deacon, Laypreacher, Colleyville, Texas

WWJD! HAVE YOU SEEN IT? It's everywhere. It's on necklaces, bracelets, bumper stickers, Bible covers, coffee mugs, T-shirts. There's even a CD entitled *What Would Jesus Do?* But WWJD means different things to different people. If you're a Dallas Cowboys fan, it probably means "What Will Jerry Do?" Some local high school students say it stands for "Why Waste Jack Daniels?" They go to Christian bookstores and buy their WWJD bracelets and give these letters a whole new meaning. What would Jesus do?

The new year is almost here. If you haven't accomplished what you set out to do this past year, you have a brand-new year ahead. As I thought about the new year coming, I concluded that it would be nice to be reminded to ask each day, "What would Jesus do?" Whatever we tried to do this year that didn't go the way we desired, this is ancient history. We must put the past behind us. Now is the time to look forward to the new year.

The apostle Paul gave some good words that apply to all of us: "Forgetting what is behind and reaching forward to what is ahead" (Phil. 3:13). What was Paul forgetting? He wanted to forget that he had persecuted Christians, that he had stood there consenting to the stoning of Stephen. He wanted to forget past mistakes but past successes as well. He was the greatest evangelist and missionary of his day. But even the successes had to be put behind him. He wanted to put it all behind him. He said, "Whatever I've done, I'm going to forget what lies behind. I'm going to reach forward to what lies ahead." "I pursue as my goal the prize promised by God's heavenly call in Christ Jesus"(Phil. 3:14).

Paul determined to go into the future focused on what Jesus would do. It's not just a fashion statement; it's a statement of faith. Many people wear WWJD because it's the thing to do, but to Paul it was a statement of faith.

Let's look at four things Jesus would do and what He wants us to do in the year ahead.

I. Jesus Wants Us to Respond Rather Than React

Our tendency is just to react to people. We get upset, frustrated, or angry about the situation. We go into a reaction mode. And guess what? If you are walking around in a reaction mode, get ready because God will send you a test. It could be your spouse, it could be a friend, it could be a worker at the office—but you will get a test.

Ephesians 4:31 says, "Stop being mean, bad-tempered and angry. Quarreling, harsh words, and dislike of others should have no place in your lives" (LB). Apply this to the relatives who are in town this week for the holidays. You know, the one who wanted to watch his TV program and didn't want to watch yours. Perhaps you're frustrated because he didn't want to come to the table to eat with everyone else when dinner was ready. Paul concludes this passage by saying, "Instead, be kind to each other, tenderhearted, forgiving one another just as God has forgiven you because you belong to Christ" (LB). We are to be kind, forgiving, loving, and tenderhearted toward others.

What would Jesus do? He would respond in love and kindness. Let me show you what He said in Luke 6:35: "But love your enemies, do good, and lend, expecting nothing in return. Then your reward will be great, and you will be sons of the Most High.

For He is gracious to the ungrateful and evil." What would Jesus do? He would respond in love and kindness.

He would respond in forgiveness. In Luke 23:34 we read the account of Jesus hanging on the cross. He looked up to the Father and said, "Father, forgive them, because they do not know what they are doing." He responded in forgiveness. We can't go forward when we are angry and resentful toward people. Such behavior means we will have a year when the glory of God is lacking in our lives.

Did you hear what Jesus said? "Forgiving one another, just as God also forgave you in Christ" (Eph. 4:32). In the Sermon on the Mount, Jesus was even more specific, "For if you forgive people their wrongdoing, your heavenly Father will forgive you as well. But if you don't forgive people, your Father will not forgive your wrong-doing" (Matt. 6:14–15). We are to forgive others as we have been forgiven. We will never have to forgive someone else of as much as God has had to forgive us! Here is the principle. If you are unforgiving, you are unforgiven. If you are forgiving, you are forgiven. A forgiving spirit is a sure sign that we have been forgiven.

Jesus would also be unselfish. Ephesians 5:2 declares, "Walk in love, as the Messiah also loved us and gave Himself for us, a sacrificial and fragrant offering to God." Jesus was unselfish. The Bible tells us that He came down from heaven, took the form of a man, and gave His life for us. He was unselfish, and He would have us respond unselfishly. He would respond in love, kindness, and forgiveness, and so should we.

II. Jesus Wants Us to Be an Influence Rather Than to Be Influenced

Christians no longer are much of an influence in society because we have lost our credibility. The divorce rate in the Christian community is as high as it is in the world. Professing Christians go to the same movies and watch the same TV programs and read the same material as the world. We have lost our credibility!

If we are going to be a strong influence for Christ this year, there must be some changes in our lives. Paul asked the ultimate question.

"For am I now trying to win the favor of people, or God? Or am I striving to please people?" (Gal. 1:10). We have to ask ourselves that question.

You know what we do? We get a yes-man to tell us that everything we are doing is OK. I have a yes-man doll that sits on the desk in my office. If I pat it on the head, it agrees with me about everything. This is the kind of dialogue I can have with it:

"I think I'll do it my way this year." The doll will respond, "*I couldn't agree with you more.*"

"Don't you think so?" "*Oh yeah, I'm behind you all the way.*"

"I just want to make a lot of money." "*I'm sure whatever you are thinking is correct.*"

"I just love controlling my own destiny." "*Good idea. I wish I'd thought of that.*"

"My way is better than God's way." "*What more can I say? When you're right, you're right.*"

"God is certainly lucky to have a guy like me." "*Right on, man!*"

All of us need a yes-man. We can do whatever we want to do if we have a yes-man. But in reality, we do have a yes-man—and his name is Satan. He stands behind us saying, "Yeah, go to that movie." "Yeah, say this back to that person." "Yeah, it's OK to do that." He's our yes-man.

But do you know what God wants us to be? He wants us to be yes-men and yes-women. He wants us to say yes to Him. He wants us to realize that we need to be an influence in the world rather than to be influenced by the world.

We influence by our character. The dictionary defines *character* as "reputation, moral excellence, ethical traits." Character is who you are when no one is looking. Character is what you are when you are at home by yourself and no one is around. That's your real character. God is looking for people of character who will be an influence in this world.

One pastor was preaching one Sunday on the evil of sin. He said, "If you love sin, stand up!" Nobody stood. He pounded the pulpit and said, "If you love sin, stand up!" A woman stood up in the back of the church. He looked at her and said, "Sister Sarah, do you love sin?" She replied, "Oh, pastor, I thought you said 'gin'!"

God wants people who will take a stand for something. If we don't do that, we will fall for anything. God wants us to take a stand for something. He wants us to be men and women who hate sin. Jesus hates sin, but He loves the sinner. We need to learn to hate sin like Jesus does and stay away from the things that drag us back into the world. We need to be people of character.

Romans 12:2 says, "And do not be conformed to this world, but be transformed by the renewing of your mind" (NASB). Phillips translates this, "Don't let the world squeeze you into its mould." That means spending time with Jesus. It is a reminder that we need to spend time with Him in His word every day.

This passage continues, calling on us to renew our mind "so that you may prove what the will of God is, that which is good and acceptable and perfect" (Rom. 12:2 NASB). That's character—not being conformed to the world.

The psalmist asked, "Who may ascend into the hill of the LORD? And who may stand in His holy place? He who has clean hands and a pure heart, who has not lifted up his soul to falsehood and has not sworn deceitfully. He shall receive a blessing from the LORD" (Ps. 24:3–5 NASB). "Clean hands"—that's our work. God wants us to have character in our work. "Pure heart"—that's our thoughts, our desires, our wills, our choices. They need to come from a pure heart. "Not lifted up his soul to falsehood"—that's our words, being a person of our word, not lying or being deceitful. Then this passage says, "Has not sworn deceitfully." The psalmist is talking about keeping our promises.

God wants us to be men and women of character. And if we are going to influence rather than to be influenced, we must influence by our character.

We also influence by our integrity. The dictionary defines *integrity* as "soundness, adherence to a code of values, utter sincerity, candor, honesty, completeness."

John 18:38 records the appearance of Jesus before Pilate. After Pilate's interrogation of Jesus, he brought Him out before the people and said, "I find no grounds for charging Him." In other words, there was nothing in Jesus that Pilate could find to justify His being crucified. Jesus was a man of integrity!

If you were put on trial for the things in your life, would somebody be able to stand and say, "I find no grounds for charging him"? I heard about a man who was filling out a job application. One of the questions was "Have you ever been convicted of a felony or a misdemeanor?" It was a yes-or-no question, so he checked no. The next question was "Why?" And he wrote, "I haven't been caught yet!"

God wants us to lead not only by our character but also by our integrity. I heard about a businessman who had accumulated two thousand dollars in cash that he planned to deposit in the bank. As he was unlocking his car, he placed the deposit slip and cash on the roof. You guessed it—he drove off without taking the money down. When he got to the bank, he had no deposit to make. He was in a panic all day, searching for the money along the road to the bank.

His banker called that afternoon and said, "Guess what? An anonymous person just made a deposit in your account for two thousand dollars. He also left a note that said, 'Merry Christmas.'"

Now that's integrity! That is someone who knows what integrity is all about. If we're going to be the influence God wants us to be, we will influence by our character and our integrity.

God also wants us to influence through encouragement. Psalm 34:1 says, "I will praise the LORD at all times; His praise will always be on my lips." In other words, if we're praising the Lord, and our praise toward Him fills our lives, His praise in us will also be directed toward other people. We need to lift people up, not cast them down. We need to build up their self-esteem, build up their positive mental attitude about themselves. We need to give praise to God, and as we do so, we should be people of encouragement.

My grandmother was one of the most positive people I have ever known. My dad was sitting at the kitchen table with her one morning. He said, "Mother, you are so positive. I believe you would even have something good to say about the devil." She thought for a few seconds and said, "Well, he is a hard worker!"

We can find something positive to say about every person we meet. If you don't believe that, God will give you a test. He will allow you to demonstrate your influence by being an encourager to others.

III. Jesus Wants Us to Intercede Rather Than Interfere

Listen to Romans chapter 8, verses 26 and 34, "In the same way the Spirit also joins to help in our weakness, because we do not know what to pray for as we should, but the Spirit Himself intercedes for us. . . . Christ Jesus is the One who died, but even more, has been raised; He also is at the right hand of God and intercedes for us." He is our example! The Holy Spirit intercedes for us. Jesus Himself intercedes for us (see John 17:20).

Jesus said to Simon Peter, "Simon, Simon, look out! Satan has asked to sift you like wheat. But I have prayed for you, that your faith may not fail, And you, when you have turned back, strengthen your brothers" (Luke 22:31–32). Jesus interceded for Simon Peter.

We need to intercede rather than interfere. Do you know what that means? To *interfere* means "to block, to hinder, to impede, to obstruct, to meddle." We need to intercede instead of interfere. Oswald Chambers said, "God gives us insight not so we can be critical, but so we can intercede."

Who's rubbing you the wrong way? Maybe someone at work or at home? Who's giving you a hard time? You are always griping about them. Maybe it's time to start praying for them instead of griping about them. God wants us to pray instead of being critical. God wants us to lift people up.

Recently I heard a story about a missionary in Africa. He worked in the jungle in a remote area. Every two weeks he would come from the jungle to the city to get some cash and supplies. One time as he went into the city, he saw two men fighting. When the fight ended, one was badly injured. The missionary went over and ministered to the injured man and shared the gospel with him. Then he left and returned to his home.

Some time later he was back in that town. He encountered the same man he had helped. "Do you remember me?" the man asked.

"Yes, you're the injured man whom I helped," the missionary replied.

"Yes, you shared Christ with me, and I just want you to know that I prayed and invited Jesus into my life," the man said. "Now I have Him in my life, and I'm a believer."

The missionary responded, "That's great!"

The man continued, "Let me tell you the rest of the story. That night when you helped me, my friends and I noticed you had money and medicine. We decided to follow you home. We were going to kill you and steal your money and medicine. But when we came to your camp where your tent was pitched, there were twenty-six armed guards standing around your tent."

The missionary laughed and said, "I was by myself; there was no one with me."

The man replied, "Oh, no, I saw them. All of my friends saw twenty-six armed guards standing guard around your tent."

The missionary shared this story with his home church the next time he was back in the United States on furlough. When he finished the story, a man stood up and asked, "What day was that?" The missionary thought a minute and told him the day.

The man said, "Well, that night in Africa was daytime over here. I was going to play golf that day. As I was putting my golf clubs in the trunk of my car, the Holy Spirit really impressed me of the need to pray for you. It was such a strong impression that I called some of the men in the church, and we met down at the church to pray. And those men are here tonight. I would like them to stand."

When they stood, the missionary counted twenty-six men!

God wants us to become interceders for one another. He wants us to intercede rather than interfere. He wants us to respond rather than react. He wants us to influence rather than be influenced.

IV. *Jesus Wants Us to Serve Rather Than to Be Served*

We live in a self-serve society. You can pump your own gasoline at the self-service island and go to the ATM machine and get your own money. You can go to a store and buy and package your own groceries. This is a self-serve society. Our idea of serving is serving ourselves.

Listen to what Jesus said as He was talking to the Pharisees. "Hypocrites! Isaiah prophesied correctly about you when he said: 'This people honors Me with their lips, but their heart is far from Me'" (Matt. 15:7–8). Maybe you are into lip service. Maybe you're always talking about what you're going to do. Maybe you're always talking about what you used to do. Maybe you're always bragging about all the big plans you have for serving God. God wants you to know that lip service is not enough. He doesn't want us to be lip servants. He wants us to serve others unconditionally.

He doesn't want us to give eye service. "Don't work only while being watched, in order to please man, but as slaves of Christ, do God's will from your heart" (Eph. 6:6). God wants heart service. "Render service with a good attitude, as to the Lord and not to men" (Eph. 6:7). Do it for Him. Maybe she's driving you crazy; maybe he's not worthy of your respect. Turn them over to the Lord!

Listen to Ephesians 6:8, "Knowing that whatever good each one does, slave or free, he will receive this back from the Lord." That is our promise from God. God doesn't want us to give lip service or eye service. He wants us to serve from the heart with good will toward others. And God promises, "If you will do that, you will receive back a blessing from the Lord." What a promise!

Service is an attitude of the heart. And service involves serving one person at the time. In Matthew 25 Jesus spoke about the coming judgment. He said:

All the nations will be gathered before Him, and He will separate them one from another, just as a shepherd separates the sheep from the goats. He will put the sheep on His right, and the goats on the left. Then the King will say to those on His right, "Come, you who are blessed by My Father, inherit the kingdom prepared for you from the foundation of the world. For I was hungry and you gave Me something to eat; I was thirsty and you gave Me something to drink; I was a stranger and you took Me in; I was naked and you clothed Me; I was sick and you took care of Me; I was in prison and you visited Me." Then the righteous will answer Him, "Lord, when did we see You hungry and feed You, or thirsty and give You something to drink? When did we see You a stranger and take You in, or without clothes and clothe You?" . . . And the King will answer them, "I assure you: Whatever you did for one of the least of these brothers of Mine, you did for Me"(Matt. 25:32–38).

We serve one person at the time. Even if it is someone insignificant in the eyes of the world, we are doing it on behalf of Jesus.

Have you seen the bumper sticker that says "Think Globally"? We live in a world where we can see what is going on in London, Tel Aviv, Baghdad, or anywhere else in the world. We have started to think globally. Our whole mindset is thinking globally. While this has positive aspects, it is also Satan's tool to defeat us. If he can get us to thinking globally, we will become frustrated because we can't save the world. And if we can't serve the whole world, then we are tempted not to serve anybody! God wants us to serve one person at the time.

While walking on the seashore one morning, a boy noticed thousands of starfish that had been washed up on the beach during the night. He knew they would die if they didn't get back into the water. So he began to pick them up and throw them back into the water as fast as he could. A man came up and asked him what he was doing.

The boy replied, "I'm saving these starfish."

"There are thousands of starfish here," the man pointed out. "What difference does it make?"

The boy held up the starfish in his hand and said, "To this one, it makes all the difference in the world!"

We are going into a new year. I don't know what happened in your life this past year, whether it was good or bad. I don't know if you were as successful as you wanted to be. I don't know if you accomplished everything you wanted to accomplish. But God reminds us that we need to serve rather than to be served. Just touch one life at a time. It will make all the difference in the world.

We don't need a New Year's resolution; we need a New Year's recommitment. In the altar of our hearts, we need to make a recommitment to be all God that wants us to be. Maybe you haven't committed your life to Christ. You can do it right now. Your New Year's commitment can be your new commitment to Christ. Many of us need to recommit our lives to the Lord and let Him work in our lives. We can do that right now.

Zig Ziglar once held up a Bible before a large conference of Christians. He asked, "How many of you believe every word of this Book is true?" Almost every hand went up. Then he held up a newspaper and asked, "How many of you believe every word in this paper is true?" Not one hand went up. Then he asked the question I am going to ask you: "Then why do we spend time more time reading what we don't believe than we do reading what we know to be true?" We spend more time reading the things we don't believe than we do reading God's Word.

God wants us to respond rather than react. He wants us to influence rather than to be influenced. He wants us to intercede rather than interfere. He wants us to serve rather than to be served. This will require spending time in God's Word, allowing His Holy Spirit to energize us. God wants us to focus on Him, putting the past behind us and moving with him into the future.

Part 3:

Preaching from a Heart of Encouragement

26

Three Certain Signs of Salvation: Consider This as You Pray for Revival!

ROMANS 8:14–16 NKJV

Tom Elliff
Senior Pastor, First Southern Baptist Church,
Del City, Oklahoma

SEVERAL YEARS AGO my family shared a vacation with another family. They were close friends, and we enjoyed a wonderful time of recreation, fellowship, and inspiration. One afternoon we decided to have some friendly family-versus-family competition. To organize the teams I said, "I want all the Elliff family to come over here." Immediately my children and wife made a circle around me on the court. I didn't see any of my children looking about or wondering, *Does that mean me? Am I an Elliff?* They knew who they were. They were part of the Elliff clan.

If the Lord Jesus came today and said, "All the people who are part of My family come and stand by Me," would you have to pause and consider whether you are part of the family of God? Or would you instantly know that He was speaking of you?

It is the singular nature of revival that it can only happen in the hearts of God's family. Others will always benefit from the effects of revival, but revival itself is a sovereign work of God among His people.

Not everyone is part of God's family. I know there is the common misconception that the entire world is part of God's family. But the Bible says there is a unique group of people on this earth who are, in fact, born into the family of God. The great revival passage in 2 Chronicles 7:14 opens by targeting a specific audience: "If My people."

Any individual, church, or nation seeking revival must first follow the admonition of the apostle Paul to "examine yourselves as to whether you are in the faith. Test yourselves" (2 Cor. 13:5). Contrary to public belief, an intense personal examination of your relationship to Christ is both a scriptural and necessary prerequisite for revival. Many churches fall into prolonged periods of spiritual deadness because they do not heed Paul's command to the church: *"Examine yourselves!"*

Over the years, I have counseled faithful church members who, despite all their dedicated activity, were keenly aware that something was desperately wrong in their relationship with God. Many of them have confessed to years of doubt about the genuineness of their salvation. Others indicate that they have slipped into the meaningless and futile habit of daily asking the Lord to save them "just in case they are not already saved." That prayer does nothing but add confusion to an already troubled heart because it is not born out of a deep conviction of sin, nor does it bring the sweet certainty of salvation.

In 1 Corinthians 11:28, Paul once again says to the members of the Corinthian church, "let a man examine himself." He is referring here to the kind of proof that comes from testing. So at the beginning of your journey to revival, it is both expedient and profitable to *examine yourself* to see if you are really targeted in the statement *"if My people"* (2 Chr. 7:14). But *what questions should you ask*? And *what evidences should you seek*? Let our text, Romans 8:14–16, serve as a simple guide.

I. Am I on an Upward Path?

Paul indicates that those who are the sons of God are those who are "led by the Spirit of God" (Romans 8:14). You should consider whether, from that moment you have identified as the point of your conversion, you can see God's leading in your life along an *upward spiritual path*. This does not mean that the pilgrimage of your life will never be marked by lapses, stumbling, moments of great failure and disappointment, or battles with besetting sin. You might think of your life's journey as being similar to that of a mountain climber whose path consists of many ups and downs. Although his general direction is upward, at times he must go downward in order to find a clearer path. From a distant vantage point, however, we would observe that, regardless of his struggles and brief descents, the basic direction of his path is upward.

There is a common perception today that *becoming* a Christian can be separated from *being* a Christian. But they are inseparable. Often, a person thinks he is saved simply because he can remember that he "prayed the prayer." But what about his life since then? Has he grown closer to the Lord, or farther apart? Has there been little or no spiritual growth in his life since the point of conversion? Would having heard him pray twenty years ago be the same as hearing him pray today? Is his devotional life different? Are his commitments different? Has his sensitivity to sin and hatred of it diminished or grown? *Change is the very essence of genuine conversion.*

This thought that *becoming* a Christian can be separated from *being* a Christian is errant and must be replaced by the correct and scriptural perspective. The Scripture clearly teaches that we are not saved by our good works (Eph. 2:8–9). But the Scripture does insist that people who are genuinely born again will give evidence of their salvation by their behavior. In other words, *belief cannot be separated from behavior.*

In the Sermon on the Mount, our Lord reminds us that *"not everyone who says to Me, 'Lord, Lord' shall enter the kingdom of heaven, but he who does the will of My Father in heaven"* (Matt. 7:21). On another occasion, He chided those who called

Him Lord and yet did not *do what He said* (see Luke 6:46). The point is that true saving faith affects the way we believe.

One of the most sobering statements in Scripture regarding the change that takes place in the life of a believer is found in 1 John 3:6–9: "Whoever abides in Him does not sin. Whoever sins has neither seen Him nor known Him. Little children, let no one deceive you. He who practices righteousness is righteous, just as He is righteous. He who sins is of the devil, for the devil has sinned from the beginning. For this purpose the Son of God was manifested, that He might destroy the works of the devil. Whoever has been born of God does not sin, for His seed remains in him; and he cannot sin, because he has been born of God."

In this passage the references to sin imply sinning in a *continual* sense. For instance, we might read the passage this way: "Whosoever abides in Him does not keep on committing the same old sins in the same old way."

For too long people have excused their spiritual deadness by including themselves in that group they call "the backslidden." But earlier in John's letter, he points out that anyone who is habitually backslidden has probably never been genuinely born into God's family. "They went out from us, but they were not of us; for if they had been of us, they would have continued with us; but they went out that they might be made manifest, that none of them were of us" (1 John 2:19).

The fact that genuine salvation produces godly behavior is irrefutably stated in Hebrews 11, the roll call of the great men and women of faith. As you read this passage, you will discover that not one of these individuals is famous simply because of what he or she thought or felt. Each one is famous for the *behavior* that characterized his or her faith; Abel *offered*, Enoch *walked*, Noah *prepared*, Abraham *went out*. In other words, though we are not saved by works, neither are we saved by the kind of faith that does not produce good works.

Some years ago, I heard the chaplain of a Rotary Club pray this prayer: "Lord, be with these Rotarians today, for we know Thy way is the Rotary way." This misguided man had reduced his expectations of the remarkable change that takes place at conversion to the point that it was no more demanding than the creed of a community service group! And, sadly, he has great company.

With all due respect to that good organization mentioned above, meeting Jesus—passing from death to life, having old things pass away and all things become new, having our destination changed from an eternity in hell to any eternity in heaven, surrendering our lives to One who is the Creator and the sustainer of the universe and acknowledging Him as King of kings and Lord of lords—will produce a life that is so different no *mere* creed can embody it. For this reason, the first certain sign of salvation is a life on an *upward path*.

II. Have I Made an Outward Profession?

"For you did not receive the spirit of bondage again to fear, but you received the Spirit of adoption by whom we cry out, 'Abba, Father'" (Rom. 8:15). *Abba* is a word of tender endearment and communion. It is more like the term *daddy* than the more formal word *father*. Paul is saying that the true believer is set free from the bondage of sin and the law and adopted as a child of God. He is not intimidated as he openly cries out to the Father on the basis of a new and intimate relationship.

In the passage above there is a sense of eagerness to confess the Lord. Jesus even indicated that the fear of *confession* before men indicates a lack of *possession* of genuine salvation. "Therefore whoever confesses Me before men, him I will also confess before My Father who is in heaven. But whoever denies Me before men, him I will also deny before My Father who is in heaven" (Matt. 10:32–33).

Many people think that anything *personal* is also meant to be kept *private*. When asked about their salvation, they will tell you that their religion is a personal matter. While it is a personal matter, it was never intended to be kept private or secret. My marriage ceremony was an intensely personal issue, but it was not private. The ring I wear on my finger is a constant visual reminder to everyone I meet that I belong to someone.

The Lord is so interested in our outward profession that He even included it as a part of His Great Commission. Disciples were not only to be *made* but were also to be *marked* by the ordinance of baptism, a striking picture of a person's death to an old life and resurrection to new. This new life is to be characterized by the behavior expected from the very first disciples: "Teaching them to observe [or do] all things that I have commanded you" (Matt. 28:20). Every believer should be unashamed to say it, show it, and share it. Jesus indicated that those who love Him will keep His commandments, and those who subscribe to His lordship will do what He says.

Many professing believers have no sense of victory in their lives because they stubbornly refuse to follow the Lord's commands regarding an outward profession of faith. I remember one prominent church leader confessing that after having been baptized as a young man, he later became deeply convinced of his sin and his need of genuine salvation. In deep brokenness he received Christ by faith. The next Sunday, when the altar call was given in his church, he started to go down the aisle and tell his pastor what had happened, but then he thought, *I'm a church leader. People would be disillusioned if they thought I had been in a position of leadership all these years and was not genuinely saved. Making this decision would cause confusion, and I certainly don't want to do that. Anyway, salvation is a personal matter, and what really matters is that I have trusted Christ.*

With tears this man confessed to me that through the ensuing years he became increasingly more concerned about what people thought of him than what God knew about him. He then admitted that *he* knew there would never be spiritual victory in his life until he made an outward profession of his faith. When he did openly confess his faith before his church family, many other men, in brokenness and with tears, came to the altar to receive Christ and follow Him in scriptural baptism.

It is precisely this reason that our Lord demands an *outward profession* on the part of those who know Him.

III. Do I Have an Inward Peace?

Romans 8:16 should encourage every believer: "The Spirit Himself bears witness with our spirit that we are children of God." Here is the crucial, final, and inescapable evidence of genuine salvation. It is the witness of God's Holy Spirit with our spirit, affirming to us that we belong to God.

When people ask me to help them discover whether they are truly born again, I often encourage them to pray, then ask God to speak to them through 1 John because John's First Epistle sheds great light on the evidences of salvation. In 1 John 4:13 we are reminded, "By this we know that we abide in Him, and He in us, because He has given us of His Spirit."

I have known people who were in such turmoil about their salvation that they would play intellectual gymnastics about the issue. "Let's see," they would say, "in Revelation 3:20 Jesus said He would come into my heart if I asked Him. I have asked Him; therefore, He must be in my heart." Unfortunately, such mental gymnastics never really help, because peace never comes, and the doubts return: *Am I really saved? Did I say the right words? Have I done the right things? Was I really sincere? Did I have enough faith?* And since every preacher they hear has a different way of describing the conversion experience, they find themselves on a spiritual merry-go-round, growing dizzy with the many suggestions of different prayers, postures, and performances.

Here is what Paul is telling us: After you strip away your "conversion experience," your good life, your church membership, and even the testimony of others who say "Well, if anybody is saved, you're saved," *the truly born-again person still has a deep underlying sense of assurance that is given to him by the Spirit of God.* None of the former will get you into heaven. In fact, there are many people who have all of those spiritual dominoes properly aligned, and yet the doubt remains. *What is missing is the witness of God's Spirit.*

While in college and dating my wife-to-be, I was perplexed to hear her say on more than one occasion, "Sometimes I wonder if I am really saved." I just knew she must be a Christian. After all, she had made her *decision* in one of the largest churches in the state and was *baptized* by one of the most noted pastors in the area. She had grown up in church and even surrendered her life to a *missionary call.* In fact, our first date was to a Wednesday night worship service where she was leading a missions group for young girls! Everything about her life indicated she was a Christian.

During the early years of our marriage, when Jeannie again expressed doubts about her salvation, I logically convinced her that she was truly born again. But God's Spirit prevailed! In the fourth year of our marriage, she told me, "It makes no difference what either of us say or think; *I don't have inward peace!* I know I am lost!" That night she became a new creature in Christ.

It would be difficult for me to describe the change that occurred in her life. I thought she was already the perfect lady, but *her transformed life became a challenge to my own.* Her insatiable hunger for the Word of God was one of the most notable changes. She also developed an earnest desire to see others come to Christ. Within hours of her conversion, she stood before the church, confessed her faith, and followed the Lord in baptism. Through the years, she has repeatedly remarked about the *wonderful peace* that the Spirit of God has brought to her heart.

Many people go through life with recurring doubts about the issue of their salvation. They often pray that prayer which I have called the Nothing Prayer: "Lord, if I'm not saved, save me." As I have already noted, such a prayer is not born out of a *genuine conviction* that they are lost. Nor does it bring *certainty* of salvation. If it did, they would have no need to repeat it again and again. *The Spirit would bear witness with their spirit that they were children of God.*

There is a great deal of prayer for revival these days—personal revival, church revival, and prayer for a national awakening. I believe we desperately need revival in each of these areas. But it is impossible to "revive" those who have never been made alive by the grace of God in the first place. The great revival prayer in 2 Chronicles 7:14 is to be offered, says God, by "*My people who are called by My name."* It may not be revival but genuine conversion that many people in our churches need to experience.

Some years ago, after preaching this message on "The Three Certain Signs of Salvation," I was confronted by an irritated church member who exclaimed, "You're just trying to sow doubt in the hearts of these fine church members. We are all right with God, and we don't need to ask any questions about our faith!"

Beneath his anger, I sensed a tinge of fear; fear that an examination of himself would prove that true faith was a missing element in his own life. Sadly, he adamantly refused such a spiritual examination. Had he done so and found himself outside the faith, it would have been a simple matter to repent of sin and unbelief and turn to Christ for His grace, mercy, and genuine salvation. But if in the process of such examination he had found himself to be a member of God's family, then he would have been a candidate for genuine revival. Genuine revival comes to those of whom the Lord says, "These are *My people.*"

One of these days Jesus *will* come to call His own family members home to Himself. *If it were today, would you be named among them?*

27

The Family Connection

GENESIS 2:21-25 NASB

Ted H. Traylor

Pastor, Olive Baptist Church
Pensacola, Florida

WE HAVE BEEN TALKING RECENTLY about connecting with God, with
our church, and with our community. The Bible tells us that the family connection is also important. Listen to these words about the
family from the second chapter of Genesis:

So the LORD God caused a deep sleep to fall upon the
man, and he slept; then He took one of his ribs, and closed
up the flesh at that place. And the LORD God fashioned into a
woman the rib which He had taken from the man, and
brought her to the man. And the man said, "This is now
bone of my bones, and flesh of my flesh; she shall be called
Woman, because she was taken out of Man." For this cause a
man shall leave his father and his mother, and be joined to his
wife; and they shall become one flesh. And the man and his
wife were both naked and were not ashamed (Gen. 2:21–25).

You will never have a great family until you have a great marriage. Having children does not make a great family unless there is a
marvelous marriage providing the bedrock to build that family on.
Here is a definition of family: one man and one woman, united in
marriage for life, and if God chooses, children either biological or
adopted.

It is a sad day in America when we have to define marriage, but we must. There are bills today being debated by legislators in the halls of state houses throughout the United States as well as in the U.S. Congress trying to define a family. Now mark this down: If one man can marry another man, what is to keep us from having laws that say one man can marry three women? Once the biblical guideline of truth is removed and no fences are built, anything is possible. When God is not in our lives, there are no restraints. When you take God out of the equation, every perversion is possible.

Without revival and moral revitalization in America, all types of perversion will be common in the family structure of our nation. That's where we're headed. We're on a slippery slope where anything goes. We have to define the family. It is not one woman and another woman. It is not one man and another man. It is not one man and a multiplicity of wives.

A family is one man and one woman, united in marriage for life, and if God chooses, children either biological or adopted. How do you have a great marriage? Out of this text I want to review four things that I call *marriage markers*. There are many others, but I want to give you these four. Then I want to focus on the family and the connection that we need to make as we make our marriages stronger.

I. Marriage Markers

Let's look at the four marriage markers that come right out of this text. The first marriage marker is *monogamy*. One man, one woman. There is no place for polygamy. Some men in the Old Testament had a multitude of wives. Polygamy was practiced, but nowhere do you find Scripture affirming or supporting polygamy. The monogamous relationship is the biblical pattern. Hear me on this: The Bible does not *support* everything that the Bible *reports*. Just because it reports a fact does not mean that it encourages or supports that fact. The biblical support is for monogamy. One man, one woman, one life. So the first marriage marker is monogamy. It is ridiculous that we have to talk about this, but we have a generation growing up where truth is so distorted that we need to go back to the essentials.

Recently the *Pensacola News Journal* reported that one company was taking a plane load of nude passengers. They were going to some island in the Caribbean. The plan was for the people to get on the plane and then disrobe. It was a nude flight. America today sees nothing wrong with that; just let everybody do what they want to do.

The culture in which we live says that all rules are gone, all fences are down. We must see marriage as monogamy. We have to come back to the basics and start right there. I cannot believe I have to take time even to discuss this, but the Bible says one man, one woman, one life. That's God's marker. It is the only way for a culture to survive. One man and one woman united for life.

Marriage marker number two is *fidelity*. Our text points out that a man and woman in marriage will become one flesh. After one man and one woman marry, they are together for one life, and they know only each other. Keep your Bibles open at Genesis chapter 2 and go to Hebrews chapter 13, verse 4: "Let marriage be held in honor among all, and let the marriage bed be undefiled; for fornicators and adulterers God will judge." The marriage bed is to be undefiled. This means that nobody else is to be in your life sexually—only your spouse.

Fornicators and adulterers God will judge. Paul went so far as to say that fornicators and adulterers will not see the kingdom of God (see 1 Cor. 6:9–10). What Paul said is that if you are a fornicator and an adulterer and that is your lifestyle, you are not saved. You are lost, and the Spirit of God does not reside in you. If you disagree, don't take it up with me. Take it up with God's Word. Sexual relationships are reserved for the confines of marriage. This is God's way.

Yesterday we had a wedding here in the worship center. One of our staff members got married. It was a beautiful wedding. In the middle of the ceremony, the bride took off her purity ring and gave it back to her father and said, "I have been true to my commitment." I wanted to stand up and shout, "Glory to God!" Somebody should have shouted.

If you want to have a great family, start with a great marriage. That marriage begins with monogamy, and it continues with fidelity. You should be faithful not only before you get married, but once you get married, you should be involved sexually only with your marriage partner because you will not defile the marriage bed.

Marriage marker number three is *longevity:* "For this cause a man shall leave his father and his mother, and shall cleave to his wife; and they shall become one flesh" (Gen. 2:24). How long do they cleave? It should be for a lifetime.

There are a lot of prenuptial agreements being written by couples today. I had a pastor call me a while back. He had been asked to officiate at a wedding for a young couple. He said, "I have a young man whose grandfather has left him a multimillion-dollar company, and he's marrying a lovely girl in our church. But his grandfather will change the will and leave him out of it if this young man does not get a prenuptial agreement saying that this multimillion-dollar company is set aside for the grandfather's descendants only."

I said, "You mean he doesn't want the girl to get half of it if they get divorced?"

He said, "That's exactly it."

I responded, "That young man needs to decide if he's marrying his grandfather or his wife."

This shows the current thinking about marriage. We know that marriages come apart all the time. But I got in my marriage for good. I told my wife if she leaves, I'm going with her! That's just the way it is. It's called longevity. God's Word says we are to cleave. Cleave and never leave. That word *cleave* means "to glue." The couple is glued together and cannot come apart. Marriage is meant for longevity. Romans 7:2 tells us that we are to be bound together until death. Ecclesiastes 5:5 warns us that it's better never to vow than to vow and not live up to the promise.

Yesterday before I came to the wedding for that lovely young couple, I went to a sixtieth wedding anniversary celebration. What a marvelous thing it was to see that wonderful, saintly, and godly couple. We prayed over them as tears fell down their cheeks. These weren't their first tears. They had experienced sixty years of joy and sadness—but sixty wonderful years.

Longevity is a marriage marker—staying together until the end. We have an entire generation among us today that has been taught by our culture that marital longevity is not the way. If we're going to have great families, we must commit ourselves for the long haul. "For better or worse, richer or poorer, in sickness or in health, until death do us part." That's what you promised when you got married. Be a person of your word.

The fourth marriage marker is *intimacy:* "And the man and his wife were both naked and were not ashamed" (Gen. 2:25). This verse speaks of intimacy. The world has sold us a bill of goods by making us think that sex is evil. Sex is God's marvelous gift to us. And God intended for sex to be experienced within the confines of marriage. Take your Bibles and turn to 1 Corinthians 7 and read the first seven verses. Paul is writing to the church at Corinth. Celibacy in and out of marriage had become the norm in that time. Celibacy had become so dominant in Paul's day that even in the church it was seen as desirable not only to be sexually pure before marriage but to abstain from intimacy in marriage.

Paul dealt with this issue when he said, "Now concerning the things about which you wrote, it is good for a man not to touch a woman" (1 Cor. 7:1–2). Now, what he means by that is the sexual relationship. He's speaking of the sexual act. It's good for a man not to touch a woman, but "because of immoralities, [let] each man have his own wife, and each woman have her own husband. Let the husband fulfill his duty to his wife, and likewise also the wife to her husband." The whole context is sexual. There is a duty and an obligation for sexual satisfaction in marriage:

> The wife does not have authority over her own body, but the husband does; and likewise also the husband does not have authority over his own body, but the wife does. Stop depriving one another, except by agreement for a time, so that you may devote yourselves to prayer, and come together again so that Satan will not tempt you because of your lack

of self-control. But this I say by way of concession, not of command. Yet I wish that all men were even as I myself am [Paul was single]. However, each man has his own gift from God, one in this manner, and another in that (1 Cor. 7:4–7).

These seven verses speak to us about the intimate, sexual relationship that a man and his wife are to enjoy. Our problem today is that we have single people who are living sexually like married people, and we have married people who are living sexually like single people. When married people come to the place that they are deprived of sex in their marriage, you can mark this down: Something is not right. In a biblical marriage you will find intimacy. The absence of true biblical intimacy in marriage has contributed to the current divorce rate in our world.

Some of you are probably asking, "Pastor, what does it mean to stop depriving? How often? When?" Every one of us is different. Every family is different. What may be depriving for one relationship would not be for another. But hear me: If you have lost the intimacy factor in your sexual relationship at home, if will affect your children and everything in our life. When your sexual drive is closed within your marriage, there will be a closure of your spirit, your mind, and your soul.

There was a time when I probably would have been fired for addressing this topic so openly in a worship service, but we in the church must deal with this issue honestly and forthrightly. Your children need to see that there is still a fire burning in your life and in your soul. You'll never have a great marriage if the intimacy factor is not a vital part of your relationship.

Now hear me on this: If you plan to get married, you will probably spend a large amount of money getting ready for a thirty-minute ceremony. You will spend hours going through all the details. You should spend some of that money and much of that time not getting ready for the *wedding* but getting prepared for the *marriage*. Spend some time in counseling and reading and getting ready for your marriage.

II. Essentials for Building a Good Marriage

Now let's move quickly to four things that you need to do if you are to build your marriage into a great marriage. These are essentials for building a good marriage relationship.

The first marriage and family essential is *growth*. Now, I do not mean numerical growth but growth between the two of you. You must be growing and stretching and knowing each other better than you knew each other last year. And how do you do that? You go to the second essential for building a good marriage. The way you grow is through *communication*.

Communication is more than just the transmission of information. A lot of men say, "Well, I can communicate." This usually means that you pass on information, but you do not communicate. This involves emotions and feelings. It's a two-pronged approach. When you deal with communication, you must deal also with emotions and feelings. Communication is important. You don't just pass on information. You reveal your true self. This is real communication.

Marriage essential number three is what I call *conflict resolution*. When conflict is properly dealt with, it becomes a growth point in marriage. There will be conflict in any relationship, whether dad to son, sibling to sibling, or husband to wife. You must learn how to deal with conflict. Anger is a part of every relationship. Most of us deal with it in one of two ways. Either we vent or we suppress. We suppress or we vent. You must learn to deal constructively with your anger. You do that through communication, and that means dialogue. Normally the woman will communicate out of her feelings, and the man will communicate from the logical side. That is not always the case, but often it is. You must bring these two different approaches together through healthy methods of conflict resolution.

Marriage essential number four is *Jesus Christ*. Look with me at Mark 15:21. Jesus is being carried to be crucified. "They pressed into service a passer-by coming from the country, Simon of Cyrene (the father of Alexander and Rufus), to bear His cross." Look at the parentheses here: (*the father of Alexander and Rufus*). They pressed this father of these two boys into service to bear the cross of Jesus.

I believe these two boys are named in this account because they were there and they saw Jesus coming with the cross. They also saw their father pick up the cross and carry it the rest of the way to the crucifixion site. Now mark this down: If you want to have a great family, let the children see their father bearing the cross of the Lord Jesus. When fathers get under the cross, the Alexanders and Rufuses of this world will never be the same again. When children see their father at the cross, the family is well on its way to supernatural living.

Maybe Alexander and Rufus said, "That man's dying for us, but let me tell you, our father helped the Messiah perform His eternal mission." When little boys see their fathers helping Jesus perform His eternal mission, the family will grow in the knowledge and grace of the Lord.

28

Perfect Peace

PHILIPPIANS 4:6–7 NASB

Claude Thomas
Senior Pastor, First Baptist Church, Euless, Texas

WE'RE IN A SERIES OF MESSAGES entitled "Great Expectations." Man would say, "Blessed is he who expects nothing, for he shall not be disappointed." That's a pessimistic view of life. But a biblical view encourages us to have expectations that are great.

I've been reading about the richest people in the world. I want you to know, they've got some bucks. I am encouraged by that because I believe that God has something to say to us about the fullness and the riches of life. Today we're going to celebrate what God offers to us. God offers something everyone wants, something everyone searches for, something everyone longs for. It is peace in life. Many of us carry heavy burdens every day. Our hearts and minds are torn apart. We are dealing with difficult things. And the question is, Is it possible for us to live in peace in the life we are experiencing right now? With the hand we've been dealt, can we deal with life in such a way that we can have peace? This is something that concerns us. We're concerned about it internationally right now.

Is it possible for the nations to have peace? We've almost come to the conclusion that it's not possible for international peace to exist. The international turmoil is so great that it's challenging our hearts and our sense of security and changing our vocabularies. In the past decade we've learned some words that we did not know before. We've learned terms like *scud,* and *stealth,* and *sorties,* and *weapons of mass destruction.* We now know that a *patriot* is more than a colorful early American. A *tomahawk* is something other than a primitive weapon used by American Indians. And a *wild weasel* isn't an untamed rodent. A *blitz* is more than a football play, and an *ordinance* is more than something that happens in the church. And *carpet bombing* isn't simply the children spilling candy all over the living room floor, and *germ warfare* is not just a new strain of the flu that we have to battle.

Our nerves have been tested, our emotions have been strained, and our hearts have been sickened because this is an uncertain hour in our world. International peace? We're very skeptical about it. We are concerned about our own national peace.

There are some things we can't do anything about, but what about personal peace? What about the possibility of experiencing personal peace? Now that's something hard to come by. It doesn't come easily. Matter of fact, if you look at America at large, you will say that America is not doing too well with personal peace. The number one drug consumed by Americans is the tranquilizer. That indicates that we're not doing too well on the matter of personal peace. You say, "Well, I'm not on the drug." OK, let's just see how we're doing. Let's take a test. Let's have a little fun with it. This is a fill-in-the-blank test. Let's see how we're relating to the struggle of finding real peace.

Complete these sentences. I'm ready to throw in the ____ (towel). I'm at the end of my ____ (rope). My life is falling ____ (apart). I'm at my wit's ____ (end). I feel like resigning from the human ____ (race). You probably are not too excited about it, but you knew the answers. This is a good indication that we are struggling; at least, we know about the struggle to find personal peace.

But here's good news. We can experience internal and spiritual peace regardless of the adversities we face in life. It doesn't matter what they are. You say, "You don't know what I'm experiencing." No, I don't. But I do know what the Bible says. We can experience internal and spiritual peace regardless of the adversities of life we experience. You say, "How do we know that?" We learn from a person in the Bible, and that's what we're going to consider today. He's a real person who has a real life, and he's in some of the most unlikely circumstances, but he brings us assurance in the midst of those uncertain circumstances. He assures us that we can have a personal, spiritual, internal peace.

Who is this man? What kind of person is this who says that? What does he know about it? His name is the apostle Paul. We will see that he's not speaking as a theorist, but he's speaking experientially. This is something that he knew about through adverse circumstances.

In our text today we find him in prison in Rome. He's facing the probability of death. But listen to what he said to his friends at Philippi: "Be anxious for nothing, but in everything by prayer and supplication with thanksgiving let your requests be made known to God. And the peace of God, which surpasses all comprehension, will guard your hearts and your minds in Christ Jesus" (Phil. 4:6–7).

Paul wrote these words to his friends to give them a confidence that they could experience a peace that was radically different, fundamentally different from the peace they ordinarily felt.

I. We Need God's Peace

The world could never provide this peace. The peace Paul talked about was different from what the world offers. It's a peace that each one of us needs. Someone may ask, "What peace is that?" The peace that we need is the peace of God. The peace that we most often seek and we most often think we need is circumstantial peace. This is a peace where there's no conflict in our lives, where we have resolved all the conflicts, and we have no turmoil and no trouble. The only problem with this is that it's dependent on something else that is usually beyond our control. If something goes wrong in this kind of peace, suddenly our lives become chaotic. Our peace is taken from us because it is dependent on circumstances. As we know, circumstances can change quickly.

My wife taught our youngest granddaughter a little game based on two words—*happy* and *sad*. Jan taught Ellie to have a happy face when she said "happy." And when she said "sad," Ellie had a sad face. Well, as time went along a little bit, Ellie took it to the extreme. She would bow her head down and get a frown on her face, and she would say, "S-a-a-a-d." "Happy!" "S-a-a-a-d." So I wanted to see how long Ellie would repeat the sequence. I said, "Happy!" And she said, "Happy!" I said, "S-a-a-a-d," and she said, "S-a-a-a-d." "Happy!" "Happy!" "S-a-a-a-d." "S-a-a-a-d." And just like that, changing quickly.

If our peace is dependent on our circumstances, it can change just like that because our circumstances can change so quickly. We need more than circumstantial peace that is determined by things beyond our control. This is what Paul said to the Philippians: "I want to assure you of something. There is a peace you can experience regardless of what you are going through. It is the peace of God." Get the picture? The peace of God. And he's saying that this peace is not determined by circumstances. It's fundamentally different, radically different from the world's peace. How is it different?

First of all, it is *supernatural peace*. It is a peace that "surpasses all comprehension" (v. 7). Now what is he talking about? What does that really mean? It means that it is a peace beyond normal human understanding. And it is a peace that is beyond normal human experience. And it is a peace that is impossible for normal human beings to produce. It is not normal peace. It is supernatural peace. When we understand that it is supernatural peace, we understand that, regardless of what happens, the peace of God is greater than the circumstances of life. He is supernatural. Above the natural adversities that we experience, God is greater, and the peace that He offers is a supernatural peace.

Second, it's not only supernatural; it is *spiritual and internal*. Regardless of what's going on in the externals of our lives, regardless of what's going on with the emotional and physical conflicts of life, there is a peace that goes beyond that. It is the peace that reaches down into the deepest parts of our lives. That's the kind of peace that Jesus gave to His followers in the upper room. He said to them just before the crucifixion: "I want to give you some news. I want to tell you what's going to happen. I'm going to be leaving you. I'm leaving you, and I'm leaving the earth" (see John 15:25–27). When they heard that, they were distraught. They were troubled. They were agitated.

Jesus wanted to encourage them and support them. He wanted them to have this peace, so He said to them: "Peace I leave with you; My peace I give to you; not as the world gives do I give to you. Do not let your heart be troubled, nor let it be fearful" (John 14:27). Jesus offered His followers a supernatural peace that was internal and spiritual. Regardless of what was going on, they would have peace. After His resurrection, He had appeared to them, and they again were troubled because things had not gone as they thought they should go. Things looked worse than they thought they had ever looked. Jesus appeared to them and said, "Peace be with you" (John 20:26). This was not normal peace. It was supernatural peace. It was internal peace. It was spiritual peace.

Understand that the apostle Paul wasn't speaking as a theorist in an ivory palace—writing this down to send it to people in the midst of the problems of life and fighting the battles of life. The apostle Paul was writing out of bad circumstances. There was conflict in the church at Philippi. There were two women in the church who couldn't get along. It was affecting the peace and harmony of the entire church. The church that Paul loved, the congregation that had been so generous with him and so good to him, was having trouble. There was church trouble.

There was also relational trouble because there were people who were not friendly to the apostle Paul and his ministry in Philippi. He also had political problems. For doing the right thing, he was put in prison. And here he is in that hole in the ground called the Mammertine Dungeon. He is chained to a rock column. That prison was wet. There was almost a river that flowed through it. Vermin were in that river, rats and rodents and all kinds of crawly creatures. The apostle Paul is not in the best of circumstances, and in all probability he is facing death.

The church that Paul loves and that has been so generous to him is having troubles. People whom he thought he could count on have misrepresented him and attacked him. He thought he could get by since he was a Roman citizen, but he ended up in prison. Everywhere he turns there is trouble in his life. Yet the apostle Paul says, "I want to tell you about a peace that passes all understanding." And he tells the Philippian Christians that this is the peace they can experience.

Not too long ago there was a movie entitled *The Perfect Storm,* based on a storm that struck the New England coastline in the early 1990s. The movie portrayed a storm that was unpredictable. There was nothing man could do to navigate it or negotiate it. It was a perfect storm. Those who study storms tell me that at the heart of the storm, there is a place called the eye. In the eye of the storm it is still and calm. There can be a whirling storm, a tumultuous storm all around, and right in the center of it there is a peaceful calm.

Here's the reality of life for us. God says there may be storms raging all around us. But at the center of our being, deep inside of us, we don't have to be torn apart. The word *anxious* means "to be torn apart." Things are happening that we don't understand, and they are pulling us one way. Things are happening that we feel badly about, and these are pulling us another way. We're being torn apart in heart and mind. Paul says, "No, you don't have to be torn apart." We can be whole at the center of our lives. There is an arena of life that we are able to control, and it's at the center of our being. It is the internal spiritual dimension of our lives. It is there that the apostle Paul says we can have a peace that is perfect peace because it is God's peace.

This peace is not something we can earn, not something we can deserve, not something we can work up, or something we can discover, or something we can make. It is something that is from God. It is peace within. Now that's the peace of God. Every person needs the peace of God. Without the peace of God, there is no peace in life. We need the peace of God that reaches inside.

II. How Can We Have God's Peace?

There are three things that I'm going to share right out of the text that tell us how we can experience the peace of God. First, we can receive Jesus as our Savior. Listen to what Paul says: "And the peace of God . . . will guard your hearts and your minds in Christ Jesus" (Phil. 4:7). Look at the last three words: "in Christ Jesus." They're the most critical words for us if we are to experience peace. Paul is telling us that the peace of God is obtained through a personal relationship. Get this. Mark this down. To have peace from God, you must be at peace with God.

We are not naturally at peace with God. We're naturally at odds with God. We're not aligned with God. Our natural inclination is to be at odds with Him. Do you want to know why so many people are not experiencing inner peace and are going through inner turmoil and conflict instead? It's because they are lacking peace with God. They are not at peace with God because of their sin. Sin separates us from God. It creates guilt in our lives. We begin to feel guilty, and in that guilt we are torn. We're pulled this way and that way. That's what guilt does to us. It tears us apart.

But Jesus is able to remove the guilt. He has the authority to remove the guilt from our lives. He also has the authority and the capability to forgive our sin. So the way to be at peace with God is for Jesus to remove our guilt and bring us forgiveness. If we are not released from the guilt of our sin, there is no peace with God.

A man went to a pastor friend and said to him, "I'm being torn to pieces by guilt. I feel so guilty."

"What do you feel guilty about?"

"Well, I just don't know if God has ever forgiven me?"

"For what?"

"Well, for anything."

The pastor said, "Tell me about it."

The man replied, "I've asked God to forgive me. I've asked Him to forgive me a thousand times."

The pastor apparently thought the man was talking about a thousand different things that he had done wrong that God needed to forgive him of, so he asked, "What do you mean you've asked Him a thousand times?"

The man replied, "I've asked God to forgive me of the same thing a thousand times."

The pastor said, "You mean you did it over and over again?"

The man said, "No. Only one time. But I've asked Him to forgive me a thousand times."

His pastor friend looked at him and said, "Let me tell you what your problem is. You've asked God 999 times too many. What you should have done is ask God to forgive you one time and thanked Him 999 times for forgiving you."

Here's what happens. We come to Jesus and say to him, "Lord this is me, and this is what's wrong in my life, and here's the problem in my life, or here's the turmoil in my life. Will you forgive me of this sin?" We don't have to ask Him a dozen times. One time is sufficient. He's not hard of hearing, and He's not incapable of forgiving, and so immediately we are forgiven, and we are at peace with God. Some people may say, "Well, I've been there, but it's sort of degenerated." We obtain peace with God through a personal faith in Jesus. But get this: You maintain peace with God through an intimate relationship with Jesus. The phrase "in Christ Jesus" not only pictures the beginning of a relationship; it pictures the continuance of a relationship, one that is becoming more and more intimate.

There will come a time in our lives when things happen that we can't control. And there will be conflict. If we're trying to find peace by eradicating the conflict, it will not come. The peace that we can count on isn't the absence of conflict, but it's the presence of the Lord in spite of the conflict. We need to understand that. We can't do enough to keep life from having its problems. We can't be wise enough, good enough, smart enough. It's a part of life. We will have our turmoils and our troubles. We will have our conflicts and circumstances that are completely adverse to anything we want. So the peace we need is not the absence of conflict. Peace will come when we are aware of the presence of the Lord.

Years ago when people rode in wagons and carriages, there was a man who owned a plantation. He had a driver for his carriage. They had been to a social gathering. After the gathering the man got into his carriage, and they were driving along when he heard his driver scream. The driver said, "You won't believe what's happening. You've got to see it. Stars are falling. The sky is falling. The world's coming to an end!" Stars were going all over the sky. The driver of the carriage was looking at a meteor shower.

The man who was riding in the carriage stuck his head outside and looked up and saw what was happening. He knew about these phenomena. He said to his driver, "I want you to fix your focus over there." And he pointed his driver toward the North Star. "You see that bright star shining in the sky?" he asked. "Just keep looking at that star, and if it falls, let me know."

When our world is coming apart and the sky is falling, we need to focus on the North Star of our lives—Jesus—and He will bring us peace. This peace is obtained through faith in Christ. It is maintained through intimacy with Christ. Have you put your faith in Christ? And if you have, are you maintaining peace in your life through an intimate relationship with Him? Peace comes to us when we accept Jesus Christ as Lord and Savior of our lives.

Second, we experience the peace of God not only when we accept Jesus but also when we ask for God's provision when we face life's conflicts. We all have things that bring emotional, physical, and spiritual conflict into our lives. Some of you are going through that right now. You're experiencing conflict. It may be in your relationships in your family. It may be with your child. Or some of you may be having conflict with your parents or your boyfriend or girlfriend. It may be conflict between husband and wife. It may be between brother or sister. It may be in the workplace, but we all know about conflict in life. I need to remind us that there are some things we can't do anything about. And the question is, "What do we do when there's nothing we can do?"

When that happens, we need to come to grips with two things. When there are conflicts, there are some things we can change.

Someone said the solution to those kinds of conflicts is perspiration. Just begin to work at it. But there are other kinds of conflict that we can't do anything about. What we do in these situations is to solve it by supplication, by prayer.

Here's what I suggest. Pray about everything. We don't know which conflicts we can settle and which we can't solve. So pray about everything. That's exactly what Paul said to the Philippians. He told them to pray when things happened that destroyed their peace. He said that they should not be anxious for anything. Don't be torn apart by the circumstances and conflicts of your life.

Paul told the Philippian Christians how to pray. He did it by using four words. First, he said, "Be anxious for nothing, but in everything by prayer" (v. 6). That's the first word: *prayer.* What does that word mean? The word *prayer* here has to do with coming before God and acknowledging who God is. In other words, it has the element of worship. Worship is coming into the presence of God and acknowledging who He is. This kind of prayer is a generic term that carries with it the awareness that we know we are in the presence of God.

Notice the second word: "By prayer and *supplication*" (v. 6). Supplication involves a definite request to God. You go before God and you make your specific requests.

Recently one of the men of our church came to me. In his family there has been enough turmoil to wreck the spirit of any man. But he's solid in his faith. He said that there was something going on in his family, with his work, and with his finances that were beyond his control. He had done everything he knew to do. He said, "I was sitting in my chair praying when the phone rang. I picked up the phone. It was a person whom I had no idea would intervene in my life to help me in any way. That person said, 'I want to tell you I can help you.' With the ring of the phone, there was a definite answer to my prayer."

If you're having challenges in your marriage, tell God it's in your marriage. If it's in your finances, tell God it's in your finances. If it's in your attitude, tell God it's your attitude. If it's in your workplace, tell God it's your workplace. Whatever it is, ask God, and be definite. Supplication is specific. Paul said, "By prayer and supplication with thanksgiving let your requests" (v. 6). Stop at that word *requests*. A request is asking God with an anticipation of an answer. We go to God and ask Him specifically about something, and we anticipate an answer. When we pray according to the Word of God and the way of God, there will always be an answer. It doesn't mean we know everything about the Word of God; it doesn't mean we know everything about the way of God. But it does mean we know enough to defer to God and His Word and His way. So you go to God and make your specific request.

Here's the way to do that. Go to God and make a specific request. Admit that you don't know everything about it. Acknowledge that you have limitations, but tell God what is happening. Tell Him about the conflict and turmoil. Tell Him that you just can't seem to get any peace. Say, "God, I'm asking You to intervene. But I'm going to defer to You, knowing that You know what's best, knowing that You will do what's best." You anticipate that God will answer in a way that He knows is best.

Let me tell you what happens. When we begin to pray like that, here's what we need to do. We need to start thanking God for answered prayer before we ever sense that the answer has come. That's why Paul says, "By prayer and supplication with *thanksgiving* let your requests be made known to God" (v. 6). If you've been a person of prayer for any time at all, you've seen God answer your past prayers. And if you walk with God in intimacy today, you know that God answers prayers in your life in the present time. Now you're asking God to do something in the future, so what you're doing is thanking Him in advance.

Paul told the people in the church at Philippi how to pray, and he told them what to pray. He said we should pray for *everything*. "But in everything by prayer and supplication with thanksgiving let your requests be made known to God" (v. 6). Pray about everything. There's nothing too large, nothing too small, nothing so profound, nothing seemingly so incidental in life that we don't pray about it.

We pray about everything. It's a good thing to do. Does it make a difference? I want to tell you it does.

I read this week about a little boy, a preschooler. He was the only child in the family. Well, he wanted a baby brother. The thing he did not know was that his mother was pregnant. But he was just aggravating his dad and mom to death. He kept saying, "I want a baby brother." When it came down to the last trimester of his mother's pregnancy, his daddy took him aside. He wanted to encourage him in prayer and teach him to become a person of prayer. He said, "I tell you what, son. Let's ask God and see if God won't answer your prayer. Now every day, you ask God to give you a baby brother."

Well, the little boy began to pray. Every day he would ask his daddy, "Has my little brother come yet? Has God given me my little brother?"

Every day the dad said, "No, but just keep praying."

After about a month the little fellow got discouraged and just quit asking God. He quit praying. About two months later, they had twin boys. They brought them home, and the father said, "Come here. I want you to see what God has done." He pulled the little blanket from one little baby's face and said, "That's your baby brother." And he pulled the blanket from the other little fellow's face and said, "And this is your other baby brother. Aren't you glad you prayed?"

The little boy looked up at his daddy and said, "Aren't you glad I quit praying?"

We are to pray about everything. Perfect peace comes to us from God, and we experience it when we connect with Christ, when we communicate with Christ and ask Him for His help.

III. God's Peace Will Protect You from All Assaults

If you accept Jesus Christ as Savior, you connect with Him. If you actively pray, you communicate with Him. I'm suggesting that you anticipate the fulfillment of His promise and have confidence in Him. We're not talking about confidence in our prayers. We're talking about confidence in Him. It's not our prayers that make it possible for God to do what He does. God is able to do what He does because God is God. So anticipate that God's peace will protect your heart and your mind against any and all assaults.

This summer while we were in Europe, my wife and I had the privilege of going to Edinburgh, Scotland. At the top of the hill on High Street there is a huge castle. We went up and through the castle. It was on a high hill, and there was a wall all around the castle. In ancient times people lived inside castles, and a part of the whole complex was a giant wall around it. And on the outside of the wall, there was a moat. The people lived inside those walls, behind those gates, and on the other side of that moat for protection from the assault of the enemies who would attack them to destroy their way of life and their peace.

Paul uses a wonderful picture to paint what God does for us and the peace He gives us. "The peace of God . . . will guard your hearts and your minds" (v. 7). The word *guard* is a military word, and it refers to a garrison of soldiers who took a stand around a city. The soldiers were there to protect the city from attack. That's the word Paul used. So Paul said to the Philippians, "The peace of God is a garrison of soldiers around your heart and your mind." Our hearts and our minds are brought together by God when we receive Jesus, when we walk closely with Christ, when we are intimate with Him. That's called wholeness. That's called peace. Then the peace of God builds a garrison around our hearts and our minds so the way we think and the way we feel are brought together. God does that.

Regardless of the conflicts we experience in life, whatever they may be, regardless of the turmoil of life, whatever it may be, there is at the center of our being a sense of peace, unity, completeness, and wholeness. And the peace of God is a garrison to protect it. Regardless of what creates turmoil externally, the peace of God is like a garrison of soldiers at our hearts and minds.

This peace is a supernatural shield. When the darts of the enemy are shot toward our minds and hearts, the peace of God does not allow them to penetrate our hearts and minds. At the core of our being, we are at peace. Our hearts and our minds can be at peace regardless of the turmoil and conflict around us. We don't have to be torn apart.

You may ask if this removes all pain? No. Does it keep us from hurting? No. But we'll not be torn apart. In the center of our being there will be peace. God can, God will, and God does give us a peace that passes all understanding. It is supernatural. It is spiritual. And it is internal. And it's given to us when we connect with Jesus, communicate with Jesus, and have confidence that He will do what He promises.

29

When Life Becomes a Puzzle

ROMANS 8:28–30 NASB

Mac Brunson

Senior Pastor, First Baptist Church, Dallas, Texas

SOMETIMES IN THE EVENING the children and I enjoy putting puzzles together. We began several years ago when I brought home one of those giant twenty-five-piece cartoon puzzles. Once the kids conquered the twenty-five-piece puzzle, I brought home a one hundred-piece puzzle that was a little more difficult. Progressively the puzzles got more complex—five-hundred-piece puzzles, then one thousand, and fifteen hundred. The complicated puzzles had smaller pieces. These were not cartoons but pictures of the countryside, city, or some intricate design.

During the course of putting these more difficult puzzles together, one of the children would become frustrated and say, "I don't know where the pieces go." Then another one would try to force the pieces together and become frustrated when they wouldn't fit. One by one they would walk away to do something less stressful. When I would finish the puzzle, I would call them back over. You could see their eyes light up and a smile crawl across their faces. Then they would call their mother to come and look at what they had done.

For many of us, that is exactly the way life becomes. There are times when life becomes a giant jigsaw puzzle. We become

349

frustrated, and we try to walk away, but we learn we can't. Then we begin to cry out to the Lord, "This just doesn't fit." There are also times when we try to force the pieces of life together and they just don't fit.

Something happens that does not fit our schedule or our plans, and it interrupts our agenda. The pieces just won't fit. Paul wrote to the church in Rome and to the Christians there who were known throughout the entire Roman Empire for their faith. Yet it was a church that was undergoing great persecution. They had kept the faith; they had labored in the face of hostility. They knew what it meant to sacrifice for the kingdom, yet they were entering a period of great persecution. Paul wrote in the eighth chapter of this great book: "We know that God causes all things to work together for good to those who love God, to those who are called according to His purpose" (Rom. 8:28).

Paul was writing to Christians who were going to be persecuted to the point that they would begin to ask, "Why is God allowing this to happen to me?" He was writing to a group of people who would begin to wonder, *Does God really care?* He was writing to a people who were going to wonder if God had abandoned them. They were going to become frustrated over the fact that they wouldn't know where the pieces went or how the pieces fit together.

Paul says that when we are faced with the puzzles of life, we need to understand that God knows where the pieces go and how they fit together. I want you to see this for yourselves in the Word of God.

I. God Assures Us That His Design for Our Lives Will Not Be Frustrated

Paul says, "We know"(Rom. 8:28). The word that he uses means that we know with an understanding, with a certainty, with an assurance that in the midst of life when adversity overtakes us, this will not frustrate the will of God for our lives. It is not a "feel so," or a "guess so," or a "suppose so"—it is a "know so" kind of knowing.

How many times have you said, "If I could only know the outcome. If only I knew what was going to happen"? You have had to make a visit to the doctor, and you wanted to know how it would turn out. Maybe you have faced surgery, and you wanted to know ahead of time how it would turn out. Perhaps you have asked, "How does this fit together in my life?" Paul tells us that when we undergo moments of adversity, when we face times of crisis, we can know that God's will for our lives will not be frustrated. We can know this in two ways.

First, *we know by revelation*. Whenever Paul uses this phrase "we know," it is always linked to the revealed Word of God. We know because God has revealed this knowledge to us through His Word. God has given us this assurance through revelation that no matter what happens, He will work it to our ultimate good. We know this by revelation.

Look at Genesis 42:36 and listen to what Jacob had to say: "You have bereaved me of my children: Joseph is no more, and Simeon is no more, and you would take Benjamin; all these things are against me." Do you feel that verse? "Everything that happens is against me!" Have you ever said that? You felt like the world had turned on you. Jacob had been told that Joseph had been killed. Reuben had been disgraced, and Judah had been dishonored. They had broken their father's heart. Dinah had been defiled; Simeon was in prison; Jacob's beloved wife Rachel was dead. Now famine threatened his family. In order to get food, the Pharaoh's chief advisor wanted Benjamin to come back to Egypt.

What Jacob did not know was that he was about to be reunited with his son, whom he thought had been dead for years, to say nothing about the fact that he and his family were about to enter into a very profitable period of their lives.

We know from God's Word that no matter how bad things may be, no matter how life seems to fall apart, no matter how puzzling it may be, nothing will ultimately frustrate God's will for our lives. Look at Israel. No one had a brighter future than these Hebrews. No one had more promise than they did, and yet they became the biggest failure in human history. They refused to enter the promised land, and they begged for a king rather than depending on God's lordship.

The kingdom split, they fell into open cultic worship, the Northern Kingdom was taken into captivity never to return, and the Southern Kingdom was invaded, but a remnant eventually returned to their homeland.

The Old Testament closed, and there was no word from God for four hundred years. Yet out of the failure, the disappointment, and the mistakes, God brought the Messiah. From revelation we know that no matter what happens, it will not frustrate, alter, or change God's ultimate will for our lives.

Second, *we also know by limitation.* Paul places a limitation on this, and it is the second way we can know that nothing will frustrate the plan of God for our lives. The limitation is that this is only for those who love the Lord. Paul makes clear that God works all things together for the good of those who love the Lord (see Pss. 63:1–3; 73:25).

This is not true for those who reject Christ and have no love for the Lord. In Romans 1:18 we read that the wrath of God is revealed against those who do not love Him. But look at Psalm 84:11: "For the LORD God is a sun and shield; the LORD gives grace and glory; no good thing does He withhold from those who walk uprightly." The psalmist says that no good thing will the Lord withhold from those who love him.

Some of you are wondering how all the pieces of your shattered lives fit together. You're frustrated and at the end of your rope. Perhaps you have thrown your hands up and tried to walk away from it all. Maybe you are asking, "How is God going to work all of this out in my life?" But no matter how bad it may seem, from revelation to limitation God wants you to know that His will for your life will not be frustrated.

II. God Promises His Sovereignty over All the Pieces

Paul says that nothing will frustrate God's plan for our lives. Perhaps you are thinking, *I don't see that.* We need to trust in His sovereignty over all the pieces of our lives. Paul says that "God causes all things to work together for good" (Rom. 8:28). I want you to see three things about this: significance, scope, and source.

First, *look at the significance* of it. God is able to take the pressure, the stress, the emergencies, the crisis, the adversity—all of it—and work it for our ultimate good. The word that Paul used which is translated "to work together" means to work something so that it produces a profit.

On July 13, 1978, Ford fired Lee Iacocca. On October 30, 1978, a little over three months later, Iacocca was named president of the Chrysler Corporation. That was the exact same day that Chrysler announced its largest-ever quarterly loss. On April 21, 1983, less than five years later, the new Chrysler Corporation triumphantly announced it earned $172.1 million in the first quarter—the highest quarterly profit in the automaker's history. Wall Street laughed, the public taunted, Congress scrutinized. Yet Iacocca was able to take what everyone considered a hopeless situation and work it all together to make the biggest profit that the company had ever experienced. If Lee Iacocca could do that with a car company, then Jesus Christ can certainly do that with your life.

Second, *look at the scope* of Paul's statement. What does he mean by "all things"? Perhaps he was thinking back on all the things that had happened in his life. Consider 2 Corinthians 11:24–27: "Five times I received from the Jews thirty-nine lashes. Three times I was beaten with rods, once I was stoned, three times I was shipwrecked . . . dangers from rivers, dangers from robbers, dangers from my countrymen, dangers from the Gentiles . . . sleepless nights, in hunger and thirst, often without food, in cold and exposure."

Then he says in the next verse, "I have to put up with the mess that church folks put me through!" Paul says God in His sovereignty was able to take all of those things and work them together so they would actually profit his life.

I don't know what the pieces of your life look like. But I do know this: If you are one of those who love the Lord, then He is sovereignly putting together all those pieces, all those hurts, all those pains, all that adversity, all that past for your good. God can even take our sin and past mistakes and make them work out for our good.

Third, *look at the source.* Paul did not say that chance, or happenstance, or coincidence, or fate did this. He specifically said the source for the working out of good in our lives is the living and reigning God. The psalmist said, "What is man, that Thou dost take thought of him?"

In March 1989 Debbie went to her doctor, who advised her to have surgery. Her mother had died three months earlier with breast cancer. Seven females in her immediate family had died with breast cancer. She was only thirty-three, and we wondered why we had to face this. There were moments when we felt like our world was coming apart.

Debbie went in for a bilateral mastectomy. She went into surgery at 6:00 that morning and did not come out until about 6:00 that evening. Before the surgery she kept asking me, "Will you be there when I wake up?" It was almost an obsession with her. She said over and over, "Make sure you are there when I wake up." I reassured her that I would be, but we both knew that all I could do was just be there. But that is what she wanted.

God knows your fears, your anxieties, your adversity, and more than anything else He wants you to know that He will be there and He can do something while He's there. He is able to take all those things that are against us and make them work for our ultimate good.

III. We Need to Allow God to Fit the Pieces Together

Many times when my children became frustrated at putting a puzzle together, they tried and tried to force the pieces together. They ended up being more frustrated, and they tore up the edges of the puzzle. There were times when they would argue, "This piece does fit here." There were times when the wrong piece looked like the right piece. But the wrong piece of the puzzle in the wrong position threw the whole picture off.

That is exactly what happens when we jump ahead of God and try to force the pieces together. God wants us to depend on Him to work all of that out in our lives. When we start trying to force issues and plans and ideas, it messes up all of life.

I want you to see this in the string of verbs that Paul used in Romans 8:29–30. We need to allow the Lord to fit the pieces together:

Because He *foreknew*. God was at work on your life in the mysterious counsels of God in eternity past. I can't explain all of this in one message, but it tells us that God was at work in our lives before the dawn of creation.

He *called* us. God's effectual call is to salvation. What God purposed to do in the counsels of eternity past, He actually did in time. At a certain time and place, He called us to salvation.

Whom God called He also *justified*. That word literally means that God as the supreme judge of all the universe declared us just, not guilty of sin when we were saved. Notice that all of these verbs are in the past tense.

Now look at the last verb: "Whom He justified, these He also *glorified*." That is also in the past tense, but it is something we will not experience until we see Him. It is what John speaks of in 1 John 3:2: "When He appears, we will be like Him."

That is what God is doing when we allow Him to fit all the pieces together. When adversity comes, He uses it to advance us. You say, "Advance us to what?" Look back at Romans 8:29: "Conformed to the image of His Son." That's the final picture of us when we allow God to put all the pieces of our lives together. God is working all the adversity, all the mistakes, all the failures, all the hurt, and all the confusion together for our ultimate good—which is to become more and more like His Son, Jesus Christ.

Charles Lang of Carson, California, has an unusual hobby. He puts together a one-thousand-piece puzzle each day, but that's not all. He has pasted 1,170 of these puzzles together and displayed them throughout his seven-room home. In 1987 he fulfilled his most ambitious dream when he hit the one-millionth-piece mark. In order to do that, he added rooms to his house so he would have the space to hang his puzzles. His biggest challenge was a seven-thousand-piece puzzle of an Italian mountain range. Charles literally lives in a house of puzzles.

Perhaps that is where you are today. Here are all the thousands of pieces. But God knows where all the pieces go and how they fit together.

30

Three Life-Changing Words

MATTHEW 11:28 NKJV

Michael Catt
Senior Pastor, Sherwood Baptist Church
Albany, Georgia

WE ARE LOOKING AT THREE LIFE-CHANGING WORDS. They are all action words. They require something of us. They are commands and invitations. Jesus said, "Come to Me, all you who labor and are heavy laden, and I will give you rest. Take My yoke upon you and learn from Me, for I am gentle and lowly in heart, and you will find rest for your souls. For My yoke is easy and My burden is light" (Matt. 11:28).

What would you do if I told you that I have an answer for all your anxieties? Would you be interested? What would you do if I told you that I have an answer for all the areas of your life where you're uptight, stressed out, burned out, and frustrated? Well, I don't, but Jesus does. I can't solve your problems, but I can introduce you to One who can. And that's the Lord Jesus Christ.

I want to take the context of these three verses, and I want you to follow with me, starting back in Matthew chapter 10. Jesus is teaching His disciples about following Him. He wants them to come to Him, take His yoke, and learn from Him. The context is important. We have to take these verses in their context.

357

In chapter 10 Jesus tells the disciples, "Fear Me, reverence Me, honor Me" (see v. 28). He says, "Confess Me" (see v. 32). After I reverence God, then I have to confess Him, not be ashamed of Him. Then He calls on them to "love Me" (see v. 37). We won't come to someone we don't confess, and we won't go to somebody we don't love. We're never going to get past the barrier of pride unless we've already gotten past the barrier of the need to confess and the need to love.

Love Me (v. 37). Follow Me (v. 38). Die for Me (v. 39). Once we have reached the point where we're willing to die for Christ, then coming to Him is not a problem. Taking His yoke is not a problem. Learning from Him is not a problem if we have come to the point where we are willing to die to self for Him.

There were four attitudes toward Jesus at the time He walked this earth. And these four attitudes are still prevalent today.

The first attitude was *the concerned*. In verses 1 through 15, we see the concerned. John the Baptist represents the concerned. By the concerned, I mean this: There are moments in our lives when we can love God, we can follow God, we can believe God, and we can trust God. But there come events, or circumstances, or health problems. Something comes into our lives, and we come to a time of doubt and fear. We wonder if God is really sufficient, or do we need to look somewhere else? Do we need to look outside of Jesus for our sufficiency?

Jesus did not rebuke John for his concern. In fact, I would say that our help comes when we're honest enough to admit that we have concerns. As long as we walk through life with pat answers that have never been tested in the fires of life, it's easier for us to say that we believe God. But when we're put in the crucible of a crisis, do we trust Him? Do we take Him at His word? And by the way, Jesus said John was the greatest man ever born of woman (Matt. 11:11). Yet John had a moment in his life when he wasn't sure that Jesus was who He said He was. So it's OK if we doubt as long as we come to Jesus with our doubts.

The second group is *the critical* (vv. 16–19). We will always have among us the critical who don't understand faith or the process of walking with God by faith. Jesus dealt with the critics in verses 16 through 19.

The third group is *the careless* (vv. 20–24). Jesus rebukes the unrepentant cities and pronounces a judgment on them. This is a sad section of Scripture. These cities had such great light and such great opportunity. And yet they missed that opportunity.

I'm convinced that God's judgment is going to be more severe on people like us, who have been in the Bible belt, who have been in Bible-believing churches, who have been in churches that practice genuine worship. It is going to be harder on us than it is on people who have been in liberal churches and in places that are dead because we know more. This means we are more accountable. Those cities of Jesus' time were going to be judged because they didn't respond to the light they were given. They didn't respond to the truth that walked among them. And their judgment was greater than that of Sodom and Gomorrah because of the simple fact that with privilege comes responsibility. And with opportunity comes accountability.

We cannot be careless with all that God has given us and all the things that we've heard. The things we have heard weren't given to us just to disseminate information, to impress us, and to help us fill out note sheets. God has given us information so we can act on it and take a stand on what we have heard.

And so there are the careless, and there will always be the careless. They think they will have another time, another opportunity, another day, another event when they can get their act together. Jesus reminds us that a day will come when the opportunity will be gone.

The fourth group is *the childlike* (vv. 25–30). Only ten prayers of Jesus are recorded in the Gospels, and this is one of the first. If we look at verses 25 and 26, we find an acknowledgement of rejoicing. In verse 27 we find a declaration of deity and of revelation. In verses 28 through 30 we discover His invitation to freedom.

Now there's rejoicing, there's revelation, and there's freedom. This invitation that Jesus gave to those people in that day is just as viable for us today, offering liberty, life, hope, and freedom as it was to them. These words were recorded for us to hear. Somebody may say, "Well, you know, God has never spoken to me. God has never said *come* to me." God is speaking. The question is, Are we listening?

I. Come

God has always been speaking. He speaks through His Word. He speaks through other people. He speaks through events and circumstances. He's speaking all around us. But are we listening? Now, why is He speaking? Because He wants us to come to Him. And who is He telling to come to Him? Those of us who are weary, heavy laden, worn out, frustrated, burdened, burned out, tired, and weary.

What will happen when we come to Jesus? He will give us rest. The three key words are *come, take,* and *learn.* We must not get them out of order. We have to come to Jesus first. It's a comprehensive word. Jesus was speaking, and all kinds of people were listening to Him. To the lost He says, "Come for salvation." To the saved, to those who believe in Him, He is saying, "Come to me for sanctification." Come to Christ. Those three words summarize His life. Why? Because we come to holiness and we come to hope. And there is no hope without holiness, and there is no holiness without hope. Jesus summarizes everything about His life and His teachings in these three words, "Come to me," for He is holy and He is our only hope.

Some of you work in manufacturing jobs and have to wear hard hats. There may be signs in your plant that say, "Safety First." One of the problems with the church today is that we're playing it safe. We want safety first. But to come to Christ is to throw ourselves on His mercy, to be desperate enough to admit that we can't do it on our own. We can't live the Christian life in our own strength. We can't tackle this problem. Congratulations! Now we are at a point where God can work with us.

God is trying to get us out of our comfort zone so we will throw ourselves in abandonment on Him. Not to events, programs, or feelings—not to anything else but Him. He said, "Come to me." Any time there is something in our lives that says to us or implies to us or pushes us to say that we don't really have to come to Christ, that we can stop somewhere along the line, that is sin. It is sin because it's settling for less than God's best for our lives.

Jesus said, "Come to me." He didn't say, "If it's convenient, or if it fits in your schedule." Here's why. Because every day of our lives, we are either moving toward Jesus, or we are moving away from Him. If we're standing still, we're backsliding. We are either moving toward Him, or we're moving away from Him.

This is a constant invitation to the Holy One, to the spotless Lamb. He didn't say for us to come to religion, or come to a denomination. He didn't say for us to come to anything but Him.

Some of us worship God as He is, and others of us will worship God as we have created Him in our image, made Him like we want Him to be. But when we come to Jesus, we break through all the facades, all the barriers, all the stuff, and a lot of junk just to get to the true One who can set us free.

Holiness is not a burden. Coming to Jesus is not a burden. In fact, it releases us from a burden. He did not say, "Come to be religious." He said, "Come to Me." That's intimacy. He wants us to have an intimate relationship with Him. If we are weary, heavy laden, burdened, and stressed out, the only way we're going to overcome these problems is to come to Christ in an intimate relationship. When we do, He will lift these burdens from us.

Jesus said, "I am gentle and humble." Jesus did not say, "That's the way I act." He said, "That's the way I am. I'm gentle, and I'm humble." Some of us have the idea that God is ready to poke us in the face! We think that if we come to Jesus, He is going to attack us. He's really going to let us have it!

Jesus said, "Come to me." Who is supposed to come? People who are weary, heavy laden, burdened, stressed out, uptight. Does He say that He will just sit there with His arms folded and make us beg? Is that what He said? No! He said, "Come to me, for I am gentle and humble."

By the way, do you know who else He said should come to Him? The little children! One of the great joys I have as a pastor is when little kids run up to me. And sometimes they grab me around my kneecap and hold on. They have an attitude of trust and love. They haven't picked up all the baggage that we adults have picked up that causes us to build walls and fences around ourselves. You have to have an attitude of trust.

Jesus says, "I want you to trust Me enough to come to Me because I am gentle and humble." Now who is He inviting to come? All who are weary and heavy laden. Those who are having difficulties, troubles, and trials.

Here's the rest that Jesus promises. He gives us rest from an accusing conscience. Satan is the accuser of the brethren. God says, "I forgive you," and Satan says, "You haven't done enough to be forgiven yet." And every time we try to step out in faith, and every time we try to come to Jesus, Satan comes up and whispers in our ear, "You know, as much stuff as you've done and as bad as you are, I don't believe I would go into the presence of God. I think He's probably mad at you."

We can ask God to forgive us, but the problem is, sometimes we can't forget it, or we've got some people around us who want to be our thorn in the flesh, and they don't want us to forget it. Jesus tells us to come to Him, and He will deliver us from an accusing conscience.

When we come to Jesus, we also receive rest from guilt. If the devil has done anything, he has taken millions of believers on guilt trips. Jesus did not say, "Come to Me, and I'll smack you upside the head." He didn't say, "Come to Me, and I'll put a whipping on you." He said, "Come to Me, . . . and I will give you rest" (Matt. 11:28). He gives us rest from the situations that wear us down. Even in the midst of troubling situations, we find strength and energy that comes from the Lord.

Jesus also gives us rest from fear. One of the things the enemy tells us is that we shouldn't throw ourselves totally on the Lord. We don't want to be totally abandoned to God because we don't know what He's going to ask us to do. That's right, but I can tell you this: Anything God asks us to do is for our good and for His glory. And it's always consistent with His Word.

Think about the people He told to come to Him. These were agricultural people. They were the poorest of the poor. Israel was an impoverished nation. Everywhere they turned they saw signs of the Roman Empire reigning and ruling over them. Everywhere they turned they saw bondage. They had to work long, they had to work hard, and they had nothing to show for it. Just think about the taxes they paid. And we think *we* pay taxes.

They paid a produce tax, a census tax, a tax for being alive. If you were alive, you had to pay a tax. They paid property taxes, and property taxes included their livestock. If they had one goat or one sheep or one chicken, they had to pay taxes on that livestock. They had to pay an import tax, a city tax, a national tax, and a Roman tax. If we want to talk about a nation that would have elected somebody for tax relief, they would have done it. And on top of being burdened and oppressed by the society, by their circumstances, and by the government of Rome, the Pharisees were placing all kinds of burdens on them.

Mark down this reference: Matthew 23:4. Jesus is speaking of the Pharisees, and He says that they bind heavy burdens that are hard to bear and lay them on people's shoulders. The world is pressing them down, their circumstances are pressing them down, their finances are pressing them down, and now the religious establishment is pressing them down. There are heavy burdens on them. And Jesus stands up and says, "I've come to help."

"Sounds like a good plan to me! You mean, you're going to help me out from under all these burdens?"

"Yes, if you'll come to Me."

Note that nothing changed about the political situation in the book of Acts. But everything changed in the spiritual realm. And they went from the bondage of trying to jump through hoops and going through a system to the freedom of walking with the person of Christ. Christianity is not about a creed or a ceremony or a tradition. It is about Christ. And I know somebody in that crowd said when they were thinking about all the things going on around them: "Who is He kidding? Rest? We can't get any rest!"

Jesus promises that He can give rest. What He promises, He produces. Rest in our spirits. Rest in our minds. Rest in our hearts. Rest in our souls. God wants to give us rest.

II. Take

The second thing Jesus says is for us to take. "Take My yoke upon you" (Matt. 11:29). A yoke doesn't sound restful, but it is one of the most common figures of speech in the Hebrew language. A yoke indicated submission to an obligation or an occupation. A yoke was a sign of submission. It was to an occupation or an obligation. Jesus was saying, "You need to take the yoke as a free and deliberate choice of your will. I'm not going to come and cram this thing on you. I'm not going to force you with this. You need to take it on yourself and put your head in it." And by the way, we cannot get in a yoke unless we bow our heads. It's a sign of humility, a sign of surrender.

Jesus didn't offer a pillow. He didn't offer a massage, although my back could use one right now! He didn't offer a recliner. He offered a yoke—something that is used for labor. Sounds like He was just adding to the labor. But the yoke was not a way to get out of work. The yoke was a way to make the work lighter. And Jesus is saying, "If you yoke up with Me, we will do this together."

A yoke has to have two animals in it to work. When Jesus says that His yoke is easy, it means that His yoke fits well. One tradition says that Jesus, as a carpenter, was excellent at making yokes, that Joseph taught Him how to make these agricultural implements. Yokes were made out of wood. The owner would bring his ox in, and the carpenter would design the yoke to fit that particular animal. Farmers didn't just go down to Home Depot and ask for any old yoke.

No, yokes were designed, carved, cut, and shaped to fit the particular animal that was being used in the plowing process. And Jesus says, "If you'll take My yoke, it is easy and will fit you well." God never intended for us to be yoked up with Him and for it be a burden. God intended for us to yoke up with Him and for it to be a blessing. He said that His burden is light, which means that it is easy to carry. Why? Because this yoke is not placed on us by a slave driver. This yoke is placed on us by a Savior who invites us to come to Him. He said for us to take His yoke—and it is easy.

God never expects or demands that we do this on our own. He says, "Yoke up with Me, and get in partnership with Me, and together we will face your burdens. We will face your problems and your obstacles together." Only when we yoke up with Him do we find that He helps us in carrying the burden.

There are two things we should note about this. If we want to take the two sides of the yoke, there is the power of the Holy Spirit, and there is your personal discipline. We need the power of the Spirit to walk in the fullness of Christ. But we've got to be disciplined to live in the power. We must be obedient and disciplined to live the life that is filled with the Holy Spirit. We can't just do whatever we want to do because then the yoke does not fit well, and we're not going to get anywhere we're supposed to go. We have to have the power of the Spirit and personal discipline. And those two things together yoke us up with Christ, and Christ begins to work in our lives.

Now here's an important assumption, and don't miss it. Jesus is assuming that we understand it is His yoke. The assumption of these verses is that we understand it is His yoke, which means He is setting the direction, He is determining the pace, and He is deciding how far and how much we do.

We must not go out and run ahead of God and then ask Him to catch up with us and bail us out. We walk step-by-step with Him, not pulling against Him, not pulling away from Him, not resisting His leadership, but working in this light and easy, well-fitting yoke, walking side by side with Him. Why? Because He's the lead ox. He is the One leading us into the work. He is the One in charge of the pace. He is the One in charge of the direction. When we yoke up with Christ, it's not so much us asking God to help us out; it's us learning to join Him in His work.

One of the reasons church work is so frustrating for people, and one of the reasons pastors get out of the ministry every month by the hundreds, and one of the reasons people work for a while in a church and then quit, is that they are trying to do God's work in the energy of their flesh rather than yoking up with Christ. Our prayer should be, "Lord, what do You want me to do? Where do You want me to serve? How do You want me to walk beside You so that I can accomplish Your work, not my ideas. I'm not interested in my ideas about how You're going to get the work done in this church. I want to know Your ideas about how I'm going to get the work done in this church."

Now I want to tell you something. In more than twelve years of pastoring this church, I've had some dumb ideas. S-T-U-P-I-D, stupid ideas. I've had some real hair-brained ideas, but I've never had a bad idea when I was yoked up with Christ. The half-baked ideas were only when I tried to get ahead of God, or I tried to pull back and say, "Now, Lord, maybe we don't want to do that." But when I yoke up with Him, I go at His pace at His direction in His stride, His way, His path—and it's easy.

Now confession is good for the soul, but it's bad for the reputation. There have been times when I've wanted to get out of this yoke and get ahead of God and say, "Now God, let me help You see where we need to be going. If you knew this church and this community the way I know them, You would understand what we need to be doing." When I stop and listen, Jesus always says to me, "Michael, get back in the yoke. I'm in charge; you're not. Get in the yoke. Walk with Me."

There have been days, weeks, and months when pastoring this church has been a burden to me. It's been frustrating to me. But when I'm in the yoke, it's not. I don't know how to explain that, except to tell you that the yoke God made for me fits me well. And when I am yoked up with Him, I am walking in His power, not mine.

III. Learn

Come, take, learn. "Learn from me." Jesus is the teacher. First you come, then you take, then you learn. And by the way, we never graduate from the school of learning. I've met people who tell me they are too old to learn, too old to memorize Scripture. You're never too old to do what's right. "Learn from Me," Jesus says. He is both the lesson and the teacher.

The Bible is the only book that we can sit down and read where the author or the subject of the book is there to teach us what it says. I'm now reading the biography of John Adams. He thought at one point about going into the ministry. You know, for the life of me, I can't get the subject of this book to return my call. I'd like to ask him a question. But he won't return my call. I sat down in a recliner yesterday and read a little bit, and John Adams wasn't in the room with me.

But when I sat down this week with this Bible, the Holy Spirit came into the room with me to say, "If you listen to Me, I'll teach you what this Bible says." He is not only the lesson; He is the Teacher of the lesson. He's the Author, the Perfecter, the Finisher, the Teacher, the Educator, the One who gets us through. He teaches us what He did, and He did what He taught. He's consistent.

So let me give you some suggestions from this lesson. First of all, learn His mind. Philippians tells us, "Let this mind be in you which was also in Christ Jesus" (Phil. 2:5). Second, learn His life, taking the form of a bond servant. We will never have a servant's heart if we never lower our heads to get in the yoke. We may think we're too good for that. We're better than that. We don't need to do that. That's good for other people, but it's not good for us. If this is our attitude, we'll never experience what Jesus has promised.

Third, learn from His life, learn from His humility. He humbled Himself (Phil. 2:8). If we want to have power with God, we have to humble ourselves.

Fourth, we must learn from His heart. Jesus wept over Jerusalem. He cared about children. He sat down by a well with a woman nobody else would have talked to. He went to the house of a Pharisee. Jesus went where nobody else would go because He knew that the healthy didn't need a physician. The sick needed a physician. And so we learn from His heart.

And one of the things I pray for my life is, "Lord, give me a heart that is like Yours. Help me to see this community the way You see it.

Give me a burden for people, to not get angry because of what I see in the news but to be broken and burdened because of what I see."

Fifth, learn to exhibit the fruit of the Spirit. If we're going to learn from Jesus, we need to exhibit the fruit of the Spirit. If we're exhibiting the fruit of the Spirit, we no longer use that standard line, "Well, that's just the way I am." Jesus came to make us new creations in Christ. He came to make us new in Christ. "Well," we say, "that's the way we were raised." Well, we need to get over our raising! Your life should give evidence of the fruit of the Spirit. Many Christians give more evidence of the works of the flesh than they do of the fruit of the Spirit (Gal. 5:16–25).

Sixth, learn to discipline your life. In personal Bible study, just sit at His feet. My favorite story in all of Scripture is the account of the sisters Mary and Martha. Mary chose the best part. Jesus said to Martha, "You are worried and troubled about many things" (Luke 10:41). Mary was worried about one thing. And Jesus said that she had chosen the "good part" (v. 42). That phrase means the prime cut of meat, the choice morsel. And what she had chosen would not be taken away from her. Now here's the principle of the Mary and Martha story: Jesus could have survived if Martha didn't get supper on the table. But Martha would not survive unless she sat at the feet of Jesus and learned from Him.

It is imperative for us to spend time with God, stopping long enough just to sit and listen, just sit at His feet. In personal Bible study, in worship, in prayer, in forgiving others. Jesus often tied forgiveness, faith, and answered prayer together. He says, "If you have faith, you can move mountains" (see Matt. 17:20). By the way, if we want to have mountain-moving faith, we had better forgive people. Mountain-moving faith is not just saying to a mountain, "Hey, get on, move." Mountain-moving faith is tied to the willingness of our hearts to forgive people.

We cannot live this life of following Jesus on our own. I was raised in a church where my pastor told me every week, "Try harder. Don't you need to rededicate your life?" Well, folks, you can't rededicate something you've never dedicated. And I thought that *rededicate* was the same thing as *redecorate*. And I would go to redecorate my life for a while. One day I woke up to the reality that I couldn't live up to the standard, but God could. It is not Michael Catt trying as hard as he can to live the Christian life, hoping that at the end he can finish the race well. It is Christ in me, the hope of glory. We can't do anything but cooperate. And when we cooperate, we find that we have yoked up with the One who will teach us, and lead us, and walk with us.

Jesus knows us. He created us. And He says, "Come, take, learn." And look at what He promises. We will find rest for our souls. He didn't say one out of twenty of us would find rest. He didn't say a percentage of us would find rest. He said, if we come, if we take, and if we learn, *all* of us will find rest.

Now, one last thought. Look at Simon Peter. I love Simon Peter. There were two things that Simon Peter could never do—sit still and shut up—which is a problem for all of us who are type A's. Jesus comes to Simon Peter one day and says, "Simon, I'm going to make you into a rock" (see Matt. 16:18). And when He said it, Simon Peter didn't say a word, which was a rare occasion in his life. Jesus said, "I'm going to make you into a rock." It shocked Peter. Why? Because Peter, although he always tried hard, knew his weaknesses. He knew his thoughts. And as he looked into the mirror of his life, he realized that Jesus was promising him something he could never do on his own. "I'm going to make you a rock. You're not much right now. You're kind of like a mud pie right now, but I'm going to make you into a rock."

Simon Peter knew he couldn't make himself into a rock. He would try to help Jesus along. Then he would stick his foot in his mouth, and Jesus would have to rebuke him (Luke 22:34). He had to be sifted. He denied the Lord. He went through all that embarrassment. Then Jesus came to him. Jesus didn't ask Simon, "Peter, do you promise Me that you'll never deny Me again?" No, Jesus said, "Peter, the only issue I'm concerned about now before I go to heaven is, do you love Me? That's the only thing I want to know. Do you really love Me?" (see John 21:15–17).

Simon Peter did not hear what he was expecting. He had denied the Lord. He had been an embarrassment to the disciples. Then he decided that he would just go back to fishing. He had made every mistake he could make. Yet Jesus said, "I'm going to make you a rock." Some rock. I mean, he was sinking fast. And Jesus came to him and said, "Simon, do you love Me? All I want to know is, Do you love Me?"

You know what Jesus did to Simon Peter at that moment? He did exactly what He promised in Matthew 11. "Come to Me, and I'll give you rest." He did not lecture Simon Peter on his failures. He just gave Simon Peter another job to do. Isn't that just like Jesus, and so unlike us? I mean, we want to remember everyone's failures. And Jesus says, "OK, everybody knows you failed. Now what are you going to do from here? What are you going to do from this point on?"

"Simon, if you love Me, feed My sheep." God trusted Simon Peter and gave him a job to do. Peter wasn't perfect. But God trusted him enough that when it came time for the Holy Spirit to fall and for the church to disperse into the world, He laid his hand on Simon Peter and said, "Peter, you're the evangelist for today." And three thousand people were saved (see Acts 2:14–41).

Simon Peter did in a ten-minute sermon what he couldn't do for three and one-half years. He saw the glory of God fall on his life. He had tried, he had tried, and he had tried. But in an atmosphere of forgiveness, faith, and prayer, suddenly everything changed about Simon Peter.

Do we need to come to Jesus? If we come, we need to take. And once we take, we need to learn.

31

The Counseling Secret

ROMANS 15:14 NASB

Ed Young

Senior Pastor, Second Baptist Church
Houston, Texas

THE LOSS OF THE SPACE SHUTTLE *COLUMBIA* is a great tragedy for America and for the world. Our hearts go out to the many who grieve this tragedy. We take things for granted, and we trust those who work in the area of science and the science of travel in outer space. But this reminds us again of how dangerous these flights are. So we pray for these families, and certainly we'll pray for our president, for the chairman of the joint chiefs of staff, for all of our military.

We do not want to be known just as a large church, a missionary church, or even a Bible-believing church. We want to be known as a house of prayer. That's the power of God to His gathered community. We will pray about the direction our nation is going as we seek to bring freedom to all the world. To whom much is given, much is required. We cannot sit back in the face of demonic, evil terrorism. I'm proud of our nation, and we pray for our leadership as we do what has to be done. We pray for peace, but we do what has to be done in order to defend ourselves.

Open your Bibles with me to our text, Romans 15:14. We are looking at relationships that enhance and relationships that bless, especially those that we develop in the household of faith, the church. Paul writes: "And concerning you, my brethren, I myself also am convinced that you yourselves are full of goodness, filled with all knowledge, and able also to admonish one another."

The word *admonish* may be translated as "counsel." It's an accurate translation. This verse tells us that Christians are full of knowledge and goodness. Therefore, we are able to counsel one another.

There are a lot of phobias around. I never cease to be amazed at the different kinds of fears all of us have. They crop up all the time. Claustrophobia we know, acrophobia we know—a lot of different phobias. We are afraid of things. We are frightened of things. Many times it's hospitals. Sometimes it's people of different backgrounds. We could build a big list of all the different phobias we have.

But I heard of one this past week that I've never heard of before. I thought I knew most of the fears. This person has a fear of open doors. Have you ever heard of that one? If the door is closed, he has no problem opening it. If the door is cracked, he can go on. But a door that's entirely open, he just can't move; he can't go through it. And he has a brother who got so disgusted with his phobia that he once threatened him and said if he didn't quit this silly thing, he was going to lock him in a room with all the doors open. I love that phrase, "locked in a room with all the doors open."

Some of us are something like that, but we may never have put it in those words. We have a tough time making decisions. We wait, we're not sure, or we overly plan, overly think, get too much information, and we just don't know which door to go through and what to do. Some of us live our lives, in one sense, locked in a room, because of our indecision, with all the doors open. So we need a voice that will give us a clear word of counsel.

Now let me put over to one side professional counseling. I believe that certainly there are times in the lives of individuals in which everything is so knotted up, and so convoluted, and so confusing that they may need to go to a Christian psychiatrist or a Christian counselor. We have many wonderful Christian counselors in our church who are professionally trained. We even have a psychiatrist who sings in our choir on Saturday night. And we have a lot of Christian psychotherapists here. There are times when we need to get professional counseling from trained men and women.

But putting that to one side, the way I'm using counseling today is in a different genre. That is what this passage in Romans says. Paul says to the church in Rome, "You are full of goodness. You are full of knowledge. Therefore you are to admonish, you are to counsel one another." This is within the family of faith.

Why do you think you come to church and sit in a Bible study class to get biblical insights from God? Why do you think we come to worship and sit here, sing, praise, and feel lifted up to the Almighty? A by-product of this, in one sense, is a large counseling session. We receive the knowledge of God, the touch of God, so we can impart that to others. And one of the best places for this to take place is in the household of faith. So we are to be counselors; we are to be "therapists," though not in the professional sense. We could call it caregiving. We could call it insight from maturity. We could call it godly wisdom.

In all the relationships we have, we are to understand that God has imparted to many of us this gift of counseling. All of us need to be engaged in some kind of relationship with others because of what God is building into our lives through the insight and experiences we have had.

I. Methodology

Now we have to ask the question of methodology. In the Bible we have many words that can be translated "counseling" or "to counsel." There are four words I want us to look at.

Conversation. Go to Deuteronomy 11:18–19: "You shall therefore impress these words of mine on your heart and on your soul; and you shall bind them as a sign on your hand, and they shall be as frontals on your forehead. You shall teach them to your sons, talking of them when you sit in your house and when you walk along the road and when you lie down and when you rise up." We counsel through conversation. That's the word for counsel here. The word *teach* means "counsel." We teach, we counsel through conversation. That's the best counseling we do!

We sit at the table. Our children and our spouses get a good idea of what we think about a lot of things by just eating a meal and listening to our conversation. Or we counsel when we're sitting in the living room. We counsel, we comment about something on television. We counsel when we're with friends. We counsel when we stand in a hall. We counsel through conversation. Most of us have learned a great deal through give-and-take conversation, whether in a dormitory room, in an organization, or in our recreation or vocation. We have conversations, and as Christians counseling is going on. We're imparting thoughts and insights to one another. We never thought about it, but that's really what's happening. This verse says that we counsel, we teach everywhere we go. When we talk, we are counseling. We counsel through conversation.

Consultation. Look at Proverbs 15:22. It says that "without consultation, plans are frustrated, but with many counselors they succeed." The word *counsel* here means "consultation." It's one thing to do casual counseling. We display things in our lives, and we share wisdom or insight, or we share foolishness. But we also counsel through consultation. This is when someone may call us to one side, or maybe two or three of us will sit down, and someone will say, "I want to bounce something off you. I want your wisdom." That is consultation. It has the idea of secrecy, that we keep this to ourselves. When someone shares things with us, it is important that we keep their confidence. How rare it is today to find someone we can totally open up our lives to, and know it will go no further. So consultation is another kind of counseling.

Correction. Proverbs 1:5 says that "a wise man will hear and increase in learning. And a man of understanding will acquire wise counsel." We counsel through correction, and the word for *counsel* here is a different Hebrew word. It describes when a person is corrected. It's the picture of someone putting a rope on an animal that is outside the pasture and taking that animal and guiding it back into the pasture. It describes the act of leading it where it needs to be.

Sometimes we sit down and say, "Look, we need to sign a contract. We need to enter into a covenant." And we write it down. We speak softly and gently and many times with a tear in our eyes, but it is a correction to get somebody back on the right path. Correction is another kind of counseling.

Confrontation. Proverbs 12:20–22 describes another kind of counseling. The fourth word for counseling is found in these verses. It is a different kind of emphasis. "Deceit is in the heart of those who devise evil, but counselors of peace have joy. No harm befalls the righteous, but the wicked are filled with trouble. Lying lips are an abomination to the LORD, but those who deal faithfully are His delight." This is when we serve as "counselors" and counsel through confrontation. We have to confront, and sometimes this is traumatic. Before we confront, we had better be prayed up. But there's a counseling through confrontation that happens in the family of faith.

Conversation, consultation, correction, and confrontation. Those are the different styles of counseling that are going on all the time by men and women who love the Lord Jesus Christ. He has given us knowledge, and our lives are filled with goodness. And we are equipped to do these types of counseling. Paul says we must be doing this. This is a part of our commission as sons and daughters of God.

II. Practicality

We have looked at methodology, and now we look at practicality. What happens when we are counseled? What do we do when we counsel others? We can see it right here. The word is *help*. We give help. We receive help.

Let's see HELP as an acrostic, because it fits perfectly for what we're about. The *H* stands for godly counselors who are wise in the things of the Lord. They *heal*. Look at it. It's right there in Proverbs 12:18. But a false witness deceives. "There is one who speaks rashly like a thrusts of a sword, but the tongue of the wise brings healing."

Haven't you talked with someone when your life was totally broken, and this person spoke healing words? Isn't that tremendous?

I've had so many times and moments of extremity in my life when someone would come to me and speak a healing word. Godly, wise men and women, even young people, who counsel others. We are to speak healing words.

The *E* in HELP is for *evangelize*. Check out the life of Jesus Christ. What did He do? He healed people. He introduced them to God and showed them how they could have eternal life through Him. And then He taught them. He healed, He evangelized, and He taught. When we are talking with someone, or they are talking with us, make sure they know what it means to be a Christian. Make sure they nail down that basic commitment in their lives. Otherwise, we're giving them standards and insights they cannot understand.

Godly, wise counselors also *listen*. This is represented by the *L* in HELP. Look at Proverbs 12:15: "The way of a fool is right in his own eyes, but a wise man is he who listens to counsel." Look at Proverbs 18:13: "He who gives an answer before he hears, it is folly and shame to him." So in counseling, what do we do? We listen! We ask questions, and we listen with our hearts. We listen with our experience. We listen with our minds.

Next is the *P* in HELP. Look at Proverbs 11:14: "Where there is no guidance the people fall, but in the abundance of counselors there is victory." In other words, we are to *point*. Let me tell you the strategy of secular, nonbelieving psychotherapists. They listen and they ask questions, and they listen and they ask questions. Your insurance runs out, and then you run out of money. And they listen, and they ask questions. But they give no answers. They may give some medication, but they will give you no answers. That's their strategy.

This is not what we are to do in the family of faith. What are we to do? We are to give guidance. We are to give insight. We point.

I read about an executive who was retiring after building a large corporation. His successor was brought in from the outside and was working with him for six months before he became CEO. The young successor to the successful CEO went to him and said, "I'd like to ask you what has been the secret of your success these many years?"

The man answered, "Two words: good decisions."

"I'd like to press that if I could, sir. How were you able to make good decisions?"

"One word: experience."

The young man said, "But I'm just starting out as CEO. I want to know how you get the experience to make good decisions?"

"Two words: bad decisions."

The reason we're there for people—ready to heal, ready to evangelize, ready to listen, and ready to point—is that in Christ we are filled with biblical knowledge and goodness, and our motives are pure. Thus we are able to give insight to those who come to us. It's wonderful to know the resources that we have in the household of faith.

The last thing I want you to see is the most important point. What if I told you that you could receive a counseling session with Almighty God, and He would sit down with you and say, "This is how you are to live for the rest of your life"? He promised to guide you through every choice you'll make from now until your death. Would you heed His words of advice? I can tell you something that may shock you. We're all terminally ill. Everybody here is terminally ill, with no exceptions. Therefore, between now and our graduation, if we could have an audience with God, we would say, "God, I want to see my life. I want to see life as You see it. So I will always make the right choices and the right decisions from this day forward." And if you sat down with Almighty God and He gave you those answers, would you follow through?

We have a clear, clean word from Him that will enable anyone who follows this path to make right decisions at every turn of his life—guaranteed. God gives us three conditions; he gives us one promise in a familiar passage of Scripture: "Trust in the LORD with all your heart [condition number 1] and do not lean on your own understanding [condition number 2]. In all your ways acknowledge Him [condition number 3], and [here is the promise] He will make your paths straight" (Prov. 3:5–6). He will direct your path. God makes this promise.

I want us to see exactly how this works. *Trust* is the first word: "Trust in the LORD with all your heart." What does it mean to trust? It means to put your full weight down on Him. It means to have total confidence in Him. It means without wavering, without hesitation we affirm that we are sure of God.

I read about a man who was trying to teach his young son some business principles. He put the guy on a little platform and held out his arms. He said, "Son, jump to your daddy, I'll catch you. Jump to your daddy." The boy jumped, and he pulled back his arms—crash! The boy was crying. But he got up on the platform again. The father said, "Jump to your daddy. You can count on me. Jump to your daddy." The little boy jumped, Dad pulled back his arms, and he crashed again. The father said, "Son, that is one of the first things I want you to learn about the business world."

God holds out his arms to us, and He says, "Jump; put your full weight down." And every single time He catches us and holds us. We can trust in the Lord with all of our hearts.

The Bible is full of promises built around that word *trust*. If we trust in God, it's amazing what this will bring to our lives. Psalm 4 talks about trust. If we trust in God, we have peace in our inner life. Just trust, and we have peace. Psalm 16 says if we trust in God, we have joy. Psalm 22 says if we trust in God, we don't have to worry about our enemies. If somebody declared war on us, if we trust in God, He'll take care of it in His timetable.

First Chronicles 5 says if we trust in God, our prayers will be answered. Sometimes God says yes; sometimes God says no (by the way, that's an answer). Sometimes God says maybe; sometimes God says wait. But those who pray in faith will have every single prayer answered.

Someone recently told me that he never trusted in God totally until the doctor said to him, "You have cancer." We are to trust in God. Now what does this involve? It means we trust in God, and God is our Lord. "Trust in the LORD with all your heart" (Prov. 3:5). That means we're Christians. And when Jesus Christ is in our lives, and we've invited Him there, guess who else is there? The third person of the Trinity—the Holy Spirit. The Holy Spirit leads us in making decisions because the Holy Spirit is in our hearts. We have received Jesus Christ into our hearts, so the Holy Spirit is in our hearts. When we trust in Him with all of our hearts, we feel the leadership of the Holy Spirit, that inner voice, the voice of God.

The first condition is trust. The second condition is, "Do not lean on your own understanding" (v. 5). What does *lean* mean? It means something "to help hold you up," "to enable you to stand," "to put you in the proper position." We lean. We lean on our understanding. All of us have had that experience. We are to lean on God's understanding.

Where do we get God's understanding? The Bible! What does the Bible say about the will, the plan, and the purpose of God? The Bible says we're to be saved, we're to know Christ. We're to be Spirit filled. We're to let the Holy Spirit lead our lives. We're to be sanctified. That doesn't mean we have halos above our heads. It means we're growing, seeking, and growing more mature in our faith day by day. We're to be submissive to those in authority above us, and we're to be serving.

God says, "This is My will. This is where you begin, and when this is operative in your life, then we can move to the other kinds of decisions." Lean on God's understanding. We lean on the Bible. Where else do we get God's understanding? Godly counselors. People who have been ahead of us. People who have been through life's experiences. People who have been there, done that, and people who have walked through, people who have made good decisions and bad decisions. Godly counselors help us get God's understanding. They help us discern through Scripture and through godly standing. We lean not on our own understanding but on God's understanding.

Then the third condition: "In all your ways acknowledge Him" (v. 6). In what kind of ways do we acknowledge God? We acknowledge Him in circumstances. We have to make a decision. There's an open door. There's a closed door. There's a little narrow door to squeeze through. There's a window that's half open. What do we do?

In the choices that we make, we acknowledge Him in those circumstances. We say, "God, You've put this before me. You've put this decision here, and I acknowledge You. You are a part of the circumstances of my life. This is a part of Your sovereign plan.

We acknowledge God in common sense. We acknowledge Him working through our thought processes. So we begin to be able to make decisions. Everybody knows the little checkpoints. We know through the leadership of the Holy Spirit, the inner voice. We know through the teaching of the Bible. We know through circumstances. We know through common sense. We know through godly counselors. If we get all those things in place, and all those lights are on, we can make good choices, good decisions.

We see how they fit in the framework of these three conditions. Trust in the Lord with all your heart. Lean not upon your own understanding. In all your ways acknowledge Him. And what does the last verse say? "He will make your paths straight" (v. 6). In other words, He will give us the ability to make the right decision and the right choices for the rest of our lives.

Let me make a bold statement. If you are joyously and completely committed to the Lord Jesus Christ, God gives you a blank check in the decisions and choices that you make. Let me say it another way. If you are committed to Jesus Christ as best you know, completely and joyously, you cannot make a wrong decision. Let me say it still another way. The Bible gives us clear directions on every decision we'll ever have to make.

Let's just say for illustration that a woman is in a department store, and she can't decide between the pink dress and the blue dress with the little wide hem on it. And the length of this one over against the cost, but the charm of that one. You say, "I've got you! I had to make a decision. I wanted to make a decision. You said the Bible gives me counsel on every decision I'll ever have to make. How does this apply to the matter of picking out a dress?" I'll tell you exactly how it works.

Number one, the Bible teaches us how to use money correctly. Number two, the Bible teaches us to discern between those things that we want, and those things that we need. The Bible teaches us if I'm rich with myself, I am also to be rich and generous with God. Doesn't the Bible teach us that? And the Bible teaches us that we are to buy clothes that are not showy and gaudy and that do not call attention to ourselves like we are in show business. We should buy clothes that display our inner character. Therefore, buy the pink dress or the blue dress. God does gives you discernment and direction in that choice.

Sometimes we make choices that we look back on and say, "I should have done this, or I should have done that." But maybe you didn't make a mistake. Perhaps God is still working out His plan, His will in your life. You can do whatever you want to do, whatever your heart, your discernment leads you to do. In any decision you face in life, you cannot and will not make a mistake—if you are trusting in the Lord, leaning on His understanding, and acknowledging Him in all your ways.

32

Bring Back the Glory

EXODUS 33:1–16 NASB

Jon Moore
Revivalist
North Richland Hills, Texas

WHEN I FIRST STARTED IN A TRAVELING MINISTRY some twenty-eight years ago, it was a surprise to me that so many of the people of God knew a great deal about the secular history of America, but few knew much about the spiritual history of the United States.

The truth is that there have been four great nationwide movings of God in our history. The first began in the late 1730s; Christian historians refer to it as the Great Awakening. The second great moving of God began in the late 1790s; it is called the Second Great Awakening. The third nationwide moving of God began in the late 1850s. Sometimes it is referred to as the Prayer Revival or the Layman's Revival. It has that name because there were no preachers prominent in that great moving of God. It began—of all places—in New York City on Manhattan Island in a little storefront church on Fulton Street.

A few years ago I had the privilege of being on Manhattan Island preaching a revival meeting. We walked down Fulton Street praying that God would begin revival again. In the original revival Pastor Jeremiah Lanphier invited business people to give up their lunch hour and come to the church and pray for revival. That was in the fall of 1857. By the turn of the new year, 1858, every church in downtown New York City was filled with men giving up their lunch hour to pray for revival. By the spring of 1858, people were being converted at the rate of ten thousand a week in New York City alone. That revival spread up and down the eastern seaboard. It began to move west until it embraced the entire country.

The next nationwide revival—and the last one we had in the United States—began in 1905. If you were paying attention to those dates, you likely noticed that sixty years separated the beginning of the first Great Awakening and the beginning of the Second Great Awakening. Approximately sixty years passed between the beginning of the Second Great Awakening and the Prayer Revival of the late 1850s. Then we had about fifty years between that revival and the revival that began in 1905. That was the last great nationwide revival we had in America, and that has been almost one hundred years ago.

We have the dubious distinction of living in a generation in America where it has been longer than any other time in the history of this country since we've had a nationwide revival. The glory of God has departed.

That brings us to our passage of Scripture. Those of you who know your Bible know from chapter 32 of the book of Exodus that the people of God had sinned a great sin. That is always the cause of the leaving of the glory of God—sin. They made a golden calf, and they bowed down and worshipped that dumb idol. God was angry. His wrath was so kindled that He threatened to destroy all of them and start over with Moses and begin a new people. But Moses stepped in between the wrath of God and the people of God. He began to intercede, and the success of His intercession is revealed in the first three verses we just read. In verse 1 the Lord said to Moses, "All right, go ahead; you take the people and lead them into the land that I promised their forefathers." Then God added something to the promise.

He said in verse 2, "I'll send an angel ahead of you and I'll give you victory over all your enemies." I haven't met very many people who wouldn't be satisfied with that. But Moses wasn't satisfied.

Moses kept on praying. In verse 3 the Lord said something that the people had not anticipated. He said, "But I will not go with you." To capture the significance of that, you have to put yourself in the place of these people. For 430 years they had been in bondage in Egypt. They knew nothing about corporate worship. They had not had time to worship. The Egyptians had kept them working, and they had not had any moments to gather together to corporately worship God.

Their faith was so weak that God sent a deliverer, a man by the name of Moses. Knowing that their faith was weak, God condescended to show Himself—by day by a pillar of cloud and by night by a pillar of fire. But suddenly because of their sin, that cloud of God's glory departed. It is precisely at this point that we see the significance of the ministry of Moses and we see the kind of ministry so needed in this hour. Every pastor, evangelist, staff member, deacon, Sunday school teacher, and every man and woman of God needs to pay attention.

What do we need to do in hopes that God's glory will once again come and rest over His people? Notice what Moses did. Notice that repentance is needed if we are to have any hope for the return of the glory of God in our generation. In verse 4 the Bible says, "When the people heard this sad word, they went into mourning, and none of them put on his ornaments." Most Baptists don't agree on what genuine repentance is. If you asked everybody here today to stand and give their own definition of repentance, we'd have scores of different definitions.

This verse reveals that there are two aspects to biblical repentance. The first aspect is hearing. Many people listen, but only a few actually hear. The people who hear do so because this ability is given to them by the Lord. One day Jesus said to His disciples, "No one knows the Son except the Father; nor does anyone know the Father except the Son, and anyone to whom the Son wills to reveal Him" (Matt. 11:27). No one knows God unless Jesus wills to reveal Him. So the privilege, the blessing, the ability to hear is a gift from God Himself. Repentance begins not just with listening, not just with intellectual understanding, but with hearing with the ear of the heart.

To get to biblical repentance you have to add heeding to hearing. The Bible says that when the people heard this sad word they did two things: they went into mourning, and they stripped themselves of their ornaments.

Verse 6 of Exodus 33 says that they "stripped themselves of their ornaments, from Mount Horeb onward." First, let's answer a couple of questions: Why was it a sad word? And why did they go into mourning? For this reason: God said they could have the promised land. They could have the land flowing with milk and honey. But He would not go with them.

That generation of God's people had enough sense to understand that milk and honey are nothing without the bread of life. What good is revival without the Reviver? So many people today have caught up in seeking *the blessing.* "Lord, give me this blessing. Lord, give me that blessing." You can have all the blessings in the world, but you don't have anything without the Blesser. When God gave the people what they wanted but declared that he would not go with them, they went into mourning.

Let me speak specifically to those who are leaders of worship, to music leaders. We've gotten to the place that all we want to do is celebrate. If any people in the world have a reason to celebrate, it's Christians. But there needs to be a place in worship for us to weep and mourn and grieve.

Grieve and mourn over what? Over our lack of Christlikeness and the sin in our lives that ensnares us and makes us incapable of reaching out to a lost and dying world. A part of worship should be reserved for grieving and mourning and weeping over our sins.

But that's not all the people did. The Bible says they stripped themselves of their ornaments. Why did they do that? That's what had gotten them in trouble. They didn't get those ornaments just by coincidence. God put the fear of God into their Egyptian masters, and they said, "Take our gold. Take our silver. Take our best garments. Just get out of the country." The Egyptians had just lost the firstborn in every household. The fear of God was on their hearts. It ought to put the fear of God into our hearts when we understand that we can so use, and so misuse, and so abuse the blessings of God that they become a snare to us. And so the people stripped themselves of their ornaments.

In the Second Great Awakening the frontier at that time was Kentucky. Can you imagine a United States of America and the western frontier is Kentucky? The revival that began earlier on the eastern coast in the late 1790s didn't reach Kentucky until 1800. In the summer of 1800 the old camp meetings that began in Kentucky and Tennessee spread over into North and South Carolina. Thousands of people were converted in those camp meetings.

There happened to be a Presbyterian minister in Logan County, Kentucky, who kept a journal, a diary. In his diary he recorded some things about the winter of 1799. The revival hadn't gotten to Kentucky yet. Listen to what this man of God recorded in his journal. He said the winter of 1799 was filled with weeping and mourning by the people of God.

It could be that the reason we don't have national revival is that we're so busy celebrating and feeling good about ourselves and putting a positive spin on everything that we've lost the ability to weep and mourn before God. But we will never see the return of the glory of God until we understand that it requires repentance.

The Bible says in verse 7: "Now Moses used to take the tent and pitch it outside the camp, a good distance from the camp, and he called it the tent of meeting."

What is this tent of meeting? When the tabernacle in the wilderness was built, it was referred to often as the tent of meeting. But at this point the tabernacle hadn't been built. God hadn't yet told Moses to build it. So even before the tabernacle was built in the wilderness, there was an understanding of a need for a tent of meeting.

If it was a tent of meeting, who met there? First, it was a place of consecration. It was consecrated for one purpose. This is where people could go to meet God. For these days of revival, think of this church building as a tent of meeting. Your church facility should not be a place of entertainment. It should not be a place to transact business. It should be a tent of meeting—a place where you can go and meet God.

But if the church building is the only place you ever go to meet with God, you will miss much of what He has to say to you. Every Christian needs a "pup tent." Every child of God needs a place where he can retreat and meet personally and privately with God— a tent of meeting.

You know what's so wonderful about the tent of meeting? All you need for entrance is a personal hunger for God. It doesn't make any difference how big your bank account is. It doesn't make any difference whether you have any degrees behind your name. It doesn't make any difference about the color of your skin. It doesn't make any difference about your race or ethnicity. All you need is a hunger for God, and you're welcome at the tent of meeting. It's reserved and consecrated for those who want to meet with God.

But not only is it a place of consecration; it's also a place of intercession. The Bible says in verse 8, "Whenever Moses went out to the tent all the people would arise and stand, each at the entrance of his tent, and gaze after Moses until he entered the tent."

If it was a tent of meeting, if it was consecrated specifically for the purpose of meeting with God, why were those people still at their tent, and why were they just watching? Let me answer that by asking you a question. Do you have any people in your church like that? They just watch. They just look. I'm not going to comment any further. We'll just leave it at that.

Did you ever think about who Moses was praying for in that tent? One of the most precious commodities in the modern church— and there is a lack of it—is discernment. Perhaps God has given you an element of discernment. You have got enough spiritual sense to recognize that regardless of what everybody else is saying and regardless of all the fluff in the organization, something is missing. This is good, but you need to understand that God never gives discernment for the purpose of condemnation. God always gives discernment for the purpose of intercession. Moses and Joshua went to that tent to pray for those irresponsible people, to pray for those people who never participated, who never gave, who were not involved.

Some years ago an elderly pastor was asked to give his testimony at a meeting of preachers. He told about how his heart had just dried up. He was in a wilderness time in his personal life in ministry. He knew that he couldn't continue like he was. He went out into the woods and spent the entire day—didn't eat or drink, just took his Bible and prayed and wept and read the Word—and God met with him. He told that crowd of preachers what God had done in his heart. How He revived his heart and gave him a new vision and a new sense of direction and a new zeal.

Afterwards one of the young preachers came up to him and said, "Sir, I bear witness with everything you said. I'm there in my life, and I need what you've found. Would you please help me?"

The old pastor replied, "Why don't we go out into the woods together? I could take you to the same place where God met with me. If God met with me, He can meet with you. Do you want to do that?"

The young man said he would like that. So they got in the car and drove out into the country. They walked out into the woods. They began to climb a hill. They got to the top of a hill with a beautiful view of the surrounding countryside. The young man asked, "Is this the place?" The old man replied that they had to go further.

Then they went down the other side of the hill to a beautiful meadow. The young man asked, "Is this the place?" The old man said, "No, we have to go farther."

They went up another hill and down another hill and up another hill and down another hill. Finally the young man protested, "I can't go one step farther. God has got to do something in my life. I can't continue."

The old man said, "Then this is the place!"

I wonder how many of us are in the wilderness of our wanderings. Your heart is dry. You may have a lot of activities going on. There may be a vast organization. But in your heart you know that the cloud of God's glory has departed. Are you ready to come to the place where you are not willing to take one step farther?

The question has to be: Is it worth it? Yes, it's worth it. Look at verse 9: "Whenever Moses entered the tent, the pillar of cloud would descend and stand at the entrance of the tent; and the LORD would speak with Moses." What happened? The cloud of God's glory returned.

Look what happened when the cloud of God's glory returned. First of all, there was a different response. Verse 10 says, "When all the people saw the pillar of cloud standing at the entrance to the tent, all the people would arise and worship, each at the entrance of his tent." Who are those people in verse 10? They are the same group that we read about in verse 8. They weren't participating. Now in verse 10 we see them on their faces before God, worshipping.

What happened? The glory of God came down. We need to grasp the truth that the glory of God—and only the glory of God—is what changes people. This will change people even when they have no thought of changing.

I never will forget my days in what we now know as the Asbury Revival, back in the early 1970s. I remember a church service in which a young hippie got saved. He had a beard, and he hadn't taken a bath in weeks. His clothes were dirty, and he was barefoot, but somehow somebody got him to church, and he got saved. He was one of those guys who just blesses your heart because he got saved from the top of his head to the soles of his feet.

The next night he walked in the church, and I didn't know who he was! He had shaved. He had taken a bath. I questioned the people at church. Nobody had told him to get cleaned up, but he had met Jesus, and this made a difference in his life. I introduced myself, and he told me who he was. He had a young woman with him. I thought she was his girlfriend. But it turned out that she was his sister.

His sister was a witch. No, she wasn't a woman in witch clothing. She was a member of a group of witches in that town. She was upset because her little brother had gotten religion. She came that night to cast a spell on the church. She didn't disrupt anything. She sat there in the service, muttering under her breath. She was doing her satanic incantations. She was praying to the devil.

Sometime during that service she stopped praying to Satan. God began to deal with her heart. She didn't respond to the invitation, but after the service I was in the back with a group of men. I looked down, and there was this young man and his sister and a pastor, and all of a sudden they got on their knees and began to pray. In a few minutes she stood up and turned around. Nobody had to guess what had happened to her. She came into that service with a scowl on her face, with a weight on her shoulders, with anger and hatred in her heart. When she stood up, she had the glory of God on her face. She got gloriously saved.

Salvation is not about training. We need to be trained, but it's not about whether you've got training. It's not about how good your personality is. It's not about how persuasive you are. It's about the power and glory of God. If we could ever get people into the presence of the glory of God, they will get changed, whether they planned to be changed or not.

Look at verse 11: "Thus the LORD used to speak to Moses face to face, just as a man speaks to his friend." Have you ever thought about who God's friends are? God's friends are intercessors.

The prophet Isaiah in chapter 62 of his book talked about those men on the wall. They were crying out day and night, giving themselves no rest and giving the Lord no rest until He once again made His people "a praise in the earth"(Isa. 62:7). We need some men and women who will go back to their churches and stand on the wall and cry out to heaven day and night and give themselves no rest and give the Lord no rest until once again the cloud of God's glory comes back to rest over His people.

Look at verse 14 of Exodus 33: "And [the Lord] said, 'My presence shall go with you, and I will give you rest.'"

Now look at verse 15: "Then [Moses] said to [the Lord], 'If Your presence does not go with us, do not lead us up from here.'" Verse 16 says, "For how then can it be known that I have found favor in Your sight, I and Your people? Is it not by Your going with us, that we, I and Your people, may be distinguished from all the other people who are upon the face of the earth?"

The only thing that sets the local church apart from the Rotary Club or any other good service organization is the glory of God.

Without the glory of God, we are no different from any other service organization.

Edwin Booth could not escape his heritage. He was the brother of John Wilkes Booth, the person who assassinated President Abraham Lincoln. He could not change that. But what he could change and what he did change was his legacy. One day Edwin Booth stood at the train station waiting for the train to arrive. The people were jostling to get to the front so they could board the train quicker. One young man on the edge of the platform lost his footing and fell on the tracks right in front of the approaching train. Edwin Booth jumped off the platform and helped him get off the tracks just before the train would have hit him. Ironically, the name of the young man whom he saved was Robert Todd Lincoln, the son of Abraham Lincoln. Booth could not change his heritage, but he changed his legacy.

The last nationwide revival we had in the United States was long ago. There's not a person in this room who has seen nationwide revival in America. You may have seen pockets of it, but nothing nationwide. We'll never be able to change that. We can't change our heritage, but we can do something to change our legacy. We can be men and women who will not be satisfied with the status quo, who will not be satisfied with a shrinking, impotent church. We can stand on the walls and cry out to heaven day and night and give the Lord no rest and give ourselves no rest until God once again makes His people a praise in the earth.

Don't you want to be in that number? Would you not like to see another day when people started being converted at the rate of ten thousand a week? Or twenty thousand a week? Or a hundred thousand a week?

Don't misunderstand what I've said today. Only God can bring revival. But historically, both biblically and in church history, He has used His people, putting a burden on their hearts, to be men and women who have cried out for revival. I challenge you to make yourself available to be that person who calls out to God for Him to send revival throughout our land.

33

Hallelujah

REVELATION 19:1–6 HCSB

James T. Draper, Jr.

THERE IS A WONDERFUL WORD, and I want to share it with you. It's an exciting word. You can't say it and keep still. You can't say it and keep quiet. You can't say it and be unemotional and uninvolved. It is a simple word. It is the word *hallelujah*. This is a Hebrew word. *Halle* means "you (singular) praise." *Hallelu* means "you (plural), all of you praise." And then *hallelujah*, putting the little "jah" in our transliteration of it, is the word for Jehovah or God. So *hallelujah* means "praise ye the Lord."

It's a wonderful word—it's a biblical word. At least fifteen of the psalms begin or end with the word *hallelujah*. It's a word that is found throughout the prophets, throughout the psalms in particular, and even found in the New Testament, in the book of Revelation. The one place that the word *hallelujah* appears in the Greek New Testament is in Revelation 19:1–6. It appears four times. Notice first verse 5: "A voice came from the throne, saying: 'Praise our God.'"

Now that's not the word *hallelujah*; that is the Greek word for "praise" or "extol" or "bless." It's in the present active imperative second personal plural, and it means, "All of you do it." All of us are commanded to praise our God. "All you His bond servants, you who fear Him, the small and the great." That includes all of us—all of us who love God, all of us who have given ourselves in faith to Jesus Christ. Whether we are great or small, we are to praise God. God commands us to do it.

393

Praise is a response. We don't have praise unless something happens first. We do not have praise unless there is a reason for praise. Praise is first, last, and always a response of the human heart. But what kind of response? The word *praise* and the concept of praise means "a sincere acknowledgment with real conviction of someone or something's value or worth." It means that something happens or someone does something, and we have a deep and abiding conviction that the object of our praise is worthy, is of value, is virtuous, is all that it ought to be. It is a strong response of the human heart. Here in these six verses that begin the nineteenth chapter of Revelation, we have the reason, the ground for our praise.

Before we look at these verses, I want to remind you of our responsibility to praise that we find throughout the book of Psalms. There are many admonitions to praise in the Psalms. They are numerous throughout, but listen to these: "I will praise the LORD at all times; His praise will always be on my lips" (Ps. 34:1). I thought of Psalm 103: "Bless the LORD, O my soul, and all that is within me, bless His holy name" (Ps. 103:1 NASB).

How do we bless God? Is God incomplete? Does God need something that we can give to Him? How do we bless God? It becomes very apparent when we look at the Word of God here. "I will praise the LORD at all times; His praise will always be on my lips" (Ps. 34:1). We bless God when we praise God. In Psalm 145 we read, "I will praise You every day; I will honor Your name forever and ever" (Ps. 145:2). We bless God by praising God. It blesses God when we praise Him.

We can easily substitute the word *praise* for the word *bless* in the Psalms. "Praise the Lord, O my soul, and all that is within me, praise His holy name." It would be just as accurate, just as right, just as biblical, just as true to our experience with Him. We are to *praise* God because our praise blesses God. It brings joy to the heart of God. It brings happiness to Him because that is the purpose for which man was created. Man was created to praise God, to bless God, to fellowship with God.

So when we come to the matter of praise, we're talking about something that is at the very heart of all we believe and everything we are. The sad thing is that so few of us ever spend time consciously praising God. In our prayers we ask Him for things. We talk to Him about doing certain things. We sometimes thank God and express gratitude to God, but I wonder how often we set time aside to do nothing but just praise the Lord. Hallelujah! in our hearts and in our souls.

Yet over and over again, the Bible says that is what we're to do. Simon Peter wrote: "Ye are a chosen generation, a royal priesthood, an holy nation, a peculiar people" (KJV). Why are we peculiar? He tells us that we should "proclaim the praises of the One who called you out of darkness into His marvelous light" (1 Pet. 2:9). The element of praise is the one thing that sets us apart from the rest of the world. When we study the pagan world, we find a legacy of bitterness and resentment against whatever gods there may be, because of the unhappiness and lack of fulfillment and purpose in these societies and in the nations of the world. But a Christian person is unique in this world, a peculiar person, because a Christian is one who praises God, who thanks God, who blesses God.

The writer to the Hebrews said, "Therefore, through Him let us continually offer up to God a sacrifice of praise, that is, the fruit of our lips that confess His name" (Heb. 13:15). That is the purpose for God's people—to praise Him. I have a duty to God to praise Him. It blesses God when I praise Him, so I have a duty to God to praise Him. I have a duty to myself to praise God because when I praise God I lose some of my touchiness. I lose some of my resentment. I lose some of my carnality. When I praise God, something happens on the inside of me that makes my life sweeter and better and more like Him. So I have a responsibility to myself to praise God.

I have a responsibility to my fellowman to praise God, because it is by faithfully praising God publicly that people come to know Christ. It is through the praise of the people of the Lord that the lost are saved. As we praise God with our lives, with our lips, and with all that we are, we are able to bring salvation into the experience of others through our praise. So I have a duty, a responsibility to praise God. And it's commanded of me in God's Word.

What am I to praise God for? This passage from Revelation gives us four reasons we ought to praise God. From our souls there ought to come a great crescendo of praise and thanksgiving to God. "After these things I heard, as it were, a loud voice of a great multitude in heaven, saying, 'Hallelujah! Salvation, glory, and power belong to our God'" (Rev. 19:1). Then verses 2 through 6 amplify and explain those words.

I. Hallelujah for His Perfect Redemption: Salvation

There is nothing incomplete about what God gives. God's salvation is a perfect salvation. It is a salvation that brings forgiveness of sins now; it brings a sweetness to life now, but it carries us through life, through death, into eternity. His salvation is a wonderful "hallelujah" thing. When we talk about salvation, we are to praise God because of His perfect redemption.

Man's redemption, man's salvation is temporary. Every kind of salvation man has is temporary. If our lives are saved in some accident, we were saved only for another date with death. We're saved only for another time. Whatever salvation is of this world is temporary. It is not lasting. But God's salvation is eternal. God's salvation is permanent. Not only does He bring forgiveness now, but it is a forgiveness that extends into all of eternity. His salvation in us is a permanent, eternal salvation.

Now that's worth shouting about! That's worth praising God about! That's something to get excited about! Hallelujah for a salvation like that! I'm not going to lose it tomorrow. No one is going to take it away from me. No one is going to cheat me out of it. No one is going to force it away from me. It is mine. I have been given redemption by God. It is a perfect, eternal redemption. So I can say in my heart, I can cry out in my soul, "Hallelujah! Praise God for a salvation like that—eternal, perfect salvation!"

Do you know an unsaved person can't really praise God? An unsaved person may acknowledge the existence of God, the power and wisdom of God. But praise is a sincere acknowledgment of a true conviction in our hearts of the worth and value of a thing or a person. So if I praise God, it's because I've been convicted in my soul that He is what He claims to be. It is because I have accepted in my heart the message that He has delivered to me, and I have accepted it and received it. It is mine. I have salvation in my heart, and that is why I can praise God. That eternal salvation, that perfect salvation is mine. So we have a right to praise God. We have a right to say, "Hallelujah!" because God has given us a perfect salvation, a perfect redemption.

II. Hallulujah for His Perfect Righteousness: Glory

More than that, God has given us a perfect righteousness. Notice the apostle John says, "Hallelujah! Salvation [that's redemption] and glory [that's righteousness]." Then he enlarges on that in the second verse by saying that God's judgments are true and righteous. He is a God of righteousness. He is a God who demands righteousness. His is not a righteousness like this world's. The world's righteousness is false. It is trivial. It is insignificant. It is not lasting but temporary in nature. It is a false kind of righteousness. It is not what it seems to be. It looks good on the surface, but inside it is full of dead men's bones. It is something that is rotten and destructive of life.

But God's righteousness, God's judgments are true. They are what they seem to be. His judgments are true and righteous. And I can praise God for that! I can praise God because when I came to receive salvation from Him, He declared me righteous, just as if I had never sinned. The righteousness of God has been imputed to me.

Concerning the Old Testament saints, the writer of the eleventh chapter of Hebrews says that they believed God, and their faith was counted to them for righteousness. It is God's righteousness. God doesn't expect me to achieve it on my own. God doesn't expect me to try to clean up my life and do the best I can. He says, "I want you to acknowledge that you cannot live it, that you cannot hold out, you cannot do what you need to do. When you come to that place in repentance and faith, as you bow your knee to Me and reach out to Me, I will give you a righteousness that's real. I'll give you a righteousness that lasts. I'll give you a righteousness that's true, not one based on your strength. Not one based on your wisdom, not one based on your ability to keep it, but one that is eternal and true." Hallelujah for righteousness like that.

The more I think about it, the more excited I get. I can hardly stand still. The more I see of what God has done for me and what He has given to me, in my heart there wells up a hallelujah to God for His perfect righteousness.

III. Hallelujah for His Perfect Respect: Honor

We ought to praise God because of His perfect honor. That is connected with worship, with respect, with reverence. That's why I believe with all of my heart that what we do in the place of worship ought to bring praise and glory to God. That's why we ought to be attentive, why we ought to participate, and why we ought to pray for what God wants to do in that service. Every time we gather together, we are here because of the perfect respect, the perfect reverence that belongs to God.

Notice verse 4: "Then the twenty-four elders and the four living creatures fell down and worshiped God, who is seated on the throne, saying: Amen! Hallelujuh!" They worshiped God because they were confronted with One who had perfect honor, perfect respect, One who deserved their attention, One who had earned that respect. Man doesn't deserve the kind of praise we're talking about here. It is always a false praise that comes to us from other human beings. It is always an undeserved praise, but to God there wells up praise in the heart of the person who belongs to Him.

Hallelujah because of who God is! He is the One who has brought salvation to me. He is the One who has removed my sin and brought me His righteousness. He is the Creator, the Redeemer. I must praise Him! I must worship Him! I must bow in respect to Him! Hallelujah! Pass the word! That's the foundation of my praise to Him.

IV. Hallelujah for His Perfect Rule: Power

We can praise God because of His perfect power or perfect rule. Verse 6 says, "Then I heard something like the voice of a vast multitude, like the sound of cascading waters, and like the rumbling of loud thunder, saying: Hallelujah—because our Lord God, the Almighty, has begun to reign!"

And verse 16 says, "On His robe and on His thigh He has a name written: KING OF KINGS AND LORD OF LORDS." We can praise His name because He has perfect power. We can praise His name because He will carry through His rule upon this earth. He longs to rule in our hearts, and He has demonstrated His power to us by bringing forth His Son out of the grave. Men killed Jesus Christ. They sought to keep Him in the grave. They buried Him and sealed the tomb with the seal of the mighty Roman Empire. But God moved in great power, and the stone rolled away without the aid of human hands. And Jesus Christ came out alive, eternally, magnificently, victoriously—alive! Jesus Christ, God's Son, showing His perfect power, His perfect rule here on earth.

And one day He's coming again. One day He's going to return. One day this Jesus Christ, this Savior, is going to come back to this earth. One day He is going to set up His kingdom. He has promised it. He has pledged it. There have been those before Him who said they were going to establish a kingdom. There were those before Him who said they would usher in Utopia. There were those before Him and since who have said they would bring in the millennium. But only Christ has the power to do that. Man's power is inadequate. God's power is unlimited. There is nothing that God cannot do. There is nothing that God cannot bring to pass. Hallelujah for His perfect power! What a wonderful, beautiful reason to praise God!

I look at these things and see how they have been borne out in my life. I remember when God came into the chaos and the confusion of my heart and saved me and brought His perfect redemption into my experience. I remember when as a little lad I knelt beside my father and mother's bed and wept my heart out as

I invited Jesus to come into my heart. I remember that experience of redemption. So I cannot praise God enough because it is permanently etched in my mind, rooted in the past but grounded in the present and headed for the future with Him. A wonderful and perfect redemption that was good enough for then, good enough for now, and will be good enough for eternity—a perfect, wonderful salvation that God has given to me.

So in my heart I can cry out, "Hallelujah! Praise the Lord for what He's done in my heart!" He has given me a perfect righteousness—not what I deserved, not left up to my abilities—but *His* righteousness. My goodness is as filthy rags. The very best I can do stinks in His sight. The very best I can do is unacceptable in His sight. The very best I can do is nothing but filthy rags.

He gives me not my best but His best. Not my righteousness but His righteousness. He makes me eternally wealthy, eternally rich in the righteousness of God. Hallelujah! for a righteousness like that. He brings a perfect respect and honor so I can come into the place of worship and I can fall on my knees and worship Him because He alone is worthy of that kind of praise, that kind of worship.

We cannot say enough about God's power. It takes the most despicable of men, the most enslaved of men, and brings them into the glorious liberty of salvation and eternal life, and gives them a new direction. There are people all across this world who can say, "Yes, there was a time when my life was enslaved, when I was a victim of sin, when I was away from God, my heart was empty, my heart was ugly and filthy and evil—and Jesus came in and gave to me, with His power, new life."

If you can't say "Hallelujah!" about that, you just haven't been saved! If you look back at the past and remember what you used to be, then look into the present and see what you are because of the grace of God, there wells up within your soul a wonderful Hallelujah! for what God has done.

Many things in God's Book tell us to do this. For instance, look at Psalm 148. I've always wanted to be a music director, but the Lord just didn't bless me with that talent. But I'm going to lead a choir right now. Do you want to listen to it? Just look at Psalm 148. Listen to this choir. Are you ready up there? All right! Praise ye the Lord! It's just "Hallelujah!" "Hallelujah from the heavens!" "Praise Him in the heights!" Now get ready! "Praise Him, all His angels!" All right, angels, let's hear it! "Hallelujah!" It's an angelic chorus. "Praise Him all the hosts!"

All right, sun—"Praise Him, sun!" All right, moon—"Praise Him, moon!" All right, stars—"Praise Him, all ye stars of light!" All right, heavens that surround us and encompass us—"Praise Him! Hallelujah!" Let them praise the name of the Lord, for He commanded, and they were created. All right, earth, let's hear it— "Praise the Lord from the earth!" Sea monsters and all deeps— "Praise Him." All right, fire—"Hallelujah!" Hail—"Hallelujah!" Snow—"Hallelujah!" Vapors—"Hallelujah!" Stormy wind— "Hallelujah!" I believe it's harder leading singing than it is preaching. I have just about worn myself out, and we're not through yet!

All right, mountains, stand up tall. Let's hear it—"Hallelujah!" All hills—"Hallelujah!" Fruitful trees and all cedars—"Hallelujah!" Beasts and all cattle, creeping things, and flying fowls— "Hallelujah!" Kings of the earth and all people—"Hallelujah!" Princes—"Hallelujah!" Judges—"Hallelujah!" Young men— "Hallelujah!" Maidens—"Hallelujah!" Old men—"Hallelujah!" I don't know why old women aren't mentioned. Is it because women never grow old? Somehow they got left out.

Children—"Hallelujah! Let them praise the name of the Lord!" Why should we praise God? Why should we lift up our voices? Why should we do it? Because "His name alone is exalted" (Ps. 148:13). There's not another excellent name in the earth—not the name of a prophet, not the name of a teacher, not the name of a preacher, not the name of a president, not the name of a king—not any name on the earth. We can write all the names of the great men across the skies, and when we have finished, God will come with a pen dipped in blood and write "Jesus Christ."

His name is the *only* name that is worthy of praise! His name is the *only* name worthy of adoration! His name is the *only* name before which we are to bow. It is His name by which we're saved. If we do not claim that name of Christ, we are not saved. We shall not know eternal life. His name alone is excellent and brings salvation. It is the name before which men must come to be saved. It is the name that must continually be on the lips of the saints, of those who love Him—His name *only*. Praise not man. Praise not the ingenuity of man. Praise not man's organization or his genius. Praise Jesus. His name *only* is excellent! *Hallelujah!*

Look at Psalm 150. "Hallelujah!" it starts out. "Praise God in His sanctuary. Praise Him in His mighty heavens. Praise Him for His powerful acts; praise Him for His abundant greatness" (vv. 1–2). And it ends the same way: "Let every thing that breathes praise the LORD! Hallelujah!" (v. 6). *Hallelujah!*

34

Building Blocks for a Strong Family

EPHESIANS 3:14–15 NIV

Dan Hall
President, On Course Ministries

GROWING UP, I OFTEN WATCHED the television program *All in the Family* with my father. It was one of those times I watched my dad belly laugh. I think he knew some "Archie Bunkers," although he was far from one himself. Archie was the stereotypical chauvinistic bigot. Meathead was the quintessential liberal. Gloria was the whiner. And of course, Edith just floated on someone else's radar screen most of the time.

Perhaps you will recall the episode where Meathead and Gloria were getting married. They were arguing with Archie over whether to have a Polish rabbi or a Catholic priest officiate the wedding. Quite upset that a Pole would be in his home, Archie declared, "Well, I can tell you one thing! I'm not going to have some rabbi going around sprinkling *incest* all over my house!" We have to laugh at Archie's bigotry, idiocy, and butchery of the English language, all the while believing himself part of the intelligentsia.

These shows capture our hearts because they deal, although humorously, with home and family. In the first months after September 11, 2001, Home Depot's sales increased some 25 percent. Why? During difficult times, people go home. People intuitively move toward family when things get tough. We look for a refuge.

Even the History Channel gets into the arena. One recent program *Family Tree* told the story of someone attempting to trace the lineage of William Wallace. Another was tracing his own family origin. Why does that intrigue us? Because we feel a rootedness, a sense of belonging, in our family.

Over the years, however, family shows on television have evolved into more and more dysfunction. It began with the idyllic *Father Knows Best* and *Leave It to Beaver*. These programs gave way to the stereotypical *All in the Family* and *Good Times*. Entertainment evolution led to the politically correct *Home Improvement, The Cosby Show,* and the morally impotent *Everyone Loves Raymond,* where the man's buffoonery is continually accentuated by a condescending woman. The demise has continued with the cynical despair of *Frazier, Friends,* and *Sex and the City,* propagating singleness as a satisfying lifestyle.

Our children are being deluged with this dysfunction through programming that specifically targets them. MTV and VH1 push the envelope further by affirming not only singleness but casual sex. From *Real World* to *Blind Date,* from *Sorority House* to *Sex in Rock 'n Roll,* these channels portray the sexual perversions of our time.

MTV's *Y2Sex* aired during prime time viewing in 2002. The program examined teenagers and their exploration of various sexual practices. The result was the normalization of deviant sexual behavior so that our children no longer have a reference point about right and wrong in sexual matters.

David Seal, Jr., in his article entitled "We're Not Mayberry" says: "Children are growing up in a world where the meaning of life has been reduced to shopping at a mall, where boredom is the greatest fear, and entertainment is the sole solution." I agree with his assessment. And in the midst of all this, there are really only two places of refuge left in America: godly homes and Bible-based churches. We need to fight for these!

There are many issues regarding the family. Primarily, we must understand that there is a dynamic in family that is godly, divine, and powerful. Genesis 1 gives us a snapshot of what the family should look like: "God said, 'Let us make man in our image, in our likeness, and let them rule over the fish of the sea and the birds of the air, over the livestock, over all the earth, and over all the creatures that move along the ground.' So God created man in his own image, in the image of God he created him; male and female he created them. God blessed them and said to them, 'Be fruitful and increase in number, fill the earth and subdue it'" (Gen. 1:26–28).

It has been said that politeness is a person who listens with interest to things of which he is an expert when told to him with certainty by a novice. Our culture is trying to speak to the family when it does not have a clue what it is talking about. Our nation continues to slide toward familial bankruptcy. The church has tried to be polite, but it is imperative that as we seek to relate graciously to the world, we also speak a clear word to our culture regarding God's model for the family.

I. God's Design for the Family

There are three aspects to God's design for the family. The first fundamental truth is that family begins with a male and female. That settles the sexual preference issue. *God's design for the family begins with a man and a woman.* This is an established principle in God's Word!

The second aspect of God's design is that *God brings together a man and a woman in a covenant commitment.* They are committed to each other and to each other alone. Mark Twain was arguing with a Mormon about polygamy, exchanging cultural, spiritual, and theological perspectives. Finally the Mormon said, "You can't show me one passage of Scripture that says polygamy is wrong."

Twain said, "I can, too."

"Well, what is it?"

"That's easy. 'You cannot serve two masters.'"

The family begins with a covenant commitment by a husband and a wife to each other alone, before God. This speaks to the issue of moral faithfulness, before and after marriage. Many accept that adultery is wrong. We know that if one is in a marriage and they commit adultery, it is wrong. But moral fidelity reaches further.

Fornication, or sex before the marriage relationship, is sexual immorality. It occurs outside a covenant relationship, and thus it is wrong. We cannot have God's blessing on our relationships if we violate the principles of covenant commitment, even if we love the other person.

The question is often asked, How far is too far? Here's the answer: You've gone too far when you can't do it in front of her dad. You may say, "Dan, that's awfully harsh." It isn't harsh when you are a dad! It sounds pretty reasonable to me. Every time you violate that woman, every time you violate that man, you are violating him or her in the presence of their heavenly Father.

We must gain control of our passions. A recent study demonstrated that our sex drive is the only passion that we permit people to fulfill in any way they desire. We do not let people who overeat feel good about their problem. We do not allow people to drink too much without challenging their actions. But when it comes to sex, we think that anything goes as long as it feels good and does not "hurt anyone." This attitude is disrupting and destroying marriages.

Some couples were involved sexually before they married, though maybe only with the person they married. They may never have dealt with the fact that they built on the wrong foundation. Some of the uncertainty and insecurity in their relationship today may go back to the fact that they violated God's principles and never repented. They have never had the courage to look at each other and admit their wrong and ask each other for forgiveness. If they would repent, they would find a whole new foundation on which to build their marriage. The future would be years of moral purity. This repentance disarms Satan of his ability to heap guilt on us. God forgives and wholly cleanses us.

This unrelenting passion for moral purity must also include a rejection of the increasingly acceptable arrangement of living together. It does not matter how committed a couple is to each other, if they refuse to enter the covenant relationship of marriage, they are not in a covenant commitment. This must be said in our culture. While some would accuse us of being antiquated, we are actually seeking to help them to build a successful life. They are building on the wrong foundation if they are failing to observe the principles that God has designed for the family.

The third aspect of God's design for the family is that *the family exists for God's purposes.* During a wedding ceremony, I heard a pastor say, "Love is not self-absorption in each other. Love is coming together and committing yourselves to God's purpose for your lives." God brings us together for His purposes. Our prayer should be, "God help us in this marriage to become everything You have called us to be."

One of the primary purposes in God's heart is life. Jesus said, "I have come that you might have life, and have it to the full" (see John 10:10). Genesis 1:28 tells us that God's first command to a married couple is to be fruitful and multiply. And we are not simply talking about having children. Rather, we are talking about procreating life. If a couple can't have children or have chosen not to have children, they are still called to procreate life and to procreate God's purposes in their lives.

There are many strong Christian couples who are ministering life out of their marriage. For many, it includes the immediacy of their own biological children. For others, it may be ministering to other people's children. And for many others, it is ministering to God's children in general. They understand that God has brought them together to affirm life on the earth. His command and blessing is on this arrangement. There is nothing more powerful than a man and a woman in a divine covenant commitment, fulfilling God's purposes.

So is it any wonder that the devil wants to destroy the family? It is the greatest channel of God's grace to this culture. That is why God says in Psalm 68 that He is a Father to the fatherless, a defender of widows, and that He places the lonely in families (see Ps. 68:5–6). His answer to the loneliness question is to put people in family relationships where their needs can be met. So God has both an important social design and an eternal purpose for the family.

II. Building Blocks for the Family

Now let's consider five building blocks for a strong family. Look at Psalm 78: "I will open my mouth . . . I will utter hidden things, things from of old—what we have heard and known, what our fathers have told us. We will not hide them from our children; we will tell the next generation the praiseworthy deeds of the LORD, His power, and the wonders He has done" (Ps. 78:2–4).

The first building block for the strong family is *clear values*. The psalmist declared, "I know what I've been taught, and I'm going to teach it to my children." God commanded our forefathers to teach their children so that the next generation would know them—even the children yet to be born—and they in turn would tell their children. Then they would put their trust in God and would not forget His deeds. They would keep His commandments. There are many families who have not established what is really important in life.

The beginning of our clear values must be in the Word of God, not *Oprah,* or *The O'Reilly Factor,* or the latest trendy magazine. What does God's Word say about how to build a strong family? I want to give you six values that are primary in my family. These values are the ones that my wife and I try to uphold in our family and impart to our children.

The first and most important value is a *personal relationship with God through Jesus Christ.* You can be born again. You can know God. You can talk with God. You can walk with God *today*. You don't have to wait until you have graduated from seminary, or college, or even high school. You don't have to wait until something weird happens to you.

I was saved when I was five, and my wife was saved when she was seven. I have a daughter who was saved at three, and she will tell you when she accepted Christ and what happened on that day. It is incredible. All three of us knew what we were doing when we accepted the Lord. Did we understand everything that happened to us spiritually? Of course not! But how many of us actually did? We have all grown in our walk with the Lord.

When I accepted Christ, I just didn't want to go to hell. That was my sole motivation. But I knew enough to know that He was the only way to avoid that destiny. And God honored that decision. How much more did I need to know? Later I learned I was a coheir with Christ and that all Christ is has become my identity. I learned that greater is He that is in me than he that is in the world. I learned that Christ took God's wrath and satisfied it at the cross, thus becoming sin that I might become the very righteousness of God. But when I got saved, I didn't understand any of that. I just didn't want to go to hell. I wanted to go to heaven. And here is what is incredible. Jesus saved me anyway! And He has helped me grow in the faith.

Another important value to teach our children is the *absoluteness of the Scripture as God's Word*. We need to know it. We need to understand it. We need to obey it. We need to see this conviction modeled in the home. We want our children to know the Word of God. We talk about it at the dinner table. We talk about it as situations allow for scriptural applications. I want my children to know the Word of God is foundational for life.

Another key value we need to teach in the home is that *God's will is always best*. I want my children to know that God's will is always the best option. No matter what happens, God is always working for our absolute and eternal optimum outcome. We were having a family discussion in our home a few weeks ago. One daughter was upset about something that was going on in a relationship. I simply asked, "What does God's Word say about it?" If we choose God's will, we will discover the most effective solution. She applied God's Word, and while it was initially difficult, she ended up receiving kudos from her principal for her mature behavior.

A fourth important value is that *each person is made by the Lord for a specific purpose*. I want my children to know they were shaped and fashioned by God Himself for a specific purpose. They have value, they are important, they are unique.

The next value we teach in our home is that *we are solely responsible for our lives*. We must not blame our difficulties or problems on someone else. We live in a society of victimization. The world claims that every bad thing in our lives is someone else's fault. But it is our responsibility to live our lives and to accept the consequences of our actions and decisions. I will answer for my life. No one else can do it for me. No one else should. It is part of my unique personality and who I am as a person.

The final value that we try to instill into our children is a *sense of eternity*. Ecclesiastes 3:11 says, "He [God] has set eternity in the hearts of men." I want my children to live their lives with the understanding that they are living for eternity. One day we will stand before God and answer for the paths we chose to walk. We will receive rewards for our lives on earth. I want their values and their decisions today to be based on that sense of the eternal.

The second building block is *authority*. The first authority is the parents. Many modern households are in chaos because of a lack of order in the home. This happens in too many situations because the children don't know who the parents are. Ephesians 6:1–3 says, "Children, obey your parents in the Lord, for this is right. Honor your father and mother—which is the first commandment with a promise—that it may go well with you and that you may enjoy long life on the earth."

Therefore, we must have *understood authority* in the home, and this begins with parents being parents. The situation in many homes today is tragic. There is much disorder and tension because parents are not serving as authorities. Too many children rule the home. They rule their parents with whining, tantrums, and complaints. Consequently, parents give in and don't understand why the children persist in those behaviors. *Parents need to be parents.*

Some parents fear they will damage their children if they exercise parental authority. But not disciplining them will damage them also! Paul said life will not go well with our children if they do not obey their parents. And they will not obey their parents if the parents do not demand it. If we love our children and want them to live prosperous, fulfilling lives, we must train them to obey us.

You may say, "But I was abused and mistreated as a child." If you were abused, don't scar your offspring by repeating the abuse. Help is available for those so wounded. However, we can also abuse our children by withholding the discipline they need in order to grow into responsible adults.

Another important dimension of this authority in the home is that *men are to lead.* Ephesians 5 says that as a church submits to Christ, wives should submit to their husbands (see Eph. 5:22). This is politically incorrect, but it is spiritually mandatory. Husbands are called to lead in the home. We are to love God and be men who obey Him.

Some will certainly be offended by this assertion of male leadership, but somebody has to lead. You cannot drive in a caravan unless someone is given the lead position. You cannot dance if someone does not lead. A sports team cannot win if someone does not lead. And God has mandated that responsibility to the husband. Someone has to lead.

To be sure, some women are married to men who fit the stereotype, either as sluggards or dominating jerks. But the answer is not rebellion, independence, or some kind of feminist movement. What men have done for centuries is often reprehensible. But there's still "a way that seemeth right unto man, but the end thereof are the ways of death" (Prov. 14:12 KJV). If we do not respond according to God's Word on this matter, we will only perpetuate the problem. If your husband isn't leading, you must find God's heart on this matter. Just know that He has promised that He would minister to you.

Men, we are called to lead, but it is within the context of loving our wives as Christ loved the church (see Eph. 5:25). Consider what Peter says: "Husbands, in the same way be considerate toward your wives . . . that your prayers may not be hindered" (1 Pet. 3:7 NIV). The tragedy in many family situations is that where men try to lead, they stop being considerate. They tend to be either dominating or withdrawn.

God, knowing this proclivity in men, commands them to treat their wives with respect as the weaker partner. The phrase "weaker partner" does not mean that the wife is weak physically, emotionally, or spiritually. In the context it means that she is the weaker partner *positionally*. Having thus subordinated her, God requires the man to affirm his wife by elevating her as sharer and coheir of the gracious gift of His life. He is to reach down and draw her to walk beside him. How? By considering her. By granting her emotions, her thoughts, and her perspectives influence in the decision-making process. It is true that men will stand before God for the decisions in the home. But if we do not consider our wives in those decisions, we will be limiting God's wisdom to us in that process, and we must answer to her heavenly Father on why we did not consider His life in her.

Men, when we understand our role, we will elevate our wives, not patronize them. We *husband* them. This word *husband* is a farming term. It has to do with meaningful and purposeful cultivating. It's a far cry from the dominating Archie Bunker, or the impotent Raymond, or Tim "The Tool Man" Taylor whom we see on television. Men, don't confuse leadership with domination or always being right.

One woman said, "I met 'Mr. Right.' I just didn't realize his first name was 'Always.'" Men, that is not leadership. Please show leadership by loving God and loving your wife and loving your children. One of our greatest joys is to love our wives as Christ loved the church. And how much did Christ love the church? He gave His life for it!

Building block number three for the home is that we need to have *shared responsibilities*. Ecclesiastes 4:9 says, "Two are better than one, because they have a good return for their work." John Adams, in talking about training his own children, said to his wife, "Fire them with ambition to be useful, exercising frugality and industry."

If we are going to have strong families, we need to have shared responsibilities. We need to teach our children how to work. Proverbs 14:23 says, "All hard work brings a profit." We must teach them the value of industry. We must help them develop a work ethic. We must train them to appreciate the value of making a contribution to society and instill a sense of pride and community into them.

My children are already saving money for their first car. I am helping them do this because I want them to learn the value of a dollar. Not long ago my son was begging to go to McDonald's. I had just given him a dollar. I said, "Son, you give me that dollar, and we'll go to McDonald's." Suddenly, McDonald's was not as appealing as it was when it didn't cost him anything. I want him to understand the value of that dollar he is holding in his hand.

When we get up from the table at our house, I make work assignments. "You do this, you do that, you cover the kitchen, you take the sink," and so on. I want our children to accept responsibility. I want Mom out of the kitchen. She has worked hard enough. And of course all the children are scrambling to see who is going to receive those specific assignments. They have their ideas about which jobs are the easiest.

And the truth is that it would be easier to do these things ourselves. Children can turn a five-minute job into thirty minutes. It is amazing, and they gripe the whole time. But doing these jobs ourselves would not be teaching them how to work and how to share responsibilities in the home.

Building block number four is to *value individuals* in the family. Psalm 139 says: "For You [God] created my inmost being; You knit me together in my mother's womb. Lord, I praise You because I am fearfully and wonderfully made; Your works are wonderful, I know that full well. My frame was not hidden from You when I was made in the secret place. When I was woven together in the depths of the earth, Your eyes saw my unformed body. All the days ordained for me were written in Your book before one of them came to be" (Ps. 139:13–16).

Strong families will value the individuals in the family. We need to know each member. We need to listen to them and hear their hearts. In our home we often go around the dinner table and have everybody tell about their day. No one is allowed to interrupt while others are talking. What we find when we get around the table is that we have heard one another's hearts. We have heard their interests. We have heard their goals.

My wife is good at listening to our children. Generally speaking, dads are good at telling what they know, while moms seem good at discovering things about their children they do not know, simply because they know how to listen. I listen to my wife pray for our children. She knows their hearts, and she hears what they are saying. I am trying to learn from her.

So we need to know our children. We need to encourage them. Speak positively about each child. Speak positively about each other. Build up your wife. Build up your husband in front of the children. Build up the children in front of one another. Enjoy who they are. Enjoy their expressions. Our children have different personalities. We try to affirm that personality, whether it is the organized one, the relational one, the party animal, or the strong-willed one.

We are learning to enjoy the expressions of our children. Our two-year-old has a favorite song, "Little Drummer Boy." We have been singing "rum-pa-pa-pum" since October. We are all sick of "rum-pa-pa-pum." But underneath our feigned irritation is a corporate joy in sharing these moments together. It's a fun thing. Sometimes the whole family joins in. We value this ritual because it is part of who Bethany is.

Another part of this valuing the individual is supporting our children. This involves helping them with their schoolwork and helping them with their athletics. But it is also taking the family to support them when they are participating in an athletic event or having a music recital. Support like this builds a strong family.

Building block number five for the family is to *build joyful memories*. The Jewish custom was to have ways of remembering. The Old Testament might even be considered a book of remembrance.

The Passover celebration evolved into the service of communion for the Christian church. Baptism reflects our salvation and identifies us as believers. Those are points of remembrance, things that we go back to. They remind us of important events from the past.

In our family we have Thanksgiving, Christmas, and Easter banners. My wife has organized and promoted these rituals. The banner has felt symbols that attach to the banner with Velcro. For instance, twenty-five days before Christmas we begin our Christmas banner. Each day we read Scripture related to Christ's birth and ministry, sing a song, memorize a Bible verse, and pray. After this time of celebration, someone places the symbol that corresponds to that day's story on the banner.

We have similar banners for Easter and Thanksgiving. For Easter, we make a chocolate cross cake. This helps us to remember who Jesus is and His sacrifice on our behalf.

We also make a big fuss over birthdays in our family. I didn't have many birthday parties when I was growing up. My wife taught me how to celebrate birthdays, and we do that with the children. If I ever schedule anything that conflicts with a birthday party, I am in big trouble! These birthday parties—plus all the other traditions that my wife is so good about maintaining—provide good memories for our family.

There is power in joyful memories—vacations that you take as a family, restaurants that you go to, the things that bring memories and joy. My counsel to people: "If you ever have to choose between money and a memory, go for the memory." I am not suggesting you go into debt and get into financial trouble. But sometimes in our overzealous frugality, we fail to turn an event into a wonderful memory that will stay with our children for a lifetime.

Telling stories is also a good way to build memories. At family reunions people repeat the same stories over and over again, laughing at the appropriate points. Why? These stories show our con- nection to others. They remind us that we belong to something bigger than ourselves. Have you ever noticed how children like to hear stories about themselves? Retell those stories. We can also tell them stories about how Daddy and Mommy met. We can tell them how we came to follow Christ. The children will often not care how often they hear those stories, so we are able to keep retelling them. The result is strength in the family and security in their little hearts.

Just a brief mention, grandparents are our greatest family assets for preserving and passing on memories. They can help families knit together by retelling the stories that affirm and speak of the value of people and human relationships. This affirmation is powerful in helping to root individuals and families. If grandparents are still living, find ways to include them in the lives of your children.

Clear values, authority, shared responsibilities, valued individuals, and *joyful memories* combine to create a beautiful mosaic of hope and purpose for any family. This institution of family is often maligned, misrepresented, and abused, even though it is the most important foundation of any community. It is worth our energies to build it for God's glory, whatever that may cost us.

Strong families take hard work. Poet Nikki Giovanni said, "Nothing is easy to the unwilling." We must be willing to fight for this divine institution and cultural mooring.

In conclusion, a strong family begins and continues with a personal, vibrant, growing relationship with Jesus Christ. We started with Ephesians 3:14–15. It tells us that the family was brought into being by God Himself. He will help us build a strong family if we commit ourselves to Him and pray that every member of our families will come to know Him as Lord and Savior and follow Him with all their hearts.

35

Don't Give Up the Ship

MALACHI 2:13–16; ECCLESIASTES 5:4 NIV

Jim Henry
Senior Pastor, First Baptist Church
Orlando, Florida

JAY KESSLER IS A COLLEGE PRESIDENT who also does some counseling and writing. In a recent interview, he told a reporter the following story. It was Christmastime and he was at a country club. He sat down at a table next to a friend who was sitting by himself. The man, well-loved and well-known in the community, had just gone through a divorce. He had remarried, as had his former wife. Kessler said:

My friend sat silently for several minutes, his eyes some-what misty and filled with regret. Then he said, "You know, Jay, I often see my former wife with this other man and, even though we're divorced and she has every right to be with him, I really resent him. It looks to me like they are really happy. I get a horrible, sinking feeling because I thought our divorce would solve a problem, but it didn't. I feel like I've lost it all; I'm convinced that if we had tried harder at our first marriage . . ." and his voice trailed off.

Then he said something that seemed extremely insightful. "You know, Jay, we should have tried harder." After a pause, he added, "I think we tend to marry the right person the first time around. What do you think?" I nodded yes. I answered, "I've noticed that people usually have some kind of intuitive sense when they pick their mate. Spending time to make their relationship work is far superior to giving up." He agreed. I guess every marriage starts out with all the anticipation and excitement of new love, but when things dry up or grow sour it seems somehow easier to throw it all away and then start over.[1]

We live in what someone has called a "throw-away society"—a cut-flower generation. We throw away diapers, disposable cameras, and just about everything else. I'm told Hollywood has a store that rents engagement and wedding rings. I understand that Hollywood actors and actresses average four marriages each during a lifetime. But one of every two marriages in America ends in divorce.

I'm speaking to two groups: those of you who are already married and, hopefully, not contemplating divorce—and I hope you never will. Or you may be thinking about it. I want to plug really hard for you to stay with your vows. The second group I'm talking to are those of you who are single and will be married. But before you get married, make sure you lock down the hatch and that it will be a commitment for a lifetime so you choose well and stay with your vows.

Some of you are divorced; you've already gone down that path. And some of you could speak on this subject better than I can. This is not to criticize you who are divorced. It's not to put a judgment on you. Some of my best friends and family members have walked through that valley of the death of a marriage, so I understand something of that. I'm certainly not wanting to put you down or cast aspersions on you in any way. But you'll understand as I go through this message that my call is a call that the Bible gives, and that is to keep your vows.

As your pastor, I have that responsibility, even though it might be painful to hear. I have the responsibility to challenge all of us who are married and those who will be married to keep their vows and not to let that ship sink. I believe that everybody who gets married intends for that ship of love to keep on sailing. But somewhere along the way, the love boat can get into trouble; the seas get choppy, and it becomes difficult. There comes a tendency in this throw-away society to throw away the investment of those years. Today on behalf of God's Word and His will, I want to bring this message as a challenge to you to keep your marriage ship afloat.

In the book of Malachi, chapter 2, Malachi, the last prophet in the Old Testament, is speaking to the people of Judah. He talks about covenants, beginning with the covenant of Judah and Israel with God. In verse 13, he narrows it to those who are married.

> Another thing you do: You flood the LORD's altar with tears. You weep and wail because he no longer pays attention to your offerings or accepts them with pleasure from your hands. You ask, "Why?" It is because the LORD is acting as the witness between you and the wife of your youth, because you have broken faith with her, though she is your partner, the wife of your marriage covenant.
>
> Has not the LORD made them one? In flesh and spirit they are his. And why one? Because he was seeking godly offspring. So guard yourself in your spirit, and do not break faith with the wife of your youth.
>
> "I hate divorce," says the LORD God of Israel, "and I hate a man's covering himself with violence as well as with his garment," says the LORD Almighty.
>
> "So guard yourself in your spirit and do not break faith" (Mal. 2:13–16).

I. Guard Against Leaks in the Ship

As we look at this passage and talk about not giving up the ship, I want you to notice first some caution signs that your marriage ship could be leaking. Verse 15 says, "Guard yourself in your spirit" (NIV). So there is a warning given, a commandment issued in this passage that we should be careful because marriages can get into trouble. There are some early warning signs which indicate that your marriage might be springing a leak.

We have early warning signals from military spy satellites that can tell us if there is danger from an approaching enemy. If you are swimming at the beach, the guards will warn you of impending danger. There are early warning signs for cancer, heart attacks, and other things. So we are used to early warning signs. For some of you who are married, God's Word declares first, "Guard your spirit, guard your heart."

What are some of the signs that your marriage could be heading for trouble? I want to make an acrostic of the word *divorce*.

First, let's look at the letter *D*. The first early warning sign for marriage is *Dullness*. You've been married for several years, and the routine gets to be boring. You go to work on Monday morning and you work until Monday night, and you come home, and you fix dinner, and on Monday nights it's beans. You go through the same routine the next day, and the next night it's collard greens; then another night it's pizza, and Thursday night it's spaghetti; Friday it's Taco Bell, and Saturday night you're on your own. Sunday it's sandwiches.

You go through the same routine day after day; you help the children with their homework; you're tired; you watch television or read the newspaper; and it goes on day after day after day. This brings on dullness and boredom. You begin to think, *It has to be more exciting than this.* Dullness and boredom! If you're feeling that way, it's an early warning sign for your marriage.

The *I* in *divorce* stands for *independence*—that sense of "I need my space. I've got to have my rights; I mean, after all, I'm still an individual." Some preacher has said the troubles begin when a man is busy earning his salt and forgets his sugar, and he or she goes away and they forget and become independent. *Do I really need him? Do I really need her? I think I could make it if I had to.* A sense of independence moves in. Now independence is a good thing in many ways. But the Bible declares that we are built for relationships, for family, for community. That's why I emphasize communal relationships—belonging to a church family. The Bible is clear about that. It knows little about independence but a great deal about community. Our strong American sense of independence often bleeds over into marriage.

Third, there is the *vexation* of immaturity, the V in *divorce*. Paul said in 1 Corinthians, "When I became a man, I put away childish things" (1 Cor. 13:11 KJV). Sometimes in marriage there is a lot of immaturity, and it becomes vexing to the married spouse. How do you know a person is immature or mature? There are several evidences of maturity.

A mature person accepts responsibility for his or her actions. A mature person also accepts others; he understands other people. He may not like everything about other people, but he accepts their faults. A mature person accepts reality. Mature people will accept reality, look at it, and say, "That's real; I need to deal with that."

A mature person also accepts the growing process. Everybody is going to get older, and a mature person accepts that as part of the life cycle. Does this mean that a spouse should not try to look his best, feel her best, act his best? Of course not. But a mature person accepts the reality of the cycles of life and understands that growing old and the changes that come with the passing years are inevitable.

Immaturity in any of these areas can cause problems in a marriage. The longer a person remains immature in the marriage, the deeper that problem can become, finally causing the other partner to say, "I just can't put up with this relationship any longer."

Then there's the thing I call the *omission of God,* which stands for the O in the word *divorce*. Sometimes it begins as an erosion process with a couple. They're active in church, go to Bible studies, have fellowship with friends, enjoy being at church. Then after a while they no longer have their quiet time; they don't pray or read the Bible like they used to. Perhaps they start skipping church every other Sunday; then they attend every third Sunday. One thing leads to another, and after a while their hearts have grown cold. Whenever God is left out of the triangle of marriage, trouble is lurking. Someone has compared this situation to two ticks feeding on each other. Rather than having God as a source, a giver, a renewer, a rebuilder, or as a focuser of faith and love, the couple begins to frustrate each other because they have no central source of strength and power.

The *R* in *divorce* stands for *romance fizzles.* Romance in marriage used to sizzle, but now it fizzles. I heard about a wife who was complaining to her husband. She said, "Honey, you don't love me like you used to."

"What are you talking about?"

"You used to kiss me."

"All right," he answered, "I'll kiss you." He leaned over and kissed her.

She said, "You used to hold my hand." So he reached over and grabbed her hand.

She said, "You used to bite me on the neck." He jumped up and started out of the room. She asked, "Where are you going?"

"I gotta go get my teeth."

You have to keep romance going in a marriage, and this doesn't mean sexual techniques. It means certain things you share. Communication, stories, and experience all help build the romance of our relationships. This makes physical intimacy in a marriage more meaningful because of the way you share experiences and those little things you tweak each other with. That's what builds the joy of the physical side of marriage. But if you don't make some effort to keep a marriage fresh and exciting, romance can fizzle.

The *C* in *divorce* represents *communication breakdown.* Someone has said that communication between a husband and a wife is not a luxury; it's a necessity. Sometimes spouses quit talking to each other. Why do they do that? The biggest reason is selfishness. You get tied up in your world, and you don't care enough about reaching out when you are tired. Or you need to talk to—or listen to—your spouse and don't do it. You may think, *If I told him this or shared this with him, it would hurt him—and I don't want to cause any pain.* Sometimes we don't communicate because of low self-esteem. Perhaps you think, *If I did this, or talked about this, she wouldn't think as highly of me as she ought to, so I just won't bring it up.*

These things can lead to a breakdown of communication in marriage. Men, our wives want us to talk to them about how we feel and about what is going on in our lives. It's critical to the relationship. In a communication breakdown where you don't talk, I guarantee you that someone will show up who will listen to her talk. And it's usually a person of the opposite sex.

The *E* in the word *divorce* stands for *entrapped by materialism*. A few years ago the state of Washington had eleven thousand divorces. More than half of them had to do with financial problems. Someone has said it is not the high cost of living but the cost of high living that causes problems in marriages.

If any of these things are becoming early warning signs in your marriage, don't let them get you to the edge of the cliff and push you over. If you and your mate are heading in that direction, you need to talk to someone who can help you turn things around.

II. Consequences of a Sinking Ship

The prophet Malachi also talks about the consequences if the marriage ship sinks. Look at verse 16 of Malachi 2: "'I hate divorce,'" says the LORD God of Israel, 'and I hate a man's covering himself with violence as well as with his garment,' says the LORD Almighty." Why does God hate divorce? The Bible doesn't say very often that God hates something, but when it does, it should get our attention. God hates divorce for several reasons.

First, He hates divorce because He is seeking godly offspring. Look at verse 15: "Has not the LORD made them one? In flesh and spirit they are his. And why one? Because he was seeking godly offspring."

God made Adam and God made Eve. He didn't make a bunch of Adams and a bunch of Eves. He made one man for one woman. The first institution was marriage. God intended for godly Adam and godly Eve to bring forth godly offspring. When He joins a woman and a man together in this basic institution of marriage, what does

He want? He wants Christian couples to produce godly children. This becomes much more difficult to do when divorce enters the picture. So God says, "I hate divorce because I am looking for godly offspring."

Second, divorce breaks faith and violates truth standards. In verses 14–15, Malachi talks about breaking faith. In fact, He also talks about it in verses 10–11 and 14–16. He talks about violating truth's standard. God is a God of faithfulness and truth. When divorce happens, it takes away the picture of fidelity that God is trying to portray in the marriage relationship. God keeps His Word; He keeps His vows; He keeps His covenant. Divorce violates the standards that God is trying to bring to the world as a God of truth and honesty.

Third, notice what God says in verse 16 through the prophet Malachi: "I hate a man's covering himself with violence as well as with his garment" (NIV). God uses some strong terms talking about the consequences of divorce.

Divorce brings a great deal of emotional harm—the tears, the screams, the rejection, the loneliness, the depression, the emptying of self, and the feeling of "I'm not anybody." All of these things happen in divorce. Can anyone who has gone through a divorce say it was pleasant? Nobody I know has said it was a good thing to be divorced. Nobody I know says, "We went to the divorce court, and we did it happily." Divorce brings a tremendous emotional challenge to those who go through it.

Some attorneys discussed the anger that people manufacture when they go through divorce. One of the attorneys said, "There's enough anger I have dealt with in divorce proceedings to turn the turbines at Niagara Falls." That's a lot of anger. Another of the attorneys said that in one case where there was to be a property division in a divorce, the husband brought a chain saw into the kitchen of their house and began to cut the cabinets and even the sink in half. That's how angry he was. In another case, the wife, who was a hairdresser and had taken care of her husband's toupees through their years of marriage, found out that her husband was having an affair. She took his seven thousand dollars worth of toupees, covered them in lighter fluid, and set them on fire. Another woman took everything out of the house when she moved out. She even removed all the lightbulbs so her husband could not see what was missing when he discovered she had left him.

One husband took off with a young woman to Hawaii and wired his wife to sell all their assets and split the proceeds. So she sold his $70,000 Mercedes for $250 and sent him his $125. That is anger! Divorce takes a tremendous emotional toll on people. One lawyer said that when people go through a divorce, their brains suddenly turn to bubble gum.[2]

Divorce is also harmful to personal identity. People begin to look at themselves and ask, *Who am I? Who do I belong with? What's wrong with me?* There's a profound sense of loss of personal worth when you've given yourself to someone you love and your love is rejected.

Divorce is also harmful because it affects one's friends. It puts friends in a difficult position—your neighbor friends, the people you work with, your church friends, your family friends. Whose side do they choose, or do they try to stay neutral? Usually some friends will side with the wife, and others will take the husband's side. So friends are caught in a terrible bind as they try to show their support without being manipulated to one side or the other.

Divorce also causes a great deal of economic harm, particularly for women. Generally speaking, it's tougher financially for the woman to make a go of it after she's divorced. It causes a whole new class of impoverished people. When two people go through a divorce, the only ones who come out well are their respective lawyers. I'm not putting down lawyers; they have to do a job. But I am saying that economically the cost of divorce is tremendous.

My dad worked for a judge who handled a lot of domestic cases. Dad would tell about some of the things he saw and heard. Some men would go through with a divorce and make a commitment that they would pay so much money a month in alimony and child support. Then they would become the scum of the earth by not keeping their promise to support their children and their wives. The economic consequences are horrific.

Divorce also causes a tremendous weight to fall on children who are born of that union. I was interested in reading an item in a family newsletter by a man who had gone through a divorce. Here's what he had to say about the aftermath of his divorce:

On one of the first days after the separation I went to the house to get some clothes. My youngest daughter Megan ran out to tell me our dog Beau had been hit by a car and had been taken to the animal clinic. I raced there and the veterinarian brought Beau in to see me and laid him on the examining table. I had not cried during the terrible breaking away from my wife Barbara; I had told her I was angry at my inability to cry. Now, I came apart completely; it was not weeping; it was screaming; it was despair.

The car had crushed Beau's spine, the x-ray showing irreparable damage. Beau looked up to me while the doctor handed me a piece of paper saying that she needed my signature to put Beau to sleep. I could not write my name because I could not see the paper. I leaned against the examining table and cried as I had never cried in my life. I was crying not just for Beau, but for Barbara, the children and myself. Crying for the death of a marriage, for inconsolable loss. I heard the doctor crying and Beau, in the last grand gesture of his life, dragged himself the length of the table on his two good legs and began licking the tears as they ran down my face. I lost my dog and found my metaphor in the x-ray of my dog's crushed spine. I was looking at a portrait of my broken marriage.

There are no metaphors powerful enough to describe the moment when you tell the children about the divorce. Divorces without children are minor league compared to divorces where children are involved. To look into the eyes of your children and tell them that you are mutilating their family and changing all their tomorrows is an act of desperate courage that I never want to repeat. It also reveals their parents' last act of solidarity and the absolute sign that the marriage is over. It felt as though I had doused my entire family with gasoline and struck a match. The three girls entered the room and would not look at me or Barbara; their faces with dark rings of grief and human hurt told they already knew. My betrayal of these young sweet girls filled the room. They wrote me a note of farewell since it was I who was moving out. When I read the notes I could not see how I could ever service such excruciating pain. The notes said, "I love you Daddy; I'll visit you." For months I dreamed of visiting my daughters locked in a mental hospital. The fear of damaged children was my most crippling obsession. For a year I walked around feeling as if I had undergone brain surgery.[3]

A few years ago Wallerstein, a psychologist, did a twenty-five-year study following children of divorce. The study showed that children from homes where divorce had occurred were less likely to go on for higher education; they had a lower sense of self-esteem, and they were likely to do the same thing in their own marriages. They found that these children, as they grew older, became more unstable in their emotional relationships, particularly with their father and knowing how to be a father. They had bitter memories of the legal system because they felt that it had forced them into visitation and custody and all those kinds of things, and they didn't like it. Divorce had led them to fear marriage and making a commitment.

Finally, divorce causes spiritual problems. Because two people, who have been married and committed and then break up, cause a spiritual effect. God's Word says, "Do not cause anyone to stumble whether Jew or Greek" (1 Cor. 10:32). When people are divorced, the stumbling-block effect is noticed particularly in church relationships. When people in places of leadership and trust go through divorce, it really hurts spiritually. It is difficult to try to put all that together when a person, supposedly, is walking with the Lord and then goes through a divorce.

So why does God hate divorce? Because He is seeking godly off-spring. Divorce breaks faith, violates truth standards, and harms people. It illustrates separation instead of union. Divorce speaks of damnation, not salvation. God has pictured marriage as a union between Christ and all of us who put our trust in Him. He has told us that Christ is the husband; we, the married partners, the children of faith, are the wife because the church is the bride of Christ. He made a covenant to keep us eternally secure. When we're saved, God is going to keep us saved; we're not going to lose our salvation.

But when a divorce happens, the picture that God has given of the union between a husband and a wife is broken. People can then say, "Can I trust God? Did God really mean what He said? Here's a union that has been broken. It was supposed to be a picture of God's solidarity and commitment and covenant to us. But now the husband and wife are broken apart, and it is a picture of separation—eternal separation—and God is a God who brings us to eternal life." So when God says that He hates divorce, you can see some of the things from God's heart that speak to us today.

III. How to Keep the Ship Afloat

How do we keep our marriage ship sailing? The words "break faith" in Malachi 2:14–16 are interesting. They really mean "garmenting," because this phrase goes back to a noun that means "garment." In those days in the Middle East, a person's garment was about the most important thing he had. Most people were poor, so the garment was what they wore on the outside to keep them warm. Many times poor people would use this outer garment to sleep in. That's why Jewish law said that a person could use his garment as collateral for a loan, but at nighttime he was allowed to have it back because it was possibly the only thing that might keep him from freezing to death. The word was later changed to a verb, and the verb began to mean you were scandalizing or you were taking away or cheating someone. The phrase "break faith" is taken from that word *garment*. Malachi declares that the people were taking away from someone, scandalizing, garmenting, or breaking their marriage vows.

The prophet then uses that very strange phrase "covering himself with violence as well as with his garment" (v. 16). In the Old Testament the phrase which indicated that a person was committed to marriage and physical intimacy was "spreading of the garment over the wife." For instance, in the story of Ruth, when Boaz decided Ruth was going to be his wife, he took his garment and spread it over her on the threshing room floor. That meant he was committed to her.

Now we would use the term today in the meaning of physical or sexual intimacy, saying a person "went to bed with her." In those days the husband covered the wife with a garment, which declared, "I am committed physically, emotionally, and spiritually to you, and this is the physical symbol of it." Now here is what God says, "I hate a man's covering himself with violence as well as with his garment." He is saying that if you divorce, you are breaking up a relationship; you're taking that garment away; you're taking away that intimacy between God and yourself and the bride or husband of your youth. In a sense, it is a violent taking away of something that God intended to be together. So God uses some powerful terms in talking about why He hates divorce.

To those of you who may be thinking about it before you proceed with divorce, let me ask you these questions: (1) Why did you get married in the first place? (2) What did you see in each other? (3) Why did you want to be together all the time? (4) Why did you want to commit yourselves to marriage? (5) Why did you want to share things and spend time together? There was something between you in the beginning. There was love and commitment, all of those things you thought about when you got married. And if you did then, these things can be rekindled and rebuilt, and you can keep your vows. How do you do that?

I have five little words that I think will help you. I know this is simplistic, but they will work if you work them.

1. *Forget.* Paul said in Philippians 3:13 to forget those things that are behind. You may have said some things to each other that you need to forget. Usually when people get into divorce proceedings, they go back and talk about things that happened years ago. They

never let them die. They are still live skeletons in the closet. You have to forget. Someone said that wisdom is the art of beginning to overlook. There are some things you simply have to overlook because this is a part of being married.

2. *Future.* Look to the future. Look ahead at what the potential is instead of behind at what was. Paul said in Philippians 3:14, "I stretch toward those things which are in front of me." Think about the future, and consider the damage and harm that can be done if you keep focusing on the past.

3. *Faith.* Envision a renewed faith—or a first-time faith for some of you—in Jesus Christ and pledge your commitment to Him. Keep believing that God can perform a miracle and help you in your marriage. Let your faith serve as your anchor when everything else around says, "Give it up, it's not worth it, go ahead and get a divorce." Keep your faith in the God who honored your vows.

4. *Forgive.* Somebody said there are three types of forgiveness. The easiest type of forgiveness is to accept what Jesus Christ has done for us on the cross. The only thing we can do to be saved is to say, "Lord, I am a sinner, forgive me, I trust You." That's the easiest forgiveness in the world, yet it's amazing how many people turn that down. The greatest offer in the world: eternal life, heaven, walk with God, peace with God, no guilt hanging over us from the past. People sometimes won't take the easiest forgiveness of all.

The second type of forgiveness is the forgiveness of another person. This is the next easiest type of forgiveness—to go to another person and forgive him or to accept forgiveness from him or her. Most people will accept your request for forgiveness and forgive you. What a wonderful thing it is to have forgiveness like that.

The third type of forgiveness is the hardest. Can you forgive yourself? You've got to forgive yourself of the past—forgive yourself of some things you did. You have to forgive yourself, because if you ask Christ to forgive you, He has forgiven you. You are forgiven and you will remember, but He has forgiven. The other person may remember, but that person has forgiven. But if a person can learn to forgive like Christ does, when a spouse has been unfaithful, the wronged person says—as hard as this is—"I forgive you." But the person on the other side usually ends up saying, "I can't forgive myself. Why did I treat my spouse like that?" It's the most difficult type of forgiveness, but if you will accept Christ's forgiveness, He forgives you.

5. *Firmness.* Stay committed. The most solemn vow you'll ever make in your life, except your vow to trust Jesus Christ, is your marriage vow. God considers it sacred, a covenant vow. His Word is clear on this. There is nothing more important that you will do or say in your life than when you say, "With this ring I thee wed, and I promise you and I promise God." That is a solemn vow. Be firm. "I will keep my vows, God being my helper. I'll do everything I can to keep them."

Dr. Bob Moorehead, a pastor friend, has in his church what he calls the "Stander's Prayer." Here is that "stander's" affirmation:

I am standing for the healing of my marriage. I won't give up, give in, give out, or give over until that healing takes place. I made a vow, I gave the pledge, I gave a ring, I took a ring, I gave myself, I trusted God and said and meant the words, "In sickness and in health, in sorrow and in joy, for better or for worse, for richer or for poorer, in good times and in bad."

So I am standing now and I won't sit down, let down, slow down, calm down, fall down, look down, or be down, 'til the breakdown is torn down. I refuse to put my eyes on outward circumstances or listen to prophets of doom or buy into what is trendy, worldly, popular, convenient, easy, quick, thrifty, or advantageous.

Nor will I settle for a cheap imitation of God's real thing, nor will I seek to lower God's standard, twist God's will, rewrite God's Word, violate God's covenant or accept what God hates—namely, divorce.

In a world of filth, I will stay pure; surrounded by lies, I will speak the truth; where hopelessness abounds, I will hope in God; where revenge is easy, I will bless instead of curse; and where the odds are stacked against me, I will trust in God's faithfulness. I am a stander. I won't acquiesce, compromise, quarrel, or quit. I have made the choice, set my face, entered the race, believed the Word and trusted God for all the outcome. I will allow neither the acts of my spouse, nor the urging of my friends, nor the advice of my loved ones, nor the economic hardship nor the prompting of the devil to make me let up, slow up or give up until my marriage is healed. Amen.

Now that's a commitment! That's firm, and God wants it to be that way. God declares in Ecclesiastes, chapter 5, verses 4–5: "When you make a vow to God, do not delay in fulfilling it. He has no pleasure in fools; fulfill your vow. It is better not to vow than to make a vow and not fulfill it."

So my exhortation to you is to keep your vows. Don't give up the ship. Stay the course. Do everything possible to keep your marriage intact. I want to tell you, all of heaven is on your side.

1. Jay Kessler, *Is Your Marriage Really Worth Fighting For?* (Elgin, IL: David C. Cook Publishing, 1989), 22.

2. Karen Peterson, "Hell Hath No Fury as a Divorcing Couple," *USA Today*, 27 September 1996.

3. James C. Dobson, *Focus on the Family Newsletter*, June 1991.

36

Why?

JOB 3:11–23 NKJV

James Merritt

Senior Pastor, Cross Pointe, The Church at Gwinett Center
Duluth, Georgia

EVERY GENERATION FOR THE LAST SIXTY YEARS has had an event occur that people will never forget. It is a bookmark on the hard drive of their memory. The World War II generation, still living, remembers exactly where they were on December 7, 1941, when they heard about Pearl Harbor.

For my generation, the boomer generation, the singular event we remember occurred on November 22, 1963, when President John F. Kennedy was assassinated. I still remember walking back from the library to my sixth-grade class, where another classmate came running down the hall screaming, "President Kennedy has been shot."

Then the buster generation had an event seared into their memory on January 20, 1986, when the space shuttle *Challenger* exploded in a ball of fire before a nationwide television audience.

Now the millennial generation has their own signal but tragic event and date which will always remind them where they were and what they were doing when it happened—September 11, 2001, when the greatest single tragedy ever to hit this country occurred, now known as "America under attack." Once again we are confronted with the great question: Why? Evil has once again reared its ugly head to confront those who believe in God and to impassion those who don't. The problem of evil has been called the "Achilles' heel" of Christianity. The question arises: How can a God who is all-powerful and absolutely good allow evil in His creation?

George Barna, the leading researcher of spiritual trends in the evangelical world, conducted a national survey in which he scientifically selected a cross-section of adults and asked this question: "If you could ask God only one question and you knew He would give you an answer, what would you ask?" The number-one answer was this: "Why is there pain and suffering in the world?"

Years ago after survivors of the United Airlines Flight 232 crash in Sioux City, Iowa, attributed their survival to God, an organization of atheists, known as the Freedom from Religion Foundation, issued a call for secular newspapers to quit using "Bible Belt Journalism." Ann Gaylor, leader of the group, said, "Every time a tragedy is reported our members must brace themselves for the inevitable. If there are survivors reporters will make sure 'God' will get the credit, but never the blame. . . . Why don't they ask these religionists who claim 'God' helped them why 'He' let tragedies happen in the first place?" Referring to the United crash, she asked, "Why didn't their omnipotent 'God' just fix the hydraulic system of Flight 232 and save everybody?"[1]

This question goes all the way back to the oldest book in the Bible. The first chapter of Job reads like this week's newspaper:

Now there was a day when his [Job's] sons and daughters
were eating and drinking wine in their oldest brother's
house; and a messenger came to Job and said, "The oxen
were plowing and the donkeys feeding beside them, when
the Sabeans raided them and took them away—indeed they
have killed the servants with the edge of the sword; and
I alone have escaped to tell you!"

While he was still speaking, another also came and said,
"The fire of God fell from heaven and burned up the sheep
and the servants, and consumed them; and I alone have
escaped to tell you!"

While he was still speaking, another also came and said,
"The Chaldeans formed three bands, raided the camels and

took them away, yes, and killed the servants with the edge of the sword; and I alone have escaped to tell you!"

While he was still speaking, another also came and said, "Your sons and daughters were eating and drinking wine in their oldest brother's house, and suddenly a great wind came from across the wilderness and struck the four corners of the house, and it fell on the young people, and they are dead; and I alone have escaped to tell you!" (Job 1:13–19).

Substitute "terrorists" for Sabeans and Chaldeans, and a hurricane for the wind, and we have the same situation we face today.

As we will see, Job asked the same question millions of people are asking today: "Why?" Now I want you to see how God Himself answers the question as I raise and answer three crucial questions this morning.

I. Why Do We Suffer from Evil?

Job at first tries to keep a stiff upper lip when he says, "Naked I came from my mother's womb, and naked shall I return there. The LORD gave, and the LORD has taken away; blessed be the name of the LORD" (1:21). But after Satan was allowed to take Job's health away as well, he begins to cry out in chapter 3 and raises the question over and over—"Why?" Listen to these verses:

"*Why* did I not die at birth? *Why* did I not perish when I came from the womb?" (v. 11). "*Why* did the knees receive me? Or *why* the breasts, that I should nurse?" (v. 12). "Or *why* was I not hidden like a stillborn child, like infants who never saw light?" (v. 16). "*Why* is light given to him who is in misery, and life to the bitter of soul?" (v. 20). "*Why* is light given to a man whose way is hidden, and whom God has hedged in?" (v. 23).

Now what Job is really asking is this: "Why did God allow this to happen?" He was saying in effect: "God, where are You?" Now we hit the crux of the question: If there is a God, and if this God is good, why is there evil in the world?

Thousands of years ago the Greek philosopher, Epicurus, put it this way: "God either wishes to take away evil, and is unable; or He is able and unwilling; or He is neither willing nor able; or He is both willing and able. If He's willing but unable, He is feeble, which is not in accordance with the character of God. If He is able and unwilling, He is envious, which is equally at variance with God. If He is neither willing nor able, He is both envious and feeble, and therefore not God. If He is both willing and able, which alone is suitable for God, from what source then are evils? Or why does He not remove them?"

That word *why* is not just a question. It is really an accusation. In fact, the Hebrew word for *why* is not only a cry of sorrow, it is a cry of protest. It assumes that all suffering is unjust and that God's silence is inexcusable. It is an age-old question. We're not the first ones to ask it, nor will we be the last. The prophet Habakkuk asked God, "Why do you make me look at injustice? Why do you tolerate wrong?" (Hab. 1:3 NIV). The prophet Jeremiah challenged the Lord, saying, "I would speak with you about your justice: Why does the way of the wicked prosper?" (Jer. 12:1 NIV).

Now I am going to tell you something that will probably disturb you, but it is the truth nonetheless: nobody truly and totally knows the full and final answer to the *why* question. Anyone who tells you they do is either ignorant, arrogant, or both. That's a real problem for us because we live in a the-public-has-the-right-to-know generation. We live in a society that demands an explanation for everything, and we want to be informed on everything from Jimmy Carter's hemorrhoids, to Ronald Reagan's colon, to George Bush's hatred for broccoli, to Bill Clinton's haircuts. We get frustrated because though journalists and fortune-tellers and lawmakers operate by that policy, God does not. He operates strictly on a need-to-know basis.

It's interesting that every time tragedy strikes, we call God on the carpet and demand that He explain Himself, and He had better have a good reason for doing what He did. Well, this next statement sounds hard, but it's still true—*because God is God, He doesn't need to explain His actions to anyone.* It is interesting that for thirty-seven chapters in the book of Job, God is totally silent. He doesn't say one word to His servant Job. But then in chapter 38 God asks Job the one question to end all questions: "Where were you when I laid the foundations of the earth? Tell Me, if you have understanding" (Job 38:4).

What He said to Job in effect was, "You wouldn't even be here trying to ask me a question if I hadn't decided to create you to begin with." Then in Job 40:2 he drops the final bomb: "Shall the one who contends with the Almighty correct Him? He who rebukes God, let him answer it."

Even though I don't know any truly final answers to the whole problem of evil, there are some things I do know. I know that evil is real, and I also know that for evil to exist you must also admit that good exists because without good there can be no evil. That also tells me that ultimately it must be appropriate that there is evil, or evil would not exist. Augustine said, "God judged it better to bring good out of evil, than to suffer no evil to exist."

Now please understand that to say it is good that evil exists is not the same thing as saying that evil is good. To say evil is good would itself be evil, and the Scripture plainly declares that evil is evil. But to say it is good that there is evil is simply to declare the fact that God is good, and that His providence extends to all things, including evil. In fact, God is sovereign even over evil and is able to bring good out of evil, and to use evil for His purpose and His plan for this world.

Don't miss the importance of that statement. The fact that God allows or ordains that there be evil means He deems it good to allow it. He only ordains what He wills should take place; His will is perfect and absolutely good and righteous. If God wills that evil should exist—and it could not possibly exist if He did not will it—then we must conclude that in His counsel and purpose and plan, He has good reasons for allowing evil to exist.

I freely admit that evil is a problem we have to face. But it is not fatal to the Christian faith. We must interpret the unknown in light of the known, not the known in light of the unknown. What we do know is this: God does exist, and God is good. But in my mind that raises still another question.

II. Who Should We Seek During Evil?

There are those who conclude that since there is evil in the world there can be no God because a God who is all-powerful and totally good would not allow evil to happen. Well, I, quite frankly, do not see that as the dilemma that some people do. In fact, I draw comfort from that line of thinking. Because those who complain that evil is a problem can only do so if they affirm the existence of that which is good. If you insist that evil is real, you also have to insist that good is real. But if there is no God, then you must not only account for evil, you also have to account for good.

My friend and the great apologist, Ravi Zacharias, tells of a time when he was speaking at the University of Nottingham in England when an exasperated student stood up and attacked God with this question. Zacharias used that question as an axe to chop this person's legs right out from under him. The student stood up and said, "There cannot possibly be a God with all the evil and suffering that exists in the world!" With a smug look on his face, he then waited for Zacharias to respond.

Zacharias replied, "When you say there is such a thing as evil, are you not assuming that there is such a thing as good?" The student said, "Of course." Zacharias continued, "But when you assume there is such a thing as good, are you not also assuming that there is such a thing as a moral law on the basis of which to distinguish between good and evil?" This time the student reluctantly said, "I suppose so."

So Zacharias said, "In other words, in order to have good or evil there must be a moral law, a standard by which to determine what is good and what is not." The student said, "You are right."

Zacharias then said, "If then there is a moral law, you must posit a moral lawgiver. But that is who you are trying to disprove and not prove. If there is no moral lawgiver, there is no moral law; if there is no moral law, there is no good; if there is no good, there is no evil. I'm not sure what your question is!" The student then replied, "Well, what am I asking you?"[2]

Evil, in my estimation, does not say we should run *from* the idea of God, but we should run *to* the idea of God. You think about this. We never question the good things that happen to us—only the bad. Dr. M. Scott Peck makes this observation: "It's a strange thing. Dozens of times I have been asked by patients or acquaintances: 'Dr. Peck, why is there evil in the world?' Yet no one has asked me in all these years, 'Why is there good in the world?'"[3]

Let me ask the question another way. Why is it we blame God only for the bad things that happen to us? Why do insurance companies describe natural disasters and catastrophes as "acts of God"? We never question the positive points of life, only the bad. We are not amazed at God's goodness; we take that for granted, as though God owes it to us. Badness surprises us; goodness does not.[4]

The point I'm making is this: to try to get rid of God and eliminate God because of evil is to make the discussion totally unnecessary. We have problems with evil in this world not because of our unbelief but because of our faith! The great British Bible teacher, G. Campbell Morgan, said it this way: "Men of faith are always the men that have to confront problems. Block God out and your problems are all ended. If there is no God in heaven, then we have no problem with sin and suffering. . . . But the moment that you admit the existence of an all-powerful governing God, you are face to face with your problems. If you say that you have none, I question the strength of your faith."[5]

Evil should not force us to turn *away* from God; it should force us to turn *to* God. Indeed that is *always* one purpose of evil. It not only challenges our faith; it changes our focus. C. S. Lewis once said, "God whispers to us in our pleasure, speaks to us in our conscience, but shouts to us in our pains; it is His megaphone to rouse a deaf world."[6]

But this raises a question: To what God should we turn? In my estimation, there is only one God we can turn to, and it's certainly not a god who would reward cowardly, murderous attacks with a heaven surrounded by beautiful virgin women. No, the only God we can turn to is the God of the cross. It is the cross that tells me that

God cares. It is the cross that tells me that God is good. It is the cross that tells me that God is love. It is the cross that tells me that God can even use evil for His good purpose. As a matter of fact, you will never make any sense out of evil—indeed, you will never make any sense out of life—without the cross of Jesus Christ.

How can anybody in a world of pain worship a God who is immune to pain? If you ever go to a Buddhist temple, you will see a statue of the Buddha; his legs crossed, arms folded, eyes closed, the ghost of a smile framing his mouth, a remote look on his face; totally detached from what's going on in the world. That is not the God I turn to. The God I turn to is a God whose Son was nailed to a cross, back lacerated, limbs torn from their socket, brow bleeding from a crown of thorns, mouth dry, intolerably thirsty, forsaken by God the Father Himself for sins He did not even commit. That is the God whom I turn to. Yes, there is a question mark about human suffering. But over it we can boldly stamp the exclamation point of the cross, which symbolizes divine suffering and tells us that God does care. This raises our third and final question:

III. What Should We Say about Evil?

There is one thing we must remember: When the sky is black, God seems to be silent, and we are in the deepest throes of the darkest disaster, God is always in complete control. When God permits Satan to light the furnace, He always keeps His own hand on the thermostat. That's why he says to Job, "Who then is able to stand against Me? Who has preceded Me, that I should pay him? Everything under heaven is Mine" (41:10b–11).

Jesus Himself said something interesting about evil. He told a parable of the wheat and the tares. He told how the "enemy came and sowed tares among the wheat" (Matt. 13:25). Now "among the wheat" in the Greek is a strong expression meaning "all through the midst of the wheat, between the wheat, and on top of the wheat." The roots had become so inextricably intertwined that any attempt to pull them out would have torn out the wheat as well.

So Jesus said, "'No, lest while you gather up the tares you also uproot the wheat with them. Let both grow together until the harvest, and at the time of the harvest I will say to the reapers, 'First gather together the tares and bind them in bundles to burn them, but gather the wheat into my barn'" (Matt. 13:29–30). Jesus said, "You can't root out the bad without rooting out the good. Wait until harvest when they will all be rooted out, and then separate the good and the bad."

Remember this: The tares of evil do not worry the Master. He will take care of them in due time. Make no mistake about it: God's control is never interrupted. His sovereignty is never challenged. The world is *His* field, and He will tend it properly.

How do I really know this is true? Because history tells us that God can take the greatest evil and bring out of it the greatest good. Exhibit A once again is the cross of Jesus Christ. Humanity cannot and will not ever experience any greater depth of evil than that exhibited by the crucifixion of Jesus Christ. Yet, because of the cross and because of the empty tomb, out of Satan's greatest strike against God, God brought man's eternal salvation. Therefore, "We know that all things work together for good to those who love God" (Rom. 8:28).

As many of you know, Barbara Olson, the former federal prosecutor and TV commentator, married to Solicitor General Ted Olson, called her husband twice in the final minutes of her tragic final flight. In her first call her last words were, "What do I tell the pilot to do?" She was cut off. She called him back and again with her last words said, "What should I tell the pilot?" Well, I would have told the pilot as well as everyone on board that plane, "Believe on the Lord Jesus Christ, and you will be saved" (Acts 16:31). I believe more than anything this is God's wake-up call for the church to be more urgent about the business of making sure a lost world knows Jesus Christ as Lord.

I want to close with a final answer to the question I have raised in this message with a poem entitled, "The Lord Knows Why."

I may not know the reason why
Dark clouds so often veil the sky,
But tho' my sea be smooth or rough;
The Lord knows why, and that's enough.

I may not know why I am led
So often in the paths I dread,
But trusting Him I'll press my way;
The Lord knows why; I will obey.

I may not know why death should come
To take the dear ones from my home,
But tho' mine eyes with tear be dim,
The Lord knows why; I'll trust in Him.

So tho' I may not understand
The leading of my Father's hand,
I know to all He has the key—
He understands each mystery.

Oh yes, He knows, the Lord knows why
These things are ordered from on high.
Tho' dark clouds may hide the sun,
The Lord knows why; His will be done.

1. "News Report's Mention of God Angers Atheists," *Atlanta Constitution*, August 12, 1989.

2. Ravi Zacharias, *Cries of the Heart* (Nashville: Word, 2002), 66–67.

3. Cited by Ron Dunn, *When Heaven Is Silent: Live by Faith, Not by Sight* (Nashville: Thomas Nelson), 67.

4. Ibid., 68.

5. Ibid., 22–23.

6. Cited by Alister McGrath, *Intellectuals Don't Need God: Building Bridges to Faith Through Apologetics* (Grand Rapids: Zondervan, 1993), 104.

37

Getting the Right Perspective

LUKE 5:27–32 NIV

O. Damon Shook

Senior Pastor, Champion Forest Baptist Church
Houston, Texas

I'M GOING TO BE TALKING TO YOU ABOUT SUCCESS and how to have a successful life. And I've been looking through some magazines, trying to find the answer. I'm confused. I don't think any of those people interviewed about the meaning of life know what they're talking about. In fact, they contradict one another. But I know what the answer is. The answer to successful living is found in one book—the Holy Bible, the Word of God. We are going to open up this book and look at the qualities that are necessary for a successful life.

Now let me give you a definition for successful living. This is my own—take it or leave it. But I've thought about it a lot, and my conclusion is that successful living is living to please God and through that, blessing others. You know, when you really get through all of life, wouldn't you like to be able to say, "Lord, I really pleased You most of the time, and I blessed others by pleasing You"? I think that's what really matters.

There are some qualities that we must have if we're going to live to please God and bless others. The most important quality is the quality of perspective. This enables us to value what's important, to have the right priorities, and to share what's valuable with others.

443

I. Perspective Enables Us to Value What Is Important

Some of you who follow baseball know that the playoffs are now going on. There are two teams in the American League and two teams in the National League that are battling it out for who's going to be in the World Series. The winner of the two teams from each league will be in the series. And one of the teams that has surprised everybody this year is the Minnesota Twins. They are battling for the American League championship. Now the Twins were not expected to do well. To everyone's surprise, they won their division, and now they're fighting for the pennant and the right to be in the World Series.

I remember back a number of years ago when the Minnesota Twins won their first American League pennant. When they came home from Detroit after winning the pennant, thousands of Minneapolis and St. Paul fans gathered to celebrate with them! And as they got off the plane, the reporters were there. One of the players for the Twins was Greg Gagney. He was the shortstop. And one of the reporters rushed up and said, "Greg, this has to be the greatest day of your life!" Greg replied, "No, it really isn't. It's a wonderful day to win the pennant and to get to play in the World Series. It's a dream come true, and I'm excited about it, but it's certainly not the greatest day of my life. The greatest day of my life was the day I received Jesus Christ as my personal Lord and Savior."

Greg Gagney was a good baseball player, but he had perspective enough to know what was really important. Baseball was his vocation and his livelihood, and he loved the game, and he liked to play, and he wanted to win. He was glad his team was in the World Series, but it wasn't the most important thing. Most of us don't have that kind of perspective.

I want to show you in the Bible some people whom you would have thought would have had perspective on the most important things in life, but they didn't. And I want to show you someone you would have thought would have had no perspective on such things, but he did. Turn with me to the fifth chapter of the Gospel of Luke, beginning at verse 27. Jesus is in Capernaum, and the Scripture says:

> After this, Jesus went out and saw a tax collector by the name of Levi sitting at his tax booth. "Follow me," Jesus said to him, and Levi got up, left everything and followed him. Then Levi held a great banquet for Jesus at his house, and a large crowd of tax collectors and others were eating with them. But the Pharisees and the teachers of the law who belonged to their sect complained to his disciples. "Why do you eat and drink with tax collectors and 'sinners'"? Jesus answered them, "It is not the healthy who need a doctor, but the sick. I have not come to call the righteous, but sinners to repentance" (Luke 5:27–32).

Perspective is the God-given ability to see truth and reality. To know what is true, and to know what is real, and to know what is really important. And it's a God-given ability that God offers to everyone who will ask Him. It's something you need to ask for on a daily basis. As you walk with Him, as you trust Him, as you depend on Him, as you go to His Word, He will constantly be opening up your perspective. He will sharpen your ability to see the truth, to see the real, to know what is not phony, not sinful, not wrong, not useless, but important.

Of all the people who should have had this perspective were the Pharisees. The Pharisees were religious people. They were religious leaders. They had been trained in the Old Testament Scriptures. They knew a lot about God, a lot about the Old Testament, but they didn't have a personal relationship with God. To them, it was all ritual and legalism and going about keeping rules. And they had no perspective. Listen to this: They had so little perspective that when God came down from heaven in the person of His Son and pitched His tent among them, they didn't even recognize Him. They thought He was an imposter, and they killed Him.

But the man who had perspective on what was really important was a fellow named Levi. Jesus changed his name later to Matthew. Levi was a tax collector. Now Levi was one of those people who decided that money is all-important, and you did what you had to do to get it. He had committed himself to serve with the Roman government, which was over Israel. Because he was a Jewish citizen who had committed to serve with the Romans, he was hated by his fellow Jews. But he didn't care! His pockets were full of money. His bank account was bulging. His house was big. He probably had a villa on the Sea of Galilee. His position was powerful. Money and power and all of the things that go along with them were his. But suddenly he developed some perspective about what was really important.

Levi had thought it was money that was important. He thought power, prestige, place, prominence, and position were important. But suddenly all of these things became insignificant because they didn't satisfy something deep inside his inner being. And all the money he could cram in his life and all the position and power he craved choked him and made him more miserable and unhappy.

No doubt Levi, who came from the tribe of Levi in Israel, grew up as most Jewish boys. He was probably schooled in the Old Testament at the synagogue and by his parents. And no doubt he knew a lot about God's Word. Later when he, as Matthew, wrote the Gospel of Matthew, he had ninety-nine references in his twenty-eight chapters to the Old Testament. So he knew a lot about the Old Testament. But he had probably forgotten, forsaken, and removed himself from the truth of the Bible. He had run from God's Word, from God's truth, and from a relationship with God, until a man named Jesus crossed his path.

When Jesus crossed his path, Levi had never seen, heard, or talked to anyone like Jesus. Jesus made his headquarters in Capernaum, where Levi was a tax collector. No doubt many times he had heard Jesus preach. No doubt he saw a lot of Jesus' miracles. No doubt he knew much about Jesus, but he could not explain Jesus in terms that his human mind could grasp except to say, "He's from God."

So suddenly Levi began to have perspective about the important issues of life. His money didn't cut it anymore. His power wasn't enough anymore. His position wasn't what counted anymore. He needed something that would satisfy the deep longing of his heart. Have you ever come to that place where you've really begun to see what is important? All of us have been confused at times. All of us have had warped views about what really matters. All of us have thought this or that was important. And when we began to ask God, He started to show us what really matters.

I remember years ago when God showed me and my wife what really mattered. I said, "God, with all of my heart, I want to make You my first priority, my wife my second priority, and my family and my kids my third priority." I haven't accomplished that perfectly, even today, but I keep trying.

That commitment years ago changed my life. It changed my family. It made a great impact because God was constantly telling me that my job, even as a pastor, is not as important as my relationship with Him. And if I fail in my personal relationship with God, I will fail as a pastor. If I fail in my relationship with my family, everything else is insignificant, no matter what kind of church I am a part of. If I cannot say, "God, here are my kids and here's my wife, and we walk with You," what difference does it make? We have to see with perspective about what really matters in life.

Years ago the leader of the country of Prussia, Frederick Wilhelm III, was in trouble. The nation had been through a terrible war, and their country was almost bankrupt. There was no money to feed the people and meet the basic needs of the country. He didn't know what to do. Finally, he came up with the solution. He asked the women of Prussia if they would bring their gold and silver jewelry, their precious stones, and give them to the commonwealth, give them to the king, to buy the basic commodities the people needed to rebuild the country.

The women responded unbelievably. By the thousands they came, bringing their silver and their gold jewelry to be melted down, to be traded for other commodities. In exchange for their jewelry, they were given an iron cross that said, "This gold traded for iron, 1813."

A strange thing happened in Prussia over the next few years. Women quit wearing gold and silver jewelry and precious stones. To them the most beautiful jewelry was an iron cross worn around their necks that said, "Gold given for iron, 1813." They had made a sacrifice for their country. It's all a matter of perspective about what really matters in life.

What is valuable is the worth of something in our eyes. The world says money, possessions, prestige, and power are all that matter. But God says, "No, it's not all that matters. Pleasing Me and blessing others is what matters." Perspective enables us to see what is really important.

II. Perspective Enables Us to Choose the Right Priorities

One day Jesus came by the booth where Levi was collecting taxes. Now this is what the Scripture says: "'Follow me,' Jesus said to him, and Levi got up, left everything and followed him" (Luke 5:27–28). The Scripture says that Jesus *saw* Levi. The word *saw* here is not a word that describes casually glancing. It is a word that means Jesus looked at him with interest and love. He focused His eyes and attention on Levi. Levi caught His eyes, and their eyes locked together. Then Jesus said, "Follow me." Levi got up, left everything, and followed Him.

What an amazing thing! Certainly Levi already knew who Jesus was. He had probably already had encounters with Jesus. He was already aware of some things going on in his own heart, and now Levi's perspective, his ability to see who Jesus was, his ability to recognize the importance of Christ enabled him to make the life-changing decision to leave everything and follow Christ.

When Peter, James, John, and Andrew followed Jesus, they were fishermen. And they gave up their fishing business, their boats, and their nets. And they followed Him full-time. They began to live with Him every day. But they could have gone back to their fishing business if they chose to do so. But when Levi followed Jesus, he couldn't go back to his fishing business. He didn't have a fishing business. His was a once-for-all kind of decision. This was a leaving-everything kind of decision, and it was all linked to not following some principles, not committing himself to some ideals, not getting involved in rule-keeping and religious activity. It was a relationship with a person—Jesus Christ.

That's what it's all about. "Follow me," Jesus said. Jesus didn't say, "Live better." Jesus didn't say, "Do right." Jesus didn't say, "Join that group." Jesus didn't say, "Follow that ritual." Jesus said, "Follow Me. I want you to come into a relationship with Me." Have you come into a relationship with Him? When you do that, it means you have enough perspective to determine your priorities.

Following Jesus as your number-one priority in life will help you make some hard decisions. This week I have received e-mails from two men in our church who have had to make some hard decisions about their jobs because their jobs were hindering them from meeting the spiritual needs of their families. Their jobs enabled them to meet the physical needs of their families, but that was not enough for these men.

One of them said he had worked for a company for thirteen years. Not long ago he got the promotion he had been longing for, planning for, praying for, and looking forward to. But that promotion meant that he had to be gone almost all week every week. He had also made a commitment after he became a Christian that he was going to put his family first. He was going to meet their spiritual needs—let the Lord meet them through him. He said he became more and more miserable, more and more unhappy, and more and more dissatisfied over the weeks that followed because he knew he wasn't doing that. Finally he had to quit his job and get another job because he realized what was important.

The other man had a job that required him to travel most of the time. And it all came to a head around September 11 of this year when we had our big memorial celebration. Our buildings were filled that Wednesday night. He wanted to be here. He had planned to be here. He was in the music part of the program, but his business required him to be gone all week. He would not be able to be here for that worship service.

He asked his boss, "Can I just wait until Thursday to leave?"

His boss replied, "No, you have to go before then."

He talked to his wife. He prayed about it. She had recently been laid off. She had no job either, but he told me, "I just knew I couldn't live that way anymore. I have to give God more of a place in my life." So he quit. A few days later the Lord opened up another job where he could stay in town, take care of his wife, take care of his family, take care of his needs, take care of his church—the things that are important in his life. He had the courage to choose his priorities wisely.

My daughter Romana was a good basketball player. In fact, when she was in the seventh grade, she set a scoring record for the seventh-grade girls' basketball team in her school. Nobody had ever scored as many points in a season as she scored that year. And she played well all through junior high and early high school. I thought she had a lot of potential to be an outstanding basketball player.

But I remember one day in early high school. She came home with a serious look on her face. "Dad, I quit basketball today," she told me.

"What?"

"I quit basketball today."

I told her, "You love basketball! It's great exercise, you love the game, you're good at it, and you quit?"

"Yes, Dad, I quit," she replied. "For several weeks now our coach has been telling us that basketball has to be number one in our lives. We have to eat basketball, sleep basketball, drink basketball, live basketball. Basketball has to be the most important thing we do, the most important thing we think, the most important thing we are. I've been debating this for a couple of weeks." Then she said, "Basketball is not the most important thing in my life. Jesus Christ is." She continued, "I really thought I had an alternative, and so I quit. And I have a real peace about it."

Wow! I went back and talked to myself. I wonder what I would have done in high school if that had been my choice. I'm not saying that everybody ought to quit basketball, that everybody ought to quit their jobs. All I'm saying is sometimes we have to do things that aren't normal that are out of the ordinary, that are extreme because we have the perspective to see that we must have our priorities right.

III. Perspective Enables Us to Share What Is Valuable with Others

As soon as Matthew met Jesus, he had to share his good news with others. Listen to what the Scripture says: "Levi held a great banquet for Jesus at his house, and a large crowd of tax collectors and others were eating with them" (Luke 5:29). He wanted his friends, his fellow tax collectors, to know what Jesus could do for them, so immediately Jesus was the guest of honor for a banquet. Levi invited all his friends to come over and celebrate and share with him. His commitment to Jesus was special.

Somebody has said that a truly converted person will not be able to go to heaven alone. If you really know Christ and He's so important in your life, you have to tell others about Him. You have to share something of Him with those around you.

Yesterday I called a number of people who had been attending our church as guests to tell them how special they are and how wonderful it is to have them attend our services. Almost every one of them said that they came with somebody from our church, and they named someone who brought them or invited them. That's what it's all about! We have to share Christ with others because He's so valuable!

I got a letter three or four weeks ago from a man who had been attending our church for four weeks. He said, "I was invited by an acquaintance and one of your members to come to your church. And I've been there four times. I haven't seen him yet!" He went on to say, "You have a beautiful new building. And you have so much room now. It's not full, and you have those two services. If everybody in your church would bring somebody else, you would fill it up."

And I thought, *You're right on, man. That's the answer.* It's always been the answer. It's one beggar sharing with another beggar where he found bread. That's what it's all about. It's not the preacher who draws people. It's each of us letting Christ use us.

That's what John Wanamaker did. He made quite an impression on people in the city of Philadelphia some years ago. A multi-millionnaire, he owned a huge department store in that city. At one time he was postmaster general of the United States. But he also started a Sunday school for poor kids in a tough section of town. And he had four thousand poor kids coming to Sunday school to hear about Jesus every Sunday.

Somebody asked him one day, "Wanamaker, how do you do all those things? You run those businesses, do all those other things, and then you have that Sunday school for all those kids. How do you do it? How do you take care of all that business?"

He replied, "My real business is that Sunday school. I learned a long time ago to seek first the kingdom of God and His righteousness, and all these other things will be added unto you." This man had perspective. And perspective enables us to value what's important, to have the right priorities, and to share what's valuable with others.

Let me finish up by pointing out some people who didn't have any perspective. The Pharisees and teachers of the law complained to Jesus' disciples, "Why do you eat and drink with tax collectors and 'sinners'?" (Luke 5:30).

Many people have no perspective about who Jesus is or why He came. Jesus, overhearing them, said, "I have not come to call the righteous, but sinners to repentance" (Luke 5:32). "Hey," Jesus said, "you don't find a physician who hangs out with all the well people. The physician associates with sick people so he can help them get well. I didn't come here to find the best people and congratulate them. I came here to find all the sinners and forgive them and take them home to heaven one day."

What kind of perspective do you have about the purpose of the church? It has more than one purpose, but one of its major purposes is to make a difference in the lives of people who have never been inside its doors, who've never heard His message, who've never met

Christ, who don't know anything about the gospel. That's part of our responsibility. These religious leaders saw no need in themselves. They were self-righteous and pious and full of sin. Jesus said they were like a bowl that was clean on the outside but filthy on the inside, and they didn't even know it (Luke 11:39).

God the Father and Jesus were saying, "I've come for those who know they need Me, like a Levi who has perspective, who can face up to his sins, who can come to grips with his need, who can realize that he's not what he thought he was or not what he claimed to be. But he wants God to do something in his life."

Robert Munger said the church is the only fellowship in the world where the one requirement for membership is the absolute unworthiness of the candidate. I've joined some clubs in my time— social clubs and various organizations that do a lot of good. But I remember I had to fill out all this information, all these sheets of paper, telling how good I was. Telling all the nice things I had done, listing all the people who would recommend me, proving I was worthy to be a member of this club or organization.

But the church of Jesus Christ doesn't have you fill out anything like that. The church has just one requirement. You admit you're a sinner who needs a Savior. That's the requirement. God is not looking for some good people whom He can pat on the back and take home to heaven. He's looking for those who will admit they're not good enough. They're sinners, and they can never measure up to His holiness. And they want to be saved. Many of us have no perspective on true salvation. We're blind to why Jesus came.

The Pharisees were. They missed the Son of God. They will spend eternity in hell rather than heaven because they thought they were good enough. If there's one thing I want our church to be, I want it to be a place where the worst sinners in the world can come and meet Christ. He died for sinners, and this is the faithful saying that we must share with the world.

Perspective is based on truth. Levi, who seemed to have no perspective up to this point, suddenly was able to see truth and reality. The Pharisees had spent all their lives being religious, but they could not see past their own self-righteous noses. Judgment day will be a surprise for some people.

I want to be personal with you today, and I want to talk right to your heart. Do you have perspective? Do you know what's really valuable? Do you realize what's important? Do you recognize the right priority? Matthew wrote the first Gospel in the New Testament. He was a committed follower of Jesus Christ. His life was changed because God gave him perspective. He will also give such perspective to you today.

38

A Man and His Word

MATTHEW 13:18–23 NKJV

George Harris
Pastor Emeritus, Castle Hills First Baptist Church
San Antonio, Texas

NEVER IN MY LIFETIME have I seen such a need for the church of the living God to sound a clear, definite, positive message for a world that is in darkness. And much of that world is composed of religious people who are confused by those who have been reluctant to speak and perplexed by those whose compromise makes them less than credible. Our world and our churches need a clear, sound voice giving direction for the new millennium.

Delivering the message is not for the timid, the cowardly, those who are afraid to take a stand and be counted, or for those who are looking for an easy way out, refusing to be involved. It's time to draw a line and take a stand for what we believe to be truth.

When Jesus made His ministry debut, He spoke in parables because His message was easy to understand in parable form. The parable in Matthew 13 is the one I want to address. It's called the parable of the sower. Jesus was speaking to an agricultural society that understood about planting crops. In His parable He described a sower who went forth to plant his seed. Some of the seed fell by the wayside, and some fell on stony ground. Some fell on thorns and thistles, and some fell on good ground.

The seed that fell on the wayside was carried away by the birds. The seed that fell on the stony ground took root quickly but wilted and died in the strong sunlight. The seed that fell among the thorns was choked out, and that which fell on the good ground bore fruit— some thirtyfold, some sixtyfold, some one hundredfold.

"Therefore hear the parable of the sower: When anyone hears the word of the kingdom, and does not understand it, then the wicked one comes and snatches away what was sown in his heart. This is he who received seed by the wayside. But he who received the seed on stony places, this is he who hears the word and immediately receives it with joy; yet he has no root in himself, but endures only for a while. For when tribulation or persecution arises because of the word, immediately he stumbles. Now he who received seed among the thorns is he who hears the word, and the cares of this world and the deceitfulness of riches choke the word, and he becomes unfruitful. But he who received seed on the good ground is he who hears the word and understands it, who indeed bears fruit and produces: some a hundredfold, some sixty, some thirty" (Matt. 13:18–23).

When I was a boy, my Dad made a strong statement to me. He said, "Son, when you make a promise to someone, you must keep your word. A man is no better than his word." I grew up with that principle instilled in my heart. Twenty-eight years ago, when I came to Castle Hills First Baptist Church, one of the search committee was concerned about our not being able to buy a home before the one in Arizona sold. I said I didn't have the money. He replied, "Don't worry about it. You find a house you want, and I'll loan you the money for the down payment, and when your house sells, you can pay me back." No papers were signed, no documentation whatsoever. He trusted my word that I would repay him the ten thousand dollar loan. Six months later, when my house sold, I repaid him.

This man worked in the lumber business, and, as I understood it, lumbermen buy and sell lumber over the telephone. It's done on the basis of the word of one man on the end of the phone line taking the word of the man on the other end. It's all about being a "man of your word."

I want to speak to you about "A Man and His Word." I want to address the critical issues facing us as children of God, as Southern Baptists, and as local churches. Jesus had a word for His disciples that is clearly for us today as well. We need to have an exposure to the Word, to experience the Word, and to see the expression of the Word.

I. Exposure to the Word

First, the parable speaks to us of several different ways in which a person is exposed to the Word. Jesus described the "stolen" Word, the seed that fell on stony ground and was stolen by the birds. The Word is still "stolen" in our society. Let there be no mistake. Let's not live in denial. We are in a war, and we have been provided with the armor we need for protection from the enemy. Paul wrote that the sword of the spirit is the Word of God (Eph. 6:17).

The battle for the Word has been going on for at least half a century since liberal theology from Germany made its way to our country. One exponent, Harry Emerson Fosdick of New York City, said from his pulpit, "Some day we will find the ancient tomb in which we will discover the bones of Jesus."

German rationalism and later neoorthodoxy permeated theological institutions in America which began to turn out preachers who believed in humanism rather than the inspired, infallible, inerrant Word of God.

My son Jeff recently returned from Johannesburg, where he preached for fourteen days. He returned elated because he saw five hundred young people stand up to trust Jesus as Savior in one public school meeting. He said that after the meeting, the principal stood and said to the student body, "For all of you who have trusted Christ today, if you do not have a Bible, come by my office, and I will see that you're given one."

What a contrast to one of our newest San Antonio high schools, where last week one of our young people was told by the principal to wear his necklace on the inside of his shirt because the cross was offensive to some. What is wrong with this picture? Free to preach the Word in Africa but not free in the United States of America, a nation founded on Christian principles? As religious leaders, we must be aware that we're at war with an enemy who is attempting to steal the Word from our schools, from the media, and eventually from our pulpits if we don't take a stand against him now.

Many, including one messenger in the 2000 Southern Baptist Convention, assert that the Bible is inspired and points to Christ but is, nonetheless, just a book. These people believe that the Word of God is a book with the biases and traditions of the days in which it was written—a book to guide us, but nevertheless, just a book. We must be vigilant and outspoken about what we believe, lest we be drawn into compromise with these who would "steal" the Word.

Jesus not only spoke about the "stolen" Word, but He also spoke about a "shallow" Word that was illustrated by the seed that fell on stony ground: the seed that took root quickly and began to grow but was wilted by the sun. This seed represents those who received the word but perished when persecution came. I'm afraid we have some shallow people around today, many of them preaching in pulpits across the land. This shallow preaching has spawned a generation of "listeners" who hear but don't practice their beliefs. They come to church to be entertained, to have their emotions stirred rather than to study the Word of God.

This shallowness becomes evident when the time comes to take a courageous position on moral issues. Those who don't have a tap-root grown from reaching down into the Word of God have no biblical principles on which to face issues such as abortion. They're unable to take a stand because they are tolerant of the world's ideas and intolerant of the Word.

Ministers who are guilty of shallow preaching are responsible for how they deliver the Word of God. Preaching is not public speaking or entertainment. The definition for preaching is found in Nehemiah 8:5–8: "And Ezra opened the book in the sight of all the people . . . and they read from the book, from the Law of God, translating to give the sense so that they understood the reading." Preaching is reading from the Word of God and giving the sense thereof, not cute jokes off the Internet, headlines from the newspaper, shaggy-dog tales, or entertainment.

When I was a young preacher, my pastor told me, "George, don't worry about telling your people about Shakespeare. Don't try to be up on the newest thing in science. Take refuge in the Word of God because most of them don't know much about that." It's time we stopped trying to meet the culture where it is and become like it. We need to bring people to the standards of the Word of God.

There are also those who have stifled the Word of God represented by the seed that fell among thorns and was strangled by the weeds. If we carefully read the Scripture here, we find Jesus saying that this illustrates the people who became entangled in the world and the deceptiveness of riches. I would say that this is a warning against one of the great sins of those in ministry today—preoccupation with lesser things.

When we come to the pulpit with a message that burns deeply within us, the Word is set on fire from heaven. It's not our role to be cute or contemporary but to be empowered by the Holy Spirit of God. We need to mine our own gold right from the Word rather than creating an assimilation by taking bits and pieces of other people's sermons.

Our church members are hungry for a Word from God, not the stolen Word, or the shallow Word, or the stifled Word, but a clear, sound voice from the Holy Spirit of God through His messenger. Is it any wonder that the devil would steal away the Word to keep people from coming to know Christ? Is it any wonder that we have a health-and-wealth mentality because of shallowness? We have a generation of people who have been misled into thinking that the Christian life is a life without any suffering. But many great Christians, great preachers, and great churches have suffered because they refused to apologize for the Word of God.

Why did God give us the Word in the first place? So that we can learn to be fruitful. Hebrews 4:12 says, "For the word of God is living and powerful, and sharper than any two-edged sword, piercing even to the division of soul and spirit, and of joints and marrow, and is a discerner of the thoughts and intents of the heart."

The Bible is more than a book because it is the only book that gives birth to those who are dead in their trespasses and sins. It is the only book that gives deliverance from demonic oppression and gives light in the midst of darkness. You may argue that you were saved by Jesus Christ, not by a book, but you wouldn't know there was a Jesus Christ without the Bible. We read in John 1:1: "In the beginning was the Word, and the Word was with God, and the Word was God," and in verse 14, "the Word became flesh and dwelt among us."

How are we saved? "For by grace you have been saved through faith, and that not of yourselves; it is the gift of God, not of works, lest anyone should boast" (Eph. 2:8). By faith! Then how do we have faith? "Faith comes by hearing, and hearing by the word of God" (Rom. 10:17). It is by this book that you know Jesus Christ. The Man and his Word are the same. Call me a "bibliolater" if you like, but I worship the Book that introduced me to the Savior. People say, "Paul got saved, and he didn't have a Bible." But they need to read that the incarnate Word spoke to him from heaven one day and called him by name and introduced him to the Word face-to-face. Paul didn't get saved without the Word. You may say, "I could get saved without the Bible." Yes, you could, without having it present, but not without hearing its message.

II. The Experience of the Word

"Of His own will He brought us forth by the word *(logos)* of truth, that we might be a kind of firstfruits of His creatures" (James 1:18). There are three dimensions of the Word. There is the word *(Logos)*, which speaks of the incarnate Word, Jesus. There is the written Word *(logos* again), which we use when we speak of the Book, the written record of God. And there is the *remah* of God, which is translated in Ephesians when Paul wrote of the sword of the Spirit as the Word (the *remah)* of God, the spoken Word of God (Eph. 6:17).

We have such a shallow mentality today about the Word that we could quote "Mary had a little lamb," and some would think it was Scripture. I hear people say, "Well, Scripture says that God helps those who help themselves." While this may be true, God didn't say it—Benjamin Franklin did.

We need to experience the Word of God. In 1 Peter 1:23, we read: "For you have been born again not of seed which is perishable but imperishable, that is, through the living and enduring word of God" (NASB). The word for "seed" here is the Greek word *spora*. It is the word from which we get the word *sperm*. It carries the meaning of conception. It means that when the Word of God is mingled with the faith of man, conception takes place, and we are born into the kingdom of God. Now there is an experience! Until a person has had an experience with the gospel of Jesus Christ, until he has heard the gospel and responded to that Word by repenting of his sins, he will not have a *conversion* experience.

There must be a *conviction* experience. In 2 Timothy 3:16, Paul wrote, "All Scripture is given by inspiration of God." He says *all* Scripture. He was at that time talking about the Old Testament. He was *writing* the New Testament, although he didn't know it. The Holy Spirit of God was moving upon him in a marvelous way, inspiring the Word of God in word and in thought. Listen to these words:
But it is written:
   "Eye has not seen, nor ear heard, Nor have entered into
   the heart of man
   The things which God has prepared
   for those who love Him."
But God has revealed them to us through His Spirit. For the Spirit searches all things, yes, the deep things of God. For what man knows the things of a man except the spirit of the man which is in him? Even so no one knows the things of God except the Spirit of God. Now we have received, not the spirit of the world, but the Spirit who is from God, that we might know the things that have been freely given to us by God.

These things we also speak, not in words which man's wisdom teaches but which the Holy Spirit teaches, comparing spiritual things with spiritual (1 Cor. 2:9–13).

Let me remind you of something you may already know. Comparing spiritual "thoughts" with spiritual "words" is the way the original language reads. Some say, "I believe the Bible is inspired in thought, but not in word." Let's have a little game. I challenge you to have a thought without words to express that thought!

It isn't even intelligent or theologically astute to say, "I believe the Bible is inspired in thought but not in word." You can't have a thought and give it expression without words! This means that when the Holy Spirit breathed on Paul, Matthew, Mark, Luke, and all the rest, and poured in His thoughts, He may have accommodated the ideas to their words. But it was the Holy Spirit of God choosing the words of a man and putting the thoughts of God with the words of a man to express the very Word of God. Just a Book! I tell you it is a Book and a Book that time has not been able to erase, a Book that persecution has not been able to extinguish, a Book that critics have not been able to explain away, and a Book that scientists have not been able to understand or discredit. Yes, it's a Book, but it is *the* Book that you and I must preach and proclaim if the world is going to be saved. Without it there is no hope.

III. The Expression of the Word

When we've been exposed to the Word and experienced the Word, there naturally follows an *expression of the Word*. In fact, when we've put our roots down deeply into it and experience it daily, there is no way under heaven that we can *keep* from expressing it. A beautiful example of a man who was unable to keep from expressing his faith in the Word is the life of Watchman Nee, a Chinese Christian who lived under Communism. After his conversion, he became a dynamic witness for the Lord. So powerful was his testimony that he was thrown in prison and guards were assigned to watch him 24-7. But each guard would be won to Christ by Watchman Nee and flee into the interior of China, taking with him messages from Nee. So the officials said, "We must change the guards more often." They changed the guards monthly, then weekly, and then daily, and finally, hour by hour. This only gave Nee more prospects to win to Christ. Watchman Nee died in prison in 1972, but he remained a faithful witness for Jesus Christ until the end. Twenty years of persecution and imprisonment under the Communist regime failed to weaken his commitment to the Savior. He was exposed to the Word, experienced the Word, and spent his life expressing the Word. May God help us to sound a clear, definite, positive message, declaring the Word to our world.

39

Rock Solid: How to Build a Life That Lasts

MATTHEW 7:24–29 NKJV

Jack Graham

Senior Pastor, Prestonwood Baptist Church
Dallas, Texas

WE LIVE IN A WORLD where we want everything in a hurry. I've seen folks stand in front of a microwave and complain that it takes a full minute to heat up a cup of coffee! Can you relate? We like drive-thru convenience, all things disposable, and cell phone availability.

And never have so many complained of having so little time to enjoy life.

Too often we sacrifice quality for convenience. We say we don't have time. We say we can't wait. We've embraced a "just do it" philosophy. More and more people are sacrificing enduring truth for quick fixes.

But if we want to ensure that we can weather life's greatest storms no matter how strong the winds or how torrential the rains, we need to step out of the quicksand of convenience and step onto the bedrock of lasting truth.

Storms are an inevitable part of life. It's simply a reality that our lives will experience a train wreck or two. You may be on the brink of a storm or in the middle of one today. And you may be tempted to jump to a quick-fix solution. But before you act, let me show you how you can build a life that lasts—a rock-solid life.

Jesus, a carpenter and the builder of mankind, provides clear instruction on how you and I can build a rock-solid foundation for our lives. At the end of the Sermon on the Mount, in Matthew 7, Jesus talks about a man who builds his house on rock and another who builds on sand. In this story, Jesus gives us three building blocks for a life that will last.

> Therefore whoever hears these sayings of Mine, and does
> them, I will liken him to a wise man who built his house on
> the rock: and the rain descended, the floods came, and the
> winds blew and beat on that house; and it did not fall, for it
> was founded on the rock.
>
> But everyone who hears these sayings of Mine, and does
> not do them, will be like a foolish man who built his house
> on the sand: and the rain descended, the floods came, and
> the winds blew and beat on that house; and it fell. And great
> was its fall (Matt. 7:24–27).

The Importance of the Basics

Jesus focused on the fundamentals of faith. Forget the complexities, forget the enigmas, forget the theological twisters that all too many of today's teachers focus on. The faith that Jesus taught was profound enough to set the religious establishment of His day on edge, yet so simple that a child could understand it.

It's time that we all got back to the basics of faith.

John Wooden is a man who practiced the basics. Wooden was a great builder of basketball players and teams who led the UCLA Bruins basketball team to championship after championship.

He was an old-school coach. He did all kinds of things that his players considered unusual, and he had all kinds of policies that his players thought were odd. But he won. Why? Because coach Wooden taught the basics, building a solid foundation for an unprecedented string of victories.

The game for Wooden was always about fundamentals. And many of America's finest high school players would go on to play college ball under renowned coach John Wooden at UCLA. It was from Wooden that players like Lou Alcindor, who later became the great Kareem Abdul-Jabbar, would learn the basics of the game.

At every season-opening practice, Wooden would gather the players that he had recruited from America's best high school basketball teams and instruct them—on how to put their socks on. Imagine what these young men must have been thinking! "What! I've come to UCLA to learn how to put my socks on? This is the coach of the best basketball program in the country?" And Wooden would make very clear to them that, yes, learning to put their socks on was precisely what he was going to teach them before they bounced a ball and did a drill.

Speaking rhetorically, Wooden would ask, "You know why you gotta put your socks on in the right way? Because if you don't put your socks on properly there will be wrinkles in your socks, and wrinkles cause blisters, and you can't play with blisters."

And so Wooden would teach his players step-by-step how to put their socks on, first the right foot and then the left foot. Physically grown men training to put on their socks, one foot at a time! That's teaching the basics! By emphasizing the fundamentals, Wooden built a foundation to last the season and, for many of these youthful stars, throughout their professional careers into their personal lives.

He showed how much he cared for them by teaching them old-school discipline. He cared nothing for the unnecessary and the frivolous. For Wooden, showboating by dribbling behind your back or between your legs to show up your opponent was not a part of the game.

Among the other things that Wooden demanded of his players was that they have short hair and be clean shaven. Why? Because long hair would stay wet longer after a shower, heightening their chances of catching a cold and preventing them from playing. During an era when long hair and beards were the "in-thing," especially in trend-setting California, this particular policy drove some of his players crazy.

The story goes that after a summer break future NBA great Bill Walton returned to UCLA sporting a lengthy beard and long hair. John Wooden took one look and said, "Bill, you're gonna have to cut that." Walton, in turn, responded, "No. You have no right to tell me that. I have a right to wear my hair like this."

Wooden paused before responding and then asked Walton, "Do you believe that, Bill? Do you believe it very strongly, Bill?" And Walton stated, "I absolutely do!" "Well," said Wooden, "I like men that believe in things very strongly, who will stand up for what they believe and stay with it." Then Wooden added, "It's been nice having you on our team, Bill. We're going to miss you."

Bill Walton cut his hair and his beard and learned how to play ball like few men before or since. And to this day, he calls Coach Wooden, who is now more than 90 years old, every week just to tell him how much he loves him. Wooden, you see, was much more than a coach to his players. He became their father figure. Of the 188 or so players that he coached during his career, he knows the whereabouts of 172.

Coach Wooden was committed to the basics. He taught his players the importance of building a solid foundation for success—in basketball and in life.

There is great opportunity today to complicate our lives and to miss out on the basics. Yet it is my belief that Jesus wants us to focus on the basics as we seek to build our lives on the rock-solid truth revealed to us in His life and in God's Word.

Building a Strong Foundation

Jesus' Sermon on the Mount is the most significant sermon ever delivered. Recorded in Matthew's fifth, sixth, and seventh chapters, it is a masterful exposition of the law, a potent assault on religious legalism, and a clarion call to true faith and salvation.

Those who heard Jesus deliver the Sermon on the Mount were amazed with its relevance. In fact, the crowd's response to this incredible teaching is recorded in the last sentence of Matthew 7: "And so it was, when Jesus had ended these sayings, that the people were astonished at His teaching, for He taught them as one having authority, and not as the scribes" (Matt. 7:28–29).

The scribes quoted others to establish the authority of their teachings, but Jesus was His own authority (Matt. 28:18). He taught with such force and clarity that it was obvious to all that He was the source of the truth He taught.

Among the many things that Jesus teaches in the Sermon on the Mount is the absolute need to build our faith on a sound foundation. He offers us a simple yet powerful illustration of two home builders to drive home His point. The houses in His illustration represent religious life, and the wind and rain are divine judgment:

> Therefore whoever hears these sayings of Mine, and does them, I will liken him to a wise man who built his house on the rock: and the rain descended, the floods came, and the winds blew and beat on that house; and it did not fall, for it was founded on the rock.

> But everyone who hears these sayings of Mine, and does not do them, will be like a foolish man who built his house on the sand: and the rain descended, the floods came, and the winds blew and beat on that house; and it fell. And great was its fall (Matt. 7:24–27).

Two men. Two houses. One founded on rock. The other built on sand. Both buffeted by wind and pelted with rain. The house with a solid foundation remains standing. The other collapses.

Jesus uses this easy-to-understand yet profoundly vivid picture to direct us in building the right foundation for our lives. You can have two houses, but the one with the strongest foundation will outlast the one with weaker underpinnings.

Likewise, you can have two people, two churchgoers, if you will. They dress similarly, live in the same neighborhood, speak the same language, carry the same Bible, and maybe even sing the same hymns with the same enthusiasm. Yet there's a distinct difference between them. One actually hears and internalizes the good news of Jesus.

The other, if he or she even hears the Word, fails to acknowledge it in his or her life.

The former is building a life founded on the rock that is the Word. The latter leads a life as insubstantial as sand, pursuing a self-indulgent and fleeting existence. Amid the tempests of life, which will fare better? And when we enter that ultimate of storms, which of these two lives will be wanting—the life whose foundation is fixed in God, the rock of ages, or the life without foundation?

Building Block #1: The Reality in Jesus Christ

Building your life on the rock is essential, now and forever, if you are to build a life that will last. How do you do that? The first building block is in the reality that is Jesus Christ.

The "therefore" that Jesus uses to begin His illustration of the man who builds his house on rock signals a summation of the points that he has just made. Key among them is the point Jesus makes to the people who will stand before God on judgment day and assume that past actions alone will be sufficient for entry to heaven: "Many will say to Me in that day, 'Lord, Lord, have we not prophesied in Your name, cast out demons in Your name, and done many wonders in Your name?'" (Matt. 7:22).

To these, Jesus tells us, He will say, "I never knew you; depart from Me" (Matt. 7:23a).

His choice of phrases here is interesting. To know someone in the biblical sense suggests an intimacy akin to marriage. So Jesus is telling us that access to heaven hinges upon our really knowing Him through a deep personal relationship that, in turn, makes Him know us. It's one thing to say, "I know Jesus," and another to say that He knows you. The latter is crucial.

We live in a celebrity-crazed time, when fans assume that they know their favorite stars. People go gaga over what these famous people wear and eat and say and do. And many write to their favorite celebrity. Well, you may know a lot of superficial things about your star, but the star hasn't got a clue who you are. So don't expect return mail. You're just another crazed fan.

In the same way, there are a lot of people who claim to know Jesus. Simply knowing His name, however, without committing to a deep personal relationship with Him does not mean that He knows your name. A person whose life displays the reality of Jesus and the Christian faith as preached and proclaimed by Jesus in the Sermon on the Mount is far different from the anemic Christianity often preached and proclaimed in some churches today.

Jesus preaches a personal relationship that is far deeper than the rhetoric often heard in some so-called Christian circles today. He is describing a relationship and a fellowship with God that is life changing.

Sadly, a lot of the people who profess Jesus in their lives through surveys and polls lead lives barely different from people who don't profess Christ. These self-professed Christians do not reveal their faith at their workplaces or in their marriages or in their academic pursuits and places—because it's not real. And rest assured, Jesus does not allow for superficiality or artificiality. He won't let you get away with that.

It's like the guy I heard about who was stuck in traffic behind a lady who was talking on her cell phone. He was one of these self-professed Christians, as proclaimed by the myriad bumper stickers on his car. Well, this man was becoming increasingly incensed as the woman in front of him missed two lights, distracted as she was by her conversation on the telephone. He began raising his hands, shaking his fists, honking his horn, and turning the air blue with profanity at such a volume that you could hear it outside the car.

When he could take it no more, he accelerated around the woman's vehicle, only to be pulled over by a police officer who had observed his antics. The officer insisted that the man get out of his vehicle and sit in the police cruiser. Stunned, the man exclaimed, "What are you talking about? All I did was try to get through this traffic! You can't pull me over for yelling at that woman!"

As the officer checked out the man's license and registration, the officer gave the man a real good looking-over. When the officer released him, the irate man assured the officer that he would never hear the end of it—that he had been pulled over for no reason. To which the officer responded, "I'll tell you why I pulled you over, sir. When I saw your car and the bumper stickers and the way you acted, I thought you must have stolen the car."

A person's actions do indeed speak louder than a person's words. As Matthew 7:20 states, "Therefore by their fruits you will know them." The fruits our lives yield are what others will judge us by.

John also talks about the basic truth of knowing Jesus. John, in fact, even defines some of the spiritual fruit that shows we are saved. He states, "Whoever confesses that Jesus is the Son of God, God abides in him, and he in God"(1 John 4:15).

So my first question to you is, Have you confessed Jesus as your Lord and Savior? If you haven't, you are not a Christian. You can invoke the name of God all you like, but it is impossible to be saved without confessing Jesus Christ as your Lord by personally and publicly identifying yourself as a follower of Jesus.

You must believe in who He is—the Savior, the sinless and spotless Lamb of God, and in what He did for you—dying on the cross for your sins and rising again on the third day. But only if we confess with our mouths the Lord Jesus Christ and believe in our hearts that God has raised Him from the dead will we be saved (Rom. 10:9).

Knowing Jesus as your Savior is the first building block of a life that lasts. That reality is the basic truth to a rock-solid life.

Building Block #2: The Stability in Jesus Christ

If the first building block to a life that lasts is knowing the reality of Jesus, the second building block is relying on the stability that is in Christ Jesus.

Take a look at 1 John 3:9: "Whoever has been born of God does not sin, for His seed remains in him; and he cannot sin, because he has been born of God."

What that means, literally, is that a real, confessing Christian does not sin. But, of course, we all know believers who sin. I wish I could tell you that I never sin or that I'll never sin again. But I'm not all that confident, because I know my nature, and I know the temptations. And, yes, we all sin (Rom. 3:23).

But there's a difference between the true child of God who is building a life upon the rock and a person who isn't. The difference is that the person whose life has been or is being changed by the power of Jesus Christ does not continue to live and practice and embrace sin. There's a discomfort when we sin caused by the conviction of the indwelling presence of the Holy Spirit.

Somebody once said that when we are saved Jesus fixes it not so we can't sin anymore but that we can't enjoy it anymore. There is a grain of truth in that thought. When we are saved we gain conviction and a check is placed upon us—like the warning light that lights up on the dashboard of a car—when we cross the line. The Holy Spirit lives within us, and we can't continue to do what we used to do. We're transformed. We're changed by the power of Jesus Christ. We're founded on the bedrock of Christianity.

By contrast, a person who blatantly persists in sin is building a life on sand. That person does not acknowledge the reality of Jesus and has no foundation on the rock of a substantial relationship with and in Christ.

Jesus is to be the foundation of our lives. In fact, the Bible often refers to Christ as the chief cornerstone—the indispensable and fundamental component to build our lives upon.

> Now, therefore, you are no longer strangers and foreigners, but fellow citizens with the saints and members of the household of God, having been built on the foundation of the apostles and prophets, Jesus Christ Himself being the chief cornerstone, in whom the whole building, being fitted together, grows into a holy temple in the Lord, in whom you also are being built together for a dwelling place of God in the Spirit (Eph. 2:19–22).

There is no other way than to found your life upon the rock. Only in this way can Jesus change our lives. And not only that, but our belief and our confession in Jesus will result in Jesus' changing how we relate to other people. People that we hated, we will love.

Check out 1 John 5:1: "Whoever believes that Jesus is the Christ is born of God, and everyone who loves Him who begot also loves him who is begotten of Him."

Simply put, it means that when you are born again you become a new person in Christ and a member of a family, all of whose members you love (2 Cor. 5:17). Once Jesus Christ enters your life, you'll discover a love for those you hated and will embrace other believers as your brothers and sisters in Christ.

It saddens me to hear people say that they get their spiritual nourishment solely through the radio or television or the Internet. Church is so much more than sermons and Bible study. It is fellowship among the members of a family who believe in and encourage and bless and strengthen one another. The church is a place where we can serve as the salt and light of the culture of our community. It's a place to share Christ, a place where we function as a body.

We each have spiritual gifts we need to share with one another. And that's why God created the church. If you love Jesus, you'll love the people who love Jesus and will long to be with them—in His church.

I want to mention one more fruit by which you can distinguish between the real Christian and churchgoer. Look at 1 John 2:5: "But whoever keeps His word, truly the love of God is perfected in him. By this we know that we are in Him." Now ask yourself, "Do I live in obedience to the Word of God?"

We must keep God's Word, abide in God's Word, love God's Word, and live God's Word. Founding your life upon the rock is to build your life upon the Word of God. As it is with loving people you once disliked, becoming a Christian enables you to understand a book that once made no sense to you. What gave you no sustenance before becomes living bread. You want to be with and of the Word. You develop an appetite for spiritual truth in your life because you know Jesus, and the more you know the more you grow in Him.

I'm concerned about the professing Christians in America who think the Christian life is solely an esoteric religious experience. Even some evangelical churches try to make it all about the experience, the emotion, rather than about building foundations: a trust in God's Word. Test the average high school student on the fundamental truths and personalities and events of the Bible, and he or she fails miserably. Many are growing up and merely adopting the religion of their parents instead of having a personal relationship with Christ and growing in the Word.

If you are to build a life that lasts, you need a foundation for your life. The point is that if you love Jesus and know Him, you're going to love His word and its truth. That's why Jesus said that those who build their houses on the rock are the ones who hear His word and keep His commandments and do what He says. To build your life to last means building on the reality of Jesus Christ.

And that, in turn, implies building on the stability that is Jesus Christ. Every builder knows the importance of laying sturdy foundations. The bigger the building, the sturdier the base must be. Months can be spent digging and laying out iron and steel and pouring concrete before the actual structure begins to rise.

A good foundation is essential, for buildings and for lives. For the storms will come. Just as a Texas tornado can come up out of nowhere to buffet a building, problems and tragedies can arise unexpectedly in the happiest lives. Jesus tells us that the rain falls upon the just and the unjust, so dispense with the idea that somehow you're going to escape the storms of life (Matt. 5:45).

The storms that Jesus teaches us about can take many forms. They can be the storm of thunderous judgment in the future or the periodic and temporary storms that arise in all lives. The latter encompass all kinds of tests that try our lives in varying degrees. These can be a financial crisis, a family crisis, a marital crisis. They can even involve a trial of unanswered prayer. But you know what? A faith that can't withstand the tests thrown at it by life is a faith that can't be trusted. So take those storms in stride. A good storm will demonstrate the reality and the stability of your faith's foundation.

Over the years, I've had numerous church members tell me, "Pastor, we're in a storm, and it's hard. But somehow, I'm not sure how, we're still standing. We're still trusting in God, and there is peace in His presence in this storm, and we couldn't live without it."

The fact is that people whose lives lack a foundation built upon the rock of the reality of Jesus don't survive. They have no stability. If you build your life around toys and trinkets and selfish pursuits, around anything other than Jesus Christ, one of these days a storm is going to strike and tear your life apart. You'll have nothing to stand on. You'll have no strength of support and stability in your life. We all need to heed what that great old gospel song proclaims:

> On Christ the solid Rock I stand,
> All other ground is sinking sand;
> All other ground is sinking sand.
> (Edward Mote)

To confront the seasons and the storms of life, we must stand on the rock that is Jesus. This is how we build a life to last.

Building Block #3: The Eternity in Jesus Christ

The final building block of a life that lasts is the eternity that is in Jesus Christ. I'm talking about a life that lasts forever beyond this physical life in the company of Christ. Building a solid foundation on the rock of Christ in our physical lifetime leads, ultimately, to an eternal future with God.

You were built to live forever. God has set eternity in our hearts.

Life is brief. It's described in the Bible, in fact, as little more than a vapor, a mist, a dew in the morning that comes up and quickly disappears (James 4:14). We're going to spend far more time in eternity then on this earth. That's why Jesus instructs against the foolishness of building a life for here and now without thought of eternity.

The Christian lives for eternity, and that priority is life changing. We're to seek first the kingdom of God and His righteousness (Matt. 6:33). This aim alters our values. It revises the way we live, because we recognize that the here and now isn't all there is. We live knowing that we have so terrific a future and a promise with God in heaven that it defies comprehension.

Paul alludes to this in 1 Corinthian 2:9: "Eye has not seen, nor ear heard, nor have entered into the heart of man the things which God has prepared for those who love Him."

We can only imagine what awaits us from the glimpses Scripture gives us of this great glory. And it is these glimpses of our prize that keep us steadfastly anchored to the rock that is our foundation.

The Bible tells us that in heaven we will rejoice and revel in God's presence. That's what makes heaven, heaven. In heaven, we're going to be reunited with family and friends, all the loved ones who've gone before us in Christ. In heaven, we're going to be restored and renewed and completed in Jesus Christ, given immortal, glorified bodies, and serve Him day and night.

We're not going to sit in heaven and waste eternity away. We're going to be serving God forever. We're going to walk with Him always.

That's why we live for eternity. Because we know that death isn't the end. Death for the Christian is a doorway—the exit from life and the entrance to eternity.

In knowing this, we must know, too, that there are eternal consequences to everything we do in the here and now. We have so many choices in life. But for the afterlife, we get only two choices: heaven or hell!

Isn't it interesting that Jesus, who is love incarnate, ended the Sermon on the Mount with a good, healthy, holy dose of fear? He talks about judgment. He talks about the broad road that leads to destruction. He tells us that while we have many choices there are consequences to every choice, that the decision we make today determines our destiny, forever. Choose to live without God in life, and you choose to live without God in the afterlife.

That's why Jesus came to earth. He arrived to save us from making the wrong choice, from being judged and found wanting and delivered to hell and its eternal death. He came to offer eternal life instead to all who believe, to all who build a life to last on the bedrock of His reality. He came to show us that the life we know now is but preparation for the eternity to come. Thus, the words of the prophet who admonishes: "Prepare to meet your God" (Amos 4:12).

To build your life to last means building for eternity on a foundation of Jesus Christ. Do you know Christ? Or do you just know the name and a few things about Christ? Does Christ know you? Are you living as a child of God? Do you exhibit the character of the kingdom? Again, do you know Christ? Is Jesus living in you? Are you seeking first the kingdom of God and His righteousness?

Conclusion

San Francisco's iconic and oft-photographed Golden Gate Bridge is absolutely essential to meeting the transportation needs of the Bay area. So much so that it is one of the first things in America to receive increased attention when the terrorism alert level escalates.

Did you know that the Golden Gate Bridge is built directly over the San Andreas Fault? During an earthquake, the bridge is built to sway some twenty feet at the center of its one-mile span.

The secret to the bridge's durability, however, lies in more than just its flexibility. By design, every part of the bridge—its concrete roadway, its steel railings, its cross beams—is integrated, from one welded joint to the other up through the vast cable system to two great towers and two great land-anchor piers. The towers, which bear most of the weight, are deeply embedded in the rock foundation beneath the sea. The Golden Gate Bridge stands today because of its solid foundation.

Our lives are an even greater engineering marvel than the Golden Gate Bridge. After all, we are God's workmanship (Eph. 2:10).

Follow these three simple building blocks to construct a life that lasts:

1. Build your life on the reality that is in Jesus Christ. Jesus hated phony religion. Why? Because it kept people from a real relationship with Him. In Matthew 7:20–23, Jesus makes clear that there are many who think they have favor with God but don't, for one simple reason: They don't know Him.

To really know Jesus is to have a personal relationship with Him. It's not about the superficiality of merely making an appearance at church and going through the motions of doing religious things. It's a personal, intimate friendship with Jesus. That is the first building block for a life that lasts.

2. *Build your life on the stability that is in Jesus Christ.* Every contractor knows just how critical laying a strong foundation is to the stability of a building. Life is no different. You and I must dig deep into the bedrock of Jesus Christ if we are to weather the storms that will hit our lives.

What does that mean? It means knowing Christ and His word and doing what we know. That's why Jesus says in Matthew 7:24, "Whoever hears these sayings of Mine, and does them, I will liken him to a wise man who built his house on the rock." That's the second building block.

3. *Build your life on the eternity that is in Jesus Christ.* You must understand that you were built to live forever. At the same time, you must realize that your physical life is but a vapor and that you will spend infinitely more time in eternity then you spend on this earth.

This knowledge will lead you to live for eternity and to reorder the priorities of your life based on that truth. With that commitment, you have put in place the third building block for a life that lasts.

If you want a life that will last, build upon the stability that is Christ. Build upon the reality of a personal relationship with Jesus with an eye to the eternity that is just around the corner.

Part 4:

Preaching from a Heart for the Kingdom

40

The Church's Main Business

MATTHEW 28:16–20 KJV

Jerry Vines
Senior Pastor, First Baptist Church
Jacksonville, Florida

WHAT IS THE CHURCH'S MAIN BUSINESS? Or why is the church here? Our text in Matthew 28 comes after the resurrection of Jesus. He is getting ready to go back to heaven. This passage of Scripture says:

> Then the eleven disciples went away into Galilee, into a mountain where Jesus had appointed them. And when they saw him, they worshipped him: but some doubted. And Jesus came and spake unto them, saying, All power is given unto me in heaven and in earth. Go ye therefore, and teach all nations, baptizing them in the name of the Father, and of the Son, and of the Holy Ghost: teaching them to observe all things whatsoever I have commanded you: and lo, I am with you alway, even unto the end of the world. Amen (Matt. 28:16–20).

Any organization, institution, or business justifies its existence only insofar as it carries out the purpose for which it was founded. This is certainly true in every area of life. A grocery store justifies its existence if it continues to make groceries available to people. Suppose we walked into a grocery store and asked to buy a dozen bananas. If they said, "We're sorry, we don't sell food here, but we've got some motor oil if you'd like to have that," it wouldn't be long until they would be out of existence.

Suppose we went into a college, into a university, and walked into the registrar's office and said, "We would like to sign up for some courses. We would like to educate ourselves in several areas." Suppose they should say to us, "We don't have any courses available for you, but if you'd like a dozen bananas, we have plenty of those." It wouldn't be long until that institution would be out of existence.

So any organization, any institution, any business justifies its existence only as long as it accomplishes the purpose for which it is intended. Now that is true also of the church of the Lord Jesus Christ. What is the main purpose of the church? Why is the church here?

I want you to follow with me certain statements from Jesus which I believe give us the irresistible logic of the main business of the church. If there is a heaven—and there is—and if there is a hell— and there is—and if Jesus died on the cross to make it possible for people to go to heaven and not go to hell, then the most important business of the church is to let people know that they do not have to go to hell. They can go to heaven. Because Jesus died on the cross for their sins, it is possible for them to go to heaven. That is the irresistible logic of what I call "evangelism," and it is the irresistible logic of the main business of the church.

The main business of the church is evangelism. The word *evangelism* is taken from a Greek verb that means "to tell good news." The noun is the word *evangelion,* which is translated "gospel" in many passages in the Bible.

Evangelism is the work of telling the good news that Jesus died on the cross, that He was buried, that He rose again, and that those people who will turn from their sins by repentance, and by faith will turn to the Lord Jesus Christ, receiving Him as their personal Savior, will not go to hell, but they can go to heaven. That is the work of evangelism, and it is the main business of the church.

I was reading an article recently in the newspaper about a wealthy man who has announced his intentions to begin an institution. It was interesting to read what he had to say about it. He was going to start this institution because he believed the most important thing in the world is to get people ready to go to heaven. Then he said that the best way to do that was through education. While I commend his efforts to build an institution of higher education, and though he seems to understand what the main purpose of it all is, the main purpose of the church is not education. That is one factor, certainly, but the main purpose of the church is evangelism, telling people the story of the Lord Jesus and how people can be saved through Him. That's the main business of the church.

It is sometimes easy for us to misunderstand the main business and to get a little concerned when things are changed. I read a number of years ago about a buggy business. They were successful until the automobile was invented. People started riding in automobiles instead of buggies, and the company refused to change. They continued to try to sell buggies and went out of business. They made the crucial mistake of thinking they were in the buggy business, when they were actually in the transportation business.

I'm afraid there are many churches that are reluctant to change because they think they are in the buggy business, when they are really in the transportation business. We need to understand that we're not riding in buggies anymore. We're in the jet age and flying on jet airplanes. Our business is to win people to faith in the Lord Jesus Christ. We must never be detoured from that.

Now having said that, I want to tell you that it's the easiest thing in the world for a church to get involved in all kinds of secondary trivialities. Ever heard of a doodlebug? When I was a boy, we would go up under a house where there was a lot of loose dirt and take a stick and begin to dig in the ground. And we would say, "Doodlebug, doodlebug, come get your supper." After a little while, a little doodlebug would come up.

We spent a lot of time looking for doodlebugs. And there are a lot of churches today that are involved in what I call the "doodlebug business." They're just digging, digging, digging for doodlebugs, and they get excited and carried away and worked up about a number of activities. But when you really boil it down, they are in the doodle-bug business. Our main business is to tell people about the Lord Jesus Christ and get them ready to go to heaven when they die. That's the main business of the church.

We know that evangelism is our main business because Jesus founded the church, and He knows what the business of His church ought to be. He has given it to us in a beautiful way in the verses of our text. It is called the Great Commission. Unfortunately, for a lot of churches, it is the great omission.

Jesus has told us in these verses exactly what He wants the church to do. I want to reassert this truth. I'm talking about why we are here as a church. I'm talking about what my role is. I'm talking about what the role of the staff is. I'm talking about what the deacons are to do. I'm talking about what all the workers of our fellowship and what all the members of our church ought to do. I'm talking about the main business of the church—evangelism—and I want us to see this truth from the words of Jesus just before He went back to heaven.

I. Jesus Set Forth His Power

Jesus said, "*All power* is given unto me in heaven and in earth" (v. 18). The word *power* speaks of the right to use power. Jesus is referring to His *authority*, the right to exercise power. Jesus already had power. At the end of the Sermon on the Mount, the Bible says that when the people heard the words of Jesus, they were astonished at His sayings, "For he taught them as one having *authority*, and not as the scribes" (Matt. 7:29). He had authority in His teaching.

In the ninth chapter of Matthew, a sick man was brought to Jesus. Jesus said, "That ye may know that the Son of Man hath power [authority] on earth to forgive sins" (Matt 9:6). He already had authority to teach; He already had authority to forgive sins, yet now He says, "All authority is given to me." Why is there some new statement of the authority of Jesus given?

The night before Jesus went to the cross, the religious leaders came to arrest Him. He said, "This is your hour, and the power of darkness" (Luke 22:53). But when Jesus died on that old rugged cross the next day, all the powers of hell joined themselves against the Lord Jesus Christ. On that cross of Calvary, we are told that He spoiled powers and principalities, and now He has all authority. Total power, total authority belongs to the Lord Jesus Christ. The hands that were pierced with the nails of the cross are the hands that hold the scepter of this universe. He has all authority—total power, total authority!

But then notice that He has universal authority. He says, "All power is given unto me in heaven and in earth" (v. 18). This means that angels, cherubim, and seraphim gladly do His bidding. This means that the demonic powers of the world are held in check by Him. This means that He has total universal power—power in heaven, power on the earth. Jesus Christ has the authority to tell the church what to do. It's His church. It's not my church. It's not your church. It is His church. Jesus said, "Upon this rock I will build my church" (Matt. 16:18). He's the One who founded the church. He's the One who says, "All power, all authority is given to me." And the good news is that the power to carry out this Great Commission has been provided for us in the Lord Jesus.

Now put this statement in its context. Jesus was talking to some disciples who had just been scared out of their wits. The cross of Calvary had come. They all forsook Him and fled. Now they understand that Jesus Christ has been raised again from the dead, and yet Jesus says to that motley group of disciples, "I want you to go into all the world and preach the gospel. Go into all the world and make disciples. Go into all the world and win people to faith in the Lord Jesus Christ."

There they were like little specks in the world. There they were like little drops in an ocean of humanity, and yet Jesus said, "Go into all the world and tell them about me." And they must have wondered how they could do that. Because He said, "All power is given unto me."

When these early disciples went out, the Lord said, "Ye shall receive power, after that the Holy Ghost is come upon you: and ye shall be witnesses unto me . . . unto the uttermost part of the earth" (Acts 1:8). That's an encouragement to us today.

In just a moment I will get specifically into this matter of winning people to Christ, making disciples, soul winning, and witnessing. It's going to frighten some of you. And you're going to say, "Well, I can't possibly do that." Jesus said, "All power is given unto Me." And He said, "I'll give that power to you. I'll give you the power to do what I've commanded you to do."

That's what I like about Jesus. He never asked us to do something without providing us the power to do it. It is such an encouragement to us to see all power. But notice that all power means all authority. That means Jesus is in charge. Now we must stop right here for a moment and solve the authority question.

Have you yielded yourself to the authority of Jesus? Have you committed to Him in your mind and heart? Not only is He the Savior of your life; He is the Lord of your life. He is the final authority in your life. You can't go further in the Great Commission until you solve the authority question. So I'm going to ask every believer right now in your own hearts to say to the Lord Jesus Christ, "Jesus Christ, You are not my Savior alone; You are also my Lord. I yield my life today to Your authority. I'll do whatever You command me to do."

II. Jesus Set Forth His Plan

Any business that is going to accomplish its purpose must have a good business plan. That is the only way to accomplish the mission of a business. So what Jesus does now, in verses 19 and 20, is to lay before His church His business plan. Here's how we will accomplish the mission He has assigned us to accomplish. And there are four parts to this plan.

The first part is *going:* "Go ye therefore" (v. 19). The verb here is not an imperative. It has the force of an imperative, but really the idea here is "as you are going" or "having gone." It is assumed by the Lord Jesus Christ that those who follow Him will be going.

I heard about a country preacher one time who said to his congregation, "Now beloved, if we're going to do what the Lord called us to do, the church has got to walk."

And the congregation said, "Amen, let the church walk."

Then he said, "Folks, if we're going to do what the Lord called us to do, we've got to run."

And the people responded, "Amen, preacher! Let the church run!"

The preacher said, "If we are going to do what the Lord wants us to do, the church has got to fly!"

And they cried, "Amen, preacher, let the church fly!"

Then he said, "Now if the church is going to fly, you folks are going to have to give more money than you've been giving."

And the people said, "Amen, preacher. Let the church *walk*."

We're on a walk, and Jesus assumed that believers along the way would be witnesses for Him. Jesus took this seriously. He said, "The Son of man is come to seek and to save that which was lost" (Luke 19:10). Jesus Christ was on a journey. He journeyed all the way from heaven to this earth. Everywhere Jesus went, He was on a walk to tell others how they could be saved. When Jesus went fishing, He told the fishermen how they could be saved, and they followed Him. When He sat down beside a well to refresh Himself with the cool water, He won the woman at the well to faith in Him. Even as He was dying on the cross, He stopped dying long enough to win a thief and get that thief out of hell into heaven! Jesus took His own commission seriously.

The early Christians also took this Great Commission seriously. On the day of Pentecost, Simon Peter stood and preached the pentecostal sermon. When it was over, he gave an invitation. On that one day, three thousand people were saved and baptized into the fellowship of the church (see Acts 2). The early Christians took Jesus' orders seriously.

They took it seriously as individuals. In Acts 8, the Spirit of God said to the deacon Philip, "Arise and go into the desert" (see Acts 8:26). Philip went and met a man riding in a chariot. And the Lord used Philip to win that man to faith in the Lord Jesus Christ, "as they went on their way" (Acts 8:36). It is assumed that we as believers are to go. So the church must have plans to go into the world to win the lost to Christ.

We do that in basically two ways in our church. We have an organized visitation program. That's one of the reasons it is so important for every member to become a part of a Bible fellowship class in our church. All of these classes are organized to get involved in a weekly program of going out and telling people about Jesus. It's time for us to get back into organized visitation. It's time for us to get involved in knocking on doors.

We not only need to participate in organized visitation; we need to practice lifestyle visitation. Wherever we are, as we go, try to be witnesses for the Lord Jesus Christ. There are different kinds of contributions to this plan. Some people are unusually gifted in actually "closing the deal," so to speak. They know how to lead people to accept Jesus Christ as Lord and Savior.

We have several hundred people in our church who are gifted in closing the deal. But that's just a part of the process. There are others who are gifted in inviting people to church. Some of you are gifted in prayer. Some of you are gifted when you go into stores to pass out tracts. It is all a part of the process of lifestyle evangelism. Wherever God has placed you, whatever the circle in which you move, it is your circle of influence. It is your sphere of influence. And as you go, be a witness.

I read an interesting article about the head coaches at the University of Georgia and Florida State—Mark Richt and Bobby Bowden. Richt, who is a fine young Christian coach, told about how when he was on the coaching staff of Bobby Bowden, one of the players on the team died. Coach Bowden called the team and coaches together and shared with them how they could be saved. He asked, "If that boy had been you, would you be in heaven or hell now?" Mark Richt said that was the day he received Jesus Christ as his Lord and Savior.

You probably are never going to have the chance to witness to a football team. You probably are never going to have the opportunity to move in certain circles that other people will move in. But as you go, wherever you are, do whatever you can to obey the Great Commission of our Lord to get involved in this "going" business of making disciples.

Not only is there going; there is also *winning*. Jesus says, "Go ye therefore, and teach all nations" (Matt. 28:19). And literally the word used here is "make disciples of all nations." What does it mean to "make a disciple?" To make a disciple means to win someone to faith in the Lord Jesus Christ. Then this person begins to follow Jesus Christ as his Lord and Master. That's what it means to make a disciple. Go and make disciples. That's the main business of the church. That's why we are here.

R. O. Stone was minister of music at Dauphin Way Baptist Church in Mobile, Alabama. He was a vibrant, outgoing Christian and a great soul winner. As Stone was being overcome by cancer, his mind was not always clear. Some mornings he would get up and get fully dressed—suit and tie and everything. And he would say to his wife, "It's time to go to church!" Of course, it wasn't time to go to church, but she went along with him.

They would get in the car as if they were going to church and would just ride around. After a while, he would drop off to sleep in the car. Then his wife would drive back to the house and pull up in the driveway. In a little while Stone would wake up and say, "Are we home?"

She would reply, "Oh, yes, we're home."

Then he would ask, "How many got saved in the services today?"

Even in his condition he understood that the main purpose of the church is to win people to faith in the Lord Jesus Christ.

Listen to what Jesus says! *Make disciples*. This is imperative. It is a command of the Lord Jesus. Make disciples. Win people to faith in Christ. That's our command—that's not a suggestion. That's a command! This is mandatory. It is not optional. This is the command of the Lord Jesus Christ—to make disciples. Have you obeyed the command?

Go *ye*—that's plural. A lot of people think it's just go *you*—singular. A lot of people think winning others to the Lord is just the pastor's job. And if he doesn't win many lost people to faith in Christ, they think it's time for him to change jobs. Ladies and gentlemen, in the church of the Lord Jesus Christ, this is a command for every member of the church. It's not just the pastor's job. It's not just the staff's job. Go *ye*—every one of us, a vast army of us—telling the good news of Jesus, getting people saved.

This is the job of every believer—going, winning. I'm here to tell you a church that does not win souls does not deserve the land on which the building stands. I'm here to tell you that a Bible class that does not win souls is not worth the electricity, the heat, the lights, the carpet, and the paint that goes into that room. Are you winning people to Christ in your Bible class? If not, get busy. It's time for you to do that. Put a chair in your class that's empty. Say to the members of your class, "This chair represents some person who needs to know Jesus Christ. Get him here next Sunday."

Notice there's a third part to this game plan. Jesus says going, making disciples, winning, and then he says *baptizing* them "in the name of the Father, and of the Son, and of the Holy Ghost" (Matt. 28:19). We haven't done New Testament evangelism until we have taken this third step.

When we are asked to support missionary endeavors in other parts of the world and missionaries tell us they had five thousand people saved, the next question we need to ask is, "How many of those have been baptized and are in the fellowship of the church?" We haven't completed the job until we obey this command: Baptizing them! It's not enough to get people to sign a card. It's not enough to get them to raise a hand. We've got to win them to Christ, and then we are to baptize them in the name of the Father, the Son, and the Holy Spirit.

Baptism doesn't save anybody, but baptism is an outward expression of an inward experience. Baptism is a way of giving open testimony that a person has indeed received Jesus Christ as his Savior, that Jesus is not only Savior but He's also Lord. It reveals that we intend to follow Him and live for Him.

Baptism is an act of illustration. It illustrates the death, burial, and resurrection of Jesus. That's why we immerse. It's also an illustration of what happened to us. It's a picture of our death to our sins, our old way of life, and our resurrection to a brand-new way of life. It's an illustration. Baptism is also an act of appreciation. By being baptized, we're saying to the Lord, "I appreciate what You did for me in saving me, and I'm not ashamed to do what You have commanded me to do." It is an act of appreciation. Baptism is also an act of identification. We are identifying ourselves with the local church. Have you been saved? If so, have you been baptized? It is an act of identification.

In the New Testament we discover that when people were saved, when they received Christ as their Savior, they were baptized. You didn't have to write them a letter. You didn't have to call them on the phone. You didn't have to persuade them. You didn't have to cajole them. You didn't have to try to trick them. The moment they received Jesus Christ, they were like the eunuch in the book of Acts. He said, "Here is water; what doth hinder me to be baptized?" (Acts 8:36).

When I was pastor at Bethesda Baptist Church, there was a little lady attending our revival services who had nine children. Her name was Mrs. Screws. I went to the little house where she lived. She had to do her washing outside because they didn't have running water. She had a big black kettle, and she was washing clothes for those nine children.

I asked her, "Have you accepted Christ?"

"Oh, yes, preacher, I've accepted Christ."

"Have you been baptized?"

"Preacher, I'm afraid to be baptized. I don't know if I can be baptized."

I said, "Mrs. Screws, I'll tell you what you do. This afternoon before the evening service, you ask Jesus what He wants you to do. Will you do whatever Jesus wants you to do?"

She said, "I will."

I got to the church a little early that night. And soon after I got there, Mrs. Screws and all her children arrived. She walked up to me with a big smile on her face. "Preacher, I did exactly what you told me to do this afternoon," she said. "I asked Jesus what He wanted me to do. And He told me to be baptized. I'm a-joinin' the church tonight."

Ladies and gentlemen—going, winning, baptizing! But there is another dimension to Jesus' Great Commssion: "Teaching them to observe all things whatsoever I have commanded you" (Matt. 28:20). We need to get people involved. We should teach new Christians to live the Christian life. The Christian life is not something that's just a matter of information; it's a matter of *application*. It's not just a matter of what you believe; it's how you behave!

After you accept Christ and have been baptized and are in the fellowship of the church, you should be more pleasant at home. You should be a better worker on the job. You should behave better at school. Your life should be better if you are a disciple, a follower of the Lord Jesus.

III. Jesus Set Forth His Promise

Here's the third dimension of the Great Commission. Jesus set forth *His promise*. He said, "Lo, I am with you alway, even unto the end of the world" (Matt. 28:20). What a promise!

If you obey Jesus' "go," you can claim His "lo." Now we know that Jesus is with us always. But here He is making a special promise that when we go, when we witness, when we seek to win people to faith in the Lord Jesus in a special way, He's with us—always, all the days of our lives.

This has been a difficult week for me. When I was pastor at Dauphin Way Baptist Church in Mobile, Alabama, we had a fine young doctor in our church. She was my oldest daughter's Sunday school teacher. She was a witnessing Christian who won many people to Christ. I saw her bring forward many people whom she had personally led to Christ. She eventually felt the call of God to go to the foreign mission field. She left our church and went to one of the most dangerous places on the planet. She has served there for twenty-five years.

Four years ago she was driving back up through the hill country to immunize boys and girls and to deliver babies. She had become so loved by the people, yet some people hated what she was doing. They kidnapped her and put her in the back of her car. They said to her, "You say anything, and we'll kill you!" The car stalled, and they abandoned her. Her life was spared.

Somebody asked her, "If you had been shot and had known you were going to be shot, would you have gone to this dangerous place?"

She said without hesitation, "Oh yes."

On Monday of this week, a Muslim extremist with ties to Al Qaeda broke into the hospital room where this doctor has been ministering to the people of Yemen. The man shot her in the head. She died instantly. President Bush said she was rendering humanitarian assistance. This is certainly true, but there is more to it than that. She was not only rendering humanitarian assistance in ways that would be respectful to the land in which she served; she was making disciples. She was winning people to faith in Jesus.

Her dad, a highly respected doctor in Alabama, said: "She's in heaven for sure. That's why Christians have nothing to fear." From that standpoint, we will see her again. It's a matter of who gets to heaven first.

Do you remember the old saying, "The blood of the martyrs is the seed of the church"? Already the reports are that the people of Yemen have had their hearts broken and they are especially tender. I believe the result of her death will be thousands and thousands of people in Yemen coming to know Jesus Christ as their personal Savior.

You may ask, "Preacher, why was she over there in such a dangerous place?"

I'll tell you why. It's because she took seriously these words: "Go and make disciples of all the nations, baptizing them and teaching them." She was willing to die to obey the Lord's command and to perform the main business of the church.

If this doctor was willing to die to carry out the church's main business, what are you willing to do?

41

Do You Hear That Plea?

LUKE 16:19–28 HCSB

Gene Mims

Vice President, LifeWay Christian Resources
of the Southern Baptist Convention

EVERY TIME I COME INTO A CHURCH, I'm reminded that nobody ever comes to church by accident; they always come on purpose. I'm also reminded that God never does anything by accident. He always does what He does on purpose. It's no accident that you are here today. By the providence of God and the plan and the will of God for your life and by your taking time and making yourself available on your schedule, you and the will of God have met.

I want us to look at a familiar passage of Scripture. I'll make some comments about that passage. Then I want to tell you about a man whom I led to Christ. That encounter changed my life forever. Then I'm going to tell you about a plea, a plea that I hear sometimes at night, and it wakes me up—a plea that motivates me and drives me like nothing else in my life. God has a kingdom agenda, and you're part of that right now. It's the will of God and the agenda of God that every person in the world know His love for them.

God wants people to know that He loves them. He doesn't hate them. He's not ready just to judge them. He created them, and He wants to redeem them in Christ and put them into an eternal love

497

relationship with Him. Sometimes, though, for us who know Christ, we need to hear the plea that would motivate us to be used of God to fulfill His kingdom agenda.

Let's spend this time together and enjoy what the Bible says. Enjoy His story together and enjoy this plea, and, I promise you, it will change your life.

The Bible is filled with incredible stories. Jesus was the master storyteller. He tells one story that I will read in a moment. It talks about a plea that I want you to hear, a plea that if you hear it well, it will change your life. I think about the various pleas and how powerful they are. Have you ever thought about the plea of a young child to a mother? That child can speak, and a mother will respond to satisfy the need of her child. I think about the plea from heaven. You remember in Isaiah where the Lord was pleading for someone to go. "Whom shall I send, and who will go for us?" Isaiah said, "Here am I Lord, send me" (Isa. 6:8).

Pleas are important. Pleas move our hearts. They affect our wills. They put us in motion. They get us to do the right thing. They satisfy needs. But there's a plea that I want you to hear from Scripture. This plea from Scripture can change your life. I know it has changed mine. It's the most powerful story I have ever read. Jesus is telling the story of the rich man and Lazarus. You know that story well. It's found in the sixteenth chapter of the Gospel of Luke. Now listen to all of it. You might think that you hear a plea—and you will initially—but that's not the plea I want you to hear. Follow with me now as I read.

"There was a rich man who would dress in purple and
fine linen, feasting lavishly every day. But at his gate was left
a poor man named Lazarus, covered with sores. He longed
to be filled with what fell from the rich man's table, but
instead the dogs would come and lick his sores. One day the
poor man died and was carried away by the angels to
Abraham's side. The rich man also died and was buried. And
being in torment in Hades, he looked up and saw Abraham
a long way off, with Lazarus at his side. 'Father Abraham!'

he called out, 'Have mercy on me and send Lazarus to dip
the tip of his finger in water and cool my tongue, because
I am in agony in this flame!'

"'Son,' Abraham said, 'remember that during your life
you received your good things, just as Lazarus received bad
things; but now he is comforted here, while you are in
agony. Besides all this, a great chasm has been fixed between
us and you, so that those who want to pass over from here
to you cannot; neither can those from there cross over to us.'

"'Father,' he said, 'then I beg you to send him to my
father's house—because I have five brothers—to warn them,
so they won't also come to this place of torment'"
(Luke 16:19–28).

When I read that story, I'm confronted with a number of things
that are important for us to remember. If we're going to make a
difference in our world and if we're going to be trained so we can
train others to fulfill God's kingdom agenda, we need to be aware of
the truth of what God says in His Word.

The Lord Jesus knew that one day we would be together like
this, and He would want us to remember and to know some important things. Let me tell you something that is true about our lives.
At this moment it's true about our lives together, and it's also true
about everybody whom you've seen today and everybody whom
you've ever known. The person whom you saw today when you
were coming here—maybe to the right at the traffic light when
you were stopped or standing in line at the supermarket—every
person that you know, including yourself, including me, has this to
face. There is a fatal moment coming for every one of us.

One of these days you're going to face your final moment. One
of these days I'm going to experience my final moment. I can't live
forever. I can be rich on earth, or I can be poor on earth. I can be as
rich as the rich man or as poor as Lazarus, but one day we're all
going to die. That moment has been appointed to every one of us.

The Bible says it's appointed for a man once to die and after that
the judgment (see Heb. 9:27). Think about that for a moment. It's

appointed for a man once to die. Every man, every woman, every little boy or girl you know, every young person has a date with destiny. You didn't choose the day of your birth, and you haven't chosen the day of your death, but it has been chosen for you. A fatal moment is coming for all of us.

When I read in Scripture about Lazarus and the rich man, I'm also reminded that most of life is futile. It's futile because everything in eternity seems to be reversed from things on earth. Think about this: This man who was rich is now in hell. He was not only rich, but he lived any way he wanted to live and had more than enough. I can imagine that he was a man of wealth and influence and power. I can imagine that he could speak to people, and they would do whatever he wanted them to do.

But in eternity everything was reversed. He was comfortable on earth but in agony in eternity. Lazarus had nothing on earth but everything in eternity. The rich man didn't lack for anything until he died, and then he didn't have anything. Lazarus didn't have anything until he died, and then he had everything.

So much of our lives is spent in futility, hanging on to things that are important here but have no bearing in eternity. Things that you can touch and feel, powerful things here on earth but things of weakness in eternity. Things of great magnitude here, but in eternity they're of no consequence.

Life has a fatal moment, and much of life is futile. But the thing I would really like for you to see before we get to that plea that I think could change your life forever is the fact that not only is life fatal and futile, but it's also final. When you die, nothing changes in eternity. Everything can change on earth. Here you can be poor and become rich. Or you can be rich and become poor. But in eternity nothing changes.

Those are chilling words that Abraham said to the rich man. Listen to them again: "'Son,' Abraham said, 'remember that during your life you received your good things, just as Lazarus received bad things; but now he is being comforted here, and you are in agony. Besides all this, a great chasm has been fixed between us and you, so that those who want to pass over from here to you cannot; neither can those from there cross over to us'" (vv. 25–26). There are no second chances in eternity. It's fixed. It's final. Nothing ever changes in eternity.

That leads me to this plea that the rich man makes. The rich man first asks for just one drop of water, but his eternity is fixed and water won't come. He asks for some sort of relief from the agony he's in, but relief is not going to come. He would like for anything to come and relieve him for just a second, but that flame burns forever, and nothing ever changes. The good news about this is for Lazarus, our friend. Nothing is going to change for him either. He had a tough life on earth, but he's comforted in heaven. He's comforted in the presence of Abraham. Everything is for his comfort forever. And that will never change.

I'm reminded that whatever we're going to do for the Lord on earth, we have to do because this is the only place it can change. Do you know something? Not even God Almighty can change what happens in eternity. If a person is separated from God today and dies, he's going to be separated for all of eternity. No second chances. No absolution. No purgatory to get out of. Everything is fixed. Whatever we're going to do for the Lord to establish His kingdom agenda for people is going to have to be established right now because one day it will never change.

But now listen to the rich man's plea. "'Father,' he said, 'then I beg you to send him to my father's—because I have five brothers— to warn them, so they won't also come to this place of torment'" (vv. 27–28). That's the plea that I can't get around. That's the plea that became something in my life that I never would have expected.

Now I want to tell you about Paul, a man whom I led to Christ. In leading him to Christ, I heard a plea that changed my life forever.

Not far from the spot where I am standing now, I had the privilege of serving as interim pastor of a church. At this church I met a man whose story became my story and really changed my life. His name was Paul. One Sunday morning after I had finished preaching, he came up to me and said, "The things that you say sometimes trouble me, and I'd like to talk to you about them."

I told him that we would talk, but we just never could find a time to do that. Time after time over a period of months, he would come up to me and say, "I sure would like to talk to you." I would respond, "Well how about now?" He would reply, "Well, I can't right now." Then he would walk away. We just never seemed to be able to get together.

At the end of my time at that church, when the people had called a permanent pastor, I knew I had to get with Paul. God gave us two events that brought us together. I was in the Nashville airport, and I just happened to see Paul. Unfortunately, he was flying to his mother's funeral. I prayed with him and asked the Lord to give me the opportunity to share Christ with Paul. God did that. The airline announced that our flight would be delayed for one hour.

We sat down together, and I said, "Paul, I want to ask you a question." Then I went through the entire FAITH outline, telling him how to be saved. Each point seemed to move Paul and grip him. When I came to the part where he could receive Christ, he said, "I'm not ready to do that. I'm upset over my mother's death, and I just need to take care of that above all else right now." What made that more interesting is that not only was Paul an unbeliever; he was also Jewish. So he was going through a lot of conflicting emotions.

I asked my wife at a later time to get with his wife and to arrange our schedules for a time together. On Good Friday before Easter, they came to our home. We began to talk about Paul's spiritual condition. He knew why he was there. In fact, he had even told some friends around the church that he was coming to our home and that we would probably be talking about salvation. I told him, "Paul, you can ask me any question you want to, and I'll answer as best I can. Then I want to ask you one question." We talked for maybe an hour or so. He asked me everything he could think of, and God gave grace. Everything Paul asked I either knew the answer to, or I gave him enough of an answer to satisfy him. What a wonderful man and a good friend he is, and what a great time we had.

When he was through with his questions, I said, "Paul, here's the question that I would like to ask you. Why do you think God is moving in your life? You have family members who aren't interested in these matters, but God is really moving in your life."

He replied, "I don't know." So I went through the FAITH outline again with him.

He told me, "I don't think I'm ready to do that. I don't know if I really understand it."

I said, "Paul, I think you really understand it. The night I became a Christian I was reading Romans 10:9–10. And I read that I had to believe in my heart that God raised Jesus Christ from the dead. Then I had to confess with my mouth that Jesus is Lord."

Paul told me, "I believe that in my heart, but I can't say it with my mouth."

I responded, "Sure you can."

"No, I can't."

"Sure you can."

"No, I can't."

We went back and forth like that for a moment. Then I said, "Paul, the only reason a person wouldn't say that Jesus is Lord is because he really doesn't believe it or maybe pride or something is holding him back."

He asked what that something might be.

I responded, "It could be Satan. Maybe the devil is holding you back, not wanting you to have what God is offering you."

Paul looked down in his lap for a moment. Then he looked back and me and said, "If you're telling me the truth, then my mother is probably in hell. And I don't know if I want to go to heaven if my mother is in hell."

I thought about that for a moment. I picked up this Bible that I just read from and opened it to the story of Lazarus and the rich man. I read it and looked at Paul and said, "I don't know where your mother is tonight. Only God really knows. But if she is in hell, I know what she's telling me to tell you. She's pleading with me to tell you something."

He asked, "What's that?"

"She's pleading with me to tell you not to come down there. I hear her saying to me, 'Gene, don't let my son come to this place.'"

Paul looked back down at his lap for a moment. He looked at me. Looked down. Looked at his wife. Looked down. Looked at my wife. Looked down. Then he looked at his wife and said these amazing words: "Jesus is Lord."

Do you hear that plea? I hear people right now in my mind's ear saying, "Gene, don't let my son come here. Don't let my daughter be in this place. Don't let those people whom I love come to this place of agony and torment." Do you hear that plea? Pastor, do you hear that plea? Do you hear the plea of those in your community whose loved ones have gone on? And those loved ones are calling out to you and your congregation, "Don't let my children come here. Don't let my grandchild come here. Don't let my wife come here." Do you hear it, pastor? Youth leader, do you hear it? Do you hear it from the friends of those who have gone on from your youth and who are in eternity tonight? "Don't let my friend come here."

I hear that plea everywhere I go, even when I'm standing in line with people in front of me. I can hear their relatives saying, "Don't let him come here." I hear it when I'm driving along and look to my left and there's a car driving along beside me. I think there may be a relative somewhere in eternity saying, "Could you do something to reach them?" To respond to a plea like that is to set yourself up to achieve the kingdom agenda. That plea troubles me and in a way delights me because it motivates me to reach out to people with the love of God and this plan that we call FAITH and to lead them to Christ so they will never go to hell.

I've wondered sometimes if there might be more soul winners in hell than in some of our churches. Wouldn't that be a sad thing? More people in eternity crying out for the salvation of their loved ones and their friends than people in our churches. You've chosen to make a difference. I really don't believe that there are any accidents in the kingdom of God. I believe it's the purpose of God and the will of God for you to be here and to answer that plea. Pastor, take responsibility to train your laypeople to answer the pleas of those in eternity and to lead men and women to Christ. Youth leader, you can lead young people to Christ. Laymen, learn to lead your family members to Christ. That's why in God's timing your life is about to change. I don't believe you'll go away from here not hearing what I hear.

Can you hear that plea? That plea changed my life. I'm praying that God will help you to hear that plea and to answer it with the ministry of this incredible thing we call FAITH. May God use all of us to answer that plea from eternity.

42

Making by Breaking

GENESIS 32:24–31 NASB

Hayes Wicker
Senior Pastor, First Baptist Church
Naples, Florida

OLD LEGENDS NEVER DIE; THEY JUST FADE AWAY. In 1973 I stayed in the home of Dave Hollinger, head coach of the UCLA wrestling team. As we drove into the faculty parking lot, a craggy old man checked our pass. Dave said, "That's Gorgeous George!" He was the most famous professional wrestler of the 1940s, now no longer a muscleman with Goldilocks hair but broken by life's body slams.

The outrageous pretension and depravity of professional wrestling has once again captured the culture. The original "wrestler" was not Gorgeous George but Jacob. God told Jacob that if he would "go home again," He would bring him prosperity.

This wrestler's arena is a rocky valley. The leaves of the twisted trees glisten like teardrops under the glow of the moon. Jacob feels the cold slap of the wind. His caravan has now passed the Jabbok ford safely, yet he is troubled and hopes to somehow touch the face of God, whom he has neglected for years. He has sent a messenger of reconciliation to his estranged brother, Esau. Years before Jacob had deceitfully taken his brother's birthright and his father's blessing, and now he fears that Esau is coming to meet him with an army, intent on revenge.

The match begins! A hand grabs him! Jacob wrestles in the shadows with an unknown person. On the screen of God's Word, we see a wrestling match that is deadly serious and one that all of us are engaged in at some time in our lives. It is intense. The Hebrew word for *wrestle* means "to roll in the dust."

Who seized Jacob? An assassin from Esau? The rabbis thought it was Jacob's guardian angel (not "touched" but mugged "by an angel"). But I believe this was a theophany, the preincarnate form of Jesus. After all, Jacob later called Him "God." Hosea called Him both an "angel" and "the LORD" (Hos. 12:4–5).

You have heard the phrase "make or break." God is making by breaking. Just as Jacob desired, God wants to bless us. I was moved to faith in Christ as a teenager when a man at my church said at a New Year's Eve party: "God bless you, Hayes." I saw the reality of sin contrasted with the possibility of blessing. We often flippantly say, "God bless America," but blessing only happens when we are broken.

The Hebrew word for blessing (*barak*) here is used only of God's work for and with us as He pours out His life and shares His goodness. In the Old Testament the intensive form of the verb is usually used; God gives a big-time, industrial-strength blessing. As Billy Graham used to say, "God bless you real good." God's wrestling and breaking are designed to help, not hurt. When a broken bone heals properly, we are stronger in the broken place. But how does God use brokenness to bring blessing?

I. Brokenness Allows Failure So That Success Might Be Found

Jacob, the wrestler, had been a phony for years. Life was a stage, and he was the strutting star, always coming out on top, able to outwit Esau, Isaac, and Laban.

David said, "I am like a broken vessel" (Ps. 31:12). He used a Hebrew word (*shabar*) that means "to burst." The time will come when you will feel as if you have exploded, but it is then that God is picking up the pieces and finally putting them together His way. As Roy Hession, the English preacher, often said: "Revival is not so much the top blowing off as the bottom falling out."

It's hard to learn this when you are young. I pastored my first church in college during the hippie movement of the early 1970s. We were a cool church. There was a dove painted with a black light over my head in the baptistry. When the lights were turned out, the dove and the robes glowed. Groovy, man!

Of course, ministry is not about entertaining but winning and discipling. The cross doesn't need glitz. Water baptism pictures death, burial, and resurrection. God will allow your dreams to go through death and burial before resurrection, but then you can glow in the dark!

After one and a half years in that pastorate, I became enticed by some of the things of the world and considered changing my major and leaving the ministry—even though I was having outward success. In that "dark night of the soul," I wrestled with the authority and inerrancy of God's Word as well as the inadequacy of my own personal life. I knelt on the college baseball field one night and prayed, "Lord, even if I never achieve any of the world's success, I will follow Your call; I will believe Your Word; I will do Your will." The burden was lifted. Brokenness brought blessing.

Alexander Solzhenitsyn understood this principle, surviving Stalin's Gulag to become a Christian prophet to the Western culture: "Bless you, prison, for having been in my life." But God has another maneuver.

II. Brokenness Crucifies Self So the Spirit Might Win

The name *Jacob* means "heel catcher." His name pictures his self-centeredness and lust for more: "I will grab for whatever I want. I can do it myself."

God's desire for us is the testimony of Paul, "I have been crucified with Christ" (Gal. 2:20), and of David, "I am like a broken vessel" (Ps. 31:12). This Hebrew word means "to lose one's self." You say, "I'm a self-made man." Well, self-made man, create life with no raw materials, the air you breathe, the water you drink, the blood in your body.

God is trying to get the "Jacob" out of us. It is self that can destroy your marriage. It is self that can make you rely on your abilities and education. It is self-conceit, self-sufficiency, self-will that splits churches. Self proclaims, "I'm the devil's advocate," instead of saying, "I'm the Lord's servant." It is self that feels rejected and neglected. Humility is not despising yourself; it is distrusting yourself.

Just as water seeks to fill the lowest places, so God is looking for a truly broken person to be His riverbed so that out of your inner being will flow "rivers of living water" (John 7:38). Jesus wants to fill, to flood, and to flow through you! We, like Jacob, want to *get* a blessing, but God wants to *make* us a blessing so we sing, "Make me a blessing; out of my life may Jesus shine." He is making by breaking.

I hope that you announce with Paul, "I joyfully concur with the law of God in the inner man" (Rom. 7:22). If you are a Christian, the Holy Spirit is in you in the inner person: "Our inner man is being renewed day by day" (2 Cor. 4:16).

A distinctive, mysterious something bubbles up to the surface and gives impressions to others, usually of our dominant features. I was convicted in the early 1980s by a friend who said, "Whenever I am around you, I sense ambition." She was out of line but not off base in that blunt comment. Then and now I want to be like the Shunammite said of Elisha: "This is a holy man of God passing by us continually" (2 Kings 4:9). He didn't conduct a chapel, teach a Bible class, or work a miracle, yet holiness came forth.

We know the apostle John as "the disciple whom Jesus loved." When He called the Twelve, Jesus nicknamed John a "son of thunder," literally, "the soon-angry one." John and his brother James wanted to call down fire on the prejudiced Samaritans: "Nuke those suckers!" The thunder rolled! The lightning flashed! But Jesus rebuked them and said, "You do not know what kind of spirit you are of" (Luke 9:55). Ultimately, the pushy personality and hair-trigger anger was not just changed but exchanged—Christ loving through John.

What spirit comes from you? Does ambition flow? Does anger flash? Or do people say, "This is a holy man . . . this is a holy woman of God passing by"? But God uses another wrestling move.

III. Brokenness Brings Desperation So That Faith Might Be Supreme

Jacob wrestled until God dislocated his thigh. God wanted His will to win, and He wanted Jacob purged of self-sufficiency. He wants to pin our wills to the mat of submission so we don't cry "uncle!" but "Lord!"

My dad once met the famous actor, John Wayne, in a store in New Mexico.

"John, how are you doing?"

"I'm not doin' very well; I guess I got the flu."

"A big guy like you ought to be able to whip it."

"I'm doin' the best I can."

John Wayne had cancer and didn't know it. Hopefully, the Duke turned to the King, with "true grit" becoming true faith.

The way to win is to surrender. The way up is down. The way to gain your life is to lose it. The way to get is to give. The way to live is to die. In brokenness you distrust your best and embrace Christ's best.

But God has to touch us at the source of our strength so that we no longer fight but cling. No wonder we read, "Cease striving and know that I am God" (Ps. 46:10). It's not our striving and struggling, but our clinging, tenacious faith that says, "I will not let you go unless you bless me" (Gen. 32:26). Then and only then could the God-Man promise, "You have prevailed."

Every difficulty is a call *from* God, and every call from God is a call *to* God—to trust Him, to seek His face, to desire His person even more than His blessing.

When twenty-eight-year-old Billy Graham was preaching in England in the early years of his ministry, he didn't see much fruit. When the young English expositor, Stephen Olford, met the young evangelist, Graham was wearing a pink suit and preached a twenty-minute sermon full of jokes. An unknown Welshman stood in a worship service and rebuked Graham. He began to be broken. Then Dr. Olford shared privately with him about the power of the Holy Spirit. At the end of three days, in desperation, Graham (even with tear ducts not working) prayed those words of Jacob: "I will not let thee go, except thou bless me"(Gen. 32:26 KJV). He poured out his heart in full surrender to the Lord and was filled with the Spirit. He began pacing back and forth saying, "I am filled. This is the turning point of my life!"

In other words, "Blessed are those who hunger and thirst for righteousness, for they shall be satisfied" (Matt. 5:6). Indeed, blessed are those who wrestle, for they shall win. But God is not finished with us until we understand that brokenness leads to change.

IV. Brokenness Confesses Need So That Change Might Be Real

The Lord asked Jacob, "What is your name?" (Gen. 32:27). To the Jews a person's name represented character. Jacob admitted his name, which meant "deceitful," "the one who trips up." As Jeremiah said, "The heart is . . . deceitful" (Jer. 17:9), literally, "a Jacob." In essence, Jacob confessed: "Lord, this is who I am. I have played the game and faked it. I am full of self."

Jacob left the riverbank, not strutting but limping and made new, as indicated by his new name, *Israel,* meaning, "God rules." Is Jesus Lord, and is there an evident limp in your life?

When interviewing prospective ministers for our church, I look for something that is not in the résumé. I look for a time of failure and brokenness in a person's life that has led him or her to the point of "leaning on . . . his staff" (Heb. 11:21), a time when that person has "met God face to face" (Gen. 32:30), when the Champion's hand has been raised in victory in the ring of that person's life. What's next after you have been broken?

V. Brokenness Results in Service So That God Might Be Glorified

In Genesis 32:20, we see the culmination of Jacob's conniving to try to appease Esau. He sends messengers ahead to make a flattering, fawning message by calling himself "your servant Jacob." He gives gifts to find favor. But he is on to something, though he is ignorant of the need and nature of service.

We make a choice to either exist or really live, and even the world loves those who serve. Jesus said that if we "keep our lives," we "lose them" for eternal life (see John 12:25). He used a word that actually speaks in the present tense: "You are actually gaining right now, not just later in heaven." Also, you who love your life are destroying it right now. In service we gain by giving. We particularly become like our Master.

Suppose you are the head of a personnel department and our Savior visits you for a job interview:

"What's your name?"

"Jesus."

"I detect an accent. I don't think you're from around these parts. Where did you use to live?"

"Heaven."

"Mr. Jesus, do you have any references?"

"The heavenly Father and the Holy Spirit."

"Sir, do you go by any other names?"

"Jesus Christ, Son of God, Prince of peace, Emmanuel. You can call me 'Lord.'"

"What was your previous job?"

"CEO of the universe."

'What position do you desire?"

"Servant."

Would He fit your personnel agency's profile? Jesus came to get down and dirty with the poor and needy and to die for the sins of His creation. He took the "form of a bondservant" (Phil. 2:7).

Jacob understood service only after his time of brokenness. When he did meet Esau (see Gen. 33), his service was acceptable. In verse 11, he said, "Please take my gift . . . because God has dealt graciously with me." Only then could he truly be Esau's servant, because he was the Lord's servant. Only when he met "God face to face" (Gen. 32:30) could he help his brother.

Service is not to gain leverage but to give a blessing. Without brokenness your spiritual gifts, personality profiles, and natural talents present Jacob and not Israel. Service to God and man is only because of God's gracious dealings with us and workings through us.

One of God's special servants, aged author and missionary Wesley Duewel, visited our church and told our staff about the Welsh Revival of 1904. In the 1970s Dr. Duewel went to the little town in Wales and met the last living people—brothers, ages eighty-six and eighty-four—who were there with Evan Roberts when it all began. They related the thirteen-year prayer of Evan, "Lord, bend me." It was his way of saying, "Make me by breaking."

They shared with Duewel how twenty-six-year-old Evan went the pastor of his home church and said: "God has given me a vision to see a hundred thousand people saved. Would you let me preach to the young people?"

The pastor reluctantly agreed. After the pastor's benediction and departure, seventeen teenagers stayed behind. Roberts put them on a row of pews. He then locked the door, turned to the first young man, and said: "Stand up. Now pray this prayer: 'Lord Jesus, forgive me of my sins and fill me with Your Spirit.' Now sit down." He went to one after the other, having each teenager say the exact same words three times. That technique isn't taught in seminaries and distributed in bookstores! Finally, in the front, one person began to weep and truly repented of his sins. As the old Welshman told Wesley Duewel, "That's when the fire fell. That's where I was when the fire fell!"

Evan Roberts was asked years later, "What sustained you those thirteen years?" He replied, "You will never quit seeking after that which consumes you." Will you say, "God, I will not let you go unless you bless me. Make me to be like you, even if it you have to break me?"

43

Our Addition to God's Provision

2 PETER 1:5–9 NKJV

Johnny Hunt
Senior Pastor, First Baptist Church
Woodstock, Georgia

I WANT YOU TO PAY careful attention to this title, because I'm living where I'm preaching. I've nearly finished with Henry Blackaby's book about Abraham, *Created to Be God's Friend.* As I was reading this morning, the author talked about how the ultimate test for Abraham came after God had been working in his life. God finally told him to offer his son Isaac as a sacrifice on Mount Moriah. Mount Moriah is where Mount Calvary is, and where God told Abraham to go and take his son, his only son, and offer him up as a sacrifice.

God used the experience to work in Abraham's life. And there are times in our lives when God takes us to a new level. God does something significant when He says, "I want you to add to this." So listen carefully to the reading of the Word of God.

"For this very reason . . . add to your faith virtue" (2 Pet. 1:5). God gave you faith. You placed your faith in grace. But now He says add to your faith. He says to add virtue. And then to your virtue, add "knowledge, to knowledge self-control, to self-control perseverance, to perseverance godliness, to godliness brotherly kindness, and to brotherly kindness love. For if these things are yours and abound, you will be neither barren nor unfruitful in the knowledge of our Lord Jesus Christ" (2 Pet. 1:5–8). It means, "If this happens in your life and you begin to grow, you will have additions to what God has given in His provision; you will not be useless."

It is frightening that we have the potential to be useless as it pertains to the kingdom of God. Peter continues, "For he who lacks these things is shortsighted, even to blindness, and has forgotten that he was cleansed from his old sins" (2 Pet. 1:9).

I want to ask you a question: What good would I be to the kingdom of God if I did not even know I had been purged from my sins? As we talk about God's provision for Christian growth and now our addition to God's provision, we have seen that cooperation with God is required and the application of spiritual diligence and spiritual discipline is needed.

Two hundred and thirty-six pastors in a twelve-month period failed morally, and we have a record of these failures in books like Steve Farrar's *On Finishing Strong*. You may ask, What happened to those men? They got to the place where they were no longer cooperating with God, and there was no longer the application of spiritual diligence and discipline. The foundation of our personal relationship with Jesus Christ is based on faith. And this speaks of our initial acceptance of God's grace, as offered in the gospel.

Peter speaks of building on faith. Where there is life, there must be growth. The new birth is not the end; it is the beginning. In God's grace God blesses our homes with children. All that they need—this is incredible and encouraging—is to live godly lives. But His children must apply themselves and be diligent to use the means of grace He has provided. So spiritual growth is not automatic.

Peter listed seven characteristics of the godly life in the verses I read. But we must not think of them as seven beads on a string, or even seven stages of development. The word translated "add" literally means "to supply generously." In other words, we develop one quality as we exercise another. So these graces that Peter refers to relate to one another the way the branch relates to the trunk of a tree, and the twigs to the branches, like the fruit of the spirit in

Galatians 5:22. These qualities grow out of a vital relationship with Jesus Christ. So it's not enough for the Christian to let go and let God, as though spiritual growth were God's work alone.

Literally, here's what Peter is saying in these verses: "Make every effort to bring alongside your faith these characteristics." So the father and the child work together. God, the heavenly Father, and God's child are cooperating in working together. And God is adding to their spiritual progress.

This is the same principle we find in Philippians 2:12: "Therefore, my beloved, as you have always obeyed, not as in my presence only, but now much more in my absence, work out your own salvation with fear and trembling." It means to work continually to bring something to fulfillment or completion. When I got saved, God placed His divine nature in me. And for the last thirty years, I've been working out in cooperation with God what His work did to me. And it is God who is producing it. I'm not the one producing it. God is producing it. But I'm cooperating with Him, and He's working it out.

Now this does not refer to salvation by works, but it does refer to the believer's responsibility for active pursuit of obedience in the process of being set aside for the purpose of your life—glorifying God. The big word we use is the word *sanctification*. When I came to Jesus Christ in faith, God worked the work of salvation in me. Ever since then God has been working in and through and out of me. It's a process of being set apart, particularly, specifically, uniquely, and conspicuously for Jesus Christ. That is sanctification.

Philippians 2:13 makes this statement to give greater clarity. "For it is God who works in you both to will and to do for His good pleasure." I want you to listen carefully because I'm taking a little extra time to introduce this sermon. Although the believer is responsible for working, it is the Lord who actually produces the good works and the spiritual fruit in the lives of the believer. This is accomplished because He works through us with His indwelling Spirit. The Bible says that He works to do His will and His good pleasure.

Listen to this. God energizes both the believer's desires and his actions. I begin to say to God, "I've come to know You. I'm changed now. I've got a new desire in my heart." God energizes the believer's desires and his actions. And God's power makes His church willing to live godly lives.

I preached for a men's conference recently. One of my best friends has been away from the Lord. You know, people do get away from the Lord. My friend was away from God. I mean distant. But I knew that in the past he had walked with God and was a godly influence in my life. He got right with God the other night. About seven or eight men got saved, and about thirty men got right with God. He stood to his feet and told me, "I want you to come by my business tomorrow."

On my way home I dropped by his place, and he took me out to an old shed. And he said, "I want you to know just moments before you got here that God radically changed my life. And there's a want-to and a desire in my heart once again to serve Him. I went back there in the back room and poured out all the liquor I had bought, and I want to live my life for God." Listen, God energizes a man! But it happens when that man cooperates with God. You can be saved and live like a hellion, unless you desire to grow and be what God wants you to be. Either you believe that, or you believe that everybody who is not living right has never been saved. I believe there's a great host of people who haven't been saved. But I also believe there are many who have been saved but have not grown.

When I walked the aisle on January 7, 1973, to receive Jesus Christ, right behind me was my dear wife. My wife had been saved as a thirteen-year-old teenager through the godly influence of her grandmother. But my wife had experienced no growth in her life. She had come to Christ, received him, knew things had changed, but she did not grow. I've heard that story a thousand times.

The Bible says that God wants to work in believers "to will and to do for His good pleasure" (Phil. 2:13). God wants Christians to do what satisfies Him. We're living in a day when we're trying to build our churches so we can do what satisfies the people who hear us. Instead, the people who hear us should be attempting to satisfy the God whom we glorify and magnify.

There is an inner dynamic, an inner principle, an inner power, as the divine nature impels us to a holy life. The Holy Spirit gives us both the desire and the power to do God's will. I never desired to do God's will or had the power to do God's will until I came to Jesus Christ, and God placed in me a new dynamic and a divine nature.

We must be sure that the various Christian virtues are included in our lives. The divine nature is not an automatic, self-propelling machine that will turn out a Christian life for us, no matter what we do or the attitude we take toward the salvation that God has provided. The divine nature always produces a change in the life of the sinner who receives the Lord Jesus Christ. But greater change comes during the living out of the new life that God has placed in you as you submit to growth.

Salvation works at its best when the believer cooperates with it, not only determining to live a life pleasing to God, but stepping out in faith and depending on God who has implanted new life within.

Faith does not exempt a person from works. There is a "grace" theology out there that basically says that the goal of grace is to get a person saved—and that's it. You never talk about works. Martin Luther struggled with this concept. He was not sure the book of James was inspired or should be a part of the New Testament. The problem was that Luther could not reconcile faith and works. Listen carefully. I am not preaching a faith-and-works salvation. I am preaching a faith that works.

When Christ came into my life, there was a new dynamic, a new desire, a new dimension, a new principle, a new power that wanted to serve the Son of God. And as I began to serve Him, to study His Word, and to apply His principles to assimilate Him into my life and to appropriate Him into my daily walk, God began to grow me. Faith does not exempt a person from works.

Salvation is also a work of grace. That divine nature implanted within my heart, inputing to me God's righteousness, is a work of grace and grace alone. And sanctification, just as much as salvation, is a work of grace. Sanctification is a will to grow. Sanctification is the process that Jesus Christ began in my life the day salvation became a reality. God began to grow me. And so as He's growing me, I am being sanctified, which literally could be translated "being made holy." You are being made more and more like Jesus every day you live.

Let's talk about the characteristics of a growing life. It begins with the challenge to complete obedience. Because of all the God-given blessings that Peter mentions in 2 Peter 1:3–4, the believer cannot be indifferent or self-satisfied. Such an abundance of divine grace calls for total obedience.

God has given this marvelous grace, this abundant grace, and it calls for total devotion. So because of the new birth and God's promises, we have a part to play in living out that salvation. The gifts spoken of in 2 Peter 1:4 are to have their logical outcome in my personal character. The phrase "giving all diligence" (2 Pet. 1:5) may best be translated as "making maximum effort." In other words, the Christian life is not lived to the honor of God without effort. Even though God has poured His divine power into the believer, the Christian is required to make every disciplined effort to add to what God has done.

Paul puts it like this: "Him we preach, warning every man and teaching every man in all wisdom, that we may present every man perfect [or mature] in Christ Jesus" (Col. 1:28). That's the same duty Pastor Johnny Hunt has. I pray that one day when you stand before Jesus Christ, it will be known that you got saved down here and that we preachers challenged you in such a way that you were presented mature at the coming of Jesus Christ.

And then Paul goes a step further. He says, "To this end I also labor, striving according to His working which works in me mightily" (Col. 1:29). He says he is laboring, working with every fiber of his being, to present all believers mature in the Lord Jesus Christ. He says, "I want you to be perfect, I want you to be complete, I want you to be mature. I want you to be like Jesus. I don't want anything to be lacking."

Paul gave the effort to serve and honor God with all his might. When he uses the word *labor,* it refers to working to the point of exhaustion. "Striving" gives us the word *agonize,* and it refers to the effort required to compete in athletic events. At the same time Paul knew that effective striving or working led to eternal results being done by God through him. I can't change a life, but I know someone who can. I preach a gospel that has the power and the dynamite to change the lives of those who will receive it and appropriate it in their daily lives.

Listen to Paul again. He says, "By the grace of God I am what I am, and His grace toward me was not in vain; but I labored more abundantly than they all, yet not I, but the grace of God which was with me" (1 Cor. 15:10). Paul is saying that God placed grace in him, and he appropriated that grace, and he worked as hard as he knew how to be everything God wanted him to be. It was God who produced it, but he was cooperating with God.

In verse 5 of 2 Peter 1, Peter makes this statement: "Add to your faith." The word *add* means to "give lavishly and generously." It means to outfit with additional supplies, to provide more than is needed, to provide beyond basic needs. What does it mean to provide more than you need?

In Greek culture the word *add* was "supply." In the Greek New Testament, this is the word for "choirmaster," the person who was responsible for supplying everything that was needed for his choir. The word never meant to equip sparingly. God has given us faith and all the grace necessary for godliness (2 Pet. 1:3–4). We add to those by our diligent devotion to personal righteousness.

Now, with that in mind, let me show you how God is working in my own life. It begins with the calling to be committed to this type of ministry. That is the challenge. But according to the apostle Peter, it continues with seven characteristics that should mark the lives of believers. He says, "I want you to just let God work in you. Cooperate with Him if He's working in you, and these seven characteristics will be lavishly supplied." They will become a reality in your own personal walk with the Lord.

I. Virtue

First, God adds virtue. You know what virtue is? It is moral power. America needs a dose of this. If it's true that 25 percent of the men in our evangelical churches are hooked on Internet pornography, I'll tell you why: They are not cooperating with God. God adds moral power. It translates as "moral energy." It is vigor of the soul. It is a power that performs deeds of excellence. The God-given ability to perform heroic deeds is the quality of life that makes someone stand out as excellent. Remember, it is energy that Christians are able to exhibit as God places His energy in them.

I'm ashamed to say this, but I started abusing alcohol when I was in the eighth grade. When I quit school in the eleventh grade, I probably had about an eighth-grade education. Four years later I got saved. God gave me purpose and direction in life and called me to be a gospel preacher. Thank God for the gospel!

Then I went off to college. I received a government grant for one semester just to see if I could make the grade. Do you know how I made it in college? Most of the students weren't really committed, so I excelled! I was at the top of the class! Sometimes the reason somebody has energy to live on a level of excellence is not because they've got something you don't have. It is because they've applied themselves and God has rewarded their dedication. They have given themselves to the God who moved within them.

When anything in nature fulfills its purpose, that is virtue, moral excellence. One great commentator said, "The land that produces crops, that is virtuous. That's excellence, because it's fulfilling its purpose." Ladies and gentlemen, where have we come from? Where are we going? What are we here for? What is virtue in my life? Is it making a living? Is it making a name for myself? Or is it actually fulfilling the purpose for which God created me and placed me here? That's it! Virtue reflects right conduct under discipline. In a virtuous person, good habits are established and fleshy desires are dissipated.

II. Knowledge

Peter's second word is *knowledge*. This is truth properly understood and applied. Knowledge involves diligent study and pursuit of truth in the Word of God. It refers to the ability to handle life successfully. It comes from obedience to the will of God. Jesus said it well: "If anyone wills to do His will, he shall know concerning the doctrine, whether it is from God or whether I speak on My own authority" (John 7:17). It's the ability to apply to particular situations the ultimate knowledge that wisdom gives.

III. Self-Control

Peter's third word is *self-control*. A good translation is "holding oneself in." You know what we're doing in America? We're saying, "Oh, just let yourself go. Enjoy it!" But the Word of God says to hold it in. Someone says, "I am just weaker than you in this area." You're not weaker in an area than I am. You just have not held yourself in. You decided to let yourself go. Believers are to control the flesh, the passions, and the bodily desires.

Self-control refers to the ability to take a grip of yourself. Get a grip! And then when you get the grip, you realize that God will give you the energy to sustain that grip.

Proverbs 16:32 says, "He who is slow to anger is better than the mighty, and he who rules his spirit than he who takes a city." Proverbs 25:28 says, "Whoever has no rule over his own spirit is like a city broken down, without walls." And if there are no walls, there is no protection, and you will be raped and consumed as an individual. But God says, "If you cooperate with Me, I will build your life. I will add to your faith. You will have self-control. You will be a person who masters his desires and passions, especially his sensual appetites." The Greeks used this word as "one who has his sex passions under control." So listen: virtue, guided by knowledge, disciplines desires and makes it desire servitude and not a mastering of one's life.

IV. Perseverance

Peter's fourth word is *perseverance*. God is teaching me something here. What does it mean to persevere? It's patience or endurance in doing what is right, never giving in to temptation or trial. It is the spiritual staying power that will die before it gives in. Have you ever prayed, "Oh, God, before I give in to sensual appetites—oh, God, that I might die!" And do you mean it to the point that you have such fear of God in your life that you would actually calculate in your mind that you would probably go to a premature grave if you did this thing? Pretty strong, isn't it? It's the virtue that can endure. Listen to this. You endure not simply with resignation but with vibrant hope. Not just resigning yourself and saying, "I can't do anything about it! I'm just going to persevere!" You can do something about it! You believe God's in it, and so you endure with vibrant hope that God will come through.

The apostle Peter reminds us to remain under trials and testings in a way that honors God. Perseverance is the heroic, brave patience with which a Christian not only bears but contends. Here's a great verse to help you understand perseverance: "Looking unto Jesus, the author and finisher of our faith, who for the joy that was set before Him endured the cross, despising the shame" (Heb. 12:2). Joy? Yes, joy! Jesus had vibrant hope, brave patience. He despised the shame. Have you ever been in something you despised but you stayed in it anyway? You didn't have to. You could have checked out. You could have gone south, but you stayed in it with a brave patience. And you endured it; you endured it until your vibrant hope gave you joy!

We don't find that word *despise* much in the Bible, especially in the context of Jesus Christ. Have you ever thought about what Jesus despised? What He endured on the cross, He despised. It was despicable! And yet, thank God, with perseverance He stayed there. Jesus persevered so that He might receive the joy of accomplishment of His Father's will.

Jesus was accomplishing the will of God! Vibrant hope! He could have come down from the cross. In Matthew 26:53, He even told His enemies that He could call angels to destroy this world and set Himself free. I believe that when He was on the cross, He looked out there in time knowing who would get saved—that's foreknowledge. And God in His foreknowledge saw us out there and realized that on the cross He was purchasing our salvation. He could even look back at the cross and think, *Abraham got saved by faith, but I'm paying the price for that faith. And so I'm going to stay right here in vibrant hope.*

V. Godliness

Peter's fifth word is *godliness*. But wait a minute! If my Bible says you add godliness to your faith, it doesn't mean that when you get saved you're automatically godly. Peter says to add to your faith "godliness" (2 Pet. 1:6). It could be translated "godlikeness." We're to be like the God whom we serve as He works in our hearts.

The word for *godliness* actually means "to worship well." You know who can really come to church and worship well? Those who are godly. It describes the person who has a right relationship with God. But it goes further than that. It's good to come to church, but you can't worship well unless you are right with God and right with one another. There will be no power over my life if I am not right with God and right with you.

You can come to church and say, "I love Jesus, but I just can't stand half of this congregation." Friend, you aren't worshipping! You might be in a worship service, but you aren't getting into His presence. It is the quality of character that makes a person distinctive. Oh, God, give us distinctively Christian people!

Such a person lives above the petty things of life, the passions and pressures that control the lives of others. He seeks to do the will of God, and as he does he seeks the welfare of others. He not only wants to do it for God's glory but also to do it for the good of humanity. Godliness is a practical awareness of God in every aspect of life. Thinking about buying a home? Did you talk to God? Going to trade cars? Did you talk to God? Thinking about taking a new job? Did you talk to God? Every aspect of your life is touched by God.

VI. Brotherly Kindness and Love

Here are two other characteristics mentioned by Peter: *brotherly kindness* and *love*. Do you know what brotherly kindness is? It's a choice to love people who are unlovely. It gives us our word Philadelphia—"brotherly love." Not only does God want us to add the kind of love that loves people by choice, but He's also talking about *agape* love, the kind of love that God showed toward us.

I tried to write a summation statement when I prepared this sermon this week. We have the divine nature because we got that when we got saved. That's how I know I'm saved. God put something inside me. It's a new principle, a new power, a new desire. I want to serve God.

Because we have the divine nature, we can grow spiritually and develop this kind of Christian character. This growth takes place through the power of God and the precious promises of God. So the divine genetic structure is already there. God wants us to be conformed to the image of His Son (Rom. 8:29). The life within us will produce that image if we will cooperate with God and use the means He has given us.

44

God's Plan Is Abundant Victory

ROMANS 8:37–39; 2 KINGS 13:14–19 KJV

Adrian Rogers
Senior Pastor, Bellevue Baptist Church
Memphis, Tennessee

WE ARE IN A WAR. And from every vantage point, it would seem that Satan is winning. A flicker of fiery revival rises up, and soon only smoke remains. A church springs up and then dies on the vine. By and large Christians are becoming discouraged and battle-fatigued in the fight. Some have been beaten so badly by the devil that they are like the cat that had its tail stepped on so many times he expected it. When someone came into the room, he would stick his tail out and wait. That is the way we seem to be—just wondering what Satan is going to do next.

But I want to tell you that God's plan for me, for you, and for His church is *abundant victory*. In the Lord Jesus Christ, we are more than conquerors. We must stand on the promises of God's Word that proclaims: "Nay, in all these things we are more than conquerors through him that loved us. For I am persuaded, that neither death, nor life, nor angels, nor principalities, nor powers, nor things present, nor things to come, nor height, nor depth, nor any other creature, shall be able to separate us from the love of God, which is in Christ Jesus our Lord" (Rom. 8:37–39).

And we are to say, "Thanks be unto God, which always causeth us to triumph in Christ, and maketh manifest the savour of his knowledge by us in every place" (2 Cor. 2:14). It is time for every child of God not simply to believe in what God has said and what God has done, but we must move forward and believe that victory is what God *is saying* and what God *wants to do*. Let's look at an illustration of this present victory God promises in the life of Elisha in 2 Kings 13:14–19:

> Now Elisha was fallen sick of his sickness whereof he died. And Joash the king of Israel came down unto him, and wept over his face, and said, O my father, my father, the chariot of Israel, and the horsemen thereof. And Elisha said unto him, Take bow and arrows. And he took unto him bow and arrows. And he said to the king of Israel, Put thine hand upon the bow. And he put his hand upon it: and Elisha put his hands upon the king's hands. And he said, Open the window eastward. And he opened it. Then Elisha said, Shoot. And he shot. And he said, The arrow of the LORD's deliverance, and the arrow of deliverance from Syria: for thou shalt smite the Syrians in Aphek, till thou have consumed them. And he said, Take the arrows. And he took them. And he said unto the king of Israel, Smite upon the ground. And he smote thrice, and stayed. And the man of God was wroth with him, and said, Thou shouldest have smitten five or six times; then hadst thou smitten Syria till thou hadst consumed it: whereas now thou shalt smite Syria but thrice.

At the time of this story, Elisha is about eighty years of age. He has ministered as a prophet of God through the reign of four kings. And now he is old and sick in a little cottage in the capital city of Samaria. It is a serious situation—so serious that 2 Kings tells us his sickness is going to take his life.

And not only is his sickness serious, but his finances are not in the best of shape either. More than likely Elisha has not made enough money during his lifetime to have a retirement fund to use in his final days. He is like the preacher who went to the bank to cash his annuity check. The teller said, "I hate to pay you with these dirty bills, but they are all I have."

He replied, "Don't worry about it. No germs could live on my salary."

Now, back to the story. There is a knock on the door. A young king named Joash enters the cottage of Elisha, the prophet of God. Joash explains to Elisha that he is frightened because his army—the army of Israel—has been reduced to almost nothing. Furthermore, the king of Syria has mobilized a mighty army toward the north and the east, and all they are waiting for is for this young, inexperienced king to come to the throne.

Joash looks at this frail, sick, old man and falls across his bed weeping and saying: "O my father, my father, the chariot of Israel, and the horsemen thereof" (2 Kings 13:14). The man whom Joash had trusted now looks like he is about to die, and Joash feels great despair. He knows he is powerless against the imposing Syrian army.

Have you ever wept because you felt powerless over a seemingly impossible situation? Well, if you haven't, you should! There is nothing wrong with weeping when situations become overwhelming. You see, we are up against the organized, mobilized, demonized forces of hell! But there is good news for those who weep in despair.

I. The Mandate for Victory

Elisha said, "Open the window eastward. And he [Joash] opened it. Then Elisha said, Shoot. And he shot. And he said, The arrow of the Lord's deliverance, and the arrow of deliverance from Syria: for thou shalt smite the Syrians in Aphek, till thou have consumed them" (2 Kings 13:17). Elisha said, "Do this and you shall have victory."

My preacher brother, when you were born again, you were born to fight in a battle. And not only fight. When you were born again, you were born to win! That is more than rhetoric. That is truth! Did you read what Elisha called the arrow that Joash shot? "The arrow of the Lord's deliverance" (13:17). God wants to give us ultimate victory. In this day and age we are not to survive; we are to thrive. And it is high time that we stopped singing "Hold the Fort," and began singing "Onward Christian Soldiers!" God is calling you to victory.

Let me share with you the burden of my heart. I see the upcoming generation of preachers, and I am praying, "Oh God, give us some young soldiers. Give us some young spiritual kings. Give us some champions. Give us some men of God who are Spirit-filled, Bible-drilled, and victory-thrilled. Oh God, give us some men who have a positive attitude, who believe: "If God be for us who can be against us." When you were born again, you were born to win.

Now let me tell you about the enemy. The enemy is not Hollywood or the pornographer. The enemy is not the dope pusher or the liquor baron. The enemy is not the IRS or your mother-in-law. The enemy is not the Democratic Party or the Republican Party. Job professions do not determine the eternal state of a person. Faith professions determine where a person spends eternity. Every person needs to repent and get right with God!

It is half past late, and every believer needs to wake up and gear up for war. I know a lot of people will respond, "I am tired of all this battle talk. I want to be at ease. It is time we stopped fighting." And these people are right! It is time we stopped fighting—fighting one another, that is. God's Word tells us, "For we wrestle not against flesh and blood, but against principalities, against powers, against the rulers of the darkness of this world, against spiritual wickedness in high places" (Eph. 6:12).

I am going to take this battle cry one step higher and say that if every believer does not get into the battle, he or she has sinned against the Lord. Numbers 32:23 says, "But if ye will not do so, behold, ye have sinned against the Lord: and be sure your sin will find you out." Now what is the sin that will surely find you out?

If you examine the context of this passage, you will learn that the children of Israel were about to cross the Jordan River and the tribes of Reuben and Gad wanted to stay where the grass was tall and lush for their cattle. Moses said, "Well, that's fine. But, when we go into the land, there is going to be a battle. And when the battle begins, you are going to have to cross over Jordan and fight with us. If you do not, you will sin against the Lord."

Some people may say, "Well, I just don't want to get involved." Listen, the message from God's Word is clear: no believer has a right to be at peace when his brothers are at war. We have a job to do, and it is a job we cannot ignore. There is a raging battle of unbelief, liberalism, and postmodernism. And the fight will never be over until Jesus comes.

If you think I am being belligerent, I am not. But I have a burning message in my heart that I need to share with you. There have been generally three steps to every great fortune that has ever been earned. One generation generates, another generation speculates, then the third generation dissipates. I am afraid that we have speculators in the church today. And in ten or fifteen years we will have some dissipaters. If you read Paul's Epistles, you will see that we are at war, and we will always be at war. We simply must eradicate the idea that life is going to be all honey and no bees. There is a mandate for victory.

II. The Method for Victory

The Weapon We Must Employ

Elisha told Joash to "take bow and arrows" (2 Kings 13:15). This is highly symbolic, as 2 Kings 13:17 explains that this arrow was "the arrow of the LORD's deliverance." The weapons we must employ for victory are spiritual because our enemy is a spirit being of unbelief. Second Corinthians 10:4–5 says, "(For the weapons of our warfare are not carnal, but mighty through God to the pulling down of strong holds;) casting down imaginations, and every high thing that exalteth itself against the knowledge of God, and bringing into captivity every thought to the obedience of Christ."

An apostasy is primarily an idea, and you cannot shoot down an idea with a bullet or even with a literal arrow. Our battle-ax is the Word of God. Our artillery is prayer. Our ally is the Holy Spirit. Our shield is faith. We cannot rely on the artillery of man, such as philosophy and psychology, to clean up the world. Philosophy has a place. Psychology has a place. Politics has a place. Organization has a place. But the devil has outgunned us in every one of these areas. And if you try to build your church with those things, you are going to fail.

We hear a lot about being "seeker sensitive" churches, and I believe we ought to be. We ought not to be rude to unsaved people. We ought to be like the businessman who said business goes where it is welcome and stays where it is treated well. But seeking to be sensitive in our message is not the same thing as being welcoming in our method. It is not the preachers' job to fill the pew; it is our job to fill the pulpit and to preach the Word of God.

The victory is sure. We have the Holy Spirit, and it is time we dropped the H-bomb. It is time we depended on God and what God alone can do.

The Weakness We Must Empower

The young king came to the old prophet, who told him to take up a bow and arrow. When the young king put his hands on the bow and arrow, the prophet of God put his hands over the hands of that young king.

You see, we are naturally weak. We are incapable of winning this battle on our own. We must have the hand of Almighty God over our hands as we labor to bring His truth to the world. Perhaps you are feeling a little inferior today. Maybe you have read books, attended seminars, listened to tapes, and said, "I am not as good as he is in teaching the Word." I have a word for you: Your weakness is not a liability; it is an asset.

Oswald Chambers said, "An unguarded strength is a double weakness." And I would add that a dependent weakness is double strength. Let God put His hand upon your hand. Paul discovered this when God said to him, "My grace is sufficient for thee: for my strength is made perfect in weakness" (2 Cor. 12:9). And Paul responded, "Most gladly therefore will I rather glory in my infirmities, that the power of Christ may rest upon me" (2 Cor. 12:9). It is not your scholarship; it is your relationship. It is not your fame; it is your faith. It is not who you know; it is whose you are.

Whatever you may think of him, Billy Sunday knew the anointing of God. He was known to place his sermon notes on Isaiah 61:1, which says: "The Spirit of the Lord GOD is upon me; because the LORD hath anointed me to preach good tidings unto the meek; he hath sent me to bind up the brokenhearted, to proclaim liberty to the captives, and the opening of the prison to them that are bound."

God called me to preach when I was a young man playing football in high school. At the time I couldn't tell you who came first in Bible chronology—Abraham or Moses. I knew little about the Bible, but I knew that God called me to preach, and I wanted His power upon my life.

One summer night I walked out on the football field where I used to practice and I prayed, "Oh God, I want You to use me." That just didn't seem right, so I got down on my knees and prayed, "Oh God, I want You to use me." But I still didn't feel right about approaching God in that way, so I lay face down on the ground and prayed, "Oh God, I want You to use me." Now I know you will think what I did next was odd, but I made a little hole in the dirt and I stuck my nose down in that hole and I prayed, "Oh God, I am as low as I know how to get. Oh God, I want You to use me."

On that starry summer night in the middle of that football field, I couldn't tell you much about the theology of the Holy Spirit, but the power of God moved into my life in a life-changing way. I didn't speak in tongues; I didn't see beams of heavenly light. But I was forever changed.

Years ago I found some of my old sermons. I was so ashamed of them that I tore them up. I didn't want anybody to see them. But I would be dishonest if I didn't tell you that God had anointed those messages. God *did* anoint, and God *did* bless. And I bless His holy name that when I take up "the arrow of the LORD's deliverance" (2 Kings 13:17), God puts His hands upon my hands and says, "Shoot." I have felt the touch of God upon my life. I had rather die than be sentenced to preach without the anointing and power of God.

My brother in Christ, this is what I want for you. In the name of God, take up the weapon of God—but do so in God's strength. God always identifies Himself with obedient weakness.

The Wickedness We Must Encounter

Elisha told Joash to "open the window eastward" (2 Kings 13:17). What was eastward from where they stood? Israel's wicked foe, Syria. Elisha wanted Joash to confront his fear and encounter the wickedness that lay ahead of him. In the same way, we must encounter wickedness. We can't hide from it. We need to open the windows and expose our sins, fears, failures, and defeat. Is there anything of which you are afraid? Let me give you some promises of God:

> For God hath not given us the spirit of fear; but of power, and of love, and of a sound mind (2 Tim. 1:7).

> And in nothing terrified by your adversaries: which is to them an evident token of perdition, but to you of salvation, and that of God (Phil. 1:28).

> Ye are of God, little children, and have overcome them: because greater is he that is in you, than he that is in the world (1 John 4:4).

Before you can gain the victory, you must open the window. Victory's arrows cannot be shot through closed windows. Don't let the sinister minister of fear intimidate you. You say, "Well, I am not afraid of the devil." That is not the question. Is the devil afraid of you? He ought to be.

The Warfare We Must Engage

When Elisha told Joash to shoot the arrow out the window, do you think the Syrians saw it? Probably not, but that didn't matter. The devil saw it. God saw it. And remember, this arrow was symbolic. In the time when this took place, nations declared war by shooting an arrow toward the land of the enemy. It was an act of aggression and a challenge—much like when a man takes off his gloves and slaps another man in the face.

Now I know that some people may not want to be at war. You simply do not want to open the window and shoot the arrow. You would rather go back into your stained-glass religious haven. But I have a word of warning for you. If you feel this way, you are saying more or less to the devil: "If you leave me alone, I will leave you alone."

There was a hunter who went out one day to hunt bear. As he was walking through the woods, he saw a great grizzly bear. He raised his gun to shoot, and the bear put up his hands and said, "Hold it, don't shoot me. Let's talk. There's no reason for you to resort to violence. After all, what you really want is a fur coat. And all I really want is a good meal." When it was over, the man had a fur coat, and the bear had a good meal.

Now that is the rationale of the devil. He wants us to say, "You leave me alone, and I will leave you alone." But we must not give him the satisfaction. Preacher, I beg of you: Never, never, never lay down the sword. Open the window, shoot the arrow, declare war. Remember what Isaac Watts wrote in his hymn "Am I Soldier of the Cross?"

> Must I be carried to the skies
> On flowery beds of ease,
> While others fought to win the prize,
> And sailed through bloody seas?
>
> Are there no foes for me to face?
> Must I not stem the flood?
> Is this vile world a friend to grace,
> To help me on to God?
>
> Sure I must fight if I would reign;
> Increase my courage, Lord.
> I'll bear the toil, endure the pain,
> Supported by Thy Word.

III. The Measure of Victory

And Elisha said to Joash: "Take the arrows. And he took them. And he said unto the king of Israel, Smite upon the ground. And he smote thrice, and stayed. And the man of God was wroth with him, and said, Thou shouldest have smitten five or six times; then hadst thou smitten Syria till thou hadst consumed it: whereas now thou shalt smite Syria but thrice" (2 Kings 13:18–19).

Joash picked up the arrow and seemed to gingerly, almost half-heartedly strike the ground. This greatly upset Elisha as he looked at Joash and said, "Why did you quit? Why didn't you keep striking the ground?"

Why do we not gain the complete victory? Because all we do is showcase our form. We fail to exert God's holy force against the enemy. If I have learned one thing in my ministry, it is that God does business with those who mean business. And I will tell you something else: you will measure your own victory. Did that sink in? Let me repeat it: You will measure your own victory. Joash settled for a limited victory; he defeated Syria three times and that was all. Do you want the complete victory, or only one that gets you through the day? The measuring cup is in your hands.

These days there is a lot of talk in the church about being moderate. That is exactly what Joash did—he struck the ground moderately. Now I don't mind moderation about the right things, such as eating, spending money, and using leisure time. That is a favorable character quality. But there are some things we should not be moderate about.

What if I asked you, "How do you feel about the inspiration of the Word of God?" And you said, "I am moderate about that." What if I asked you, "Do you love Jesus?" And you said, "Moderately." A man and his word may be different, but God and His Word are not to be separated. He is the Word of God and the God of that Word. We can't be moderate about these things. If my wife asked me, "Adrian, do you love me?" and I said, "Well, I love you moderately," then I am in big trouble! Here's my point: moderate heat never boiled water.

The great preacher, Vance Havner, once preached a sermon entitled "The Menace of Moderatism." He said: "The great peril we face today is not extremism, serious as that is, but moderatism. By moderatism I do not mean moderation; the Scriptures teach moderation. Temperament avoids excess, but moderatism is something else. The only colors that Charles Haddon Spurgeon knew were black and white. In all things he was definite. With Spurgeon you were either up or down, in or out, alive or dead. As for middle zones, graded lines, light compounded with shadow in a graceful exercise of give-and-take, he only looked down upon them as implacable enemies of the Metropolitan Tabernacle. I say may his tribe increase."

Now someone may read this and tell someone, "Adrian Rogers told preachers to be belligerent." Let me set the record straight before it has a chance to bend: I am telling you to be militant.

I am always willing to apologize. I am willing to repent. I am willing to forgive. I am willing to negotiate. I am willing to counsel. I am willing to dialogue. But the Word of God is not up for negotiation. And by the grace of God, I will not, if He will only help me, ever compromise His Word or be moderate about the Word of God.

I am calling you to have a burning, blazing, passionate, emotional love for Christ and His Word. Nothing pleases God more than to be greatly trusted. He wants to do for us "exceeding abundantly above all that we ask or think, according to the power that worketh in us" (Eph. 3:20).

A young African was martyred for his faith. This text was found in his room:

I'm a part of the fellowship of the unashamed. The die has been cast, I have stepped over the line, the decision has been made. I am a disciple of Jesus Christ. I won't look back, let up, slow down, back away, or be still. My past is redeemed, my present makes sense, my future is secure. I'm finished and done with low living, sight walking, smooth knees, colorless dreams, tamed visions, worldly talking, cheap giving, and dwarfed goals. My face is set, my gait is fast, my goal is heaven, my road is narrow, my way is rough, my companions are few, my guide is reliable, my mission is clear. I won't give up, shut up, let up until I have stayed up, stored up, prayed up for the cause of Jesus Christ. I must go till He comes, give till I drop, preach till everyone knows, work till He stops me, and when He comes for His own, He will have no trouble recognizing me because my banner will have been clear.

Don't just strike the ground three times. Get out of the boat with both feet and go for God with all that is in you. If you will lift up the Lord Jesus, He will give you arrows of deliverance. You need nothing else. You should settle for nothing less.

Oh God, give us men of passion. Give us men of emotion. Give us men of resolution. Give us men of determination.

45

Zebedee: A Believer Who Changed History

MATTHEW 4:18–22 NKJV

Jerry Sutton
Senior Pastor, Two Rivers Baptist Church
Nashville, Tennessee

GOD'S INTENTION FOR OUR LIVES is that each of us will have such an impact in the world that we will be able to change it either in a small way or a large way, depending on the call of God upon our lives. Today I want to talk to you about a believer who changed history. Zebedee is a man in the Bible who is somewhat obscure. On the other hand, two of his sons made a great impact on the world. Matthew's Gospel reads:

And Jesus, walking by the Sea of Galilee, saw two brothers, Simon called Peter, and Andrew his brother, casting a net into the sea; for they were fishermen. Then He said to them, "Follow Me, and I will make you fishers of men." They immediately left their nets and followed Him.

Going on from there, He saw two other brothers, James the son of Zebedee, and John his brother, in the boat with Zebedee their father, mending their nets. He called them, and immediately they left their boat and their father, and followed Him (Matt. 4:18–22).

One of the greatest tasks in life is preparing the next generation. Zebedee, although little known himself, was a man whom God used

539

to prepare two men who became disciples and followers of Jesus Christ. Although we dare not minimize the role of the mother of James and John, what I would like to do is to glean from the pages of Scripture some insight about Zebedee, their father, and the role he played.

I realize that all of us have had a dad. He was either present or absent. He was a good dad or a lousy dad. All of us have memories of what our relationship to our father was or maybe some anxiety over what we wish it had been. What I want to do with you today is share from God's Word what God wants a dad to be like. We're using one man as an example. Was Zebedee perfect? Certainly not. Was he used by the Lord? Absolutely. God doesn't expect us to be perfect, but He does expect us to seek Him. When we seek Him, and when we desire to walk with Him, this will make an impact on the lives of our families.

I. Zebedee Was a Strong Influence on His Sons

The first thing I want to point out is that Zebedee was influential in the lives of his sons. Our text tells us that Jesus was walking along the Sea of Galilee. He was calling men to follow Him. Along the way He saw two brothers, "James the son of Zebedee, and John his brother, in the boat with Zebedee their father" (v. 21).

Now obviously Zebedee had some kind of influence with his sons. He had influenced them as little boys, as teenagers, and he exercised influence on them as far as their choice of work. His sons said, "Dad, we want to work with you." We know that he influenced their lives.

Probably the best definition of *leadership* is this: Leadership is influence. Zebedee was a leader in the lives of his sons. Often in the Scripture we find James and John either with their dad, which is the case here in our text, or we find them identified as the sons of Zebedee.

John was a prolific writer. He wrote the Gospel of John, 1, 2, and 3 John, and the book of Revelation. In the only reference to his father, speaking of those who were disciples and followers of Jesus

Christ, John identifies both himself and his brother James as "the sons of Zebedee" (John 21:2). So obviously, Zebedee was an influence in their lives.

Now let me ask you this question: Who are you influencing in life? When you influence people, how do you influence them? Do you influence them in a positive way or a negative way? Do you build people up or tear people down? Do you have an encouraging spirit or a critical spirit? Zebedee influenced his sons for better and not for worse.

We know little about Zebedee. There are a few things that we do know, but for the most part, we know him because of his sons. James and John were part of the inner circle of Jesus' disciples. They were there with Jesus on the Mount of Transfiguration. They were sent out to preach. They were men who watched Jesus' miracles unfold. They were men of God. James became the first Christian martyr. The book of Acts tells us that Herod Antipas went on a tirade against the apostles and the disciples, and James was killed. He was the first of the disciples to be martyred for his faith.

On the other hand, John was the last living apostle. He was placed on the Isle of Patmos, and it was there that he had the vision from God to write the book of Revelation. Although Zebedee is somewhat obscure, we know that his sons, James and John, were incredibly influential. We may not be influential in a big way, but we can influence our children, and our children may well have an incredible impact in life.

Perhaps many of you didn't have a good dad, and you're carrying around the emotional scars of the influence of your father. Some of you never heard your dad say, "Son, I'm proud of you," or "Sweetheart, I love you." You never heard a word of encouragement from your dad like, "God's going to do great things through your life." You never heard your dad say, "Honey, I'm proud of you."

Some of us live with those emotional scars. And the problem is that because we've been wounded emotionally, we take that same wound and inflict it on our kids. Sometimes it's conscious; sometimes it's unconscious. You may have grown up in a family where your dad told you, "Son, you'll never amount to anything." Then when you try to relate to your children, you find yourself saying the same thing. You're trying to motivate them to be better, but you may be discouraging them.

What I want to say to you is this: Like it or not, as a parent or a grandparent, you have incredible opportunities to influence your children and grandchildren. And I want to encourage you to influence them in such a way that they will have a heart for God and a heart for God's work.

II. Zebedee Taught Values to His Sons

The second insight about Zebedee is that he imparted qualities into the lives of his sons. The first thing I notice here is that he taught them how to work. "Going on from there, He [Jesus] saw two other brothers, James the son of Zebedee, and John his brother, in the boat with Zebedee their father, mending their nets" (v. 21).

A boat in Jesus' day was spelled W-O-R-K. It meant work. One thing I notice about Zebedee is that he taught his sons to work. They were workers. They earned their living from the boat. One of the things that we dads need to do is to teach our children how to work. Teach them there's a price to pay and that we need to work. If a father does not teach his children how to work, it seriously impairs them for the rest of their lives. So the first thing I see here is that Zebedee taught his sons how to work.

Not only did he teach them how to work; he taught them how to work together. "Going on from there, He saw two other brothers, James the son of Zebedee, and John his brother, in the boat with Zebedee their father, mending their nets" (v. 21). They learned to work together. It's one thing to learn how to work. It's another thing to learn to work together. It's one thing to fly solo; it's another thing to be able to work together as a team. And it's just as important to learn how to get along with people and to work with people as it is to learn to work.

I've known some people who were incredible workers, but they were just misery to be around. We need to learn not only to work, but we need to learn to work together. Zebedee did that with James and John.

Third, notice that Zebedee taught them how to solve problems. Look what the Scripture says here in verse 21: They were "in the boat with Zebedee their father, mending their nets." Now what does that mean? When nets were used, they would get torn. Maybe the net would catch a piece of driftwood or a large number of fish, and the nets would tear. Here we find James and John mending the nets. There had been a tear, and now they are mending the nets. They are learning to solve problems.

Have you ever noticed in Scripture how the occupations that people have often picture what God is going to do in their public ministry, in their service to God? Some people may ask, "Why would you say that?" For several reasons. First of all, God gives each of us different talents. Some folks have a gift of teaching; others have a gift of service. Others have a gift of discernment. There is a variety of gifts. But what I discover is that the gifts God gives you, the way He made you, is the way He wants to use you.

Let me give you an example. What was Peter's great gift? He was the great evangelist. He stood up on Pentecost and preached. He gave the invitation, and thousands of people came to Christ. Thousands were added to the church on that day. But when we first see Peter, he's fishing. And then he becomes a fisher of men. He was used to harvesting. God used him to harvest.

Then consider the apostle Paul. When Paul was first called, he was a rabbi, a scholar, an intense persecutor of the church, but his father had taught him to do what? To build what? To make what? Tents! He was a tent maker. That was his occupation. And that was what sustained him on his missionary journeys.

Now it just so happens that with every disciple, no matter what kind of ministry or service to God they had, they were taught some kind of trade so they could have something to fall back on. Paul was a tent maker. He understood how to construct tents. You know what Paul's ministry was overall? Someone will say that he was an evangelist. Yes, he was. Someone will say that he was a theologian. Yes, he was. Some people will say that he was a thinker who was used by God to pen Scripture. Yes, he was. But overall God used Paul to build the church. That was his work in evangelism; that was his work in missions. That was his overall work. He was used by God to build the church. He was a tent maker by trade, but he was a church maker by calling. And he built the local church.

I want us to notice what happened with James and John. I'm thinking particularly of John. When he was called, he wasn't fishing. He was mending nets. What was his calling in ministry? The reason he wrote the Gospel of John, the reason he wrote the epistles of 1, 2, and 3 John, and the reason he wrote the book of Revelation from the human perspective is that there were heresies and false teaching rising up in the church. And God used him to pen those writings for the singular purpose of shoring up what Satan was trying to tear down.

John's calling was to mend the nets. We see that Zebedee taught his sons about the work of fishing, working from the boat. He wanted them to learn to work. He wanted them to learn to work together, but he also wanted them to learn to solve problems. That's what they're doing. They're learning to solve problems. They're thinking ahead. If they don't repair the holes in the net, the fish are going to swim right on through. James and John are learning to solve problems.

Not only are they learning to solve problems, they're learning to plan ahead. They are thinking that tomorrow when they go out to fish, it will be too late to decide to mend the nets. So Zebedee is teaching them to solve problems, and he's teaching them to plan. He's teaching them how to be decisive. "And immediately they left the boat and their father" (v. 22). That is being decisive. He taught them how to make decisions.

Something that all of us need to learn how to do, something we need to teach our children, is how to solve problems, how to make decisions, and how to plan. Solving problems looks to the past. What was wrong? How do we fix it? Decision making is in the present. What decision needs to be made right now? Planning looks to the future. Zebedee taught all three of these matters to his sons, and we need to do the same thing. We need to teach our children how to solve problems, how to be decisive, and how to plan.

Verse 22 says, "And immediately they left the boat and their father, and followed Him." They had learned about Jesus. Early in the Gospel of John, it is reported that James and John spent some time with Jesus. They wanted to understand who He was and what He was about. When the call of God came, when the conviction came, when Jesus said, "Follow Me, and I will make you fishers of men" (v. 19), they didn't hesitate, they didn't back up, they didn't argue about it, they didn't debate it. They immediately followed Him.

You may have never had a dad who taught you how to make decisions. All of your life you may have been taught by example to put things off, to procrastinate. All of your life you may have been taught by example, either positively or negatively, that the best decision is no decision. But when it comes to spiritual things, to make no decision is to make the wrong decision.

God's desire for us is that when He speaks and calls us to come and follow Him, we need to be decisive. Can you imagine what it was like? Here is Dad Zebedee, who was running a business. Peter worked with him. He was a partner. There were hired workers whom he was responsible for, and his sons were part of the business. Zebedee was not some fly-by-night operator. He was a man with a big operation. He had lots of people working for him. He had to worry about logistics. He had to worry about capital. He had to worry about taking the fish that were caught and getting them to market. He had the entire responsibility. But he had taught his sons to be decisive. And when the call of God came, they didn't hesitate.

Not only did he teach them how to be decisive; obviously he taught them to put God first in everything. Immediately they left their boat and their father, and they followed Jesus. Zebedee had taught them how to put God first, and when the call of God came, they responded.

There are some of us to whom God has spoken time and time again. We thought we needed to make some kind of decision, that we needed to surrender to God. But every time we have thought that, the devil has whispered to us that it is a great idea, but just wait and put that off until tomorrow. Let me tell you a secret: Tomorrow never comes. Tomorrow is a mental construct that never comes. When God calls us to make a decision, He always says that today is the day of decision (see 2 Cor. 6:2). If we're going to make a decision, it must be today.

Now I'm asking if you would do the same thing Jesus asked those disciples to do? Would you say, "Lord, I want to follow you"? Notice they didn't just do it in their minds. There are several instances in Scripture where people were called to follow Jesus, and they became what we might call "secret disciples." Nicodemus was a secret disciple. Joseph of Arimathea was a secret disciple. But sooner or later those who followed Jesus in secret finally came out in public. They said, "We want to stand up and be counted." And they stood up, and they were counted.

Jesus doesn't call us to follow Him secretly. He calls us to follow Him publicly. God does not want us to be secret disciples, keeping our lights hidden under a bushel. Jesus put it this way. "Let your light so shine before men, that they may see your good works and glorify your Father in heaven" (Matt. 5:16). God wants us to follow him publicly. Zebedee gave his sons permission to follow Jesus publicly, and they *immediately* followed Jesus. He taught them how to be decisive. He also taught them to put God first.

One other thing is that Zebedee taught his sons his values. The only way they would have been willing to follow Jesus, the only way they would have been willing to leave the family business, was that Zebedee had taught his sons the values that matter. This is what is important. This is what counts.

What kind of values are you teaching your children? The values that you have will be communicated. And many times it's not just what's taught, but it's what's caught. I've heard it said that until about the age of sixteen, our children are going to do what we as parents say. After that, they're going to do what you do. Values are as much caught as they are taught.

What's important to you? What is your value system? What are you communicating to your children? The same things that Zebedee taught his sons are the very things that God wants us to impart to our children. He wants us to teach our children how to work. He wants us to teach them how to work together. He wants us to teach our children how to solve problems. He wants us to teach our children how to plan. He wants us to teach our children to be decisive.

Zebedee taught his sons to plan, to be decisive, to put God first. He taught them his values. And he imparted these qualities into the lives of his sons. God expects us to impart those same qualities into the lives of our children.

III. *Zebedee Was Involved in the Lives of His Sons*

Notice also that Zebedee was involved in his sons' lives. There's no place for an absentee dad. Some of the greatest emotional wounds we have in our society are caused by absentee dads. Maybe your dad walked out on your mom. Maybe your dad never showed up. Maybe he was married to your mom and they were in the home, but he never had any kind of positive impact or interaction with you. God expects us to be involved in the lives of our children. There is no place for absentee dads and no place for passive dads. God expects us to be involved in the lives of our kids.

I want to make sure my kids turn out right because they spent time with me. That's why I coached ball. It's not because I had all this extra time. I did it because I wanted to spend time with my kids.

What kind of time are you spending with your children? And what kind of time are you spending with your grandchildren? There's a myth that goes like this: "I may not be spending quantity time with my child, but I'm spending quality time." No matter how you slice that, it is still baloney. Your kids need time with you. They need you as a role model. They need you to interact with them. They need you to pray with them. They need you to spend time with them. They need *you*.

We live in a culture where the role of the father has been criticized and minimized. Look at popular TV shows, the movies, or magazines, and we will see that the role of the father has been minimized. Don't get your information from the media. Don't let the sitcoms define what kind of dad you're supposed to be. Let God's Word define the father you should be and the relationship you should have with your children.

IV. Zebedee Taught His Sons Independence

Zebedee was influential in his sons' lives. He imparted qualities into his sons' lives. He was involved in their lives. But notice also that he gave them permission to be independent of himself. Some dads want to control their children. Even after the kids are grown, their father may still be trying to control them. He's either holding the purse strings or he has some kind of unhealthy emotional attachment to his children, and he is trying to dominate them. There are three things that every dad needs to give his child.

First, you need to move your children from being absolutely dependent on you to being absolutely dependent on God. I didn't say independent of you, though that's part of it. But there is a point where you need to say, "Son, as you grow older, I'm going to give you more responsibility. And the more responsibility you can handle, the more I'm going to give you." And as children, we need to move from the place where we are accountable and obedient to our parents to the place where they become our counselors.

Scripture tells children to obey their parents in the Lord, for this is right (see Eph. 6:1). And for a child who is in the formative years, that is absolutely true. Children, obey your parents.

Now on the other hand, as our children grow to maturity, we as parents need to bring them along, helping them to make decisions, teaching them how to solve problems and how to trust God for their needs. And we need to lead our children from absolute dependence upon us to absolute dependence on God. I don't want my children to be dependent on me. Someday I may not have the resources to take care of them. On top of that, I'm not always right. I want to help them go from being absolutely dependent on me to being absolutely dependent on God.

There's a point when our children will be grown and mature. They know why they have obeyed what we say. On the other hand, our children should always be able to come to us for counsel. There was a point in my life that whatever my dad said was law. If he said it, then it was done. To disobey my dad was a serious infraction in my home, and there were no exceptions.

On the other hand, when I grew up, when I matured, I was no longer living under his roof. I was responsible for my own decisions and my own life. Yet I would still go back to my dad and ask his counsel. We need to help our children move from being absolutely dependent on us to being absolutely dependent on God. We need to teach them to move from being absolutely obedient to us to the point of seeing us as a source of wise counsel. That's the first thing we need to do as parents.

Second, we must give our children roots. To be your son or to be your daughter needs to mean something. If we study the name Zebedee, we discover that it comes from a Hebrew word which means "gift," "gift of God," or "gift from God." James and John understood that their father was a gift. He was a gift from God. There was a root system there. Dad was a rock. Dad was consistent. Dad could be counted on. Dad was a role model. Dad was a godly man, and he gave his children roots.

We need to give our children roots, or a secure foundation. One reason so many people live emotionally disturbed lives is that they have no root system. When they look back, all they see is regret. All they see is disappointment. But just because that's the kind of experience you had growing up does not give you permission to treat your children the same way.

I had one of the greatest grandmothers that anybody could ever have. She loved us, and she encouraged us. We would go and cut her grass and take care of her yard. She would pay us more than we were worth, I'm sure. She would always ask if she could get us a cold drink. I have all kinds of wonderful memories of my grandmother. It was not until I was well into my adult life that we discovered that when my grandmother was four years old, her dad put all the kids in the Methodist Children's Home in Selma, Alabama. Their mother had died. He remarried, and his new wife did not want the children. He just put them in the children's home. And every year he would promise to visit on Christmas. But he never came. He would say every year that he would come to see them on their birthdays. But he never came. They would get word that dad was going to come, but daddy never came.

My grandmother had one of the greatest disappointments of anybody I know. From the time she was four years old until the time she was an adult, it was promises made, promises broken. Just because she was wounded emotionally as a child did not mean that she had to wound emotionally as an adult. And just because you were wounded as a child does not mean that you have permission to wound anybody else, no matter what your background, your experience, your heartbreak, or your disappointment. If you have a relationship with Jesus Christ, you have no basis, no reason, no authority, and no permission to mistreat your children. Our job is to give our children roots.

Third, we need to teach our children to move from absolute dependence on us to absolute dependence on God. Zebedee gave his sons permission to be independent from him. He moved them from dependence upon himself to dependence upon God. He gave his sons roots, but he also gave his sons wings.

I can just imagine that James and John as little boys would be watching their dad fish. Probably the first five to ten years they were in the boat with dad, all they did was get in the way. Now I can just imagine what it was like when I was growing up and dad would let me cut the yard. The first several years that I tried it, I'm sure I made a major mess out of it. But dad let me have the opportunity.

So James and John watched dad fish, and they learned by watching him. They learned more than just by watching him; they learned more than just fishing. I can hear their conversation: "Well, James, what do you think God wants to do in your life when you grow up?"

"I don't know, Dad, but I want to be just like you."

Zebedee probably said something like, "Well, Son, nothing would honor me more than for you to be like me. Now, John, what do you want to do when you grow up?"

"Well, Dad, I work real hard when I go to synagogue, and I'm trying to learn. Someday I want to write some things that make a difference in people's lives."

Zebedee replies, "Son, you can become whatever you want to be. You can become whatever God wants you to be. You can make a difference in people's lives by what you write. I hope you do that."

Then Zebedee turns and asks, "James, what do you want to do?"

James replies, "Dad, I want my life to count. I want to stand up and be counted for God."

Zebedee says, "Son, that's going to happen in your life."

By the way they talk and the way Zebedee lifts their vision to what they might become, he not only gives them roots, but he gives them wings. Many times dads are the world's best at clipping wings. "You'll never become anything." "You want to do what?" "Son, you've got to be kidding!" And by our words we can destroy our kids. We can make them emotional dwarfs.

God says, "I want you to teach your children how to move from absolute dependence on you to absolute dependence on me. I want you to teach your children in such a way that you'll give them roots! I also want you to teach them in such a way that you'll give them wings to help them fly, to help them to succeed, to help them make a difference in life."

Satan keeps whispering in our ears, "Oh, that's a great idea. Just wait and do it another time." I want to say to you that whatever you choose to do for God, do it now. It could be that you're a parent and the truth is that you have been a poor parent. Perhaps you live with regret, and you think over and over again about your many mistakes. There's not a better time than right now to start over. You cannot erase the past, but you can start right now to have a brand-new beginning and write a brand-new ending in the lives of your children.

46

How to Contend with Conflict

JAMES 4:1–10 NKJV

Keith Thomas

Senior Pastor, Cottage Hill Baptist Church
Mobile, Alabama

"WHERE DO WARS AND FIGHTS come from among you?" (James 4:1). In light of our current world situation, James's question is relevant for us. War has been a part of every era of human history. Even the Lord Jesus spoke about wars and rumors of wars (see Matt. 24:6). These are critical days for us as a nation. The House of Representatives and the Senate have both agreed that our president has latitude to move forward in protecting our world from men like Saddam Hussein. Our world seems to be coming closer and closer to global war. A world on the brink of an apocalyptic war ought to pay close attention to what James is saying in this verse.

But James is not really talking to the world. He is talking to believers. He asks, "Where do wars and fights come from among you?" There are at least three wars we need to be aware of that have an intensely personal application for us. We need to see how we can avoid fighting all these wars, battles, and conflicts. I want to speak about how we can contend with these conflicts.

One of the conflicts that we are inevitably going to face is the Civil War. That is the war that we fight with one another. We are family. We are friends. But we still have conflicts, and the collateral damage is huge. This civil war is where character assassinations take place. It is where we talk about other people behind their backs—those covert, backstabbing, betraying operations. Everybody gets damaged in this kind of war. Our relationships get damaged, our marriages get damaged, our friendships get damaged, our careers get damaged, and everything becomes part of the battle.

Another type of war in which we engage is the World War I model. This war is fought internally but also causes external fights. The battle is a contrast of doing things God's way and fulfilling His desires or doing things our way and fulfilling our own desires. It is a constant battle that goes on inside us. I have discovered I am in fairly good shape as long as people do what I want them to do and people talk about what I want them to talk about. As long as I am in control, there is not much conflict in my life. We encounter problems when we face those who may challenge us or those who do not want to bow to our wishes. This is when conflict happens.

Then there is even the Holy War model, where we challenge God by walking with one foot in the world and one foot in heaven. It is here that we end up in conflict with God. Understand that this is one war that we will never win. The consequences of this war are devastating. James reveals two significant things to show us how to contend with these conflicts that inevitably come our way. He shows us how these conflicts develop, and then he shows us how we can diffuse those conflicts.

I. The Development of Conflicts

What is it that causes these conflicts? These fights? These quarrels? I want you to think right now about the person who causes the most conflict in your life. James shows us how to contend with the conflicts that we have with these people. He shows us four things that can cause a conflict to develop into a full-scale war.

Unbridled Selfishness

James shows us first the sin of *unbridled selfishness*. Why do we find ourselves in conflict with people with whom we ought to be in concert? It is simply because of unbridled selfishness. Notice in verse 1: "Where do wars and fights come from among you? Do they not come from your desires for pleasure that war in your members? You lust and do not have. You murder and covet and cannot obtain. You fight and war." In this passage the word *war* refers to a perpetual state of conflict. Conflict of this magnitude goes on and on and is never resolved. The word *fight* refers to those separate little skirmishes within that long-range campaign. Whether the conflicts are long, drawn-out resentments that are like war, or whether they are those sudden explosions of dislike or disagreement, they all issue from the same source. We tend to be selfish. Thus our feelings get frustrated and our desires conflict with somebody else's. Those frustrated feelings often result in fights.

Have you ever noticed that marriages have built-in conditions for conflict? Just think back about what you expected from your spouse before you got married. How unrealistic, how idealistic you were about marriage. Husbands, you thought she would always wait on you hand and foot. You thought she would follow every well-intended idea that you had, and that she would prepare three meals a day, with variety, and that whenever you came home from work she would always be seductive and sexy. Wives, you thought your husband would always come home and would love to cook supper with you. You thought he would love to do the dishes with you after supper. You thought he would want to help clean house. And finally, you thought he would love just being your partner in domestic duties, and then you would sit by the fireplace and talk for three hours. Marriage is just one example of how conflicts can begin, but you must realize that the underlying root of conflict is selfishness.

As you examine other areas of your life, you will discover that unbridled selfishness is at the core of all conflicts. James says, "You lust and do not have" (v. 2). He is not talking about a sexual issue here. Instead, he is focusing on what you want—deeply desiring something and those feelings and desires being frustrated. When you focus on self, the by-product is lust. Lust then produces discontent, and discontent results in disharmony. That word *lust* is the Greek word *hedonae;* we get our word *hedonism* from it. It is that unbridled search for pleasure, the spirit that wants immediate satisfaction right now. *Self* wants to please itself at the expense of everyone else. Nothing else matters. It has an insatiable appetite for possessions, for power, for popularity, for position, and for passion. Then these pleasures begin to dominate and drive our lives.

James says selfishness can even lead to things like murder and covetousness. Our unbridled selfishness will give us an insatiable desire for pleasure and things. God created things for us to use and enjoy, and because of this, we are to use things and love people. But the problem is that whenever we start to love things, it causes us to get the equation backwards. We start to love things and use people instead of loving people and using things. We start to manipulate and try to seek to control things in order to get what we want. We always seem to want what we cannot have. Sometimes we even want what does not belong to us. This wanting is never satisfied because worldly, selfish things never bring permanent satisfaction. So James says that unbridled selfishness causes conflict.

Unchecked Prayerlessness

Next, we see in this passage that the sin of *unchecked prayerlessness* also leads to conflict. James says, "Yet you do not have because you do not ask. You ask and do not receive, because you ask amiss, that you may spend it on your pleasures" (vv. 2–3). Unbridled selfishness ultimately leads to a prayerless life, a life where we do not ask for the right things. If there is anything we need as Christians, it is to learn how to pray. The believer who can pray with the right heart can do anything! Why? Because prayer can do anything that God can do, and God can do anything. Our desperate need is to link our lives with the omnipotent God who has called upon us to pray.

There is not one failure in our lives that is not a prayer failure. Every sin in our lives could have been prevented by prayer. We do not have a genuine need that fervent, believing prayer cannot meet. Many people are spiritually frustrated, empty, and missing out on all God has for them because they have not learned how to connect with God in prayer. It is as though they are spiritually asleep. They are oblivious to what God wants to do in their lives.

Many people who claim to know the Lord Jesus are sleeping their way through the abundant life that He desires for them to enjoy. They are missing out on so many wonderful blessings. They live their lives in the grip of guilt. They know they have blown it. But they are not willing to release that guilt to a loving God who wants to bring forgiveness. They live their lives with worry and fear instead of the peace and joy that only Jesus can give. His peace gives us inner security that is possible only through Him!

Prayer is the main factor in determining the spiritual blessings we experience. Our spiritual life is where it is because of the condition of our prayer life. The measure of the fullness of our lives is directly related to the health of our prayer lives. Notice the problem again. James declares that we have the *wrong method*. "You do not have because you do not ask" (v. 2). Prayerlessness is not just some kind of weakness we have; it is wickedness. Not to pray is a sin! It is not a matter of simply missing a blessing and doing without the things God wants us to have; it is sinning against God.

James goes on to say that we not only have the wrong method, but we ask and do not receive because we "ask amiss," that we may spend it on our "pleasures" (v. 3).

Sometimes people pray and get no answer because their prayers are based on the *wrong motivation* (asking "amiss"). They are willing to sacrifice the answer to their prayer on the altar of their own selfish desires. These people are not asking for the glory of God; they are asking for the fulfillment of their lusts. What we are asking God to do is to change our lives but in essence to leave us alone. God will not answer a wrongly motivated prayer. He will not subsidize our sins. He will not underwrite our selfishness. He will, however, meet our needs, and we have the right to ask Him to meet our needs. But understand our desires may be denied if we do not come to the Lord in the right way. We cannot pray for sinful, selfish desires and expect God to answer our prayers.

Unguarded Worldliness

James illustrates the sin of *unguarded worldliness* in verse 4: "Adulterers and adulteresses! Do you not know that friendship with the world is enmity with God? Whoever therefore wants to be a friend to the world makes himself an enemy of God. Or do you think that the Scripture says in vain, 'The Spirit who dwells in us yearns jealously'?"

How can a Christian be at war with God? This is the picture painted of Jesus. Whenever we came to Christ to be a part of the family of God, we turned from our sin, placed our faith in Jesus alone to save us, and became a part of Christ's church. The church is the bride of Christ (2 Cor. 11:2). That describes our relationship with Jesus. He is the bridegroom; we are the bride.

Just as a bride should be pure and give herself to her husband alone, so we should belong to the Lord Jesus and Him alone. We should give our love to no one else. No other lovers come before Him; He alone is Supreme. We are married to Him. We made a pledge to Him openly and publicly that we would be faithful. That is the figure of speech that James is using in this verse.

The problem: Although we belong to Christ as His bride, another suitor comes calling. It is the world. The world schemes for our affection. Satan comes on soft and suave. He just wants to be our friend. He is not looking for a deep and intimate relationship. Then this enemy begins to connive. He is a perverted adulteress and suitor, trying to seduce and manipulate a wife away from her husband. You need to know that "friendship with the world" always leads to a love of the world. The Bible says that when we turn from Jesus and become friends with the world, we commit spiritual adultery.

Let me illustrate it this way. Suppose you take your wife to a restaurant, and you get her the best table possible. She is excited because this is an unbelievably expensive, romantic restaurant. You get her seated, but you don't sit down. You say to her, "Honey, I don't want you to worry about a thing, but I am not going to eat with you. Don't be anxious; I am going to be just across the room at that table over there."

Your wife looks over and says, "Who's that beautiful woman?"

You say, "Honey, that's my girlfriend. I have been meaning to tell you; I have fallen in love with her, too. But you don't need to worry about a thing because I still love you. I am going to have dinner with her because she doesn't know about you, and I don't want her to know. But everything is OK. We'll have dinner over there, and I'll take care of your dinner here. Don't worry, Honey. I love you, too."

That is a recipe for disaster! You can't have two lovers. And God won't either. *God will not tolerate two lovers.*

Are any of us guilty of the sin of unguarded worldliness that leads to spiritual adultery? We have made a commitment to the Lord Jesus, and we should be as faithful to God as a faithful woman is to her husband. But what has happened is that we have become friends with the world, and some of us have climbed into bed with other gods such as materialism. We just love things; we have to have them. Like consumerism. It is always about *us*. What are you going to do for *me*? What's in it for *me*? Whatever makes you feel good, that's what you do.

Whenever we begin to desire worldly things more than we desire God, we are committing spiritual adultery. We are like a married woman who goes after other men, flirting and seducing them. James lets us know that there is a holy, loving jealousy that a wife and a husband should have toward each other. Likewise, there is the Spirit of God who lives within us and yearns jealously for our lives to be dominated by the lordship of Jesus. This Spirit keeps crying out, "Be devoted to Jesus! Be devoted to Jesus!" You see, God does not want just a *place* in our lives; he wants *preeminence*.

Unbroken Haughtiness

As we try to get in on all of God's grace, a huge obstacle is set before us. It is called pride. This sin has brought more heartache to our lives than any other sin. God resists pride. I am not referring to self-respect, conscientiousness, or receiving proper honor. We need self-esteem in understanding who we are in Christ. The grace of God will exalt a person without inflating him and debase a person without humiliating him. But pride is the attitude that functions without regard to who God is or what He wants. It shows itself in an attitude that makes us blind to our own needs. It makes us see other people and their faults, but it does not let us see the big beam in our own eyes.

Proverbs 16:5 says, "Everyone proud in heart is an abomination to the LORD; though they join forces, none will go unpunished." Proverbs 11:2 says, "When pride comes, then comes shame; but with the humble is wisdom." James must have had Proverbs 3:34 in mind: "Surely He scorns the scornful, but gives grace to the humble."

This unbroken haughtiness causes God to resist us. That word *resist* means "to set in battle array." God says, "You're not going to go forward; you're not going to get by with this. I am going to resist you."

How does God resist the proud? First of all, by *refusing to speak*. Luke 23:8–9 says, "Now when Herod saw Jesus, he was exceedingly glad; for he had desired for a long time to see Him, because he had heard many things about Him, and had hoped to see some miracle done by Him. Then he questioned Him with many words, but He answered him nothing." Herod was noted for his pride and arrogance, and it was received by the Master's silence. Jesus said nothing. He refused to speak. In Romans chapter 1, God describes a reprobate mindset. In their arrogant, rebellious, prideful lust, they find God comes to the place where He no longer has anything to say to them. He does nothing to stop them, and He has nothing more to do with them (see Rom. 1:21–26). That is a scary, dangerous consequence of holding on to our pride.

God also resists the proud by *ridiculing their schemes*. Psalm 2:1–4 says, "Why do the nations rage, and the people plot a vain thing? The kings of the earth set themselves, and the rulers take counsel together, against the LORD and against His Anointed, saying, 'Let us break Their bonds in pieces and cast away their cords from us.' He who sits in the heavens shall laugh; the LORD shall hold them in derision."

Men and nations can move independently and rebelliously against God, but He responds with derisive laughter. He laughs at them. He brings their schemes to nothing.

Another way God resists the proud is by *removing their status.* Daniel speaks of Belshazzar: "But when his heart was lifted up, and his spirit was hardened in pride, he was deposed from his kingly throne, and they took his glory from him" (Dan. 5:20). God can take our positions away. He can give them, and He can take them away. Nothing we have is so secure that God cannot take if we don't hold it in humility.

The remedy for this is humility. He "gives grace to the humble" (James 4:6). The humble are those who recognize and confess to God, "I am undone. I'm lost without you. I need your sovereign rule over every capacity of my life. I choose brokenness before you. I yield all that I know about myself to all that I know about you. And God, if you'll just take my life and use it, it is yours." God begins to enrich people like this, and He begins to show His favor toward them.

II. Diffusing Conflicts

Not only does James show us how conflicts develop, but he also shows us how to diffuse them. "Therefore submit to God. Resist the devil and he will flee from you. Draw near to God and He will draw near to you. Cleanse your hands, you sinners; and purify your hearts, you double-minded. Lament and mourn and weep! Let your laughter be turned to mourning and your joy to gloom. Humble yourselves in the sight of the Lord, and He will lift you up" (James 4:7–10).

If we are serious about ending the conflicts and the wars in our lives, there are several things we can do.

Submit to the Father

First, there needs to be submission to the Father. Whether the conflict is at home, at your workplace, or in your heart, it all starts to be diffused when you submit to the Father. Verse 7 says, "Therefore submit to God." The word *submit* is a military word which means to get into your proper rank underneath your commanding officer. Can you imagine a private coming to a general and saying, "I know I am in your army, but I am going to determine what I do, when I do it, and how I do it. If I need any help from you, I'll call you." That will never work!

James has a name for those who think they know better than God and who don't want to submit to His authority. He calls them the proud. He is referring to that spirit that makes us blind to our own weaknesses and needs. In essence, this spirit says, "I know the way I should go. I don't need any help from you. I can handle my own life. I am capable of taking care of myself."

The starting point for achieving peace on the inside is to submit to the Father. When you have peace on the inside, you can have peace on the outside. There is no peace inside or outside until there is submission to God's authority over our lives. If we are in charge, here's what's going to happen. Anytime something does not go the way we want it to go, we are going to get irritable, frustrated, and upset. But if God is in charge of our lives, we can have peace even in the midst of disappointment.

Stand Against the Devil

In addition to submitting to God, we also need to stand against the devil. "Therefore submit to God. Resist the devil and he will flee from you" (v. 7). For some time the United States gathered intelligence reports about Saddam Hussein. They analyzed all of his capabilities in order to wage a successful military campaign against him if he did not comply with disarmament demands. The same is true for us in waging a successful spiritual war. We need to gather some intelligence reports from God's Word about our enemy.

The Bible makes clear that our enemy Satan is *real*. He is not imaginary. He is a powerful force in this world. We do not need to become obsessed with him, but neither do we need to ignore him. If we do, it will be to our detriment. We must not be like spiritual

Don Quixotes—fighting spiritual windmills because we don't have a clue as to who our real enemy is. So we fight with our wives, we have conflicts with our husbands, we have conflicts with our bosses and conflicts with our friends. Who do you think is behind all that? It is the enemy. Satan is a real enemy who needs to be resisted.

Not only is he real; he is also *rebellious*. He is doing everything he can to derail us and sabotage what God wants to do in our lives. He hates you. His real war is with God. Because God loves us, Satan hates us. He wants to disorient us, to discourage us, and to deceive us so that he might destroy us. It may not be physical destruction. It may be emotional. He will try to derail us spiritually with attitudes and actions that are destructive to our spiritual well-being. He loves to use deceit. If he can get us to believe something that is not based on truth, he can begin to control our behavior.

Satan loves to give partial truth. He loves to take part of the truth and twist it to deceive us. The Scriptures give us an example of this with the disciples. Jesus told them to take the boat to the other side of the Sea of Galilee. Being tired, He lay down in the boat and went to sleep. While he was asleep in the boat, a big storm came up. The disciples were afraid they were going to die. So they woke up the Lord as if to say, "Don't you care about us?" Jesus rebuked the wind, and then He rebuked them (see Mark 4:34–41). Why? The disciples had bought a lie, and their faith was floundering due to the deception of the wicked one.

The truth of the matter is they were not going to die. Jesus told them to go to the other side. He was the master of the waves. The disciples thought otherwise because their circumstances were controlling their thinking and Satan was feeding them lies.

Satan also loves confusion. He loves to confuse us about what is truly righteous and who is true to the Lord and about what values and priorities we ought to live by. He will confuse us about the joy of submission and make us think that our lives will be ruined if we do not submit. He tries to tell us that we need to pray, "Lord, change that person," instead of, "Lord, change me." He loves to confuse us.

Consequently we never work on ourselves, and we wonder why we keep getting into the same problems over and over again. We have been confused into thinking our conflict was all about our circumstances. We believe that our circumstances are making us frustrated and upset when in reality it was something inside us that needs to be changed.

Now how does Satan do this? He plays on our pride, especially our wounded pride. He is the master at telling us what we want to hear. He will suggest to us, "You don't have to take that." "Who does she think she is?" "You don't have to put up with that." "Retaliate." He tells us things our pride wants to hear. We need to recognize his voice and resist it with truth.

Satan is also *relentless*. He never gives up. He is like a roaring lion constantly prowling about. He will continue to lie to us, tempt us, confuse us, and urge us to pursue only what we want out of life. That is why we need to resist him and take our stand against him.

Separate from the World

It is clear we need to submit to the Father and to stand against the devil. But in addition to this, we also need to be separate from the world. James declared, "Draw near to God and He will draw near to you. Cleanse your hands, you sinners; and purify your hearts, you double-minded" (v. 8). James uses a priestly concept in this passage because priests were the ones who drew near to God and they understood what was necessary for them to do this. They knew it meant they had to be separate from the world. One could not come to God with unresolved, unrepented sin. James says, "You draw near to God; He will draw near to you."

God is where He has always been. We are the ones who have drifted away. James reminds us that if we want to diffuse the conflict in our lives, we need to come back to God. We need to draw near to God. As we drift away from Him, we lose the intimacy factor in our relationship. Then the battles in our lives begin to increase.

When I was in high school, we used to go to the beach and surf. We would go out and catch a couple of sets of waves and look back to the shore where our car was parked. A few minutes later, we would look back and see that the tide had pulled us away a little bit, but we weren't concerned because we really hadn't drifted that far. We could still see where we got in the water. We could still see the car; it was no big deal. We would catch a couple of more waves, and before we knew it, we were way down the beach, and we couldn't see the car. It was a lot of work and a lot of agony to try to paddle against that current to get back to where we got in the water.

The same is true spiritually. We will always have the pull of the flesh, pulling us away from intimacy. But we think, *It is no big deal. I'm fine. I'm not that far away from the Lord.* But the reality is, you're in trouble. Why? Your intimacy has diminished. You are not where you used to be spiritually. You *think* you're OK. James says that if we really want to end these conflicts, we need to draw near to God. Then He will draw near to us.

Hebrews 10:22 says that conflicts will not be resolved unless we "draw near with a true heart in full assurance of faith, having our hearts sprinkled from an evil conscience and our bodies washed with pure water." Second Chronicles 15:2 says, "The LORD is with you while you are with Him. If you seek Him, He will be found by you; but if you forsake Him, He will forsake you." If we seek Him, He will draw near to us.

I have discovered that the more time I spend with God, the better I get along with other people. Some people only get close to God when they are in trouble. If we could just discipline ourselves to draw near to God every day, we would find ourselves getting along better with other people. We would find conflicts diminishing and relationships beginning to grow sweeter. The conflicts in our lives are in direct proportion to the amount of time we spend with God.

III. Seriousness in Our Repentance

James says there also needs to be a seriousness in our repentance. Being submissive to the Father and standing against the devil will enable us to know the sweetness of grace that God delights to give us.

In order to receive that grace, we must draw near. We need to be serious about drawing near to Him and possess a seriousness about dealing with our own personal sin. Notice what James says in verse 9, "Lament and mourn and weep! Let your laughter be turned to mourning and your joy to gloom." *We have to get serious about our sin!* We can't just laugh it off. It is just too serious. Sin is what is keeping us from the blessings of God.

James uses the word *lament*. That describes a soldier who has voluntarily given up some of the things other people have because he has been called to be a soldier. James says that we must voluntarily give up some things that the world wants us to have. These things will lure us away from God and seduce us spiritually. We must lament over the spiritual conditions that seek to pull us under and plunder us spiritually.

Look at verse 10: "Humble yourselves in the sight of the Lord, and He will lift you up." It is possible to submit outwardly and yet not be inwardly humble. Let me ask some questions. Do you find it difficult to back down in an argument? Do you find it difficult to admit when you are wrong? Looking back, you see that there used to be an excitement about your walk with God. It is just not there anymore. You have drifted. As a result, you are not spending time with God like you used to. You are not sharing your faith like you used to. You are trying to fix things on your own and to your own advantage without seeking the face of God. You are leaning on your own understanding, and things have become disjointed. James says we need to humble ourselves. We must admit that we need God and humble ourselves before Him. If we do this, the Lord will exalt us. He will lift us up.

There was a conflict between the prodigal son and his father (Luke 15:11–24). Such a conflict that the son went to his father and demanded, "I want my inheritance. Give it to me now." He became the consummate party animal. Wasting it, buying anything he wanted, doing anything he wished. But all of this caught up with him, and he eventually found himself broken and impoverished. He came out of his spiritual insanity, and he began to realize, *I am the one with the problem. I need to go home. I'm going to humble myself before my dad, hoping he'll take me back and let me be his son again. I would even settle for being a servant.*

The father sees a figure in the distance. *Who's that coming? He looks familiar.* He gets a little closer. *I recognize his walk!* He gets a little closer. *That's my boy!* He starts running toward his son. He didn't shame him; he restored him. And then?

The conflict was over.

47

After These Things

GENESIS 22:1–19 NASB

Ken Hemphill

National Strategist for Empowering Kingdom Growth
Southern Baptist Convention

MANY OF US HOPED that church attendance would continue the spiral of growth it had enjoyed in the months immediately after 9/11. We all know now that it quickly returned to the pre-9/11 status. But even so, there is a subtle message from Ground Zero that reminds us of the significant role of the church and what it must play in the healing of our land. Prior to that unforgettable day, few people walking those blocks in New York City would have noticed the cross streets that ran next to those majestic towers. Back then street signs seemed inconsequential when you were looking up at the buildings that soared about a quarter of a mile above the pavement.

But now with everything at ground level, the names of those streets should gain far more attention than before. The posted names of those two streets are simply Church and Liberty. The atrocities of September 11 are incredible, yet the avenue to liberty from our grief, anger, and fears is found in God's victorious church.

I want to invite you to turn to Genesis 22. As we look at these circumstances and these events, I want to declare to you, first of all, that God does not cause the evil circumstance. He is a good God. But God does use circumstances to build the character of His children. I want to take you on a pilgrimage of faith. We often talk about Abraham as the example of faith, as the model of faith. So I want us to go back and take a bit of a journey because it was not always the case. We are going to start at the end of the passage and then circle and come back. This is among the most familiar of all Old Testament passages. It is one of those passages that catches our imagination. For those of us who are parents, it tugs at our hearts because we find this incredible moment when God says to Abraham, this father of the faith community, that He wants him to sacrifice his son, Isaac.

We begin to ask the question, What is God doing? And the answer is: God is revealing Himself. God uses difficult circumstances as the platform on which He reveals His own character and His own nature. Someone recently said that the greatest need that we have in America right now is to understand the nature and character of God. We are going to discover five of the incredible Old Testament names of God as He reveals Himself through His name and through His character.

> Now it came about after these things, that God tested Abraham, and said to him, "Abraham!" And he said, "Here I am." And He said, "Take now your son, your only son, whom you love, Isaac, and go to the land of Moriah; and offer him there as a burnt offering on one of the mountains of which I will tell you." So Abraham rose early in the morning and saddled his donkey, and took two of his young men with him and Isaac his son (Gen. 22:1–3).

Isn't that the most incredible statement you have ever read? How brief it is! It doesn't even seem to catch our attention, but if we read it with the eyes of our hearts, it begins not only to catch our attention but to catch our hearts. Here is a man who had been struggling to have a son of his own. That was emotion enough, but this son is a unique son because he is the son through whom the covenant promise of God was to flow. Now all of a sudden in Abraham's old age, God has fulfilled His promise. Now it appears to the outward eye that God has reneged, that He is demanding that Abraham take his son and kill him.

Well, I want us to understand this, so I want us to go all the way back to Genesis 12. We are going to take a journey.

I. The Call to Obedience

Step 1 is what I call "The Step of the Call to Obedience." I want you to underline the phrase "after these things" in your mind. What had occurred to bring Abraham to this point and time? Many of you are like me, saying, "I don't know if I could do that, even if God were to command it. I know who God is, but I am not sure I could do that. I'm not sure I could place the most precious thing I have on that altar before God." So we ask the question: How did Abraham get there? The answer is through these steps of general prodding through circumstances.

> Now the LORD said to Abram, "Go forth from your country, and from your relatives and from your father's house, to the land which I will show you; and I will make you a great nation, and I will bless you, and make your name great; and so you shall be a blessing; and I will bless those who bless you, and the one who curses you I will curse. And in you all the families of the earth shall be blessed" (Gen. 12:1–3).

Here is an incredible moment in time. Abram is being called on a journey. It is a journey to leave the familiar and to follow God. It's pretty simple. There is actually in this command no hint as to where he is going. Have you ever thought of that? Here Abraham is in his father's homeland. He is with all the things that are familiar to him. And God said, "I want you to go to a place that I'm going to show you. And when I do, I am going to bless you and make you a blessing to all the nations of the earth." In a sense this is the beginning of the Great Commission. But Abram had nothing to go on except God's Word. He demonstrated absolute faith in God's Word.

Today God is taking our nation into some unfamiliar territory. There are all sorts of fears about what may happen. But I want you to know that in spite of those fears, God is sovereignly controlling the universe. No matter where God moves us, no matter what the circumstances we face, God is in control, and He is going to use those circumstances to conform His children to His image.

II. The Lesson of Dependence

Now, let's move down a couple of chapters, and we will pick up step 2 in chapter 14 of Genesis. Remember that Abraham had a nephew, Lot, traveling with him. Abraham and Lot are moving together. Their crops, their people are together. Their flocks are together. And Lot, being a little young and impetuous, sees a land that he thinks looks fertile. It was not the way God had directed, but so many times we are like Lot. We see with our eyes that something looks appealing. It looks like greener grass is on the other side. And all of a sudden, we begin to move ahead of God, and we move apart from Him.

And Lot says to his uncle Abram, "Listen, I am going to take all of my possessions, and I am going this direction." Now, you remember where he ends up. He ends up in Sodom and Gomorrah. Anytime you quit following God, no matter how difficult it is to follow Him, the other way is worse. No matter where it is. I tell my students when they are struggling with where God may call them that the safest place in the world is in the will of God. We have a daughter right now in Southeast Asia, in a dangerous part of the country, a dangerous part of the world. I always told her that, and she told me, "Anywhere in the will of God is safer than anywhere else out of the will of God."

Lot doesn't understand that. He looks with his eyes. He looks with the flesh, and he concludes that there is fertile land and he should take his people and go that way. But Abram continues to follow God. Now Lot gets into trouble there because, in the midst of all this, there is a rebellion taking place against the king in that area by the name of Chedorlaomer.

Now look at verse 8: "The king of Sodom and the king of Gomorrah and the king of Admah and the king of Zeboiim and the king of Bela (that is, Zoar) came out; and they arrayed for battle against them in the valley of Siddim" (Gen. 14:8). In other words, these five small kings were paying taxes to Chedorlaomer, and they determined that they had had enough. They decide to rebel. Now we probably never would have heard anything about this story had it not been for one key issue. We find this in verse 12: "And they also took Lot, Abram's nephew, and his possessions and departed, for he was living in Sodom."

So when this rebellion takes place, Lot and all of his people are taken into captivity, and uncle Abram has to come to the rescue. We find that whole story beginning in verse 14:

When Abram heard that his relative had been taken captive, he led out his trained men, born in his house, three hundred and eighteen, and went in pursuit as far as Dan. And he divided his forces against them by night, he and his servants, and defeated them, and pursued them as far as Hobah, which is north of Damascus. And he brought back all the goods, and also brought back his relative Lot with his possessions, and also the women, and the people (Gen. 14:14–16).

What occurs now is fascinating. When Abram returns victorious from this battle, two kings come out to meet him—the king of Sodom, who is a defeated, deposed king, and the king of Salem, Melchizedek. This name Melchizedek ought to strike a little attention because we find him also pictured in the New Testament, almost as a prefiguring of the Lord Jesus Christ. He is the king of Salem, the king of peace. He is the priest of El Elyon. Now watch what happens in verse 17.

Then after his [Abraham's] return from the defeat of Chedorlaomer and the kings who were with him, the king of Sodom went out to meet him at the valley of Shaveh (that is, the King's Valley). And Melchizedek king of Salem brought out bread and wine; now he was a priest of God Most High. And he blessed him and said, "Blessed be Abram of God Most High, possessor of heaven and earth; and blessed be God Most High, who has delivered your enemies into your hand!" And [Abram] gave him a tenth of all. And the king of Sodom said to Abram, "Give the people to me and take the goods for yourself." And Abram said to the king of Sodom, "I have sworn to the LORD God Most High" (Gen. 14:17–22).

That name is El Elyon. It means "possessor of the heavens and the earth." Abram would not take a thread or a sandal thong, or anything because the king might say, "I have made Abram rich."

In this name God is saying something to Abram. This name *El Elyon* is often used when we find Israel among pagan nations. There is a declaration here that God, the sovereign God of the universe, is the possessor of the heavens and earth. It doesn't matter where He is; He is still in control. During that time there was the idea that God was localized. Everywhere one went across the valley, there was another god of this people, and there was another god in this territory. The assumption may have been that now that they are down in Sodom and Gomorrah, other gods are in control.

But God says, "I want you to understand something through this prophet, through this priest, this king of Salem, Melchizedek. I want you to understand something about My nature you may not have understood. I possess the heavens and the earth. I created them. They are mine. Every resource is mine."

Notice what the two kings do. One wants to make a deal. Now the one wanting to make a deal has nothing to deal with. Sodom has been defeated. And the king comes out almost whining and says, "You just keep all the gold and all the silver, and all the spoils of war. All I ask from you is my people." He had no right to ask anything.

Listen carefully to me. Satan is a defeated adversary. He was defeated on the cross and Calvary. Now he has nothing to bargain with, yet he still tries to bargain every day. The only way he can do anything is through deception. He is the author of lies. That is all he can do. He will lie to you about what he can provide. He can provide nothing. He possesses nothing. He is defeated. He was absolutely defeated on the cross. The only way he can deal with you is through deceit, deception, and lying.

Abram is incredible here. He said, "I don't want anything you have. I don't even want a piece of thong for a sandal. We have been marching, and some of our shoestrings are worn out. I am not going to take anything from you because you might say I made Abram great." That is one of the reasons that we function by grace only. If any one of us ever claims we could do something for God on our own, we would do it and claim that we have made God great.

The other king is also fascinating. Melchizedek, king of Salem, comes out with an offering for Abram. He comes out bringing wine and bread. He comes out to give him sustenance as he returns from this fierce battle. By the way, Abram immediately gives him a tithe of everything he had. I have heard people say, "I don't tithe because that's a principle of the law, and I am under grace." Notice that the law has not yet been given. Tithing is the response of grace to the fact that God is the possessor of the heavens and the earth. In fact, if we have been released from the law through grace, then we ought to do more than the law asks, not less. That is what Jesus always taught!

Abram comes to understand that God possesses everything. There is a lesson of dependence here. There has been, first of all, this step of obedience. Now Abram learns the lesson of dependence. In your own spiritual life through the circumstances God has brought into your life, have you made this first step of obedience? Now, will you move further to depend on Him? "I refuse to take even a shoe-string from the adversary. I will not take anything in his hand because he may say that he made me great."

III. The Need to Surrender

Step 3, the need to surrender, occurs in chapter 15. Did you notice the phrase I told you to look for?

After these things the word of the LORD came to Abram
in a vision, saying, "Do not fear, Abram, I am a shield to
you; your reward shall be very great." And Abram said,
"O Lord GOD, what wilt Thou give me, since I am childless,
and the heir of my house is Eliezer of Damascus?" And
Abram said, "Since Thou hast given no offspring to me, one
born in my house is my heir." Then behold, the word of the
LORD came to him, saying, "This man will not be your heir;
but one who shall come forth from your own body, he shall
be your heir." And He took him outside and said, "Now
look toward the heavens, and count the stars, if you are able

to count them." And He said to him, "So shall your descendants be." Then he believed in the LORD; and He reckoned it to him as righteousness" (Gen. 15:1–6).

The name *Lord* translates the Hebrew word *Adonai*. In fact, there are two names here. One is Yahweh. This is the one we get the English word *Jehovah* from. Abram declares, "Yahweh is my Adonai." Now you may remember that the name *Yahweh* came later at the Exodus. It had already been mentioned, but it appears again in its most significant time when Moses is at the burning bush (Exod. 3). There the Lord reveals the fact that He knows the plight of His people. He has heard their cries. Some of us may have been asking since 9/11, Does God know what's happening? Does He hear our cries? Does He care? And God said to Moses, "I have heard. I know. I do care. And I'm coming to deliver."

Moses, of course, wants to debate how God is going to do this. God said, "I will tell you how I am going to do it. I am going to use you." Moses still wants to debate. He says, "But I'm not very qualified to do this kind of deliverance." He finally asked God one question. He said, "If I go, what shall I tell them your name is?" God said, "I'm glad you asked Me because My name is 'I am!'" This is imperfect in the Hebrew. So let me translate. God said, "I am who I have been, and I will continue to be." He reveals an action that began in the past. It is still going on in the present. It will not change in the future. In other words, all the way back, God revealed that He is unchanging. By His very nature, He is the same yesterday, today, and forever. He alone is the eternal covenant God. *I am!*

Now Abram declares that the "I am" is his Lord. In this "Lord" there is both a cry of doubt and surrender because Abram says, "I don't have an heir yet." All of this covenant promise was based on his children. There is the doubt, but there is the surrender because Genesis 15:6 says, "He believed in the LORD; and He reckoned it to him as righteousness." Have you come to the point of absolute surrender?

I have been asked by many people, "What do you think the issue of lordship means?" I want to give you a definition. It is real simple.

When you come to the issue of lordship, you place revelation over reason. That's as simple a definition as I can give you. You come to the place where the issue in your life is, What does the Word say? What has God said? Now that's a struggle for many people because they may find themselves in a difficult marital situation. We would like to do something, but it's contrary to the Word of God, and so we have to deal with this question: Do I believe revelation or do I believe my reason? Do I follow my reason or my emotion?

We can deal with an issue as simple as stewardship to illustrate. You look at the budget, and you look at the month, and you have more month left than you have money. Now you know what God says about stewardship. And you can conclude rationally and reasonably that you are not able to tithe. But the Word of God says you must do it.

I remember when my daughter Rachel was away in college. She was in one of her early classes in personal finance. The professor gave them a salary figure, and they had to write out a budget. In her budget she put her tithe. Her college professor marked it wrong. I hate to tell you it was a Baptist school, but she marked it wrong. And so Rachel came back to the professor and said, "Excuse me, my dad has always told me that the Word of God says we must do this."

The professor replied, "Honey, you can't balance your budget with it."

Rachel said, "Look, I did balance it."

The professor said, "Well, you can't eat on that much."

Rachel said, "This is what God says." And then she looked at the teacher and said, "My dad has always told me that 90 percent with God is more than 100 percent without Him." How did she know that? Because of revelation, not because of reason.

A rational person can't believe that. That was the greatest struggle Nicodemus had. Nicodemus was a rational man. He could not believe a revelation. Some of you are struggling with all of this. You are trying to find some hope in the church, but you are not sure yet because you are just like Nicodemus. When he came to

Jesus, Jesus said, "I am going to solve all of this problem for you. All you have to do is be born again."

Nicodemus, being a rational, reasonable man, said, "That's not possible. I can't get back in my mother's womb."

Jesus said, "No, Nicodemus, you must be born of water and the Spirit. You had a physical birth. You need a spiritual birth."

Some of you are struggling with that step of faith. It really is an issue of lordship because lordship and redemption are tied together. They are not separate parts.

I want to say a word to you Christians. You can't say, "No, Lord," in the same breath. It is not an option. When you come to the issue of lordship, you can't say, "Well, I'll go if . . ." or, "I'll go when . . ." or, "I'll go but. . . ." There is no "but." There is no "if." There is no "when." There is "Yes, Lord." If you do not know Christ as Savior and Lord, then the first step is to say, "I don't understand how from God's vantage point He can take an old sinner like me, change his heart, give him a new future. But by the Word of God, I'm going to believe it this morning, and by faith I'm going to appropriate that in my life."

We still have a little way to go to step 4 because we do have a few "glitches" going on. First of all, even though Abram had made this kind of faith step, he still struggled. All of us Christians do, don't we? You may be thinking, "I would love to do that, but I don't know if I could live up to it." I am going to promise you that you can't, but God can through you. In essence, Abram said, "OK, God, I know You have got a big promise here, and I want to help You because I am going to adopt Eliezer."

Now Sarai gets into the story here because she did not believe she could have a child. She decided to send in Hagar, a young handmaiden, to Abram so he could have a son by her. By the way, the conflict between Jews and Arabs is the result of this sin. You see, man's sin always creates catastrophe on earth. God is the sovereign God of the universe. He does not need our help. He only wants our participation.

IV. The Move to Full Reliance

Now we go to step 4, the move to full reliance. Let's read this incredible story. Turn over to chapter 17 of Genesis:

When Abram was ninety-nine years old, the LORD appeared to Abram, and said to him, "I am God Almighty; walk before Me, and be blameless. And I will establish My covenant between Me and you, and I will multiply you exceedingly." And Abram fell on his face, and God talked with him, saying, "As for Me, behold, My covenant is with you, and you shall be the father of a multitude of nations. No longer shall your name be called Abram, but your name shall be Abraham; for I will make you the father of a multitude of nations. And I will make you exceedingly fruitful" (Gen. 17:1–6).

The name *El Shaddai* (God Almighty) is interesting. It comes from a Hebrew root *Shad,* which translates "breast." That's a rather curious translation, isn't it? And then you wonder what the point of it is. Well, most of the deities in those territories in those days were goddesses, fertility goddesses. Most of the religions were fertility religions. If you have ever been to museums, you may have seen these goddesses with multiple breasts literally surrounding their whole body.

And there was this idea of the rising and dying cycle of fertility. God said, "By the way, if you want to know who I am, I am El Shaddai," God Almighty to nourish. Now a young twenty-one-year-old girl may get pregnant, and it has nothing to do with a fertility goddess. But I want to tell you something: no fertility goddess can put a child in a ninety-year-old barren womb. And no fertility goddess can put a child in a virgin's womb. Only El Shaddai can do that.

God majors on the impossible, not the probable. This is an impossible story. This is impossible by every calculation in every nation at every time. Sarai is beyond the age of bearing children. And God said that He would do something bigger than anyone could imagine. I don't know if you noticed it, but God changed Abram's name. Names are critical in the Old Testament. The psalmist says in Psalm 9:10, "Those who know Thy name will put their trust in Thee." And here is a revelation of that name, and God changes Abram's name.

Abram's name meant "exalted father." Abram had spent the entirety of his life being in reproach because of his own name. Every time he met someone in the marketplace, they would say, "Hi, I'm Ken. What is your name?"

Abram would reply, "Well, I am exalted dad."

"Oh, really, got any pictures of your kids?"

"Well, the truth of the matter is, I don't have any kids."

"Oh yeah, exalted daddy, big deal, no kids."

It was scorn to Abram, literally every time he had to use his name; it was a disgrace to him. So God said, "I am going to change your name. Your first name wasn't big enough to really get the idea of what I am going to do because I am going to make you a father of a multitude of nations."

Abram was ninety-nine years old. Did God do what He promised? Absolutely. God's promises are absolute. And so we begin to understand this move to full reliance, and now we are going to take the last step here in Genesis 22.

V. A Step of Faith

Now we understand why Abraham is prepared to listen to God. In all these circumstances God wastes nothing. I remember several years back when seven young people were gunned down at a church about one and one-half miles from our campus. Those who were shot included three of our precious students who were there to rally at the flag. I remember as we had that memorial service in TCU Stadium that a young priest came to pray as a part of that community prayer. I'll never forget what he said. He stepped to the microphone and in a short prayer he said, "Thank You, Lord, that you waste nothing." A lot of commentators were talking about "what a waste of life." He said, "God wastes nothing."

I want you to understand something. Circumstances are not a waste to God. He does not cause evil circumstances, but He takes the circumstances and conforms His people to His image. Isn't that what He said in Romans 8? That those whom He loves He conforms to the image of His Son. In everything God is at work.

So He has been at work in Abram's life, and he comes now to this final hurdle—this last dash to the finish line. And he says, "After these things." The drama in this story is unparalleled. "On the third day Abraham raised his eyes." He saw the place from a distance. Can you imagine how his heart is palpitating? He has been traveling for three days with his son and his servants. Abram said to them, "Stay here with the donkey, and I and the lad will go yonder; and we will worship and return to you." I want you to notice, first of all, the faith statement found in verse 5. Isn't that incredible? He tells the men to stay put. "The boy and I are going to worship. We are going to come back."

The book of Hebrews tells us that Abraham dared to believe that God could raise Isaac from the dead. Nobody had ever said anything about someone being raised from the dead. Jesus hadn't been raised. On this side of the cross, it's easy to understand this statement. On this side of Calvary, on this side of the resurrection, we know that there are firstfruits. There was One who has been raised from the dead. Abraham did not have that knowledge. He had only the promise of God that this was the son of the covenant. So he concluded that if God gave him this son of the covenant and then took him back, God would raise him up. That's what Abraham believed. This is an incredible statement of faith.

I want you to watch this because in Genesis 22:6–8 we get a little picture frame: "So the two of them walked on together." It appears first in verse 6 and is repeated in verse 8, which means that the Holy Spirit is trying to draw our attention to it, and there is a dialogue here you cannot miss: "Abraham took the wood of the burnt offering and laid it on Isaac his son, and he took in his hand the fire and the knife. So the two of them walked on together" (v. 6).

Wouldn't you have loved to have been there? We get only a glimpse of what was being said. Isaac spoke to Abraham, his father. He said, "Dad."

Abraham answered, "Here I am, my son."

He said to him, "Behold, I see the fire and the wood. Where is the lamb for the burnt offering?"

And Abraham said, "God will provide for Himself the lamb for the burnt offering, my son."

The result is that the two of them walked on together. Here is this incredible statement, this revelation moment. I reminded you a while ago that lordship requires revelation not reason. Now Abraham is moving by revelation not by reason. This does not sound like a reasonable request. It doesn't sound like a reasonable request when you understand that this is the child of the covenant and that Abraham is elderly. He probably could not have another child. It appears to him that this is God's last hope. What does Abraham say? "The Lord sees."

Now go back to verse 8 because it is the Hebrew word *Jireh* which means "to see." His answer is not exactly the way it's translated in English. His answer is: "God's watching." God sees this. God's eye is on us. God is omniscient. That means He knows everything. He knows even the future at this moment.

Now, do you know the rest of the story? Here we find faith in action. They came to the place where God had told him to go. Abraham built the altar there, arranged the wood, bound his son Isaac, and laid him on the altar on top of the wood. Abraham stretched out his hand and took the knife to kill his son. Any doubt what is going to happen here? There is no doubt that Abraham is going to be obedient to the Lord.

But the angel of the LORD called to him from heaven, and said, "Abraham, Abraham!" And he said, "Here I am."
And he said, "Do not stretch out your hand against the lad, and do nothing to him; for now I know that you fear God, since you have not withheld your son, your only son, from Me." Then Abraham raised his eyes and looked, and behold,

behind him a ram caught in the thicket by his horns; and Abraham went and took the ram, and offered him up for a burnt offering in the place of his son. And Abraham called the name of that place The LORD Will Provide [Jehovah Jireh], as it is said to this day, "In the mount of the LORD it will be provided" (Gen. 22:11–14).

Now what we don't always see in the text is this: The ram was already in place. God didn't ship this animal down from heaven. He didn't beam it down like they do on *Star Trek*. The lamb was already there. The difference was that Abram could not see the lamb until he took the final step of faith.

Let me give you a statement here. God's pre-vision always dictates His pro-vision. You ought to write that one down. It's worth it. God's pre-vision dictates His pro-vision. The Lord saw beforehand that Abraham would need a sacrifice in place of his son, and the ram was already in the thicket. Do you understand where I'm going? Before the foundation of the world, God knew that all of us Abrahams in our sinfulness would need a sacrifice for our sins. He knew that man created in His image, given free will, would fall and descend and desecrate the image of God in his own life, and that there would have to be a sacrifice, One to pay the penalty of our sin. And God's pre-vision led to His pro-vision.

Do you understand what I am saying? God's Son was sacrificed in the heart of God before the foundation of the world. Isn't that an incredible concept? God loved us so much that even before He took the risk of creating us, knowing that we would fall into sin, He sent His Son, tangled Him in a bush on Calvary, and the Lamb was provided.

I don't know where you are in your walk with God today, but if you have never taken that first step to surrender, I want to tell you something: God has provided the Lamb. You have to come to the point of understanding this sacrifice, this place of beginning, to accept revelation over reason. If you are still struggling like Nicodemus was and saying, "I can't get back into my mother's womb," don't worry about it. God has already provided the way through His Son for you to be born again.

But now I want to say a word to us believers because there is a message in this. Have you come to the point where you trust God enough to put your Isaac on the altar? Your Isaac may be your notion of success. It may be your idea of security. Some of us right now are nearing retirement or are at retirement and are wondering about whether there is any security in the financial markets. There isn't. The only security is in the Lord. Have you come to the point where you trust Him with your life? Have you come to the point where you trust Him with your family, with your children, with the stewardship of your life?

I was with a group at Ridgecrest, and there was a young lady there. She was vibrant, excited, and open because she was headed to seminary and to the mission field. Following behind her was her mother with her shoulders all slumped over saying, "I just can't give her up." I said to her, "You don't have her until you give her up. Listen, if she is in the will of God, she'll be safer there than she will with you." Give her up. Put her there.

Abraham had to come to the point where the most precious thing could be sacrificed. Think about this man who had been traveling this journey. Finally God gives him a son in his old age out of his own loins. And it's not just a son whom he loves like a dad would a son, but it's a covenant son of promise on which the hope of Israel and the world resides. And God said to give him up. And Abraham said, "Yes, Sir."

How is it in your life today? Are you going to move "after these things"? If you are going to take that "after these things" step, where is God speaking to you? For some of you, it may be a call to service in the life of this church. It may be a call to stewardship. It may be a call to witnessing, as you realize that people around you are open to a witness. But you have never actively shared your faith. For some of you, it may be a decision regarding church membership. God may be calling some of you into full-time Christian ministry. You may say, "I'm too old." Listen. Abraham was ninety-nine. Are you dealing with reason, or are you dealing with revelation? If God is calling you, I promise you that you are not too old.

If God is calling you, I promise you He will provide the security. God has never failed a single person who has been obedient to follow Him. What is your Isaac? Will you place him on the altar to discover that Jehovah Jireh is the Lord who provides?

48

Chained to the Chariot

2 CORINTHIANS 2

Ronald Dunn (1936–2001)
President, LifeStyle Ministries
Pastor and Minister-at-Large, MacArthur Boulevard
Baptist Church, Irving, Texas, and a popular Bible conference
preacher and evangelist

HAS IT EVER BOTHERED YOU that there seems to be a great discrepancy between what the Bible says believers are and what we really are in our daily living? You read all of those great things in the New Testament about those of us who are in Christ. But when you turn to observe the lives of believers, you have to shake your head and say, "Well, I see the picture in the Bible of what you ought to be, but you don't look a thing like your picture."

Is this just a glamour photo that God has made, where we're specially made over and made up so that we're not presented as we really are? Or is it something else? For instance, here's one picture the Bible gives of a believer. In Romans 8 Paul talks about all the terrible things that can happen to a person—all the fears and terrors that we face in life. He declares, "In all these things we are *more than conquerors* through him who loved us" (Rom. 8:37). That's the only time the words "more than conquerors" appear in the New Testament. It means we are *supraconquerors*. We not only conquer, but we conquer by an overwhelming margin. And this isn't just a promise; this is a statement of fact. Paul said, "We are more than conquerors through Him who loved us." Simply because Christ loved us and we know Christ, we win by an overwhelming margin.

I suppose every Christian believes we're going to win eventually. But they also think it's going to be close. They think the margin of victory will be narrow—that we're barely going to squeak by. In the last three seconds, they surmise, the Christians are going to kick a field goal and beat the devil 17 to 14. We're going to win, but it's going to be by a slim, narrow victory.

That's not what the Bible says. The Bible says we don't win by a narrow margin; we win by an overwhelming margin! We are *supra-conquerors* through Him who loved us! Well, I see the description in the Bible of what you're supposed to look like, but you don't look a thing like your picture!

In John 4, Jesus was talking to the woman at the well. And He said, "Whoever drinks of the water that you have will thirst again. But whoever drinks of the water that I give him shall *not never* [notice the double negative] thirst again" (John 4:13–14). In other words, Jesus said that whoever took a drink of the eternal life that He offered would never thirst again.

And yet, everywhere I go I find Christians who are thirsting and living lives that are filled with emptiness. I see in the Bible what you're supposed to be but you don't look a thing like the picture.

The apostle John declared, "This is the victory that overcomes the world, even our faith" (1 John 5:4). I used to read that, and I would think, *That's why I'm not overcoming the world. I don't have enough faith. If I just had more faith, I could overcome the world.* But then I realized that that's not what John is talking about. John goes on to say, "Who is victor over the world but he who believes that Jesus is the Son of God?" (1 John 5:5 NEB). It's not how much faith you have. It's the kind of faith you have. It's faith centered on Jesus Christ.

Now if I were to ask how many of you believe that Jesus is the Son of God, I'm confident we'd get 100 percent affirmation. But the positive response would be much lower if I were to ask, "How many of you have overcome the world?"

I believe the reason we do not look like our photograph is that we are either ignorant of a certain truth, or knowing it, we have failed to obey it. Let's take a close look at 2 Corinthians 2:12–17.

Beginning in 2 Corinthians 2:12 and continuing all the way through verse 11 of chapter 6, Paul diverts from his main thought and defends and describes his apostleship. Some people were casting doubt upon his authenticity as an apostle. What we're about to read is an introduction to that entire section. So Paul said:

"Now when I went to Troas to preach the gospel of Christ and found that the Lord had opened a door for me, I still had no peace of mind, because I did not find my brother Titus there. So I said good-by to them and went on to Macedonia.

But thanks be to God, who always leads us in triumphal procession in Christ and through us spreads everywhere the fragrance of the knowledge of him. For we are to God the aroma of Christ among those who are being saved and those who are perishing. To the one we are the smell of death; to the other, the fragrance of life. And who is equal to such a task? Unlike so many, we do not peddle the Word of God for profit. On the contrary. on Christ we speak before God with sincerity, like men sent from God" (2 Cor. 2:12–17).

I want to call your attention to the first part of verse 14: "But thanks be to God, who always leads us in triumphal procession in Christ." In this statement Paul gives us the truth, the principle, the key, the secret to living the victorious life that God has presented for us in the Bible.

The apostle does this in other places, of course, but here he does it in a special way. Notice the phrase "thanks be to God, who always leads us in triumphal procession in Christ." Those words "always leads us in triumphal procession" are the translation of one Greek word. This was a technical term for a custom that was common among the Roman armies of that day. When Paul wrote these words to the Corinthians and they saw that word, they immediately knew what it was. They got the picture, they got the application, and they got the message.

But today, we are so far removed from Paul's time that we miss what Paul is saying here. "Triumphant procession" refers to a custom that was common among the Roman armies. As soon as the soldiers had won the victory, they dispatched a herald who would run all the way back to the city of Rome. He would run through the streets of the city, announcing that the victory had been won. The word *preach* comes from that word *herald,* and that's what preaching is. It is going ahead of our conquering hero and announcing to everybody that the victory has been won.

When the people of the city heard the news, they began to make preparation for what they called a *triumphant processional.* It was a magnificent victory celebration. A particular type of incense was burned in the temples for those occasions. And that's why Paul refers to the perfume, or the fragrance. If you had been a citizen of Rome in those days, and you had stepped out of your house one morning and breathed the air and smelled that particular incense, you would have said, "Hey, we're going to have a party! We're going to have a celebration. There's going to be a parade!"

When a commanding general—the conquering hero—returned to Rome, the people would line the streets, waiting for the appearance of their hero. The procession would be led by a priest swinging censors, burning that special incense. He would be followed by musicians and others. The main figure in that drama was the commanding general, the victorious military leader. He would be riding in a gold-plated chariot drawn by white horses. Right behind that chariot were the officers of the defeated army who were chained to that chariot. These men would later be executed, so they were being dragged to their death. The enemy soldiers who had been captured would be brought in later, and they would be enslaved.

When the people saw their hero in that chariot, they would cheer and shout. They would throw garlands and confetti into the air. But when they saw the officers of that defeated army chained to that chariot and being dragged along behind, they would really go wild.

This was a demonstration of the power of their hero. Paul was referring to that custom when he said, "Thanks be to God, who always leads us in his triumphant procession." In other words, Paul was *Christianizing* that custom. He was saying there was a time when he was at war with Jesus Christ. There were hostilities between God and Paul. But the Lord Jesus had conquered him, and he had yielded to Him in unconditional surrender. And He had put Paul in the chains of His lordship, and he was chained to His chariot. And everywhere Paul went, Christ led him in His triumphant procession.

The New English Bible really brings it out well by saying, "Thanks be to God, who continually leads us about, captives in Christ's triumphant procession." Paul was saying, "I came to Jesus Christ. He overcame me, and I yielded to Him in unconditional surrender. He placed my hands in the chains of His lordship and chained me to His chariot. And now thanks be to God, everywhere I go and in every place I am being led in His triumphant procession."

Paul was wanting everybody to know this before he detailed his apostleship, because when you get over to chapter 4 of 2 Corinthians, he will speak about some bad things happening to him. He is saying in anticipation, "Now I'm going to tell you some things that some of you are going to think reveals failure and defeat. But I want you to know at the outset, thanks be to God. He always leads me in His triumph in Christ, and wherever I go, it may look like defeat to you; it may look like failure to you. But I'm chained to His chariot, and that means that everywhere I go, I am following in his own triumphant victory in Christ!"

Paul, how is it that you can say everywhere you go there's victory? "Because I've been conquered by Jesus Christ. I'm chained to His chariot, and I'm simply following along in the wake of His victory." Here is the principle, the secret. If you want to be a conqueror, you must first be conquered. If you want to be an overcomer, you must first be overcome. If you want to be a master, you must first be mastered. If you want to exercise authority, you must first submit to authority.

I was preaching in Florida a few years ago, and a man got to talking about my sermon. He said, "Preacher, that was a good sermon." I thanked him and told him I was glad he enjoyed it. But he went on to say there was one thing about it he didn't like. I asked what it was. "I didn't like that idea of being chained to the chariot," he replied. "I think if you would take that out, it would be a better sermon."

I said, "Brother, that *is* the sermon. That's the sermon right there! If I take it out, I don't have a sermon."

He said, "Well, it just seems degrading and humiliating to be chained to a chariot."

"Absolutely, Absolutely!" I replied. "I know why you don't like it. I don't like it either. None of us like it."

You know what I want to do? I want to ride up front with the Lord! I don't want to be chained back there. I want to ride up front, helping drag others along. Well, heaven knows He needs some help from time to time. Sometimes I say to Him, "Lord, why are we going so slow? Everybody else has passed us up. Can't you put the pedal to the metal on this thing?"

Other times I say, "Lord, why did You take this road? It's so bumpy, and it's got potholes in it. And we passed up a good superhighway." Sometimes I say, "Lord, I'm tired of traveling. Let's pull over at this roadside park and have a picnic." I like to help the Lord drive, don't you? That's where I want to be—up front.

But Paul says if you want to be a conqueror, you must first be conquered. And I say to you that you are only experiencing as much victory in Jesus as Jesus is experiencing in you. If there is an area of repeated failure in your life, that's a good sign there is an area of your life over which Jesus Christ is not yet Lord. If we want to be conquerors, we must first be conquered.

The best illustration I've ever seen of this occurs in the encounter of Jesus and the centurion who had a sick servant. He came to Jesus and he said, "Lord, my servant is sick."

Jesus said, "I'll come to your house and heal him."

The centurion said, "Oh, no, Lord, don't do that. I'm not worthy to have you come under my roof. Just speak the word, and my servant will live, for I also am a man under authority with soldiers under me. And I say to this one, go, and he goes. And to this one, do this, and he does it."

When Jesus heard that, he marveled and said, "I have never seen such great faith, not even in all of Israel" (see Matt. 8:5–10).

Now I have great respect for the Word of God. But I must confess to you that for a long time I couldn't see what was so great about what that man said. I didn't understand it. What did he say? He said, "I also am a man under authority with soldiers under me. And I say to this one, go, and he goes. And to this one, do this, and he does it."

Jesus was amazed. He said, "I have never seen such great faith." I couldn't see what that had to do with faith. But I got to thinking. *If it amazed Jesus, it ought to amaze me.* I would think it would take a lot to amaze Jesus. He was amazed twice in the Bible. Both times He expressed amazement at the faith of a Gentile. What could you show Jesus, or what could you tell Jesus that would amaze Him? He's seen it all! He made it all!

If this encounter with a Gentile amazed Jesus, it ought to do something to me. I thought to myself that I must be missing something. Let's look at their encounter again. Jesus told the centurion that He would come to his house and heal his servant. But the centurion replied, "Oh, no, Lord, don't do that. I'm not worthy to have you come under my roof. Just speak the word, and my servant will live, for I also am a man under authority." Now I would expect his next words to be, "And if I am told to go somewhere, I go somewhere, and when I am told to do something, I do something." But that's not what the centurion said.

He said, "For I also am a man under authority with soldiers under me. And I say to this one, go, and he goes. And to this one, do this, and he does it." The centurion was saying, "I live under authority; therefore, I have authority." And he did. He had authority over one hundred soldiers. That's why they called him a centurion.

As long as that centurion was submitted to the authority of the emperor, he had the emperor's authority over those one hundred soldiers. If he rebelled against the authority of the emperor, he lost his authority over those one hundred soldiers. So that was the principle by which he was living. But that's still not what amazed Jesus. What amazed Jesus was one little word that the man said. Some translations say "also." Some say "too." And unfortunately, some translations leave it out. But it belongs there.

Now listen to me as I quote it: "He came to Jesus and he said, 'Lord, my servant is sick.' Jesus said, 'I'll come to your house and heal him.' The centurion said, 'Oh, no, Lord, don't do that. I'm not worthy to have you come under my roof. Just speak the word, and my servant will live, for I also am a man under authority.'" In other words, "I don't have to run my own errands. If I want something done, I tell others to do it, and it's done for me. And Lord, I understand that You live by the same principle I live by." When he said, "I, too," or "I, also, am a man under authority," this is what amazed Jesus—that this centurion had such great insight into the truth that Jesus Himself lived by that same principle. He said, "I have never seen such faith."

But the point I want you to get is that this was the principle by which Jesus Christ lived. He lived under the authority of His Father; therefore, He had His Father's authority. That's the principle by which the centurion lived. He was under the authority of the emperor; therefore, he had the emperor's authority. That's the principle by which Paul lived. That's the principle by which we should live if we want to experience victory in the Christian life. Let's look at three brief things about this victory.

I. This Victory Is God's Victory through His Son

This victory that Paul talked about is God's victory through His Son. Paul was saying, "Thanks be to God, who always leads us in his triumphant procession in Christ." It's not we who are triumphing; it's not we who are riding in that chariot. No, He doesn't cause us to triumph. He *leads* us in His triumph. It is God's victory through His Son. I'm trying to say that the responsibility for victory in the Christian life is not mine; it is God's. I realize that many of us use the expression "win the victory." I've got to go out there and "win the victory," to overcome the devil, and win over temptation.

But I want you to know that there are no victories to be won. Christ Jesus won every victory two thousand years ago when He died for us on the cross! The truth of the matter is that every temptation you will face has already been overcome by Jesus. The responsibility for victory is not ours. It's important for us to know that, because most Christians feel, *It's up to me. So I didn't do good, I did bad yesterday, but I'm going to do better today. So I climb out of bed, grit my teeth, tense my muscles, and say, "I'm going out there and win the victory today, if it kills me!"* And it usually does! The responsibility for victory in the Christian life does not rest with us. It's not *our* victory; it is *God's* victory through Christ.

I like the story of David and Goliath in 1 Samuel 17. They must have fought funny wars back in those days. Israel was fighting the Philistines. One day David's dad said, "David, here's a sack lunch. Your brothers are at war. Take them lunch." It just seems strange to me that David just walked into the war and said to his brothers, "Here's your lunch from home."

When he got to the front lines, David saw this giant mocking Israel and Israel's God. And Israel was hiding over behind the bushes, scared to death. Little David said, "I want you to do something about that guy."

"Son," they replied, "just leave the lunch and go back home. Play your harp and write your poetry."

"Well, it's not right to let him get by with this," David said. "Why don't you do something about it?"

"You don't understand the situation. Go home. We'll handle this."

"Well, you're not handling it well, it seems to me. I'd take care of him."

"Huh! You'd what?"

"I'd take care of him."

"Go ahead and try."

They started to put Saul's armor on David. "Oh, no, I don't want Saul's armor," he cried. "It would swallow me up. I don't need anything. I've got my slingshot and five smooth stones."

They said, "Good-bye, brother. Been nice knowing you."

And remember what happened? Little David marched out to meet Goliath. He stopped and looked the giant straight in the kneecap. He said to Goliath, "The battle is the Lord's. He has delivered you into my hands."

The battle was not David's—why, of course it wasn't. He wouldn't have been there if it had been! Neither was the battle Israel's. That's why the Israelite soldiers were hiding behind the bushes. The battle was the Lord's. What I need to learn to do is stand in front of the Goliaths in my life and say to them, "The battle is the Lord's. He has delivered you into my hands." It's God's victory through His Son.

I'm a Southern Baptist, and in my denomination we have a bad habit of calling the church by the pastor's name. When I was pastor, people would say "Brother Dunn's church." Or last week I was at "Brother Ken's church!"

We know it's not the pastor's church, but you hear that so much and for so long that you begin to think maybe it is. You're the pastor, and you've got all those people out there, and they're your responsibility. And you've got to take care of them. When they hurt, you've got to heal them. And when they're angry, you've got to soothe them. And you have to make sure you have more people in attendance this Sunday than you had Sunday a year ago, or it won't look good in the statistics. And we're behind on our budget. This whole thing is mine. This is my church, and I'm responsible for it. I've got to build it, and I've got to take care of it. It's just too much. That's why in our denomination we have about a thousand ministers a year quitting the ministry. It's just too much.

Well, that's the way I felt about my church. Once I was preaching through the book of Matthew, and I came to Matthew 16 where Jesus said, "On this rock I will build my church" (Matt. 16:18). And

I saw a little word there that I had not paid much attention to before: *my*. Jesus said, "I will build *My* church."

I said, "Lord, do You mean to tell me this is Your church?"

"Yes, sir!"

"Welcome to it!"

I was never so glad to get rid of anything in all my life! A great weight was lifted from my shoulders. This is the Lord's church!

Then Jesus said, "Upon this rock *I will build* My church."

"Lord, I thought I was supposed to build it. That's been one of my problems. You mean to tell me that You will build the church? This is Your church, and You will build it?"

"Yes."

What a deal! I don't know of anything that liberated me any more as a pastor than this. Now I understand that it is not *my* responsibility to get people to walk down the aisle and join the church. It's not *my* responsibility to get the people to give. It's not *my* responsibility to build the church. This is God's responsibility. I have a responsibility, and we'll get to that in a moment. But building the church is not my responsibility! It is the Lord's church, and He does the building. I do what God tells me to do as faithfully as I know how. And the rest is up to Him. This is God's victory through His Son.

You may be thinking that I am preaching a religion of passivity. No, not at all. We do have a responsibility, a great responsibility, but I think it is essential that we understand that it is God's responsibility to give the victory and to give the growth. Let's understand that first.

II. This Victory Is Ours Through Submission

Now we come to our responsibility. This is God's victory through His Son, but it becomes mine through submission. How do I enter into this victory? By submission, by living "chained to the chariot." You may say, "Oh, is that all?" Well, if you say that, I know you've never tried it.

We have a lot of "Houdini" Christians in the church, and they can get out of those chains. My number-one responsibility is to make certain that moment by moment, day by day, I am living under His lordship, and I am living chained to His chariot. Every other responsibility I have flows from that.

A seminary student was interviewing several pastors in our area about our philosophy of ministry. One of the questions he asked me was, "What is your primary responsibility as pastor of this church?"

I said, "Me. Write it down. M-E, me!" He looked at me, and I admit it did sound like an egotistical and irresponsible answer. I said, "You want to know what my top priority is as pastor of this church?"

"Yes."

I said, "It's to me. Let me explain. My number-one priority as pastor of this church is not to the lost of this community. My number-one priority is not to the members of this church. My number-one priority is to *me*. To make certain that I am living filled with His Spirit, chained to His chariot. Because when I am filled with His Spirit and living under His lordship, then the lost of this community and the members of my church will be ministered to by the overflow of my life."

In 2 Corinthians 2, Paul makes this point clear. These men who were chained were being led to their death. And Paul put himself in that position: "Thanks be to God, who always leads [me] in his triumphant procession" (2 Cor. 2:14). Yes, but that's leading to death. And in chapter 4 he tells us what kind of death. He says, "I bear about in my body the dying of the Lord Jesus so that the life of Jesus might be made manifest through me. So then death works in me, that life may work in you" (2 Cor. 4:10, 12).

Now I want you to focus on that. I bear about in my body the dying of the Lord Jesus. Why? So the life of Jesus that dwells in me can manifest itself through my mortal flesh.

The only thing that will bless anybody is the life of Jesus. When I stand to preach to my congregation, I cannot bless anyone. I cannot minister to anyone. I may tell a few jokes and get a few laughs, and I may come up with two or three clever little thoughts, but nobody's going to break out of their chains. No hearts are going to be healed. No wounds are going to be ministered to. No lives are going to be touched. The only thing I have to offer anybody is the life of Jesus that dwells in me. And the only way that you people are going to be ministered to is if somehow the life of Jesus that is in me will manifest itself through my mortal flesh and touch your lives. That's what ministry is all about.

I must make certain that you understand. It's not the preacher. It's not me. I don't bless anybody. I don't minister to anybody. It is the life of Jesus in me. That's what people need. People don't need to hear my opinions. They don't need to hear my advice. What people need is to be touched with the life of Jesus. The life of Jesus is in me, and I must make certain that I live in such a way that His life can manifest itself through my human personality and touch others. Then people will be blessed.

Jesus said, "If any man come to me and drink, out of his innermost being shall flow rivers of living water" (John 7:37–38). I like to think of myself as the riverbed. And He supplies the river. Nobody's ever been blessed by an old, dry, crusty riverbed. No, it's the river running along it. So this victory is God's victory through His Son. It becomes mine through submission.

III. *This Victory Is Ours in Any Situation*

There are two phrases in 2 Corinthians 2:14 that I want you to notice. First, Paul said, "Thanks be to God, who *always*." At the end of that verse he said, "He manifests through us the sweet aroma of him in *every place*." So we have *always* and *every place*. Always—that's time. Every place—that's space. We are time-space creatures. Everything we do is in time and space. Here's what Paul is saying: "Thanks be to God who always, anytime, every time, all the time, leads me in His triumph in Christ. And every place, all places, any place, you name the place."

Now I don't say this lightly. I've thought about this before saying it. If we can learn how to live chained to the chariot, there is no conceivable situation in life in which God cannot give us victory. This may require us to redefine the word *victory*.

I won't say I've *learned* it; I'll say I'm *learning*. When I wake up and find myself in some trial, some difficulty, some adversity, the first thing I do is check to see if I'm "chained to the chariot." I check to see if as far as I can tell, I'm still living under His lordship. And if I am, then I can say two things about that situation. First, He led me into it. If I'm chained to His chariot, I couldn't have gotten there any other way! He led me into it.

Second, Jesus has already overcome it. Well, of course, because I'm following in the wake of His triumph. You may find this hard to believe, but when you live chained to the chariot, do you realize that you walk on conquered ground? That every time you put your foot down, you place it on territory that Jesus Christ has already conquered? He's leading you along, and you're simply following in His triumphant train!

There is no conceivable situation in life in which God cannot give us victory. When I was in college, I pastored a little country church in Oklahoma. I lived in Fort Smith, Arkansas, so I would drive down there every weekend. This church was about thirty miles over on the Oklahoma side. To get to this little church, I first took a main highway, a good highway, a big superslab. But then, after a while, I got off on a secondary road, a nice, smooth, asphalt road. After that, I got off on a road that had been acquainted at one time with asphalt, and it was pretty rough. And finally I got off on a dirt road. This dirt road wound through the foothills and mountains for about three or four miles to the church.

Three times on this dirt road I crossed a little, crystal-clear stream about an inch deep. And I didn't think anything about it. I just splashed right through it.

One Sunday morning I was driving to the church. It had been raining all week, but God had given us a beautiful sunshiny Easter Sunday. I had on a new suit and a new pair of shoes. And I was driving my 1946 Ford.

Back in those days when I drove to a preaching appointment, I would practice my sermon. I was trying to make it last forty-five minutes. I figured that if I could go for forty-five minutes in the car, when I got up before the people I could at least go for twenty-five minutes.

So I was driving along and preaching my sermon. It was coming along pretty good, as I remember. Suddenly, my car began to buck like it had hit a brick wall. Then it just stopped! I felt my feet getting wet. I looked down, and water was coming through the floorboard. Then I noticed that this little stream that was usually about an inch deep was about knee-deep. I hadn't even paid any attention to it.

There wasn't anything to do except get out of the car, take off my new shoes, roll up my pants legs, and walk the last mile and a half to the church. You may be saying, "Preacher, does this story go anywhere?" Yes. One day I came to Jesus Christ, and I surrendered my life to Him. He put me in the chains of His lordship, and He took off! And I was happy. Praise God. Hallelujah. It's fun to be a Christian! Just trust in Jesus every minute of life! Praise God!

We went along like that for a while. Then we got off that smooth highway and got on that secondary highway that wasn't quite as nice and smooth. But that doesn't bother me, man. I'm chained to His chariot. Trust in Jesus. Bless God. Hallelujah! It's fun to be a Christian! Amen! Bless God!

And after a while we got on the third road that had potholes and bumps. But it doesn't bother me! I'm chained to His chariot! Praise God! Hallelujah! Trust in Jesus all the way. It's fun being a Christian! I'm having the greatest time of my life!

Finally, we got on that dirt road. Well, that doesn't bother me either. There's just a little dust in my eyes and grit in my teeth. And right there I can sacrifice for Jesus—chained to His chariot! Bless God! Hallelujah! Praise the Lord! Amen! I'm having a wonderful time! It's fun being a Christian!

Well, after a while, I feel my feet getting wet. I look down, and I am passing over one of those little streams. The water is about toe high. Well, that doesn't bother me! Bless God! Hallelujah! Praise the Lord! Trust in Jesus all the way! Man, it's fun being a Christian!

I keep on going along, and after a while the water gets up to my knees. Doesn't bother me. I'm chained to His chariot. Praise God! Hallelujah! Bless the Lord! Amen! It's fun being a Christian!

Then the water gets up to my waist. Well . . . amen. And then the water gets up to my shoulders. Oh, Jesus! And then the water gets up to my chin. And I say, "If I don't get out of these chains, He's going to drown me!"

Do you know what victory is? Victory is staying chained to the chariot, even if the water covers your head. Victory doesn't always mean that the Lord will lead you on dry land or drain the swamp. Sometimes He will take you into water that covers your head. Victory is staying chained to that chariot, no matter how deep the water gets, no matter where the chariot leads.

I go back to what the apostle John said in his first epistle. He said, "Faith is the victory" (1 John 5:4). He didn't say, "Faith brings the victory," or, "Faith gains the victory." He said, "Faith *is* the victory."

You come into my office, and you say, "Preacher, I've got to have surgery. The doctor says there's a malignant tumor. And it doesn't look good." I ask you, "Do you still believe?" "Yes," you reply. That's victory.

Later I stand beside your bed. They've done the surgery, but all they could do was sew you back up and send you home to die. I ask again, "Do you still believe?" You reply, "Yes, I still believe." That's victory.

And then I stand beside your grave, and I turn to your wife and ask, "Do you still believe?" And she says, "Yes, I still believe." That's victory. This is God's victory through His Son. It becomes ours through submission and remains ours in any situation. And if we learn how to live chained to the chariot, there is no situation in life in which He cannot give us victory.

49

How to Finish Well

2 TIMOTHY 4:6–11 NKJV

Roger Spradlin
Senior Pastor, Valley Baptist Church
Bakersfield, California

"FOR I AM ALREADY BEING POURED OUT as a drink offering, and the time of my departure is at hand. I have fought the good fight, I have finished the race, I have kept the faith. Finally, there is laid up for me the crown of righteousness which the Lord, the righteous Judge, will give to me on that Day; and not to me only but also to all who have loved His appearing" (2 Tim. 4:6–8).

I once heard John Bisagno share in a sermon a personal illustration from his college days. That illustration became a haunting story for me. He said that, while attending Oklahoma Baptist University in order to prepare for the ministry, he met a girl there, and they were married. His father-in-law, who was also a pastor, said to him, "You'd better be careful and guard your spiritual life because, out of twenty young men like you starting out in the ministry, all but one will not make it to the end." By "not make it," he meant that some kind of moral failure, discouragement, disillusionment, or bitterness would push them out of the ministry.

Bisagno said he didn't believe that! So he wrote in the flyleaf of his Bible the names of twenty-four young men who were on fire for God, just like him. They were soul winners. The ambition of their lives was to serve God vocationally. He said that, one by one, through the years he has scratched names off the list because of failure, discouragement, or other reasons that have driven them from the ministry. He held up his Bible at the conference where I heard him speak and said, "There are only three names left on that list."

That was shocking to me, but I'm not sure that it should have been. The fact is that beginners are a dime a dozen. It's terminators who are rare. We are good at starting things. If you don't believe that, just look in your garage! Most of our garages are filled with projects that we have started but never completed. Our culture puts a premium on starting but not so much on finishing.

The sad illustration of this, culturally, is the breakdown of marriage. There is a jewelry store in Hollywood that has a sign in the front window that reads, "We rent wedding rings." That's sad, isn't it? In our Baptist life the emphasis today is nearly exclusively on the *initial* step of Christianity. We speak in terms of how many people have accepted Jesus, or how many have walked down the aisle. We present the gospel of a good start. But the truth is, not all who start well finish well.

Chapter 4 of 2 Timothy is about *finishing well*. When the apostle Paul wrote these words, he was in prison in Rome for the second time. He was not under house arrest this time. He was in a dark, dank dungeon—kind of a hole in the ground—under the sentence of death, waiting each day for his execution. He wrote to his young associate, Timothy, and sought to motivate him to persevere. He said to Timothy, in essence, "I am going to disappear from this earth. I am going to be with God. Don't you give up!"

It's as though Paul pulled out all the stops to motivate Timothy. He used every metaphor he could about serving God. He challenged Timothy to be a steward—that is, to guard the gospel as a treasure. He told him to be a soldier and fight the battle, to be an athlete who strives for victory. He compared him to a husbandman who labors in the Lord's vineyard. He reminded him to be a student who gives himself to a lifetime of study and to be a servant.

Paul motivated Timothy not only with his words but also with his life. He became retrospective as he looked back over his life and then prospective as he looked beyond death to the crown that was awaiting him. By the world's standards Paul's life had been a dismal failure. As a young man, he had thrown away the prospects of a bright future. He had jettisoned the prestige of being a renowned rabbi. He had often been beaten throughout his life. He had labored to the point of exhaustion. He had been hunted, despised, derided, ridiculed, and laughed at. Now he was cast into prison awaiting execution.

In verse 6, Paul gives two images—one of *pouring out* and one of *packing up*. He said, "For I am already being poured out as a drink offering," a reference to the libation offering where the pagans would pour wine on the animal sacrifice, or the Hebrews would pour out the drink offering alongside the sacrifice. Maybe he was referring to the violent nature of his own impending death by being beheaded. That was an awful death! The executioners would take a man who was struggling and fighting and tie him down. Then they would take a double-bladed axe and sever his head. His body, limp and trembling, would spray out blood. Maybe Paul is thinking about his own death and the literal pouring out of his life. Perhaps he is thinking about the nature of his entire life—that his whole life had been like a libation offering, poured out to God as a living sacrifice of service to Him.

Paul said, "The time of my departure is at hand." We could translate the word *time* as "season"—"the season of my departure is at hand." In the spring of his life, Paul had met Jesus on the road to Damascus. He had experienced that long summer run of ministry. Then in the fall of his life, he had been arrested and taken from court to court. Now the winter of his life is before him. He said, "The season of my *departure* is at hand." The word he used means "to loose," like unfastening the moorings of a ship. It means to cut its tethers so it is free to sail. It was a word that was used of soldiers breaking camp, as they would loosen the tent stakes. He is saying, "I am ready to be loosed. I am ready to pack up. I am being poured out." These are the valedictory words of Paul's life, the benediction of a life well lived, as he motivates Timothy.

Paul began to reminisce about his own life. It is in this reminiscing that we see the principles that enabled Paul to finish well. The spiritual landscape today is littered with the broken lives of ministers who had great talents but ruined their ministries. Maybe there is a personal word of application for us as we look at the life of Paul and how he finished.

I. In Order to Finish Well, We Need to Fight for the Faith

The first principle that enabled Paul to finish well is that he "fought for the faith." Don't misunderstand Paul's statement as egotistical. It is not braggadocio. It is not *I* have fought the good fight, or *I* have finished the race, or *I* have kept the faith. In fact, the personal pronoun is not only *not* emphatic; it's not even there! It is simply understood. Paul is not bragging. He is emphasizing the nature of the Christian life and ministry. When we look at Paul's life, we see a life of maturity. We are spiritually envious of this man who has weathered the storms. He is like spiritual leather. There is a toughness about his life. We want Paul's maturity that speaks of unspeakable joy and peace that passes understanding. We want the ability to be content in whatever state we find ourselves. We look at his ministry that is expansive and persuasive, and we want to be like Paul. We want his maturity. We want his ministry. We want the product of his life.

But this passage is not a description of the *product* of his life. He is speaking of the *process* that produced such maturity. He is saying that the nature of the Christian life is a fight. The nature of the Christian life is not an invitation to prosperity and health. It is not an invitation to a life of ease that is free from struggle and pain. He says, "It is a fight." We get our word *agony* from the word that is translated "fight." It's an athletic word. Paul says that we have to be tough to finish. There is, of course, the constant battle against the temptation of Satan. Paul is also the one who said, "That which I want to do I end up not doing; that which I don't want to do I end up doing" (Rom. 7:19). He constantly fought a battle with the flesh.

Then there is the battle against culture. All of his life he was out of step with culture. If we are to live for God, we will be out of step with the world. There will be no end to the line of people who will try to talk us out of doing what we should do.

Paul said, "I have finished the race" (2 Tim. 4:7). Paul is like a marathon runner who has run through the streets, and now he is entering the stadium for the final lap. Every muscle is being strained. His lungs are burning, but he refuses to quit.

The most enduring image, I suppose, from the Barcelona Olympics was that of the young British sprinter, Derek Redmond, who, in the midst of the race, pulled a hamstring and began to limp toward the finish line. The camera was on his face as he grimaced in pain. His father crawled over the railing onto the track and put his arms around his young son, and together they limped toward the finish line. The security guards came, but Derek's father waved them off. Together, as the world cheered, the two of them crossed the finish line.

Sometimes that's what the Christian life is about. It is not always about soaring like an eagle, or running and not being weary. Sometimes it is walking and simply not fainting. The ministry is not about how fast we run or about the size of the crowds to whom we minister. It is about *perseverance,* about enduring to the end.

Fighting the fight and running the race were Paul's illustrations for what he declared next. In verse 7, Paul says, "I have kept the faith." The word *kept* means "to guard as a sacred deposit." The faith had been entrusted to him, and he had carefully guarded it. Life had been full of voices urging him to give up the faith. There had been the bribes and threats of the old nature and the constant whispers of the world, but he had kept the faith. Paul uses "faith" in the sense of the message of the gospel or the doctrine that had been entrusted to him.

If Paul had not "kept the faith," maybe there would be no faith for us to keep. We are only one generation away from the faith becoming extinct. That's why we are to guard it like a treasure. It's as though we are in this long relay race, and the baton has now been handed to us. We hold it in our hands as a sacred treasure that we are to guard, and we are to be careful that it is still intact as we hand it on to the next generation.

That's why we need to be willing to fight for the inerrancy and authority of Scripture. We are to be willing to fight for the fundamentals of the faith because the nature of the Christian life is that it is a fight or a race. Alexander McClaren said, "The Christian life is not a garden of ease, nor is it a desert devoid of joy. But it's a gymnasium—a place of struggle." We look at Paul's life, and we like the *product* of his life, but we are not so sure that we welcome the *process* of sanctification that was in Paul's life.

I have often visited the giant sequoia redwood trees located about seventy miles north of where I live. I can't even begin to describe how large they are. It's an amazing experience to stand at the foot of one of these massive trees, look up, and realize that it has been growing for hundreds of years! If God wants to grow a giant sequoia tree, it takes hundreds of years. If He wants to grow a daisy or a pansy, it takes just a few days. The problem is that we are content to be "daisy" or "pansy" Christians rather than being spiritual giants. We want the *product* of spiritual maturity, but we don't want the *process* that produces that maturity within our lives. Paul describes the process that produces maturity as being a fight and a race!

II. In Order to Finish Well, We Need to Focus on the Future

Paul speaks of focusing on the future as the motivation of the Christian life in verse 8. He said, "Finally, there is laid up for me the crown of righteousness which the Lord, the righteous Judge, will give to me on that Day." The word *crown* does not refer to the emblem of a king but rather to the emblem of a victor. It is the laurel wreath that was to be placed upon the head of those who won the race. It was the most prized possession in the ancient athletic world. As the runners ran the marathon, they would run through the streets and then enter the coliseum for the final laps. The crown was always placed in a prominent place so the runners could see it. If it was a sprint, it was at the end of the race. If it was a marathon, it was high up so as they entered the stadium they could see the crown before them. Paul is like a runner whose legs are aching, his side is splitting, and his lungs are burning. But he thought, *I will not quit because the motivation of service to God is yet ahead in the future. There is a crown laid up for me.*

As good as the Christian life is, as profitable as it is to serve God, the motivation that we have at the end of the race ultimately is the Lord Jesus and the crown He has reserved for us. The crown was not placed at mile fifteen or at mile twenty. The crown was at the *end* of the race. Paul tells Timothy, "I see the tape. I see the finish line, and there is a crown waiting for me." He is motivating Timothy by saying, "Don't get bogged down in the fight and the hassle of the race. The reward is at the end."

III. *In Order to Finish Well, We Need the Fellowship of Friends*

Not only did Paul focus on the future, but he also maintained a fellowship of friends. He said, "This crown is to be given not to me only but also to all who have loved His appearing (v. 8). Immediately he begins to think about his companions. He says to Timothy, "Be diligent to come to me quickly; for Demas has forsaken me, having loved this present world, and has departed for Thessalonica—Crescens for Galatia, Titus for Dalmatia. Only Luke is with me. Get Mark and bring him with you, for he is useful to me for ministry. And Tychicus I have sent to Ephesus" (vv. 9–12).

The word translated *come* that Paul uses, means "come with velocity." It's a picture of a lonely old man in prison that desires the fellowship of his friends. You will not likely finish well *alone*. When we look at Paul's life, we see that there was always an entourage of people around him. There were the "Timothys" in whom he was investing, but they were investing back. There was a kind of mutual accountability.

God has designed us so that we are to serve Him in concert and coordination with one another. We need one another. We are too weak to go it alone. There are those who want to be "Lone Ranger Christians." They want to serve God alone. They don't want to let anyone into their lives because they have been hurt or wounded. The fact is that the church is filled with people with imperfections and even leaders sometimes who are weak and immature, not to mention those whose lifestyles betray their confession.

In spite of the differences, in spite of the irritations, the imperfections and the hurts, we will not make it to the end alone. All of us need the fellowship of kindred spirits. We need to be open and honest with others. We need other people to hold us accountable.

IV. In Order to Finish Well, We Need to Forget the Failures of Others

One last principle in Paul's life that enabled him to finish well is that he *forgot* the failures of others. "Only Luke is with me. Get Mark and bring him with you, for he is useful to me for ministry" (v. 11). We know the story of Mark on that first missionary journey. When Paul and Barnabas started out from Antioch with the call of God in their hearts and the message of the gospel on their lips, they took a young man, John Mark, with them. But along the way, John Mark quit and went home. We don't know if he was sick. We don't know what happened, but he turned back. As Paul and Barnabas planned the second missionary journey, Barnabas suggested that they take Mark with them, but Paul refused. Barnabas pleaded with Paul to give him another chance. Paul considered him a quitter, and a disagreement broke up the gospel team. Paul took Silas, and Barnabas took Mark.

As the months stretched into years, and the years into decades, we find Paul, now an old man, writing to Timothy. He said, "Get Mark and bring him with you, for he is useful to me for ministry" (v. 11). Somehow in the expanse of those years, Paul had forgotten, or at least forgiven Mark's failures.

Some people live their lives as though no slight will ever escape them. No injury is ever forgotten. They move from place to place in ministry, but tucked away within their hearts is a long list of everyone who has ever wronged them. If you want a formula for absolute misery, then try to settle every score in the ministry. Bitterness comes from unhealed wounds. Bitterness produces a critical or caustic spirit that eventually becomes a cynical spirit. It poisons your prayer life. It ruins your home life. It wrecks your ministry and destroys your spiritual life. If the nature of the Christian life is a fight, then you are going to get hurt. If it's a race, you will, at some point, be bumped in the race.

In the Los Angeles Olympics, Mary Decker was favored to win the women's eight hundred meters. As the race started, all of the commentators said that she was sure to win. As they came to the first curve, a girl from South Africa bumped Mary Decker, and she fell. As the camera focused on Mary's face, you could see the hurt of the injury of falling, and the hope of winning the race suddenly drained from her face. She sat there and cried.

It reminded me of another Olympic runner, the great Presbyterian missionary Eric Liddell. In the movie about his life, *Chariots of Fire*, he, too, was bumped during a race, and he fell. For a moment he sat on the track. Then he got up and began running in his unorthodox style with his arms flailing and his face pointed toward heaven. He ran and ran—and he not only finished the race, but he actually won. Do you know why? Because he did not stay down. The fact is, you are going to get hurt in ministry. Those in whom you invest the most will sometimes yield a paltry return. There will be people who will turn on you—those you never expected to hurt you. You will be hurt! You will be bumped! Not everyone will love you! Sometimes you have to go where the band doesn't play, but the key is to get back up!

I remember when my first child was born. I had never thought that babies were all that pretty, that is, until we had *our* first baby. We named her Charity—a little girl with blonde hair and blue eyes! She brought so much joy into our hearts. She reminded me of a doll that my sister had when she was a kid. When she was in first grade, her school had an open house. It was a time when students could take their parents to school in order to show off all the little things they were doing and to meet their teacher. I was preaching across town in a revival meeting that week. At dinner, I sat down with Charity and explained to her that I wasn't going to be able to go that night. I told her that her mom would go, and that I would love to be there more than anything, but I was going to be telling people about Jesus. She seemed to understand.

As I was preaching in the little church, toward the end of the message, a phone began ringing in the back of the church. An usher went to answer the phone. As I was extending the invitation, he stepped in the back door and waved at me, indicating the phone was for me. I finished the invitation and went to pick up the phone. A voice said, "Your little girl, Charity, has been hit by a car." I rushed to the hospital, arriving ahead of the ambulance.

The ambulance came to a halt at the emergency entrance. When the ambulance doors opened, I could clearly see an attractive woman in a black dress leaning over a child. She was well dressed, but her hair was disheveled, and there was a smudge of blood on her face. Later I found out that she had given Charity CPR. As they brought the patient out, she appeared pale. She had a tube in her mouth and an IV in her hand. She was wearing a tattered red dress. It was Charity.

She is dead, was my first thought. Then, just as quickly, I thought, *Charity is really going to be upset when she finds out that her favorite red dress was torn from the neck to the waist so CPR could be administered.*

Charity was taken to an emergency room while my wife and I were ushered into a waiting room. A young doctor entered our room with a nurse. The doctor was Asian and spoke in broken English. It was obvious that he was extremely uncomfortable with his duty. He said, "I'm sorry, but your daughter didn't make it." He droned on about doing all that they could but how nothing could be done.

Ironically, I remember feeling sorry for him. I thought how much I would hate to tell anyone such awful news. She was dead. Those words, even now, are difficult to write, and it turns my stomach to say them. The truth is often painful. This time the truth was *devastating*. There is perhaps no more wrenching word that can be said than *dead*. I cannot explain to you the pain of losing a child. It is difficult to hold the broken body of a little blonde-haired, blue-eyed girl and to close the casket on your first child.

A few days later there was a knock at my door. I opened the door and a woman was standing there—the woman who had been driving recklessly that night, the woman who had been a hit-and-run driver and who later turned herself in. She introduced herself and said to me, "Will you forgive me?" Under my breath I asked the Lord, "Give me grace." Somehow I found the strength to say, "I forgive you."

Looking back on that day, I know now that if I had not forgiven her, then someone, somewhere would have scratched my name off a list, as my life would have devolved into bitterness.

The fact is that people are going to fail you. There are going to be hurts and bruises in life. The apostle Paul forgot those things. His final day on earth came perhaps a few days after he wrote these words to young Timothy—or maybe it was weeks or months. I don't know if Mark got there. I don't know if Timothy was there. But there was a day when the soldiers came and pulled the apostle out of that hole in the ground. He probably covered his face from the sun, which he had not seen for some time. In his shackles he walked between two soldiers to the south of Rome. There was a chopping block. He said a few words to his close friends—Mark, Luke, and Timothy, or whoever was there. He was strapped down, and then a burly soldier raised the two-bladed ax above his head. Perhaps Paul, for a moment, thought he saw the glint of the sun upon the ax. Then he realized in the next moment that it was the sheen on Jesus' face when the Master said, "Well done, thou good and faithful soldier" (see Matt. 25:16).

Paul had *finished well!*

50

Why I Am a Southern Baptist

Hebrews 10:23–25 HCSB

J. T. Reed
Senior Pastor, First Baptist Church
Fair Oaks, California

WHAT I AM GOING TO SHARE with you is not an exposition of Scripture but a personal testimony and an account of history. It is scriptural, biblical, very much based on the Word.

I want to tell you three things about myself. First, I am by commitment a Christian. I am by conviction a Baptist, and I am by choice a Southern Baptist.

I. By Commitment a Christian

I am by commitment a Christian. What does that mean? It does not mean that I am a churchgoer, though obviously I am. Being a Christian means more than just going to church. Neither does it simply mean that I'm an American, though sometimes we call our nation a "Christian nation." The reality is that many of our founding fathers were Christians. Many who came here to America came looking for religious liberty, and many of the foundation stones of our country are based on Christian principles. Sometimes people identify Christianity with America, or America with Christianity. But being a Christian and being an American are not synonymous.

To say that I am a Christian does not mean that I am religious, although I have and do participate in religious activities. Religion is a way to express one's beliefs. But there is much more to being a Christian than just those expressions. I have gone through the ritual of baptism, and I participate in the Lord's Supper and all of those things. But being a Christian is more than that.

There is one other thing that being a Christian doesn't mean. It doesn't mean that I simply believe in God. There is much more to it than just believing in God. The book of James tells us that Satan himself believes in God, but it does him no good. He knows God much closer and much more face-to-face than we do, but that doesn't make him right with God.

What does it mean? To be a Christian means I have some specific beliefs about a man called Jesus Christ. I believe that He appeared on this earth about two thousand years ago, was known as Jesus from Nazareth, and was the Christ, the promised Messiah. I believe that Jesus is the Christ. I believe that He was God, that this Jesus before He was known on earth, in all eternity was with God and was God. And then one night in Bethlehem, He was born. He was incarnate. He came to earth to live life as a man.

He lived a perfect life. Although He was tempted, He never sinned. He never lied. He never stole. He never broke any of the Ten Commandments. He never did anything that would mark Him as a sinner. This man lived a perfect life. When He died on the cross, it was God's plan that He would die as the substitute for our sins. The Scripture says that God "made the One who did not know sin to be sin for us, so that we might become the righteousness of God in Him" (2 Cor. 5:21).

I believe that is true because He came back to life. He died, was buried, and came back to life. He is risen! He is alive today. I accept that not only as a fact of history, but my acceptance has resulted in a personal commitment of my life to the lordship of Jesus Christ.

But now the dilemma begins. In His Word God says, "Let us hold on to the confession of our hope without wavering, for He who promised is faithful. And let us be concerned about one another in order to promote love and good works, not staying away from our meetings, as some habitually do, but encouraging each other, and all the more as you see the day drawing near" (Heb. 10:23–25). I understand these verses to say that I'm to fellowship with other Christians. I need to meet with other Christians. Now the dilemma begins—what church, what group of Christians do I meet with?

In the first century it was easy. You simply looked for the people with the sign of the fish, and they were all unified. There had not been a deterioration, a delusion, and all kinds of heresies and errors to mix in with the faith at that point. But now what church do I go to? Do I go to the church that calls themselves Scientists, who say that the Christ spirit who came upon Jesus at His baptism and left Him at the cross came upon a woman in the 1800s and inspired her to write a key to the Scriptures? Is that the church I want to go to? Or do I go to the Church of Scientology, or to the Church of Religious Science, which speaks of pyramid power and crystal power and consulting the dead? You see, all the people who claim to be Christian aren't, and every group that calls itself a church is not necessarily so. How do I know what group of people to identify with?

II. By Conviction a Baptist

I am by conviction a Baptist. I chose to identify with the people known as Baptists. I did not say I am by conviction a Protestant. Our society tends to categorize everyone as Protestant, Catholic, Jewish, etc. If a person is not Jewish or Catholic, then he is probably Protestant unless he is an atheist. But technically Baptists are not Protestants. Protestants protested against the Catholic Church. True Protestants are the Episcopal Church, Presbyterian, Lutheran, etc., but Baptists come out of English Separatists. Protestants broke from the Catholic Church. Baptists emerged from the English Separatists. In the history of England, the Anglican church separated. They were Protestants. They separated from the Catholic Church, and then out of this there came two groups. The Puritans, who thought they could remain in the church. They thought they could stay in the faith and purify the church. That's why they were known as Puritans.

The other group thought the best thing to do was to separate from the Church of England, and so they were called Separatists. A group of them separated and went to Holland. There in Holland they began to look at the Scriptures and say, "This is the type of people we need to be. These are the things we need to be doing." And they became known as Baptists, primarily because they practiced baptism by immersion. Ever since apostolic ages there have always been those who have said, "We need to go by the Scripture and by nothing else."

Some of the English Separatists went to Holland, where they came under the influence of the Anabaptists. The Anabaptists had sprung up in the 1500s, soon after the invention of the printing press and publication of Bible in the common language. Before that time, all copies of the Bible were handwritten, so they were very expensive. The Catholic Church used only the Latin Bible in Mass, but few people understood Latin.

After the invention of the printing press, the Bible was translated and published in the common language of the people. People began to get their own copies and began to study the Bible. They began to understand what the New Testament taught about faith in Christ and Christ alone for righteousness. Some began to understand the need to be baptized after receiving Christ by faith, but the Catholic Church objected, claiming that infant baptism was sufficient. Those who practiced believer's baptism were condemned as "rebaptizers," or Anabaptists. These Anabaptists joined with the English Separatists, and out of that union came what we know as Baptists.

Baptists have some distinctive beliefs. All of these together make a person a Baptist. Let me give you five of these Baptist distinctives.

The first is *the authority of the Bible and its sufficiency for faith and practice.* Baptists are known as people of the Book. We believe that the Bible is the Word of God. We do not believe that it contains the word of God. We believe that it is the Word of God. There are many denominations that believe this is the Word of God, but Baptists go one step further. Baptists say not only that the Bible is authoritative but also that it is sufficient for faith and practice. The

Bible determines how we should be a church. Many churches believe that the Bible is the Word of God but think that history and other things shape how they should conduct themselves as a church. Baptists say the Bible is not only the Word of God and the authority for our lives, but it is also sufficient for our faith and practice.

I have a brother who is ten years older than I. When he lived in Gilroy, California, he and his wife were part of a new church. Their intent was to do everything according to the Bible. Often we would discuss things, and they said to me one day, "You know, every week we are becoming more Baptist."

The second Baptist distinctive is *the competency of the soul.* Competency of the soul means that every person is competent to go to God directly. We don't have confessional booths. You don't have to confess your sins to me. You go directly to God. As you pray, you don't have to pray through me. You go directly to God. This is known as the priesthood of the believer. Every one of us is a priest. But this means not only that I go directly to God in prayer; this also means that I have ministry responsibilities. Every one of us is a minister. All of us have ministry responsibilities. We are all called in this together.

Baptists also believe in *immersion baptism of believers only.* The Greek word for "baptize" *(baptizo)* means "to immerse in water." A Greek historical document tells us that a battle was lost because of a hold in a ship. The ship sank into the Mediterranean Sea; it was "baptized" because it went down into the water.

But Baptists believe not only in immersion baptism but immersion baptism of believers only. The proper sequence is confession of Jesus Christ as Lord and then baptism to symbolize the death, burial, and resurrection of Jesus Christ, and also what has happened in our lives.

Baptism means I have died to an old life. I have been resurrected to a new life in Jesus Christ. Baptism also proclaims my future. After my body has been laid in the grave, I will be resurrected in all eternity with Jesus Christ. We believe in immersion baptism of believers. That's why we don't baptize babies. We dedicate the parents to raise their children in the things of God. But we wait until people are old enough to understand that they have personal sin and have received Jesus Christ as their personal Savior before we baptize them.

Baptists also believe in *the complete independence of the local church and its voluntary cooperation with other Baptist churches.* Every Baptist church is an independent church. We own our own property. We choose our own pastors. We choose our own literature. We choose our own programs. We choose to cooperate with other churches, or we choose not to cooperate with other churches.

And then the fifth Baptist distinctive is *absolute separation of church and state.* We do not believe that the state should run the church; neither do we believe the church should run the state.

I am a Baptist because these principles are the closest to what I believe the Scripture reveals. Let me conclude this section with a quote from Robert A. Baker, a Baptist historian. He said:

The pattern for Baptists, then, is that which is said out of the New Testament. Baptists believe that it is authoritative for every generation. Some Christian people have felt that this pattern was only meant for the generation to whom it was given. They think that succeeding generations may modify or replace the pattern so that the needs of a new day can be met adequately. Others have counted themselves superior to the New Testament in authority and have openly altered or eliminated specific teachings. Still others have claimed that the New Testament plus the traditions of the first five centuries of Christian history constitute the pattern and authority for Christianity. These things Baptists deny. They believe that the effort of Christians today should be directed not toward modifying but toward reproducing the pattern of the New Testament. Only to the extent in which they hold to this principle and put it into a practice can Baptists or any other group claim the name New Testament Christians.[1]

III. By Choice a Southern Baptist

I am by commitment a Christian. I am by conviction a Baptist. I am a fourth-generation Baptist. However, each succeeding generation has had to make the choice for themselves about whether to remain Baptist or what kind of Baptist to be. My great grandmother was a Primitive Baptist, a group that did not believe in missions. They were so local church oriented that they thought there should not be any missionary enterprises. I choose not to be identified with that kind of belief. Of my Baptist grandparents who were Southern Baptists, two sons remained Southern Baptists, my uncle in Oklahoma and my father. One son chose to become an American Baptist, and one son chose to become Church of Christ, which originally sprang from among Baptists. Of Baptists there are many types. Some are Missionary Baptists, Independent Baptists, General Baptists, American Baptists, Southern Baptists, Seventh-Day Baptists, and a host of others.

Why did I choose to be a Southern Baptist? I am by choice a Southern Baptist. Let me clear up first some mistaken notions of what it means to be a Southern Baptist. One is the idea of Southern Baptists as having an affinity for the racism that the historic South is identified with.

Southern Baptists are the most racially, ethnically diverse denomination of all the denominations. Since 1945 after the end of World War II, Southern Baptists have broken out of the sectionalism that centered in the South and have spread all over the nation.

Let me give you a little information about Southern Baptists. First, Southern Baptists are missionary minded. It is their spirit of missions destiny that draws me to be a Southern Baptist. I am by heritage a Southern Baptist. But I have wrestled with this, and I made a conscious choice to be a Southern Baptist, primarily because of its spirit of destiny—missions destiny.

Baptists in general began to be missionary in England in the late 1700s. A man named William Carey was the heart and soul of the initial missionary enterprise of Baptists. He was an English shoe cobbler. England at that time was divided between the Particular Baptists and the General Baptists. They were the two main Baptist groups. The Particular Baptists said that Jesus died only for the elect. They emphasized the limited atonement of Calvinism. The General

Baptists said that Jesus died for all, the general atonement. The Particular Baptists were opposed to mission enterprises and evangelism. They claimed it was wrong to try to convert someone for whom Jesus did not die.

Carey, although he was a Particular Baptist, challenged this idea and presented the idea that the Great Commission had application for the current day and not just for the first disciples. One man stood up in an associational meeting to rebuke Carey. He said, "Sit down, young man. When God wants to convert the heathen, He will do it without your help or mine. You are a miserable enthusiast for even asking such a question." But Carey persisted. He was instrumental in forming the first missionary board, known as the Particular Baptist Society for the Propagation of the Gospel among the Heathen. The first missionary they sent was William Carey. He went to Calcutta, India. He arrived in 1793 and baptized his first convert in 1800. Soon other missionary societies began to spring up.

On American soil, Baptist missionary societies began to develop, as well as similar societies for other denominations. In 1812 the Congregationalists formed the American Board of Commissioners for Foreign Missions. It sent Adoniram and Ann Judson, along with Luther Rice, to India as Congregationalist missionaries. The Judsons and Rice traveled on separate ships. They knew they were going to confront Carey, who was a Baptist. They knew they were going to have to defend why they were not Baptists. So they studied their New Testament on the journey over there.

During the voyage they became convinced that believer's baptism by immersion was the proper mode of baptism. After arriving in India, the Judsons declared themselves Baptists and were immersed. Rice made the same declaration about two months later. They did not feel right about being Baptists and being supported by Congregationalists, so they resigned. Rice returned to America to raise funds to support the Judsons as Baptist missionaries. Out of this effort was formed the General Missionary Convention of the Baptist Denomination in the United States for Foreign Missions. It was called the Triennial Convention because it met every three years.

The Triennial Convention continued to meet, but in the 1840s it declared that no missionary could take his slaves with him to the mission field; it would not be right for the mission board to appoint a man who was a slave owner. The Baptists in the South felt that this placed the denomination over the church. They felt it was a denomination telling the church what they could believe. And so in 1845, the Southern Baptist Convention was formed. Southern Baptists strongly defended the independence of local churches, and they wondered how they could unify their churches without dictating doctrine. They said that their purpose was to organize a plan for eliciting, combining, and directing the energies of the whole denomination in one sacred effort for the propagation of the gospel.

That's our history, and I'm not at all proud of the slavery part. But I think you need to understand in the 1860s there were not only Southern Baptists and Northern Baptists, there were also Southern Methodists and Northern Methodists, Southern Presbyterians and Northern Presbyterians. And the whole nation was split North and South. After the Civil War many of those groups began to meet together and no longer divide themselves into North and South. But Northern and Southern Baptists were moving in different directions concerning church polity and missions. By the way, in the 1950s the Northern Baptists changed their name to American Baptists.

The SBC missionary purpose has today produced a denomination with 5,500 missionaries in 130 countries through our International Mission Board. Our North American Mission Board has 5,100 missionaries. We have the largest missionary force of any denomination.

We support missionaries. One of the primary ways of doing that is through the Cooperative Program. Our Southern Baptist Convention (SBC) began in 1845. To fund the various entities of the SBC, each organization would send speakers to the churches to appeal for money. Many churches had someone giving one of these special appeals almost every week, and this was damaging the churches. Money would flow to the more prominent ministries, but some of the less visible ministries were not being adequately supported. The dynamic speakers would get better offerings. There was a great problem of funding all the different things that Southern Baptists were doing. So in 1925 we devised what is called the Cooperative Program.

The idea is that each church would take a portion of its weekly offerings and designate a portion of that—10 percent, 5 percent, 8 percent, 20 percent, whatever they felt of the Lord to designate— to the Cooperative Program. The Cooperative Program involves cooperation between the state conventions and the SBC.

This is how it works. We collect the tithes and offerings in our church. We send a portion of that to the state convention office. The state convention keeps a portion of that for funding missionaries and ministries in the state and forwards the rest of the funds to the Southern Baptist Convention Executive Committee in Nashville, Tennessee. The Executive Committee then puts those funds in a budget, a portion of which goes to the North American Mission Board, the International Mission Board, seminaries, etc. Since 1925, we have grown in our missionary force because it is a reliable, predictable source of funding. We do not have missionaries to come before our church and ask for special offerings because we support them though the Cooperative Program.

Some of you may have been in churches where a missionary would come and show his slides, tell his story, and then ask, "Will this church pledge for the next two years $50 a month to my ministry, or $25 a month, or $100 a month?" Those missionaries make their way around to different churches issuing these appeals. And after they get enough funding, they go back to their mission field and do their work. Then at different times they come back to the United States and make the appeal for funds again. Not only are they missionaries; they also have to be fund-raisers.

Our SBC missionaries never have to worry about fund-raising. Our missionaries receive full salaries and benefits. They never have to worry about coming back and drumming up funds. They never have to worry about those funds drying up. Our missionaries are the envy of the whole evangelical world. Because of this predictability and consistency, individuals are able to devote their entire careers to missions. Yes, they do come back on furlough. They spend a year traveling about speaking to the churches, not to raise money for their mission but to share about what the Cooperative Program does and what their ministry is accomplishing.

The Cooperative Program not only supports our missionaries but our seminaries as well. In the United States, we have six seminaries. These schools train missionaries, pastors, and other staff leaders for Christian service. Two of our seminaries are the largest in the world—Southwestern Baptist Theological Seminary in Fort Worth, Texas, and The Southern Baptist Theological Seminary in Louisville, Kentucky. If you are a Southern Baptist and you sense that God has called you into the ministry, our denomination wants you to get an education. So the SBC supplements your tuition. You have to be endorsed or approved by a Southern Baptist church. Other students attend and pay full tuition. That's what our denomination is, and we are a part of that. We are a part of training pastors and missionaries all over the United States. We are a part of those missionaries around the world through the Cooperative Program.

In addition to the Cooperative Program, we as Southern Baptists also emphasize two special offerings. One is the Annie Armstrong Easter Offering for home missions, named after a godly woman who devoted her life to promoting missions. The other is the Lottie Moon Christmas Offering for overseas missions. Lottie Moon was one of the first missionaries to China. She devoted her entire life to the Chinese people. In fact, she gave much of herself and gave away her food during a famine time. She basically starved herself to death and died in Japan on the way back to the United States one Christmas Eve. With these two offerings—the Annie Armstrong and the Lottie Moon—all the funds that are collected go directly to mission projects on the mission field. They don't go to administration. They don't go to salaries. They go to supporting our mission efforts. They go to specific essential projects.

Our denomination has recently undergone some structural changes. The Home Mission Board is no longer called the Home Mission Board. It is now called the North American Mission Board.

The Foreign Mission Board is now called the International Mission Board. Together, SBC churches are starting an average of four churches a day in the United States. There are now over forty-two thousand Southern Baptist churches. Someone has said that if all sixteen million Southern Baptists stood shoulder to shoulder, we would reach from Miami to Juno. That's how many Southern Baptists there are.

In 2002, 420,000 people were baptized in Southern Baptist churches in the U.S. And 450,000 people were baptized in Southern Baptist-related churches overseas. That means one baptism every fifty-one seconds. That's like Pentecost happening every week—one baptism every fifty-one seconds.

The heart of the Southern Baptist Convention is wrapped up in its logo. The Southern Baptist logo is an open Bible. That open Bible emphasizes we are a people of the Book. And then above the open Book is a world. We have the world in view. And then intersecting both the Bible and the world is the cross of Jesus Christ. We believe that the good news of the gospel—the death, burial, and resurrection of Jesus Christ—is the only way the world will be transformed. It is the only hope for the world. The cross is central. The Bible is foundational. And the world is in our view.

I am proud to be a Southern Baptist. I am a Christian by commitment. I am a Baptist by conviction. And I am Southern Baptist by choice. All of us as Christians follow the footsteps of the One who gave us the Great Commission and said, "Go . . . and make disciples of all nations" (Matt. 28:19). We as Southern Baptists follow the footsteps of our mission-minded forebears. My challenge is that we remain true to that call and be involved in missions—not only around the world but also in Fair Oaks, and in Carmichael, and Folsom, and Orangevale, East Sacramento, and North Sacramento. Wherever we have impact, we will be mission-minded people, because Jesus Christ is the only hope for our world.

1. Robert A. Baker, *The Baptist March in History* (Nashville: Convention Press, 1958), 9–10.

Contributors

Daniel Akin, President, Southeastern Baptist Theological Seminary

Mac Brunson, Senior Pastor, First Baptist Church, Dallas, Texas

Michael Catt, Senior Pastor, Sherwood Baptist Church, Albany, Georgia

Morris H. Chapman, President and Chief Executive Officer, Executive Committee of the Southern Baptist Convention

William Crews, President, Golden Gate Baptist Theological Seminary

Charles W. Draper, Associate Professor of Biblical Studies, Boyce College, The Southern Baptist Theological Seminary, Louisville, Kentucky

James T. Draper, Sr. (1913–1966), Pastor, First Baptist Church, Warren, Arkansas

James T. Draper, Jr., President, LifeWay Christian Resources of the Southern Baptist Convention

Randy Draper, Deacon, Lay Preacher, Colleyville, Texas

Ronald Dunn (1936–2001), Pastor and Minister-at-Large, MacArthur Boulevard Baptist Church, Irving, Texas, and popular Bible conference speaker

Tom Elliff, Pastor, First Southern Baptist Church, Del City, Oklahoma

Jack Graham, Pastor, Prestonwood Baptist Church, Plano, Texas

Dan Hall, President, On Course Ministries

George Harris, Minister at Large, Castle Hills First Baptist Church, San Antonio, Texas

O. S. Hawkins, President, Annuity Board of the Southern Baptist Convention

Ken Hemphill, National Strategist for Empowering Kingdom Growth, Southern Baptist Convention

Jim Henry, Senior Pastor, First Baptist Church, Orlando, Florida.

Johnny Hunt, Senior Pastor, First Baptist Church, Woodstock, Georgia

Chuck Kelley, President, New Orleans Baptist Theological Seminary

Richard Land, President, The Ethics & Religious Liberty Commission of the Southern Baptist Convention

James Merritt, Senior Pastor, Cross Pointe, The Church at Gwinett Center, Duluth, Georgia

Gene Mims, Vice President, LifeWay Christian Resources of the Southern Baptist Convention

R. Albert Mohler, Jr., President, The Southern Baptist Theological Seminary

Jon Moore, Revivalist, North Richland Hills, Texas

Paige Patterson, President, Southwestern Baptist Theological Seminary

Jerry Rankin, President, International Mission Board of the Southern Baptist Convention

Robert E. Reccord, President, North American Mission Board of the Southern Baptist Convention

J. T. Reed, Senior Pastor, First Baptist Church, Fair Oaks, California

R. Philip Roberts, President, Midwestern Baptist Theological Seminary

Adrian Rogers, Senior Pastor, Bellevue Baptist Church, Memphis, Tennessee

O. Damon Shook, Senior Pastor, Champion Forest Baptist Church, Houston, Texas

Roger Spradlin, Senior Pastor, Valley Baptist Church, Bakersfield, California

Jerry Sutton, Senior Pastor, Two Rivers Baptist Church, Nashville, Tennessee

Claude Thomas, Senior Pastor, First Batist Church, Euless, Texas

Keith Thomas, Senior Pastor, Cottage Hill Baptist Church, Mobile, Alabama

Ted H. Traylor, Pastor, Olive Baptist Church, Pensacola, Florida

Jerry Vines, Senior Pastor, First Baptist Church, Jacksonville, Florida

Hayes Wicker, Senior Pastor, First Baptist Church, Naples, Florida

Ed Young, Senior Pastor, Second Baptist Church, Houston, Texas

ATTENTION LIBRARY STAFF
Please check for
Accompanying CD

DEMCO